The L.L.BEAN® BOOK of NEW NEW ENGLAND COOKERY

The L.L.BEAN® BOOK of NEW NEW ENGLAND COOKERY

Judith and Evan Jones

ILLUSTRATIONS by LAUREN JARRETT

Random House　　New York

*Grateful acknowledgment is made to the following for permission to
reprint previously printed material:*

Harper & Row, Publishers, Inc.: "Popovers" and "Green Mountain
Green Tomato Bread" from *The Book of Bread* by Judith and Evan
Jones. Copyright © 1982 by Judith Jones and Evan Jones. Reprinted
by permission of Harper & Row, Publishers, Inc.
Alfred A. Knopf, Inc.: "Squash Cornbread" from *The Victory
Garden Cookbook* by Marian Morash. Copyright © 1982 by
Marian Morash and WGBH Educational Foundation. "Nut Sauce
II" from *Eat Right, Eat Well—The Italian Way* by Edward Giobbi
and Richard Wolff, M.D. Copyright © 1985 by Edward Giobbi and
Richard Wolff, M.D. "Nasturtium Radish Cheese Canapés" and
"Ripe Tomato and Green Oregano Pizza" from *A Cook's Guide to
Growing Herbs, Greens and Aromatics* by Millie Owen. Copyright
© 1978 by Mildred Ziegler Owen. Reprinted by permission
of Alfred A. Knopf, Inc.
Random House, Inc.: "Perciattelli with Fresh Sardines and Fennel
Sauce" from *Italian Family Cooking* by Edward Giobbi. Copyright
© 1971 by Edward Giobbi. Reprinted by permission
of Random House, Inc.
Viking Penguin, Inc.: "Dandelion Tempura" and "Zucchini
Pancakes" from *Health, Happiness, and the Pursuit of Herbs* by
Adele G. Dawson (Brattleboro, Vermont: The Stephen Green Press).
Copyright © 1980 by Adele Dawson. Reprinted courtesy of
Viking Penguin, Inc.

Library of Congress Cataloging-in-Publication Data

Jones, Judith.
The L.L. Bean book of new New England cookery.

Includes index.
1. Cookery, American—New England style.
I. Jones, Evan, 1915– . II. Title.
TX715.J775   1987   641.5974   87-314
ISBN 0-394-54456-0

Manufactured in the United States of America

2 4 6 8 9 7 5 3

FIRST EDITION

Book design by Carole Lowenstein

Dedicated to the memory of
our seventeenth-century Yankee forebears
John Bayley and Eleanor Bayley

FOREWORD

New England is a land of diverse seasons. Nature shapes the land throughout the year, and in the process shapes the people who live here. To live in New England is to adapt to the changing seasons and to enjoy the special qualities each change brings.

We at L. L. Bean have witnessed the cycle of New England's seasons for three quarters of a century, and we've seen New Englanders adapt their proud traditions in response to the changing times as well as the variable weather. The cooks of New England have developed foods to greet the seasons, creating as much variety in their cooking as in the weather itself. From hearty midwinter stews and chowders to light soups for summer afternoons, meals are planned to please the palate, sustain the spirit and make use of seasonal foods. These cooks have reacted with equal creativity to the waves of immigrants into the region. All have contributed the influence of their native foods and have become true New Englanders in spirit, integrating their traditional cuisines into their adoptive settings. Perhaps nowhere else can so many ethnic styles of cooking be found flourishing.

It seems particularly appropriate, then, that on our seventy-fifth anniversary we are bringing you this book of today's New England cookery. The response to *The L. L. Bean Game and Fish Cookbook* demonstrated a continuing desire for practical recipes that are easy to prepare and uncommonly flavorful—recipes that reflect the flavor of a region known for its good taste! To compile a collection that would mirror the varied and enduring culinary skills of the "new" New England cooks, we turned to two of the country's leading food writers, Judith Jones (who co-authored *The L. L. Bean Game and Fish Cookbook*) and her husband, Evan Jones. Judith and Evan, who own a house in Vermont where they garden avidly, crisscrossed New England, talking to many people and gathering ideas for recipes that capture the nature of the region and its cooking—unexpected, down-to-earth, diverse, traditional, yet constantly changing. In that spirit —the spirit of New England—we hope you will use this book as a guide to creating your own menus, adapting the recipes to the special qualities of the land and climate where you live.

CONTENTS

INTRODUCTION

This is not a collection of nostalgic recipes, but a book of New England cooking for our times. It's a book about enjoying food. New Englanders, like Americans in every other region, change—Yankees may see themselves as having been characteristic of what it is to be American longer than most, but the fact is that New Englanders are no more entrenched in the past than anyone else.

Food that can be described as New England in style is still straightforward—as it was for Priscilla and John Alden and the middle class of the seventeenth century. It's far more interesting, however, because the twentieth-century cooks have incorporated many more ethnic influences than the bland English tastes that took hold at Plymouth Rock.

It's a long time, indeed, since New Englanders have led provincial lives. And cooking has reflected that. "We breathed the air of foreign countries, curiously interblended with our own," Lucy Larcom wrote of her mid-nineteenth-century girlhood. "Men talked about a voyage to Calcutta, or Hongkong, or up the Straits—meaning Gibralter and the Mediterranean—as if it were not much more than going to the next village." When she was a child, Miss Larcom wrote, jars of tropical fruits, tamarinds, ginger root, and other spicily appetizing tidbits were as common in Beverly, Massachusetts, pantries as barberries and cranberries.

Evidence of such "air of foreign countries" is most easily recognizable in the 1980s in the restaurants that thrive from the great Yankee ports on the Atlantic to such villages in the Champlain Valley as Ferrisburg, where an Indian restaurant could prevail as successfully as a similar place in Portland, Maine. In home kitchens, as well, New Englanders don't habitually reject flavors that might surprise the palate. Many a contemporary cook is as much a globe-trotter as any schooner crewman in the days of sail.

Not only has the region not changed in that sense, but any semblance of chip-on-shoulder feistiness is gone. "Frederic's pressed duck at the Tour d'Argent isn't bad," a Yankee wrote a couple of generations back, "but it can't hold a candle to coot stew. . . ." *Boeuf à la mode* as served in Paris could be a pretty good dish, the same writer asserted, "but my grandmother's corned beef hash was better—much better."

In this century there is crusty, mellow corned beef hash to be had, even if there isn't much Yankee pressed duck, and many who take pride in traditional dishes such as New England boiled dinner make it a point to be adept at classic cooking styles that often reflect the cuisine of Escoffier. Young culinary professionals we happen to know—one of them in Portland —have gone abroad for advance training and returned to their home precincts, and, equally important, to the regional ingredients that they have learned, as experts, to respect anew.

We set out to put this book together after years of crisscrossing New England, eating in private homes as well as restaurants, and becoming steadily impressed with the evidence we found: regional cooking doesn't have to be dully provincial and often is prepared with finesse and is faithful to the nineteenth-century traditions that made Boston's Parker House and other hostelries internationally admired. More people are eating out than ever before, and more of them are inspired enough by restaurant fare to reflect such experience in meals they prepare for themselves.

The variety is wide-ranging. No hunter friend has yet sat us down to a meal of coot stew, yet we're comforted to know of Rhode Island places where the snail salad, decidedly not French, is composed of garlic-scented sliced conch (the local gastropod). More simply, the creamed chicken in patty shells that we had not long ago for lunch at the Philbrook family's farm in the White Mountains may have seemed to be of standard country style—in fact, the chicken dish was one of the great variety of traditional North Country dishes of which many cooks have developed their own versions.

Thousands of young New Englanders, like pioneer homesteaders, have made a serious decision to establish themselves as families, and some of them thrive in unaffected ways, raising goats and sheep and producing cheeses never before made in this country—others champion natural foods or are dedicated to vegetarianism, determined to minimize the effects of pollution. Bread baking as a commercial enterprise is among many ways that the young are fencing off the technological encroachments.

There's not much news here—New England has always been eclectic. The trouble may be that we have been myopic about the region. Assessing the Yankee psyche, we've seen only what we wanted to see—as if Currier and Ives lithographs were the reality of village and hill-farm life, as if black wood-burning stoves and biscuits rising, and beans cooking gently overnight, were as definitive today as a century ago.

Variety that reflects individuality still characterizes New England cookery, much as it did in the past. The difference may be that more influence from several ethnic heritages is admitted openly. Yankee food is still dependent on ingredients at hand, but it is sparked by seasoning that can be both more imaginative and more subtle. The complaint that Harriet Beecher Stowe once made from Paris about the excessive use most New England cooks made of a few all-too-common spices is forgotten in the current concentration on lighter dishes, more delicacy in sauces, and the deft seasoning that springs from both the increasing number of kitchen gardens and herb patches and the proliferating farmer's markets that bring fresh produce to village greens and shopping malls alike.

The *new* New England cooking style is as much a mosaic of ethnic heritage, as are the Red Sox fans that fill Fenway Park. The assertion that all immigrants were crowded into congested sections of industrial towns is a distortion. In the countryside of Maine, New Hampshire, and Vermont, Scotch and Welsh settlers, so assimilated that few outsiders recognize the differences in their backgrounds, still bake scones and oatmeal bread and grow leeks alongside other vegetables. Many French, having moved down from Canada, for several generations have been responsible for the popularity of split pea soup, as well as various forms of pork pies. Settling in central Massachusetts and in Maine more than four generations ago, Germans have been producing their own kinds of sausages and have made sauerkraut a favorite item in many kitchens north of Portland. And there are Czechs, Greeks, Lebanese, Hungarians, Irish, Italians, Lithuanians, Poles, Russians, Scandinavians, and Swiss, not to say American Indians and black Americans, whose contributions to New England we've sought to include in this book.

We have not collected "old country" recipes, but rather we've tried to pack these pages with the ideas that show how Yankee eating habits are changing, as reflected in recipes that are so contemporary that they represent the times. Just as we have found much exemplary cooking in all the six states through which we've traveled, so you will discover surprises and new culinary ideas. Here, then, is New England—from blueberry pancakes to the salt-meadow lamb of Block Island. Cheers!

—JUDITH AND EVAN JONES
Bryn Teg, 1987

APPETIZERS

To START with appetizers seems a proper way to begin a book about food, but the word—in a climate that encouraged abundant meals—isn't a part of the Yankee tradition. As Fannie Farmer knew when she published her first cookbook, Bostonians and other North Country citizens were real eaters, and they liked to pull up a chair and begin without any shilly-shallying.

Each of the dinner menus in Miss Farmer's first book starts off with a hearty soup; only full-course dinners, as she planned them for turn-of-the-century parties, called for the beginning flourish of oysters, clams, or anchovy canapés before the soup. "For a gentleman's dinner," she instructed her followers, "canapés with sherry wine are frequently served before the guests enter the dining room."

In our own Yankee view, things haven't changed all that much. Although cosmopolitan cocktail parties may still demand dainty "finger food" to help in the precarious business of balancing drinks for a guest or two, real North Country hosts and hostesses are as often as not content to offer a cracker topped with sizzling store cheese (the local cheddar). In restaurants, and sometimes in inns, we find ourselves ushered to salad bars to make our own first courses, which incidentally uses up some of the time spent waiting for the kitchen to get the main course ready (the old relish tray used to serve the same function).

So our suggestions in this first chapter reflect some of the eating attitudes that are new in New England. There are no luxurious avocado halves with 8 or 10 (per person) shrimp in a Russian dressing. We recommend appetizers that are light and tempting. "In a way"—as Elsie Masterson once put it—"they are teasers, a beginning kind of food."

Baked Clam Appetizer

1 scant cup minced fresh clams, or one 7½-ounce can minced clams
4 tablespoons vegetable oil
1½ tablespoons minced scallions, including tender greens
3 tablespoons minced parsley
1 teaspoon capers, drained and chopped
¼ cup finely chopped mushrooms
2 tablespoons fresh lemon juice
4 tablespoons common cracker crumbs (page 34)
½ hard-boiled egg
Salt
Freshly ground pepper

Drain the clams and set aside on a paper towel. Heat the oil in a skillet and sauté the scallions, parsley, capers, and mushrooms over medium heat for about 5 minutes. Remove from the stove and stir in the lemon juice and the cracker crumbs. Mash the egg half, both white and yolk, and stir it into the sauté mixture along with clams. Season to taste with salt and pepper. Lightly grease 4 scallop shells, and fill with clam mixture. Heat for 4 or 5 minutes in a preheated 400-degree oven, and serve immediately.
SERVES 4

Clams (or Oysters or Mussels) Casino

Some Yankee loyalists remember Clams Casino as a classic opener on Boston's Locke-Ober menu, and others assert that Oysters Casino can be traced back to Newport's Casino Club—small matter for contemporaries who find them today on many restaurant menus. Aside from that, there is at least one home cook we know who has her own version of Mussels Casino.

2 dozen fresh cherrystone clams (or plump oysters or mussels)
Rock salt
6 strips bacon
6 tablespoons butter
½ cup finely chopped shallots or scallion bulbs
½ cup finely chopped fresh herbs (three-quarters parsley, one-quarter fresh dill, tarragon, or chervil, if available; otherwise all parsley)
½ cup finely chopped green pepper
A few drops Tabasco sauce
2 tablespoons lemon juice
1 teaspoon Worcestershire sauce
Freshly ground pepper

Open the clams (or oysters or mussels) and set aside the best 2 dozen shells. Spread a layer of rock salt in pie pans, and nestle the selected shells in the salt. Fry the bacon gently until it has rendered all its fat, then drain on paper towels. Mix the butter with the shallots, parsley and herbs, green pepper, Tabasco to taste, lemon juice, and Worcestershire. Put a clam (or

oyster or mussel) in each shell and top with a dollop of the butter mixture. Grind a little pepper over each. Break up the bacon into 24 pieces, and set a piece on top of each shell. Broil 4 inches under a hot broiler for 6–8 minutes, until the herb butter is sizzling and the bacon is crisp.
SERVES 4

Broiled Oysters with Radishes and Butter Sauce

1 tablespoon butter
10 fat radishes, trimmed and cut in julienne
16 large oysters, or 2 dozen or more small oysters

BUTTER SAUCE:
½ cup dry vermouth
3 shallots, or 4 scallion bulbs, chopped

Salt
Freshly ground pepper
8 drops Tabasco sauce
¾ cup fresh bread crumbs
2 tablespoons chopped parsley

1 tablespoon lemon juice
4 tablespoons (½ stick) cold butter

Heat 1 tablespoon butter in a small pan and sauté the radishes until they bleed and are just lightly cooked, about 2–3 minutes. Open the oysters and scrape them from the shell, reserving the juice in a small saucepan. Spread the radishes in the bottom of half of the emptied shells (if there is any remaining radish juice, put that in the small saucepan too), and place oysters on top (2 to a shell, if they are small); shake a drop of Tabasco over each oyster. Mix the bread crumbs with the parsley, and sprinkle over the oysters. Broil 5–6 minutes, until browned on top.

Make the Butter Sauce: Add the vermouth, shallots, and lemon juice to the juices in the small saucepan and boil them down to 1 tablespoon. Whisk in the butter, 1 tablespoon at a time, until you have a smooth sauce. Spoon a little of the sauce over the broiled oysters.
SERVES 4

Mussels "Rockefeller"

3 pounds mussels
1½ pounds fresh spinach, or one 10-ounce box frozen
½ cup heavy cream
3 shallots, minced
Salt
Freshly ground pepper

Freshly ground nutmeg
2 garlic cloves
3 tablespoons softened butter
4 ounces fresh goat cheese or ricotta or mozzarella
About ½ cup fresh bread crumbs
Olive oil

Scrub the mussels and steam them in a large covered pot with ¼ cup water until they open. Remove the mussels from the shells and pick out about 20

of the largest shell halves and arrange them in one layer in a large pan (discard the rest of the shells). Put 1 mussel in each of the half shells, if they are large plump ones; if smaller, put 2 in a shell. Cook the spinach in boiling water to cover until just tender, about 4–5 minutes. Drain, cool, squeeze dry, and then chop fine. Put the spinach in a pan with the cream and shallots and cook gently until the cream is absorbed, about 8 minutes, stirring occasionally. Season with a little salt, pepper, and nutmeg. Smash the garlic with the flat of a large knife, remove the peel, and then chop. Add ½ teaspoon salt, then mash with the flat side of the knife until the garlic is almost a purée. Work the butter into the garlic mixture. Now cover each mussel with a spoonful of spinach, smear a little of the garlic butter over, lay a piece of goat cheese on top, and sprinkle with bread crumbs. Drizzle just a little olive oil over the tops just before putting the mussels about 8 inches under a hot broiler. Broil until they are sizzling and browned on top.
SERVES 5–6

Smoked Mussels in Grape Leaves

Louise Andrews Kent, aka "Mrs. Appleyard," is just one New Englander who believed in bringing grape leaves into the kitchen. She recommended that cooks who have grape arbors "pick the biggest and the best leaves." Wash them, then boil them in water until they lose their fresh green color, about 5 minutes. Failing a crop of your own, you may use leaves packed in brine, but wash them before filling.

20 vine leaves
½ pound spinach
½ pound (1 cup) ricotta cheese
1 cup chopped fresh mushrooms, or about 1 dozen dried*
½ pint (about 1 cup) smoked mussels

2 tablespoons chopped fresh coriander
1 tablespoon chopped shallots or scallion bulbs
½ teaspoon mace
¼ teaspoon cayenne
Salt

* If you use dried mushrooms, soak them 30 minutes in warm water to reconstitute. Drain.

Wash fresh vine leaves and boil as directed above. If using canned leaves, remove them from the brine and soak them in cold water about 1 hour, then rinse under cold running water. Unfold the creases in the leaves and spread them, rough side up, on paper towels to drain. Blanch the spinach in lightly salted boiling water until just tender; drain, chop fine, and squeeze out excess water. In a mixing bowl, mix together the ricotta, chopped mushrooms, mussels, coriander, shallots, and chopped spinach. Season with the spices and salt to taste. Chill the mixture 1 hour. To assemble, put a little of the chilled mixture in the center of a leaf, partially roll the stem end up, fold in the sides, and continue rolling to the point of the leaf. Each leaf should be firmly packed and tightly rolled. Arrange the rolled leaves in the top of a steamer and steam them for about 30 minutes. Serve warm, or, better, chill overnight and serve cold.

SERVES 4–5

Oriental Baked Shrimp

The appreciation of so-called Oriental seasonings inspires many cooks to experiment with recipes of their own. This is a delicious first course that we like to serve.

2 pounds Maine shrimp, peeled and cleaned
1/3 cup applejack or sherry or brandy
1/3 cup soy sauce
2 teaspoons vegetable oil
1 large garlic clove, chopped fine
2 teaspoons finely chopped candied ginger

Put the shrimp in a mixing bowl. Mix or shake together the applejack or other liquor, soy sauce, oil, chopped garlic, and candied ginger. Pour this marinade over the shrimp and set aside for 2 hours or more, stirring occasionally. In a shallow baking dish just large enough to hold the shrimp in one layer, arrange the shrimp, then pour the marinade over. Bake in a preheated 400-degree oven for 8 minutes.

SERVES 8

Sea Urchins in Their Shells

Our friend Claudia Roden first introduced us to sea urchins while recalling her youth in Egypt, when she used to swim out from Alexandria to find spiky jewel-like balls clinging to the rocks. She would bring them home to relish the salmon-colored roe, scooped out with crusty bread and seasoned only with a little lemon juice. The "subtle, iodized taste" she favored has only recently been discovered by lovers of good food—because it *does* take a certain amount of courage to slice off a circle of the porcupinelike exterior and spoon out the coral surrounded by a dark liquid. But sea urchins eaten in their shells as an appetizer have become chic nowadays around Block Island and the Connecticut coast, especially at Christmastime when the cold weather makes them easier to bring to market. One taste of this ambrosia and you're likely to become addicted. Count on 6–10 sea urchins per person, and arrange them on individual plates with wedges of lemon as a festive way to start a meal. For another way to use sea urchins, try them in a pasta (see page 357).

Mussels in Snail Butter

As early as 1763, Mrs. Sylvester Gardiner and other Back Bay hostesses who entertained in Maine and Boston often served the native mussels that were found along the shore. Here's a contemporary way of one-upping those who start a meal with *escargots à la Bourguignonne*.

24 mussels
1/2 cup (1 stick) softened butter
1 tablespoon chopped shallots
2 large garlic cloves, chopped very fine

1 tablespoon chopped parsley
1 tablespoon very dry white wine
Salt
Freshly ground pepper

Steam the mussels (page 5), remove from the shells, and select 24 half shells that will stand as close to level as possible. Mix the butter with the shallots, garlic, parsley, and wine. Put 1/2 teaspoon of the butter mixture in each of the selected shells. Place a mussel on top, then cover with more of the butter. Arrange the shells in a shallow baking dish and place in a preheated 400-degree oven for 15–20 minutes. Serve sizzling hot on escargot plates or on soup plates filled with rock salt, or napkin-lined plates. (Prepare ahead of time if you choose and freeze, then transfer to the hot oven.)
SERVES 4

Cold Salmon Mousse

This may also be made with cooked, or even canned, salmon, but we found making a mousse out of leftover scraps from a side of smoked salmon made a delicious achievement. If you have a fish-shaped mold, here is your chance to use it; otherwise use a ring mold.

1 envelope gelatin
1/4 cup cold water
1/2 cup fish broth, see page 69, or
   1/4 cup clam juice mixed with
   1/4 cup water
1/3 cup mayonnaise
1 tablespoon fresh lemon juice
2 scallions, including tender greens, minced

1/2 teaspoon paprika
2 cups finely flaked smoked salmon, or cooked or drained canned salmon
About 12 shakes Tabasco sauce
1 tablespoon capers, chopped
1/2 teaspoon or more salt
2/3 cup heavy cream

GARNISHES: *dill, lemon slices, radishes*
Cucumber-Radish Sour Cream Sauce (page 634)

Dissolve the gelatin in the water. Bring the fish broth to a boil, then pour on top of gelatin, and stir until dissolved. Let cool. Stir in the mayonnaise, lemon juice, scallions, paprika, salmon, Tabasco, capers, and salt (use more

to taste if not using smoked salmon). Whip the cream until it forms soft peaks, then fold it into the mousse mixture. Transfer to a lightly oiled fish mold or ring mold that holds 1–1½ quarts, pressing the mousse down firmly and evenly. Refrigerate, covered with plastic wrap, for several hours or overnight. To unmold, dip the bottom of the mold into hot water for about 30 seconds and loosen the edges with a knife, then flip onto a serving platter. If it doesn't come clean, repeat the procedure. Decorate with sprigs of dill, lemon slices, and radishes, and serve the sauce on the side.
SERVES 8

Fish Mousse

This is the kind of elegant first course one is apt to encounter in a good restaurant today that seems too tricky to try to reproduce at home. But it is a deceptively simple dish to make if you have a food processor; otherwise we don't recommend trying to do it.

¼–½ pound white-fleshed fish, such as sole, halibut, catfish, or cod
½–¾ pound scallops
1 whole egg
2 cups heavy cream, very cold
1 cup fresh bread crumbs
1½ tablespoons chopped scallions, including tender greens

1½ tablespoons chopped fresh tarragon, or 1 tablespoon fresh dill
⅛ teaspoon grated nutmeg
Salt
2 egg whites
½ pound (about 2 cups) cooked shrimp, lobster, or crab, or a combination, cut in small chunks

In a food processor, spin the fish and scallops with the whole egg until puréed, scraping down the sides of the bowl with a spatula as necessary. With the machine going, add the cream in a steady stream, then the bread crumbs. Mix in the seasonings and add salt to taste. In a bowl, beat the egg whites until they form firm peaks, then fold them into the fish mixture.

To make individual molds or a ring mold: Butter lightly twelve 5-ounce Pyrex cups or a 2-quart ring mold, plop a spoonful of the mousse into the bottom of each cup or all around the bottom of the ring mold, arrange pieces of the cooked seafood on top, then fill the cups or ring mold three-quarters full with the mousse. Put the cups or ring mold in a pan and pour enough boiling water to come about two thirds up the sides. Bake in a preheated 350-degree oven for 30–35 minutes, until set.

To make a loaf: Butter an 8-inch loaf pan, spread one-third of the mousse on the bottom, arrange half the seafood in a layer on top, then make a layer of the mousse, another of seafood, and a final layer of mousse. Place the loaf in a pan of simmering water and bake in a preheated 350-degree oven for 50–60 minutes, or until a skewer plunged into the middle comes out clean.

Fish Mousse (continued)

To serve: Let the mousse rest in its mold(s) 10 minutes. Turn the individual molds out onto warm plates—allowing 1 or 2 molds per person—or unmold the ring or loaf onto a warm serving platter. Serve garnished with watercress or with a little Hollandaise (page 632) poured over or passed in a sauceboat. Or chill and serve with lemon quarters and Green Mayonnaise (page 347).
SERVES 6–12

Crayfish in Licorice-Flavored Cream

3 tablespoons butter
2 tablespoons minced shallots or scallions bulbs
½ cup minced fennel
About 2½ cups cooked, shelled crayfish (see box opposite)
3 tablespoons Pernod or anisette or, if unavailable, dry sherry

1–2 tablespoons chopped fresh tarragon (depending on its strength), or 1 teaspoon dried
¾ cup heavy cream
Salt
Freshly ground pepper
1 tablespoon chopped parsley

Heat the butter in a skillet and sauté the shallots and fennel gently until tender, about 5 minutes. Add the crayfish and sprinkle on the Pernod or other liquor and the tarragon. Heat through, tossing, then add the cream and cook rapidly until it thickens slightly. Add salt and pepper to taste, and sprinkle parsley on top. Serve with toast points or in prebaked small pastry shells (page 565).
SERVES 4

Salt Cod Cocktail Fritters

1 pound salt codfish
5 tablespoons finely chopped scallions, including tender greens
Freshly ground pepper
Tabasco sauce

1 egg, well beaten
1 cup flour
1 cup milk
Oil or fat for frying

Prepare the fish by soaking in water overnight, changing water occasionally. Drain and flake the fish coarsely. Stir in the scallions, blending thoroughly, and add several turns of the pepper grinder and a small splash of Tabasco. Combine the fish mixture with the egg, flour, and milk, making a rather light batter. Drop by heaping teaspoonfuls into hot deep fat (375 degrees) and fry until crisp on both sides. The fritters should be very thin and crunchy.
SERVES 6–8

Yankee Crayfish

Some time after World War II, a fisherman here and there in New England started to use the freshwater crustacean called crayfish as bait in some of the deep, cold lakes of the Northeast. As the crayfish thrived, slightly modified minnow traps were set out to reduce their multiplying numbers; and as the crayfish thus caught increased, the small, somewhat shrimplike creatures began to attract cooks. An enterprising neighbor of ours managed to develop a market for them among restaurant chefs in and around Burlington, and a friend on Caspian Lake is one of the wily hostesses who persuades guests to peel the cooked crayfish that she serves with a side dish of dill-flavored mayonnaise. When guests prepare their own, she says, it cuts down on liquor consumption.

The chore of extracting the crayfish meat is labor-intensive, to say the least. Crayfish of New England's deep freshwater ponds yield only about ½ inch of meat apiece, and digging it out requires breaking through the undershells—a painstaking chore. However, the preparation of an elegant shellfish hors d'oeuvre or a crayfish pasta for family and friends is a labor of love, and one that is really rewarding on a leisurely summer afternoon.

We have found that it is not necessary to go through any special disgorging operation, as some cookbooks recommend. We prepare our crayfish by letting them rest a day, then washing them in several changes of water. To cook, we plunge them into a large pot of lightly salted water and boil them 10–12 minutes (fish one out and taste after 10 minutes —the flesh should no longer cling tenaciously to the shell and it should taste tender). When they are cool enough to handle, cut the undershell with a small sharp knife or scissors, and then extract the meat in one piece. Save the shells (see below). You'll need about 5 pounds of crayfish to make about 2 cups of meat. The cooked crayfish are attractive—they look like small lobsters—so save some of them to garnish your dish.

Crayfish Bisque

The meaty shells and succulent legs will make a simple, delicious bisque. Simply dump all the debris after you've extracted the tail meat into a pot, cover with cold water, add 1 large sliced onion, and a big pinch of salt, and boil them for 20 minutes. To get more substance into the broth, scoop out the shells and grind them up, in batches, in the food processor, then return the grindings to the broth. In a separate saucepan cook 2 tablespoons butter and 2 tablespoons flour together, stirring, until golden. Stir in 4 cups strained crayfish broth, pushing through the strainer as much of the solids as possible. Cook about 20 minutes, until fairly thick and intense in flavor. Add about ¼ cup heavy cream per serving, season with salt as necessary and a dash of Tabasco, and serve with chopped parsley on top and a whole crayfish or two floating in the soup.
SERVES 4

Albert's Hot Crabmeat Lorenzo

"This can be an appetizer or a light luncheon entrée served with a tossed green salad," Albert Stockli told us when, as chef-proprietor of Stonehenge, in Ridgefield, Connecticut, he shared this recipe with us.

One 7¾-ounce can crabmeat
1 egg yolk
1 teaspoon prepared mustard
2 tablespoons mayonnaise
1 teaspoon chili sauce
1 teaspoon grated horseradish
1 tablespoon softened butter

½ garlic clove, minced
½ cup grated Parmesan cheese
½ teaspoon pepper, preferably white
Pinch of cayenne
4 slices white bread, toasted

Drain the crabmeat and reserve 2½ tablespoons of the liquid. Pick out any shells, and flake the crabmeat. Mix together the reserved liquid, egg yolk, mustard, mayonnaise, chili sauce, horseradish, butter, garlic, cheese, pepper, and cayenne until well blended. Stir in the crabmeat. Spread even amounts of this mixture on the toasted bread slices, place on a baking sheet, and bake in a preheated 400-degree oven for 10 minutes, or until lightly browned.

SERVES 4

Frogs' Legs Marinated and Grilled

"Frogs herald the end of maple sugaring," Gale Lawrence wrote in *The Beginning Naturalist*. In summer, hundreds of leopard frogs can be seen in New England fields or crossing roads. They are considered as much of a delicacy among wild foods as freshwater crayfish; and frogs' legs are also flash-frozen and sold in small packages in supermarkets in many Yankee communities. These aren't the ones known by country folk as "swamp pigeons," but they make a fine beginning course or a hot nibble with drinks around a barbecue grill.

8 frogs' legs
3 tablespoons lemon juice
1 tablespoon olive oil

Salt
Freshly ground pepper

GARNISHES: *lettuce leaves, lemon slices, and black olives*

Run cold water over the frogs' legs, and dry well. Mix the lemon juice with the oil and a little salt and freshly ground pepper. Put the frogs' legs in a flat-bottomed dish, and pour the marinade over them, rubbing it well, then set aside for an hour or more. When the coals on the grill are glowing without flame, put the frogs' legs in a folding wire grill, and place over the heat, turning frequently, for 10–12 minutes, until they are evenly cooked.

(This process may be adapted to an indoor broiler.) Put the frog's legs on plates with lettuce leaves, lemon slices, and black olives.
SERVES 4–6

---

8 small plum tomatoes
½ cup heavy cream
2 shallots, chopped
4 ounces smoked mussels

1 tablespoon chopped chives
Freshly ground pepper
2 tablespoons fresh bread crumbs

Baked Plum Tomatoes Stuffed with Smoked Mussels

Cut the tops off the tomatoes and hollow out the centers. Set them upside down on paper towels to drain. Put the cream in a small saucepan with the shallots and boil until reduced by more than half and quite thick. If the smoked mussels are canned, drain them on paper towels. Cut them in half if large, and add them to the reduced cream. Season with chives and a little pepper. Spoon equal amounts of this filling into the tomatoes, then place the tomatoes upright in a small, shallow casserole that has been rubbed with a little olive oil, and sprinkle the bread crumbs on top. Bake in a preheated 350-degree oven for 20 minutes.
SERVES 4

Morels, found in mid- to late May, are perhaps the most sought-after of the wild mushrooms for their rich woodsy flavor. They can, of course, be simply sautéed, but since they are so precious it is fun to treat them royally, as in this recipe.

2 slices white bread, crusts removed
1 egg
2 ounces raw salmon
¼ cup heavy cream
Salt
Freshly ground pepper

A few gratings of nutmeg
1 sprig parsley, or 2 tablespoons
    chopped
About 12 good-size morels
1 tablespoon softened butter

Morels Stuffed with Salmon Mousse

Put the slices of bread in the bowl of a food processor or blender and spin until you have soft crumbs. Add the egg, raw salmon, cream, a pinch of salt and a couple of turns of the pepper mill, the nutmeg and parsley, and spin until you have a smooth paste. Or put the bread and the salmon through the fine blade of a meat grinder, then mix in the other ingredients and beat until smooth. Slosh the morels in a bowl of lightly salted cold water, then shake and pat dry. Trim off any tough areas at the end of the stems. Now, using either a pastry bag or a demitasse spoon, pipe the salmon mixture through the stems and into the hollows of the morels. Liberally butter a casserole just large enough to hold the stuffed mushrooms—upright if you like—in one layer. Bake in a preheated 375-degree oven for 25 minutes.

SERVES 4 AS AN APPETIZER; 3 AS A LUNCH COURSE

Stuffed Mushrooms

12 good-size mushrooms
3 tablespoons olive oil
5 scallions, including tender greens, chopped fine
¼ cup fresh bread crumbs
¼ cup finely chopped watercress leaves

1 teaspoon chopped fresh rosemary, or ½ teaspoon dried, crumbled
Salt
Freshly ground pepper
3 tablespoons grated Parmesan or aged cheddar

Remove the stems from the mushroom caps. Rub the outside of the caps with 2 tablespoons oil. Trim off any dark or hard spots from the stems and discard. Chop the stems, then mix them with the scallions, bread crumbs, chopped watercress and rosemary, and salt and pepper to taste. Fill the caps generously with this mixture, drizzle the remaining 1 tablespoon olive oil over the top, and sprinkle cheese over them. Set in a shallow baking dish and bake in a preheated 400-degree oven for 20 minutes, until browned on top and just tender.

SERVES 4

VARIATION: Use the Jerusalem artichoke filling on page 16. You will need at least twice the amount to fill 12 mushroom caps.

Sardine-Stuffed Mushrooms

Among recipes collected in the Maine coastal area are numerous interesting ones in which the region's sardines are a dominant accent.

12 large mushrooms
4 tablespoons olive oil and/or vegetable oil or butter
1 garlic clove, peeled
3–4 scallions, including tender greens, chopped

2 cans Maine sardines, mashed
⅓–½ cup fresh bread crumbs
Fresh lemon juice
Freshly ground pepper
1 tablespoon chopped fresh basil

Wipe the mushroom caps with a damp cloth and remove the stems. Heat half the oil and/or butter in a large skillet with the garlic clove, then add the mushroom caps, round tops down, and cook over moderate heat for about 3 minutes. Turn the caps, cover the pan, and cook 2 minutes more. Remove the caps, discarding the garlic. Meanwhile, chop the mushroom stems. Heat the remaining oil or butter, add the chopped stems and scallions, and cook 1 minute. Remove from the heat and stir in the sardines, bread crumbs, and a light sprinkling of lemon juice and pepper. Taste and correct the seasoning if necessary (salt should not be needed). With a teaspoon, stuff the sardine filling into the hollows of the mushroom caps, pressing it down lightly and mounding it up in the center. Chill in the refrigerator. Sprinkle the chopped basil on top and serve with sliced tomatoes or peeled red peppers as an hors d'oeuvre.

SERVES 4

Snails in Mushroom Caps

There's a time-honored way of cooking snails with finely minced salt pork, but such a delicacy was uncommon except at the great hotels of nineteenth-century Boston. It's only since young chefs have begun to have their way with New England ingredients that diners-out find snails among the hors d'oeuvre. This combination turns up now and then in upper Connecticut Valley restaurants. You could use local conch instead of snails.

24 large mushrooms
2 tablespoons butter
1–2 tablespoons vegetable oil

Salt
Freshly ground pepper

FOR THE SNAILS:
24 medium to large snails
8 tablespoons (1 stick) butter, softened
4 garlic cloves, chopped fine

5–6 scallions, chopped fine
¾ cup chopped parsley
2 tablespoons chopped fresh basil
1 tablespoon applejack or Cognac

Remove the stems from the mushrooms carefully (save stems for another use). Heat the butter and oil and sauté the mushroom caps, turning to cook outside and in, for about 5 minutes. Sprinkle the caps lightly with salt and a turn or two of the pepper grinder. Put a snail in each mushroom. Mix the 8 tablespoons butter with the garlic, scallions, parsley, basil, and applejack, and sprinkle lightly with salt and pepper. Top each snail with an equal amount of the garlic butter, pushing it down into the mushroom. Put 6 stuffed mushrooms on each of 4 ovenproof serving dishes and put them in a preheated 350-degree oven for about 15 minutes. Bring them sizzling to the table as a first course.

SERVES 4

Artichoke Bottoms Stuffed with Puréed Jerusalem Artichokes

Though both bear the name artichoke, the Jerusalem artichoke is a root vegetable native to America that grows so abundantly in the Northeast that when you plant it, it's wise to do so far from your garden, or it will take over. The globe artichoke is another species that needs more months of sun than New England provides, but one finds it readily in supermarkets. Both vegetables do have an unusual and delicious affinity, we discovered when we stuffed some scooped-out artichoke bottoms with Jerusalem artichoke purée. (Incidentally, one can often pick up California artichokes that look a bit browned, maybe even a little moldy on the outside, but when you pare down to the interior, the heart will still be untainted.)

4 good-size artichokes
1 lemon
3–4 Jerusalem artichokes (about ¼ pound)
2 tablespoons butter
2 tablespoons cottage cheese or moist farmer cheese

2 tablespoons lightly beaten egg
Salt
Freshly ground pepper
1 tablespoon grated Parmesan

Pull all the leaves off the artichokes and trim the stem level with the base. As you work, rub all the cut surfaces with lemon. Slice the remaining leaves off down to the choke, then pare all around the base until you get down to the light-green flesh. Steam the artichoke bottoms for about 20 minutes until just tender. Scrape out the thistle or choke.

While the bottoms are steaming, peel the Jerusalem artichokes and cut them into thin slices. Drop them immediately into lightly salted boiling water into which you have squeezed about 1 teaspoon fresh lemon juice. Boil until tender. Drain and purée through a vegetable mill or in a food processor. Blend in the butter, cottage or farmer cheese, egg, and salt and pepper to taste. Fill the artichoke bottoms with equal amounts of this mixture, sprinkle a little Parmesan on top of each, and bake in a preheated 400-degree oven for 20 minutes.
SERVES 4

Swiss Chard Leaves Stuffed with Lamb

12 large Swiss chard leaves

STUFFING:
2 tablespoons olive or vegetable oil
1 medium onion, chopped
2 garlic cloves, chopped
1 cup cooked, finely minced or ground lamb
½ cup cooked barley
Salt to taste

Freshly ground pepper to taste
1 teaspoon chopped fresh rosemary, or ½ teaspoon dried, crumbled
6–8 mint leaves, chopped, or ½ teaspoon dried, crumbled
¼ teaspoon cinnamon

BRAISING LIQUID: *½ cup leftover lamb gravy, thinned with water or lamb marinade, or, lacking either, ½ cup canned tomatoes with their juice*

Cook the chard leaves in boiling water for 30 seconds, drain, and spread them out to dry on paper towels. Heat the oil in a skillet and sauté the onion gently until translucent, adding the garlic the last minute of cooking. Mix together with the remaining stuffing ingredients.

Snip the stems off the chard leaves and remove a little of the rib if the leaf seems tough and unyielding. Place a heaping teaspoon of the stuffing mixture in the center of each leaf, roll it up, tucking the ends in as you do so, and place in a shallow baking dish, seam sides down. Pour the braising liquid around, drape foil over the top, and then cover the pan. Bake in a preheated 350-degree oven for about 15 minutes, until just heated through (longer cooking will turn the chard leaves black). Serve hot with a little braising liquid poured over, or cold with a drizzling of olive oil and a slice of lemon on top.

SERVES 4

Stuffed Squash Blossoms in Beer Batter

In picking summer squash blossoms for stuffing, look for male blossoms—the ones without fruit developing on the stem. You want to use these because it would be wasteful to pick the female blossoms, which are going to produce squash.

2 ounces (about ¼ cup) Portuguese
  sausage (lingüiça or chouriço) or
  country ham
2 minced shallots or scallion bulbs
1 teaspoon vegetable oil
1 cup fresh bread crumbs
2 tablespoons chopped parsley

Salt
Freshly ground pepper
1 egg, lightly beaten
About 16–20 male squash
  blossoms
1 recipe for beer batter (page 141)
Frying oil

GARNISH: *lemon wedges*

Sauté the sausage and shallots or scallions with the oil in a small skillet for 1 minute, then mix with the bread crumbs, parsley, and salt and pepper to taste. Stir in the egg to bind the mixture. Spoon a little of the stuffing into each blossom. Leave enough room to fold the tips of the petals over one another. Then heat enough oil in a skillet or frying kettle to cover the bottom by 1 inch. When hot enough so that a bread crumb dropped into the oil quickly sizzles and browns, drag each stuffed petal gently through the beer batter, and drop them into the frying pan. Don't crowd. When the bottoms are browned, turn and brown the other side. Remove and drain on paper towels and keep warm. Serve with lemon wedges.

SERVES 4

With a Grain of Salt—or Less

Salt was important in the Yankee past—widely used as a preservative, it was, therefore, considered at least as desirable a flavoring by cooks in New England as anywhere else in the world.

The common winter diet of previous generations was often based on weekly menus in which New England boiled dinner prepared with corned (salt) beef might be followed the next day by a salt fish dinner, Cape Cod turkey (salt cod) on the next, Boston baked beans flavored with salt pork, finnan haddie newburg, macaroni-haddie casserole, barbecued oysters, codfish balls, corned beef hash—salt ad infinitum.

No longer. Salt in a measured teaspoon contains 5 grams of sodium (pure salt). Independent medical research groups recommend a daily intake of 3 to 8 grams a day—an amount supplied in a varied, well-balanced diet, according to Jane Brody, "even if you eat no obviously salty foods and add no salt in cooking or at the table." The recommended daily minimum amount of sodium is a natural component in ordinary untreated foods that make up your usual diet.

The trouble is that typical Americans, including those without the excuse of New Englanders' seaboard heritage, consume two to three times the recommended amounts. Much of this consumption is unconscious, because food manufacturers add salt liberally to all kinds of products, even to sweet breakfast cereals. Sodium occurs in a variety of common ingredients—bicarbonate of soda, monosodium glutamate (MSG), soy sauce, and in numerous preservatives; it is found in most cheeses, in beef and chicken bouillion cubes, in yeast extract, and, of course, in such things as bacon, ham, sausage of all kinds, and smoked fish. A large percentage of salt consumed—more than three-quarters—comes from processed, highly refined foods, which makes it difficult for some, whose lives have been oversalted, to cut down precipitously.

As a vital shift toward the new New England cookery, recipes in this book make light of salt. Amounts of salt are minimal; in many cases we suggest that salt be sprinkled *lightly,* or that you add salt to taste, leaving it to your palate and informed discretion to depend less and less on the risky liberal use of salt to "heighten flavor." Try to avoid overuse of processed food—we have called for fresh ingredients almost everywhere and wherever possible. In our own kitchen, we use unsalted butter and polyunsaturated oils and/or pure olive oil. Many vegetables (particularly root vegetables), we believe, have so much natural flavor that they need no added salt. Herbs and well-chosen spices often replace the need for any salt or for the use of salty bottled condiments.

Country cooks know how good cooked milkweed can be in its many variations. Found in open fields and along backroads, pendulant clusters of milkweed flowers turn lavender, pink, and brown in midsummer, and in late summer the green seed pods are evident on the tall, large-leaved stalks. The pods are ready to eat when they feel plump and are a light, slightly grayish green in color.

Stuffed Milkweed Pods

STUFFING:
1/4 cup minced country ham
1/4 cup minced mushrooms
1/2 cup fresh bread crumbs
1 egg, lightly beaten
2 tablespoons minced parsley
About 12 fresh sage leaves,
   chopped, or 1 teaspoon dried,
   crumbled

Salt
Freshly ground pepper
About 24 fresh plump milkweed
   pods

Mix all the stuffing ingredients together, being careful to season only lightly with salt because of the ham; taste to make sure. Slit the milkweed pods lengthwise and remove the seeds and pithy interior. Fill the pods with the stuffing, using just enough so that the openings you have cut will stay closed. Place on a steamer tray and steam for about 7 minutes, until just tender.
SERVES 6

VARIATION: Dip the stuffed milkweed pods into beer batter (page 141), and fry as you would squash blossoms (page 171). Squash blossoms are also good stuffed with the above filling, and it's nice occasionally to serve some pods and squash blossoms together, either steamed or fried.

These fritters are particularly good with chopped fresh tomatoes, seasoned with scallions and a little hot pepper.

Goat Cheese Fritters

1 cup fresh goat cheese
1/2 cup fresh bread crumbs
2 tablespoons chives
1–2 tablespoons other fresh herb,
   such as tarragon, marjoram,
   basil, or one-half dried herb and
   1 tablespoon chopped fresh
   parsley

1 egg yolk
1 egg, lightly beaten
About 3/4 cup flour
Oil for frying

Mix the goat cheese with the bread crumbs, herbs, and egg yolk. Form into about 10–12 balls, then roll each first in the beaten egg, then in flour. Heat

1 inch of oil in a skillet to frying heat (about 360 degrees), and slide the cheese balls into the hot oil. Fry about 30 seconds on each side, until browned, drain on paper towels, and serve immediately.

SERVES 6

Eggplant Slices Broiled with Ham and Cheese

1 eggplant (about 1 pound), cut into ½-inch slices
Salt, preferably kosher
Olive oil
Very thin slices country ham (enough to cover the eggplant slices)

¼-inch slices mild melting cheese, such as Monterey Jack or mozzarella (enough to cover the eggplant slices)
Cayenne

Sprinkle both sides of the eggplant slices with salt, and place on a rack or in a colander to sweat for about 30 minutes. Pat the eggplant thoroughly dry by slapping each piece between paper towels. Arrange the slices on a broiler rack or cookie sheet, brush with olive oil, and place about 9 inches below a hot broiler. When lightly browned on the top—in about 10 minutes—turn the slices, brush the other side with oil, and broil another 5 minutes. Now cover the eggplant with thin slices of ham and top with cheese slices, and return to the broiler until the cheese has melted and is bubbly. Sprinkle a little cayenne on top of each piece.

SERVES 4

Eggplant and/or Zucchini Rolls Filled with Herbed Cheese

These are good made with both thin eggplant and zucchini slices, or use one or the other. You'll need a very large zucchini—a good use for one of those giants that seem to spring up overnight in the garden. The appetizer may be served hot with tomato sauce or tepid with cold salsa.

1 medium eggplant
½ very large zucchini
Olive oil
Salt
About ¾ pound fresh mozzarella, sliced, or goat cheese or a combination

4–5 tablespoons chopped fresh herbs, such as parsley and chives with chervil, or basil with marjoram and thyme
Freshly ground pepper to taste
1 cup Homemade Tomato Sauce (page 630) or Salsa (page 634)

Trim off the root and rounded head of the eggplant, then stand it on one end. Slice off just enough skin and flesh from either side to make a flat surface, then cut lengthwise into ⅛-inch slices. Do the same with the fatter half of the zucchini; you want to make thin slices of about the same dimension. Rub both sides of the slices with olive oil, salt lightly, and place on a baking sheet. Broil 4 inches from the source of heat until just soft but not brown, then turn and broil on the other side to soften. Lift the slices up carefully and place a slice of mozzarella and/or a spoonful of goat cheese on one end, sprinkle with the herbs, season with pepper, and roll up. To serve hot (and it is best in this case to use the mozzarella), place the rolls in a baking dish, drizzle spoonfuls of tomato sauce over, and put in a preheated 450-degree oven until bubbling. To serve at room temperature (better for the goat cheese filling), arrange on individual plates with a few spoonfuls of salsa on the side.

SERVES 6

Chicken Liver Pâté

We have neighbors who bring us the chicken livers when they slaughter a batch of chickens to freeze for the winter. They just don't care for them, but maybe if they knew how to make this simple pâté, they might not be so generous.

1 pound chicken livers
4 tablespoons butter
3 tablespoons minced shallots or
*   scallion bulbs or spring onions*
3 tablespoons brandy or dry sherry
1/3 cup heavy cream

Salt
Freshly ground pepper
About 3 tablespoons chopped fresh
*   herbs, such as chives, tarragon,*
*   chervil, or sage*

Trim the chicken livers, removing any greenish spots, connective tissue, and fat. Cut each liver into quarters. Heat the butter in a skillet, add the livers and shallots, and cook rapidly over medium-high heat, tossing, for about 5 minutes, or until the livers have exuded their blood but are still rosy inside. Pour the brandy or sherry into the pan and cook quickly a few seconds to burn off the alcohol. Put the mixture into a food processor or blender and purée, adding the heavy cream. Season to taste with salt and pepper. Pack the purée into a lightly oiled bowl and chill. Unmold and sprinkle the herbs all over the top.

Note: We find that the pâté keeps better if you do not mix the fresh herbs into it; however, if you are planning to eat it all right away, fold the herbs in before chilling and add additional sprigs on top for garnish. Serve with melba toast or hot crusty French bread.

SERVES 10–12

Puréed Broccoli First Course

We find this a surprisingly springlike appetizer to serve in fall or winter.

3 cups broccoli florets (use stems
  for stir-fries, see page 310)
6 slices lean bacon

4 anchovy fillets
2 tablespoons heavy cream
Freshly ground pepper

Cook the broccoli florets in 1 inch of boiling water, uncovered. Meanwhile, cut the bacon in thin crosswise strips, and fry until crisp, then drain on paper towels. Drain the broccoli but don't press out the water, and put the florets in a food processor with the anchovy fillets. Spin until puréed, adding the cream. Season liberally with pepper. Put the purée in 4 small dishes, and make a hollow with a spoon in each serving. Divide the bacon, putting some of the strips in each hollow, and serve immediately.

SERVES 4

Curried Crab Pâté

During Provincetown summers, the late cooking-school teacher Michael Field often served this on buttered toast as an accompaniment to drinks.

½ pound fresh or frozen crabmeat
½ cup chopped onion
½ cup heavy cream
⅓ cup softened butter
1 teaspoon curry powder

¼ teaspoon salt
¼ teaspoon white pepper
1 teaspoon fresh lemon juice
½ teaspoon Tabasco sauce

Shred the crabmeat, making sure it is free of any hard pieces. Put it in a food processor with the chopped onion and some of the cream. Spin the blade for about 1 minute, then scrape the mixture from the sides of the container, add the remaining cream, and blend the mixture until it is smoothly puréed. Add the butter and the curry powder and blend for about 10 seconds, then sprinkle in the salt and pepper with the lemon juice and Tabasco and continue blending the mixture for about 10 seconds more. Turn the curried crabmeat into a 2-cup rectangular container and pack it down lightly. Chill for about 3 hours, until it is firm. When you're ready to serve, place the container in hot water just long enough to loosen the bottom and sides, and invert the pâté onto a serving dish.

SERVES 4–6

Potato Chips and Company

Serving drinks to guests is a friendly act that, often as not, seems to call for crunchy accompaniments of which potato chips have been the most popular for a century. Tons of the best commercial chips are made by a Maine family, or in a small factory on Cape Cod. Some of us proud New Englanders, however, make our own from potatoes that have been produced in Aroostook County and other parts of the region since the first Irish "invasion" during the eighteenth century. In addition—and a marvelous stretch of the possibilities—crisp, paper-thin chips can be made with Jerusalem artichokes, celery root, or even parsnips. A mandolin slicer, designed especially to ensure thin, even slices, will persuade you there's *nothing* like homemade party chips to serve with drinks, whether they be soft or hard. Even better, potato chips fresh from the stove make a wonderful surprise when served as a dinner accompaniment.

> *3 large potatoes*
> *Frying oil or lard*
> *Salt*

Peel the potatoes and cut them into paper-thin slices (if you have a mandolin slicer, it will do a fast, even job; otherwise use a vegetable peeler). Drop the slices immediately into a bowl of cold water and refrigerate for 2 hours. Heat slowly a good 2 inches of oil or lard in a frying kettle. Drain the potato slices and pat them thoroughly dry. When the oil reaches 325–330 degrees, scatter a handful of potato slices into the oil (don't crowd the pan; you want to have just one layer of chips at a time floating on the top of the fat). Stir the chips around with a slotted spoon, let the heat of the oil come up to about 350 degrees, and as soon as they turn golden remove them to paper towels to drain; they shouldn't take more than a minute and a half to cook and you don't want them to turn brown. Repeat with the remaining slices. When all are done, sprinkle salt over them and serve in a napkin-lined basket.
SERVES 6–8

VARIATIONS: Prepare Jerusalem artichoke, celery root, or parsnip chips in the same way (you need soak them only about 30 minutes), and the oil should be 350 degrees when you drop these vegetable chips into it. Go easy on the salt because such root vegetables have a natural saltiness.

Smoked Bluefish Pâté

Bluefish have challenged Yankee anglers for so long, that going after them has been described as the oldest sport on Martha's Vineyard. John Hersey has written a fine book on the subject, called *Blues*, and the actress Jane Alexander is co-author of a recipe collection exclusively devoted to bluefish. Here is a "new" recipe to use for a party.

2 teaspoons finely chopped onion
½ pound skinned and boned
  smoked bluefish, flaked
½ pound unsalted butter at room
  temperature
5 ounces cream cheese at room
  temperature

2 teaspoons anchovy paste
2½ teaspoons brandy
½ teaspoon Worcestershire sauce
Juice of ½ lemon

Blend with a fork or in a food processor the onion and the bluefish with the butter, cream cheese, anchovy paste, brandy, Worcestershire, and lemon juice. When entirely smooth and well mixed, put the pâté in a serving bowl and chill. Remove from the refrigerator 10 minutes before serving. Serve with melba toast or unflavored crackers.
SERVES 8–10

Chilled Cod in Horseradish Cream

No White House occupant seems safe from recipe hunters. It's been reported that John F. Kennedy's family made this dish a favorite of the Hyannis summer colony, and since then the recipe has traveled through Cape Cod and most of the six New England states.

4 cod fillets (about 2 pounds)
4 tablespoons prepared
  horseradish, drained
2 cups sour cream
½ cup chopped scallions, including
  tender greens
1 teaspoon cider or white wine
  vinegar

3 tablespoons chopped fresh dill, or
  2 teaspoons dried
Salt
Freshly ground pepper
4 lettuce leaves

GARNISHES: 2 hard-boiled eggs, quartered
           2 tomatoes, peeled and quartered

Wipe the fillets with a damp cloth. Steam the fish in a covered pan for about 8 minutes, until it flakes when touched with a fork. Cool. Meanwhile, mix the horseradish with the sour cream, adding the scallions, vinegar, dill, a light sprinkling of salt, and a few turns of the pepper grinder. Blend the mixture well, and spread half of it to cover the bottom of a large shallow

dish big enough to hold the fillets snugly. Arrange the cooled fillets in a single layer on top of the horseradish mixture. Spread them with the remaining horseradish mixture, cover, and chill for at least 1 hour. Place a lettuce leaf on each of 4 plates, and fill it with 1 fillet and some of the horseradish cream. Garnish with eggs and tomatoes.
SERVES 4

Crabbing is an amateur sport for some families with easy access to Vineyard Sound, but if fresh crabmeat isn't at hand, this dish can be made with any kind you buy. It can be served as a light appetizer or spooned into avocado halves for a lunch dish.

Martha's Vineyard Crab and Avocado Appetizer

1 pound crabmeat
4 canned water chestnuts, drained and sliced

1 hard-boiled egg, chopped
¾ cup Green Mayonnaise (page 347), made with basil

GARNISHES: *tomato and cucumber slices*
sprigs watercress (optional)
avocado halves (optional)

Mix the crabmeat, water chestnuts, and chopped egg lightly with a fork. Mix some of the mayonnaise into the crabmeat mixture, reserving enough to top each serving. Arrange tomato and cucumber slices on plates, spooning the crabmeat mixture into the center. Garnish with watercress and, if you like, spoon into avocado halves for a more substantial dish.
SERVES 6 AS AN HORS D'OEUVRE; 4 AS A LUNCH DISH

A splendid first course, as prepared in the Madison, Connecticut, home of Jacques and Gloria Pepin.

Gloria Pepin's Roasted Pepper Hors d'Oeuvre

2–3 green or red peppers
3–4 garlic cloves, minced
About ½ cup olive oil

Salt
Freshly ground pepper

Spear a pepper with a long-handled fork and carefully hold over a high flame, turning to blacken the skin all over. This can also be done under a broiler. As soon as they are black, immediately pop the peppers into a paper bag and twist the top to close it securely. Leave about 5 minutes (the steaming in the bag will help loosen the skin). Remove and pull off the blackened skin. Cut open the peppers and remove the seeds and ribs. Cut the pepper into strips about ¼ inch wide, then put them in a bowl with the minced garlic. Pour in the oil, season well with salt and pepper, and set aside to chill for several hours. Remove from the refrigerator about a half hour before dinner.

SERVES 4

Mozzarella and Tomato Salad with Nasturtium Flowers

This is a handsome first-course salad of Italian origin, inspired by the good fresh mozzarella that is being made around New England today. Nasturtiums are in flower when tomatoes are ripe, and the two complement each other on the plate. (They're edible, too—see box opposite.)

2 large, very ripe tomatoes
½ pound fresh mozzarella
½ cup coarsely chopped fresh basil

Freshly ground pepper
½ cup Vinaigrette (page 346)
4–8 nasturtium flowers

Slice the tomatoes ¼-inch thick, using a very sharp knife. Slice the cheese to make neat pieces of equal size. Arrange both on 4 salad plates, alternating and slightly overlapping slices of tomatoes and cheese, then sprinkle the basil over all. Season with freshly ground pepper, and spoon the vinaigrette over each salad. Let stand about 15 minutes at room temperature. Just before serving, arrange 1 or 2 flowers on each plate.

SERVES 4

Cold Bean Salad with Red and Yellow Peppers

This colorful midsummer salad, which makes the most of different kinds of snap beans and peppers as they ripen in your garden or as you find them in farmers' markets, is best served as a first course, where it warrants full attention.

About ¾ pound green beans
About ¾ pound purple or yellow beans
3 scallions, including tender greens, sliced thin
3 tablespoons chopped parsley
3 tablespoons chopped fresh summer savory and/or tarragon, or ½ teaspoon dried (use both kinds of fresh herbs if you have them)

¾ cup Vinaigrette (page 346)
1 medium sweet red pepper, charred and skinned (page 25), cut into strips
1 medium sweet yellow pepper, ribs and seeds removed, cut into strips

GARNISHES: *lettuce leaves, 1 dozen blanched sugar snap or snow peas, tomato wedges, small black olives*

Choose beans of approximately the same size—not too large—snap off the stem ends, and leave them whole. Cook them together in a large pot of boiling salted water until just tender, about 5 minutes, but taste them to make sure; they should be tender but still have some snap to them. Drain and separate the two kinds. Marinate each kind of bean for 10 minutes in a separate bowl with ¼ cup of the vinaigrette and half the fresh herbs (if you have two kinds of fresh herbs, use a different one for each kind of bean). Marinate the two kinds of pepper strips in the remaining vinaigrette. To assemble: arrange lettuce leaves around a large platter. Arrange the beans in mounds at either end. Place the pepper strips on top and around the edge, along with the other garnishes.

SERVES 6

Please Learn to Eat the Daisies

Much too young to know of the Broadway hit warning all and sundry to refrain from nibbling on daisies, a young Vermont waitress smilingly encouraged the diners she served the other night to eat the brilliant flowers that brightened their plates. At long last, there's a return to the old understanding of Yankee cooks that food can be enhanced by both the color and taste of garden blossoms.

Puritan contemporaries of Charles Lamb, the essayist, often had marigolds floating in their soup, and fried squash blossoms have been more or less common for generations. So have marigolds (called by Dorothy Hartley "the most useful cookery plant") and nasturtiums, both often mixed in salads. The spiky, spheroid blossoms of chives owe much to Shaker kitchens, where the subtle and colorful Blue Flower Omelet was created.

For apprehensive eaters, it is good to realize that no restaurateur worthy of the title puts anything inedible in his servings; and it's also good to remember to wash the nasturtium, or rose, or other petals you use—and don't use those that have been sprayed with insecticides.

One cook, lucky enough to live in the country, writes, "We put marigold petals into beef stews, scatter them into glazed vegetables, put them into cheese sauce and use them to decorate both cooked dishes and salads." Sliced tomatoes can be enhanced by nasturtium flowers filled with cream cheese, and there are numerous culinary uses for elderflowers, rose hips, borage, day lilies, white roquette blossoms, violets, or scented geranium leaves.

Scallops and Roasted Red Pepper Salad

2 tablespoons freshly squeezed lemon juice

6–7 tablespoons olive oil or combination of vegetable and olive oils

1/4 cup chopped fresh herbs, such as parsley, chives, tarragon, or chervil

4 scallions, including tender greens, sliced thin

Salt

Freshly ground pepper

3 cups lightly cooked scallops*

1 large sweet red pepper, roasted, skin removed (page 25), and cut into strips

1/2 small semi-hot green pepper, seeds removed, sliced thin (optional, or use less to taste)

About 24 sugar snap peas, strings removed, cooked 1 minute, drained, and cut on the diagonal into thirds

3 teaspoons capers

GARNISHES: *black olives, quartered tomatoes, and/or slices of avocado, nasturtium flowers, lettuce leaves*

* See page 137 for flavorful way of cooking large sea scallops (perhaps when you make that recipe, you may want to plan for leftovers for this salad). Otherwise, sauté raw scallops lightly in a little butter in a large pan, tossing—2 minutes for small scallops, 4 minutes for large.

Mix the lemon juice, oil, herbs, scallions, and a little salt and pepper together. Pour over the scallops and peppers in a bowl, mix well, and let sit about 10 minutes, tossing occasionally. Fold in the peas, scatter the capers on top, and arrange on a platter or on separate plates. Garnish attractively as desired.

SERVES 4 AS AN APPETIZER; 3 AS A LIGHT MAIN COURSE

Sardines with State o' Maine Sauce

Down East cooks rallied to help Maine celebrate 150 years of statehood in 1970, and this appetizer was among the harvest of ideas emphasizing such Maine products as canned sardines.

4 large canned sardines

4 slices tomato

4 slices lemon

4 slices dill pickle

2 cloves garlic, chopped very fine

1 tablespoon finely chopped onion

1 tablespoon finely chopped green pepper

1 tablespoon mustard seed

1 teaspoon grated horseradish

1 tablespoon water

2 tablespoons olive oil

Salt

Freshly ground pepper

1/2 teaspoon celery salt

1/4 teaspoon paprika

1/4 teaspoon cayenne

Drain the sardines and arrange them on a serving dish with the tomato, lemon slices, and pickle. In a bowl, blend the garlic with the onion and green pepper, whipping in the mustard, horseradish, water, and oil. Sprinkle lightly with salt and pepper, and stir in the celery salt, paprika and cayenne. Mix this dressing thoroughly, and pour it carefully over the sardines and the tomato slices.

SERVES 4

Mussel Salad

5 scallions, including tender greens, chopped
½ green pepper, chopped
1 small cucumber, peeled, split, seeds removed, chopped

parsley, chives, dill, chervil, or tarragon
½ cup Vinaigrette (page 346)

GARNISHES: *lettuce leaves, tomato wedges, quartered hard-boiled eggs, or a few blanched sugar snap peas or radishes*

Mix all the solid ingredients together with all but 2 tablespoons of the vinaigrette, and let marinate a couple of hours before serving. Arrange on a platter or on separate plates on a bed of lettuce, garnish as you wish, and drizzle the remaining vinaigrette over.

SERVES 6 AS AN APPETIZER; 4 AS A LIGHT MAIN COURSE

Sardines of Port Clyde

We remember a literary light of the 1930s, who had a fine wine cellar, all right, but the real passion of his connoisseur heart was sardines. He treasured his sardine *cave's* canned goods in the same way he did his wines—by the year of maturity and the provenance of fishing grounds. The memory surfaced with the announcement in 1983 that Port Clyde sardines had tied with an entry from France in a tasting competition.

Tasters gathered in a Manhattan restaurant and sampled fifteen brands from Canada, Norway, Portugal, Yugoslavia, and other countries, but only the sardines of Port Clyde, Maine (packed in Eastport, Rockland, and Stonington) were considered equals of the French brand, Rodel, which cost ten times as much as Port Clyde's in the retail market.

Reporting the competition, James Villas described sardines as a "neglected food that is highly nutritious, blessedly inexpensive, and delectable to eat, simply by itself or incorporated into numerous dishes. Ounce for ounce," Villas summed up, "sardines provide more calcium and phosphorous than milk, more protein than steak, more potassium than bananas, and more iron than cooked spinach."

Sardine Appetizer

4 ounces canned Maine sardines
4 ounces cream cheese
2 tablespoons chopped onion
2 tablespoons finely chopped green
  pepper

½ teaspoon Dijon mustard
(optional)

Mash the sardines with the cream cheese in a mixing bowl. Add the onion, green pepper, and mustard, and stir until thoroughly blended. Turn out in an attractive bowl, and serve the mixture with wheat crackers.
SERVES 4–6

Hot Artichoke Dip

Carole Evans—a Greek-American who has taught Dover, New Hampshire, children history through cooking—sometimes serves this recipe when she gets together with fellow members of a food-loving group who share interesting dinner parties regularly. This recipe serves a generous number for a party, but leftovers can be frozen and reheated.

One 15½-ounce can artichoke
  hearts
½ cup mayonnaise
8 ounces softened cream cheese

4 ounces shredded mozzarella
1 cup freshly grated Parmesan
1 small garlic clove, minced fine

Drain the artichoke hearts and chop them fine, then mix them with the mayonnaise, the three cheeses, and the garlic. When the ingredients are thoroughly blended, turn the mixture into a lightly buttered 10-inch pie plate or a shallow casserole. Bake in a preheated 350-degree oven for 15 minutes, or until hot and bubbly. During the baking, stir the mixture once after 7 or 8 minutes. Serve hot with crackers or toasted triangles of pita bread.
SERVES 25

Humus

2 cups cooked chick-peas
¼ cup tahini
¼ cup water
Juice of 2 lemons (about ¼ cup)
2 fat garlic cloves, minced

Salt
Freshly ground pepper
2 tablespoons pine nuts, toasted
Parsley sprigs

Mash the chick-peas or purée in a blender (if using canned chick-peas, rinse them off before puréeing). Blend the tahini paste with the water and lemon juice until smooth, then mix into the chick-peas along with the garlic.

Season with salt and pepper to taste. Serve on salad plates in a circle about ¼ inch deep, and sprinkle pine nuts on top, garnishing with parsley sprigs. Or serve as a dip with crisp raw vegetables and squares of Syrian bread.
SERVES 8

Ralph Ray's Lebanese Eggplant Appetizer

All over New England there are Middle Eastern families whose cooking style is much appreciated by their neighbors. This delicious appetizer, known as *baba ghanough*, and humus (see opposite) are both made with tahini or sesame paste that can be readily found in specialty food shops, come from Washington County, Maine.

1 medium eggplant
Salt
Freshly ground pepper
1 tablespoon tahini
2 tablespoons water
Juice of 1 lemon

2 garlic cloves, minced
2 tablespoons olive oil
2 tablespoons pine nuts, toasted*
Parsley sprigs
Syrian pita or pocket bread
Celery ribs (optional)

* Found in specialty food shops.

Pierce the eggplant with a fork in two or three places. Trim away the stem end. Broil the eggplant, turning repeatedly to char it evenly. When soft inside, peel off the skin. The pulp should be a dull yellowish-green and of pudding consistency. Remove any discolored seeds, and mash the pulp in a mixing bowl, preferably with a wooden pestle. Season lightly with salt and pepper. Mix the tahini paste with the water, and add the lemon juice and minced garlic. Stir this mixture into the mashed eggplant. Serve in small amounts on salad plates, topping each serving with a drizzling of olive oil and a scattering of pine nuts. Garnish with parsley sprigs and pieces of Syrian bread. Or make a mound, topped with parsley sprigs and surrounded by bread and celery ribs trimmed into sticks to serve with drinks.
SERVES 8

Ham and Cheese Spread

1 cup finely chopped smoked ham
8 ounces cream cheese
¼ cup finely chopped onion

¼ cup finely chopped green pepper
Freshly ground pepper

Mix all the ingredients in a bowl, adding pepper to taste (you won't need salt). Serve with celery sticks or crackers, or spread on top of thin slices of rye or pumpernickel bread.
SERVES 4

Bedeviled Ham Spread

Yankee colonists, frugal as they were, made use of scraps of food in ways their descendants often adapted—witness this version of the British potted ham, sometimes better known in Puritan precincts as deviled ham.

1½ cups ham trimmings
1 hard-boiled egg
1 tablespoon soya mayonnaise*

1½ tablespoons plain yogurt
1 teaspoon mild prepared mustard
Freshly ground pepper

* Mayonnaise made with soya oil, either commercial or homemade. Regular mayonnaise may be substituted.

If possible, use sugar-cured cob-smoked ham. Put all the ingredients in the container of a food processor (if ham pieces are somewhat large, cut them up). Process until you have a very smooth, finely textured paste. Keep covered in the refrigerator.

MAKES ABOUT 2 CUPS

Yogurt-Mushroom Stem Spread

2 tablespoons safflower oil
4 ounces mushroom stems, finely chopped
4 scallions, including some of the tender greens, finely chopped
1 small garlic clove, finely chopped

2 tablespoons grated cheddar
½ cup plain yogurt
2 tablespoons finely chopped parsley
½ teaspoon ground mace

Heat the oil in a skillet, add the mushrooms, scallions, and garlic, and cook until they are soft, stirring frequently. In a mixing bowl, combine the vegetables with the cheese and add the yogurt, parsley, and mace, stirring thoroughly. This is especially good on sesame cocktail crackers.

MAKES 1½ CUPS

Millie Owen's Nasturtium and Radish Spread

"If you've never tasted nasturtiums," Millie Owen wrote in her book *Cooking with Herbs, Greens, and Aromatics,* "nibble one of the young leaves. They taste like mild pepper and are a bit salty at the same time—something like watercress and similarly high in vitamin C. . . . The best part of nasturtiums, the little tender leaves, can be used in sandwiches or chopped fine to add to salad dressings or to scatter over food as a pepper substitute."

1 bunch or handful small red radishes
1 tablespoon finely chopped nasturtium leaves

1 teaspoon lemon juice
8 ounces goat cheese, cream or yogurt cheese, at room temperature

Wash the radishes well, removing the tops and the tail-like roots. Slice several of the radishes very thin, and set them aside to use as a garnish. Coarsely grate the remaining radishes. Quickly blend the grated radishes and the chopped nasturtium leaves with the lemon juice, and mash them into the cheese with a fork, mixing thoroughly. Spread this mixture on thin slices of pumpernickel or other dark bread. Serve as a canapé, topped with whole nasturtium leaves.

MAKES ABOUT 1 CUP

Yogurt

Although more than 90 percent of yogurt in the American diet is consumed either on the North Atlantic or Pacific coasts as of the 1980s, it was virtually unknown in the United States until Dr. James Empringham published *Intestinal Gardening for the Prolongation of Youth* in 1926. The first commercial yogurt was produced only five years later by the Columbosian family in Andover, Massachusetts. Selling first as a health food, a mass market wasn't found until a manufacturer added strawberry preserves. Between 1955 and 1980, consumption increased by a factor of 35, and plain yogurt's worthiness as a substitute for sour cream was noted by James Beard in the 1960s.

Yogurt can be made so easily at home that if you use it frequently, it is well worth your while to make it yourself so that it is always on hand. You will notice that we call for it often in recipes, in an effort to make for lighter cooking.

To make yogurt: Heat 1 quart of milk to the boiling point. Cool to 110 degrees (you should be able to plunge your finger into it and hold it there comfortably while you count to 10). Beat about ½ cup of the warm milk with 2 tablespoons yogurt (your "starter") until very smooth, then pour this into the remaining milk and mix well. Pour into a crockery bowl or individual cups, cover with plastic wrap, and set in an oven with a pilot light; or wrap the bowl in a blanket and set it over a pilot light on top of the range or on a radiator (the ideal temperature should be about 110 degrees). Leave for 8 hours to set, then refrigerate.

For a nonfat yogurt, use skim milk, and when you beat in the yogurt starter, beat in ⅓ cup nonfat dry milk for enrichment.

To make yogurt cheese: Put 1 quart of yogurt—more or less depending on how much cheese you want to make—into a strainer lined with a double layer of cheesecloth and set over a bowl. Let the yogurt drain for 8 hours. Discard the whey (or use it as a liquid when making bread) and refrigerate the cheese, wrapped in its cheesecloth, until ready to use. It will keep fresh up to 10 days. Serve lightly salted as is or mixed with chopped scallions and/or chives and chopped fresh herbs. Yogurt cheese is delicious as an appetizer or in salads; it may also be used instead of cream in dips, cheesecakes, etc.

Common Crackers

Vermont common crackers became abundant again in the 1980s when Vrest Orton, the first entrepreneur (he would have eschewed that word) to revive the typical Yankee country store of the nineteenth century, bought the C. H. Cross machinery and moved it to Rockingham, in the Williams River Valley, to produce the all-American biscuit called common crackers.

Generations back, they were known as "Montpelier biscuits," because many people believed they had to be made with water piped out of hill springs around the Vermont capitol. Creamy white in color, with layers "thin and crackly as old parchment," they were puffed out with Green Mountain air. They are used in many traditional recipes calling for crackers, but they are at their best when split in the traditional way—with thumbs and fingers—buttered and toasted under the broiler, particularly with a topping of Yankee cheddar cheese, which turns sizzling and golden and almost too hot to eat without the accompaniment of hard cider or a more contemporary imbibement.

Cheddar Sesame Appetizers

Among New England cheeesemakers, "Uncle Abe" and "Aunt Debbie" Manchester of Adamsville, Rhode Island, produced cheddar of such quality that day-long carriage drives from Newport, Providence, and New Bedford were de rigueur among socialites in the nineteenth century. Decades later, Adamsville's golden cheddar was served at the White House by Mrs. John F. Kennedy, whose wedding took place in Newport.

1 cup flour
¼ teaspoon dry mustard
Cayenne
⅓ cup cold butter

1½ cups grated sharp cheddar
2 tablespoons water
1 tablespoon sesame seeds

Sift the flour, mustard, and a generous sprinkling of cayenne into a bowl, and cut in the butter and ½ cup of the cheese, as you would for biscuits or pie dough. When the mixture resembles the texture of fresh bread crumbs, drizzle in the water, a little at a time, mixing with a fork. Gather the mixture up and form into a flat cake. Sprinkle a working surface with flour, and roll the dough out into a long rectagular shape ⅛ inch thick. Sprinkle the surface of the dough with ½ cup cheese, then fold the dough over and roll out again into a rectangle not quite as thin. Sprinkle the remaining ½ cup cheese on top. Cut the dough into strips ½–¾ inch wide and 2–3 inches long, and sprinkle them evenly with sesame seeds. Arrange the strips slightly apart on an ungreased baking sheet and bake in a preheated 350-degree oven for 12–15 minutes.

MAKES ABOUT 4 DOZEN

Cheese Wafers

Among the traditional Yankee cheeses produced in the six New England states are fine cheddars from Cabot, Shelburne, and Grafton, Vermont, and from Barrington, New Hampshire—any of which can enrich wafers to nibble with drinks.

½ cup butter at room temperature
8 ounces aged cheddar, grated
1 cup flour

½ teaspoon dry mustard
½ teaspoon paprika
¼ teaspoon Worcestershire sauce

Using a food processor, an electric beater, or a large wooden spoon, beat the butter until it is light and airy. Add the cheese and continue beating until the mixture is thoroughly blended. Stir in the flour, mustard, paprika, and Worcestershire, and beat slowly to make a thick, thoroughly blended batter. Spread this on a floured surface and form into 3 or 4 long rolls about 1¼ inches in diameter. Wrap the rolls in wax paper and place in the refrigerator for several hours or overnight. To bake, preheat the oven to 475 degrees. Cut the rolls into slices ⅛ inch thick. Arrange slices in rows on cookie sheets, and bake 7–8 minutes, until lightly golden.

MAKES ABOUT 6 DOZEN

Smoked Corn Snacks

½ pound kielbasa or other smoked
    sausage, sliced ¼ inch thick
2 cups white cornmeal
1 teaspoon salt

½ teaspoon baking soda
1 teaspoon baking powder
1¼ cups buttermilk
2 eggs, beaten

Arrange the thinly sliced sausage in even rows on the bottom of a 9-inch-square pan, and place in a preheated 450-degree oven. Toss together the cornmeal, salt, baking soda, and baking powder. Stir in the buttermilk and beaten eggs, and mix thoroughly with the cornmeal to make a lump-free batter. Remove the baking pan from the oven and turn over the sausage slices. Pour the batter on top, being careful to keep the slices in regular rows. Bake for about 20 minutes. Remove from the oven and let rest a few minutes, then cut into squares, with 1 slice of sausage in the center of each piece.

SERVES 8

SOUPS
and CHOWDERS

NEW ENGLAND soups, like those of other regions, reflect the current trends and idiosyncrasies as well as the local provender. The hearty soup called chowder seems to have derived its name from the French word *chaudière,* meaning cauldron. In the middle eighteenth century, French-speaking Channel Islanders from Guernsey and Jersey settled along Massachusetts's North Shore and soon were cooking seafood in iron pots filled with milk from their dairy cattle

Flavored with onions, salt pork, and root vegetables, Yankee chowders became the favorite New England soup. They remained pale and soothing, until some Rhode Islander—or was it an Italian in Boston or on Long Island Sound?—changed the color of clam chowder by adding tomatoes. On Martha's Vineyard they say it was John Pease of Edgartown who added potatoes to seafood brew, and when no fish was at hand there were intrepid cooks who made chowder with corn and little else.

It was on the Vineyard, as well as other stretches of Yankee coastline, that wives of Portuguese fishermen turned garden-fresh kale soup with potatoes and spicy sausage into an American dish. French cooks moved down from Quebec and helped transform *habitant* soup, thick with split peas, salt pork or ham bone, into a potage that hits the spot when skiers come in from the cold.

It's the recent New England summers (most of our neighbors think that northern Vermont is a lot hotter than it used to be in July and August) that have seen cool fruit soups become popular—the influence of Scandinavian Yankees is to be noted here. Think of liquid blueberries and cool melon soups. Thus, knowing New England in all kinds of weather as we do, the variety and popularity of its regional soups is easy to understand. Cold winters inspire sturdy mixtures, and even in midsummer there may be an occasional spot of chilly rain that cries out for bowls of broth and seasonal vegetables to chase away the blues. At his Blue Strawbery restaurant in Portsmouth, James Heller combined an onion, an apple, and a tomato with bouillon and wine to make a summer broth he serves either chilled or hot.

Someone has said that a woman who can't make soup shouldn't be allowed to marry. As unacceptable as that is in a time when both men and women are at home in the kitchen, it may be noted that good New England soups are often turned out by culinary whizzes who know how—as Beatrice Vaughan wrote in *Yankee Country Cooking*—to use "Every scrap of meat or vegetables, every bit of goodness from bones and leftover gravy. Nothing," she added, "is easier to make without great expense than good soup, and soups seem to lend themselves to variation and experiment—an ingredient casually added or omitted, more of this and less of that; and perhaps the result will be a subtle new combination to be repeated intentionally the next time."

VEGETABLE SOUPS

Onion-Patch Soup

English colonists didn't neglect the onion family when they chose seeds for their New World gardens, and they also found that Indian cooks gathered wild onions—in fact, in northern Vermont, the Abnakis gave the name Winooski (or onion) to the stream over which the state's bright gold capitol dome shines. A creative contemporary Boston cook, Don Balcom, gathered six varieties of onions when he developed the soup on which the following recipe is based.

3 tablespoons butter
1 red onion, thinly sliced
2 leeks, white part only, thinly sliced
2 silverskin onions, thinly sliced
2 shallots, sliced
2 garlic cloves, sliced
1 tablespoon chopped chives

2 scallions, including tender greens, chopped
1 quart chicken broth
½ teaspoon chopped fresh rosemary, or ⅛ teaspoon dried
1 teaspoon minced fresh dill
Salt
Freshly ground pepper

Heat the butter in a large heavy saucepan and stir in the red onion, leeks, silverskin onions, shallots, and garlic. Cook 2–3 minutes. Add the chives and scallions, and stir while cooking 1 minute more. Pour in the chicken broth, add the herbs, and bring to the boiling point. Taste, add salt if needed, and simmer a few minutes. Serve hot.
SERVES 4

Fort Fairfield, Maine, claims it produces more potatoes than any other town in the world, and its cooks have reason to be proud of their variations-on-potato themes.

Aroostook Potato and Fresh Pea Soup

2 medium potatoes, peeled and cut up
1 onion, sliced
2 cups boiling water
1 cup cooked fresh peas
1 teaspoon chopped fresh rosemary, or ½ teaspoon dried, crumbled

½ teaspon dried thyme
2 tablespoons butter
2 tablespoons flour
3 cups milk, heated
Salt
Freshly ground pepper
Finely chopped parsley and/or chives

Boil the potatoes and onions in the water for about 20 minutes, until both are soft. Add the peas and the rosemary and thyme. Pour a little of the soup at a time into a blender or food processor and spin until it is smoothly puréed. Melt the butter in the soup pan and stir in the flour. Blend carefully with the hot milk and cook, stirring, until lightly thickened. Stir in the puréed vegetables, add a sprinkling of salt to taste and several turns of the pepper grinder. Sprinkle with chopped parsley and/or chives.
SERVES 4–6

An old-fashioned soothing soup made with rich milk and fresh tomatoes. Smart cooks learned long ago that if you add a bit of baking soda, the tomatoes won't curdle in the milk.

Tomato Bisque

2½ cups milk or half-and-half or a combination
1 bay leaf
1 spring onion, sliced
About 6 celery leaves
¼ teaspoon baking soda
2 pounds ripe tomatoes, roughly chopped

¾ to 1 teaspoon sugar
¾ cup fresh bread crumbs or torn-apart crustless bread
Salt
2–3 tablespoons butter

Simmer the milk, bay leaf, onion, and celery leaves very gently for 10 minutes. Add the baking soda, tomatoes, ¾ teaspoon sugar, and bread crumbs and simmer, covered, for 15 minutes. Put the soup through a vegetable mill or strainer. Season with salt and a little more sugar, if necessary. Serve hot in warm bowls with a little butter floated on top.
SERVES 4

Essence of Pea Soup

The development of the sugar snap pea has been a joy to gardeners and cooks alike. Not only does one get the pleasure of eating the pea and the pod, but the cook doesn't have to do all the work of shelling peas. This is a thick, brilliant-green soup that tastes so sweetly of the essence of peas that it needs no seasoning. You can float some heavy cream on top, but why?

4 cups sugar snap peas, strings
   removed
2½ cups water

1 spring onion, slivered
Heavy cream (optional)

If some of the sugar snap peas are slightly over the hill, shell them and discard the slightly withered pod. Otherwise, simply cut them in half and toss them into the water with the slivered onion. Simmer until the pods are tender, about 15–20 minutes. Dump the contents of the pan into a food processor or blender and process for a few seconds (if you use a blender turn off and on quickly so you don't get too much of a baby-food purée; you want some texture). Reheat. No seasoning is necessary, but for those who wish it, float a spoonful of heavy cream on top of each serving.
SERVES 4

Cream of Mushroom Stem Soup

A fine soup to make when you have used mushroom caps for stuffing or some other purpose.

Stems from 1 pound of mushrooms
2 scallion bulbs
1 cup chicken broth
2 tablespoons butter
2 tablespoons flour
1 cup light cream or condensed
   milk or whole milk
Salt

Freshly ground pepper
2 teaspoons fresh thyme (with
   flowers if flowering), or 1
   teaspoon dried
About 1½ cups sour cream or plain
   yogurt, at room temperature
1–2 tablespoons chopped chives or
   parsley or a combination

Put the mushroom stems in a food processor. Cut the scallion bulbs in small pieces, and add to the mushroom stems. Spin until well ground, then add the chicken broth and spin about 30 seconds. Heat the butter in a 2-quart saucepan, and stir in the flour until the mixture is smooth. Cook gently 1 minute, then add a little of the liquified mushroom mixture, stirring well, and continue until all of it is incorporated. Stir in the cream or milk, and add salt and pepper to taste and the thyme. Simmer gently about 10 minutes. Just before serving, float a tablespoon of sour cream or yogurt on top of each serving, and sprinkle with chives and/or parsley.
SERVES 4

2 cups fresh string beans cut about
   1 inch long
1/3 cup coarsely chopped leeks
1 medium potato, peeled and diced
2 cups lamb or chicken broth

Salt
Freshly ground pepper
2 tablespoons chopped fresh
   savory, or 1 teaspoon dried
1/2 cup heavy cream

Creamy String Bean Soup

Put the vegetables in a saucepan and cover with broth; add a little water, if necessary, to cover. Season lightly with salt, a few turns of the pepper grinder, and the savory. Simmer for about 30 minutes, but do not overcook —the vegetables should still have texture. Add the cream and reheat just before serving.

SERVES 4

---

1 1/2 cups chopped onion
4 tablespoons vegetable oil
2 teaspoons finely chopped garlic
1–1 1/4 pounds eggplant, peeled and
   diced
1 large tomato, peeled and seeded
1 bay leaf

1 teaspoon chopped fresh
   rosemary, or 1/2 teaspoon dried,
   crumbled
4 tablespoons uncooked rice
4 cups chicken broth
1/2 cup plain yogurt

Eggplant-Tomato Soup

Cook the onions in the vegetable oil until they are translucent. Stir in the garlic and cook gently 1 minute. Add the eggplant and cook, stirring and tossing, until the eggplant is lightly browned. Add the bay leaf and the rosemary. Chop the tomato and stir into the eggplant with the raw rice and the broth. Bring the mixture to a boil and cook about 20 minutes; do not let the rice get mushy. Remove the bay leaf and turn the soup into a food processor or blender. When the soup is puréed, return it to the pot and reheat. Serve in bowls, topped with a spoonful of yogurt.

SERVES 4–6

Fiddler's Greens

Perhaps there is nothing that is both more "old Yankee" and "new New England" to the same degree as the wild greens of late spring that are known as fiddleheads, cinnamon fern and ostrich fern, and sometimes bracken.

In Maine, fiddlehead greens in general (before unfurling, the young tender fronds are shaped like the end of a violin) have been annually gathered in great quantities ever since the first settlers began to emulate the Indian cooks along the Tobique River. In Aroostook County, whole villages are known to join in fiddleheads hunts in May. Throughout the Northeast, the stately ferns grow along streams and other soggy places in woods and semi-shaded areas, and though they have been known as highly edible to rural Yankees for many generations, they've eluded the cookbooks, as well as restaurant menus, until recently.

But now supermarkets sell them fresh and frozen, and there are processors who put them up in cans for wide distribution. But we know that fiddleheads are best when they are as fresh as possible. Their flavor resembles a combination of asparagus, broccoli, and artichokes, and they are always good either cold with a vinaigrette dressing or warm on toast with hollandaise. But we have found a variety of other ways to use them—in soups, in stir-frys, with pasta, cooked with meats, chicken, and fish (check the index for recipes). We urge you to try them.

To prepare fiddleheads: Fiddleheads always need cleaning. There is a brown, dry leaflike covering that nestles into the coils, which must be rubbed off as you slosh them in cold water.

To cook fiddleheads: There is disagreement as to how long fiddleheads should be cooked. Some cooks like to steam them for only 2 to 3 minutes, but we find that leaves them crunchily undercooked and their flavor not fully developed. Sometimes recipes call for blanched fiddleheads, which means they are dropped into a large pot of boiling water for 1 minute, drained, and then cooked further along with other ingredients in the recipe. To fully cook fiddleheads, boil them in a good quantity of boiling water or cook them in a steamer for about 7 to 8 minutes (or to your taste).

To freeze fiddleheads: This is the best way to preserve them. Drain after the initial 1-minute blanching, and pack in freezer bags.

Fiddlehead-Spinach Soup

1 cup cooked fiddleheads (see opposite)
2/3 cup cooked chopped spinach
1 cup beef stock
1 cup water
3/4 cup plain yogurt
Salt
Freshly ground pepper

In a blender or food processor, spin the fiddleheads, spinach, and stock until smooth. Empty the mixture into a saucepan, then pour the water into the blender or processor to remove any clinging vegetables, and add to the saucepan. Heat to the boiling point, and blend in the yogurt. Taste, and add a little salt only if needed. Season with freshly ground pepper.
SERVES 4

Beet Soup

With sugar and raisins and yeast cakes, wily Yankees once made wine with garden beets. Borrowing a little from today's Russian and Polish influences, new New Englanders make a hearty soup of scrumptious color and very little fuss. A delicious first course.

1 quart strong poultry or meat broth or a combination
2 cups peeled, quartered, and thinly sliced beets
3–4 tablespoons sweet vermouth
4 slices lemon or lime

Put the stock in a large saucepan, add the sliced beets, and bring to a boil. Simmer for about 20 minutes, until the beets are tender but not soggy. Stir in the vermouth, reheat, and serve in bouillon cups with slices of lemon or lime.
SERVES 4

Radish-Top Soup

You've probably been throwing away radish tops for years, but you'll find them a surprising treasure in this good soup.

2 tablespoons butter
1 large onion, chopped
2 medium new potatoes, sliced thin
4 cups tender radish greens, washed and roughly chopped
4 cups chicken broth
Salt
Freshly ground pepper
About 1/3 cup heavy cream (optional)
4–6 good-size radishes, sliced thin

Melt the butter in a heavy saucepan, add the onion, and sauté about 5 minutes. Add the potatoes and radish greens and stir for about 30 seconds. Pour in the broth, bring to a boil, reduce heat, and simmer, partially cov-

ered, for 25–30 minutes, or until the vegetables are tender. Purée in a food processor or put through a food mill. Heat, season to taste with salt and pepper, and add cream, if you wish. Serve hot, and top each bowl with a scattering of thinly sliced radishes.
SERVES 6

Jerusalem Artichoke Soup

An old Yankee first course, sometimes known frivolously as "Palestine Soup," that has been brought up to date.

½ pound Jerusalem artichokes
1 small onion, sliced
2 tablespoons butter
2½ cups chicken stock

Salt
Freshly ground pepper
1 cup watercress
1 cup heavy cream

Scrub and peel the artichoke roots, and cut them in slices. Heat the butter in a saucepan and cook the vegetables for about 5 minutes. Add the stock, bring it to a boil, reduce heat, and simmer with the vegetables for 30–40 minutes. Let cool, then add a little salt and pepper to taste. Pour the mixture and the watercress into a food processor to purée. Add the cream and simmer for 15–30 minutes.
SERVES 4

Zucchini and Swiss Chard Soup

1 pound fresh young zucchini
½ pound Swiss chard leaves
½ cup chopped onions
2 tablespoons vegetable oil or
* butter*

1 cup cooked brown rice
5–6 cups chicken or beef broth
Salt
Freshly ground pepper
Freshly grated Parmesan

Wash, trim, and grate the zucchini. Wash the chard leaves, cutting away any tough ribs, and shred the leaves. Put the chopped onions and the oil in a large heavy soup pot and cook 4–5 minutes over gentle heat, stirring occasionally. Add the grated zucchini and shredded chard and cook about 5 minutes, then stir in the rice and the broth. Taste for seasoning, and add salt and pepper as necessary. Bring to a boil, then pour into a soup terrine or ladle it into individual warm bowls. Have grated cheese in a bowl to sprinkle on the soup as desired.
SERVES 6–8

Parsnip Soup

Vegetarian trends in New England have a way of reviving enthusiasm for dishes pushed to the back burner a couple of generations ago. This is an up-to-the-minute version—very light on fat—of an old favorite.

4 tablespoons butter
1 pound parsnips, peeled and sliced
1 garlic clove, minced
3–4 scallion bulbs, chopped
1 cup chopped celery, with some
    leaves
2 tablespoons flour

3 cups chicken broth
1–2 cups water
½ teaspoon ground coriander
Salt
Freshly ground pepper
¼ cup chopped parsley
2–3 scallion tops, chopped fine

In a heavy soup pot, melt the butter and cook the parsnips about 10 minutes, coating thoroughly with butter. Stir in the garlic, scallion bulbs, and celery, and cook about 5 minutes, covered. Stir in the flour, add the broth, a little at a time, and add water a little at a time, stirring continuously. Use a cup to ladle the parsnip mixture into a food processor or blender. Spin long enough to eliminate lumps. When all has been puréed, return the soup to the pot, adding the coriander and a little salt and pepper to taste, and reheat. Sprinkle each serving with parsley and scallion tops.
SERVES 4–6

Swiss Chard Soup

This is unusually good made with the red-stalked Swiss chard, sometimes known as rhubarb chard, because it gives tempting color to the soup.

2 cups water
2 cups beef, chicken, or vegetable
    broth
1 large potato, peeled and sliced
    thin
1 large onion, sliced thin
1 garlic clove, chopped
4–5 cups Swiss chard leaves,
    shredded, with tender stalks
    chopped

⅓ cup country ham chopped or cut
    in small strips
Salt (optional)
Freshly ground pepper
About 4 tablespoons grated
    Parmesan or other aged cheese

Bring the water and broth to a boil, add the potato, onion, and garlic, and cook, semi-covered, about 15 minutes. Add the chard and cook another 10 minutes. Stir in the ham and heat through. Taste to see if salt is needed, and add several turns of the pepper grinder. Serve with grated cheese sprinkled over the top of each bowl.
SERVES 4

Corn Chowder

In the old days, this recipe would call for diced salt pork to provide both fat and flavor. Of course, bacon may be used as well. But corn oil makes a lighter chowder. This can be made with cooked or blanched frozen corn and is good at any time of the year, but if you are making it at the height of the corn season, it is even better made with fresh kernels scraped from the cob, along with any accumulated juice.

1½ tablespoons corn oil
1 onion, coarsely chopped
1 Italian sweet red pepper, seeded and chopped
2 medium potatoes, peeled and diced
1 cup water
1 small bay leaf

1 teaspoon chopped fresh parsley
1 small sprig thyme
1½ cups cooked or blanched corn kernels or fresh kernels
2 cups milk, heated
1 cup heavy cream, heated
About ½ cup plain yogurt
Chopped chives

Heat the corn oil and cook the onion and pepper about 5 minutes. Add the potatoes and water, bring to a boil, cover the pan, reduce heat, and cook gently until the potatoes are tender. Stir in the herbs and add the corn and the hot milk and cream. Bring the chowder to the simmering point for a minute or so. If you are using blanched or fresh corn, cook a few minutes longer, until just tender. Serve very hot, adding a dollop of yogurt and a sprinkling of chives to each bowl.
SERVES 4–6

Mady's Vegetable Soup with Basil and Garlic

Mady Wolkenstein is a contemporary painter who finds time to cook special dinners at the Old Inn on the Green at New Marlboro, Massachusetts. Her sense of color is a match for her palate, and we found proof of this when dinner at the Berkshires inn began with the New England garden soup, accented by Mady's own *pistou* sauce (*pistou* is the French provençal version of *pesto*—the Italian mixture of mashed garlic and fresh basil with olive oil and pine nuts or walnuts that has become so popular in recent years as a sauce for pasta).

¾ cup cauliflower in ½-inch dice
¾ cup potatoes in ½-inch dice
¾ cup scraped carrots in ½-inch dice
¾ cup celery (strings removed) in ½-inch dice
¾ cup green beans in ¼-inch slices
¾ cup Belgian endive cut in 1 x ¼-inch strips

¾ cup leeks (washed and trimmed) cut in 1 x ¼-inch strips
¾ cup peeled, seeded, and chopped tomatoes
¾ cup summer squash in ½-inch dice
10 cups chicken stock (undersalted)

PISTOU:

10 garlic cloves, peeled
1½ cups tightly packed basil leaves
Extra-virgin olive oil

Salt
Freshly ground pepper
Freshly grated Parmesan cheese

Put all the cut-up vegetables in a large pot with the stock, bring to a boil, and cook until the potatoes are cooked through. To make the pistou, purée the garlic with the basil, adding the olive oil, a little at a time, until a consistency of loose paste is obtained. Season lightly with salt and pepper. Pour the soup into 8 warm bowls, and heap each with the *pistou*. Sprinkle liberally with grated cheese.

SERVES 8

8 ribs celery
2 tablespoons safflower oil
4 scallions
½ tablespoon flour
2 medium carrots, grated

4 cups chicken or beef stock, heated
1 cup cooked wild rice
½ cup plain yogurt
3 tablespoons grated cheddar

Celery, Carrot, and Wild Rice Soup

Trim the celery and chop fine. Heat the oil and stir in the celery, cooking, covered, for 5 minutes. Chop the scallions, including the tender greens, and stir into the celery and oil. Cook 1 minute, stir in the flour, and continue cooking 1 minute more, stirring. Add the grated carrots, whisk in the hot stock, and bring to a boil. Reduce heat and simmer about 20 minutes. Stir in the wild rice and bring the soup to a boil. Fold in the yogurt. Serve with grated cheese.

SERVES 4

Cooking with Herbs

New England Shakers have model communities at Sabbathday Lake, Maine, in New Hampshire, and in several places in Massachusetts. There they maintain the sect's reputation for nurturing scores of different kinds of herbs and encouraging other people to use them in cooking, as well as in medicinal ways. Today, more than ever, cooks seem to be heeding the Shaker message, growing their own fresh herbs and foraging for wild ones to enhance their cooking.

We urge you to grow some of the herbs that can be grown in a small plot near your kitchen or even on a sunny windowsill. In our own recipes those most commonly used are: parsley (the flat-leaved variety is the most flavorful, although the curly-leaved is more decorative); chives (they will come back every spring); tarragon (be sure you get the French tarragon plant and it, too, will serve you year after year); dill (plant it early—it grows abundantly); chervil; savory; rosemary (it won't survive a severe New England winter, so bring in the plant at the first frost); sage; sorrel; thyme; mint; basil; marjoram; and oregano.

With the exception of thyme and possibly rosemary and oregano, almost all herbs are more delicious when fresh. Obviously that's not possible year round, but at least you can preserve your herbs either by drying them, or by making herb butters (see box, page 219).

One learns to cook with herbs by tasting and making your own judgments about what goes best with what (see page 434). For instance, avoid mixing too many different herbs in one dish, because too many competing flavors cancel each other out.

Determining how much to use of a single herb is again a question of taste. There are no hard and fast rules, particularly because the flavor of any single herb is apt to be stronger as it deepens during the warm months of summer, and the conditions under which it was grown also have a lot to do with the intensity of flavor. Tarragon grown in northern New England is not going to have the same pungency as that nurtured under a Mediterranean sun, and there are some herbs, like basil, that simply don't make it in the Northeast Kingdom unless you pot them and baby them by bringing them in at night (even so, you'll never make a pesto that tastes like the Italian pesto).

In cooking any kind of herb, it is difficult to give absolute equivalents for the proportionate amount of dried herbs you should use when substituting them for fresh. So treat our suggested amounts only as guidelines, and always taste. Other herbs, like sorrel, keep so beautifully when frozen that they taste like summer all winter long. When putting it up, sometimes we mix in a little of the small-leaved wild sorrel that grows around us.

To prepare sorrel: Wash the leaves and pat or spin them dry. Pull the stems off large leaves, going up into the center of the leaf, and discard. For 1 pound of leaves, melt about 1½ tablespoons butter in a nonaluminum saucepan and cook the the sorrel gently, stirring, for 3–4 minutes. It will reduce considerably and turn into an olive-green purée.

To freeze sorrel: Spoon ½ or ¼ cup of the sorrel purée into plastic freezing pouches, seal, and freeze immediately.

CHEESE SOUPS

3 large onions, sliced thin
2 tablespoons butter
2 tablespoons flour
2 cups milk
2 cups chicken broth
½ teaspoon salt
½ teaspoon pepper
½ teaspoon mace
1 egg yolk, well beaten
1 cup grated cheddar
Chopped parsley

Onion-Cheese Soup

Sauté the onions in the butter until they are lightly browned. Stir in the flour so that it blends smoothly with the butter, then gradually add the milk, stirring until the mixture is smooth, then add the broth. Add the seasonings and simmer about 5 minutes. Take the pan from the heat and stir in the beaten egg yolk and the cheese. Heat the soup just to the simmering point, and sprinkle with the parsley.
SERVES 4

1 small cauliflower, trimmed and
  cut in small pieces
1 small onion, sliced
4–5 cups chicken stock (page 69),
  or canned
1 bay leaf
1 tablespoon butter
1 tablespoon flour
1 cup milk
¾ cup loosely packed grated
  cheddar
Salt
Freshly ground pepper

Cheese-flavored Cauliflower Soup

Cook the cauliflower and the onion in the stock for about 30 minutes, adding the bay leaf but no other seasoning. Remove the bay leaf and pour the cauliflower and its liquid, a little at a time, into a blender or food processor and spin long enough to purée. Heat the butter in the same saucepan and blend in the flour; cook gently a minute, stirring, then carefully stir in the milk until blended. Add the puréed cauliflower, heat the soup to a simmer, and blend in the cheese. Taste and add salt as necessary and a few turns of the pepper grinder.
SERVES 4

Northpack Cheese Soup

As Vermont is identified with cheddar-type cheeses produced in several Green Mountain villages, New Hampshire is proud of the tangy cheese made by Lowell and Edith Reinheimer at South Lyndeboro.

6 ounces Northpack cheese, grated (1½ cups)
½ cup heavy cream
2 eggs, well beaten

3 large slices stale caraway rye bread, crumbled
6 cups beef broth, heated
Chopped parsley

GARNISH: *caraway seeds*

Blend the grated cheese with the cream, and divide equally among 4 warmed soup dishes. Mix beaten eggs with the crumbled rye bread, and add to the hot broth. Bring to a boil and pour immediately over cheese mixture in soup dishes. Sprinkle with chopped parsley, and serve caraway seeds separately to be sprinkled over soup.
SERVES 4

Celery Soup Garnished with Smoked Cheese

In her vegetable book, our friend Jane Grigson says that her choice of the most delicious of celery soups is a Danish version in which "creamed blue cheese gives a savoury yet tactful richness to the light flavour of celery." With her inspiration, and the State of Maine Cheese Company as the source of one of the best smoked cheeses we've found, we contrived a variation that is a genuine New England first course.

1 head celery, chopped
2 medium onions, chopped
2 tablespoons butter
1 tablespoon flour
4 cups chicken stock

Freshly ground pepper
3–4 ounces Cumberland smoked cheese
Chopped celery leaves

In a covered pan, simmer the celery and onions in the butter for about 10 minutes. Stir in the flour and add the stock, a little at a time, stirring constantly. Season with freshly ground pepper, but add no salt until the end, if at all. (The saltiness of the cheese and the stock should be enough.) Cover the pan and simmer the soup about 30 minutes. Meanwhile, cut the cheese into a tiny dice. Just before serving, add the cheese to the soup over low heat and stir until it is melted. Sprinkle chopped celery leaves over each bowl.
SERVES 4

½ cup scraped and chopped carrots
½ cup chopped onion
½ cup seeded and chopped green
  pepper
¼ cup seeded and chopped sweet
  red pepper
½ cup chopped celery
4 tablespoons butter or vegetable
  oil or a combination
3 tablespoons flour

Salt
3 cups chicken stock
2 cups crumbled Vermont cheese or
  other cheddar
½ teaspoon Worcestershire sauce
Freshly grated pepper
1 teaspoon chervil
2 cups shredded cabbage
1 cup milk, scalded

Vermont Cheese Soup

Put the chopped vegetables in a large pot with the butter and/or oil and cook over low heat for 7 or 8 minutes, until the vegetables have begun to soften, but do not let them brown. Sprinkle in the flour and a little salt, and stir constantly for 2 minutes. Stir in the chicken stock, a little at a time, blending well with the cooked flour, until the mixture becomes thick. Cover and simmer about 4 minutes—the vegetables shouldn't lose their crunchiness. Stir in the cheese and seasonings, and cook just long enough for the cheese to blend with the liquid. Add the shredded cabbage, stir in the scalded milk, and cook for 1 minute over low heat. Don't let the cabbage become soggy.

SERVES 4

HOT or COLD SOUPS

2 tablespoons butter
1 large onion, chopped
3–4 cups chopped zucchini (about
  2 pounds)
2½ cups chicken broth

Salt
Freshly ground pepper
Heavy cream (optional)
½ teaspoon curry powder
  (optional)

Zucchini Soup

Melt the butter in a heavy saucepan and sauté the onion and zucchini gently, stirring occasionally, for about 5 minutes to bring out their flavors. Add the chicken broth and cook over medium heat, partially covered, for about 20 minutes, until the vegetables are soft. Put through a food mill or spin in a food processor to purée. Return the soup to the heat, season to taste with salt and pepper, and stir in a little heavy cream (about ½ cup) if you wish, although the soup is delicious just as is. To serve cold, chill the soup thoroughly, and stir in about ⅔ cup heavy cream and the curry powder.

SERVES **4**

Puréed Cream of Corn Soup

1½ cups chopped leeks, including a little of the tender greens
1½ cups chopped green peppers
3 tablespoons vegetable oil
8–10 good-size ears tender corn
Salt

Freshly ground pepper
About 1 cup milk
1 teaspoon curry powder
2 cups evaporated milk or heavy cream
4 teaspoons chopped fresh basil

Put the chopped leeks, green peppers, and vegetable oil in a skillet and sauté over medium heat for 4–5 minutes, stirring often. Use a sharp knife to slice off the kernels from the corncobs, and stir them into the skillet, continuing to cook the mixed vegetables 3–4 minutes longer. Do not let them burn. Sprinkle lightly with salt and pepper, stir in most of the milk, and scrape the mixture into the bowl of a food processor. Spin about 1 minute, then add the curry powder, evaporated milk or cream, and fresh basil. Continue to spin in spurts until puréed. If the soup seems too thick, add a little more milk. Reheat if serving hot. Or chill to serve cold.

SERVES **4**

A Garden Soup

3 cups chicken stock (page 69), or use canned
4 small boiled potatoes
½ cup lightly cooked green beans
1 small zucchini, chopped
2 stalks celery, chopped
2 tablespoons butter
1 tablespoon chopped fresh savory, or 1 teaspoon dried

Salt
Freshly ground pepper
1 cup cream, light or heavy, as preferred
2 tablespoons minced fresh tarragon

Put the stock in a blender or food processor and add the potatoes and beans. Spin until puréed. Braise the zucchini and celery in the butter for 5 minutes, then add to the food processor, spinning again until all the vegetables are puréed. Add the savory, and season very lightly with salt and pepper. Stir in the cream. Serve hot, or refrigerate until cold. In either case, sprinkle fresh tarragon on top after ladling out.

SERVES **4**

1 tablespoon vegetable oil
1 cup plus 2 tablespoons finely
   chopped green peppers
½ cup chopped onion
2 cups chicken broth
1 tablespoon chopped fresh
   summer savory, or ½ teaspoon
   dried

1 tablespoon butter
1 tablespoon flour
1 cup milk
Salt
Freshly ground pepper
1 cup whipped cream

Green Pepper Soup

Heat the oil and sauté 1 cup chopped green peppers and the onion until soft. Add the chicken broth and savory and simmer for about 20 minutes. Meanwhile, in a separate saucepan, heat the butter and stir in the flour. Cook gently for a minute, stirring, then off heat stir in the milk. Return to the heat and whisk until smooth and lightly thickened. Season with a little salt and pepper, and blend the cream sauce into the pepper-onion broth. You may purée the soup in a blender or food processor or serve as is. To serve hot, add a dollop of unsweetened whipped cream to each bowl and sprinkle on some of the remaining chopped pepper. To serve chilled, add the extra green pepper and fold in the whipped cream when the soup is cold.
SERVES 4–6

1½–2 pounds spinach
2 tablespoons vegetable oil
6 scallions, including tender greens,
   finely chopped
½ green pepper, seeded, trimmed,
   and cut into chunks
1 large potato, peeled and diced

4 cups chicken broth
Salt
Freshly ground pepper
1 tablespoon chopped fresh
   tarragon, or 1 teaspoon dried
½ cup plain yogurt or sour cream

Spinach Soup

Wash the spinach, trimming away any brown parts or very tough stems. Heat the oil in a large heavy saucepan and cook the scallions and green pepper until soft. Shake the spinach to remove excess moisture, and add it to the saucepan along with the potato. When the spinach is limp, add the broth and cook 20 minutes, seasoning with a little salt, a few grinds of the pepper mill, and the tarragon. Turn off the heat, and when the soup is cool, spin a few times in the food processor or blender, just enough to break up the spinach and potatoes without puréeing them. If the soup is to be served cold, refrigerate for several hours, then stir in the yogurt. If you want hot soup, reheat it, pour into warm soup bowls, and top each serving with a couple of spoonfuls of yogurt or sour cream.
SERVES 4

Fiddlehead Soup

2 fat leeks, cleaned and sliced, including about one-third of the tender green leaves
1 onion, sliced
2 medium-small potatoes, peeled and sliced

About 3 dozen fiddleheads, cleaned (see page 44)
6 cups water
Salt
Freshly ground pepper
½ cup heavy cream

GARNISH: 4 fiddleheads, cooked 6–7 minutes in water to cover

Put all of the vegetables in a pot, cover with the water, and bring to a boil. Skim off any scum that rises to the surface. Add a little salt and pepper, cover, and simmer about 40 minutes, until everything is very tender. Purée in a blender or food processor (the blender will make a smooth soup; the food processor a coarser-textured soup, which we prefer). Serve hot as is or with cream blended in at the last minute and brought to the simmer, garnishing each bowl with a fiddlehead. Or serve cold stirring in as much of the cream as desired.
SERVES 4–6

VARIATION: Substitute an extra onion for the leeks and a scraped carrot for one of the potatoes.

Sorrel Soup

Stalkers of wild edibles have long appreciated the delightful sourness of wild sorrel and more gardeners are now planting it, if only to have the treat of sorrel soup. It is one of the great pleasures of early spring. Years ago in Alstead Center, New Hampshire, where we rented our first Yankee house together, our benefactor was a wise woman who made us sorrel soup just before she departed her woodland premises. "That's just sour grass?" we said, hoping disdain didn't show up in the question. The word *sorrel* may derive from the Greek word for sour, but the small leaves are deliciously transformed into both soups and sauces (see index for other recipes). This soup can be made more simply like the Turnip Greens Soup on page 58, using only potatoes for a thickener and eliminating the eggs and cream, but this richer version is based on a classic French dish and shows sorrel off at its very best.

1 small potato, peeled and chopped
1 medium onion, sliced
3 cups chicken broth
3 egg yolks
½ cup heavy cream
2 cups sorrel leaves, stems removed, cut into strips

1 tablespoon butter
2 tablespoons water
Salt
Freshly ground pepper

Simmer the potato and onion in chicken broth until very tender, about 40 minutes; then purée in a food processor or blender. Return the purée to the heat. Beat the egg yolks with the cream, and add 1 cup of the hot soup to temper the egg yolks, then return the egg-cream mixture to the purée and keep under a simmer, stirring until thickened. In a small nonaluminum pot, cook the sorrel leaves in the butter and water for 1–2 minutes, stirring until they turn a grayish-khaki color, then stir them into the soup. Correct seasoning with salt, if necessary, add a little pepper, and heat through but don't boil. Serve in warm bowls. Or chill and serve cold.
SERVES 4

Spiced Cream of Broccoli Soup

2 cups fresh or cooked chopped broccoli
½ cup chopped onion
¾ cup chopped green peppers
3 tablespoons butter
¼ teaspoon mace
½ teaspoon grated fresh ginger
½ teaspoon turmeric
Freshly ground pepper
About 1 cup milk
½ cup plain yogurt

GARNISH: 2 teaspoons chopped scallions

Put the chopped vegetables in a heavy saucepan with the butter, cover the pan tightly, and steam the vegetables over low heat 10 minutes or more, until they are tender but still have texture. Process them in a food processor with the seasonings, thinning them with the milk to produce a smooth purée. Add the yogurt and spin until it is absorbed and the color of the soup is a fresh spring green. Serve hot or cold, with scallions sprinkled on top.
SERVES 4

Puréed Green Bean Soup with Curry

1 large onion, diced
1 pound green beans, trimmed and roughly cut up
3 cups light chicken broth or water or a combination
Salt
1 cup light cream
1 teaspoon curry
⅛ teaspoon freshly grated nutmeg

GARNISH: chopped chives and fresh summer savory

Cook the onions and beans in the broth and/or water with a good pinch of salt, until tender. Purée in a food processor or blender. Stir in the remaining ingredients, correct the seasoning, and reheat. Ladle into warm bowls and sprinkle the fresh herbs on top. Or serve cold, sprinkled with herbs.
SERVES 4

Turnip Greens Soup

2 medium onions, sliced
2 medium potatoes, peeled and
    sliced
About 7 cups water
About 16–20 tiny turnips
4 cups roughly chopped young
    turnip greens
Salt

Freshly ground pepper
½ teaspoon fresh thyme, or a pinch
    dried
2 tablespoons sweet butter
    (optional) (for hot soup)
2 teaspoons chopped chives
4 dollops sour cream (for cold
    soup)

Cook the onions and potatoes in a large pot in 6 cups of the water for about 20 minutes. Meanwhile, put the trimmed tiny whole turnips in a small pot with lightly salted water to cover and boil until tender, adding a small handful of the chopped turnip greens for the last 5 minutes of cooking. Add the remaining turnip greens to the onion-potato base, along with a little salt and pepper and the thyme, and cook for another 15 minutes, until everything is very tender. Purée the onion-potato-turnip-green base in a food processor or blender, or put through a food mill. Taste and correct the seasoning; if the soup seems thick, thin with a little of the water in which you cooked the whole turnips and swirl in the optional butter enrichment. To serve, ladle portions into warm soup bowls, garnish with tiny turnips and greens, and sprinkle chives on top. To serve cold, don't add butter; chill and serve with the same garnish plus a dollop of sour cream sprinkled with chives.

SERVES 4

Cranberry-Tomato Soup

2½ cups cooked tomatoes
2 cups jellied cranberry sauce

Sour cream
Grated lemon rind

Put the cooked tomatoes and cranberry sauce in a blender or food processor and spin until the tomatoes are puréed. Heat the mixture in a saucepan until it begins to simmer. Do not boil. Serve hot with dollops of sour cream and a sprinkling of grated lemon rind. Or chill in the refrigerator for several hours, and serve cold with a lemon slice in each bowl.

SERVES 4

At the Governor's Inn, near Okemo Mountain, we discovered Deedy Marble's Sweet Potato Vichyssoise, a stimulating combination of leeks and candied sweet potatoes, and we went home to adapt her recipe, using plain boiled sweet potatoes in a soup that is equally good served hot or cold.

3 tablespoons butter
3 large leeks, white part only, chopped
3–4 cups chicken stock
1 cup dry white wine or very dry hard cider

2 cooked sweet potatoes, peeled
1 small cooked white potato, peeled
Plain yogurt

Heat the butter and cook the chopped leeks very gently for about 5 minutes, until limp. Add the chicken stock and wine and simmer for 20–25 minutes. Chop both kinds of potatoes, and mash them into the soup, stirring with a whisk. Simmer for 5 minutes or more. Cool the soup, and purée it in a food processor or blender. Chill, and serve with a dollop of yogurt as a garnish. Or reheat and serve hot.
SERVES 4

COLD SOUPS

Many Armenians have been New Englanders for several generations, and they share family recipes, especially with cooks interested in "natural food." In his privately printed *Recipes from Armenia*, Tomas Azarian of Cabot, Vermont, tells us this is "a good soup during humid or 'dog days' when your body craves a light meal."

4 cups cold water
½ cup barley
2½ cups plain yogurt

Salt
Mint leaves

Bring the water to a boil, stir in the barley, and cook until soft. Set aside to cool. Beat the yogurt until smooth and stir it into the cooled barley. Season with a little salt and the mint leaves. Chill.
SERVES 2–4

Chicopee Chilled Beet Soup

Thousands gather each September in Chicopee, Massachusetts, to celebrate at the "World's Greatest Kielbasa Festival," staged by Yankees of Polish heritage. Here's one of the recipes frequently served.

1 cup chopped boiled kielbasa
2–3 cups plain yogurt
¾ cup heavy cream
1 cup beef stock
1 cup diced cooked beets
2½ cups beet juice
2 hard-boiled eggs, chopped

1 medium cucumber, peeled and diced
Juice ½ lemon
¼ teaspoon ground bay leaf
2 tablespoons chopped fresh dill
Salt
Freshly ground pepper

Put all the ingredients in a large mixing bowl. Stir well, then refrigerate 3 hours or more. Ladle into chilled soup bowls.
SERVES 4–6

Gazpacho

Gazpacho has become as ubiquitous a summer soup as jellied consommé once was, but the quality varies. Too often restaurants will gussy it up with tomato juice or V-8 so that the natural goodness of the fresh summer vegetables is lost. We condone the addition of a little sugar because New England tomatoes can never possess the bursting sweetness of those grown under a Mediterranean sun, so you aren't corrupting a flavor but simply making the Yankee counterpart more like the Spanish classic.

2½ pounds ripe tomatoes, peeled
1 medium cucumber, peeled
1 small-medium green pepper, seeds and ribs removed
1 small-medium sweet red pepper, seeds and ribs removed
1 large sweet onion
½–1 teaspoon hot red pepper sauce, or a few drops Tabasco sauce

1–2 teaspoons sugar
Ice cubes
Salt
2 scallions, including tender greens, chopped

Cut 1 of the tomatoes in half and squeeze out the seeds and juice, then cut into a small dice. Cut one-quarter of the cucumber and one-quarter of the green and red peppers into the same-size dice, and reserve all these as a garnish. Coarsely chop the remaining tomatoes, peppers, and sweet onion, and spin them in a food processor until they are reduced to pulp. Season with pepper sauce, sugar, and salt to taste. Chill. To serve, ladle into chilled soup bowls over a cube of ice. If the soup has thickened too much in the refrigerator (so that it's almost like applesauce), put 2–3 ice cubes into each

bowl. Mix the scallions with the other reserved diced vegetables and either sprinkle them on top of each serving or pass them in a separate bowl.
SERVES 4

Blueberry Soup

A handsome New England inn on a warm summer evening may be an ideal place to find such a rewarding recipe as Cynthia Giarraputo's lavender-blue blueberry soup.

1 quart cleaned fresh blueberries
½ cup maple syrup
Juice of 1 orange
¼ teaspoon cinammon
Lemon juice
1 quart half-and-half

Place the blueberries, maple syrup, orange juice, and cinnamon in a saucepan and bring to a boil. Remove and purée in a blender or food processor. Add lemon juice to taste. Chill, and stir in the half-and-half before serving.
SERVES 8

Cold Watermelon Soup

4 pounds juicy watermelon
½ cup Chablis
1 tablespoon lime juice
About ¼ cup chopped fresh mint

GARNISHES: lime slices and mint sprigs

Cut off the watermelon rind (you can use it for pickles). With a melon baller, cut out 8 balls of watermelon fruit and reserve them for the garnish. Remove all the seeds, cut the watermelon into rough chunks, and spin them in a food processor or blender. Add the wine, lime juice, and chopped mint and purée until smooth. Chill for several hours. Ladle into chilled bowls, and garnish with reserved melon balls, lime slices, and mint sprigs.
SERVES 4

Cold Cucumber and Yogurt Soup

2 medium cucumbers (about 2 pounds)
4 scallions
1 slice fresh ginger about the size of a quarter, peeled
1½ cups chicken broth
⅔ cup plain yogurt
Salt
Freshly ground pepper
2 tablespoons chopped fresh dill
2 tablespoons chopped fresh chives

Peel the cucumbers, split them lengthwise, scoop out the seeds, and cut them in rough pieces. Roughly cut the scallions, using some of the tender

Cold Cucumber and Yogurt Soup (continued)
greens, and roughly chop the ginger. Put the cucumbers, scallions, and ginger in a food processor or blender along with the chicken broth and yogurt, and spin until blended. Add salt and pepper to taste. Chill thoroughly, and serve sprinkled with dill and chives.

SERVES 4

Cold Salmon and Cucumber Soup

2 cups fish stock (page 69)
¾ cup chopped peeled cucumber
3 scallions, chopped
1 cup cooked or smoked salmon

2 tablespoons plain yogurt
Salt
Freshly ground pepper

Put all the ingredients in a food processor and reduce to a smooth liquid consistency, sprinkling in the seasoning a little at a time; you may need no salt at all if using smoked salmon. Chill the soup for several hours before serving.

SERVES 4

Chilled Clam and Scallop Soup

Boothbay Harbor's Annual Fisherman's Festival is just one of the ways New Englanders remind themselves of coastal gifts to the kitchen. In April on this Maine beach, the games include shrimp picking, clam shucking, scallop shucking, and lobster picking, and inspired cooks go home to put together new combinations of seafood, such as this soup for a warm day.

1 cup shucked bay scallops
Juice of 2 limes
1½ cups clam juice, chilled

1 cup half-and-half, chilled
About 2 teaspoons capers, drained

Cut the small scallops into coinlike pieces, then cover them with lime juice and chill overnight. When preparing the soup, rinse the scallop coins and drain them. Blend together the cold clam juice with the half-and-half, and pour it into a chilled serving bowl. Add the drained scallop pieces and the capers. Serve in chilled bowls.

SERVES 4

SUBSTANTIAL SOUPS

It seems fair enough that the state where Rhode Island Red chickens originated should also be one of those famous for chowder variations. And it's also satisfying that this version of chicken chowder can be augmented by corn kernels, which make it, more than ever, a meal in itself.

4 tablespoons corn or other
* vegetable oil*
1 onion, diced
2–3 celery ribs, peeled and diced
2–3 potatoes, peeled and diced
2 tablespoons chopped parsley
2 teaspoons chopped fresh savory,
* or 1 teaspoon dried (optional)*

2 tablespoons flour
1 cup milk or light cream
2 cups chicken broth
2 cups diced cooked chicken
Salt
Freshly ground pepper
1 cup fresh corn kernels or canned
* or frozen (optional)*

Heat the oil in a large pot and stir in the onion and celery, continuing to stir for about 5 minutes, before adding the potatoes. Cover and cook over low heat for about 10 minutes, and stir in the herbs. Mix the flour with the milk to make a thin paste, then add the milk and broth to the soup pot and bring to a boil. Simmer until the vegetables are tender but not mushy. Stir in the chicken and optional corn, and sprinkle lightly with salt and pepper to taste. Cook gently 5 minutes and serve very hot.
SERVES 4

Old-Fashioned Pawtucket Chicken Chowder (With or Without Corn)

Olive oil
6 cups chicken broth
4 tablespoons ham or Canadian
* bacon, cut into strips*

4 eggs, at room temperature
6–8 garlic cloves, chopped very fine
4 thick slices stale bread

GARNISH: *chopped parsley or watercress*

Put 1 teaspoon olive oil in each of 4 ovenproof bowls and leave them in a preheated 450-degree oven for about 5 minutes. Heat the chicken broth to the boiling point. In a small skillet, sauté the ham or Canadian bacon in a

Ham and Egg Soup

little oil, stirring, for about 3 minutes. Remove the bowls from the oven and place 1 piece of bread in each. Break 1 egg into each. Divide the garlic evenly among the bowls, and pour in 1½ cups simmering stock. Add the ham or bacon, and return the bowls to the oven for 2–3 minutes. The egg will cook in the stock. Serve bubbling hot, garnished with chopped parsley or watercress.

SERVES 4

Ham-Flavored Rutabaga Bisque

Rutabagas, yellow turnips, or Swedes, as they are sometimes called, are too often neglected, considering the possibilities that their good earthy taste offers.

½ pound rutabaga, peeled and shredded
1–1½ tablespoons butter
1 large onion, sliced

¼ pound country ham, chopped
4–6 cups chicken broth
2 teaspoons chopped fresh rosemary, or 1 teaspoon dried

Put the shredded rutabaga in a large saucepan with the butter, stirring until the butter melts. Stir in the onion and the chopped ham, mixing thoroughly with the rutabaga, and cook over low heat until the vegetables are soft. Pour in the broth, add the rosemary, and simmer for 10 minutes. Spin the soup in a food processor or blender in batches, if necessary, until it is smooth. Good country ham will probably make seasoning with salt unnecessary.

SERVES 4–6

The Maine Way Gamebird Soup

As the wife of a game warden in West Gardiner, Maine, Judy Marsh noted "the lack of a good, convenient cookbook" for families fond of wild food. As a result, she collaborated in compiling a collection of fish and game recipes, titled *The Maine Way* and published by the state Department of Inland Fisheries and Wild Life. Here we've adapted Mrs. Marsh's method of making soup from upland birds.

1 pheasant or grouse
1 woodcock
1 tablespoon butter
2 sprigs parsley
¼ teaspoon dried tarragon or thyme
2 bay leaves
6–8 peppercorns

2–3 stalks celery
2 onions, chopped
½ green pepper, chopped
2 cups chopped tomatoes
2 carrots, scraped and chunked
Salt
Chicken broth
Small noodles

Cut up the birds and brown them in the butter in a large pot, then remove. Put the herbs and vegetables in the pot and cook about 2 minutes, stirring. Return the meat to the pot, sprinkle lightly with salt, and add water to cover and the peppercorns. Cover the pot and simmer about 1 hour, until the meat is tender. Remove the bones from the birds, and add enough chicken broth to make 8 cups. Bring to a boil and add noodles. Cook about 8 minutes more, until the noodles are tender.

SERVES 6–8

Mr. Bean's Bean Soup

L. L. Bean of Freeport, Maine, was known to give friends a favorite recipe now and then. We have it on good authority that this is his camp-style method of brewing bean soup.

1 cup dried beans
Fresh water
2 medium potatoes, diced
1 medium onion, coarsely chopped

¼ pound salt pork or bacon, finely chopped
Salt
Pepper

Soak the beans overnight. Drain, pour into a soup kettle, and cover with the fresh water. Add the potatoes and onion. Fry the chopped salt pork until it crackles, and add to the pot. Sprinkle the soup lightly with salt and pepper to taste, bring to a boil, and let it bubble for 1 hour.

SERVES 4

Traditional Boston Bean Soup

"A bean," a Yankee philosopher once wrote, "is a serious culinary study. . . . Each bean is complete unto itself and should be treated like a voter in an election." New Englanders treasure dozens of kinds of beans with specific kinds bearing names that conjure up the past. The preference in this recipe is for Jacob's Cattle beans, but the soup may be made with pinto or red beans, or another variety (see box, page 447).

1 cup cooked Jacob's Cattle beans or other baking beans
1 cup chopped celery (in early spring substitute fiddlehead ferns)

1 cup chopped onion
1 medium tomato, chopped
3 cups beef broth
Salt
Freshly ground pepper

In a soup pot, simmer the beans, celery (or fiddleheads), onion, and tomato in a little of the broth, until tender. Pour the mixture into a food processor or blender and spin, adding more broth, a little at a time, until smooth. Reheat, and season to taste with salt and pepper.

SERVES 4

Yankee Habitant Pea Soup

Any French-American housewife with a recipe for *habitant* soup from Canada might insist that authentic flavor comes from salt pork (1–2 pounds fat-and-lean for 1 pound of peas). In Maine's French country, some cooks prefer the marrow from a ham bone, if they can get it. We find it suits our taste to use ham hocks, but more often than not we're glad to have the ham bone, with some meat still clinging; that is an extra reward for buying (and using in many ways) the country ham of a neighbor.

1 pound yellow or green split peas
8 cups water
1½ cups chopped onions
½ cup chopped celery
1 garlic clove, chopped (optional)
1 bay leaf
1 teaspoon dried savory, or more to taste

1 ham bone with meat, or ¼–½ pound salt pork, cut in pieces
1 cup chopped carrots
Salt
Freshly ground pepper

Rinse or pick over the peas, and then soak them overnight in water to cover. Drain them and cover with the cold water in a large pot. Add the onions, celery, garlic, bay leaf, savory, and the ham bone or salt pork. Bring the pot to a boil, reduce heat and simmer, covered, for 1 hour. Skim as necessary, and add the carrots. Continue simmering for about 45 minutes longer. Stir and add salt and pepper to taste. If necessary, cook the peas a little longer and add a little more water.
SERVES 6–8

Cod and Green Pepper Chowder

1½ pounds fresh cod fillets
4 potatoes, peeled and diced
½ cup diced green pepper
1 cup chopped onion
1 bay leaf
1½ teaspoons salt
Freshly ground pepper to taste
4 tablespoons butter

2 cups boiling water
3 cloves
1 large garlic clove, minced
¼ teaspoon dried dill weed
½ cup dry vermouth
1 cup heavy cream or milk
Chopped parsley

In a large casserole, place the pieces of fish, the potatoes, green peppers, and all the remaining ingredients except the cream and parsley. Cover and bake in a preheated 375-degree oven about 45 minutes. Meanwhile, let the cream come to room temperature while the chowder is cooking. Add the cream or milk to the chowder, and stir to break up the fish. Sprinkle with chopped parsley.
SERVES 4–6

On fall weekends in Groton Long Point, Connecticut, Gretchen Higgins has been apt to make this soup to feed hungry teenage sons—and it is *good*. She evolved it, as so many good things are invented, when she had some strong lobster stock on hand and several cooked vegetables, like a few ears of corn, new potatoes, and some rice.

Lobster-Vegetable Chowder

2 strips of bacon or salt pork
1 rib celery, chopped
1 medium onion, chopped
3–4 ears cooked corn, kernels
  scraped off
2 cups chicken stock
½ teaspoon dried savory
½ teaspoon dried thyme
2 tablespoons chopped flat-leaved
  parsley

4 small red potatoes, boiled and
  peeled
2 cups strong lobster stock (see
  page 80)
1 cup milk
¼ cup cooked rice
2 tablespoons butter

GARNISH: *unsweetened whipped cream (optional)*

Cut the bacon or salt pork into small pieces, and fry out the fat. Stir in the vegetables and cook 3–4 minutes, continuing to stir. Add the chicken stock and simmer about 15 minutes with the herbs. Cut the cooked potatoes into ½-inch dice, and add them to the chowder. Stir in the lobster stock and the milk, then add the rice. Return to the simmering point and swirl in the butter. Pour into warm bowls, and add a dollop of whipped cream to each serving, if desired.
SERVES 4

The first "American cookbook," published in Hartford in 1796, emphasized New England's interest in legumes by listing nine kinds of beans and seven dried-pea varieties. This is a recent variation on traditional bean soup.

Chick-pea Soup

2 cups dried chick-peas
1 ham bone
2 quarts water
1 onion, unpeeled
2 teaspoons chopped fresh savory,
  or 1 teaspoon dried

2 teaspoons chopped fresh
  tarragon, or ½ teaspoon dried
Salt
Freshly ground pepper
6–8 ounces small, dry smoked
  sausages, cut into coins

Put the chick-peas in a pot with the ham bone and cover with the water. Bring slowly to a boil, add the unpeeled onion, and simmer 3–4 hours. When the chick-peas have begun to soften, stir in the herbs, a sprinkling of salt, and several turns of the pepper grinder, and continue to simmer, adding a little more water if necessary, until the legumes are very tender. Remove about two-thirds of the chick-peas with a slotted spoon, put them in a blender or food processor along with a little of the broth, and spin until puréed. Return this purée to the soup. Add the sausage slices and heat through.

SERVES 4–6

Vegetable Stock

Peels from 4 large potatoes
1 medium onion, peeled and quartered
2 carrots, scraped and cut up
1 small stalk celery, coarsely chopped

1½ quarts water
1 garlic clove, chopped
Salt
Freshly ground pepper

Make the stock by putting the potato peelings, including about ¼ inch of potato pulp, in a large pot. Add all the vegetables and the water and simmer, covered, over low heat, for 1–2 hours, until the vegetables are very soft. Add salt and pepper to taste. Strain to produce a clear stock.

MAKES ABOUT 1 QUART

Parsnip Chowder with Green Pepper and Chicken

2 tablespoons vegetable oil
½ cup chopped onion
1 cup chopped green peppers
1 pound parsnips
½ pound potatoes

3 cups chicken broth
Salt
Freshly ground pepper
1 cup cream (optional)
1½–2 cups cubed cooked chicken

GARNISH: *chopped parsley*

Heat the oil in a saucepan and sauté the onion and green peppers over very low heat for about 5 minutes. Peel the parsnips and the potatoes, and cut them into small cubes. Add them to the onions and peppers, and pour the broth over them immediately. Salt lightly and season with a few turns of the pepper grinder. Bring the chowder to a boil, reduce the heat, and simmer gently for about 10 minutes, until the parsnips and the potatoes are just tender. Add the optional cream and the cubed chicken and return to the simmering point. Ladle into warm bowls, and sprinkle liberally with parsley.

SERVES 4–6

Broth or Stock

Most of us don't have an old wood- or coal-burning stove with a soup pot simmering at the back, ready to receive all those bones and scraps that make a nourishing broth. But that's no reason not to make our own stock, particularly when it's so easy today to put away bones and carcasses and leftover gravies in the freezer until there's enough to make a sufficiently rich broth. Not only is it economical to make your own, but it tastes so good compared to what you get in a can or from a cube.

There are no hard and fast rules about the proportion of bone and marrow to liquid. Taste is what counts, and if your broth is thin, you can always boil it down until it is flavorful. But here are a few guidelines.

Chicken broth or stock (we use the terms interchangeably): Cover 3 pounds chicken necks, backs, carcasses from cooked chicken, gizzards, and leftover gravy, if available, with about 2½ quarts of water. For seasoning, you could add 1 unpeeled onion, 1 small peeled carrot, 1 leek, and 1 sprig of parsley. Bring to a boil and skim off the scum that rises to the surface, then reduce the heat, partially cover the pot, and simmer for 2 hours or more. Add salt at the end—about 1 teaspoon per quart, or to taste, if you are serving as is; otherwise use less. Strain and chill. Remove the fat from the top before using. *Makes about 2 quarts*

Beef broth or stock: To have a rich stock, it is necessary to brown the bones and vegetables first. Put about 3–4 pounds beef marrow bones (shank is good) with 1 large onion, 1 large peeled carrot, 1 rib celery, and 1 leek, if available, all cut in rough chunks, into a large roasting pan and broil about 6 inches from the source of heat until well browned on all sides. Pour off the excess fat, turn the bones and vegetables into a large kettle, and cover with 4 quarts water (use a little of the water to wash out the pan, scraping up all browned bits). Add a bay leaf and a pinch of dried thyme, and use the above procedure for cooking, but simmer 3½ hours.

Fish stock: Cover 2–3 pounds of bones and heads of white-fleshed fish with 6 cups water and 2 cups dry white wine or vermouth (optional—you can use all water). Add 1 peeled onion, 2–3 sprigs parsley, 1 rib celery, and cook only 30 minutes, skimming as necessary.

For Vegetable Stock, see opposite; for Pork Stock, see page 234; and for lobster broth, page 80.

Note:
· It is wise to salt stocks at the end of cooking and to undersalt, in case you want to reduce them for a sauce.
· A little caramel will give a meat stock a deeper color.
· Stocks will keep 2–3 days in the refrigerator. If you want to keep them a few days longer, boil up the broth, cool it, and return it to the refrigerator. For longer storage, freeze in a covered container.

Parsnip, Potato, and Salt Pork Chowder

1/4 pound salt pork, diced
2 medium onions, chopped
2 medium potatoes, peeled and
  diced
2 cups peeled and diced parsnips
2 cups chicken stock
Freshly ground pepper

1 teaspoon chopped fresh savory,
  or 1/2 teaspoon dried
1/2 teaspoon dried thyme
3 cups milk
1/2 cup chopped green pepper
2 scallions, with some of the tender
  greens, chopped

Fry the salt pork in a large saucepan. Add the onions and sauté 3 or 4 minutes. Put in the potatoes and the parsnips and cover with the chicken stock. Bring to a boil and cook, covered, about 25 minutes, or until the vegetables are soft. Season with pepper, savory, and thyme, pour in the milk, bring to a boil, then add the chopped green pepper and scallions and cook gently 4 or 5 minutes.
SERVES 4

Meatless Black Bean Soup

Several regions take credit for the origin of black bean soup, but New England's claim is as old as coastwise sailing. Various cooks do various things, subtle and otherwise—one Mexican version is adorned with rosy shrimp. In simpler terms, Maria Parloa, who taught at the Boston Cooking School, called for cloves and allspice, cinnamon and turnips. Other Yankees are partial to the old-fashioned porridge in which enhancement comes from a vegetable stock, as it does in the much-admired staple on the menu of the Horn of the Moon restaurant in Montpelier.

2 cups black beans
1 1/2 quarts Vegetable Stock
  (page 68)
1 large onion, sliced
2–3 stalks celery, coarsely chopped
6 medium carrots, scraped and cut
  up
1 garlic clove

2 bay leaves
About 1 1/2 teaspoons salt
Freshly ground pepper
1/2 teaspoon ground mustard
4 tablespoons vegetable oil
1 tablespoon lemon or orange juice
1/4 cup sherry
1 lemon, sliced

Soak the beans in water to cover overnight. Drain, place in a large pot, and pour the vegetable stock over them. Add the onion, celery, carrots, garlic, and bay leaves, cooking until soft. Season with salt and pepper to taste, and stir in the mustard, oil, and lemon juice. (The Horn of the Moon suggests orange juice.) Just before serving, remove the bay leaves and stir in the sherry; place a slice of lemon in each dish.
SERVES 6

Lots of cooks have played around with the ingredients of this vegetable soup, brought to the New England coast many generations ago. Originally known as *caldo verde* or *sopa de couvres*, its essentials are fresh kale, preferably after the frost has been on it, and beans, usually dried, and sausage of Portuguese persuasion, preferably *chouriço* and/or *lingüiça*. Italian sausage is sometimes substituted, or even kielbasa. It's a grand meal-in-a-bowl, one to be varied according to your own taste.

Coastwise Kale Soup

1 cup coarsely chopped onion
½ pound chouriço *sausage, thickly sliced*
½ pound lingüiça *sausage, thickly sliced*
10 cups beef broth

1 cup pea beans, soaked overnight
2 cups potatoes, peeled and cut into 1-inch cubes
1 pound fresh kale, shredded, with stems removed
Fresh mint sprigs

Cook the onion with the sausages, stirring frequently, until the onion is tender. Heat the broth to the boiling point, add the drained beans, and when the broth begins to bubble again, cook about 1 hour over low heat, until the beans are almost soft. Stir in the potatoes and continue simmering about 15 minutes. Stir in the shredded kale and the sausage-onion mixture. Bring the soup back to the boiling point, then cook over very low heat, about 10 minutes. The potatoes and beans should be soft and the kale fresh-tasting and just a little crunchy. Ladle the soup into wide bowls, adding a sprig of mint to each.
SERVES 8–10

Among reasons to have a country ham on hand is the dividend of hearty flavor that comes from adding the bones to soup.

Lentil-Hambone Soup

1 ham bone
4–5 quarts water
1 pound lentils
1 bay leaf
½ teaspoon fresh tarragon
½ teaspoon dried rosemary
1 tablespoon salt

2 large carrots, sliced ½ inch thick
1 large stalk celery, sliced ½ inch thick
4 tablespoons vegetable oil
4 onions, chopped
2 garlic cloves, chopped
¼ cup chopped parsley

Put the ham bone in a large kettle, cover with the water, and boil about 30 minutes to reduce the liquid by about one-third (to about 6 cups). Add the lentils, herbs, and salt and simmer 30 minutes. Add the sliced carrots and celery and cook 30 minutes more. Meanwhile, heat the oil in a skillet and

sauté the chopped onions and garlic until the onions are translucent but not brown; add to the soup and simmer a few minutes to blend flavors. Remove the ham bone, trimming off the meat bits and adding them to the soup. Sprinkle the soup with parsley at the last minute.
SERVES 4–6

Alstead Lentil Soup

An adaptation of a soup served one cold day not far from Alstead Center, New Hampshire.

1 tablespoon peanut oil
1 onion, chopped
1 cup lentils
½ pound Polish or Portuguese sausage (kielbasa or lingüiça)
2 cups water

2 cups beef stock
1 tomato, chopped, or ½ cup tomato juice
1 carrot, chopped
Freshly ground pepper to taste
1 teaspoon dried spearmint leaves

Heat the oil in a heavy saucepan, stir in the onion and lentils, and cook over moderate heat for about 3 minutes. Meanwhile, cut the sausage into coins, and add them to the saucepan, cooking just long enough to brown slightly. Add the water and the stock and simmer about 15 minutes. Add the tomato or tomato juice and the carrot and continue cooking for 15 minutes. Just before serving, season with pepper (the sausage should provide sufficient salt) and spearmint.
SERVES 4

Baked-Bean Soup

2 cups baked beans
4 cups water or stock
2 tablespoons finely chopped onion
4 cooked frankfurters

2 tablespoons sherry
2 hard-boiled eggs, sliced
1 lemon, sliced

In a blender or a food processor, spin some of the beans with some of the water or stock until both are transformed into porridge consistency. Simmer in a soup pot along with the onion, about 5 minutes to cook the onion. Slice the frankfurters and add, simmering 1 minute more. Stir in the sherry. In each soup dish, put several slices of egg and a slice of lemon, and pour in the piping-hot soup.
SERVES 4

An oxtail may be an awkward-looking piece of meat, someone said, but there is sweet meat between the joints, as well as a gelatin protein that comes forth during long, slow cooking. It may be eaten as a stew with the sauce lightly thickened, or served as is in large soup plates with crusty bread to sop up the juices.

Old-Fashioned Oxtail Soup or Stew

1 large onion, sliced thin
2 tablespoons vegetable oil
1 oxtail, jointed
6 cups beef broth
1 cup cider, preferably about to turn
1 cup peeled parsnips, cut into pieces about 1 inch long and of even thickness

1 cup diced turnips
1 cup diced carrots
3 medium potatoes, peeled and quartered
Salt
Freshly ground pepper
1 tablespoon cornstarch, dissolved in 2 tablespoons cold water (optional)

About 3½ hours before serving, put the onion slices and the butter in a heavy stewpot and cook them very gently for about 10 minutes. Add oxtail pieces and brown them on all surfaces. Heat the broth and add it to the pot with the cider. Simmer very gently, covered, for 2½ hours. Add the vegetables, cover, and simmer another 40–45 minutes, until tender. Taste, and add salt, if necessary, and several turns of the pepper grinder. If you want to thicken the sauce, stir in the dissolved cornstarch and simmer another minute, until lightly thickened.

SERVES 4

Barley Soup

2–3 tablespoons butter or vegetable oil or a combination
1 cup chopped onion
1½ cups diced broccoli stems
4 cups beef broth
1 bay leaf
1 tablespoon chopped fresh tarragon, or 1 teaspoon dried

1 cup quick-cooking barley
½ cup milk
Salt
Freshly ground pepper
3–4 tablespoons finely chopped sweet red pepper

Heat the butter and/or oil in a saucepan and sauté the onion and broccoli stems over low heat about 10 minutes, stirring frequently. Pour in the beef broth, add the bay leaf and tarragon, and bring to a boil. Stir in the barley and simmer about 15 minutes, or until the barley is tender. Add the milk and heat through. Season to taste with salt and pepper. Serve in hot soup bowls with a sprinkling of chopped red pepper on top of each bowl.

SERVES 4

Mussel and Tomato Soup

2 pounds mussels, scrubbed
2 tablespoons olive oil
2 large garlic cloves, crushed
¾ pound tomatoes, peeled, or an equivalent amount of drained canned tomatoes

Freshly ground pepper
Sugar
Tomato paste
Croutons fried in olive oil

Open the mussels by boiling them, covered, in ¼ inch of water in a large pan. Remove them from the shells, straining the liquid into a measuring cup, and add enough water to make 4 cups. Put the oil in another pan, add the garlic and tomatoes, and cook 5–10 minutes, pressing the vegetables into a purée without too many large lumps. Add the mussel liquid and sprinkle with a little pepper. Simmer 15 minutes, then stir in a little sugar and tomato paste to suit your taste. Add the mussels and reheat only for a few seconds (or they will turn rubbery). Pour into a warm tureen. Serve with croutons added at last moment.
SERVES 4

VARIATION: For a more delicate mussel soup, instead of tomatoes and garlic, sauté a small diced potato, ½ cup chopped celery, ¼ cup chopped shallots or scallion bulbs, and ⅓ cup chopped sweet red pepper in butter in place of olive oil. Substitute 1 cup of white wine for 1 of the 4 cups water and add the mussel liquid in the same way, eliminating the tomato paste and sugar. Purée all but 4 of the cooked mussels in a food processor and add to the soup to thicken. Use the remaining mussels as a garnish along with the croutons.

Pumpkin and Mussel Soup

1 small pumpkin
2 pounds mussels, scrubbed
3 shallots, or 1 small onion, chopped
2 garlic cloves, chopped
¼ cup dry white wine
2 cups fish broth, or 1 cup clam juice and 1 cup water

2 cups chicken broth
1 tablespoon tapioca
Freshly ground pepper
4 toasted rounds dry French bread rubbed with garlic
2 tablespoons chopped parsley

Cut the pumpkin in half and place on a baking sheet, flesh side down. Bake in a preheated 350-degree oven for about 50 minutes, or until soft. Let cool enough to tear off the charred skin, then mash the flesh (it need not be a smooth purée).

Scrub the mussels thoroughly and scrape off their beards, discarding any open ones. In a heavy pot, bring the shallots, garlic, and wine to a boil, then add the mussels, cover, and boil until the shells open, just a few minutes.

Meanwhile, bring the 2 broths to a boil, stir in the tapioca, add the pumpkin, and cook gently, 5 to 6 minutes. When the mussels are cool enough to handle, remove them from their shells. Strain the mussel cooking liquid into the pumpkin soup. Finally, add the mussels and heat through. Season with freshly ground pepper (it won't need salt). Serve in warm bowls with rounds of the bread sprinkled with parsley, floating on top.

SERVES 4

Wickford Point Mussel Chowder

Rhode Island fishermen's wives devised this gallimaufry when their gardens first gave them inspiration—and it remains an inspired dish.

¼ pound salt pork, chopped fine
2 large onions, chopped
¼ cup chopped green pepper
3 cups peeled and diced potatoes
2 cups mussel broth
3 cups steamed mussels (opposite)
1 bay leaf

1 teaspoon chopped fresh savory
   (optional)
1 cup chopped peeled tomatoes
2 cups tomato juice
Salt
Freshly ground pepper

Brown the salt pork in a large pot; remove when crisp and set aside. Stir the onions into the salt pork fat and sauté until they are translucent. Add the green pepper and potatoes with the mussel broth, cover, and simmer until the potatoes are tender. Stir in the mussels, the bay leaf and savory, and the tomatoes and tomato juice. Simmer, covered, for about 30 minutes. Sprinkle lightly with salt and pepper to taste, and garnish with the reserved crisp salt pork.

SERVES 6–8

Bay Scallops Chowder

On a brisk April day in 1960, there appeared in the *Vineyard Gazette* of Edgartown, Massachusetts, this cautionary note about what is perhaps the oldest of New England cooking techniques: ". . . chowder, if built with due respect for both clock and calendar, improves with age. In many chowder recipes one encounters the phrase 'remove to the back of the stove,' and there is a good deal of eloquence there. On the back of the stove is where much of the perfection comes in." Among the most delicate of fish chowders may be those that get both texture and special flavor from scallops.

1 pint bay scallops, including liquor
2 ounces salt pork or smoked bacon, diced
1 medium onion, chopped
1 cup cubed peeled potatoes (in ½-inch cubes)
1 medium stalk celery, chopped

About ¼ cup clam juice, diluted by half with water (optional)
2 cups milk
1 tablespoon minced fresh herbs, basil and thyme, or chervil
Salt
Freshly ground pepper

Use a slotted spoon to lift scallops from their liquor. Put salt pork or bacon in a saucepan and cook gently over low heat to release the fat. Add the chopped onion, potatoes, and celery and sauté about 5 minutes, until the vegetables are almost tender. Pour in the scallop liquor, adding a little diluted clam juice if there is not much scallop juice; add the milk and bring to a boil. Simmer about 5 minutes, stirring in the herbs (thyme and basil

For Chowderheads

Scholars seem to agree that the word *chowder* comes from a French word for kettle, used by North Atlantic fishermen, but there is precious little agreement on the subject of properly filling the kettle with the right ingredients. Most New England members of chowder-and-marching societies insist that clam chowder is a milk-based soup or stew made with quahaugs and potatoes, and accented by salt pork. That goes for Block Island Chowder, into which some cooks stir onions, parsley, bay leaf, cloves, and minced thyme. Rhode Island clam chowder, as well as that of the part of Long Island that is truly Yankee in heritage, is dependent upon the addition of tomatoes.

Some say the red vegetable intruded on the all-white stew sometime after a Rhode Island painter named Michele Felice Corne ate the first tomato. (There's a plaque in memory of this brave man in Newport.) Another theory is that the addition of tomato in flavoring clam chowder—now often known as the Manhattan version—is the result of the mad enthusiasm for dousing everything with ketchup. Red or white, however, clam chowder has a generations-old place in fundamental American cooking styles.

are a good combination), a little salt depending upon saltiness of pork or bacon, and a few turns of pepper grinder. Ladle into hot soup bowls.
SERVES 4

Menemsha Clam Chowder

50 soft-shell clams, well scrubbed
1 cup water
1/4 pound salt pork, chopped fine
1 medium onion, chopped fine
3 cups diced potatoes
1/2 teaspoon minced fresh thyme, or 1/4 teaspoon dried
1 bay leaf
1 whole clove
2 sprigs parsley
2 cups boiling water
1 quart milk (use part half-and-half, if desired)
2 tablespoons butter
Salt
Freshly ground pepper

Steam the clams in 1 cup water, covered, until they open. Remove the clams from their shells over the cooking pot, to catch any extra juices. Separate the soft flesh of the clams from the hard, and chop the hard part up fine. Strain the clam juice through a fine cheesecloth and reserve. In a good-size heavy pot, fry the salt pork until it releases some fat, then add the onion and fry until golden; pour off the excess fat. Add the potatoes, thyme, bay leaf, clove, parsley, and the chopped hard part of the clams. Pour the boiling water over, and simmer until the potatoes are tender, about 15 minutes. Add the soft clams, set aside to cool, then refrigerate overnight.

Next day remove the parsley sprigs and bay leaf, and stir in the reserved clam juice and milk. Bring to the simmer, float the butter on top, and season to taste with a little salt and several grindings of pepper. Serve hot.
SERVES 4–6

Bronwyn's Clam Chowder

2 cups water
4 medium new potatoes, peeled and chopped
2 medium onions, chopped
5 tablespoons butter
1 pint chopped clams
2 cups milk
24 littleneck or small quahaug clams
Salt
Freshly ground pepper

GARNISHES: chopped parsley and chives

Bring the water to a boil and start cooking the potatoes. Meanwhile, sauté the onions in 2 tablespoons butter until translucent. When the potatoes are partially cooked, add the onions and their cooking butter, the chopped clams and their juice, plus an additional 1 tablespoon butter. Cook until tender. Now open the littlenecks or quahaugs over the simmering soup so that their juices drop into the soup pot and mingle. Poach the raw clams

for just 1 minute in the soup. Taste—it may not need salt but add a generous amount of pepper. Serve in warm bowls with a little of the remaining butter floated on top and a sprinkling of parsley and chives.
SERVES 6

A Light Littleneck Clam Chowder

1 large potato, peeled and sliced
1 large onion, sliced
2½ cups cold water
2 ribs celery, chopped

About 40 littleneck clams
1½ cups milk
Salt
Freshly ground pepper

GARNISH: *dusting of paprika and/or 2 tablespoons chopped parsley and chives*

Boil the potato and onion in 2 cups water. After 10 minutes, add the celery and continue cooking another 5 minutes or so, until the onion and potato are soft and the celery just done *al dente*. Meanwhile, scrub the clams thoroughly and put them in a pot with ½ cup water. Cover and let cook until the clams open. Remove the clams from their broth, and strain the broth into the potato-onion base, using a cheesecloth if there is any sand at the bottom. Remove the clams from their shells; do this over the soup pot so that the clam juice from the shells falls into the soup. Stir in the milk and bring to the simmer, then add the clams and just heat through. Add a little salt, if necessary, and a few grindings of pepper. Serve with a dusting of paprika and/or fresh herbs on top.
SERVES 4

Never-Changing New England

Fortunately the Parker House in Boston is able to broil scrod and tripe the way my grandmother did, and the Copley Plaza in Boston is as adept at finnan haddie as she was; so when the skeptics deafen me with their shouting, I only need to drive to Boston in order to prove to my own satisfaction that they're wrong. And on Saturdays, the Congress Hotel in Portland serves a pea soup made just as my grandmother used to make it. When I'm able, I go to Portland on Saturdays, so that I can sit high above the city, look off across that green and rolling country to the far sharp peaks of the White Mountains, fill myself to the brim with pea soup, and think pitying thoughts of the benighted people who believe there's nothing like French cooking."
—Kenneth Roberts, *Trending into Maine*

Rhode Island Clam Chowder

¼ pound salt pork, cubed
2 onions, sliced
1 cup cold water
1 quart shelled quahaugs with juice
3 cups peeled potatoes, cubed (in ½-inch cubes)
2 cups boiling water
1 cup peeled, seeded, and diced fresh tomatoes or strained stewed tomatoes
¼ teaspoon baking soda
½ teaspoon oregano, fresh or dried
1 cup scalded cream
1 cup scalded milk
Salt
Freshly ground pepper
6 saltine crackers
½ cup cold milk

Put the salt pork cubes, the sliced onion, and the cold water in a pan, bring to a boil, and simmer 10 minutes; drain and reserve the liquid. Wash the clams; reserve the clam juice. Parboil the potato cubes for 7 minutes in the boiling water, then stir in the reserved salt pork and onion broth. Chop the clams fine, and add them to the pot along with the reserved juice. Simmer until the potatoes are just done. Mix the tomatoes with the baking soda, and add to the chowder along with the oregano. Bring to a boil and simmer 1 minute. Stir in the scalded cream and milk, and sprinkle very lightly with salt and a little pepper. Crumble the crackers into the cold milk and stir into the hot chowder at the last minute.

SERVES 8

Pantry Clam Chowder

When you can't find fresh clams on a gloomy day, you can still turn out a quick and cheering bowl.

1 thin 2 x 3-inch piece salt pork, or ½ strip bacon
½ cup chopped onion
½ cup chicken stock
4 medium potatoes, cut into ½-inch cubes
2 cups (1 large can) chopped clams in broth
Freshly ground pepper
3–4 cups milk

GARNISH: dusting of paprika

Gently fry the salt pork or bacon in a heavy saucepan for 5 minutes, or until it begins to crisp. Remove the salt pork, and cook the onions in the fat for 2–3 minutes. Stir in the stock and the potatoes, cover, and simmer 10 minutes, just long enough to soften the potatoes. Stir in the clams and their broth, and season to taste with pepper. Add the milk and bring to a boil. Taste for seasoning, and add salt only if necessary. Dust a little paprika over each serving.

SERVES 4

The Anatomy of a Clam

Clams appeal to gourmets of the New World (especially New England) far more than to those of other places. Among Indian culinary legacies that indicate appreciative palates among the Algonquins are enormous shell mounds or kitchen middens, accumulated over many centuries in what is now Maine and Massachusetts. The English colonists were saved from starvation by Indians who introduced them to the *Venus mercenaria*, the creature that Yankees call quahaugs, and clams have been characteristic of New England gastronomical inclinations ever since.

"When I say clams," a Maine chauvinist wrote, "I mean clams. I don't mean what New Yorkers miscall clams. I don't mean littlenecks or cherrystones. Those round bivalves are nothing but quahaugs . . . the correct Abnaki word for them."

To be more specific, quahaugs are divided by New Englanders into three classifications, according to size: The large "chowders" that can be as much as 4 inches at the widest point are preferred for chopping as the basis of the fundamental Yankee stew. The smallest and most tender are the littlenecks, measuring about 2 inches, and the not much bigger cherrystones are half-grown clams. The latter two are popular and are served, often as not, raw on the half shell; they're also good when baked or broiled in the shell, or fried in batter—as in recipes in this chapter and the "Appetizers" chapter as well.

Soft-shell clams, exposed at low tide in vast beds, are ideal in size for steaming, to be cooked 6 to 10 minutes in a ½ inch of boiling water, and they're often served with their broth, in soup bowls—melted butter on the side.

Lobster Bisque

This is a soup to make after you have had a lobster feast and have leftover shells from 2 or 3 lobsters with perhaps a few little scraps of lobster meat in hidden crevices. You should also have a small piece of lobster meat for garnish, so try to set some aside, or get extra to add a fillip to this very special bisque.

2 or 3 lobster shells
6 cups water
3 tablespoons butter
1 rib celery, chopped
1 carrot, scraped and chopped
1 or 2 leeks, depending on the size, cleaned, trimmed, and sliced

1 medium onion, chopped
2 tablespoons flour
1¼ cups heavy cream
Salt
Dash cayenne

GARNISH: *about ½ cup lobster meat, cut in bite-size pieces and a sprinkling of paprika*

Make a lobster broth: You will get more out of the lobster shells if you crack them or grind them up a bit. If you have a food processor, break the shells up and put in a few pieces at a time, spinning until they break up into relatively small pieces. Cover the shells with the water and cook over medium heat for about 25 minutes. Strain. You should have about 4½ cups lobster broth.

In a heavy saucepan, melt the butter and sauté the vegetables gently, stirring, for about 5 minutes. Stir in the flour and cook, stirring 1 minute, then add the strained lobster broth and whisk until smooth. Cook gently about 20 minutes, until the vegetables are tender. Either put the soup through a vegetable mill or purée in a blender or food processor. Return it to the heat and add the cream. Season with salt to taste and a little cayenne. Heat the lobster meat in the soup; then ladle equal amounts into 4 warm bowls, and sprinkle a little paprika on top.

SERVES 4

This hearty soup makes a meal in itself served with crusty bread or cornsticks.

New England Fish Soup

2 pounds mussels, cleaned and debearded
12 littleneck clams, cleaned
½ cup dry white wine
About 1½ cups fish stock, or ¾ cup clam juice mixed with ¾ cup water
¾ cup chopped onion
½ cup finely diced carrots
3 tablespoons butter or olive oil
2 garlic cloves, minced
2½ cups canned tomatoes, chopped, and their juices

2 tablespoons fresh basil, or ¾ teaspoon dried
1½ pounds firm fish such as haddock, cod, monkfish, cut in large hunks
⅓ pound small scallops or large ones cut in quarters (optional)
Freshly ground pepper
¼ cup chopped parsley

GARNISH: *about 1 dozen ½-inch slices French or Italian bread, toasted and rubbed with olive oil and garlic*

Put the cleaned mussels and clams in a large pot with the wine. Cover and cook over lively heat until the shells open. Remove with a slotted spoon and strain the liquid into a large measuring cup. Add enough fish stock to make 2½ cups. Sauté the onion and carrots gently in the butter or olive oil until limp, adding the garlic for the last minute of cooking. Combine this mixture with the seafood liquid and the tomatoes and their juice in the large pot. Add the basil now if using dried. Simmer, covered, 15 minutes, then add the fish and simmer 6–10 minutes, until opaque (the longer time

New England Fish Soup (continued)

for monkfish). Add the optional scallops for the last 2 minutes of cooking. Return the clams and mussels in their shells to the pot and simmer 1 minute more to heat through. Season liberally with pepper (no salt apt to be needed) and serve in warm, wide bowls with the croutons floating on top. Sprinkle with basil, if using fresh, and parsley.

SERVES 4–6

FISH and SHELLFISH

CONSIDERING how far the coastline runs from north to south, how wiggly it is with bays, coves, and inlets—and how many lakes, ponds, and rivers groove the terrain—it might seem easy to contrive a Yankee cookbook virtually inundated by fish and shellfish recipes. Another possibility might be to limit this section to dishes that were originated by fishermen's wives whose families first settled the New England shores. But as ethnic influences continue to change just about everything else, so new and often imaginative ways of preparing fish have become commonly accepted—and so, too, much more fish is being served, often by cooks who recognize that food from either fresh or salt waters is considered by experts to be healthier than red meat.

Fish farming is increasing in New England. (Indeed, our pond at Bryn Teg is stocked with fifty brook trout and fifty rainbows, as are other family fishing waters throughout the six states.) Mussels, once hard to find at local fishmongers, have been made popular by Italian and other ethnic restaurants, and cultivated mussels are being marketed through Yankee enterprise from Tenant's Harbor, Maine, to Newport, Rhode Island, and beyond.

In a recent year, Kathy McGee of Massachusetts's seafood marketing office, told us that her group found a 38 percent preference for mussels over a 32 percent preference for clams, while 30 percent said they liked both. In another taste test, she said, only 9 percent maintained a dislike of mussels, indicating that the prejudice of the early part of the twentieth century had almost disappeared. Once, our friend Edward Giobbi recalls, that prejudice was so deep that even during the Depression, when most New England working people were short on food, Italians who gathered mussels were said to be eating "dirt" or trash.

Now there is acceptance of seafare that isn't expensive. People who spend as much time as possible in coastal New England look forward to the springtime temptation of fresh sardines—they are wonderful with a sauce of fresh tomatoes, if you're lucky enough to have them close at hand. They aren't quite as celebrated, however, among fishermen keen on Yankee traditions, as are smelts. In spawning time, hundreds of anglers make a festive celebration of lining up for the first run of smelts on coastal rivers, and inland at such places as Lake Memphremagog as well. Cooks in the same areas have made the spring fish into various creative dishes (see pages 116 and 117).

New England fishermen have begun to provide the market with "underutilized species" of considerable range, and the change is fostered by many home cooks and professionals alike. Raquel and Peter Boehmer of Monhegan Island, in their publication *Seafood Soundings,* are among those to hail the new availability of such fish as cusk, eel, hake, pollack, shark, and squid, once considered "ethnic" rather than mainline Yankee food.

The Boehmers have also pointed out that restaurants specializing in fried clams, fried shrimp, and fisherman's platters are being supplanted by chefs who veer away from health-threatening fats and who turn out dishes in which, for instance, fresh broiled halibut and fresh haddock may be served "in a tantalizing lemon-broccoli sauce with fresh scallops and shrimp." It's important, the Boehmers write, to develop new methods that emphasize, in this way, the attractive potentialities of seafood that has heretofore been neglected.

Surely, fish cookery, as much as any other kind has moved with the times, and we're all the more interestingly nourished as a result.

FISH

Steamed Black Bass with Sorrel Sauce

The best way to steam this kind of whole fish is to put it on a heatproof platter so that as it steams you can catch the juices, which will then go into the sauce. You can improvise a steamer by placing the platter on top of some empty tuna fish cans in a roaster or wok with a cover. Black bass, which are found in cold, deep Atlantic waters, have big heads, so a lot of the weight is taken up by the head. Cook them with the heads on and serve them whole—some of the sweetest morsels are in the cheeks.

Salt
Freshly ground pepper
2 whole black bass (about 1½
    pounds each), gutted and cleaned

½ cup heavy cream
⅓ cup cooked fresh or frozen sorrel
    (page 50)

Salt and pepper the bass, and place them on a heatproof platter that will just accommodate the 2 fish. Steam, covered, over boiling water 12–15 minutes. Test for doneness by lifting a little of the flesh close to the bone with the tip of a knife; if it is opaque and comes away from the bone easily, the fish is done. Pour off the juices into a small saucepan, keeping the fish warm on the platter. Boil the juices down to about ⅓ cup. Add the cream and boil further, until lightly thickened. Stir in the sorrel, add a little salt and pepper to taste, then taste critically; you may want a little more sorrel —the sauce should have a good, sharp flavor, which softens as it blends into the fish. Pour the hot sauce over the black bass.

SERVES 4

Foil-Steamed Whole Fish

Steaming in foil is a convenient way to cook a whole fish so that it remains intact and all its juices and whatever flavors you add are trapped inside. Striped bass, with its inimitable flavor, is particularly delicious done this way; but now that striped bass fishing in North Atlantic waters has been curtailed, you might want to try tilefish or bluefish or salmon this way.

1 whole fish, such as tilefish, bluefish, or salmon (about 4 pounds), cleaned, gutted, not beheaded

STUFFING:
¼ cup finely chopped sweet red pepper
¼ cup finely chopped sweet green pepper
1 teaspoon chopped red or green hot pepper (more or less to taste)
¼ cup finely chopped fennel

¼ cup cubed water chestnuts
4 scallions, including most of the tender greens, sliced thin
2 tablespoons chopped fresh coriander or, if unavailable, parsley
¾ cup fresh bread crumbs
1 tablespoon vegetable oil
½ teaspoon Chinese sesame oil
Salt
Freshly ground pepper

GARNISHES: lemon quarters and watercress

Rinse the fish inside and out and pat dry. Mix all of the stuffing ingredients together, using salt and pepper to taste (the stuffing should be well seasoned). Spoon the stuffing into the cavity of the fish, including the head (this is one of the reasons that it is important to retain the head because that way you can get more stuffing in). Skewer closed the openings and lace string around the skewers, so that the stuffing won't burst out. Wrap securely in foil, using 2 layers if the foil isn't heavy-duty, and place in a large pan. Bake in a preheated 425-degree oven for 40 minutes. Remove the foil, lacings, and skewers, and serve on a large platter with lemon wedges and watercress.

SERVES 6–8

Bluefish in Molho (Portuguese Tomato Sauce)

MOLHO SAUCE:

3 tablespoons olive oil
1 medium onion, chopped
1 small green pepper, or ½ large, chopped
2 garlic cloves, chopped
⅓ cup red wine
¼ cup chopped parsley
1 tablespoon chopped fresh basil, or ⅛ teaspoon dried
⅛ teaspoon dried thyme

⅛ teaspoon cumin, crushed
⅓ cup water
2 teaspoons vinegar
1 teaspoon sugar
⅛ teaspoon dried hot red pepper flakes
One 1-pound can whole tomatoes in juice
Salt
Freshly ground pepper

About 1¾ pounds bluefish fillets (in 2 pieces)

Heat the olive oil in a heavy saucepan, add the onion and sauté 1 minute. Add the green pepper and garlic and sauté gently another minute. Add the red wine, bring to a boil, and stir in the herbs. Add the water, vinegar, sugar, red pepper flakes, and tomatoes, breaking them up into pieces with a fork. Bring to a boil again, cover, and simmer gently for 1 hour, stirring occasionally. Taste, and add salt and pepper as necessary. Lay the bluefish fillets in a lightly oiled shallow baking dish large enough to hold them in one layer. Salt and pepper them lightly, then pour the hot sauce over, cover, and bake in a preheated 400-degree oven for 15 minutes.
SERVES 4

Look the Fish in the Eye...

If you want to know whether a fish is fresh, look it in the eye, says Julia Child, who awakened a whole generation of Americans to the pleasures and proper techniques of good cooking, just as her fellow Bostonian Fannie Farmer had done almost one hundred years before. As *The French Chef,* on the Boston public television show that launched her, she instructed us not only to look for clear eyes in fish (and they should never be sunken) but also to touch the flesh to make sure it's not slimy, and to inspect the gills for good color. If the fish is already beheaded and wrapped in plastic when you buy it, tear off the package and sniff the fish at the checkout counter before you bring it home. Once you are home, store it on ice and eat it as soon as possible.

3 tablespoons butter
About 3–4 good-size leeks,
    trimmed of tough leaves, washed
    and chopped (1½ cups)
1½ pounds Maine (or other
    boiling) potatoes, peeled and
    sliced thin

Salt
Freshly ground pepper
¾ cup milk
1½ pounds bluefish fillets (2 large
    or 4 small)
2 tablespoons chopped parsley

GARNISH: *lemon wedges*

Bluefish Fillets Broiled with Potatoes and Leeks

Smear 1 tablespoon of the butter on the bottom of a flameproof shallow baking dish, large enough to accommodate the fish fillets later in one layer. Strew half the leeks and potatoes over the bottom, salt lightly, grind a few turns of the pepper grinder, and dot with butter. Add the remaining leeks and potatoes, and season again. Pour in the milk. Bring to a simmer on top of the stove, cover with foil, and bake in a 400-degree oven about 30 minutes, until the potatoes are just tender. Remove the dish and preheat the broiler. Lay the bluefish fillets, skin side down, on top of the potatoes and leeks. Smear the remaining butter on top, and season with salt and pepper. Place the dish as close to the source of heat as possible and broil 5 minutes. Sprinkle with chopped parsley, and serve with lemon wedges.
SERVES 4

It seems to have taken immigrant cooks who talked about the *scarola* grown in Italian gardens to realize that escarole has many possibilities in cooked dishes, as well as in salads.

Salt Cod Baked with Escarole

1 pound salt cod
2–3 garlic cloves
2 tablespoons vegetable oil
1 head escarole (1½ pounds),
    rinsed and trimmed

½ cup raisins
2 teaspoons capers or marinated
    fiddleheads, chopped
¼ cup fresh lemon juice

Prepare the salt cod by soaking overnight in a large bowl of cold water. Drain, and toss the cod into simmering water to cover for about 15 minutes, until it flakes easily. Drain, and rinse under running cold water. Check for bones and remove any that may remain. Chop the garlic, and cook it in the oil until it softens. Pat the escarole dry, shred it coarsely, then add it to the garlic, along with the raisins and capers. Stir the mixture while cooking over moderate heat for about 3 minutes. Break up the fish and stir it into the escarole-garlic mixture to coat with oil, before turning it all into a casserole. Add the lemon juice and about ¼ cup of boiling water, and put the casserole in a preheated 350-degree oven for about 50 minutes.
SERVES 4

Golden Sautéed Cod

New England cooks with Scandinavian heritage—there are Norwegians, for instance, in Billerica, Massachusetts—have their own old-country way with traditional fish like salt cod.

1 pound dried cod, soaked
   overnight
1 whole egg, beaten
3 tablespoons vegetable oil
1 medium onion, finely chopped

1 tablespoon minced parsley
1 small leek or 2 shallots, finely
   chopped
2 egg yolks
1 tablespoon vinegar

Simmer the soaked cod in fresh water to cover, until soft but still in whole pieces. Reserve the broth. Drain the cod, dip each piece in the beaten egg, and sauté in 2 tablespoons oil for 4–5 minutes on each side. Put the pieces on a hot platter in a preheated 175-degree oven. In the remaining 1 tablespoon oil, sauté the onion, parsley, and leek or shallots for about 5 minutes, until golden brown. Stir into the pan about 4 tablespoons of the reserved fish broth, bringing it to a boil before removing the pan from the heat. Beat the 2 egg yolks with the vinegar, and stir this mixture into the pan of broth, off heat. Return the sauce to medium heat, then stir constantly until it is smoothly blended, and pour over the hot pieces of cod.
SERVES 4

Salt Cod with Green Tomatoes, Leeks, Red Peppers, and Rice

2 tablespoons olive oil
1 cup chopped onions
3 garlic cloves, minced
1 pound salt cod, soaked overnight
1 cup roughly chopped green
   tomatoes
¼ cup dry sherry
¼ cup water

2 leeks, cleaned and cut into ½-inch
   pieces
1 sweet red pepper, seeded and
   sliced
One 8-ounce bottle clam juice
¾ cup uncooked rice
1–2 tablespoons chopped parsley

Heat the olive oil in an attractive, fairly large, shallow flameproof pan with a cover, if you have one (otherwise use a skillet), and sauté the onions until almost tender. Add the garlic and sauté another 30 seconds. Drain the cod, pat dry, and cut into bite-size pieces. Then add the cod and chopped green tomatoes and cook, tossing and stirring, for 5 minutes. Add the sherry, water, and leeks, cover, and let steam-cook gently for 45 minutes, stirring in the red pepper after 40 minutes. Pour in the clam juice, bring to a boil, and stir in the rice. Cover and simmer for 20 minutes. If the pan can come to the table, sprinkle chopped parsley on top and serve; otherwise turn out onto a hot platter, and then sprinkle parsley over.
SERVES 4

1 pound salt cod, soaked overnight
¾ pound grated sharp cheddar
2 tablespoons flour
1 cup milk
4 potatoes (about 1 pound), peeled
    and cut into ½-inch cubes

5 teaspoons butter
Freshly ground pepper
Pinch of salt (optional)

Salt Cod Casserole with Potatoes and Cheese

Drain the cod and cut into 1-inch pieces, removing any bones. Mix the grated cheese and the flour together. Heat the milk to the simmering point. Use 1 teaspoon butter to grease a 2-quart casserole. Distribute the cod and the potatoes over the bottom, sprinkle with the cheese-flour mixture, pour in the hot milk, and dot with the remaining 4 teaspoons butter. Grind a little pepper over and add a pinch of salt, but taste first—it may not be necessary with the salted cod. Cover and bake in a preheated 350-degree oven for 35 minutes, then uncover and bake another 15 minutes.
SERVES 4

Boston's North End is distinguished by cooks with the heritage of Abruzzi and Sicily. This is an excellent way to dress up Yankee salt cod, as we found it served on Hanover Street.

Baccalla Messinese Cafe Paradiso

1½ cups olive oil
2 onions, sliced
2 ribs celery, diced
1 pound ripe tomatoes, peeled,
    seeded, and chopped
2 pounds fresh salt cod, soaked
    overnight
1 pound potatoes, peeled and
    quartered

8–10 large green olives, pitted
2½ tablespoons capers
2½ tablespoons pine nuts
¼ cup seedless raisins
Salt
Chili powder

Heat the oil in a deep skillet and sauté the onions and celery until almost soft. Add the tomatoes and about ½ cup water and bring the mixture to a boil. Remove any skin from the fish, cut it in serving pieces, and add it to the skillet along with the potatoes, olives, capers, pine nuts, and raisins. Sprinkle lightly with salt and a good deal of chili powder, to taste. Cook gently for 30 minutes, adding a little more water if needed to keep the sauce fairly liquid. Serve very hot.
SERVES 6

Portuguese Fisherman's Stew

Among Little Compton's attractions on Narragansett Bay are its white-clapboard streetscapes reflective of seventeenth-century New England and its quiet community of Portuguese, whose boats rock in the harbor to the east. Wherever they have settled among Yankees, Portuguese cooks have helped to popularize imaginative ways of cooking local provender, with salt cod high on the list.

1 pound salt codfish
1 cup olive oil
2 large onions, chopped
2–3 garlic cloves, chopped
3 medium potatoes, peeled and
  diced
1/4 cup chopped black olives

4–5 tomatoes, peeled, seeded, and
  sliced
1/2 cup chopped parsley
3/4 cup white wine
Freshly ground pepper to taste
1 teaspoon dried thyme

GARNISH: *pimiento strips*

Cover the codfish with water for about 24 hours, changing the water two or three times. Drain, cut the fish in 2- to 3-inch rectangles, cover with boiling water, and simmer, covered, for 15 minutes, or until tender. Drain the pieces and remove the skin and any small bones, then break the fish into flakes and set aside. Heat the oil in a skillet and when a haze can be seen over it, stir in the chopped onions and garlic and the diced potatoes. Cook gently until the onions are translucent, then add the fish, olives, tomatoes, parsley, and wine. Season with thyme and pepper—no salt should be needed. Cover the pan and simmer very slowly for about 2½ hours, until the fish is very tender. Decorate each serving with pimiento strips.
SERVES 4

Codfish Cakes with Cheese and Spinach

Rural New Englanders pack a lot of spinach from kitchen gardens into freezers, and one of the rewards of the following winter is this way of perking up a classic, unpretentious meal.

1 pound salt cod
1 pound potatoes
1½ cups finely chopped cooked
  spinach
3 tablespoons freshly grated
  cheddar

2 eggs, well beaten
1/4 teaspoon freshly ground pepper
3 tablespoons butter
2 tablespoons olive oil

Soak the salt cod in water overnight. In a saucepan, cover the fish with fresh water and boil about 45 minutes. Drain thoroughly and flake the fish. Boil the potatoes in salted water, drain and peel them, and mash well.

Combine the potatoes with the flaked fish, and stir in the spinach, cheese, eggs, and pepper. Form into flat cakes about 3 inches in diameter. Heat the butter and the oil in a skillet, and cook the cakes about 3–4 minutes on each side until they are lightly browned.

SERVES 4

Salt cod has for generations provided us with some of the tastiest fish cakes, often served for breakfast or supper, or made in small fritters as an appetizer (see page 10). Usually the cakes would be made of leftover cooked salt cod and some leftover mashed potatoes, but if you don't happen to have those ingredients on hand, the cakes are even better made from scratch.

Codfish Cakes

1 pound salt cod
1 onion, sliced
1 rib celery
1 small carrot
1 pound potatoes, peeled and diced
4 tablespoons butter
1 teaspoon ground ginger, or 1 tablespoon finely minced fresh ginger

3 scallions, including tender greens, chopped fine
2 eggs, beaten
Freshly ground pepper
4 tablespoons bacon fat or oil

Soak the salt cod overnight in several changes of water. Drain and put in a saucepan with fresh water to cover. Add the sliced onion, celery, and carrot, and cook for 15 minutes. Drain thoroughly and flake the fish when cool. Meanwhile, cook the potatoes in lightly salted water until tender, then drain, and mash with the butter. Mix the mashed potatoes and cod together, along with the ginger, scallions, beaten eggs, and pepper to taste. Form into 8 cakes, and fry in hot bacon fat or oil about 3–4 minutes on each side, until browned and crisp. Serve with ketchup, preferably unsweetened (see page 628), or tomato sauce.

SERVES 4–6

Fried eels or eels with spicy stuffings were popular dishes in old Boston, and new New Englanders have adapted recipes from the Mediterranean area. Eel fishing is a Lake Champlain sport—and if you bring home your own, you'll have to kill it and skin it yourself. Whack the eel on the head, then cut the skin around the neck and peel if off—it will come off in one piece, like a glove, but you will have to use a pair of pliers to get it started. One of the best traditional Yankee recipes—one we've often used—is for eel stifle, a favorite meal for hungry artists of the Provincetown artists colony early in this century.

Eel Stifle

Eel Stifle (continued)

*2 pounds potatoes, peeled and
  sliced thin*
6 medium onions, sliced thin
Flour
Salt

Freshly ground pepper
*2 pounds eels, cut into 3-inch
  pieces*
¼ pound salt pork, diced
2 cups milk

Butter a casserole large enough to hold all the ingredients. Scatter one-third of the potatoes and onions on the bottom, sprinkle a little flour on top, salt lightly, and season with a few turns of the pepper grinder, then lay half the pieces of eel on top. Repeat with another layer of one-third of the potatoes and onions, the seasonings, the remaining eel, half the salt pork, and finish with the remaining potatoes and onions. Top with the remaining salt pork. Pour in the milk and cook in a preheated 350-degree oven for 1 hour to 1 hour and 10 minutes, or until tender.

SERVES 6

Eels Broiled with Sage

2 pounds eels, skinned
6 tablespoons olive oil
Pinch of paprika
*About 10 fresh sage leaves,
  chopped*

Salt
Freshly ground pepper

GARNISH: *watercress*

Cut the eels into 3–4-inch pieces and wipe them with a damp cloth. Blend the olive oil with the paprika and chopped sage. Dip the eel pieces in the seasoned oil, and sprinkle lightly with salt and pepper. Preheat the broiler or get a fire going in the grill until it turns to hot coals. Arrange the eel pieces on a broiler rack 4 inches below the source of heat or on the grill 4 inches above the hot coals. Broil or grill 10 minutes and turn the pieces. Baste with the seasoned oil and cook 10 minutes more, until golden brown. Garnish with watercress.

SERVES 4–6

1½ pounds fish fillets, such as
    haddock, scup, monkfish, etc.
Salt
Freshly ground pepper
2 small yellow summer squash,
    sliced thin

2–3 tablespoons chopped shallots
½ cup fresh bread crumbs
2 tablespoons vegetable oil
Juice of ½ lemon
½ cup freshly grated Swiss cheese

Baked Fish Fillets with Yellow Squash

Butter a shallow baking dish in which the fillets will fit snugly in one layer and lay them in. Sprinkle lightly with salt and a few turns of the pepper grinder. Arrange the squash slices to cover the fish, and scatter chopped shallots over them. Season lightly with salt and a little more pepper. Spread the fresh bread crumbs over, sprinkle with the oil and lemon juice, and top with grated cheese. Bake in a preheated 425-degree oven about 25 minutes, until the fish separates easily with a fork and the cheese is bubbling.
SERVES 4

Fried Fish Fillets in Batter

Use fillets of haddock, pollack, flounder, or sole. Leftover batter from the morning's griddle cakes can be substituted for the recipe below.

1½ pounds fish fillets
2½ tablespoons vegetable oil
1 tablespoon white wine
1 tablespoon lemon juice

Salt
Freshly ground pepper
3–4 scallions, chopped

BATTER:
1 cup flour
1 cup milk

1 beaten egg

Oil for frying

Cut the fillets in thirds or in halves, depending on their size. Mix together the oil, wine, lemon juice, about ¼ teaspoon salt, and several turns of the pepper grinder. Place the fish pieces in a flat-bottomed dish and pour the marinade over them, sprinkling the scallions on top. Let marinate for 1 hour or more. To cook, remove the fish and pat off the excess liquid, discarding the scallions. Mix the batter ingredients, seasoning to taste with salt and pepper. Dip each fish piece in the batter, pushing it down to cover it thoroughly. Heat ½ inch of oil in a large pan. Lift out the fish pieces and hold them over the batter bowl to drain slightly. Fry the fish over moderately high heat for about 3 minutes, until the batter browns; then flip them over and brown on the other side. Serve with a freshly made tartar sauce, page 633.
SERVES 4

Shrimp-Stuffed Fillets

½ pound medium shrimp
1 cup water
½ cup dry white wine or vermouth
Salt
4 scallions, including some tender greens, chopped
1 tablespoon chopped fresh tarragon, or ½ teaspoon dried

1 teaspoon minced fresh ginger
2 tablespoons chopped sweet red pepper
2 tablespoons parsley (Chinese, i.e., fresh coriander, or Italian preferred)
Freshly ground pepper
4 slices thin scrod or flounder fillets

Cook the shrimp in the water and wine with a pinch of salt for 2 minutes. Remove with a slotted spoon, and when cool enough to handle, remove the shells. Reserve the cooking liquid. Chop the shrimp into very small pieces, and mix with the scallions, tarragon, ginger, red pepper, parsley, and salt and pepper to taste. Place equal portions of this filling on each of the fillets, and roll them up. Place, flap side down, in a flameproof dish just large enough to accommodate the rolled fillets comfortably, sprinkle them with salt and pepper, and then pour the reserved shrimp cooking liquid over and around them. Bring to a simmer on top of the stove, then cover loosely with foil and bake in a preheated 400-degree oven for 10 minutes.
SERVES 4

Broiled Flounder with Sardine Butter

Small whole flounder are delicate and delicious broiled or grilled quickly, and you can serve them simply with lemon or butter. But try them with this pungent sardine butter spread over the charred flesh and you'll find the flavor greatly enhanced.

Salt
Freshly ground pepper
4 whole small flounder (about ½ pound each after heads have been removed)
3 canned sardines with skins on, packed in oil

3 tablespoons butter
1 teaspoon chopped fresh or dried rosemary
1 teaspoon fresh lemon juice

GARNISH: *lemon quarters*

Preheat the broiler or, if you are grilling, prepare the fire well ahead so you have hot glowing coals. Salt and pepper the flounder lightly on both sides, and broil, skin side down, as close to the flame as possible (if necessary, set on a pan to bring the fish closer to the broiling element). Meanwhile, mash the sardines with the butter, then work in the rosemary and lemon juice. After 3–4 minutes the fish should be charred. Spread the sardine butter over the surface, and let cook another minute, lowering the fish a few inches

from the flame. If you are grilling, cook the fish, flesh side down, about 2–3 minutes until charred, then turn, spread the sardine butter on top, and grill another minute, skin side down. Serve immediately garnished with lemon wedges.
SERVES 4

Orrs Island Skillet Fish Dinner

This top-of-the-stove casserole dish of fish fillets and seasoned vegetables is adapted from a Maine community cookbook.

½ cup uncooked rice
⅔ cup chopped celery
½ cup chopped carrots
1 medium onion, chopped
2 tablespoons butter
1 cup peeled, seeded, and chopped tomatoes, or canned, drained
2 teaspoons chopped fresh tarragon, or ½ teaspoon dried
Freshly grated nutmeg
Salt
Freshly ground pepper
1 cup water
1 pound fish fillets
2 tablespoons chopped parsley and/or chives

Put a large skillet over low heat and pour in the rice, adding the celery, carrots, chopped onion, and butter. Stir as the butter melts, then add the tomatoes, tarragon, a few gratings of nutmeg (about ⅛ teaspoon), a little salt to taste, plenty of freshly ground pepper, and the water. Bring to a boil, cover, and simmer for about 12 minutes. Do not stir. Lift the cover and place the fish fillets on top, add a little more water if dry, then cover again and simmer for 10 minutes, or until the fillets are just cooked through and the liquid is absorbed by the rice. Sprinkle parsley and chives on top.
SERVES 3–4

Finnan Haddie

1 pound finnan haddie
1 cup milk
2 tablespoons heavy cream
3 good-size leeks *, white part only, washed and cut into ½-inch slices
Freshly ground pepper
2 tablespoons chopped parsley

* If leeks aren't available, use 2 medium sweet onions, sliced.

Soak the finnan haddie in cold water to cover for about 1 hour, then drain, and simmer in fresh water to cover for 10 minutes. Meanwhile, in a large shallow baking dish, bring the milk and cream and leeks to a boil, reduce heat, and simmer for 5 minutes. Drain the fish, remove any skin and bones, and flake it. Add to the dish, grind pepper to taste over all, cover with foil, and bake in a preheated 400-degree oven for 30 minutes, basting three or four times. Sprinkle parsley over the top, and serve with steamed or boiled new potatoes.

SERVES 4

Baked Finnan Haddie

A big plow of a boat called *Ptarmigan* squatted next to the Stonington dock the other day, but the birds squalling and circling above were gulls, of course, some of them hungry for the haddock still to be found on the Connecticut shoreline. Somewhat different from most ways of serving smoked fish, this Stonington recipe can reward any fisherman who gets to the haddock ahead of the birds.

1 pound finnan haddie
4 tablespoons butter
3 tablespoons flour
1½ cups milk
Salt

Freshly ground pepper
1 cup diced boiled potatoes
1 tablespoon chopped fresh dill
1 tablespoon chopped parsley

Put the smoked fish in a pan and cover with water. Bring to a boil over medium heat and cook for 10 minutes. Remove from the pan and drain. Remove the skin and bones and flake the fish. Heat 3 tablespoons butter in a saucepan, stir in the flour, and cook gently 2 minutes, continuing to stir. Off heat, add the milk, then return to the heat and stir constantly, until the sauce thickens. Add salt and pepper to taste, reduce the heat, and simmer, stirring often, for about 12–15 minutes. Combine the flaked fish with the sauce, and add the potatoes and dill. Pour the mixture into a shallow baking dish and dot the surface with the remaining 1 tablespoon butter. Bake in a preheated 350-degree oven for about 15 minutes, until lightly browned. Sprinkle with chopped parsley.

SERVES 4

Haddock Baked in Cream

1½ pounds haddock or halibut
3 tablespoons finely chopped
*   scallions or shallots*
2 tablespoons butter
1 tablespoon chopped parsley
*   and/or fresh tarragon*

Salt
Freshly ground pepper
½ cup heavy cream

Rinse the fish and pat dry with paper towels. Sauté the scallions or shallots in butter, reserving enough butter to grease a baking dish in which the fish

will lie flat in one layer. Place the fish in the prepared dish and sprinkle with herbs, salt, and freshly ground pepper, and pour the cream over. Sprinkle in the chopped scallions or shallots. Cover the baking dish and put it in a preheated 350-degree oven for 35 minutes, depending on the thickness of the fish, removing the cover for the last 10 minutes of baking.
SERVES 4

Net Result–Style Baked Haddock

In Burlington, on Lake Champlain, the Net Result fish market of Sally and Denis Turpin is a source of very fresh fish and of an occasional recipe as well. This way of cooking haddock follows their lead; the cooking may be done on an outdoor grill or in an oven at 450 degrees.

1 pound haddock fillet
1/8 lemon
Freshly ground pepper
1/4 cup low-fat cottage cheese
2 tablespoons finely minced
    scallions

1 teaspoon chopped fresh summer
    savory, or 1/2 teaspoon dried
Cracker crumbs

Line a shallow baking dish with foil (or put the foil on the grill). Place the fish, skin side down, on the foil and sprinkle well with lemon juice and some freshly ground pepper. Mix the cottage cheese with the scallions and savory, and spread it over the fish. Sprinkle well with cracker crumbs. Cook on an outdoor grill over glowing coals or bake in a preheated 450-degree oven 10 minutes per inch of thickness, without turning.
SERVES 2

Haddock in Saffron Wine

1 tablespoon softened butter
2 pounds haddock fillets
1/2 cup dry white wine
4–5 saffron threads

Salt
Freshly ground pepper
2 tablespoons chopped celery leaves

Use the butter to grease a shallow baking dish big enough to accommodate the fillets in one layer; lay the fish in. Heat the wine, and crumble the saffron into it; let steep 2–3 minutes, then pour over the fish. Sprinkle with salt and pepper to taste and the chopped celery leaves. Cover the dish and bake in a 375-degree oven for 15–20 minutes, or until the fish is opaque and tender.
SERVES 4

Haddock Steaks Topped with Yogurt and Baked over a Bed of Spinach

2 pounds spinach, cooked until tender, chopped
Salt
Freshly ground pepper
4 haddock steaks (about ½ pound each)
1 cup plain yogurt
4–5 scallions, including tender greens, chopped
⅛ teaspoon dried hot red pepper flakes, or a few drops Tabasco sauce
⅛ teaspoon dark oriental sesame oil
½ cup fresh bread crumbs

Spread the spinach over the bottom of a shallow baking dish just large enough to hold the fish in one layer. Salt and pepper the fish steaks on both sides, and place them on top of the spinach. Mix the yogurt with the scallions, hot pepper flakes, sesame oil, and salt to taste; spread this mixture evenly over the fish steaks, and cover with foil. Bake in a preheated 400-degree oven for 20–25 minutes, until the fish comes easily away from the bone. Uncover, sprinkle the bread crumbs on top of the fish, and put under the broiler until lightly browned on top.
SERVES 4

Provincetown Haddock Stifle

The word *stifle* suggests the act of smothering or enveloping a principal ingredient by simmering it in a blanket of an aromatic mixture until it is gently transformed. Numerous variations on that antique method have been developed by Provincetown cooks over several generations, as in this vegetable-smothered casserole.

4 slices bacon
2 onions, sliced thin
½ cup chopped green pepper
1 garlic clove, chopped fine
4 potatoes, peeled and sliced ¼ inch thick
1½ pounds haddock, cut into bite-size pieces
Salt
1 teaspoon chopped fresh savory
Flour
2 tablespoons unsweetened tomato ketchup (page 628)
Cayenne

In a flameproof casserole, cook the bacon over moderate heat until barely crisp. Remove the bacon and drain on paper towels. In the bacon fat, cook the onions, green pepper, and garlic about 3 minutes. Remove these vegetables with a slotted spoon, and arrange a layer of one-third of the sliced potatoes in the bottom of the casserole. Add a layer of haddock and a little of the onion-pepper-garlic plus a sprinkling of salt and savory. Repeat the layers, sprinkling with a little flour and topping with potatoes. Spread on the ketchup, and pour in enough water to barely cover the layers. Sprinkle

on a little cayenne and lay the bacon slices on top. Cover the casserole and bake in a preheated 350-degree oven for about 1 hour.
SERVES 4–6

Hake Baked with Vegetables and Sherry

Around Gloucester, Massachusetts, cooks are apt to know hake as "frost fish," because it begins to cluster around piers when freezing weather comes in the fall. The silvery fish are then most often simply boiled in heavily salted water and served with fried salt pork and accompanied by beets and boiled potatoes. Here, perhaps, is a more refined way of treating this good fish.

3 tablespoons butter
1 onion, chopped
2 ribs celery, chopped
1/2 pound mushrooms, chopped
3/4 cup dry sherry
1 tablespoon fresh basil, or 1/4 teaspoon dried

1 cup fish broth, or 1/2 cup clam broth and 1/2 cup water
2 pounds hake fillets
Salt
Freshly ground pepper
1/2 cup fresh bread crumbs
2 tablespoons chopped parsley

Heat 2 tablespoons of the butter in a medium skillet, add the onion, and sauté until translucent. Add the celery and mushrooms and cook, stirring, over moderate heat, 3 or 4 minutes. Pour in the sherry and boil rapidly for 1 minute, sprinkling in the basil. Add the fish broth and heat. Using a slotted spoon, spread the vegetables on the bottom of a shallow casserole large enough to hold the fish in one layer. Put the fish on top, salt and pepper it, then pour the liquid from the vegetables over all. Mix the bread crumbs with the parsley, and sprinkle over the hake. Dot the remaining 1 tablespoon butter on top. Bake in a preheated 450-degree oven for 25 minutes.
SERVES 4

Halibut with Scallops and Peas

It can't be sworn to, but this feast may have been inspired by Maine's Vinalhaven scalloping grounds.

1 1/2 pounds halibut fillets
1/2 pound scallops
1/4 cup dry white wine
1/4 cup finely sliced scallions, including most of the tender greens
2 tablespoons finely chopped fresh ginger

Salt
Freshly ground pepper
1 cup fresh garden peas, boiled 2 minutes and drained
1 tablespoon chopped fresh coriander leaves or, if unavailable, Italian flat-leaved parsley

Put the fillets in a large shallow buttered baking dish, and distribute the scallops all around. Pour the wine around the fish and sprinkle the scallions and ginger over, then season with salt and pepper. Bring the dish to a boil on top of the stove, then cover with foil and place in a preheated 375-degree oven for 10 minutes. Add the peas and sprinkle coriander leaves on top. Bake, covered, another 2 minutes.

SERVES 4

Old Parker House Halibut

Simple and delicious dishes like this were the hallmark of the Parker House when it was a nineteenth-century mecca for Boston diners-out.

2 pounds halibut (4 fillets)
Salt
Freshly ground pepper

¼ cup melted butter
½ cup fresh bread crumbs

Rinse the fillets and dry well. Sprinkle with salt and pepper on both sides. Dip in melted butter, then in the bread crumbs. Scrape the excess butter into a shallow baking dish just large enough to hold the fillets flat. Place the fish pieces in the dish and bake 20 minutes in a preheated 375-degree oven. Serve with the juices and freshly boiled parsleyed potatoes.

SERVES 4

Halibut with Avocado and Mushroom Stuffing

4 halibut fillets
Salt
Freshly ground pepper
Lemon juice
2 tablespoons finely chopped mushrooms
4 scallions, finely chopped

3 tablespoons butter
2 tablespoons flour
1 tomato, peeled and chopped
1 large avocado, mashed
¼ cup dry white wine or vermouth
¾ cup chicken stock
2 egg yolks, beaten

Season the fillets lightly with salt and pepper, and sprinkle lemon juice over them. Place 2 of the fillets, side by side, in a shallow casserole. Meanwhile, sauté the chopped mushrooms and scallions in butter for 5 minutes. Stir in the flour, gently cook another minute, stirring, then add the chopped tomato and mashed avocado and blend well. Stir in the wine and chicken stock and add salt and pepper to taste. Spoon some of the hot mixture into the egg yolks to temper them, then add the eggs to the pan and cook gently, stirring, until the mixture thickens (do not let it boil). Spread the stuffing mixture over the 2 fillets in the baking dish. Place the remaining fillets on top, and cover with the rest of the stuffing. Bake in a preheated 400-degree oven for 20 minutes. Bring to the table sizzling hot.

SERVES 4

Mackerel, Sheepscot Bay Style

A century ago mackerel were first canned in Eastport, Maine, but Yankees have been relishing fresh mackerel since hordes of shining fish were first seen rippling the coastal water in the seventeenth century. Down-East cooks developed this flavorful variation of a traditional baking method.

1 large onion, chopped fine
1 large carrot, scraped and chopped
 fine
1/2 green pepper, seeds and ribs
 removed, chopped fine
1 bay leaf

3/4 cup vinegar
1 tablespoon chopped fresh parsley
1 teaspoon chopped fresh thyme, or
 1/4 teaspoon dried
Salt
4 mackerel (3/4–11/4 pounds each)

Mix the chopped vegetables with the bay leaf and vinegar, and stir in the chopped herbs and a light sprinkling of salt. Simmer over gentle heat for about 20 minutes, then remove the bay leaf. Arrange the mackerel in a greased baking dish in one layer, cover with the sauce, and bake in a preheated 400-degree oven for 25–30 minutes.

SERVES 4

Baked Stuffed Boston Mackerel

2 whole mackerel (about 11/2
 pounds each), gutted
4 tablespoons butter or oil or a
 combination
1 medium onion, chopped
1/3 cup chopped fennel or celery ribs
1 garlic clove, minced (optional)

1 cup fresh bread crumbs
1 tablespoon chopped fresh
 rosemary, or 1/2 teaspoon dried
2 tablespoons chopped parsley
Salt
Freshly ground pepper

GARNISH: lemon wedges

Rinse the mackerel and dry with paper towels. Heat 3 tablespoons butter and/or oil in a small skillet and add the onion and fennel or celery. Sauté, stirring, for about 3 minutes, then add the garlic, if desired, and sauté a few seconds more. Mix this with the bread crumbs, rosemary, and parsley, and add salt and pepper to taste. Spoon the stuffing into the cavities of the mackerel, then skewer or tie the openings closed. With the remaining 1 tablespoon butter and/or oil, grease a baking dish and place the mackerel, side by side, in it. Add a little more salt and pepper to the fish, then bake in a preheated 400-degree oven 25–30 minutes, or until the fish is opaque at the bone. Serve with lemon wedges.

SERVES 4

Monkfish with Garden Vegetables

Monkfish, known as angler, goosefish, bellyfish, and in French *lotte*, are found in cold Atlantic waters. Perhaps because of their ugliness (they have huge heads and enormous jaws) and the relatively small amount of edible flesh, they have generally been considerd trash fish. But in recent years, connoisseurs have been recognizing their firm, subtle-tasting flesh as a considerable delicacy, particularly when simmered with aromatic flavors that the fish readily absorbs. When cooked with lobster, monkfish absorbs the flavor of lobster, and it is difficult to tell, since it is of the same texture, which is the lobster meat and which is the ugly fish. Here the monkfish is simmered with fresh garden vegetables, enhanced by the flavor of all the various juices.

2 tablespoons butter
2 tablespoons vegetable or olive oil
1 large sweet red or white onion, sliced
2 medium sweet ripe peppers, turning to red, or 1 sweet red and 1 yellow, if available, seeded and sliced
2 garlic cloves, finely chopped
2–3 ripe tomatoes, peeled, seeded, and chopped
2 pounds monkfish, cut into 4 pieces

Salt
Freshly ground pepper
1/3 cup dry vermouth or white wine
About 1 tablespoon finely chopped fresh basil, tarragon, or chervil
2 small zucchini, sliced
10–12 plum tomatoes (preferably yellow), halved
3–4 scallions, including tender greens, cut into 1-inch pieces
2 tablespoons chopped parsley

Heat the butter and oil (you can use all butter or all oil if you like) in a large skillet and sauté the onion slices for 1 minute, then add the peppers and garlic and sauté another 30 seconds. Add the chopped tomatoes, stirring and tossing, until they release some of their juices. Push the vegetables aside and add the monkfish pieces, turning them in the pan juices to coat; salt and pepper everything lightly. Pour in the wine, bring to a boil, then sprinkle in the chopped herb. Spoon the vegetables over and around the fish, cover, reduce heat, and simmer 15 minutes. Add the zucchini slices, yellow tomato halves, and scallions. Cover and simmer another 4–5 minutes. The fish should be tender—to test, pierce with a fork; if the flesh is still resistant, cook a few more minutes. Remove the monkfish and the vegetables to a hot platter using a slotted spoon so that the pan juices remain in the pan. Boil these down rapidly until almost syrupy, then pour over the monkfish and vegetables. Sprinkle chopped parsley on top, and serve with small, steamed new potatoes.

SERVES 4

Après-Ski Monkfish Chili

When it comes to skiing, ours is strictly the cross-country style of slogging over Northeast Kingdom fields. But we join many New Englanders in a winter appetite for a bowl of unusual chili and a glowing fireplace at which to warm the feet.

1½ pounds monkfish fillets
Flour
4 tablespoons vegetable oil
¼ cup chopped onion
1 cup chopped celery
½ cup chopped sweet red pepper
½ cup chopped green pepper
1 teaspoon paprika

1 cup chopped cooked tomatoes
2 tablespoons cider vinegar
3 cups cooked lima or other white beans
Salt
Freshly ground pepper
1 tablespoon chili powder
2 tablespoons light rum or sherry

Rinse and dry the fish and cut in 1-inch cubes, then dredge in flour. Heat 2 tablespoons oil in a skillet and sauté the fish, stirring almost constantly, for about 3 minutes. Remove the fish and keep warm. Put the remaining 2 tablespoons oil in a saucepan and stir in the onion, chopped celery, red and green peppers, and paprika. Cook about 5 minutes, then stir in the tomatoes, vinegar, and beans. Simmer a minute or so, and season with a sprinkling of salt and pepper. Stir in the sautéed monkfish pieces, add the chili powder, the liquor, and adjust the seasoning to taste.

SERVES 4–6

Monkfish in Champagne Sauce

This is a splendid dish to make on those rare occasions when a cup or so of champagne may be left over from a party.

1¾–2 pounds monkfish, trimmed
4 shallots, or 1 small white onion, chopped
1 teaspoon chopped fresh chervil or tarragon, or ¼ teaspoon dried
Salt

1½ cups champagne
⅔ cup heavy cream
2 teaspoons softened butter blended with 2 teaspoons flour
2 tablespoons chopped parsley

Monkfish in Champagne Sauce (continued)

Cut the monkfish into ¾-inch slices, and place in a 9–10-inch heavy skillet in overlapping pattern to cover the bottom. Sprinkle the shallots and herbs on top, salt lightly, and pour the champagne over. Bring to a simmer, cover tightly, and simmer 6–7 minutes, until the monkfish pieces are tender when pierced with the point of a knife. Remove the fish with a slotted spoon and keep warm. Add the cream to the pan and boil down rapidly to reduce the sauce by half. Add the butter-and-flour mixture in small pinches, stirring, and continue to boil until the sauce has the consistency of a light cream sauce. Return the fish to the pan and heat through, basting with the sauce. Correct the seasoning, and serve with a sprinkling of parsley on top.
SERVES 4

Ocean Perch with Rum-Blueberry Sauce

Caught by the millions in the Bay of Maine, ocean perch is also known as sea perch, red perch, redfish, rosefish, and Norway haddock. By any other name it would be equally delicious, if served with this surprising but characteristic Down-East embellishment.

1½–2 pounds ocean perch fillets
Salt
Freshly ground pepper
1 cup fresh blueberries
2 tablespoons chopped scallions,
  including some tender greens

4 tablespoons lemon juice
¾ cup rum
5–6 tablespoons butter

GARNISH: *basil leaves, preferably purple*

Sprinkle the fillets with salt and pepper and lay them flat in a buttered shallow baking dish. Prepare the sauce by spinning the berries, scallions, lemon juice, and rum in a blender or food processor until smoothly puréed. Pour the sauce over the fish, and put the dish in a preheated 350-degree oven for about 8 minutes, until the fish separates easily with a fork. Remove the fillets to a warm serving dish, and turn the sauce into a small pan; reduce by half by boiling hard, then lower the heat and stir in the butter. When the sauce has thickened and is smooth, pour it over the fillets and garnish with fresh basil leaves.
SERVES 4

3½–4 pounds octopus, frozen
    (from the Azores)
2 tablespoons olive oil
1 large onion, sliced
3 fat garlic cloves, chopped
2 cups canned plum tomatoes
½ cup red wine

½ cup beer
1 teaspoon paprika
1 teaspoon saffron powder*
1 tablespoon crushed red pepper,
    preserved in a jar*
1½ pounds potatoes, peeled and
    sliced thin

Note: Portuguese saffron powder and preserved red pepper is available in Portuguese neighborhoods.

Octopus, Portuguese Style, in Red Wine and Beer Sauce

Defrost the octopus slowly in the refrigerator. Cut the tentacles off and squeeze them gently to remove any possible oil. Wash carefully in plenty of cold water, then plunge into a large pot of boiling water and boil 1 minute. Drain, and when cool enough to handle, peel off the purplish skin. Cut the tentacles and the rest of the body into 2-inch rings or pieces. Heat the oil in a large heavy casserole and sauté the onion and garlic slowly, stirring, for 5 minutes. Add the drained octopus, the tomatoes and their juice, the red wine, beer, paprika, saffron powder, and crushed pepper (no salt is needed). Bring to a boil, stir well, partially cover, and cook at moderate-to-slow heat for 3 hours, stirring occasionally to make sure that the octopus doesn't stick to the bottom. Spread the potatoes over the bottom of a large, lightly oiled shallow baking pan, and pour the hot octopus and its sauce on top. Cook in a preheated 450-degree oven for 25–30 minutes, until the potatoes are tender.

SERVES 6–8

For those who say that pollack can only be pan-fried to taste good, here is a way to make even frozen pollack turn into a colorful, flavorful dish.

Baked Pollack with Peppers and Tomatoes

1 pound pollack fillets
1 lemon
½ cup olive oil
2 green peppers, seeds and ribs
    removed, cut into strips
2 large onions, sliced
3–4 garlic cloves, chopped fine
3 large tomatoes, peeled and
    chopped

1 bay leaf
Salt
Freshly ground pepper
1 tablespoon chopped fresh thyme,
    or ¾ teaspoon dried
1 cup dry cider or white wine
½ cup applejack, rum, or bourbon

Wipe the fillets with a damp cloth and sprinkle them with the juice of ½ lemon. Cut the other ½ lemon into 4 wedges and reserve. Heat a shallow flameproof casserole, add 4 tablespoons oil, and sauté the green pepper strips, onions, and garlic for about 3 minutes. Stir in the chopped tomatoes,

Baked Pollack with Peppers and Tomatoes (continued)

the bay leaf, a light sprinkling of salt and pepper, and the thyme. Cover the casserole and simmer over low heat for about 10 minutes. Arrange the pollack fillets on top of the vegetable mixture and top each with a lemon wedge and a sprinkling of the remaining oil. Bake in a preheated 350-degree oven for 15 minutes, then add the cider or wine and the liquor. Continue baking for about 25 minutes, until the pollack is easily pierced when tested with a fork. Remove the bay leaf before serving.

SERVES 4

Sweet-and-Sour Pollack

Another good way to give some zip to the lowly pollack.

2 pounds pollack, cut into 2-inch chunks
Flour for dredging, seasoned with a little salt and pepper
3 tablespoons vegetable oil or butter or a combination

4 spring onions, chopped, or 6–8 scallions, white part chopped and tender greens sliced

SAUCE:
¼ cup vinegar (Chinese black vinegar, if available)
¼ cup soy sauce
2 tablespoons sugar

2 tablespoons vegetable oil
2 tablespoons finely chopped fresh ginger

GARNISH: *2–3 tablespoons chopped fresh coriander or parsley*

Dredge the pollack chunks in the flour as you heat up the oil and/or butter in a large skillet. Shake off the excess flour and, when the oil is hot, fry the pieces over medium-high heat for 2–3 minutes, along with the chopped onion or scallion bulbs, until the fish is lightly browned on all sides. Mix the sauce ingredients together, and pour over the fish. Cover and simmer gently about 5 minutes, stirring once or twice. For the last 30 seconds of cooking, toss in the sliced scallion greens, if using. Sprinkle coriander on top, and serve with steamed rice.

SERVES 4

½ pound mushrooms
3 tablespoons butter or oil or a
  combination
4 shallots or 6 scallion bulbs,
  chopped
2 garlic cloves, minced
⅓ cup fresh bread crumbs
Salt
¼ teaspoon or more dried hot red
  pepper flakes

2 whole sea trout or bluefish (about
  1½ pounds each), gutted
3 cups canned plum tomatoes with
  their juice
8 large green olives, pitted and
  roughly chopped
2 tablespoons chopped parsley

Mushroom-Stuffed Whole Fish with Tomatoes and Olives

Chop the mushrooms into small dice. Heat the butter and/or oil in a skillet, then add the shallots, one-half of the minced garlic, and the mushrooms and sauté for 5 minutes, shaking the pan frequently. Mix in the bread crumbs and season with the salt and a pinch of hot pepper flakes. Stuff this mixture into the cavities of the 2 fish, and lay them in a shallow baking dish, side by side. Chop the tomatoes roughly and sauté them with their juice and the remaining minced garlic in the same skillet for 2 minutes, then season with salt and another good pinch of pepper flakes. Stir in the olives, and pour this sauce around the stuffed fish. Sprinkle chopped parsley on top. Cover lightly with aluminum foil and bake in a preheated 425-degree oven for 30 minutes, or until the flesh comes easily away from the bone.
SERVES 4

2 tablespoons butter or vegetable
  oil or a combination
2 large ripe tomatoes, peeled,
  seeded, and chopped
6 scallion bulbs or 4 shallots, finely
  chopped
½ cup dry white wine or vermouth

2 cups sorrel (about ¼ pound),
  stems removed, cut in strips
4 salmon steaks (about ¾ inch)
Salt
Freshly ground pepper
½ cup heavy cream
2 tablespoons chopped parsley

Salmon Steaks with Tomatoes and Sorrel

In a large skillet, heat the butter and/or oil, then sauté the tomatoes and scallions or shallots for 2–3 minutes, tossing and stirring. Add the wine and sorrel and cook down briskly for 1 minute. Lay the salmon steaks in the pan, season with salt and pepper, and spoon the vegetables over and around the fish. Cook, covered, for 8 minutes, over a medium flame, turning once. Remove the salmon to a hot platter, add the cream and cook down the sauce over a brisk flame for 30 seconds, until lightly thickened, then pour over the fish, and sprinkle parsley on top.
SERVES 4

Salmon Sebago

The 1986 allotment for stocking Maine's salmon rivers was a grand total of 1.2 million young fish, some of which undoubtedly will be caught some future day by Angus Cameron, who recorded in the *L. L. Bean Game and Fish Cookbook* that he first tasted "fresh-caught Maine landlocks at a noon lunch at East Grand Lake; they were grilled over hot coals and they were delicious." Here's his recipe.

2½ pounds landlocked salmon
    fillets
4 tablespoons softened butter

2 tablespoons chopped parsley
Salt
Freshly ground pepper

GREEN MAYONNAISE:
1 tablespoon lemon juice
2–3 leaves of spinach, trimmed
    from stems
2 tablespoons fresh tarragon, or 1
    teaspoon dried

2 tablespoons chives or tops of
    scallions
2 tablespoons capers
1½ cups mayonnaise

Brush the fish with the butter mixed with parsley, and sprinkle lightly with salt and pepper. In a preheated broiler whose pan or rack has been greased with cooking oil, broil the fillets about 3 inches from the flame or filament for about 4 minutes for the first side. Turn and broil the second side about 5 minutes more. Meanwhile, make the green mayonnaise by tossing into a blender or food processor the lemon juice, spinach (or other greens), herbs, and capers. Purée, then mix into the mayonnaise. Serve the green mayonnaise alongside the salmon.
SERVES 4

Fourth of July Salmon with New Peas and New Potatoes

It was John Adams who urged that Independence Day be celebrated with parades and fireworks, and it was nature's timing that has made fresh salmon, the season's first peas, new potatoes, and strawberry shortcake the classic Fourth of July main course. Inland Yankees weren't always able to have freshly caught local salmon on hand, and a whole delicately pink–fleshed fish isn't easy on the budget today. But for a good-size Independence Day gathering of family or friends, the traditional celebration of the Declaration of Independence is as worthy of its own menu as is Thanksgiving.

1 whole salmon, with its head
    (about 8 pounds)
¼ cup chopped celery
¼ cup chopped carrot

1 scallion, chopped
2 bay leaves
Salt

EGG SAUCE:
6 tablespoons butter
6 tablespoons flour
1½ cups hot fish stock or
    salmon-steaming broth
1½ cups milk
Salt
Freshly ground pepper

A few drops Tabasco sauce
A few drops fresh lemon juice
3 hard-boiled eggs, chopped
1 teaspoon minced fresh dill
    or chervil
2 tablespoons chopped fresh
    parsley

In a fish steamer or a pan large enough to hold the fish whole, place the salmon on a rack and pour in boiling water to just beneath the rack; it should not touch the fish. Add the vegetables and bay leaves, and sprinkle well with salt. Cover the pan—you may use heavy-duty aluminum foil, if necessary. Steam about 45 minutes, adding more water if it threatens to boil away.

Make the egg sauce: Melt the butter in a heavy saucepan and stir in the flour. Cook over low heat, stirring, 2–3 minutes, then add 1 cup fish stock or the steaming liquid from the poached salmon. Return to the heat, stir until the sauce thickens, and add the milk, whisking until smooth. Season to taste with salt, pepper, Tabasco, and lemon juice, then fold in the chopped eggs and herbs. Heat through. Put the salmon on a platter, remove the skin, and coat with a little of the egg sauce, passing the rest in a bowl. Serve with steamed new potatoes and garden peas cooked in a little boiling water until just tender.

SERVES 12 OR MORE

Stuffed Sardines

2½ pounds fresh sardines
Salt
⅓ cup olive oil
½ cup fresh bread crumbs
½ cup pine nuts
½ cup yellow raisins
5 anchovies, chopped

3 scallion bulbs or 3 shallots, finely
    chopped
3 tablespoons chopped parsley
Freshly ground pepper
3 bay leaves
Juice of 1 lemon, or more

Wash the sardines, chop off the heads, split open the belly sides, gut, and remove the backbones. Soak in about 4 cups water with 1 teaspoon salt while you prepare the stuffing.

Heat ¼ cup olive oil in a small skillet, toss in all but 2 tablespoons of the bread crumbs and fry, stirring, until they turn golden. Add the pine nuts and brown them lightly. Mix in the raisins, anchovies, scallions or shallots, and parsley, and season with pepper. Drain the sardines and pat dry. Spoon equal amounts of the stuffing into the sardine cavities, and lay them, side by side, in a shallow oiled baking dish just large enough to hold them in one layer. Sprinkle the remaining bread crumbs on top, drizzle the remaining oil over, and strew bay leaves, broken in half, over the surface. Bake in a preheated 375-degree oven for 30 minutes. Remove the pieces of bay leaves and squeeze lemon juice over.

SERVES 4

Crusted Broiled Scrod

2 pounds scrod fillets
Salt
Freshly ground pepper
½ cup softened butter
2 cups fine cracker crumbs
4–5 tablespoons finely chopped green pepper

4 tablespoons finely chopped onion
1 tablespoon Dijon mustard
1 teaspoon Worcestershire sauce
Tabasco sauce
Juice of ½ lemon

Cut the fillets in half and sprinkle them lightly with salt and a few turns of the pepper grinder. Melt 1 tablespoon butter and keep warm, while mixing

Scrod

According to Fannie Farmer, writing back in 1896, "A young cod, split down the back and backbone removed, except for a small portion of the tail, is called a scrod." Purists might elaborate, maintaining that the true scrod is a small codfish, weighing between 1 and 2 pounds, and adding that broiled scrod is a strictly New England dish that once lured serious eaters to Boston hotels, where more than one chef increased his fame by serving it.

"The story goes," Alan Davidson's scholarly *North Atlantic Seafood* tells us, "that the Parker House, a famous old restaurant in Boston, always had the freshest fish of the day on its menu. But the manager never knew which this would be on a given day. So he invented the word scrod as a catch-all name for it. Thus, although scrod now officially means young cod, it is historically correct to use it for, e.g., young haddock too."

Begging the issue is small comfort to some authorities. One of them wrote heatedly that fish markets still "sell unsuspecting housewives 'scrodded' pollock, and hotels serve revolting chunks of 20-pound cod and haddock as 'scrod,' which is a gross insult and a piece of barefaced misrepresentation."

The moral: To cook something that deserves to be called scrod, look for young, very fresh whole codfish that is boned and split, and weighs about 2½ pounds or less.

the remaining butter with the cracker crumbs, green pepper, onion, mustard, Worcestershire, a liberal sprinkling of Tabasco, and the lemon juice. Pour the melted butter into a broiling pan and arrange the fish pieces in it. Broil 5 minutes, then turn the pieces over with a spatula and spread them with the crust mixture. Broil about 6–8 minutes, until the fish begins to flake and the crust is lightly browned.

SERVES 4

Scrod with Leeks and Sweet Red Peppers

1 large sweet red pepper, broiled
   and peeled (page 25)
3 large leeks
3 tablespoons butter or vegetable
   oil or a combination
Salt

Freshly ground pepper
2 pounds scrod, in 2 pieces
3–4 tablespoons roughly chopped
   fresh tarragon, or 1 teaspoon
   dried
1/3 cup dry white wine

Cut the red pepper into strips and remove the seeds. Cut off the top tough green portion of the leeks, then cut them into pencil-like strips; swish them in cold water to remove grit, then drain thoroughly. Heat the butter and/or oil in a heavy skillet or a shallow flameproof dish that can be used for serving (it should be big enough to accommodate the scrod) and sauté the leeks, stirring and tossing, for 5 minutes. Salt and pepper the fish on both sides, then place the pieces on top of the bed of leeks, strewing a few leeks along with the red pepper strips and tarragon on top. Pour the wine around, bring to a boil, cover with foil, then place in a preheated 450-degree oven and bake for 10–15 minutes, depending on the thickness of the scrod; don't overcook—the fish should remain juicy.

SERVES 4

Shad in Milk

The shad that runs in the spring is a bony creature, but fortunately one can buy skillfully boned sides of shad. It is always good grilled quickly over a hot fire and served with lemon, but if you are broiling it, this is a good way to keep the flesh moist.

2 sides of shad (about 2 pounds)
Juice of 1/2 lemon
Salt
Freshly ground pepper
3/4 cup milk

2 tablespoons cider vinegar
1 cup fresh bread crumbs mixed
   with 1/4 cup chopped parsley
2 tablespoons butter

Place the 2 sides of shad, skin side down, in a lightly buttered shallow flameproof dish that is large enough to hold them in one layer. Squeeze

Shad in Milk (continued)

fresh lemon juice over them and season lightly with salt and pepper. Mix the milk with the vinegar, and pour this around the fish. Bring to a simmer on top of the stove, then place 6 inches under a preheated broiler. Broil for 10 minutes, basting twice with the milk. Sprinkle the parsleyed bread crumbs on top, dot with butter, and put under the broiler again about 3–4 minutes, until lightly browned on top.

SERVES 6

Shad Cookouts

Clambakes, no doubt, are much better known and increasingly popular among regional travelers, but the outdoor feasts that celebrate spring and the running of shad are further proof of how good simple Yankee food can be. In Essex, Connecticut, the first Saturday in June has been the traditional Shad Bake Day for generations. The boned fish are pinned to hardwood planks and tilted beside glowing fires, as they are baked by volunteers and served forth to all comers. Up the Connecticut River, the Enfield Dam site was a mecca for thousands when the shad arrived and Edward T. Bement was the bake master.

The boned shad fillets are spread out and painted with lemon juice, lightly salted and peppered for an outdoor cookout. Grilled shad are cooked about 12 minutes, until golden brown, then turned over for a further cooking of 10 minutes, with the skin side down. Remove to a dish or platter and spread with butter, adding a light sprinkling of salt and cayenne. Serve with pickled walnuts or butternuts.

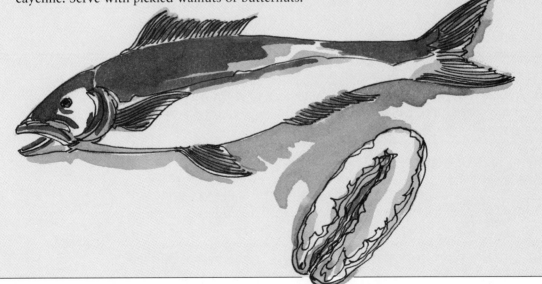

Wild sorrel and the first run of shad with its tender roe—what a way to celebrate spring in New England. Mrs. N. K. M. Lee, who signed herself "A Boston Housewife" when she published *The Cook's Own Book* in 1832, offered a method of preparing sorrel not unlike this one, but she suggested it as a sauce for an omelet.

Shad and Roe in Sorrel Sauce

1 large onion, chopped
1 cup water
1 pair shad roe
Salt
2 tablespoons softened butter

2 sides shad (about 1½ pounds)
Freshly ground pepper
Bunch of sorrel (about 1½ cups
    torn leaves)
⅓ cup heavy cream

In a medium-size saucepan or skillet, simmer the chopped onion in the water about 5 minutes. Add the shad roe and sprinkle lightly with salt. Cover and simmer very gently for 8 minutes, turning once. Remove the roe, reserving the cooking liquid. Smear 1 tablespoon butter over the bottom of a shallow baking dish just big enough to accommodate the fish in one layer. Separate the 2 halves of the roe and place one half in the center of each side of shad, opening the flaps, pressing the roe down, and then returning the flaps, which should just about cover the roe. Smear the remaining 1 tablespoon butter on the top and season with salt and pepper. Place the dish about 4 inches under a preheated broiler and cook for 10–12 minutes—be careful not to overcook the fish. Meanwhile, add the torn sorrel leaves to the roe cooking liquid and boil 4–5 minutes. Add the cream and simmer another minute, then purée in a blender or food processor. Spoon the sauce over broiled fish just before serving.
SERVES 4

8 tablespoons (1 stick) butter
4 pair shad roe
Salt
Freshly ground pepper

8 strips bacon
2 tablespoons chopped parsley or
    chives or a combination
4 lemon wedges

Shad Roe and Bacon

Melt the butter slowly in a skillet large enough to hold the 4 pair of roe in one layer. Add the roe, turning them in the butter, salt and pepper lightly, cover, and cook slowly for about 12–15 minutes, turning the pieces again several times. Meanwhile, fry or grill the bacon until crisp, and drain on paper towels. Serve the roe with the pan juices poured over and parsley and/or chives sprinkled on top, accompanied by lemon wedges and the bacon.
SERVES 4

Skate Wings in Caper Sauce

Skate is another fish that has too long been considered a trash fish—something that floated in with the tide. Fortunately it is being rediscovered (the French and Italians have long appreciated the delicacy of the skate's wings, the only part that is eaten).

1 large onion, sliced thin
1 carrot, scraped and sliced
2 ribs celery
4 whole sprigs parsley
1½ cups water
¾ cup dry vermouth
2 pounds skate wings, skinned and
  cut into 4 pieces

Salt
Freshly ground pepper
6 tablespoons cold butter, in 6
  pieces
3 tablespoons capers, drained

Place the onion, carrot, celery, parsley, water, and vermouth in a large skillet and boil about 3 minutes. Let cool for a few minutes. Add the skate wings to the broth, sprinkle with salt and pepper, cover with foil, and let simmer gently 40–45 minutes, until tender. Remove the fish and keep warm. Strain the cooking liquid and return it to the skillet. Boil until reduced to about 1 cup. Now start whisking in the butter, piece by piece, until it is all absorbed. Add the capers to heat through, then pour the sauce over the fish.

SERVES 4

Crumb-Coated Smelts with Almonds

2 pounds (18–24) smelts
Flour for dredging
Salt
Freshly ground pepper
2 eggs, lightly beaten
2 cups fresh bread crumbs

Oil for frying
3 tablespoons butter
¼ cup slivered almonds
Few drops fresh lemon juice
GARNISH: lemon wedges

Scale and gut the smelts, leaving intact the heads and any roe you may find (true smelt lovers will eat heads and all of the fried fish, and the roe is a treat for anyone). Rinse the fish and dry them thoroughly. Season the flour with salt and pepper, and just before you are ready to cook the smelts, heat about ¼ inch of oil in a large skillet. Dredge each fish in the seasoned flour, shake off the excess, then dip the fish into the egg, roll in the bread crumbs, and quickly drop into the hot oil. Repeat quickly until you have filled the skillet without crowding it (you will probably have to fry the fish in 2 batches, unless you have a very large camp-size skillet). Fry the smelts over medium-high heat 3 minutes on one side, then turn and fry on the other side 2–3 minutes, until golden. Remove from the pan and keep warm.

When all are done, pour out the frying oil and swirl in the butter. Add the almonds and brown them quickly, turning and tossing them. Sprinkle them over the fish, drizzle on what butter remains, and season with a little lemon juice. Serve with lemon wedges.

SERVES 4

Fried Smelts

The earliest chance in Maine to catch smelts is at a spot on the Kennebec River, below the Augusta dam, where lures are permitted because of the tidal water. No matter the game laws, smelts are delicious when stuffed and baked as Fannie Farmer used to make them, or they may be broiled or fried in a number of ways. Here cracker crumbs are used in traditional Yankee fashion; but a dusting of cornmeal is equally authentic in New England.

24 smelts (about 2 pounds),
   cleaned, with heads remaining
1 cup cracker crumbs
Salt
Freshly ground pepper

Paprika (optional)
⅓–½ cup butter
2 tablespoons bacon fat

GARNISH: sprigs parsley

Wipe the fish with a damp cloth. Mix the cracker crumbs with a little salt, a sprinkling of fresh pepper, and a little paprika, if desired. Roll the fish in this mixture. Heat ⅓ cup of the butter and the bacon fat in a skillet without allowing smoke to form. Add the fish and fry 3 minutes, then turn the fish, adding more butter if needed—plenty of fat is called for. Brown quickly another 2 minutes, until crust is crisp but the fish is juicy inside. Place on a heated platter and garnish with parsley sprigs. Serve very hot on hot plates.

SERVES 4

Cold Pink Snapper with Sorrel Mayonnaise

2 whole pink snappers (about 2
   pounds each), gutted and scaled,
   heads left on
Vinegar
Salt

2 cups tightly packed fresh sorrel
   leaves, strings removed if coarse
1 cup homemade mayonnaise
   (page 347)
1 hard-boiled egg, finely chopped

GARNISH: sprigs parsley or fresh coriander
        lemon slices

If you don't have a pot big enough to hold the 2 snappers in one layer, cook them one after the other. You'll need enough water to cover the fish by 1 inch. For each quart of water, add 1 tablespoon vinegar and ½ teaspoon salt. Bring to a boil, then gently lower the fish into the water, and

Cold Pink Snapper with Sorrel Mayonnaise (continued)

when the water has just returned to the boil, turn down the heat and simmer the fish very gently, covered, for 10 minutes. Remove to a platter and let cool, then refrigerate.

Meanwhile, cook the sorrel in water to cover until very tender—it will take only a minute or so if very tender. Let thoroughly drain in a colander, and when cool, mix with the mayonnaise (you won't need to chop it because the cooked leaves will dissolve easily into the sauce). Spread some of the sorrel mayonnaise over the cold fish, sprinkle chopped egg on top, and decorate the platter with parsley or coriander sprigs and lemon slices. If you have prepared the dish ahead and chilled it, remove from the refrigerator at least 15 minutes before serving.

SERVES 4–6

Sea Squabs Braised with Fennel and Mushrooms

Old-timers call them puffers or blowfish or swellfish, and today fishmongers sell them for good prices from Maine to Cape Cod and Block Island.

1 large fennel bulb
3 tablespoons butter
¼ pound mushrooms, sliced
1½ pounds sea squabs
Flour for dredging
Salt

Freshly ground pepper
¼ cup dry white wine or dry
   vermouth
2 tablespoons chopped fresh
   chervil, or 1 teaspoon dried

Remove the tough thin stalks and feathery leaves from the fennel, saving and chopping a few of the leaves for a garnish. Slice the fennel bulb lengthwise in ¼-inch slices, and separate the pieces from the root end to make sticklike pieces. Sauté the fennel in 2 tablespoons butter for 5 minutes, then add the mushrooms, sautéing and tossing for 2 minutes more. Dredge the sea squabs in flour seasoned with salt and pepper. Push the vegetables aside

and add the remaining 1 tablespoon butter to the skillet, then sauté the sea squabs, turning them, until golden on both sides. Add the wine, blanket the fish with the vegetables, cover, and cook gently for about 5 minutes, until the fish is tender. Sprinkle on the chopped fennel leaves and chervil.
SERVES 4

Sea Squabs over a Bed of Leeks

About 1¾ pounds leeks
2 tablespoons butter
¾ cup water
3 tablespoons heavy cream
1 large carrot, scraped
1 medium zucchini
1 tablespoon vegetable oil
Salt
¾ pound sea squabs
Flour for dredging
¾ tablespoon vegetable oil mixed
    with ¾ tablespoon olive oil

Slice the leeks, using only the tender part of the greens, and wash them thoroughly in cold water; drain. Heat the butter in a skillet and sauté the leeks until coated with butter, then add the water, cover, and cook slowly until tender—about 30 minutes, less if the leeks are very young. When done, the water should have evaporated; if not, boil it off quickly, uncovered, then add cream. Meanwhile, cut the carrot and zucchini into julienne strips, and stir-fry them in the vegetable oil, adding salt and a few drops of water. Cover and let them steam over moderate heat for about 1 minute; they should remain bright in color and slightly crisp. Dredge the fish in flour and sauté for 5–6 minutes in the vegetable and olive oils, turning them occasionally. Spoon the leeks onto hot serving plates, place the sea squabs on top, and garnish with the carrot and zucchini strips.
SERVES 2–3

Sea Trout with Anchovies and Herbs

4 anchovies, preserved in oil
4 tablespoons olive oil
1 tablespoon chopped fresh herbs,
    such as parsley and dill or savory
    or marjoram
2 pounds sea trout fillets
Freshly ground pepper
3 scallions, including tender greens,
    chopped

Drain the anchovies, and mash with the olive oil and herbs. Lay the sea trout fillets in a lightly oiled pan, skin side down, all in one layer. Grind fresh pepper over them, and spread the anchovy mixture on top. Place on the second rung down from the broiler and broil in a preheated broiler 10 minutes, then scatter the scallions on top and broil another 4–5 minutes, until the fish separates in the thickest part when tested with a knife.
SERVES 4

Squid, and How to Prepare Them

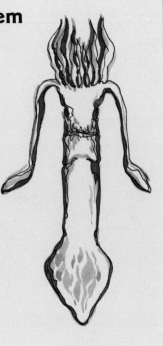

A nutritious gem of the sea," is what squid have been called, in spite of the squeamishness that exists about them. They abound in waters off Cape Cod and are prepared in many ways by New England fishermen's wives.

To prepare squid: Hold the body of the squid in one hand and the head and tentacles in the other, and pull gently to separate the two. Cut off the tentacles just beyond the eyes and reserve them. Discard the head. Remove the hard nubbin from where the tentacles were attached, and pull the thin bone that resembles a quill or a piece of cellophane out of the body and discard it. Rinse very thoroughly under running water, then peel the grayish skin from the body.

Alex Delicata's Sautéed Squid

Squid prepared by Alex Delicata (for information about him see the box on page 444) is unlike any squid you've ever tasted—or maybe not wanted to taste because the rubber-band-like rings on the plate looked so unappealing. If you cut the squid the way he recommends, the delicate pieces curl up like shavings and can be very quickly cooked, so they are wonderfully tender.

1½ pounds squid, cleaned (page 120)
1–2 fat cloves garlic, crushed and peeled
2 tablespoons butter
2 tablespoons olive oil
About 3 tablespoons chopped fresh parsley and basil
Salt
Freshly ground pepper

Slice all the squid down the length of the body and open them out flat. Cut diagonally across to get the longest possible slices, no more than ¼ to ½ inch wide. Sever the tentacles just in front of the mouth so that they can curl up like rosettes. Heat the butter and olive oil in a skillet and when bubbling, add the crushed garlic and the squid. Sprinkle on the parsley and basil and cook quickly, stirring and tossing, over medium to high heat about 5 minutes. Season to taste with salt and pepper and serve immediately.
SERVES 4

12 squid, cleaned (see box, page 120), with sacs 5–6 inches long
¼ pound lingüiça, cut into small dice
2 tablespoons minced shallots or small white onion
¼ pound mushrooms, finely chopped
¼ cup chopped parsley
1½ cups fresh bread crumbs
1 egg, lightly beaten
Salt
Freshly ground pepper
2 tablespoons olive oil
1¼ cups dry white wine or vermouth

Stuffed Squid, Portuguese Style

After you have prepared the squid, rinse out the sacs and pat dry. Chop the tentacles into very small pieces. Sauté the *lingüiça* in a skillet and when it has released some of its fat, add the shallots, mushrooms, and minced tentacles. Sauté over medium heat for 5 minutes, stirring. Remove from the heat and mix in 2 tablespoons parsley, the bread crumbs, and beaten egg, and season to taste with salt and pepper. Spoon equal amounts of this stuffing into the squid sacs, filling them about two-thirds full. Heat the olive oil in a skillet large enough to hold the squid in one layer, then lay in the stuffed sacs and brown them lightly on one side for 1–2 minutes. Turn and brown on the other side. Pour the wine into the skillet and when it bubbles up, turn the heat down and simmer gently, covered, for 1 hour. Check occasionally to make sure that the liquid has not evaporated, and add a little water if necessary. Serve hot with the remaining parsley sprinkled over the top.

SERVES 4–6

Grilled or Broiled Swordfish

Some years swordfish and summer Yankees arrive at places like Little Compton and Nantucket and Martha's Vineyard almost simultaneously— and the fish become high points of celebratory feasting. Swordfish is wonderful when grilled outdoors within scent of the sea; and similar effects can be managed when broiled indoors. With fennel turning up frequently in New England gardens, the stalks of this aromatic plant may be thrown on the fire as a bed for grilling the fish, or the fibrous seeds may be steeped in wine or hard cider for a flavorsome basting sauce.

1 teaspoon fennel seeds
¾ cup wine or cider
3 tablespoons olive oil
2 pounds swordfish steaks
3–4 tablespoons chopped fresh tarragon
Salt
Freshly ground pepper

GARNISH: lemon quarters

Crush the fennel seeds lightly, then simmer in the wine or cider for 5 minutes, reducing slightly. Stir in the oil. Bring the fish to room temperature just before cooking. Paint both sides of steaks with the wine-fennel mixture,

Grilled or Broiled Swordfish (continued)

and grill over a bed of hot coals 3–4 minutes per side, painting again as you turn the steaks, until the flesh can be easily pierced but is still moist and the exterior is marked by golden stripes from the grill. At the last minute while the fish is still cooking, sprinkle on the chopped tarragon, letting the herb absorb some of the surface juices. Sprinkle with salt and pepper, and serve with lemon quarters.

To broil indoors: Line a broiling pan with foil and grease it with 1 tablespoon butter or oil. Place the fish steaks on the foil, pour the wine-fennel-oil marinade over them, and sprinkle with salt and pepper. Place the broiling pan at the highest level under a preheated broiler and broil 5 minutes, then turn, baste with the pan juices, and broil another 4–5 minutes on the other side. Sprinkle tarragon on top and serve with lemon quarters.
SERVES 4

Oat-Crusted Brook Trout

4 trout (6–8 inches long), gutted	1/3 cup rolled oats
Salt	2 tablespoons butter
Freshly ground pepper	1 tablespoon oil

Rinse the trout, pat them dry, and season with salt and pepper inside and out. Spread out the oats and press the fish down on them, covering both sides with the oats. Heat the butter and oil in a skillet and cook the trout over moderate heat, about 5 minutes to a side, turning carefully to keep the crust of oats intact.
SERVES 4 FOR BREAKFAST; 2 FOR SUPPER WITH TOAST

Pan-Fried Brook Trout with Lettuce

A handful of cooked fiddleheads (optional) certifies the springtime aura of this combination of fish and sautéed lettuce.

4 brook trout, gutted, with head and tail intact	1 tablespoon butter
2 tablespoons flour	1 head soft lettuce (Boston, bibb, etc.), shredded
Salt	Juice of 1/2 lemon
Freshly ground pepper	About 12 cooked fiddleheads (page 44) (optional)
4 tablespoons vegetable oil	

Rinse the fish under cold water and pat dry. Sprinkle lightly with flour, salt, and pepper. In a 12-inch skillet, heat the oil and butter. When hot, arrange the fish, side by side, with a little space between them in one half of the pan, and spread the lettuce on the other half of the pan. Cook about 4 minutes over medium-high heat and turn the fish over. Use a spatula to turn the lettuce over. Squeeze lemon juice on the fish and lettuce and brown the fish on the other side for about 3 minutes. Stir the cooked fiddleheads into the lettuce and heat well. Divide the greens and arrange neatly beside the trout on heated plates.

SERVES 4

Spinach Soufflé Roll Filled with Smoked Trout

1½ pounds fresh spinach
3 tablespoons butter
⅓ cup flour
1½ cups milk
4 eggs
⅛ teaspoon mace
A few gratings fresh nutmeg
Salt
Freshly ground pepper
⅛ teaspoon cream of tartar
3 smoked trout
¾ cup sour cream
About 2 tablespoons grated horseradish
About 10 narrow, thin strips smoked salmon

Wash the spinach thoroughly and remove tough stems. Cook in boiling salted water to cover for about 5 minutes, or until tender. Drain, squeeze dry, and chop.

Melt the butter in a saucepan, stir in the flour, and cook slowly, stirring, 2 minutes. Off heat, pour in the milk, whisk to blend, then return to moderate heat and whisk until thick. One by one, separate the eggs, putting the whites in a large, clean bowl and dropping the yolks into the sauce, stirring rapidly after each addition to incorporate. Stir in the chopped spinach, season with mace, nutmeg, and salt and pepper to taste. Butter a jelly-roll pan (15 x 12 inches), fit in a piece of wax paper large enough to come up the sides, and butter that liberally. Now beat the egg whites until they foam. Add a pinch of salt and the cream of tartar and continue beating until they form firm peaks. Beat a big spoonful of whites into the cream sauce mixture to lighten it, then fold the rest of the whites in gently. Spread this mixture evenly into the prepared pan and bake in a preheated 425-degree oven for 15 minutes.

Meanwhile, remove the flesh from the trout, making sure to pick out any small bones, and break up the fish into smallish pieces. Mix the sour cream and horseradish with the trout.

Remove the soufflé from the oven and flip it over onto a dish towel that you have wet and wrung out thoroughly. Remove the pan, peel off the wax paper, and trim the edges. Spread the filling down the center. First roll the near side up over the center, then the far side. Using the towel as an aid, flip the soufflé roll onto a warm platter, and lay strips of smoked salmon over the top in a crisscross pattern. If you aren't serving the soufflé immediately (and it can be made ahead), wrap it in foil and reheat in a preheated 350-degree oven for 20 minutes.

SERVES 6–8

Trout Stuffed and Garnished with Fiddleheads

½ pound fiddleheads, cleaned and trimmed
4 scallions, including some of tender greens, chopped
2 tablespoons olive oil or butter
¾ cup fresh bread crumbs
Salt

Freshly ground pepper
2 teaspoons chopped fresh savory, or ½ teaspoon dried
4 trout, gutted and boned
2 tablespoons vegetable oil
2 tablespoons butter
Juice of ½ lemon

GARNISH: *lemon wedges*

Cook the fiddleheads in boiling salted water to cover for 7–8 minutes, until just tender. Drain, rinse, and pat dry. Set aside about 20 fiddleheads (more if very small) and chop the remaining fiddleheads, and mix these with the scallions. Heat the olive oil or butter in a small skillet and add the bread crumbs, stirring and tossing over medium heat until they turn golden brown. Mix with the chopped fiddleheads, season to taste with salt and pepper, and add the savory. Dry the trout thoroughly and spoon equal portions of the fiddlehead–bread crumb mixture into the cavities (you do not need to skewer them closed if you are careful when handling the fish). Heat the vegetable oil and butter in a large pan and when foaming, lay in the stuffed trout. Cook over medium heat 3 minutes, then carefully turn the fish and cook on the other side 3 minutes more, squeezing on the lemon juice and basting with the pan juices. Half a minute before they are done, add the reserved whole fiddleheads and let them heat through. Serve each fish with fiddleheads scattered around and lemon wedges on the side.
SERVES 4

Broiled Marinated Tuna Fish Steaks

3 tablespoons fresh lemon juice
¼ cup olive oil
3 tablespoons chopped fresh dill
2 tablespoons grated fresh ginger

1 teaspoon soy sauce
4 tuna fish steaks (about 5–6 ounces each, about ⅔ inch thick)

Mix the lemon juice, oil, dill, ginger, and soy sauce together in a shallow dish large enough to hold the fish in one layer. Score the fish steaks lightly on both sides, and place in the dish with the marinade. Let sit 30 minutes to 1 hour at room temperature, turning occasionally. Preheat the broiler and when hot, place the tuna steaks on the highest rung with some of the marinade clinging to them. Broil for 3 minutes on one side, baste liberally with the marinade, and broil 1 minute on the other side. Serve immediately with a stir-fry of lightly cooked vegetables such as zucchini, sugar snap peas, and Jerusalem artichokes (page 310).
SERVES 4

Narragansett Indians knew these fish as *squeteagues,* and Connecticut fishermen on Long Island Sound sometimes call them sea trout. Under any name, their flesh tears easily (thus is weak), but they are usually inexpensive and make good eating.

1½–2 pounds weakfish fillets
Salt
Freshly ground pepper
Flour
2 eggs, well beaten
½ cup cracker crumbs
Cooking oil
Butter

2 scallions, with some of the tender
  greens, chopped fine
¼ cup finely chopped green pepper
1 tablespoon chopped fresh
  marjoram
2–3 tablespoons chopped parsley
1–2 tablespoons prepared mustard
Dash Tabasco sauce

Wipe the fillets and dry thoroughly, season lightly with salt and pepper, and dust with flour. Dip the fish in the beaten eggs, then in the cracker crumbs. Heat equal parts of oil and butter to cover the bottom of a skillet. Cook the fish 8–10 minutes on each side, depending on thickness. Mix about 5 tablespoons butter with the chopped scallions, green pepper, and herbs, stir in the mustard, and add a dash of Tabasco. Serve the seasoned butter with the hot fish.
SERVES 4

Weakfish in Cracker Crumbs with Mustard Butter

2 cups cooked fish
¾ cup fresh bread crumbs
2 eggs
½ cup melted butter
2 teaspoons lemon juice

SAUCE:
1 medium onion, chopped fine
2 tablespoons olive or vegetable oil
1½ pounds ripe tomatoes
Pinch of sugar (optional)

2 teaspoons chopped fresh tarragon
  or dill
Salt
Tabasco sauce to taste

Salt
Freshly ground pepper
1–2 tablespoons chopped fresh
  basil

Break up the fish into small flakes, and mix with the bread crumbs. Separate the eggs, and mix the yolks with the melted butter, then add this to the fish. Season with lemon juice, herbs, salt to taste, and a few drops of Tabasco, mixing thoroughly. Beat the egg whites until they form soft peaks, then fold the egg whites into the fish mixture. Scrape into a buttered 1½–2-quart baking dish and place the dish in a large pan filled with enough hot water so that it comes about two-thirds up the sides. Bake in a preheated 325-degree oven for 45 minutes, or until set and lightly browned on top.

Baked Fish Pudding with Fresh Tomato Sauce

Meanwhile, make the tomato sauce. Sauté the onion in the olive oil until translucent. Peel the tomatoes, squeeze out most of the seeds, then chop them into dice. Add the chopped tomatoes to the onion, cover, and boil gently about 20 minutes. Season with a little sugar if the tomatoes aren't very sweet, and add salt and pepper to taste. Pour into a serving bowl and sprinkle chopped basil on top. Serve the fish pudding from its dish and pass the sauce along with it.

SERVES 4

Fish Cakes

Fish cakes can be made with any kind of leftover cooked fish, and they provide a fine way of using up all those little scraps that cling to the bone when you have served 2 large fish the night before. If you don't have quite enough to make a meal, you can always supplement leftovers with canned salmon or crabmeat. And salt cod in various guises has for generations provided some of the tastiest fish cakes, often served for breakfast or supper.

3 cups cooked fish, flaked (see suggestions above)
2 tablespoons lemon juice
3 cups boiled potatoes put through a ricer or food mill
½ cup minced onion
2 teaspoons mustard, preferably Dijon
1 tablespoon finely chopped dill
1 tablespoon finely chopped parsley
Salt
Freshly ground pepper
Dashes hot sauce or Tabasco
Oil for frying
Flour for dusting

Beat the fish with a fork to break it up and work in the lemon juice. Mix in the potatoes, onion, mustard, dill, and parsley, and add salt, pepper, and hot pepper to taste. Put in the refrigerator to chill thoroughly. Form the mixture into cakes about 3 inches in diameter. Heat ⅛ inch oil in a large frying pan, and just before dropping the fish cakes into the pan, dust each one on both sides with flour. Don't crowd the pan—you will probably have to fry the cakes in 2 batches. Cook over medium heat until browned on the bottom—about 2–3 minutes—then turn and cook the other side the same amount of time. Serve with unsweetened ketchup or tartar sauce.

MAKES 12 FISH CAKES

SHELLFISH

Fried Clams

About fried clams James Beard wrote, "These to clam lovers are as tank wine is to lovers of good Burgundy. Murder." Nevertheless fried-clam bars continue to boom along the New England coast from Connecticut to northern Maine, and it seems that most of us can't get enough of them. True aficionados will tell you that only Ipswich clams, sometimes known as belly clams, should be used for frying. In Essex, Massachusetts, purported to be the place where fried clams originated, the batter is made of cornmeal moistened with condensed milk, but we have found that finely ground cracker crumbs produce a much crisper coating. A few important rules: Always coat the clams first in flour before dunking them in the egg batter and finally the crumbs; never start coating them until your oil is hot, or they will get soggy; be sure the oil is at 375 degrees when the clams go in and don't fry too many at a time so that you can maintain that heat. Here is the recipe we have found the most successful.

*4 quarts Ipswich clams, or about ½
  quart shelled
Fresh vegetable oil for frying
About 1 cup flour
½ teaspoon salt
Several grindings of fresh pepper
Dash of cayenne
3 eggs
¼ cup condensed milk or heavy
  cream
2 cups finely ground cracker
  crumbs*

Scrub the clams and wash them thoroughly in several changes of water. Press a knife between the shell of each clam and run it around the edge; they should open easily (catch the juices and save to use in a chowder). Be sure to skin the necks; make a slit down the neck lengthwise and peel and discard the tough skin. Or, if you are lucky enough to get the clams already freshly shucked, they will probably have been cleaned, i.e., the neck skin removed. Start heating at least 2 inches of oil in a frying kettle. Season the flour with the salt, pepper, and cayenne, and spread it out on wax paper near the stove. Beat the eggs with the condensed milk or cream in a bowl and place that next to the seasoned flour. Spread the cracker crumbs on another sheet of wax paper and set that alongside the egg mixture. When the temperature of the oil has almost reached 375 degrees, pat the clams dry and dredge 5 or 6 of them in the flour (don't do this until the oil is ready for frying), then quickly dunk them in the egg mixture, shaking off the excess, and roll them in the cracker crumbs. Lower the coated clams into the fat and fry them only 1–2 minutes, or until golden brown, then retrieve them with a slotted spoon and drain on paper towels. Keep them warm while you fry the rest in batches. Serve hot with lemon wedges or Tartar Sauce (page 633).

SERVES 4–6

Yankee Cataplana Clams

A *cataplana* is a cooking vessel used by Portuguese fishing families, some of whom migrated to New England generations ago. Made of tin, aluminum, sometimes copper, a *cataplana* consists of two rounded halves that are hinged rather like a clam shell and are held tightly together by clamps. Much the same culinary effect can be achieved by using two large skillets, one to cover the other—after cooking in the lower skillet you can flip it over so the juices run downward.

4 dozen littleneck clams or mussels
¼ pound butter (1 stick)
½ pound chouriço *sausage, chopped*
½ pound lingüiça *sausage, chopped*
2 slices bacon or equal amount country ham with fat, cut up
1 cup chopped onion
1 cup chopped green pepper
3 garlic cloves, finely chopped

1 cup sliced mushrooms
1½ cups chopped parsley
1 cup sliced tomatoes
1 cup molho *sauce (page 88)*
1 cup dry white wine
4 cups fish stock or a combination of fish and chicken stock
Freshly ground pepper
Tabasco sauce to taste

Soak the clams in sea water if possible (otherwise use lightly salted water) overnight to remove all traces of sand; scrub thoroughly. Heat the butter in the cooking vessel and stir in the two kinds of sausage and the bacon or ham. Continue stirring over moderately high heat for about 5 minutes, while the sausage juices meld with the butter. Stir in the onion, green pepper, and garlic, and cook about 5 minutes. Stir in the mushrooms and cook another 5 minutes. Add the parsley, tomatoes, and *mohlo* sauce and stir well, then stir in the wine and stock, seasoning with plenty of freshly ground pepper and Tabasco to taste. No salt should be needed because both the sausage and shellfish will provide plenty. The characteristic flavor of *cataplana* dishes is peppery. Cover and simmer 15–20 minutes. Add the clams and cook covered 12–15 minutes, until the shells open. Bring the *cataplana* to the table and serve very hot in wide soup plates with crusty bread.

SERVES 4–6

Clambake for a Backyard

Rhode Islanders are recognized masters of the Yankee clambake, but the bakes have been common throughout the region since the technique was learned from the Indians. As one old account has it, "Clams, baked in the primitive style of the Indians, furnish one of the most popular dishes on those parts of the coast where they abound and constitute a main feature in the bill of fare at picnics and other festive gatherings."

To have a bake on your barbecue charcoal grill, you need 3 dozen steamer clams (or more) for 6 people. You need 6 baking potatoes, 6 medium onions, 6 ears of corn in their husks, 6 live lobsters, lemon wedges, melted butter, some seaweed or rockweed if you can get it, 12 pieces of 18 x 36-inch cheescloth, and 12 pieces of heavy-duty aluminum foil of the same size.

Wash the clams and potatoes thoroughly. Peel the onions and carefully remove the silk from the ears of corn, replacing the husks. Arrange 2 pieces of cheesecloth on top of 2 pieces of foil, and wrap the layers around ½ dozen clams, 1 lobster, 1 potato, 1 onion, 1 ear of corn, and some rockweed if you have it. Pour in 1 cup water. Repeat to make 6 packages, tying the cloth over the food, bringing the edges of the foil together to seal tightly. Place the packages on a barbecue grill about 4 inches from the hot coals. Cover all with the barbecue hood or pieces of foil tucked in all around the grill. Cook for 1 hour, turning every 15 minutes, until the potatoes are done. Serve with the lemon wedges and melted butter.

Clams Al Forno with Grilled Sausage and Mashed Potatoes

Down near the water in Providence is a restaurant called Al Forno, the source of this interesting way of roasting clams with spicy sausage.

4 large Italian hot or sweet sausages
1 pound small red potatoes
¼ cup heavy cream
7 tablespoons unsalted butter
½ teaspoon salt
24 littleneck clams, scrubbed
1 medium onion, halved and thinly sliced

1 jalapeño pepper, coarsely chopped
¼–½ teaspoon dried hot red pepper flakes, or to taste
½ cup dry white wine
¼ cup water
1 tablespoon minced fresh garlic
1 cup canned Italian plum tomatoes, chopped

Parboil the sausages 5 minutes. In a medium saucepan, cook the potatoes in lightly salted water to cover until soft, then drain. Coarsely mash the potatoes with a fork, and beat in the cream, 4 tablespoons butter, and the salt. Set aside and keep warm.

In a large baking dish, put the clams, sausages, onion, jalapeño pepper, pepper flakes, wine, water, garlic, tomatoes, and the remaining 3 tablespoons butter. Roast in a preheated 500-degree oven about 7 minutes. Turn the clams and roast about 5 minutes longer, until the clams open (discard any unopened clams). To serve, place 6 clams in each of 4 warm bowls and surround them with tomatoes and onions. Pour equal amounts of the liquid into the bowls, place a large dollop of mashed potatoes in the center, and top with a sausage.

SERVES 4

Crabmeat Cakes

6 tablespoons butter (¾ stick)
½ cup chopped green pepper, or half green and half sweet red pepper
½ cup chopped onion
1 tablespoon flour
1 cup heavy cream

1 pound fresh crabmeat
3 tablespoons finely chopped parsley
Salt
Several drops Tabasco sauce
2 eggs
About 1½ cups fresh bread crumbs

Heat 2 tablespoons of the butter in a skillet and sauté the pepper and onion until partially cooked, about 3 minutes. Stir in the flour and sauté 1 minute more. Scrape the contents of the skillet into a bowl and pour the heavy cream into the pan. Boil it down rapidly until it is really thick. Add the crabmeat to the bowl along with the reduced cream and parsley. Season to taste with a little salt and Tabasco and mix well. Refrigerate for at least 1 hour. When chilled, form the mixture into 8 cakes. Beat the eggs lightly in a wide shallow bowl, and dip the crabmeat cakes into the egg to coat thoroughly, then roll them in bread crumbs. Heat the remaining butter in a large skillet and fry the cakes fairly gently until heated through and nicely browned on both sides.

SERVES 4

Maine Crabmeat with Mushrooms and Tarragon

8 scallions
4 tablespoons butter
1/2 pound mushrooms, quartered
1/2 cup dry vermouth
1/4 cup chopped fresh tarragon
1 pound fresh Maine crabmeat

1/2 cup sour cream or plain yogurt or a combination, at room temperature
Salt
Freshly ground pepper
4 slices crisp toast, buttered

Cut the scallions in thin slices, separating the white bulb from the tender greens. Heat the butter in a skillet, add the white part of the scallions and the mushrooms, and toss and cook over medium heat 5 minutes. Pour in the vermouth and let boil a few seconds, add half the tarragon, the crabmeat, and the scallion greens, stirring. When hot, stir in the sour cream and/or yogurt, and salt and pepper to taste. Cook just long enough to heat through. Divide evenly over hot buttered toast, and scatter the remaining tarragon on top.

SERVES 4

Crabmeat with Tomato and Caper Sauce

1 pound crabmeat
1 onion, chopped
1 garlic clove, chopped
2 tablespoons vegetable oil
2 cups peeled, seeded, and chopped tomatoes
1/4 cup chopped parsley
1/2 teaspoon cinnamon

1 clove
1 teaspoon Dijon mustard
1/2 tablespoon capers with juice
1/2 cup pitted and chopped ripe olives
3 tablespoons butter
2 cups freshly cooked wild rice or other cooked rice

Flake the crabmeat and set aside. Cook the onion and garlic gently for 3–4 minutes in the oil, until tender. Add the chopped tomatoes and parsley and the spices. Stir in the mustard, capers, and olives, and cook about 8 minutes. Melt the butter in a separate saucepan and toss in the crabmeat while you heat up the rice separately, if it is not hot. When both are hot, serve the rice and the crab with the sauce on top.

SERVES 4

Soft-shell Crabs with Butternuts and Fiddleheads

3 dozen fiddleheads, cleaned and trimmed
3 tablespoons butter and/or vegetable oil
4 soft-shell crabs

Flour for dredging
Salt
Freshly ground pepper
¼ cup butternuts in pieces
½ lemon

Cook the fiddleheads in boiling salted water to cover for 7–8 minutes, until just tender. Drain and rinse. Heat the butter in a good-size skillet. Quickly dredge the crabs in flour lightly seasoned with salt and pepper, shake off excess, and sauté in the hot butter over medium-high heat, turning them after 3 minutes and sprinkling the butternuts into the pan. Cook 2 minutes more, then add the fiddleheads, salt and pepper to taste, and a little lemon juice. Stir and toss until heated through.
SERVES 4

Crabmeat and Corn Cakes

2 cups freshly cooked corn, scraped off the cob
2 cups crabmeat
3 eggs
¼ cup flour plus extra for handling
4 scallions, including tender greens, chopped fine

1–2 tablespoons chopped fresh herbs, such as parsley and chives, tarragon, chervil, or dill
Several drops Tabasco sauce
Salt
Freshly ground pepper
Oil for frying

Maine Crabs

Crabs are only marginally available in New England's Atlantic waters; the so-called red crabs of Provincetown's lobster coves have had their champions in master cook Howard Mitchum, among others, just as do the more common blue crabs, which are increasingly marketed by fishermen. In Maine, however, crab is now abundant enough to warrant Fresh Crabmeat signs on front lawns of coastal towns.

This is almost exclusively a smaller variety called rock crab (*Cancer irroratus*). Flaked crab is usually sold in 6–8-ounce containers. It should look white and opaque, plump and moist, and its aroma should be sweet. In Hancock County, where the crab industry is growing, pickers during the height of the season—April to September—can produce at the rate of 50 crabs (about 50 ounces) an hour. It's a hard way to earn a living, which makes the high price of crab, Maine or otherwise, understandable, as well as worth it.

Mix all of the ingredients together except the oil, adding salt and pepper to taste—the batter will be quite loose. Heat a large skillet with ⅛ inch of oil. Quickly, using floured hands, form 8 cakes, 1 at a time, dropping each into the skillet as it is formed. Fry over medium heat until brown, about 2 minutes, then turn and fry on the other side for 2 minutes. Serve piping hot with a little Salsa (page 634) on the side, if you wish.

SERVES 4

Lobster Steamed in Vodka

For simple steaming, of course, all water may be used, following the procedure in this recipe. But the vodka gives a faint flavor and provides a sauce.

4 lobsters (about 1¼ pounds each)
¾ cup vodka
¾ cup water
5 tablespoons cold butter, in 5 pieces

2–3 tablespoons chopped fresh tarragon, or ½ teaspoon dried

Prepare the lobsters 2 at a time. Bring the vodka and water to a boil in a large kettle that will hold the 2 lobsters, and insert a rack or 2 small ones on the bottom. Place 2 of the live lobsters on top, slap on the cover, and cook at a lively simmer for 12 minutes. Remove the lobsters and keep them warm while you steam the other 2. When all the lobsters are cooked, remove the juices in the kettle to a small saucepan, boil them rapidly down to ¾ cup, then, piece by piece, whisk in the cold butter. Add the tarragon, and serve the sauce with the lobsters.

SERVES 4

Baked Stuffed Lobster

Four 1¼–1½-pound lobsters
1 tablespoon fresh lemon juice
½ pound (2 sticks) butter
12 slices white bread, crumbled (about 2½ cups)
8 scallions, including tender greens, chopped

3 tablespoons chopped fresh chervil or tarragon, or 1 tablespoon dried
2 tablespoons chopped parsley
Salt
Freshly ground pepper

Plunge a sharp heavy knife into each lobster just below the eyes and cut through the body lengthwise (this will kill the lobster immediately, although it will continue to make reflex movements). Remove the intestinal sack and spread the tomalley and eggs, if there are any, over the flesh part of the lobster halves, then sprinkle with lemon juice. Melt 1½ sticks of the butter

Baked Stuffed Lobster (continued)

in a skillet and toss in the crumbled bread and scallions. Sauté over medium heat until the crumbs have absorbed the butter and separated. Season with the herbs and salt and pepper to taste. Spread even amounts of the crumb stuffing over the lobster halves, and crack the claws. Melt the remaining ½ stick butter, and drizzle it over the claws and stuffing. Bake in a preheated 475-degree oven for 10 minutes, uncovered, then drape foil over the tops to bake for an additional 10 minutes, at which point check to see if the lobsters are done by pulling back a little of the stuffing and making sure that the tomalley has turned greenish.

SERVES 4

North End Lobster Fra Diavolo

THE SAUCE:
1 onion, chopped
2 tablespoons vegetable oil
2 garlic cloves, minced
2 cups canned tomatoes

½ teaspoon dried hot red pepper flakes
1 teaspoon chopped fresh oregano, or ½ teaspoon dried

2 tablespoons oil
1 pound squid, cleaned, cut into ¼-inch pieces (see page 120)
2 small live lobsters, split in half lengthwise, claws cracked

12 cherrystone clams, scrubbed
1 pound mussels, scrubbed

The High Cost of Lobster

A wary explorer of Yankee waters once distilled his preference for lobster: "Your everyday lobster fished from a saltwater tank and boiled before your eyes is surely one of the great food bargains available in America today." But the annual catch is declining, and the price increases as a result. The fact is, it's hard for a lobster to make it to the table. Only about ten of a female lobster's thousands of eggs will survive in natural circumstances, and infant lobsters—all lobsters, indeed—must hold out against predators, storms, PCBs, oil spills, and other pollution. Lobstermen of this generation have to work harder, go deeper into the ocean with their traps, than their ancestors ever did. Vermont is the only state in the region without a hospitable habitat for lobsters, but its citizens make sure that plenty are trucked in daily, still alive and ready for the pot.

To make the sauce, sauté the onion in 2 tablespoons oil until almost limp, then add the garlic and sauté another 30 seconds. Add the tomatoes, hot pepper flakes, and oregano and cook over a brisk heat about 20 minutes, uncovered, until sauce is thick.

Heat 2 tablespoons oil in a large skillet, add the squid and cook, stirring and tossing, 1–2 minutes. Push to one side and place the lobster in the pan, flesh side down. If your pan is not large enough to hold the 4 lobster halves side by side, use a second skillet for the 2 other halves. Place the clams around the lobster, cover the pan, and let steam for 8 minutes. Add the mussels, cover, and steam another 3–4 minutes, until both clams and mussels have opened. Pour off some of the liquid, leaving about ¼ cup in the pan. Stir in the tomato sauce. Taste and correct seasoning. If the sauce is too thick, add a little more of the seafood juice. Serve with lots of crusty bread.

SERVES 4

Lobster or Crab Rolls

This favorite of New England coastal highways can be made with cooked lobster or crabmeat. Nowadays it is sometimes made with the packaged pink-tinted fish labeled "Sea Legs," but don't be fooled—it's not the real thing. Another heresy is to grind the seafood. Chunks are what you want, even if it does make for messy eating—after all, that's half the fun. Try serving these with homemade Potato Chips (page 23).

4 frankfurter rolls
4 tablespoons melted butter
1 pound (2 generous cups) cooked lobster or crabmeat in chunks
¾ cup mayonnaise*
4–5 tablespoons finely chopped celery

2 tablespoons finely chopped scallions, including tender greens
2 tablespoons fresh lemon juice
2 teaspoons drained capers
Salt
Freshly ground pepper

* *Note:* Aficionados prefer Hellmann's with its touch of sweetness.

Split the rolls and brush well with the butter. Grill them, butter side toward the heat. While they are grilling, toss the chopped seafood with the mayonnaise, celery, scallions, lemon juice, and capers, and season with salt and pepper to taste. When the rolls are lightly browned, spoon equal parts of the lobster mixture onto the bottoms of the rolls, cover with the tops, and serve immediately.

SERVES 4

Mussel Beach

A regional mollusk sadly neglected by many cooks of the past, the mussel is easily found within low-water areas of a New England beach—mussels attach themselves to anchors, pilings, rocks, and ledges by means of tough beards that fringe their opening edges. Somewhat resembling an elongated blue-black clam, they may grow to 6 inches in length, but are sweeter and more tender at 2–3 inches. Open a mussel and you find a pearly white interior with blue or violet shading, and the mollusk itself is a soft bright orange.

One day, visiting Clark's Cove, south of Damariscotta, we learned a good deal from Edward Meyer, Maine's pioneer mussel farmer. He had put his Princeton education behind him thirty-five years earlier to try to persuade Americans, and other mussel harvesters in Maine, Massachusetts, and Rhode Island, that this handsome shellfish is as good to eat as it has been known to be by Europeans for centuries. Cultivated mussels are more consistent in size, less gritty, and easier to harvest. Some aficionados may claim that a cultivated mussel doesn't have the same intense flavor as you get in the wild mollusk, but as long-time mussel eaters we have not found that to be true. And we're convinced the more mussels are available, the more they are promoted, the more people will take to them—as seems to be happening in New England.

Ounce for ounce, mussel meat has about the same amount of protein as beefsteak, much less fat, 25 percent of the calories, and many more mineral nutrients. Thanks to the enterprise of Ed Meyer and his Abandoned Farm operation, an increasing number of mussel cultivators are supplying markets to make mussels available for a variety of ways to cook them. We hope the recipes we've included in various chapters (see index) will whet more appetites.

Breaded Scallops

1 pound scallops
Juice of ½ lemon
1 tablespoon olive oil
Freshly ground pepper
1 egg, well beaten

½ cup dried bread crumbs
¼ cup finely minced country ham
2 tablespoons minced parsley
1 tablespoon grated cheddar
3 tablespoons vegetable oil

Rinse and dry the scallops. Mix the lemon juice, olive oil, and a few turns of freshly ground pepper; add the scallops and toss, then let stand about 30 minutes. Turn out on paper towels. Combine the bread crumbs, ham, parsley, and grated cheese. Dip the scallops in the beaten egg, then roll them in the bread crumb mixture. Heat the vegetable oil and fry scallops 3–4 minutes, shaking the pan to turn them as they brown on all sides.
SERVES 2

Over a bed of coals, sea scallops may be grilled on skewers like shish kebab meats, or in a wire grill with hinges to make it easy to hold the morsels firmly.

2 pounds sea scallops
3 tablespoons vegetable oil
3 tablespoons butter
2 large garlic cloves, peeled
1½ tablespoons finely chopped chives

2 teaspoons chopped fresh tarragon, or 1 teaspoon dried
Salt
Freshly ground pepper

Broiled or Grilled Scallops in Herb Sauce

Wash and drain the scallops on paper towels. Heat the oil and butter in a skillet and sauté the garlic until it turns slightly brown. Stir in the chives and tarragon, about ½ teaspoon salt, and several turns of the pepper grinder. Mix well and turn off the heat. Pour this sauce over the scallops and let them marinate, unrefrigerated, 1 hour or so.

The scallops may be broiled indoors placed 3–4 inches under the broiler, turning them with a spatula once or twice, until they are bubbling and slightly brown. Outdoors, thread 3 or 4 scallops on short, thin skewers, leaving ½-inch space between them to allow the heat to circulate. Grill 3–4 inches over hot glowing coals for 5–7 minutes, turning each skewer in order to cook the scallops evenly. Or place the scallops on a wire grill, secure the top part of the grill over them, and place 3–4 inches above glowing coals to grill about 3 minutes on each side.

SERVES 4

---

2 medium acorn squash, split, or butternut, using rounded end only, split,* seeds removed and pulp scraped out
4 tablespoons butter
1½ pounds sea scallops

3 scallions, including tender greens, chopped
Fresh lemon juice
Salt
Freshly ground pepper
⅓ cup fresh bread crumbs

* Note: Save the flesh of the elongated ends of butternuts for squash gratin or soup or slaw.

Scallops in Baked Winter Squash Shells

Place 1 teaspoon butter in the hollow of each squash, and bake in a preheated 400-degree oven for 40–50 minutes, or until tender. Heat the remaining butter in a large skillet and cook the scallops over medium-high heat, shaking and tossing for 5 minutes. Add the scallions for the last minute of cooking. Season with a little lemon juice, and salt and pepper to taste. Distribute the scallops and their juices in the center of the squash halves, sprinkle bread crumbs on top, and put under the broiler for 2–3 minutes, until browned.

SERVES 4

Bay Scallops in Wine Sauce

2 pounds bay scallops
About 1 cup flour for dredging
Salt
Freshly ground pepper
2 tablespoons oil, preferably olive oil
2 tablespoons butter

4 shallots, or 5–6 scallion bulbs, minced
2 garlic cloves, minced
1 cup dry vermouth or white wine
2 tablespoons chopped fresh tarragon or dill
4 tablespoons chopped parsley

Just before cooking, dry the scallops thoroughly, then toss half of them in flour seasoned with a little salt and pepper. Heat half the oil and butter in a large skillet and when sizzling, shake off the excess flour from the scallops and toss them in; cook over high heat, shaking the pan and tossing them for 1 minute (you want to brown the scallops lightly, not steam them). Remove them to a warm dish and repeat the same procedure with the remaining scallops, flouring them and then browning them in the remaining oil and butter. Remove them to the same dish. Scatter the minced shallots and garlic into the pan, stir them around, scraping up all the browned bits, then quickly add the wine. Let it come to the boil, toss in the herbs, and cook hard to reduce slightly. Return all the scallops to the pan and cook them gently in the sauce for 30 seconds. Taste, and add salt and pepper as necessary.
SERVES 4

Nickerson Tavern Stir-fry of Scallops and Snow Peas

About 10 ounces sea scallops, ligaments removed, sliced in half across the grain
Cornstarch for dredging
1/3 cup peanut oil
4 scallion bulbs, sliced 1/2 inch long
1/2 teaspoon finely minced garlic

1/2 teaspoon finely minced fresh ginger
12 thin slices water chestnuts
4 ounces or more snow peas, strings removed
2 ounces bean sprouts

SAUCE:
2 tablespoons light soy sauce
1/4 teaspoon crumbled dried red chili or pepper flakes

1 teaspoon rice vinegar or white vinegar
1/4 teaspoon sesame oil

Pat dry the scallops and toss them in the cornstarch to coat lightly. Heat the oil in a wok to the point where a piece of scallion dropped in sizzles immediately. Carefully add the scallops and stir-fry 45 seconds. Remove them and keep them warm. Drain all but 2–3 tablespoons oil from the wok. Heat it to very hot, then add the scallions and stir-fry for 10 seconds. Add the garlic, ginger, and water chestnuts and stiry-fry for 10 seconds. Add the snow peas and bean sprouts and stir-fry 15–20 seconds.

Stir the sauce ingredients together and add them to the wok, then add the scallops, tossing to coat them with the sauce. Turn off the heat and stir in the sesame oil. Toss again, and serve immediately over rice or oriental noodles.

SERVES 2

"Great Bay" Scallop Stew

2 cups milk
1 cup half-and-half
2 bay leaves
3 slices onion
3 sprigs parsley
2 tablespoons coarsely chopped celery leaves
3 tablespoons finely chopped celery stalk
Tabasco sauce
3 tablespoons unsalted butter
1 pound bay scallops
2 teaspoons chopped fresh tarragon, or ½ teaspoon dried
1 teaspoon chopped fresh summer savory, or ½ teaspoon dried
Salt
Freshly ground pepper
Unsalted crackers or fresh toast
4 teaspoons finely chopped chives

Scald the milk and the half-and-half with the bay leaves, the onion slices, parsley sprigs, and the chopped celery leaves. Cover and let stand for about 5 minutes. Strain out the bay leaf, parsley, celery leaves and onion, and add the finely chopped celery stalk, 2–3 dashes of Tabasco, and the butter. Bring the liquid to a boil again, lower the heat, and simmer gently for about 5 minutes. Add the scallops and the herbs, taste for seasoning, and add a little salt and pepper, if you think it needs it. Simmer 10–12 minutes. Put crackers or pieces of toast in each of 4 soup plates, and pour the stew over, sprinkling with finely chopped chives.

SERVES 4

Maine Shrimp

As with wild mushrooms, there are seasons for different varieties of shrimp—the tiny ones produced in the icy waters off Maine's coast are best in winter and are called bay shrimp or red shrimp. Nearly transparent when raw, they turn deep pink when cooked, and they are sweeter in flavor than southern types. About 2 inches long, they are sold with heads on and are best cooked very quickly. Averaging 40–55 shrimp per pound (not too many for a single serving), Maine shrimp take a lot of peeling, but when cooked at home and shelled at the table, they are considered by those who love them as one of the world's bargains.

Shrimp in a Green Sauce

1 pound shrimp
¾ pound green peppers
6 tablespoons vegetable oil
1 medium onion, chopped
4 garlic cloves, minced
1 tablespoon curry powder

1 tablespoon lemon juice
1 teaspoon brown sugar
1 green tomato, cut into 8 wedges
½ cup water
About 2 cups freshly cooked rice

Peel and clean the shrimp, if necessary, under running water; pat dry and set aside. Cut the peppers in strips, removing the ribs and seeds. Heat 4 tablespoons of the oil in a large skillet and fry the peppers over medium-high heat for about 5 minutes, or until their edges are slightly brown and they become limp. Remove with a slotted spoon. Put the shrimp in the skillet and fry, stirring, for 2–3 minutes. When the shrimp have turned pink, remove them with a slotted spoon. Turn the heat to low, add the remaining oil, and sauté the onion and garlic in the skillet, adding the curry powder. Cook for about 5 minutes, until the onions become translucent. Stir in the lemon juice, brown sugar, and the green tomato. Return the peppers to the skillet along with about ½ cup water and simmer very gently, covered, for 10 minutes. Remove the cover and increase the heat slightly, cooking until the sauce reduces and thickens. Stir in the shrimp and heat through. Turn out onto a hot platter and surround with freshly cooked rice.

SERVES 2

Shrimp with Green Tomatoes

2 tablespoons oil
2 garlic cloves, chopped
2 teaspoons chopped fresh ginger
1½ pounds cleaned, peeled shrimp (fresh or frozen)
4–5 green tomatoes, sliced, then cut into thin strips
6 scallions, including tender greens, chopped

10–12 mushrooms, sliced
2 tablespoons cornstarch
2 tablespoons sherry
4–6 tablespoons water
2 tablespoons chopped fresh herbs, such as parsley, cilantro, and chives

Heat the oil in a large skillet or wok, then add the garlic and ginger. Just before the garlic takes on color, add the shrimp, green tomatoes, scallions, and mushrooms, and cook over medium-high heat, stirring and tossing, about 6 minutes. Mix the cornstarch, sherry, and water (use 6 tablespoons if the pan is quite dry now—frozen shrimp will give off more water), pour into the skillet, and stir and toss until sauce is lightly thickened. Sprinkle fresh herbs on top, and serve immediately with steamed rice.

SERVES 4

3 tablespoons vegetable oil
36 fiddleheads, cleaned and
    trimmed, page 44
1/2 cup water
8–10 asparagus, trimmed, peeled,
    and cut into 1-inch pieces
Salt

1 1/2 pounds small Maine shrimp,
    peeled
1 teaspoon minced fresh ginger
4 scallions, sliced (keep tender
    green slices separate)
1 teaspoon sesame oil

Stir-fry of Small Maine Shrimp, Fiddleheads, and Asparagus

Heat 2 tablespoons oil in a large skillet or wok, then add the fiddleheads. Stir-fry 1 minute, add 1/4 cup water, cover, and let steam-cook over medium heat about 3 minutes (the water should be absorbed). Add the asparagus, stir-fry a few seconds, salt lightly, add the remaining 1/4 cup water, and steam-cook 4–5 minutes, until just tender. Add the remaining 1 tablespoon oil, and when hot, scatter in the shrimp, the ginger, and the white part of the scallions, and stir-fry quickly 1 or 2 minutes, until the shrimp are just cooked (longer and they will turn tough). Stir in the sesame oil and sprinkle on the scallion greens. Serve with steamed rice.

SERVES 4

BEER BATTER:
One 12-ounce can light domestic
    beer
1 1/2 cups flour

16–20 medium-size shrimp
Juice of 2 lemons
Salt
Freshly ground pepper

1/2 teaspoon salt
1 tablespoon paprika

Worcestershire sauce
About 1 cup flour
Oil for deep-frying

Albert Stockli's Shrimp in Beer Batter

GARNISHES: lemon wedges and Watermelon Pickles (page 628) (optional)

Pour the beer into a large bowl. Sift the flour, salt, and paprika into the beer, whisking until the batter is light and frothy. (The batter may be used immediately or stored in the refrigerator for up to 1 week, but be sure to whisk occasionally.)

Remove the shells from the shrimp, leaving the tails intact. Wash and remove the black line running down the center, if you wish (for aesthetic reasons only). Dry the shrimp and sprinkle with lemon juice, salt, pepper, and a few drops of Worcestershire. Heat at least 2 inches of oil in a frying kettle or electric fryer. Just before it reaches 375 degrees, quickly dredge the shrimp with flour, shaking off excess then dip in the beer batter, coating well, and drop them into the hot fat (do this in 2 batches). When they are

Albert Stockli's Shrimp in Beer Batter (continued)
brown on one side—less than 1 minute—turn and brown them on the other side. Drain on paper towels. Serve hot with lemon wedges and Watermelon Pickles (page 628), if you wish.

SERVES 4

POULTRY

IT'S ALL VERY WELL that there stands on Crandall Road near Adamsville, Rhode Island, the "Rhode Island Red Commemorative Monument," the world's only such memorial to a chicken; but it's equally worth noting that the fame of the Vermont turkey, once proudly featured on restaurant menus and in butcher's ads, has faded. Domestic birds have all become look-alikes, and New England cooks are among those who feel lucky when they're able to buy the free-range chickens that, in the 1980s, have become chic to serve in chic restaurants. Fashionable or not, a hen allowed to browse the natural way, it seems to most of us, is bound to have lots of flavor, and we are decidedly grateful when our neighbor Ralph Persons has enough undisciplined birds on hand (he often supplies game as well) to fill an order.

Something like three times as many meals across the country are based on poultry as on red meat, for two reasons: The medical world emphasizes that poultry makes healthier eating; and red meat is almost invariably harder on budgets. Whether nurtured on an assembly line or in a farmyard, chicken, turkey, duck, and goose are staples upon which much of New England cooking was founded—indeed, it is doubtful that the church suppers of long tradition could have become so firmly established without the plenitude of chicken. And in the 1980s, with its seasoning of ethnic culinary variations, New England cooking is exemplary when it comes to new ways of serving chicken.

In the hands of an adventurous cook, chicken can seem more succulent in a blanket of oysters and mussels, as early Yankees might have dressed it up; or pieces of white meat may be served as Baked Chicken Ruben, a contemporary New Hampshire adaptation of a delicatessen formula that mates sauerkraut, Swiss cheese, and Thousand Island dressing in a chicken casserole. With chicken and turkey packaged as drumsticks, wings, and other parts, there are dozens of new ideas for stuffing or sautéing the poultry breasts or cooking the legs, thighs, and wings in ethnic seasonings.

Domestic ducks were first raised in Connecticut after a clipper ship voyage from Peking, and the famous Watertown geese from the Boston hinterlands can be as festive as a country Christmas feast, when stuffed with chestnuts, apples, figs, and cornbread. The ubiquitous Rock Cornish game hen, whose identity has been simplified to "Cornish hens," is the result of crossing New England's Plymouth Rock chickens with Cornish game hens, and their popularity, especially as dinner-party fare, has been attributed to what one enthusiastic gastronome labeled "bunnylike breeding." As with squabs in former times, the Cornish hens served in New England may be poached and served cold, filled with pasta and goat cheese stuffing, or braised with oysters.

Time was when New Hampshire country folk used to say, "Don't plant corn until the bobwhite whistles." Bobwhite is the name used in New England for quail, or for the birds Southerners call partridge. Quail (considered the finest of game birds), as well as pheasant, have become a game-farm crop—in our neck of the woods both quail and ring-neck pheasant are raised by Tim and Amelia Fritz, of Albany, Vermont. Tim told us that 34,000 quail are raised annually on Nantucket, mostly to supply hunting preserves; but the market for the Fritzes is composed of nearby restaurants. For themselves, they pickle quail eggs—hard-boiling them and leaving them in white vinegar until the shells dissolve. Then they marinate the eggs again in a mixture that is half water and half vinegar, seasoned with about 1 tablespoon cumin seeds per quart.

Like all good cooks, New Englanders have almost inexhaustible ways of creating good food and enhancing every kind of poultry in the process. Those whose cooking we know best seem to agree with Brillat-Savarin (he hunted turkey with Yankee friends), who likened an uncooked bird to a painter's canvas—an unsullied surface on which to let your own creativity assert itself.

CHICKEN

6–7 chicken livers
4–5 chicken hearts
4 tablespoons butter or vegetable
   oil or a combination
1 medium onion, chopped
1 rib celery, chopped
1½ cups fresh bread crumbs
3 teaspoons chopped fresh thyme,
   or 1 teaspoon dried

3 tablespoons chopped parsley
Salt
Freshly ground pepper
1 roasting chicken (approximately
   3½ pounds)
1 tablespoon olive oil or softened
   butter

Roast Chicken with Giblet Stuffing

FOR THE GRAVY:
1 tablespoon flour   1 cup chicken broth

Sauté the livers and hearts in the butter and/or vegetable oil with the onion and celery for 3–4 minutes, stirring and tossing. Remove from the heat. Chop the livers and hearts into small dice, then mix with the rest of the pan ingredients, and add the bread crumbs, herbs, and salt and pepper to taste. Stuff this mixture into the cavity of the chicken, skewer or sew the opening closed, rub the chicken all over with the olive oil or butter, and roast, breast side down, in a preheated 400-degree oven for 30 minutes. Lower the heat to 375 degrees, and turn and roast another 45–50 minutes, basting occasionally with the pan juices, until done—that is, when the juices run clear after piercing deeply where the thigh is attached to the body of the chicken. Remove from the oven and let rest on a warm platter while you make some pan gravy. Skim off the excess fat from the roasting pan. Set the pan over low heat and stir in the flour, scraping up all the browned bits from the pan. Pour in the chicken broth, a little at a time, stirring to make the sauce smooth, and then let it simmer over low heat a few minutes. Taste and correct the seasoning, adding salt and pepper if necessary.
SERVES 4

Broiled or Grilled Chicken Coriander

Two diverse elements of Rhode Island's heritage are Portuguese cooks and the chickens known as Rhode Island Reds. Cooks from the Azores, scattered through Massachusetts and other Yankee regions, are often partial to the flavor of fresh coriander, which distinguishes this dish. Although the herb is apt to be found most readily in ethnic markets, it is easy to grow. By poking it under the skin of the chicken, the coriander permeates the flesh and is not burned off when the chicken is broiled or grilled on an outdoor grill.

2 small broiling chickens, quartered
4 garlic cloves
1 tablespoon kosher salt
2 tablespoons olive oil

1 bay leaf
10–12 black peppercorns
1 cup chopped coriander leaves

Wipe the chickens with a damp cloth. Smash the garlic cloves with the flat of a large knife, remove the skins, and chop them very fine. Add 2 teaspoons kosher salt and continue mincing and mashing the garlic until it is almost a purée, working in some of the olive oil. In a small mortar, crush the bay leaf with the peppercorns until pulverized, then mix this with the garlic purée, adding the remaining olive oil and salt. Rub about one-quarter of this mixture over the chicken. Mix the remaining amount with the coriander. Lift the skin of the chicken and smear the coriander mixture underneath the skin, pushing it way down to the tips of the drumsticks and into the wings, trying to distribute it evenly under the skin. Let the chicken stand at room temperature for about 30 minutes. Preheat the broiler or prepare the grill, and broil or grill the chicken about 6 inches from the source of heat, 10 minutes on each side for the white meat and 15 minutes for the dark meat.
SERVES 6–8

Chicken in Cranberry-Tomato Sauce

Two 2-pound chickens, cut up
Salt
Freshly ground pepper
1/4 cup flour
3 tablespoons oil
3 tablespoons butter
1 tablespoon finely chopped fresh rosemary, or 1 teaspoon dried, crumbled

Juice of 1 lemon
One 8-ounce can jellied cranberry sauce
2 cups cooked tomatoes

Sprinkle the chicken pieces lightly with salt and pepper and dredge them in flour, shaking off the excess. Heat the oil and butter in a very large skillet or 2 good-size skillets and brown the meat on all surfaces. Remove the chicken pieces and pour off the excess fat and sprinkle the chicken with fresh rosemary and lemon juice. Add the cranberry sauce and the tomatoes and chop them both with a spoon as the mixture comes just to the boiling point. Return the dark meat of the chicken to the skillet, baste with the sauce, cover, and simmer 20 minutes. Add the white-meat pieces, baste, cover again, and simmer another 10 minutes, until tender.

SERVES 6

Chicken with Dumplings

1 chicken (about 4–5 pounds)	Water to cover
1 rib celery	Salt
1 carrot, scraped	Freshly ground pepper
1 onion, peeled	2 tablespoons soft butter
3–4 sprigs parsley	2 tablespoons flour

DUMPLINGS:

1 cup flour, preferably cake flour	2 tablespoons chopped parsley
2 teaspoons baking powder	1 tablespoon chopped fresh dill,
½ teaspoon salt	marjoram, or savory (optional)
1 egg	1 tablespoon finely minced scallions
¼ cup milk	

GARNISHES: 12 young carrots, scraped and cooked until tender
2 cups peas, cooked until tender

Put the chicken into a pot that will hold it rather snugly along with the celery rib, carrot, and onion, cover with water, and add a good pinch of salt and several grindings of pepper. Bring to a boil, then reduce the heat, cover and simmer about 2½ hours, until very tender (if it is an old hen it will take this long). When the chicken is done, remove 4 cups of the broth to a wide pan and boil hard to reduce the broth by half. Taste and correct the seasoning. Mash the soft butter and flour together, then whisk in small pieces into the boiling broth, continuing to whisk vigorously with each addition, until smooth. Keep at a simmer.

Prepare the dumplings by sifting together the dry ingredients into a bowl. Beat the egg lightly with the milk, and stir into the dry ingredients, along with the parsley, another herb if you like, and scallions. Dip a teaspoon into the hot chicken sauce and then scoop up a rounded teaspoon of the dumpling dough. Drop it into the simmering sauce, and continue with the remaining dough, distributing the dumplings on top of the sauce a good 1½ inches apart to allow for swelling. Be sure that the pot remains just at a simmer, cover, and cook the dumplings 5 minutes on one side, then turn them carefully and cook on the other for 5 minutes. While they are cooking, cut the chicken in pieces, then pour the sauce and dumplings on top, and surround with the carrots and peas.

SERVES 6–8

Oven-Fricasseed Chicken

When serving fowl old enough to require considerable cooking time, nineteenth-century cooks either produced a stew or a variation of this dish commonly known as a fricassee. With less time in the oven, today's supermarket chickens offer similar results. Grandmother would probably have used salt pork for succulence, but fat trimmed from a country ham (or bacon similarly cured) provides saltiness and a hint of smoky flavor. Any combination of herbs that suits your taste might be substituted for sage.

¼ cup diced ham fat
1 medium onion, coarsely chopped
2½–3 pounds cut-up chicken
Freshly ground pepper
Salt (optional)
1 teaspoon dried sage leaves (not
* flakes or ground), or 2 teaspoons*
* chopped fresh sage*

2 cups hot water
2 tablespoons cold water
3 tablespoons flour

Spread the fat and onion over the bottom of a baking pan or dish just large enough to hold the chicken pieces; lay the chicken on top. Sprinkle with freshly ground pepper and the furled sage leaves (add a little salt only if the ham is not salty). Pour in the hot water and cover the dish with a close-fitting lid or with aluminum foil crumpled tightly. Bake in a preheated 400-degree oven for 15 minutes. Reduce the heat to 350 degrees and bake 30 minutes more, until the chicken is very tender. Remove the chicken to a hot platter and keep warm. Mix the cold water with the flour (or shake the water and flour together in a small sealed jar until smooth), add to the pan juices and heat, stirring, until all the lumps are gone and the juices have thickened. Pour the sauce over the warm chicken and serve.
SERVES 4

Chicken with Sausage, Peppers, and Olives

The increasing popularity of Mexican-style food is modified here by the instincts of a Portuguese-Yankee cook.

1 tablespoon vegetable or olive oil
1 pound chouriço *or other hot*
* sausage, sliced*
One 3½–4-pound chicken, cut up
2 cups chopped green peppers
1 cup chopped onion

1 garlic clove, chopped
2 tablespoons flour
1 cup chicken broth
2 cups stewed tomatoes, chopped
1 cup pitted black olives

Heat the oil in a large skillet that has a tight-fitting lid, and add the sausage. When the sausage has released some of its fat, add the chicken pieces and brown them on all surfaces. Remove the browned pieces and sausage, and cook the green peppers, onion, and garlic in the fat, until the vegetables are tender. Stir in the flour to make a paste, then add the broth, a little at a time, stirring constantly. Add the tomatoes and blend with the vegetables. Add the pitted olives and return the chicken to the pan. Cover the pan tightly and cook over the lowest possible heat about 45 minutes, until the chicken is tender. Either corn bread or rice makes a good accompaniment.

SERVES 6

A delicious meal-in-itself dish to make when you find small eggplant (about 5 inches long) and small- to medium-size artichokes in the market in early fall. The artichokes are trimmed and pared down in the Italian style so that you can eat the whole thing rather than strip them leaf by leaf—a chore that most men seem to dislike doing at the table and a messy business anyway when the artichokes are cooked in a sauce.

Chicken with Eggplant, Artichoke Hearts, and Mushrooms

4 small-medium artichokes
1/2 lemon
2 tablespoons vegetable oil
1 frying chicken, cut into 8 pieces
1 onion, chopped
1/4 cup chicken broth
1 small eggplant, cut into 1-inch
   slices

Salt
Freshly ground pepper
About 12 good-size mushrooms,
   quartered
Chopped parsley

Prepare the artichokes by bending back each leaf near the tip and snapping the leaf off; start at the bottom end and work toward the top. The tough prickly ends of the leaves at the top may be lopped off with a knife. Trim the root ends off also and rub all the cut places with lemon so there won't be any discoloration. When all the leaves have been trimmed, pare the end of the artichoke that surrounds the choke the way you would pare an apple until you get down to the tender flesh all around. Cut each artichoke in half lengthwise, and with a melon baller scoop out all the thistly part and discard it. Rub again with the lemon.

Heat the oil in a large heavy skillet and brown the chicken pieces on all sides. Remove the white meat (breast and wings) and add the onion, stirring it around to brown lightly. Pour in the chicken broth, bring to a boil, toss in the eggplant and the artichokes, salt and pepper lightly, then cover and simmer for 20 minutes. Uncover, add the white meat and mushrooms, season again, and cook gently, covered, for 10 minutes. Taste and correct the seasoning, squeezing from the cut lemon a few drops and stirring them in. Sprinkle parsley on top, and serve with rice and hot crusty bread or rolls.

SERVES 4

Chicken in Applejack

In Vermont's Northeast Kingdom, cooks with French heritage may use apple brandy or hard cider interchangeably.

One 2½-pound chicken
2–3 tablespoons vegetable oil
2 onions, chopped
2–3 potatoes, thickly sliced
2 stalks celery, coarsely chopped
1 garlic clove, chopped
2 tablespoons flour

1 cup applejack
¼ cup water
½ teaspoon salt
Freshly ground pepper
1 tablespoon chopped fresh basil,
    or ½ teaspoon dried

Cut the chicken in quarters or jointed pieces. Heat the oil in a large heavy skillet and brown the pieces well on all sides. Remove and set aside. Put the onions, potatoes, celery, and the garlic in the skillet and cook over moderate heat, turning occasionally for about 10 minutes. When the vegetables are slightly brown and partly soft, sprinkle in the flour and stir thoroughly to absorb the fat in the skillet. Pour in the applejack, stirring continuously until the liquid thickens slightly. Stir in the water and sprinkle in the salt and several turns of the pepper grinder. Add the basil and the dark meat of the chicken, cover the pan, reduce the heat to a bare simmer, and continue cooking about 20 minutes. Add the white-meat pieces, cover again, and cook another 10 minutes, or until tender.
SERVES 4

Chicken with Celeriac and Red Pepper

Celeriac or celery root, like oyster plant, was much more commonly used in the old days, and it is making a comeback as people discover it in farmers' markets or grow it in their own gardens (see page 285 for a simple celeriac braise).

1 celeriac (about ¾ pound)
1 frying chicken, cut into 8 serving
    pieces
3 tablespoons vegetable oil
Salt
Freshly ground pepper
¾ cup chicken broth or water

1 sweet red pepper, seeded and cut
    into long ⅛-inch-wide strips
4 scallions, including some of the
    tender greens, cut into 2-inch
    strips
2 tablespoons chopped parsley

Peel the celeriac and cut it into long ⅛-inch strips. Immediately toss into a pot of boiling water and blanch for 1 minute, then drain. Dry the chicken pieces. Heat the oil in a large skillet and brown the chicken pieces on all sides over medium-high heat for 5 minutes. Pour off the fat and season the chicken with salt and pepper. Remove the white-meat pieces (breast and wings) and keep them warm. Pour the chicken broth into the skillet, scatter

the celeriac over the dark meat, cover, and simmer 15 minutes. Return the white meat to the pan and simmer another 10 minutes. Toss the red pepper strips and scallions over the chicken, cover, and simmer about 5 minutes, until the vegetables are just tender. Correct the seasoning, and sprinkle parsley over the top.
SERVES 4

Sautéed Chicken with Parsnips and Cranberries

1 chicken, cut into 8 pieces
1 tablespoon butter
1 tablespoon vegetable oil
Salt
Freshly ground pepper
1 pound parsnips, peeled and cut
   into 1½-inch logs of similar
   width

½ cup cranberries
2 tablespoons water
2 tablespoons sugar

Sauté the chicken in the butter and oil as described opposite, removing the white meat after the initial browning. After 20 minutes of cooking, when returning the breast meat to the pan, scatter the parsnip logs into the pan and cook them as the chicken finishes braising. Season with salt and pepper. Meanwhile, put the cranberries in a wide pan with the water and sugar and poach quickly, shaking the pan, for only 30 seconds. Lift them out with a slotted spoon and put them on top of the chicken and parsnips to cook a final 2 minutes.
SERVES 4

Baked Honey-and-Rum Chicken

It may be that Ethan Allen or his brother Ira first mixed Vermont honey and New England rum in a hot toddy—but the person who applied the indisputably Yankee combination first to add an exotic fillip to chicken is another matter.

1 frying chicken (3½–4 pounds), in
   quarters
2 tablespoons oil, preferably
   sunflower
1 teaspoon salt

Freshly ground pepper
½ cup New England rum (or other
   rum, if you must)
½ cup fresh chicken stock
½ cup honey

Brush the chicken pieces with the oil, and sprinkle all over with the salt and several turns of the pepper grinder. Use a shallow roasting pan just large enough to hold the chicken and tuck the pieces snugly into it. Put the chicken in the preheated 400-degree oven and bake 20 minutes; turn the pieces over and continue baking 25 minutes more—total cooking time is

45 minutes. Meanwhile, combine the rum, stock, and honey. When the chicken is golden brown on both sides, use the rum-honey mixture to baste every 5 minutes for the last 30 minutes of cooking. When the drumstick turns easily without breaking the skin and the meat is moist and tender, the chicken is ready.

SERVES 4

Buttermilk-Baked Chicken with Butternuts

Be warned that this is one chicken dinner so rich it shatters every Yankee image of parsimony.

1½ sticks butter, cut up
2 cups ground butternuts *
2 teaspoons or more salt
Freshly ground pepper

2 cups buttermilk
One 3½–4-pound chicken, cut into
    serving pieces
3 tablespoons flour

* Note: Desperation may cause the substitution of walnuts.

Put the butter in a shallow baking dish large enough to hold the chicken pieces in one layer and set the dish in a preheated 350-degree oven to melt the butter. Mix the butternuts with about 2 teaspoons salt and 1½ teaspoons freshly ground pepper, and spread the mixture on a large plate. Pour the buttermilk into a large bowl and set it next to the nut mixture. Dip the chicken pieces in the buttermilk, then dredge them in the nuts to cover all surfaces. Take the hot baking dish from the oven and turn the nut-covered chicken pieces in the butter, arranging the chicken so that all the pieces lie flat. Put the now-full baking dish back in the oven and bake for 1¼–1½ hours, until the meat is very tender. At 15- or 20-minute intervals, use a bulb baster to baste the chicken with the hot butter. When the chicken is tender and slightly crusty, remove the pieces to a warm platter and keep

Chicken Parts

Many rural New Englanders are going back to raising their own chickens, or they try to buy free-range poultry. But even if you end up with mass-produced chickens, it's much thriftier to cut them up yourself, saving the backs, necks, and gizzards for chicken broth, freezing the livers until you have accumulated enough to make a chicken liver dish (see index), and using the legs, thighs, and breasts in a variety of ways that the following recipes offer.

warm. Pour about 4 tablespoons butter from the baking dish into a sauce-pan and stir in the flour to make a smooth paste. Cook 2–3 minutes over moderate heat, then add the remaining buttermilk, a little at a time, until smooth. Serve the sauce separately.

SERVES 6

Mrs. Bowles's Tandoori Chicken

Tandoor, a word used in India for oven, has become a common term in many kitchens, and one that may have been introduced in New England after Connecticut's Governor Chester Bowles and his wife returned from a stint in the U.S. Embassy in Delhi. Mrs. Bowles, at any rate, distributed her tandoori recipe as one to be easily reproduced in this country. She pointed out that the tandoori chicken could be cooked outdoors over charcoal.

1 frying chicken (about 2½–3
   pounds), skinned and quartered
1 tablespoon curry powder
2 garlic cloves, chopped
1–3 tablespoons lemon juice
1 teaspoon salt

½ cup plain yogurt
2 tablespoons vegetable oil
2 tablespoons tandoori spices *
2 tablespoons melted butter
   (optional)

   * To be found in New England shops where Indian spices are available.

Wipe the chicken with a damp cloth. Mix the curry powder, garlic, 1–2 tablespoons lemon juice, salt, yogurt, and oil, and marinate the chicken in the mixture overnight. Broil the chicken pieces for 20 minutes, turning the pieces so they don't burn. When the meat is tender, sprinkle the tandoori spices all over the pieces and, if you like, although this is not traditional, pour melted butter and the remaining 1 tablespoon lemon juice over the chicken before serving.

SERVES 4

Newport Crab-Stuffed Chicken Halves

2 chickens (2½ pounds each)
6 tablespoons butter
1 teaspoon salt
Freshly ground pepper
Freshly grated nutmeg

THE STUFFING:
¾ pound crabmeat
4 tablespoons butter
Tabasco sauce
Salt to taste

½ pound mushrooms, sliced
4 tablespoons vodka or rum
¼ cup chili sauce
1 tablespoon chopped parsley

1½ teaspoons Dijon mustard
½ teaspoon dried thyme
½ teaspoon dried marjoram
¼ teaspoon dried savory

Cut the chickens in half. Mix 2 tablespoons butter with the salt, several turns of the pepper grinder, and a generous grating of nutmeg, then rub the chicken halves with the mixture. Put the chicken pieces, skin side up, in a shallow baking pan that holds them snugly. Bake them in a preheated 350-degree oven for about 45 minutes, until they begin to turn color. Heat 4 tablespoons butter in a skillet and add the mushrooms and sauté them. Add the vodka or rum, the chili sauce, and the parsley. Pour 1 tablespoon of the mixture on each chicken half. Bake 15 minutes longer. To make the stuffing, combine the flaked crabmeat in a bowl with the remaining ingredients. Turn the chicken halves over and fill cavities with the stuffing. Top with the remaining mushroom mixture, cover lightly with foil, and bake about 15 minutes longer.
SERVES 4

Calcutta Chicken

The Young Housekeeper's Friend, published in Massachusetts in 1859, suggests that partridges, pigeons, rabbits, sweetbreads, breasts of mutton, lamb, and veal might all be used for curry. This recipe was modified for the use of battery-raised chicken.

1 chicken (about 2½ pounds)
Salt to taste
1 ounce bacon (preferably home-cured) or salt pork, cut into small dice
1 tablespoon butter

1 tablespoon vegetable oil
2 medium onions, chopped
1½ tablespoons curry powder
⅛ teaspoon cayenne
¾ cup chicken broth

Cut up the chicken into 8 parts (2 legs, 2 thighs, 2 wings with some breast meat, 2 breast pieces). Place the back, neck, and gizzard in a saucepan, cover with water, and simmer about 40 minutes to make broth. Strain, and season to taste with salt. (If you already have chicken broth, save the parts for the next time you make stock.) Fry the bacon or salt pork slowly in a large heavy skillet until brown and crisp. Remove and drain on paper towels. Remove all but 1 teaspoon bacon fat and heat it along with the butter and oil. Add the chicken parts and sauté them over high heat, turning, until all sides are brown—about 5 minutes. Add the onions and stir them around with the chicken for 2–3 minutes, then sprinkle curry powder, cayenne, and salt over and mix well. Remove breast and wing pieces and keep them warm in foil. Pour chicken broth over dark meat, bring to a boil, cover, lower heat, and simmer 20 minutes. Now add the breasts and simmer another 10 minutes.
SERVES 4

A bottle of the famous rum of Medford, Massachusetts, was described by Wine and Food Society president André Simon as "a steel fist in a velvet glove." Yankee rum has also earned much praise for numerous creations of new New England cooks, including this sweet-and-sour simmered chicken.

Rum-and-Raisin Chicken

One 3-pound chicken, in serving
  pieces
Salt
Freshly ground pepper
1/2 cup golden raisins

1/4 cup dark rum
2 tablespoons butter
2 tablespoons peanut oil
8 small onions, sliced
1 large lemon

Season the chicken pieces with salt and freshly ground pepper. Soak the raisins in the rum, adding enough water to cover the raisins with liquid; set aside for about 30 minutes.

In a heavy skillet, heat the butter and oil, then sauté the chicken pieces until they are light brown. Remove and keep warm. Sauté the sliced onions over a low heat, until they are limp. Add the warm dark-meat chicken pieces, pour the rum and the raisins over them, and stir to scatter the onions and raisins over the meat. Grate the rind of the lemon over the chicken, then cut the lemon in half and squeeze all of its juice over the chicken. Cover the skillet with aluminum foil and fit the cover tightly over the foil. Simmer for about 30 minutes, then add the white-meat chicken pieces, cover again tightly, and simmer until the chicken is very tender but not boiled—10–15 minutes.

SERVES 4

Salt
Freshly ground pepper
2 whole chicken breasts, cut into 4
  halves
6 ounces fresh goat cheese
2 scallions, including tender greens,
  minced
2 tablespoons chopped fresh
  tarragon or basil

2 tablespoons chopped parsley,
  preferably flat-leaved
1 tablespoon butter
1/2 cup dry vermouth
1/2 cup chicken broth
1 1/2 cups peeled carrots, celery, and
  peeled broccoli stems, cut in
  narrow sticks (julienned)

Chicken Breasts Stuffed with Goat Cheese

Salt and pepper the chicken breasts on both sides. Mix the goat cheese with the scallions and herbs and a little pepper and salt, only if needed. With a sharp knife, slice into each chicken breast sideways to make a deep slit, going nearly to the edges, but don't poke through. Stuff equal amounts of the seasoned goat cheese into each breast. Melt the butter in a skillet large enough to hold the stuffed breasts in one layer. Arrange them in the pan and pour the vermouth and broth around them. Bring to a boil, cover, and simmer for 5 minutes. Strew the vegetables around and over the chicken, cover again, and cook another 15 minutes, or until the vegetables are just lightly cooked and the chicken is springy to the touch. Remove the breasts and the vegetables with a slotted spoon and arrange on warm plates or a platter. Cook the juices in the pan rapidly until they become lightly thickened, then pour them over the chicken breasts.

SERVES 4

Stuffed Chicken Breasts

2 whole chicken breasts
1/2 cup finely chopped celery
1/2 cup finely chopped apples
2 shallots or scallion bulbs, finely chopped
4 tablespoons butter
1/2 cup fresh bread crumbs

1/8 teaspoon cinnamon
A few gratings of nutmeg
2 teaspoons chopped parsley
Salt
Freshly ground pepper
2 tablespoons dry sherry
1/2 cup chicken broth

Bone the chicken breasts following the directions on page 159 and divide each into 2 pieces. Pound lightly to flatten. To prepare the stuffing, sauté the celery, apples, and shallots in 2 tablespoons of the butter for 5 minutes. Stir in the bread crumbs, the spices, parsley, and salt and pepper to taste. Place equal amounts of the stuffing in the center of each of the 4 chicken pieces, roll up, and close with a skewer. Heat the remaining 2 tablespoons butter in a skillet and brown the stuffed breasts about 1 minute on each side. Splash in the sherry, then the broth, and simmer, covered, for 10 minutes. Taste and correct the seasoning. Remove the skewers, and serve with the pan sauce poured over.

SERVES 4

Libby Parlante's Chicken Breasts

About 5 tablespoons vegetable oil
1 medium onion, chopped
1 can tomato paste
1/4 cup water
One 12-ounce can tomatoes with basil
2–3 tablespoons finely chopped Italian parsley

1 tablespoon fresh chopped mint, or 1 1/2 teaspoons dried
2 whole chicken breasts, cut into 4 halves
Salt
Flour
1 egg, beaten
1/2 cup fresh bread crumbs

Put 3 tablespoons of the oil in a saucepan and cook the chopped onion 2–3 minutes, until translucent. Stir in the tomato paste, adding enough of the water to make a fluent mixture. Cook slowly for about 10 minutes. Stir in the canned tomatoes with their juices, breaking up the tomatoes with a sharp knife. Add the parsley and the mint, and cook just long enough to bring the mixture to the boiling point. Meanwhile, heat 2 tablespoons oil in a sauté pan. Salt the chicken breasts lightly, dust them in flour, dip them in the beaten egg, then in the soft bread crumbs. Cook the chicken pieces 8–10 minutes in the hot oil, until they are lightly brown and thoroughly cooked but still moist. Put them on hot plates, reheat the sauce, and pour equal amounts of it over each serving.
SERVES 4

This is a lovely dish to make should you ever happen to have a little champagne left over from a party.

Chicken Breasts in Champagne Sauce

2 whole chicken breasts, boned *
Salt
Freshly ground pepper
4 tablespoons butter
½ cup finely diced fennel or celery
½ cup finely diced white part of leeks
¾ cup finely diced mushrooms
¼ cup or more chicken broth
Flour for dusting
⅔ cup champagne
⅔ cup heavy cream

* To bone your own chicken breasts, use a sharp knife and, starting at the lower end of the rib cage, loosen the meat by scraping against the bones first on one side, then on the other, and then cut away across the top of the sternum to free the whole breast in one piece.

Cut the 2 whole chicken breasts in half to make 4 pieces. Remove the skin and any bits of fat. Season lightly with salt and pepper on both sides, then place the breasts between 2 sheets of wax paper and flatten lightly and evenly with a meat pounder or heavy bottle. In a large skillet, heat 3 tablespoons butter and sauté the diced vegetables over low heat for 1 minute, stirring, then add the broth, salt lightly, cover, and cook very gently about 5 minutes, or until almost tender; check to see if more broth is needed —the vegetables should not brown. Push the vegetables to the edges of the skillet and add the remaining 1 tablespoon butter. Quickly dredge the chicken breasts in flour, shaking off the excess, and add them to the pan. Sauté them gently 30 seconds on one side, then turn them, strew the vegetables on top, and add the champagne. After it has boiled up for a few seconds, stir in the cream, cover, reduce heat, and cook gently 5 minutes. The sauce will have thickened; if it is too thick, stir in a little more broth or cream. Taste and correct the seasoning if necessary. Serve with rice.
SERVES 4

Chicken Thighs with Fiddleheads, Whole Garlic Cloves, and Mushrooms

16–20 fat garlic cloves
3 tablespoons vegetable oil and butter or olive oil, combined
8 chicken thighs
¾ cup chicken broth
Salt

Freshly ground pepper
About 2 cups fiddleheads, cleaned and blanched (page 44)
16–20 whole medium mushrooms
Juice of ½ lemon

Boil the unpeeled whole garlic cloves in water to cover for 5 minutes, then drain. Heat the oil and butter or oils in a large skillet, then add the chicken thighs and brown all sides over quite high heat, turning frequently, for 5 minutes. Pour in ½ cup broth, scraping up any browned bits from the pan, scatter the drained garlic cloves on top, salt and pepper the chicken pieces to taste, lower the heat, cover, and cook slowly for 15 minutes. Now add fiddleheads and mushrooms to the skillet and the remaining ¼ cup broth, cover, and cook another 10–15 minutes, until the vegetables are tender and the chicken juices run clear when pricked. Squeeze the lemon juice over all, and correct the seasoning. Serve with crusty bread so that you can squeeze the soft, buttery garlic cloves onto the chunks of bread and mop up the sauce.

SERVES 4

Marinated Chicken Thighs with Mussels

2½ cups dry white wine
2 tablespoons paprika
1½ teaspoons salt
Freshly ground pepper
4 garlic cloves, peeled and cut in half
3–4 bay leaves
4 pounds chicken thighs

4 tablespoons vegetable oil
3 large onions, sliced thin
1 large sweet red pepper, ribs and seeds removed, cut into strips
3 pounds mussels, cleaned
½ cup finely chopped fresh coriander
1 lemon, cut into wedges

Pour the wine into a large bowl and stir in the paprika, salt, and pepper to taste. Add the garlic and bay leaves, then the chicken thighs, cover with a weighted plate, and marinate 4–5 hours (or overnight in the refrigerator).

Pour off the marinade through a strainer and set it aside. Discard the bay leaves, but reserve the garlic. Heat 2 tablespoons of the oil in a large skillet. Pat the chicken thighs dry with paper towels and brown them in the hot oil over medium heat 10–15 minutes, turning once. Remove the chicken and keep it warm. Pour the strained marinade into the skillet and boil over high heat, scraping up the particles of meat, until the marinade is reduced to about 2 cups. Heat the remaining 2 tablespoons oil in a flameproof casserole and stir in the onions and red pepper. Chop the reserved garlic fine, add it to the casserole, and cook gently until the vegetables are soft—about

10 minutes. Add the chicken pieces and the reduced marinade, cover, and simmer 30 minutes over very low heat. Add the cleaned mussels, cover, and cook about 5 minutes, until all the mussels are open. Sprinkle on the fresh coriander, and serve with lemon wedges.

SERVES 8

Garlic

As little as a dozen years ago garlic was not a common item on supermarket shelves throughout New England, except in ethnic neighborhoods. Yet today our local Grand Union produce buyer tells us that it is in constant demand, and there are always fat juicy heads of garlic in the vegetable bin. Still, there are a lot of New Englanders who don't understand garlic, and resist what they think is its assertive flavor.

The truth is that garlic is pungent only when it is eaten raw or when it is chopped and fried in hot fat or oil. Then all its volatile aroma fills the house, and it is indeed assertive in any dish. But if garlic is cooked gently—particularly whole, unbruised cloves still in their skins—it has a mild buttery flavor. A few cloves simmered a long time in a stew are almost indefinable, yet they give a richness and an earthiness that the milder cousins of the onion family don't have.

There is much dispute over whether garlic should be chopped or put through a press. Our own feeling is that the press extracts all the pungency of the garlic without the pulp that modifies the powerful juice. For some dishes that works well. But, in general, we prefer to whack the clove of garlic under the flat side of a large knife, which makes the skin slip off easily, then we chop it, sometimes adding a little salt if we want a fine mince or almost a purée.

Another surprisingly pleasing way to prepare garlic is to roast a whole head (or several) intact, just sprinkled with a little olive oil and salt and wrapped in foil in a 375-degree oven for about 1½ hours, or until very tender. The garlic can then be squeezed out onto pieces of warm crusty bread—and it will have a delectable flavor—or used in dishes such as the Berkshires Lentil Salad on page 338.

Interestingly, even the Boston Cooking School under the aegis of Fannie Farmer rated garlic along with chives, leeks, onions, and shallots as "an additional flavor . . . in making salads."

The varieties most likely to be available in New England are: American or Creole, a white-skinned bulb that is very strong; Italian or Mexican, with a pinkish or purplish skin; Tahitian, with bulbs 2–3 inches in diameter; and the very mild elephant, with bulbs weighing as much as 1 pound. The last is said to survive temperatures as low as 32 degrees in home gardens.

Chicken Legs with Butternut Squash, Ginger, and Hazelnuts

We use chicken legs and thighs (preferably attached) for this dish because they take just the same amount of cooking time as the squash.

3 tablespoons oil
4 chicken legs and thighs,
    preferably attached
Salt
1 medium butternut squash, peeled
    and cut into 1-inch chunks

3 tablespoons minced fresh ginger
Freshly ground pepper
1 cup or more chicken broth
1/3 cup finely chopped (but not
    ground) hazelnuts
1 tablespoon chopped chives

Heat the oil in a large skillet, add the chicken pieces, and sauté over moderately high heat until browned on both sides. Remove excess fat, and salt the chicken all over. Scatter the squash around the chicken, sprinkle the fresh ginger over, season with several turns of the pepper grinder, and pour in the broth. Bring to a simmer, cover, and cook gently for 30–35 minutes until tender, checking now and then to make sure the liquid hasn't boiled away and adding more if necessary. Toast the hazelnuts in a dry skillet, shaking over moderate heat, until they are lightly toasted and smell good. Sprinkle them over the chicken when it is done. There should be enough liquid in the pan to coat each chicken piece with several spoonfuls; if the juices are too liquid, boil them down until syrupy. Sprinkle chives over the top.
SERVES 4

Chicken Wings in Cream Gravy

2 1/2 pounds chicken wings
1/2 cup buckwheat flour
2 teaspoons chopped fresh savory,
    or 1 teaspoon dried
Salt

Freshly ground pepper
2–3 tablespoons vegetable oil or
    butter or a combination
1/2 cup milk
1/2 cup chicken broth

Remove the wing tips and cut apart the 2 remaining sections. Mix the flour with the savory, and sprinkle the mixture with a little salt and pepper. Dredge the chicken pieces in the seasoned flour, shaking off the excess. Heat the oil and/or butter in a skillet large enough to accommodate the chicken pieces and brown them on both sides over medium-high heat. Reduce the heat and continue to cook, turning the pieces occasionally, for about 30 minutes, until the meat is tender. Remove the chicken to a warm plate. Stir about 2 tablespoons of the excess seasoned buckwheat flour into the hot fat and cook, stirring, over low heat for 2 minutes. Pour in the milk, a little at a time, and mix thoroughly. Add the broth and continue stirring for about 5 minutes. When the gravy is smooth and thick, return the chicken pieces to the skillet, turning them to cover with the gravy, and reheat thoroughly. Mashed potatoes make a good accompaniment.
SERVES 4

1 cup tomato purée
1 teaspoon Worcestershire sauce
¼ cup cider vinegar
¼ cup brown sugar

2 teaspoons dried hot red pepper
 flakes
Salt
16 chicken wings

Barbecued Chicken Wings

Mix the tomato purée, Worcestershire, vinegar, sugar, and pepper flakes together. Salt the chicken wings on both sides and lay them on a foil-lined broiler pan. Spoon half the sauce over them and set them about 8 inches below a hot broiler and let them cook 10 minutes on one side, basting once or twice with the accumulated sauce. Turn them, paint them with the remaining sauce, and broil them 10 minutes on the other side. If you want to cook them over an open grill—with no foil to catch the sauce juices— paint on the sauce only a little at a time. The timing would be the same if you place them about 8 inches above glowing coals.
SERVES 4

Marinated Chicken Wings, Baked

Yankee barbecue aficionados may not deal in the most peppery of accents, but they are prolific in developing interestingly seasoned marinades.

2½ pounds chicken wings
2 cups cider vinegar
¾ cup corn oil
2 teaspoons salt

1 tablespoon lemon or lime juice
2 teaspoons chopped rosemary
 leaves, or ½ teaspoon dried

Remove the wing tips and break each wing into 2 pieces. Place in a bowl. Thoroughly mix the remaining ingredients, and pour over the chicken. Set aside to marinate 3–4 hours or longer. Arrange the chicken wings in a shallow dish and pour the marinade over them. Bake in a preheated 350-degree oven for about 1 hour.
SERVES 4

Marinated Chicken Wings, Baked or Grilled

3 pounds chicken wings
⅓ cup soy sauce
2 tablespoons molho sauce (page
 88) or chili sauce
4 tablespoons honey

1 teaspoon grated fresh ginger
1 large garlic clove, minced or put
 through a press
¼ teaspoon Tabasco sauce

Put the chicken wings in a wide-based bowl. Mix the remaining ingredients and pour over the wings. Marinate about 8 hours or overnight.
  Butter or oil a large baking pan lightly and arrange the wings in it,

reserving the marinade. Bake them in a preheated 400-degree oven for 30 minutes, then turn the meat over and paint it liberally with the marinade. Bake 20–30 minutes longer, removing the wings from the oven before they begin to char. To cook them outdoors, place the wings on a grill about 6 inches above glowing coals and follow the same procedure except that it is better to paint them several times with the marinade instead of putting it all on at once. Serve hot, tepid, or cold.

SERVES 4

Philbrook Farms Creamed Chicken in Pastry Shells

⅓ cup butter
⅓ cup flour
4 cups milk
¾ teaspoon salt
½ teaspoon curry powder
½ teaspoon pepper

2 teaspoons Sexton's seasoning salt
4 cups cubed cooked chicken
1 cup dry sherry
6 prebaked pastry shells, made with
   lard dough (page 565)

Melt the butter in a heavy saucepan and stir in the flour. Cook, stirring, over gentle heat, 2 minutes. Off heat add the milk, and then return to medium heat and whisk until the sauce thickens. Add the salt, curry powder, pepper, and seasoning salt; fold in the chicken, and transfer mixture to the top of a double boiler. Keep warm over simmering water, allowing the flavors to mellow. Just before serving, stir in the sherry and heat through. Spoon the creamed chicken into the pastry shells and serve.

SERVES 6

Farmer Cheese and Chicken Croquettes

New Englanders, like most other Americans, made their own fresh cheese in the old days, and more cooks are acquiring the habit. A big bowl of curds, white and slightly tart, once was essential to a good meal, and the fresh cheese was also often used in cooked dishes as well. This recipe pairs farmer cheese with leftover chicken. (You could use cooked shrimp or country ham as alternative meats.)

2 cups finely chopped chicken
½ cup farmer cheese *
2 scallions, finely chopped
1 teaspoon chopped fresh basil
1 teaspoon finely chopped fresh
   tarragon

Salt
Freshly ground pepper
Flour
1 egg, lightly beaten
1 cup fresh bread crumbs
Oil or lard for frying

* If unavailable, use cottage cheese left in a strainer for several hours to drain off the whey.

Mix the chicken, cheese, scallions, and herbs, and add salt and freshly ground pepper to taste. Form the mixture into 4 ovals or sausage shapes. Roll in flour to coat lightly. Dip into beaten egg, then roll in the bread crumbs to cover all surfaces. Refrigerate at least 30 minutes. Heat 2 inches of oil in a skillet or fryer to 375 degrees. Lower the croquettes into the hot fat. Fry for about 2 minutes, then turn and fry another 2 minutes, until the croquettes are crisp and golden on both sides. Drain on paper towels, and serve plain or with a mushroom sauce.

SERVES 4

Gulf House Chicken Croquettes

In a Green Mountains memoir entitled *Williamstown Branch,* R. L. Duffus, a local boy who made good, recalls a meal at the Williamstown Gulf House at which he encountered for the first time the mystery of a chicken croquette. His problem as a small boy in a public dining room lay in not knowing how to eat a carrot-shaped object that was too soft to be picked up by the fingers and too carefully formed to be broken by a fork. He sat there squirming until the waitress took away his plate. Not all croquettes are carrot-shaped; indeed, New Englanders today often prefer them when they look like hamburgers.

1¾ cups chopped cooked chicken
½ teaspoon salt
Cayenne
½ teaspoon finely grated onion
1 teaspoon lemon juice
1 teaspoon finely chopped celery
   leaves
2 teaspoons chopped parsley
1 cup half-and-half, warmed
1½ tablespoons butter
2½ tablespoons flour
1½ cups bread crumbs
2 eggs, well beaten
Oil or lard for frying

Mix the chicken with the salt, cayenne to taste, the grated onion, lemon juice, chopped celery leaves, and parsley. Heat the butter in a saucepan, stir in the flour, and cook slowly, stirring, 2–3 minutes. Off heat blend in the warm half-and-half and return to medium heat, whisking, until you have a thick white sauce. Season with a little salt and cayenne. Add the chicken mixture and mix well before spreading out on a platter to cool thoroughly and become firm (you may refrigerate). Use 1 heaping tablespoon of the mixture to form each croquette. Roll each croquette in bread crumbs, then in the beaten eggs, then bread crumbs again. Chill thoroughly. Fry in deep fat in a wire basket for about 1 minute.

MAKES 10 CROQUETTES

CORNISH GAME HENS

Roast Cornish Game Hens with Pasta and Goat Cheese Stuffing

1½ cups small shell pasta
2 Cornish game hens
2 shallots or ½ small onion, minced
2 tablespoons butter
¼ cup minced country ham
6 ounces goat cheese, broken in pieces, or, if unavailable, Swiss cheese, coarsely grated

1 tablespoon chopped chives
Salt
Freshly ground pepper
Olive oil
1 tablespoon flour

Cook the small pasta shells in a large pot of boiling salted water until done *al dente*. Meanwhile, clean out the birds and put the necks and giblets in a saucepan with about 3 cups lightly salted water and let simmer, half covered. In a skillet, sauté the livers with the shallots or onion in the butter for about 3 minutes, tossing occasionally, then remove from the heat and chop in small pieces. When the pasta is done, drain and mix with the livers, ham, goat cheese or Swiss cheese, and season with chives and salt and pepper to taste. Spoon this stuffing into the cavities of the birds, filling generously front and back. Place a piece of foil over the breast opening to hold the stuffing in place, and truss the birds. If you have a little extra stuffing, place in a small casserole and bake with the birds for the last 15 minutes of cooking. Rub the birds all over with olive oil, and salt and pepper, and place in a lightly oiled roasting pan with space between. Roast in a preheated 425-degree oven for 20 minutes, baste, and then lower the heat to 350 degrees and roast another 45 minutes, basting several more times. Remove to a warm platter and let rest while you make the gravy. Sprinkle the flour over into the roasting pan, place over low heat, and cook gently, stirring and scraping up all browned bits, for about 2 minutes. Add about 1 cup of the broth made from the giblets, bring to a boil, stirring constantly, and cook until smooth and thickened; add a little more broth if you like a thinner gravy. Remove the trussing strings from the birds, scatter any extra stuffing around, spoon a little sauce over (pass the rest at table), and garnish with a colorful vegetable such as grilled tomato halves or baked or broiled eggplant slices (page 289). Split birds in half with poultry shears to serve.
SERVES 2–4

2 Cornish hens (about 1½ pounds
   each)
½ lemon
Salt
Freshly ground pepper
1 teaspoon chopped fresh summer
   savory leaves, or ½ teaspoon
   dried

2 tablespoons butter
½ cup heavy cream
1½ pints shucked oysters

Rock Cornish Hens and Oysters

Split the hens along the back, then flatten them with the palm of your hand on the breast sides. Rub them with lemon, sprinkle with salt and pepper and savory, and lay them side by side in a shallow buttered baking pan. Dot the butter on top, pour the cream over, and bake 25 minutes in a preheated 425-degree oven. Strew the oysters around, add some oyster liquor, and return to the oven for 3 or 4 minutes, just until oysters begin to curl at the edges and are warmed through. Remove hens, cut them in half, and arrange with the oysters on a warm platter. Quickly boil down the pan juices to the consistency of a light cream sauce, add a few drops of lemon juice to taste, pour over the hens, and serve. Good with wild rice.

SERVES 4

Cornish hens are considerably larger than they were when they first came on the market, so we generally serve only half a bird per person, splitting them with poultry shears after they are roasted. However, if you have big appetites at your table, serve a whole bird per person.

Cornish Game Hens with Herbs, Flamed in Applejack

¼ ounce dried mushrooms soaked
   in ¾ cup hot water for 30
   minutes
2 Cornish game hens
Salt
2 sprigs fresh rosemary, or 1
   teaspoon dried, crumbled
2 sprigs fresh thyme, or ½ teaspoon
   dried

4 sprigs fresh parsley
Olive oil
Freshly ground pepper
1 onion, sliced
1 teaspoon cornstarch
2 teaspoons raspberry or
   blackberry or other mild vinegar
¼ cup applejack or hard cider,
   warmed

Rinse the birds and pat dry thoroughly. Put a little salt in the cavity of each, along with even amounts of the herbs. Truss, and rub with oil and a little salt and pepper. Roast in a pan for 20 minutes in a preheated 425-degree oven, then reduce the heat to 350 degrees and strew the onion slices in the bottom of the pan. Baste with a little of the mushroom soaking liquid after 10 minutes, then once or twice more with the pan juices. After roasting 40

minutes more, remove the birds to a hot platter. Scrape the pan juices into the bowl of a food processor or blender and blend until smooth. Put the sauce in a small pan, strain the remaining mushroom liquid into the pan, then add the mushrooms and simmer 5 minutes. Dissolve the cornstarch in the vinegar, and stir into the sauce. Bring just to the boil, taste, and correct the seasoning. Remove the trussing strings and pour the sauce over the birds. Bring to the table and pour the heated applejack on top, then set aflame. When the flames die down, split the birds in half and serve.
SERVES 2–4

TURKEY

Smoked Roast Turkey

One 8–10 pound turkey, eviscerated and washed thoroughly

BRINE:

4 quarts water	*½ teaspoon ground coriander*
2 cups kosher salt	*6 whole cloves*
1 cup sugar	*20 black peppercorns*
5 teaspoons saltpeter	*5 bay leaves*
½ teaspoon powdered ginger	*1 tablespoon Worcestershire sauce*
½ teaspoon mace	

Put the water in a bucket large enough to hold the turkey. Stir all the seasonings into the water and put the turkey in. Cover the bucket and place in a cool spot for 4–5 days (a cellar or mud room in chill fall weather would be fine; otherwise refrigerate if you have the room).

Remove the turkey from the brine, wipe off the excess brine, and set in your smoker. We use a Little Chief Smoker and smoke the turkey 4½ hours, using 3 pans of hickory chips. At the end of that time the temperature is about 100 degrees; adjust the time according to how hot your smoker is.

Remove the turkey from the smoker (stuff it if you wish; see pages 170–171 for some suggested stuffings). Roast, uncovered, in a preheated 425-degree oven for 1 hour, then turn the heat down to 350 degrees, cover the turkey lightly with foil, and roast another 1½ hours. Let rest 1–2 hours before carving—it will still be warm and very juicy.
SERVES 8–10

One afternoon in Manchester, New Hampshire, we sat in an apartment that drew inspiration from the view of the Merrimack River below, and we talked of the ways Greek dishes have been incorporated into Yankee cooking styles with our friend Christine Cotsibos, a member of the Daughters of Penelope. This fine way of roasting a Thanksgiving turkey is a good example of the blending of Greek and American cooking techniques.

Daughters of Penelope Stuffed Roast Turkey

1 large onion, chopped
¼ pound (1 stick) butter
1½ pounds hamburger (bottom round)
Salt
Freshly ground pepper
1 cup uncooked rice, washed, covered with boiling water, and steeped 1 hour

1 pound chestnuts, slit, baked, and peeled
½ cup pine nuts
1 cup whole almonds, toasted
1 cup seedless raisins
½ teaspoon cloves
1 teaspoon cinnamon
One 12–14-pound turkey

Sauté the onion in the butter and, when soft, add the hamburger meat. Cook, stirring and breaking up, until browned. Season to taste with salt and pepper. Stir in the drained rice, chestnuts, pine nuts, almonds, and raisins and cook, stirring, a few minutes. Mix in the spices and refrigerate, covered, overnight.

The next day stuff the bird with the stuffing, tie it up, and roast in a preheated 325-degree oven 15 minutes per pound. When the bird is done, let it rest 30 minutes on a warm platter. Remove the stuffing and put it in a pan with the turkey drippings. Mix well and, if it seems a little too dry, stir in some hot water. Bake the stuffing 10–15 minutes in a preheated 350-degree oven—it should be like a thick casserole. Serve alongside the turkey.
SERVES 8–10

Brillat – Savarin's Wild Turkey

While I was in Hartford, in Connecticut, I had the good luck to kill a wild turkey. This deed deserves to go down in history, and I shall recount it all the more eagerly since I myself am its hero.

. . . As for the turkey, which was our only roast, it was charming to look at, flattering to the sense of smell, and delicious to the taste. And, as the last morsel of it disappeared, there arose from the whole table the words: "Very good! Exceedingly good! Oh! Dear sir, what a glorious bit!"

—*Jean Anthelme Brillat-Savarin, 1795*

Stuffed Roast Turkey Breast

1 turkey breast (approximately 5 pounds)

FOR THE BROTH:
4 cups water   Salt
1 small onion, unpeeled

FOR THE STUFFING:
1 large onion, chopped   2½ cups fresh bread crumbs, made
1 medium green pepper, chopped   from rye bread
1 rib celery, strings removed,   ½ teaspoon dried thyme
   chopped   1–2 teaspoons dried rosemary,
6 ounces chouriço sausage,   crumbled
   chopped in rough dice   Freshly ground pepper

2 tablespoons soft butter   Freshly ground pepper
Salt

FOR THE ROASTING PAN:
1 medium carrot, scraped and   1 medium onion, chopped
   chopped

Remove the backbone and ribs from the turkey breast and put them in a saucepan with the water and whole onion and a pinch of salt. Simmer for 1 hour or more, until the liquid is reduced to about 1½ cups.

Meanwhile, prepare the stuffing. Sauté the chopped onion, green pepper, and celery with the sausage for about 10 minutes, or until the sausage has given off its fat and the vegetables are almost tender. Mix this with the bread crumbs, herbs, and salt and pepper to taste. Make a mound of the stuffing in the center of a shallow casserole dish or pan (preferably one that can come to the table) and place the turkey breast on top, skin side up. Rub the breast with butter and season with salt and pepper. Place in a preheated 325-degree oven for 1 hour, lightly covered with foil. Remove the foil and strew the carrot and onion pieces around, add ¼ cup of the turkey broth you have made, and continue to cook 1 hour longer. Baste occasionally with the accumulated pan juices. When done, let the turkey breast rest on

a warm platter for 20–30 minutes. Prepare the gravy by scraping up all the pan juices and vegetables and puréeing them in a food processor or blender (or mash through a strainer) and mixing with the remaining turkey broth to the consistency you like. Taste and adjust seasoning if necessary, then pour into a sauceboat. Bring the turkey breast to the table in its roasting dish or, if not presentable, remove to a warm platter and carve at the table.
SERVES 8

Alternate Turkey Stuffings *

WILD RICE STUFFING:

6 cups cooked wild rice
1 cup chopped hazelnuts
4 green apples, peeled, cored, and cut into 1-inch cubes
1 cup finely chopped onions
3–4 tablespoons crushed juniper berries
2 tablespoons chopped fresh savory, or 2 teaspoons dried
3 tablespoons chopped fresh parsley
Salt
Freshly ground pepper

Mix the wild rice with the hazelnuts, apples, and onions. Season with the juniper berries, savory, and salt and pepper to taste.
MAKES ABOUT 10 CUPS

SAUSAGE AND CHESTNUT STUFFING:

1 pound chestnuts
2 tablespoons butter
1½ cups chicken broth
2 tablespoons Madeira or sherry
½ pound country sausage
4 medium onions, chopped
2½ cups chopped celery
1 teaspoon dried thyme
1 teaspoon dried sage, crumbled
¼ cup chopped parsley
7 cups torn bread crumbs, somewhat stale
Salt
Freshly ground pepper

To prepare chestnuts: Cut a cross in the chestnuts and put them in a saucepan with cold water to cover. Bring to a boil and boil for 1 minute. Remove a few at a time and peel off both the outer and inner skin while they are still hot. Braise the peeled chestnuts in a heavy saucepan with the butter, broth, and Madeira, and gently simmer 30–40 minutes, until the liquid is absorbed.

Meanwhile, cook the sausage meat, breaking it up with a fork, until it has released its fat, about 8–10 minutes. Remove with a slotted spoon to a bowl, and pour off all but ¼ cup of the fat. Sauté the onions and celery in the fat about 5 minutes, then add them to the bowl along with the seasonings, bread crumbs, and cooked chestnuts. Season to taste with salt and pepper.
MAKES ABOUT 10 CUPS

* Note: Either of these stuffings may be used in smaller amounts for roast chicken or goose.

Braised Turkey Breast in Yogurt

Contemporary cooks translate their acceptance of the turkey breast meat that is packaged separately in supermarkets into new and imaginative main courses that sometimes are a match for traditional veal dishes. Yogurt adds a flavor of its own, and is a healthy substitute for cream.

2 pounds boneless turkey breast
2 tablespoons vegetable oil
1 large garlic clove, minced
2 tablespoons flour
2 teaspoons chopped fresh
    rosemary, or 1 teaspoon dried

½ teaspoon summer savory
Salt
Freshly ground pepper
Zest of ½ lemon
1 cup chicken stock
1 cup plain yogurt

Cut the turkey breast in chunks. Heat the oil in a pan and add the garlic, sautéing over medium heat. Toss in the turkey and brown lightly. Stir in the flour to cover the turkey pieces and stir while the flour forms a light crust on the turkey meat. Add the herbs, a light sprinkling of salt, a few turns of the pepper grinder, and the thin peeling of lemon rind shaved off with a vegetable peeler. Add the chicken stock, stir well, and cover the pan. Simmer about 45 minutes, until the meat is very tender. Just before serving, stir in the yogurt, and heat through.
SERVES 4

Turkey Fillets in Tarragon-Yogurt Sauce

2 tablespoons safflower or other
    vegetable oil
2 pounds boneless turkey breast,
    cut into 4 equal fillets
1 large shallot, minced
1 garlic clove, minced
2 tablespoons flour

1 cup chicken stock
Salt
Freshly ground pepper
1 tablespoon chopped fresh
    tarragon, or 1½ teaspoons dried
1 cup plain yogurt, at room
    temperature

Heat the oil in a skillet large enough to hold the turkey fillets in one layer. Over moderate heat, sauté the turkey pieces, turning occasionally, until well browned. Remove to a warm place. Sauté the minced shallot and garlic in the skillet juices 3–4 minutes, stirring frequently until soft. Stir in the flour, a little at a time, to make a smooth paste and cook 1 minute, stirring; then gradually stir in a little of the chicken stock, continuing until the stock is used up and the sauce is smooth and quite thick. Return the turkey pieces to the pan, season with a little salt and fresh pepper to taste, spoon the sauce over the turkey, and sprinkle tarragon on top. Cover and simmer over very low heat about 5 minutes more. Stir in the yogurt and heat, but do not boil. Spoon the sauce over the fillets, and serve with Rhode Island jonnycakes (page 377).
SERVES 4

Here is a way of using turkey breast in place of veal—Italian style, with the turkey cut into thin slices like scallopini.

Turkey Scallopini

8 thin slices boneless turkey breast
Flour for dredging
Salt
Freshly ground pepper
2 tablespoons vegetable oil
3 tablespoons butter
¼ pound mushrooms, sliced
2–3 scallion bulbs, or 1 small
   onion, chopped

3 tablespoons dry sherry
1 tablespoon chopped fresh herbs,
   such as chervil or tarragon
½ cup chicken or beef broth, or
   heavy cream
1 tablespoon or more chopped
   parsley

Pull out any tendons from the turkey and pound the slices gently to flatten. Dredge them in flour, lightly seasoned with salt and pepper, as you heat the oil and half of the butter in a large skillet. Cook the turkey over moderate to high heat (in 2 batches if your skillet can't hold them in one layer) for 30 seconds on each side. Remove them and keep warm. Add the remaining butter to the pan and toss in the mushrooms and scallions. Cook, stirring, for 2 minutes, then splash in the sherry, cook rapidly, and add the herbs and broth or cream. Cook down until you have a lightly thickened sauce. Return the turkey slices to the pan, taste and correct the seasoning, adding more salt and pepper as necessary. Cook a minute to heat through, spooning the sauce over the scallopini. Sprinkle parsley on top.
SERVES 4

Baked Turkey-Ham Hash

4 tablespoons butter
3½ tablespoons flour
2 cups milk
½ cup turkey or chicken broth
2 cups diced turkey
1 cup diced country ham

¼ cup fresh bread crumbs
¼ cup crumbled cheddar
1 cup shredded mozzarella
2 tablespoons Madeira
4 eggs

Melt the butter in a saucepan, stir in the flour, and cook 2 minutes over low heat. Remove from the heat and stir in the milk and the broth; return to heat and stir the mixture until it is thick and smooth. In a greased casserole, put the turkey and ham, evenly distributed, then pour in half the sauce; keep the remainder hot. Top the contents of the casserole with bread crumbs and the cheeses. Bake in a preheated 350-degree oven until a crusty, lightly brown surface develops, about 25 minutes. Make 4 indentations on

the surface and carefully break an egg into each, cover them with the remaining hot sauce, and return to the oven for about 18 minutes, until the eggs have set.
SERVES 4

Turkey Patties

3 fat scallions, or 1 white onion, chopped very fine
6 medium mushrooms, chopped very fine
4 tablespoons butter
1½ pounds ground turkey
1 egg white

Salt
Freshly ground pepper
2–3 tablespoons chopped fresh tarragon, or 1 teaspoon dried; or 1 tablespoon chopped fresh dill, or ½ teaspoon dried
1 tablespoon chopped parsley

SAUCE:
4–5 mushrooms,, sliced
2 scallions, including tender greens, sliced

¾ cup sour cream, or half sour cream and half plain yogurt

Paprika for dusting

Sauté the scallions or onion and mushrooms in 1 tablespoon butter until very tender. Mix with the ground turkey, add the egg white, season liberally with salt and pepper, sprinkle on the herbs, and beat with a fork to lighten the mixture. Form into 12 patties, using a light hand. Heat the remaining 3 tablespoons butter in a skillet just large enough to hold the patties in one layer, and brown them lightly on both sides. Cover and cook over low to moderate heat 10 minutes, adding the sliced mushrooms and scallions for the sauce for the last 3 minutes of cooking. When done, if there is considerable liquid in the pan, remove the patties and cook the liquid down rapidly until there is just a little left, then stir in the sour cream. Warm the sauce until heated through, taste and salt lightly if necessary; then spoon the sauce over the patties, and dust them with paprika. Serve with rice or noodles.
SERVES 4

Turkey Wing Stew

Stewed turkey wings make a nourishing and economical dish. They tend not to have much flavor, but cooking them in an aromatic tarragon-accented broth with the intense emphasis of sun-dried tomatoes and black olives gives them a special flavor. If these ingredients aren't at hand, add some root vegetables instead. Along with little white onions and carrots, use about 1 cup parsnips or rutabagas cut into 2-inch logs to give a good earthy flavor, and try a little thyme instead of the tarragon.

4 large turkey wings, split in half at the joints
3 tablespoons oil, preferably half olive and half vegetable oil
1 large onion, chopped
2 large garlic cloves, chopped
½ cup dry white wine or vermouth
2 tablespoons chopped fresh tarragon, or 2 teaspoons dried
¼ cup or slightly more chicken or turkey broth or water

Salt
Freshly ground pepper
12 small white onions, peeled
12 small carrots, trimmed and scraped
8 sun-dried tomatoes
8 black olives, preferably Mediterranean type, pitted and halved
1 tablespoon chopped parsley

In a large skillet, sauté the turkey wings in half the oil, turning them so they are golden on both sides. Remove the wings and add the remaining oil to the skillet, then sauté the chopped onion slowly until it is translucent, stirring in the garlic for the last minute of cooking. Pour in the wine and turn up the heat, as you stir in the tarragon. When the wine has reduced slightly, add the broth or water. Salt and pepper the wings on both sides, and return them to the skillet. Lower the heat, cover, and simmer very gently for 1 hour, adding a little more broth or water if the pan gets dry (there should be some liquid in the bottom but the meat shouldn't be swimming in it). Add the small onions and carrots and cook about 30 minutes more, until they are tender, adding the sun-dried tomatoes for the last 10 minutes of cooking. Stir in the olives to heat through, then taste and correct the seasoning if necessary. Sprinkle parsley on top, and serve with steamed rice.

SERVES 4

DUCK

Roast Duck with Apricot Stuffing

One 5–6-pound duck

STUFFING:
¼ pound (1 stick) butter or
* margarine*
½ cup chopped celery
3 shallots, chopped
2½ cups crumbled fresh bread
1½ cups chopped dried apricots
Grated peel of 1 orange
½ cup orange juice

Salt
Freshly ground pepper
1 tablespoon chopped fresh
* rosemary, or ½ teaspoon dried,*
* mulled*
½ teaspoon dried thyme, or 2
* teaspoons chopped fresh leaves*
½ lemon

APRICOT LIQUEUR SAUCE:
2 tablespoons duck fat
2 tablespoons flour
½ cup boiling water

½ cup dry white wine
1 cup orange juice
3–4 tablespoons apricot liqueur

Wash and dry the duck. Melt the butter and sauté the celery and shallots, stirring occasionally, over moderate heat for about 5 minutes. Put the crumbled bread in a large bowl and stir in the sautéed vegetables, the apricots, orange peel and juice, and sprinkle with a little salt and pepper. Stir in the herbs and mix well. Remove the excess fat from the duck and stuff the cavity loosely, then skewer closed, and truss the duck. Rub the skin with lemon juice, sprinkle it with a little salt, and prick all over. Place the duck, breast side up, on a rack in a shallow roasting pan. Roast in a preheated 475-degree oven for 15 minutes, then reduce heat to 350 degrees and continue roasting, drawing off the fat occasionally, for 1 hour and 20–30 minutes more, until the thigh joint turns easily. Allow the duck to rest while you make the sauce.

In a saucepan, put 2 tablespoons of the duck fat from the roasting pan and pour off the remainder. Stir the flour into the fat and cook 2–3 minutes. Pour the boiling water into the roasting pan, scrape up the brown bits, and stir this mixture into the saucepan. Continue to cook and stir, gradually adding the wine and orange juice, while the sauce thickens. Stir in the liqueur, and pour into a sauceboat. Carve the duck at table and pass the sauce.
SERVES 4

One 4-pound duck
1 small onion
Salt

Freshly ground pepper
3½ cups water
½ cup applejack

Roast Duck for Autumn

SAUCE:
2 tablespoons butter
2 tablespoons oil
1 cup chopped onion
1 garlic clove, chopped
½ pound mushrooms, sliced

1 tablespoon fresh paprika
2 tablespoons flour
¼ cup applejack
2 tomatoes, peeled, seeded, and
chopped

Remove the neck and the giblets from the duck, put them in a saucepan (reserving the liver) with a small onion and salt and pepper and 3 cups water; simmer while preparing the roast duck. Sprinkle salt and pepper inside the duck and rub the skin thoroughly, then truss, and prick the skin all over. Put the duck on a rack in a shallow roasting pan in a preheated 375-degree oven. Roast for about 30 minutes, and drain off all the accumulated fat. Mix ½ cup applejack with the remaining ½ cup water, and baste the duck with this mixture. Turn the heat down to 350 degrees and continue roasting, basting every 20 minutes or so.

Meanwhile, make a sauce by heating the butter and oil in a saucepan and sautéing the onion and garlic 3–4 minutes. Add the sliced mushrooms and continue cooking about 5 minutes. Stir in the paprika (be sure it is not stale) and the flour, and cook over low heat 2 minutes, stirring. Add 1 cup of the duck stock, a little at a time, and the wine, stirring to make a smooth sauce. Add salt and pepper to taste. Remove the gizzards from the simmering stock and chop fine before stirring into the sauce. When the duck is golden brown and crispy on all sides, after about 2 hours, remove it and set aside, keeping it warm. Remove as much fat as possible from the roasting pan. Stir in the remaining applejack and scape up all the browned bits in the pan while the brandy boils; stir this into the sauce. Add the chopped tomatoes and continue cooking—the sauce should be like gravy. Cut the duck into quarters, spoon a little sauce over each quarter, and serve with wild rice and braised carrots. Serve the remaining sauce in a sauceboat.
SERVES 4

Marinated Duck with Cranberries

Cranberries have always been common enough to Yankee coastal regions, but domesticated so-called Peking ducks haven't been around for much more than a century. When they were first raised in Stonington, Connecticut, in the 1870s, they were soon to be matched with the cranberry, and their flavor took on a bit of the wilderness. In the 1980s, however, a dish like this might be considered "nouvelle cuisine," and our recipe is actually based on one from Diane Rossen Worthington who considers it to be part of the new California cuisine.

STOCK:
Duck neck and giblets
3 cups water

Pinch of salt

MARINADE:
¾ cup cranberries
½ pear, peeled and chopped
3 tablespoons honey
½ cup orange juice

⅛ teaspoon each ground cloves,
   mace, salt, and pepper
1 duck (about 4 pounds)

STUFFING:
4 tablespoons butter
1 onion, chopped
½ rib celery, chopped
1¼ cups cubed corn bread, lightly
   toasted

½ pear, peeled and chopped
¾ cup cranberries
¼ cup hazelnuts chopped
Salt

GARNISHES: 2 tablespoons cranberries
Sprigs watercress
4 small poached or brandied Seckel pears, if available

Put the duck neck and giblets in a saucepan with the water and a pinch of salt and simmer gently, partly covered, for several hours.

Purée all the ingredients for the marinade in a blender or food processor, and pour this mixture over the ducks. Marinate for 1 or 2 hours.

Prepare the stuffing. Heat the butter in a small skillet and sauté the onion over low heat for 2 or 3 minutes, then add the celery and sauté until just tender. Mix together with the corn bread, chopped pear, cranberries, and hazelnuts, and salt lightly. Remove the duck from the marinade, pat dry, and spoon the stuffing into the duck's cavity. Skewer the opening closed and truss the duck. Roast the duck in a preheated 450-degree oven for 15 minutes, then prick it in the fatty areas, lower the heat to 350 degrees, and continue roasting 1 hour and 15 minutes, drawing off most of the fat as it accumulates in the bottom of the pan. Remove the duck to a warm platter and let rest while you prepare the sauce.

Pour 1½ cups duck stock into the roasting pan and heat, scraping up all browned bits. Add the marinade and bring to a boil. Pour off about ¾ cup sauce and keep warm. Now cut the duck in quarters, return the meat to the

roasting pan and spoon the sauce in the pan over the duck pieces. Roast about another 10–15 minutes, until nicely glazed. Serve on a platter with fresh cranberries scattered on top and garnish with watercress and small cooked pears, if you like. Serve the extra sauce in a sauceboat.
SERVES 4

Roast Duckling with Elderberry and Ginger Sauce

When Perley Fielders was the owner and chef at the Northeast Kingdom's Craftsbury Inn, his menus often featured unusual dishes that had distinct New England characteristics. Perley knew that elderberries make good Yankee wine and that the flowers were often used and served in the same manner as fried squash blossoms. As a contrary countryman, he developed a spicy elderberry sauce for duck or game that bears his own stamp.

One 5–6-pound duckling
Salt
Freshly ground pepper
¾ cup hot water

4 tablespoons maple syrup or honey
1 small onion
½ lemon

THE SAUCE:
1½ cups preserved elderberries
2 cups applejack or bourbon
½ cup Dijon mustard

Juice of 1½ lemons
Grated fresh ginger

Sprinkle the duck inside and out with salt and pepper. Mix the water well with the maple syrup or honey. Put the onion and ½ lemon in the cavity, and put the duck on a rack in an oval casserole just large enough to contain the bird. Fix the rack at a tilt so that the open cavity is uppermost. Pour the water mixture into the cavity. Carefully add a little plain water around the duck to cover the bottom of the casserole by about ¼ inch. Bring to a boil on top of the stove, reduce the heat, and cover the casserole tightly to keep in all the steam. Simmer gently for about 2 hours, turning the bird once after about 1 hour. Meanwhile, prepare the sauce. In a saucepan, heat the elderberries and the liquor, stir in the mustard, and when the mixture is simmering, add the lemon juice and grated ginger to taste. Simmer about 45 minutes, or until the sauce is reduced by one-third.

   When the drumsticks move easily, remove the duck from the casserole and put it on a tray to brown for about 15 minutes in a preheated 500-degree oven. Carve the duckling into 4 pieces, pour some of the sauce over, and serve the rest in a sauceboat.
SERVES 2–4

Hessian-Spiced Potato-Stuffed Duck

It may well be that some Yankee culinary influences can be traced to a few mercenary soldiers who stayed behind when the British forces abandoned America (see Hasenpfeffer, page 269). No matter, potato stuffings were not uncommon in early New England kitchens, and the duck in this case is enhanced by the seasonings.

2 ducks (about 4 pounds)*
3 onions, chopped
½ cup chopped celery, stalk and leaves
4 cups cubed, peeled, and parboiled potatoes

2 teaspoons dried thyme
Salt
Freshly ground pepper
Parsley
Juice of 1 lemon
¼ cup honey

* Note: If the ducks are frozen, thaw at least 24 hours slowly in the refrigerator.

Pull out the fat from the duck cavities and render over low heat. Rinse the ducks inside and out with hot tap water. Sauté the onions and celery in 2–3 tablespoons of the duck fat for about 5 minutes, then add the diced potatoes, the thyme, and a little salt and freshly ground pepper to taste. Turn the potatoes occasionally and when they are lightly brown, spoon the stuffing mixture into the 2 duck cavities. Place the ducks on a rack in a shallow roasting pan and put in a preheated 375-degree oven for 1½ hours, then draw off all the fat. Mix the lemon juice with the honey, and baste the ducks several times with the lemon-honey glaze as you roast them an additional 15–20 minutes. They should be golden brown, and the drumsticks will turn easily in their sockets when ducks are done.
SERVES 4–6

Muscovy Duck Braised with Cabbage

Muscovy ducks, even when raised domestically as our friend Ralph Person does on his farm just outside Hardwick, Vermont, taste more like wild ducks and are apt to be a bit tough in the thigh and leg. The best way to cook them is to braise them whole to keep the meat moist. Then we like to serve the breasts with the cabbage in which they have braised for one festive meal, and save the legs and thighs for further cooking in the Baked Duck and Chick-peas dish that follows or use them in a cassoulet such as the one on page 445.

2 onions
2 ribs celery with leaves
2 Muscovy ducks (about 4 pounds each)
Vegetable or olive oil
Salt
Freshly ground pepper

1 large cabbage, core removed, shredded (to make 8 cups)
2 small onions, chopped
2 small carrots, scraped and chopped
3 tablespoons caraway seeds
1 cup dry white wine or vermouth

Prick the whole onions in several places and break up the celery ribs, and place them in the duck cavities. Rub the ducks all over with oil, salt, and pepper. Place in a casserole a little larger than the 2 birds (or use 2 casseroles if necessary) and roast, uncovered, in a preheated 425-degree oven for 45 minutes to brown them. Prick in the thigh area to release some of their fat.

Meanwhile, blanch the shredded cabbage in a large pot of boiling salted water for 1 minute, then drain. Stir the cabbage into the duck casserole along with the chopped onions and carrots, mixing it in with what fat there is (Muscovy ducks have comparatively little fat). Add salt, pepper, and caraway seeds, and pour in the wine. Drape foil over the top, cover the casserole, lower the oven to 350 degrees, and braise for 1 hour and 15 minutes. When done, carve off the breasts and arrange them on a warm platter with the cabbage around them.

SERVES 6

Baked Duck and Chick-peas

1 cup dried chick-peas
3 garlic cloves
1/8 teaspoon baking soda
2 bay leaves
2 cups duck stock (see page 178)
1 large onion, chopped
2 teaspoons chopped fresh thyme, or 3/4 teaspoon dried
Legs and thighs of 1 braised Muscovy duck (see preceding recipe)
Salt
Freshly ground pepper
1/4 pound sausage meat
3 tablespoons chopped parsley

Put the chick-peas in a pot with water to cover by 1 inch. Bring to a boil, boil 1 minute, then turn off the heat and let the chick-peas stand in their cooking water 1 hour or more. Drain. Return the chick-peas to the pot, pour fresh water over them to cover by a couple of inches, add the unpeeled garlic cloves, baking soda, and bay leaves and simmer about 2 hours, or until the chick-peas are just tender. Put the chick-peas and what is left of their cooking liquid into a casserole. Scoop out the garlic flesh (discard the garlic skins as well as the bay leaves), mash, and add this to the casserole along with the duck stock, onion, thyme, and the duck pieces. Season liberally with salt and pepper.

Form the sausage meat into 8 small patties, and fry them in a skillet until most of the fat is released. Tuck the sausage patties into the casserole, cover, and bake in a preheated 325-degree oven for 2 hours. Taste: the meat and chick-peas should be very tender and the cooking liquid reduced and thickened. If necessary, cook a little longer. When done, sprinkle parsley on top.

SERVES 4

Duck Salmi

The western border farmlands of Connecticut and Massachusetts gained fame as Peking duck country a couple of generations back, and local recipes that use leftover duck in various delicious and classic ways have been in demand ever since.

1 pound cooked duck in serving
   pieces (about 2 cups)
4 tablespoons butter
1 tablespoon chopped scallions
1 stalk celery, chopped
1 small carrot, finely chopped
3 tablespoons finely chopped
   country ham

½–¾ cup small mushroom caps
4 tablespoons flour
2 cups chicken stock
½ bay leaf
¼ teaspoon mace
3 tablespoons dry sherry
Salt

Choose duck pieces that are flat and thin. Heat the butter and sauté the scallions, celery, and carrot, then stir in the ham and mushroom caps, turning frequently so the mushrooms become tender and absorb a little butter. Stir in the flour, and add the chicken stock, a little at a time, as the flour browns. Add the bay leaf and mace and cook a minute or so. Add the duck pieces and the sherry, along with a light sprinkling of salt to taste and heat through.

SERVES 4

GOOSE

Roast Goose with Chestnut, Apple, and Fig Stuffing

If you don't have any corn bread on hand, it is worth baking up a batch to make this delicious stuffing (see page 494 for a simple recipe).

1 goose (9–12 pounds)
About 1 quart water

Salt

STUFFING:
12–15 braised chestnuts (page 171)
1 large tart apple, peeled and cut
   into large dice
10 dried figs, cut in quarters
2–2½ cups crumbled corn bread

Salt to taste
Freshly ground pepper to taste
3 tablespoons chopped parsley
2 teaspoons chopped fresh savory,
   or ½ teaspoon dried

GRAVY:
1–2 tablespoons flour

About 1½ cups reserved goose
   broth

Remove the neck and gizzard from the goose and put them in a saucepan with the water and let simmer gently, partially covered, for several hours, until reduced to about 2 cups. Then season with salt.

Mix all the stuffing ingredients together, using the smaller quantities if your goose is only 9 pounds. Taste and adjust the seasoning as necessary. Fill the cavity of the goose with the stuffing, skewer closed and lace string around the skewers, then truss the bird. Roast in a preheated 325-degree oven, breast side down, for 1½ hours, drawing off the fat as it accumulates; then turn and toast another 1½ hours, or slightly more for the larger bird. When done, the juices should run clear when pricked where the thigh attaches to the body. Remove and let rest on a warm serving platter while you prepare the gravy.

Pour off all but 1 tablespoon or so of the fat, then sprinkle the flour over —1 to 2 tablespoons depending on how thick you like your gravy. Set the roasting pan over low heat and stir for a minute, scraping up all the browned bits. Add the broth and whisk until smooth. Taste, and season with salt and pepper as needed. Serve in a gravy boat alongside the goose. Remove trussing strings and skewers before carving.
SERVES 6–8

As elsewhere, retail packaging in New England includes pairing 2 meaty frozen goose legs to a package. Here's a good and simple way of cooking them.

Braised Frozen Goose Legs with Potatoes

4 frozen goose legs (about 4–4⅓ pounds)
2 tablespoons oil
2 pounds small potatoes, peeled
1 cup coarsely chopped scallions, including tender greens
2 cups cooked tomatoes

⅔ cup tomato concentrate or paste
2 garlic cloves
1 cup dry red wine
2 tablespoons wine vinegar
2 small bay leaves
1 long strip lemon or lime peel

Put the goose legs in the bottom part of the refrigerator at least 24 hours before using; they should defrost slowly and thoroughly.

Heat the oil in a heavy iron pot large enough to brown the legs as you turn them at intervals. Put in the peeled potatoes and brown them quickly. After about 20 minutes, drain off the fat in the pot. Put the scallions, tomatoes, tomato concentrate or paste, garlic, wine, and vinegar in a food processor and blend until smooth. Pour this mixture over the goose legs, add the bay leaves and the lemon or lime peel, and bring to a boil. Reduce the heat to the lowest degree, cover, and simmer for 1½–2 hours, until the meat is very tender. Remove the bay leaves before serving.
SERVES 4

GAME BIRDS

Amelia's Quail

Amelia Fritz, who raises quail in Vermont's Northeast Kingdom with her husband, Tim, believes in cooking the little birds as simply as possible to let the rich flavor speak for itself.

4 brace quail (i.e., 8 quail)
8 sprigs rosemary, thyme, or sage
8 tablespoons (1 stick) softened
   butter
Salt

Freshly ground pepper
1 medium onion, sliced
½ carrot, scraped and sliced thin
3 tablespoons port or applejack

Clean the birds and put a sprig of fresh herbs inside each (if you don't have fresh herbs, crumble just a tiny bit of dried herb inside) and salt lightly. Rub 1 tablespoon butter over each bird, salt and pepper them lightly, and place them in a roasting pan, not touching, with the vegetables scattered around. Roast in a preheated 400-degree oven 45 minutes, basting occasionally. If the vegetables are burning in the bottom of the pan, add a few tablespoons water. When done, remove the quail to a hot platter, splash the port or applejack into the pan, cook about 30 seconds, scraping up the pan juices and mashing the vegetables into them. Pour a little of this sauce over each quail, and serve. This is a dish to be eaten with fingers.
SERVES 4

Pheasant Smothered in Fresh Sauerkraut

Pheasant is apt to be dry, particulary if it is an older bird, and rather than laying strips of fat over it to keep it moist, smothering it in sauerkraut makes a light and pleasing way of cooking the birds.

2 pheasants
2 tablespoons vegetable oil
2 medium onions, chopped
2 medium tart apples, peeled and
   cut into large dice
3–4 cups fresh sauerkraut, drained
   (use 4 cups if pheasants are large)

12 juniper berries
Freshly ground pepper
2 tablespoons softened butter
Salt

Split the pheasant in half lengthwise, wash, and pat dry. Heat the oil in a large skillet and brown the pheasant pieces lightly on the skin side. Remove and set aside. Sauté the onion in the oil in the pan until limp and golden. Mix the apples, sauerkraut, juniper berries, and some freshly ground pepper. If the pheasant halves are large, cut them in half. Lay the pheasant pieces in a shallow baking dish that will hold them in one layer, flesh side down; rub softened butter over the skin, and salt lightly (the sauerkraut is salty so you need very little extra). Spread the sauerkraut mixture around and on top of the pheasant pieces, and cover the dish lightly with foil. Bake in a preheated 350-degree oven for about 55 minutes for young pheasants, and up to 1 hour and 15 minutes for older pheasants. Test by piercing at the thigh joint to see if the juices run clear.

SERVES 4–6, DEPENDING ON SIZE OF PHEASANTS

Pheasant Legs and Thighs in Red Cabbage

Often the legs and thighs of old pheasants are tough, so it is better to braise them and cook the breasts separately for a festive occasion.

4–6 pheasant legs and thighs (from good-size pheasants)
4 tablespoons chicken or goose fat, or butter and oil
Salt
Freshly ground pepper
1 good-size red cabbage, shredded
1 large onion, sliced thin

⅓ cup mild vinegar (we used blackberry, page 636)
2 tablespoons sugar
⅓ cup or more chicken broth
8–10 crushed juniper berries
2 tart apples, peeled and sliced thick
2–3 tablespoons chopped parsley

Heat the fat in a heavy saucepan or skillet and brown the pheasant on all sides. Salt and pepper the meat, then add all the remaining ingredients and cover the pan. Cook slowly for 1½ hours. Serve with braised chestnuts (page 171), if available.

SERVES 4

MEAT

OCCASIONALLY, when we visit a small farm on this side of the Quebec border, we stop for a look at the rustic pigsty set back in the woods, and talk of the ham and bacon, smoked over corncobs, that the fattening pigs will provide for the chill fall weather. Other friends (see box, page 244) in nearby Greensboro village have a smokehouse in the backyard that is large enough to provide a year's supply of breakfast meat, which they smoke over wood fires. At our house, the aroma of frying bacon from that smokehouse is often a sure way to get certain overnight guests out of bed—we even get dinner meat courses, based on smoked pork (Back Bacon with Plums, page 250).

In New England summertime, we sometimes barbecue pork tenderloin over charcoal, and this chapter includes various indoor ways of cooking almost every cut of pork. Fattest of all butchers' meats, pork can be practically self-basting, a sort of symbol of old-time Yankee frugality.

Still, like most Americans, New Englanders are partial to beef. Purebred cattle are raised on Connecticut farms and in other parts of the region, and some of the best of the meat is apt to be leaner, and more tender, with traditional flavor. The classic "New England boiled dinner," based on beef that is corned or cured in brine, is often the first thing to come to mind when certain people think of the Yankee claim to gastronomical nostalgia. Certainly this succulent meat stew was eaten frequently enough during generations of winters when it was necessary—there being no refrigeration in the kitchen—to rely on preserved foods. But today corned beef and cabbage is most often a celebratory family meal—it rates with the time-honored boiled dinners of the world, a meal anyone might serve as proudly as he or she would serve *pot-au-feu* or *bollito misto*.

Italian insinuations that helped to make manicotti a church-supper favorite in some rural bailiwicks are as responsible for the increasing acceptance of veal and of the new pasta menus that proliferate far beyond Boston and other industrial centers. "Pale" used to be the word for many veal dishes—early Yankees served veal scallops in cream sauce, or were sometimes adventurous with veal and oyster pie. In the 1980s, garlic and plum tomatoes have helped veal dishes find a way to many New England hearts. The veal raised by a 4-H farm youngster on Highway 14 may not be as softly pink as *plume de veau,* but it has proved to be delicious in the osso buco recipe we were given in Boston by a North End butcher. Even more interesting was a Fricassee of Veal with Fiddleheads (page 259).

Aside from 4-H'ers, country fairs provide visual evidence of what's happening. Sheep—and the lamb that goes to market in spring or early summer —are back in a big way, from Maine's island pastures to the Champlain Valley and southern New England. For years we've bought lamb, raised by our neighbor Roseanne Oates on the Cobb Schoolhouse Road, and more recently from Dave and Marilyn Usher of Craftsbury; friends on Martha's Vineyard fill their larders with lamb that has been nurtured on salt meadows, much as is the French *gigot pré-salé.* The number of young farmers raising sheep in the 1980s has increased steadily.

On the Vineyard, as in much of northern New England, there is a great variety of wild meat, including squirrels in the fall that are already stuffed with acorns and nuts, as well as plenty of rabbits and deer. Hunting accounts for much of the region's winter meat supply, and North Country cooks make use of every bit of the meat in sausage and mincemeat recipes that are adaptations of methods used for domestic meat. They rate deer liver as a great delicacy and bear meat fit to be roasted like pork. Mr. Bean, who was a fine hunter, preferred to cut his venison steaks about 1½ inches thick and to sear them in a smoking hot frying pan, turning and cooking them to the tastes of his fellow hunters. We have deliberately limited the number of recipes for game here because *The L.L. Bean Game and Fish Cookbook* offers such an abundant variety.

Whatever the source of meat, new New England cooks (some in the interest of good health) tend to manage budgets by putting less emphasis on meat. Instead of roasts and steaks, smaller amounts of all kinds of meat are being used; the new appreciation of vegetables calls for meals in which meat is a modest balance. The stir-fry technique borrowed from Oriental Yankees has become important in the new kitchen as a way of combining small amounts of meat and fish with crisply cooked vegetables. Similarly, the diversity of ethnic contributions has helped to change regional cooking with creative ideas for combination dishes and stuffed things, in which meat is a subtle factor. One man's meat has become just another ingredient.

BEEF

Steaks known as butcher's steaks are the cheaper but delicious cuts that butchers were supposed to save for themselves—the flank, the skirt, and the hanging tenderloin.

1 flank steak (about 10–12 ounces)
2 garlic cloves
½ teaspoon coarse salt
1 teaspoon cracked pepper
¼ cup freshly squeezed lemon juice

¼ cup vegetable or olive oil or a combination
1 tablespoon butter
¼ pound mushrooms, sliced

Make a light crisscross pattern with the tip of a knife on both sides of the flank steak, and place in a shallow dish. Squeeze the garlic cloves through a press onto each side of the steak and rub into the meat along with the salt and cracked pepper. Pour the lemon juice and oil over and let marinate 1 hour, turning a couple of times.

When ready to broil or grill, pour off the marinade into a skillet, add the butter, and quickly sauté the mushrooms 5 minutes. Meanwhile, broil the steak under a preheated broiler or over hot coals 3 minutes on each side. Spread the mushrooms on top and serve, slicing the steak on the diagonal against the grain.

SERVES 4

Broiled or Grilled Marinated Butcher's Steak with Cracked Pepper and Mushrooms

---

If you broil this flank steak for just two people one night the way we often do, you'll have enough leftover to make the Gratin of Steak Slices and Mushrooms that follows. It's worth it.

1 flank or skirt steak (about ¾ pound)
1 tablespoon finely minced fresh ginger

2–3 fat garlic cloves, chopped
Freshly ground pepper
¼ cup soy sauce
¼ cup dry sherry

Rub the flank steak with the fresh ginger, garlic, and freshly ground pepper on both sides. Place in a shallow dish and pour the soy sauce and sherry

Broiled or Grilled Flank or Skirt Steak

over the steak. Marinate 30 minutes to 1 hour. Broil the steak under a preheated broiler as close to the heat as you can get it for 2–3 minutes on one side, brush the other side with the marinade and broil 2–3 minutes more. Or grill the same amount of time over hot coals, turning once. Let rest a couple of minutes, then cut in thin, diagonal strips against the grain.

SERVES 2 (SEE NOTE ABOVE) OR 4

Gratin of Steak Slices and Mushrooms

¾ *pound mushrooms, chopped quite fine*
3 *fat garlic cloves, minced fine*
6 *shallots or scallion bulbs, chopped fine*
¼ *cup chopped parsley, preferably flat-leaved Italian parsley*
1–2 *tablespoons chopped fresh herbs, such as thyme, savory, or tarragon, or the equivalent dried*

¾ *cup fresh bread crumbs*
Salt
Freshly ground pepper
¼ *cup olive oil*
8 *thin, rare slices broiled flank or other steak (see preceding recipe)*
2 *tablespoons red wine*

Mix the mushrooms, garlic, shallots, parsley, and herbs with ½ cup bread crumbs. Add salt and pepper to taste, then mix in 1 tablespoon olive oil. Rub the bottom of a shallow casserole with a little olive oil. Distribute half the mushroom-crumb mixture over the bottom in an even layer. Lay the steak slices in a single layer on top; season with salt and pepper and drizzle the wine over. Spread the remaining mushroom mixture over the beef slices, and top with the last of the bread crumbs. Drizzle the remaining olive oil on top, and bake, uncovered, in a preheated 375-degree oven for 25 minutes.

SERVES 2–3

Pot Roast

One 3-*pound whole chuck, with fat on one side*
1 *tablespoon flour*
2 *cups water*
1 *onion, chopped*
1 *carrot, scraped and chopped*
2–3 *garlic cloves peeled (optional)*
Salt
Freshly ground pepper
2 *bay leaves*

1 *teaspoon dried thyme*
4–5 *small turnips, peeled and quartered*
2 *medium parsnips, peeled and cut into 2-inch pieces (the thick parts quartered or halved to make equal pieces)*
10 *small carrots, scraped, or 2 large, cut as for parsnips*
2 *tablespoons chopped parsley*

In a heavy pot, sear the pot roast all over, starting with the fat side to provide some grease to brown the other sides. If there isn't a fat side to your cut, film the pot first with a little vegetable oil. When the meat is brown all over, remove. Stir the flour into the pot and cook slowly, stirring, for a couple of minutes, then add the water, a little at a time, stirring. Toss in the chopped onion, chopped carrot, and the optional garlic. Return the meat to the pot, salt and pepper it lightly all over, add the herbs, and bring to a boil. Drape a piece of foil over the meat, lower the heat, then cover the pot and simmer ever so gently for 2 hours. Add the cutup vegetables and simmer another 40 minutes, covered, until the vegetables are just tender.

SERVES 6–8

Pot Roast with Cider

3–4 pounds beef chuck, well larded with fat
2–3 ounces salt pork or bacon
2 onions, chopped
3 cloves
1 stick cinnamon
½ teaspoon grated fresh ginger
2 cups hard cider*
Salt
Freshly ground pepper

Flour
1 garlic clove, finely chopped
1 tablespoon finely chopped parsley
4 large carrots, scraped and cut into chunks
8 small new potatoes
Vegetable oil
8 small white turnips
12 tiny white onions

* Note: If you have only sweet cider, add 2 tablespoons vinegar to it.

Cut incisions in the pot roast and insert 3 or 4 strips of the salt pork deeply into the cuts. Combine the chopped onions, cloves, cinnamon stick, and ginger with the cider, and pour over the meat. Set aside for several hours to marinate.

About 3 hours before serving the pot roast, drain off the liquid and pat the meat dry with paper towels. Fry a slice of salt pork in a heavy iron pot, then sear the roast on all sides. Remove, season with salt and pepper and dredge with flour. Return the roast to the pot, sprinkle with garlic and parsley and the remaining strips of salt pork, cover, and simmer about 3 hours, until the meat is very tender. About 1 hour before it is done, add the carrots.

Meanwhile, boil the potatoes until almost done, dredge them in seasoned flour, and brown them in vegetable oil. Blanch the turnips in a pot of boiling water for 1 minute, and drain. Add the potatoes, turnips, and small onions to the pot roast for the last 30 minutes of cooking. To serve, remove the pot roast to a warm platter and surround the meat with the vegetables. Skim the fat off the cooking juices, pour some of the juices over the meat, and serve the rest in a sauceboat.

SERVES 8

Pot Roast with Cranberries and Horseradish

¾ cup fresh cranberries
¼ cup sugar
2 tablespoons flour
Salt
Freshly ground pepper
One 2½-pound piece of bottom
    round beef
2 tablespoons vegetable oil or lard
⅓ cup freshly grated horseradish,
    or one 3-ounce jar prepared
    horseradish, drained

3 cloves
1 stick cinnamon
1 cup beef broth
12 small onions
12 small carrots, or equivalent
    amount of larger carrots, scraped
    and trimmed into 2-inch lengths
3 white turnips, peeled and cut into
    2-inch lengths
Drops of fresh lemon juice

Cook the fresh cranberries with the sugar in a little water for 10 minutes. Meanwhile, season the flour lightly with salt and pepper, and then pound it into the meat all over (the traditional way is to use the edge of a saucer to pound it in). Heat the oil or lard in a heavy casserole and brown the floured meat on all sides. Add the horseradish, cranberries, spices, and beef broth, cover, and cook gently for 2 hours, adding a little water if necessary. Toss in the onions, carrots, and turnips, cover again, and continue to cook until the vegetables are tender, 30–40 minutes more. Taste, and add salt and pepper as necessary and a few drops of lemon juice. Let rest 15 minutes before you slice the meat.

SERVES 6

Beef Braised in Beer with Wild Rice

This recipe, brought south from the Gaspé Peninsula, is a version of the classic *boeuf à la Carbonnade* that substitutes wild rice for boiled noodles or new potatoes.

2 pounds lean beef
1½ tablespoons vegetable oil
1 pound onions, coarsely chopped
2 fat garlic cloves, chopped
1½ cups dark beer
Salt
Freshly ground pepper
2 bay leaves

½ teaspoon dried thyme
1½ tablespoons brown sugar
2 tablespoons flour
4 tablespoons water
2 tablespoons cider vinegar
3 cups cooked wild rice (see
    page 331)

Cut the beef into 1½-inch cubes. Heat the oil in a skillet and sauté the beef in several batches to brown all surfaces. Transfer the meat to a stewpot or casserole, then add the onions to the skillet and cook gently about 8 minutes, adding the garlic for the last 2 minutes of cooking. Pour the beer into the skillet and stir briskly to scrape up any browned bits before transferring the onions, garlic, and beer to the stewpot. Sprinkle lightly with salt and several turns of the pepper grinder, and stir in the bay leaves, thyme, and sugar. Bring to a boil, cover, and simmer for 1½–2 hours, or until tender. Mix the flour and water together to make a smooth paste, then blend this into the stew. Continue cooking, stirring, for about 3 minutes to thicken the sauce slightly. Blend in the vinegar, then spoon the stew over hot wild rice.

SERVES 4

Beef Portuguese

3 ounces bacon, cut across the slice in narrow strips
4 tablespoons oil, half vegetable and half olive
2 pounds brisket or skirt steak, cut in 2-inch-long x 1-inch-wide pieces
2 large onions, sliced
2–3 garlic cloves
1 cup dry white wine or dry vermouth
3–4 strands saffron (optional)
¼ teaspoon dried thyme
2 bay leaves
One 14-ounce can plum tomatoes, put through sieve
2 cups beef broth
Salt
Freshly ground pepper
1 cup rice
2 cups coarsely grated mild cheese, such as Swiss

Brown the bacon strips in a good-size skillet, then remove them with a slotted spoon to a flameproof casserole. Leave only 1 tablespoon bacon fat in the skillet and add to it 2 tablespoons oil. Brown the pieces of meat on all sides, doing them in several batches to brown well and removing them to the skillet after. Add the remaining oil to the skillet and sauté the onions until they take on color, adding the garlic for the last minute, then remove to the casserole. Pour the wine into the skillet, bring it to a boil, add the saffron and herbs, boil hard for 30 seconds, then pour over the meat along with the sieved tomatoes (you can sieve them right into the casserole) and beef broth. Salt and pepper to taste and simmer gently, covered, for about 1¼ hours. Taste: the meat should be almost tender; if not, cook a bit longer. Now stir in the rice, cover, and cook over low to moderate heat for 25–30 minutes, until the rice is tender. Stir in the cheese, and serve from the casserole.

SERVES 4

New England Boiled Dinner

Old-timers will tell you that the best cut for corned beef must be brisket, but a New England farm–raised piece of beef that has been cured for New England winter consumption was undoubtedly not as fat as the one found in supermarkets, wrapped in a plastic pouch and bathed in its brine. In our kitchen we've found that the corned round of beef has less fat and it slices better. If you do use the fattier cut, it's best to cook the vegetables separately; they will seem fresher and less greasy. But when you choose the round, all the vegetables (except the beets) are delicious when simmered in the traditional way. Be sure to cook extra beets and potatoes, so you'll have enough left over for Bryn Teg Red Flannel Hash (opposite).

1 corned beef (about 5–6 pounds),
   round or brisket or combination
1 dried hot red pepper (optional)
2 whole garlic cloves, unpeeled
18 beets
18 small white onions, peeled
8–10 medium-sized potatoes,
   peeled and cut in half

12–18 carrots, depending on size,
   scraped and trimmed
6 medium parsnips, peeled and
   trimmed
1 green cabbage (about 2 pounds),
   cut in 6 wedges
A small handful chopped parsley

Put the corned beef in a large pot with enough cold water to cover it by 1 inch; include some of the pickling spices that come with it, particularly the hot red pepper if you like a peppery taste (or if the brine lacks pepper, add 1 hot pepper to the pot, if you wish). Toss in the garlic, bring to a boil, then lower the heat, cover, and simmer very gently 2½–3 hours (test by poking a fork into the center; it shouldn't fall apart but the fork should penetrate easily). In the meantime, boil the beets in a separate saucepan in

An Oriental-Looking Dish

Red flannel hash is one of those plebian culinary achievements that sometimes persuades strong, silent men to emote in public. Years ago, the New Hampshire columnist Haydn S. Pearson wrote movingly about the recipe. 'It is unfortunate,' he told his readers, "that the word hash has fallen into some disrepute . . . it is good, solid, everyday grub. Red-flannel-hash, however, is on a different plane. It is an Oriental-looking taste-tantalizing dish. It's color is exciting. It has allure and snap. A frying pan full of it on the kitchen stove sends a nostril-tickling aroma through the room . . . As a man comes through the wood shed with the milk pails on his arm, he inhales the smell and a smile lights his face. What better rewards for a long day's work digging potatoes or picking apples?"

water to cover until tender; drain, peel, and keep them warm. About 30 minutes before you think the meat is done, add the white onions, potatoes, carrots, and parsnips, and continue simmering until they are almost tender —about 20–25 minutes. Remove the corned beef, wrap it in foil to keep it warm (if any of the vegetables are fork-tender, remove them at this point, too). Bring the cooking liquid to a rapid boil, drop in the cabbage wedges, and cook about 10 minutes. Arrange the corned beef on a warm platter with the vegetables around (hold back on some of the potatoes and beets for tomorrow's hash), and scatter parsley over all. Bring to the table to carve, and pass mustard or mustard pickles or grated horseradish. You could also serve Ed Giobbi's sauce for boiled meats on the side (see page 632), which may not be old New England traditional, but it makes a delicious accompaniment.

SERVES 6 WITH AMPLE LEFTOVERS

Bryn Teg Red Flannel Hash

We always make a red flannel hash after we have served a New England Boiled Dinner, making sure that we have enough leftover corned beef and vegetables. We often poach an egg per serving to put on top of the hash.

1 cup or more chopped cooked
   corned beef
½ cup chopped cooked vegetables,
   such as carrots, parsnips, green
   cabbage, and onions
1 cup chopped cooked beets

2 cups chopped boiled potatoes
Bacon fat or vegetable shortening
About ½ cup beef broth
1 tablespoon chopped parsley
4 poached eggs (optional)

Toss the chopped meat and vegetables in a mixing bowl. Heat a skillet containing fat or shortening about ¼ inch deep. Spread the hash smoothly to cover the bottom of the pan, tamping it down a bit and adding a little broth. Cook without stirring over very low heat, until the hash begins to brown at the edges, at least 30 minutes. Fold it as you would an omelet and slide it onto a hot platter. Sprinkle with parsley.

SERVES 4

Corned Beef Pancakes

Leftover corned beef (or canned corned beef) can be transformed into moist meat patties to serve with scrambled eggs—a New England variety of a hamburger on a bun.

12 ounces cooked corned beef
1 medium onion
¼ green pepper, ribs and seeds
   removed

2 tablespoons chopped parsley
1 tablespoon bread crumbs
1 large egg

Corned Beef Pancakes (continued)

Chop the corned beef coarsely, and put it in a food processor with the onion and green pepper, then spin until all is well mixed (a meat grinder may be substituted). Add the parsley, bread crumbs, and egg and spin until well mixed. Shape the mixture into 8 small or 4 large patties, and fry slowly in a heavy skillet without grease, about 3 minutes per side.

SERVES 4

Greek Beef Stew

New England cooks who exchange recipes include Penelope Society members in towns where Greeks settled several generations ago. We found variations of this dish being served in Manchester, Sanbornton, and Dover, New Hampshire, and in Massachusetts, among other Northeastern states.

5 tablespoons olive oil	2–3 pounds small white (pearl) onions
4 pounds beef chuck and round, cut into 1½-inch pieces	1 medium onion, chopped
Salt	1 tablespoon brown sugar
Freshly ground pepper	3 garlic cloves, crushed
2 cups tomato juice	1 cinnamon stick
¼ cup red wine vinegar	¼ teaspoon ground cloves
½ cup red wine	⅓ teaspoon ground cumin
2 cups or more boiling water	2 tablespoons currants or raisins
2 bay leaves	¼ cup chopped parsley

In a heavy flameproof casserole, sear the meat in half of the olive oil, browning it in several batches. Return all the browned meat to the casserole and season it lightly with salt and pepper. Add the tomato juice, vinegar, and wine, and heat to the simmering point. Add 1 cup boiling water and the bay leaves, cover, and simmer gently for 2½ hours.

Drop the pearl onions into boiling water to cover for 1 minute. Remove and, when cool enough to handle, peel away the skins and cut a cross in the root end. Sauté the chopped onion in the remaining olive oil, add the peeled pearl onions, and brown lightly. Stir in 1 cup boiling water, the sugar, garlic, cinnamon, cloves, and cumin, and cook uncovered until the onions are almost tender. Scrape the onions and seasonings into the simmering stew for a final 30 minutes of cooking, adding a little more boiling water if too much of the sauce has cooked away. Total cooking time should be about 3 hours. Before serving, stir in the currants or raisins to heat through and sprinkle parsley on top. Serve with orzo (the small pasta in the shape of rice), rice, or other small pasta.

SERVES 8

Hard-working old-timers knew by instinct that stews combined flavor and nutrients, and home cooks recognized that a really good stew should be simmered in a heavy iron pot, on the back of the stove (where the heat was gentle). Stews can be such a great source of energy it's no wonder Yankees served them for breakfast.

1½ pounds beef with some fat, cut in small pieces
Flour for dredging
Salt
Freshly ground pepper

2–3 tablespoons vegetable shortening
4 cups boiling water
3 medium onions, chopped
1 teaspoon dried thyme

CORNMEAL DUMPLINGS:
1 cup flour
2 tablespoons cornmeal
2 teaspoons baking powder
½ teaspoon salt

½ teaspoon sugar
1 tablespoon butter
⅔ cup milk

1 small rutabaga, peeled and cut into small even-size logs
4 parsnips, peeled and cut into small even-size logs

12 small carrots, trimmed and scraped, or 3 large ones cut in even-size logs
8 small new potatoes, peeled

Dredge the beef pieces in the flour, which has been seasoned lightly with salt and pepper. Heat the oil in a Dutch oven or other heavy pot, and when it is about to sizzle, stir in the meat a few pieces at a time, covering them with hot fat and browning them evenly on all sides. Pour the boiling water into the pot. Add the onions and thyme, and simmer, covered.

As soon as you have put the stew on, prepare the dumplings. Mix thoroughly the flour, cornmeal, baking powder, salt, and sugar together. Cut in the butter until the dough is the consistency of crumbs, then add the milk a little at a time, stirring until the dough is evenly moistened. Cover and chill for 2 hours.

After the stew has cooked about 2 hours and is almost tender, add the rutabaga, parsnips, carrots, and potatoes and continue cooking until they are tender—about 30 minutes. Taste and correct the seasoning if necessary. While the stew is still simmering, drop the dumpling batter from a tablespoon at intervals over the top of the stew, cover, and cook gently for 15 minutes longer.

SERVES 4–6

Bean-Pot Beef Stew

Yankee bean pots come in handy for many kinds of casserole dishes, including stews that call for long, slow cooking. Any stewing meat may be used; in this recipe we found thick slices of beef shank to be especially succulent because of the marrow that adds richness to the stew.

2½ pounds beef shanks (whole pieces cut through the bone), or about 2 pounds other beef stewing meat
2 tablespoons vegetable oil
2 cups chopped onions
2 fat garlic cloves, chopped fine
1 cup red wine

3 large carrots, scraped and diced
1 cup diced raw potatoes
2 teaspoons chopped fresh summer savory, or 1 teaspoon dried
2 cups boiling water
3 tablespoons pearl tapioca
Salt
Freshly ground pepper

Heat half the oil in a heavy skillet and sauté the meat, a few pieces at a time, until brown on all sides. Remove to a bean pot or casserole. Add the remaining oil to the skillet and sauté the onions for about 3 minutes, stirring, until lightly browned; then add the garlic and cook 1 minute more, being careful not to burn it. Scrape the contents of the skillet into the bean pot. Pour the wine into the skillet, bring to a boil, scraping up any browned bits, and pour that into the bean pot. Add the carrots, potatoes, savory, boiling water, and tapioca. Season very lightly with salt and pepper and cover the pot. Put it in a preheated 275-degree oven and cook for about 3½ hours.
SERVES 4

Note: This recipe can be made in an electric bean pot.

Braised Short Ribs in Wine

Any American red wine, including those made from Foch grapes in New Hampshire, will add flavor to this robust stew.

3–4 pounds beef short ribs, cut in serving pieces
Flour
Salt
Freshly ground pepper
3 tablespoons vegetable oil
12 small white (pearl) onions, peeled

1 cup coarsely chopped celery
½ cup coarsely chopped green pepper
2 cups red wine
1 tablespoon chopped fresh summer savory

Rinse the meat and wipe it dry, then dredge it in flour seasoned with salt and pepper. Heat the oil in a heavy stewpot and sear the meat on all surfaces. Stir in the vegetables and cook, stirring, about 8 minutes. Add the wine and the savory, and sprinkle lightly with salt and freshly ground pepper. Bring the liquid to a boil, reduce heat, and simmer the stew 1 hour, or until the meat is tender. Skim off the excess fat, and serve with mashed potatoes or cornmeal mush.

SERVES 4

Stovetop Short Ribs

This rich, old-fashioned meat dish is based on one originated by the Fairfield, Connecticut, housewife who founded a renowned farmhouse bakery and later wrote a recipe-packed culinary memoir titled *The Margaret Rudkin Pepperidge Farm Cookbook*. The success of the dish depends on using the lowest possible heat to prevent burning and keeping an eye on it as it cooks. Try Baked New Potatoes in Cream (page 303) as an accompaniment.

3 pounds beef short ribs, cut in
   chunks
1/4 cup flour
2 tablespoons shortening or
   vegetable oil
1 cup dried apricots
1 can condensed beef broth, or 1 1/4
   cups strong beef stock

2 tablespoons brown sugar
2 tablespoons cider vinegar
1/4 teaspoon cinnamon
1/4 teaspoon ground cloves
1/4 teaspoon ground allspice

Dredge the ribs in flour. Heat the fat in a large heavy saucepan or a deep skillet and brown the ribs on all sides. Drain off all of the fat in the pan. Stir in the apricots with the meat. Mix together the beef broth, sugar, vinegar, and spices, and pour them over the meat. Cover and cook very slowly about 2 hours, turning the ribs a few times, until very tender; make sure that the liquid has not burned off and, if necessary, add a little more broth or water. When done, the sauce should be no more than a thick glaze over the ribs.

SERVES 4

Oven-Baked Beef Shanks with Prunes

"A good recipe to use when the oven is on for other baking," said a cook descended from a long Yankee heritage, "because the pot may be tucked in the very back and requires little attention."

1/2 pound uncooked prunes
4 pounds beef shanks, cut into 2-
   inch pieces
Flour for dredging
1/2 teaspoon dried basil
3 tablespoons vegetable oil

3 medium onions, sliced
Salt
Freshly ground pepper
1 1/2 cups water
1/4 cup cider vinegar
4 whole cloves

Soak the prunes in water to cover for 6–8 hours. Trim the excess fat from the shanks and dredge them in flour seasoned with the basil. Heat 2 tablespoons oil in a skillet and brown the meat on all sides. Remove the seared meat to a baking dish with a tight-fitting lid. Add the remaining 1 tablespoon oil to the skillet and cook the sliced onions until lightly browned, then scrape the onions and browned bits into the baking dish. Sprinkle the contents lightly with salt and pepper. Drain the prunes and arrange them around the meat. Add the water, vinegar, and cloves. Cover the baking dish and bake in a preheated 325-degree oven for 3–3½ hours, until the meat is very tender. Skim off the excess fat from the surface, and bring the dish to the table.

SERVES 4–6

Hamburger Royal

Instead of the Yankee accent of salt pork, try a little bacon—and the further enhancement of a little vegetable zest.

2 strips bacon, cut in half
⅔ cup chopped sweet red pepper
⅔ cup chopped celery
⅔ cup chopped onion

1 pound ground bottom round
Salt
Freshly ground pepper
4 kaiser rolls

Fry the 4 pieces of bacon until crisp. Remove them to a paper towel and drain off all but 2 tablespoons of the fat. Over moderate heat, sauté the finely chopped vegetables. Mix them with the ground beef, season with salt and pepper, and shape the meat into 4 patties. Increase the heat and sear the hamburgers on both sides. Finish cooking according to taste. Split 4 kaiser rolls and toast the cut sides. Put 1 hamburger patty on each of 4 bottom halves, put a strip of bacon on top, and close with the top halves. Try these without mustard or ketchup and taste the difference.

SERVES 4

Polish-American Hamburgers

1 pound ground beef
1 tablespoon chopped scallions
1 cooked beet, chopped fine

1 teaspoon caraway seeds
Salt
Freshly ground pepper

Mix the beef with the scallions, beet, and caraway seeds, and season lightly with salt and pepper. Set aside for 1 hour or more. Shape into 4 hamburger patties, and sear on a hot griddle or skillet. Turn, reduce the heat, and cook about 3 minutes. Turn and sprinkle with salt and freshly ground pepper, and cook about 1 minute for medium-rare.

SERVES 4

Janice Vogan of Craftsbury, Vermont, has insisted that her family's enthusiasm for Porcupine Meatballs is purely coincidental to the fact that the exotic earrings and necklaces she creates and sells at craft fairs depend upon a continuing supply of quills from New England hedgehogs.

Porcupine Meatballs

1 recipe Quick Tomato Sauce (page 631)
1 pound lean ground beef
¼ cup uncooked long-grain rice
1 egg, lightly beaten
1 tablespoon chopped parsley
2 tablespoons finely chopped onion

¼ teaspoon nutmeg
½ teaspoon salt
Freshly ground pepper
1 teaspoon Worcestershire sauce
About ½ cup water
½ beef bouillon cube

Mix ¼ cup tomato sauce with the ground beef and the rice. Add the beaten egg, parsley, onion, nutmeg, salt, and a few turns of the pepper grinder. Shape this mixture into about 20 meatballs, and brown them by shaking in a hot skillet slightly filmed with oil for about 1 minute over high heat. Dissolve the ½ bouillon cube in ½ cup water and add to the remaining tomato sauce, pour over the meatballs, bring to a boil, then reduce the heat. Cover and simmer 30–35 minutes, shaking the pan occasionally.
SERVES 4

An old family favorite that for some reason acquired a Russian name.

Bitki

6 slices white bread
1 cup milk
3 very large white onions, sliced
3 tablespoons butter
1½ pounds top round of beef or beefalo, ground
½ teaspoon dry mustard
5–6 drops Worcestershire sauce
2–3 tablespoons chopped fresh herbs, such as parsley, savory, a little thyme, or just parsley and ½ teaspoon dried herbs

Salt
Freshly ground pepper
1 cup sour cream, at room temperature
Sprinkling of paprika

Put the bread slices, roughly torn up, into a bowl and cover them with the milk. Let soak while you sauté the onions with the butter very slowly in a large skillet. Cover after a minute of tossing and continue to cook slowly about 20 minutes, until very soft, checking occasionally to make sure they are not sticking. When the bread is soft, squeeze out the milk and discard it. Mix the bread with the ground meat, beating well with a fork to lighten

Bitki (continued)
it and distribute the bread evenly throughout. Add the mustard, Worcestershire, and herbs, and season liberally with salt and pepper. Shape the meat into balls the size of a golf ball, and put them in the pan with the onions. Cook slowly, covered, turning now and then, for about 20 minutes. Stir in the sour cream and let it heat through. Sprinkle paprika on top, and serve with rice or noodles.
SERVES 4

Greek Meatballs

Another of the dishes that Christine Cotsibos shared with us that has become a favorite dish at Greek festivals around Manchester, New Hampshire, where there are more than 9,000 Greek residents.

2 slices golden-brown toast, crusts removed
1 medium onion, chopped
1 fat garlic clove, chopped
1 cup tomato sauce, homemade or canned (Mrs. Cotsibos uses Hunt's)
2 eggs
½ cup chopped fresh spearmint, or about 2 tablespoons dried, rubbed between the palms of the hands

Salt
Freshly ground pepper
1 pound ground beef
About 1½ cups oil for frying (Wesson was recommended) plus ½ cup olive oil

THE SAUCE:
1 tablespoon flour
2 tablespoons drippings or lard
About 1 cup tomato sauce, homemade or canned (see above)

1 garlic clove, minced
1 bay leaf

Put the toast torn in pieces, onion, garlic, tomato sauce, eggs, and spearmint in a food processor and process until the mixture is mushy—like a thick, thick sauce. Season to taste with salt and a lot of freshly ground pepper. Let this stand until the bread is moistened, about 30 minutes. Add the meat and mix thoroughly with your hands.

Heat the oil in a frying pan or kettle (you want the oil to be about 1½ inches deep). Wet your hands and shape the meat into about 30 small balls. When the oils reach 320 degrees, slip the meatballs in and fry for about 2 minutes on one side. Check to see if they are golden underneath, then turn them and fry 2 minutes more on the other side. Remove and drain.

To make the sauce, toast the flour in a small skillet, stirring, until it turns

golden. Mix in the drippings, stir until smooth, then add enough tomato sauce to make a sauce, stirring again until smooth. Add the garlic and bay leaf and simmer for 8 minutes. Put the meatballs in the sauce and heat them through for 1–2 minutes. Remove the bay leaf, and serve with orzo or rice.
SERVES 6

Filled Meat Loaf Ring

Here's a Down-East variation to make "the daily grind" more interesting, even festive, as a one-dish *pièce de résistance*.

2 large onions
3–4 medium tomatoes
3 tablespoons vegetable oil
1½ pounds ground chuck or
    bottom round
1 cup soft bread crumbs
1 tablespoon chopped parsley
2 eggs
½ cup beef broth

½ teaspoon dried oregano
½ teaspoon salt
Freshly ground pepper
1 cup freshly cooked peas
12 freshly cooked tiny white (pearl)
    onions
¼ pound mushrooms, quartered
Watercress

Peel the large onions and the tomatoes, and chop them coarsely. Use a little of the oil to coat a 9-inch ring mold. Heat the remainder in a large skillet and cook the onions and tomatoes, stirring constantly, for 3–4 minutes. In a large bowl, thoroughly blend the ground beef, bread crumbs, and parsley with the eggs. Stir in the broth, oregano, salt, and a few turns of pepper, and add the mixture to the vegetables in the skillet. Scoop this into the ring mold and press down, then cover with a piece of aluminum foil. Set the mold in a pan of cold water and cook in a preheated 325-degree oven for about 1¾ hours. Remove the foil and invert the cooked ring onto a warm round platter. Fill the center with the hot cooked peas and onions, and garnish the ring with watercress.
SERVES 6–8

Spicy Meat Loaf

With a spectrum of aromatic powders and other savory spices and herbs easily available on supermarket shelves, the seasoning of ground meat is sometimes a Yankee indoor sport these days. Here are working notes from a recent Saturday afternoon.

½ green pepper, chopped
2 medium onions, chopped
1 rib celery, chopped
1 shallot, chopped
1½ tablespoons vegetable oil
2 tablespoons chopped fresh
  parsley
1 tablespoon chopped fresh basil,
  or 1½ teaspoon dried
½ teaspoon freshly grated nutmeg
¼ teaspoon allspice
¼ teaspoon cayenne
¼ teaspoon chili powder

½ teaspon cinnamon
½ teaspoon salt
Freshly ground pepper
1 teaspoon Worcestershire sauce
Tabasco sauce
½ cup puréed tomatoes
½ cup condensed milk
½ pound ground pork
1 pound ground veal
1 pound ground beef
1½ cups fresh bread crumbs
1 egg, beaten
2 strips bacon

Put the green pepper, onions, celery, and shallot in a saucepan with the vegetable oil. Sauté, stirring occasionally, for about 5 minutes, and stir the parsley, basil, nutmeg, allspice, cayenne, chili powder, and cinnamon into the hot mixture. Season with salt and pepper. Add the Worcestershire, a few drops of Tabasco, the puréed tomatoes and condensed milk, and stir for a minute or less. Combine this mixture with the three meats, bread crumbs, and egg and mix by hand until thoroughly blended. Turn into an ungreased 8-inch loaf pan, arrange the strips of bacon across the top, and bake 1½ hours in a preheated 325-degree oven. Remove from the oven and let the meat loaf rest about 15 minutes in a warm place. Pour off the accumulated juices and skim off the fat. Turn the meat loaf out onto a hot platter, and pour the defatted juices over the top.
SERVES 5–6

Top-of-the-Stove Meat Loaves

¼ cup finely chopped celery
2 tablespoons vegetable oil
¼ cup finely chopped green pepper
¼ cup chopped scallions
⅓ cup finely chopped mushrooms
2 eggs, lightly beaten

Juice of 1 large lemon or 2 limes
2 pounds very lean ground beef
½ cup fresh bread crumbs
½ teaspoon salt
Freshly ground pepper

Sauté the celery in the oil about 3 minutes; add the green pepper and cook 1 minute more; stir in the scallions and the mushrooms and continue cook-

ing about 2 minutes, until all the vegetables are *al dente*. Stir the beaten eggs and half of the lemon or lime juice in a mixing bowl, add the beef and bread crumbs and blend well, then stir in the sautéed vegetables. Mix in the salt and pepper. With flour-dusted hands, shape the meat mixture into 2 small loaves. Brown the loaves in the skillet in which the vegetables were cooked, turning several times. Cover the pan and cook over moderate heat about 20 minutes. Remove the loaves to a hot plate. Stir the remaining lemon or lime juice into the pan and scrape up the brown bits, then pour this sauce over the meat before slicing.

SERVES 4

Where the Beefalo Roam

Seldom is heard a discouraging word among Yankee farmers who, in the 1980s, began specializing in raising beefalo—a cross between Bill Cody's Wild West animals and U.S. beef cattle. For cooking, the meat is leaner (freer of fat), has more protein and fewer calories—and less cholesterol. It's not easy to find at your local supermarket or even at the butcher, but more retailers are providing outlets for beefalo farmers throughout the region.

Sally Mole, a beefalo producer, told of supplying markets and restaurants in Williams-town, Massachusetts. "Customers want to be assured that beefalo is not a chemical product—they want the special flavor of meat finished on good grass that makes every cut tender." Beefalo makes top-notch steaks, corned beef, standing rib roasts (with Yorkshire pudding, of course), and lean hamburger. "For cross-country skier friends," Sally Mole said, "the festive winter dish is beefalo as *fondue bourguignonne*. The grass-fed flavor of beefalo results in something special when I put pots of bubbling vegetable oil [to cook the skewered slivers of meat in] at each end of my harvest table. Fondue was never better."

Daphne Hamead's Beefalo "Cigars"

Daphne Hamead grows her own herbs on a Green Mountain slope near the Canadian border and uses Oriental spices she gets in Montreal for her version of Indian kebabs—for which she prefers to use ground beefalo meat (it's tenderer and sweeter). But the following recipe can be well used when you have lean ground beef or lamb on hand.

2 pounds ground beefalo or lean
    beef or lamb
2 slices white bread, soaked in
    water and squeezed dry
½ teaspoon hot chili pepper
One 1-inch piece fresh ginger,
    peeled and minced
1 teaspoon ground cloves

1 teaspoon ground cumin
1 tablespoon ground coriander
1 tablespoon or more red wine
1 teaspoon soy sauce
1 egg, lightly beaten
About 1 tablespoon vegetable oil
    for frying

Regrind the meat in a food processor or put through the fine blade of a grinder. If using the food processor, add all the remaining ingredients and spin until thoroughly mixed; otherwise, beat thoroughly in a bowl to combine. Set aside to rest 2 hours, or overnight in the refrigerator if you have the time.

Shape the meat into as many "cigar" shapes as you have skewers. Insert the skewers into the shaped meat patties. Film a nonstick pan with oil and fry the "cigars" over medium heat, turning them often, until they are cooked through and lightly browned on all surfaces, about 10–15 minutes. You may also cook them under a broiler or over a grill.

SERVES 6–8

Yankee Chili with Ground Beef

Après-ski parties and church suppers, two incontestably New England occasions, have made what Texans sometimes call "a bowl of red" a must in almost any Northeastern cook's repertoire.

2 tablespoons oil
2 medium onions, chopped
1 small green pepper, chopped
1 fat garlic clove, chopped
2 ribs celery, chopped
1½ pounds ground chuck
2 cups canned tomatoes
½ cup ketchup (preferably Yankee
    Sugarless, page 628)

1 tablespoon or more chili powder
1 teaspoon cumin
1 teaspoon dried marjoram
1 teaspoon dried oregano
Tabasco sauce
Salt
2 cups canned kidney beans

Heat the oil in a large skillet and gently cook the onions, green pepper, garlic, and celery for a few minutes, until the onion and celery soften. Break

New England Chili

Spirited Yankee cooks can be as competitive as Texans when the bone of contention is known as chili. Annual "Chili Bake-Offs" staged in Hardwick, in Vermont's Northeast Kingdom, challenge men and women to come up with the ultimate recipe, and those who record their formulas guard them as hot properties. Ann Chandler of Amherst, New Hampshire, mixes beef and pork with pinto beans and ⅓ cup chili powder. Another New Hampshire cook adds corn and winter squash to shell beans and fires the mixture with green *aji* chili peppers. The recipe above is a method that stands on its own, or submits to lightning-inspired embellishments.

up the meat and stir it into the vegetables, cooking until brown and continuing to break it up with a fork. Stir in the tomatoes with their juice, breaking up the pulp. Stir in the ketchup, the spices, and the herbs. Sprinkle lightly with Tabasco and a little salt. Simmer very gently for about 1 hour. Taste and add more chili powder and/or Tabasco, as desired. Set aside to let the flavors blend. About 20 minutes before serving, drain the beans and stir them in. Heat thoroughly, and serve over rice.

SERVES 4

Baked Flank Steak Slices in Pumpkin-Cheese Sauce

A "made dish" based on the inspiration of James Haller, chef-proprietor of Portsmouth's outstanding Blue Strawbery Restaurant.

10–12 *thin slices cooked flank steak*
10–12 *slices North Pack cheese or New England cheddar*
⅓–½ *cup thinly sliced shallots*
4 *tablespoons butter*
4 *tablespoons safflower or vegetable oil*
½ *cup flour*
2 *tablespoons concentrated chicken broth*

Freshly ground pepper
1 *tablespoon soy sauce*
½ *teaspoon dried basil*
2 *cups white wine*
2 *cups cooked pumpkin purée*
2 *eggs*
1 *cup heavy cream*
1 *cup grated North Pack cheese or New England cheddar*

Arrange the flank steak in a shallow ovenproof serving dish and cover each slice with a thin layer of the cheese. In a good-size saucepan, brown the shallots in the butter and oil, being careful not to let them burn. Stir in the flour until you have a very smooth mixture, and continue to stir as you add the chicken broth, pepper, soy sauce, and basil. Add the wine, a little at a time, to blend it into the sauce, then stir in the puréed pumpkin. Simmer the sauce for about 1 hour, stirring occasionally so that it doesn't stick on the bottom. Mix the eggs and the cream, and stir them into the sauce, blending thoroughly. Pour the sauce over the cheese and steak slices, and sprinkle the surface with the grated cheese. Bake about 30 minutes in a preheated 375-degree oven.

SERVES 4

Braised Stuffed Flank Steak

The flank is a tasty economical cut of beef that not only goes further when it is stuffed, but makes a handsome presentation. This is equally delicious made with a beefalo flank steak.

1 flank steak (about 1½–1¾ pounds)
2 tablespoons butter or vegetable oil
1 medium onion, chopped
¼ pound mushrooms, chopped
¾ cup chopped green and red peppers, if available; otherwise use only green

1¼ cups fresh white bread crumbs or crumbled corn bread
Salt
Freshly ground pepper
2 tablespoons chopped parsley
1 tablespoon chopped fresh savory, or 1 teaspoon dried
1 tablespoon chopped fresh thyme, or ¾ teaspoon dried

BRAISING LIQUID:
½ cup red wine
½ cup beef broth
1 small onion, sliced

Sprigs parsley and thyme and/or savory
1 bay leaf

Remove the excess fat from the flank steak and pound it to flatten it and enlarge it slightly. Heat the butter or oil in a skillet and sauté the chopped onion for 3 minutes, then add the mushrooms and peppers and continue to cook for 1 minute. Mix in the bread crumbs, salt and pepper to taste, and the herbs. Spoon this stuffing mixture down the center of the flank steak, molding it with your hands into a cylinder so that it holds together, then pull the meat up around the stuffing. Skewer the ends of the steak together where they overlap and lace with a string. Make sure to tuck the end pieces up and skewer and lace them together, too, so the stuffing doesn't spill out at the ends. Put the stuffed steak into a baking dish, preferably oval and only a little larger than the rolled steak. Pour the wine and broth around, scatter the onion slices, and drape the herb sprigs and bay leaf on top. Bring to the simmer on top of the stove, then braise in a preheated 325-degree oven, covered lightly with foil, for 2 hours, basting occasionally with the braising liquid. Let rest about 15 minutes before removing skewers and string, then carve in thick slices.

SERVES 4–6

Supermarket packages of beef marked "specially sliced for stir-fry" show how housewives of the Northeast have taken to the quick-cooking Far East styles that produce light combinations of meat and vegetables. Here is an adaptation of a recipe published in Bangor, Maine. And three more recipes follow, using beef strips with different combinations of vegetables and oriental seasonings.

Oriental Beef and Vegetables, Maine Style

1 pound lean beef, cut into thin
 strips
4 tablespoons vodka or sake
1/3 cup soy sauce
1 1/2 tablespoons sugar
3/4 teaspoon ground ginger
1 garlic clove, crushed

1/2 lemon, thinly sliced
2 tablespoons vegetable oil
1 medium green pepper, trimmed
 and cut into matchstick pieces
3/4 cup leeks cut into matchstick
 pieces

Put the meat in a small bowl. Mix the liquor, soy sauce, sugar, and ginger and stir until the sugar dissolves; add the garlic clove and lemon slices and pour the mixture over the meat. Set aside to marinate for 1 hour or longer.

Heat the oil in a skillet or wok and quickly fry the meat strips in the hot oil until lightly browned. Remove the meat from the oil and stir in the vegetable sticks, cooking quickly until the leeks are almost limp. Return the meat and juice to the skillet, toss quickly with the vegetables, and serve with rice.

SERVES 4

---

2 cups fresh fiddleheads, cleaned
 (see page 44), or frozen
 fiddleheads
1/4 cup vegetable oil
1 garlic clove, crushed
2 coin-sized slices fresh ginger
1 large onion, sliced thin
Salt

1/4 cup water
About 8 medium mushrooms,
 sliced
2 cups beef or leftover rare steak,
 cut into thin strips
1 1/2 tablespoons soy sauce
1/2 teaspoon dried hot red pepper
 flakes

Stir-fry of Beef with Fiddleheads

If the fiddleheads are fresh, blanch them in a large pot of boiling salted water for 1 minute. If they are frozen, cover them with boiling water and let stand 1 minute. Drain. In a wok or large skillet, heat 3 tablespoons oil, then add the garlic and ginger and sauté for about 1 minute, until the garlic begins to turn golden. Add the onion and the fiddleheads, sprinkle lightly with salt, stir and toss for a minute, then add the water and cover. Cook gently for 5 minutes. Uncover and add the mushrooms, stir and toss for 2–3 minutes.

Remove contents of the pan to a warm bowl. Add the remaining oil to the pan and when hot, toss in the strips of beef. Stir-fry about 1 minute, until seared on the outside and rosy within. Return the vegetables to the pan, add the soy sauce and pepper flakes, and cook just enough to heat through. Serve with rice.

SERVES 4

Stir-fry of Beef and Vegetables

1½ *pounds beef, cut into thin strips less than ¼-inch thick and about 2 inches long* *

1 *tablespoon soy sauce*

1 *tablespoon cornstarch dissolved in 1½ tablespoons water*

4 *tablespoons vegetable oil*

2 *garlic cloves, minced*

1 *medium sweet red pepper, seeded and cut into ¼-inch strips*

¼ *pound mushrooms, sliced, then cut into ¼-inch strips*

1 *pound zucchini or yellow squash, cut into strips ¼ inch thick x 2 inches long*

Salt

10–12 *scallions, white parts cut into 2-inch pieces and split lengthwise, tender greens chopped*

2 *tablespoons dry sherry*

2 *tablespoons oyster sauce* †

Freshly ground pepper

* If bought ready-cut in the supermarket, cut the thicker strips of beef in half.

† Like soy sauce, oyster sauce can usually be found in supermarkets today. If unavailable, use another tablespoon or so of soy sauce instead.

Put the beef strips in a bowl and pour the soy sauce, dissolved cornstarch, and 1 tablespoon oil over them. Mix thoroughly and refrigerate for 30 minutes to 1 hour.

Heat 2 tablespoons of the remaining oil in a large heavy skillet or wok and stir in the garlic. Before it begins to brown, add the red pepper, stir-fry for 30 seconds, then add the mushrooms and squash. Salt lightly and stir-fry over medium heat for 1 minute, adding 2–3 tablespoons water to keep the vegetables from sticking. Add the white scallion pieces and stir-fry another 30 seconds; the vegetables should be just tender with a little crispness. Remove them and their juices to a warm platter. Now heat the remaining 1 tablespoon oil, lift the beef slices from their marinade with a slotted spoon, and add them to the pan, quickly stir-frying them over high heat for about 30 seconds. Return the vegetables and their juices to the pan, add the beef marinade, the sherry and oyster sauce, and heat through, tossing constantly. Grind fresh pepper over and sprinkle the chopped scallion greens on top. Serve with steamed rice.

SERVES 4

New England's Own Wines

There are professional kitchens like that of the Cafe in the Barn outside Providence and near Seekonk, Massachusetts, where Nashoba Valley pear wine is used in vinaigrettes and Sakonet Riesling enhances the steaming of mussels, and there are other New England chefs who recommend regional table wines without hesitation as accompaniments for good meals.

The efforts to produce wines to rival those of Europe, which began as early as 1632, are now, in the twentieth century, the foundation of thriving vineyards in each of the states. Even Vermont ski country is turning out a light, dry, drinkable apple essence that is admired as an aperitif wine, produced by the North River Winery at Jacksonville, near Brattleboro.

Sakonet Vineyards near Little Compton, Rhode Island, has a microclimate closely resembling that of Bordeaux and Burgundy, and since 1975 its Chardonnay, Riesling, Pinot Noir, Seyval, Foch-Millot, Vidal, and Aurora grapes have been transformed into wines that are increasingly acceptable among restaurateurs and private hosts and hostesses. Four more serious winemakers are established in Rhode Island, and a dozen in Connecticut, including the Haight Vineyard in the Litchfield Mills, and Hamlet Hill, not far from Pomfret. Chicama Vineyards (on the island of Martha's Vineyard) is among a dozen or so in Massachusetts, and there is another handful producing good wines in New Hampshire and in Maine, where the state's highly touted blueberries grow much more abundantly than grapes.

Stir-fried Rare Steak Strips with Okra

1/2 pound okra
2 tablespoons vegetable oil
1 garlic clove, crushed, skin removed
1 slice ginger the size of a quarter
4 scallions, cut into thin slices, separating white part from green

1 1/2 cups sliced rare steak, cut into thin strips
2 teaspoons soy sauce
1 tablespoon dry sherry
A few drops fresh lemon juice

Blanch the okra 1 minute in a pot of boiling water. Drain, and cut into 1/2-inch rounds. Heat the oil in a skillet or wok, add the garlic and ginger, and sauté until the garlic just starts to brown. Add the sliced okra, toss and cook 30 seconds, then add the white part of the scallions and the steak strips, and stir-fry another 30 seconds. Stir in the soy sauce and sherry and toss and cook another minute. Sprinkle scallion greens on top and season with a few drops of lemon juice. Serve immediately with steamed rice. SERVES 4

Beefsteak and Kidney Pie

2 tablespoons or more vegetable oil
2 pounds beef chuck, cut in bite-size pieces, fat removed
1 medium onion, diced
1 beef kidney, or 2 veal kidneys, cut in segments, fat removed
1 1/2 cups beef broth
1 bay leaf

1/2 teaspoon dried thyme
8–10 small white onions, peeled
1–2 tablespoons or more butter
1/2 teaspoon sugar
1 tablespoon cornstarch
2 tablespoons dry sherry
Salt
Freshly ground pepper

BISCUIT DOUGH TOPPING:
1 1/2 cups flour
2 teaspoons baking powder
2/3 teaspoon salt
1/3 cup vegetable shortening
1/3–1/2 cup buttermilk or skim milk mixed with 2 tablespoons plain yogurt

4 tablespoons chopped parsley and chives, combined

Heat the oil in a skillet, then brown the pieces of beef on all sides; do this in several batches so they brown well rather than steam. When they have browned, remove the pieces of beef to a flameproof casserole. Add the diced onion with the last batch. If you are using beef kidney, now is the time to sauté it (if using veal kidneys, do not add them at this stage because they should not cook as long). Add a little more oil to the skillet and brown the beef kidney lightly, then add it to the casserole. Pour the beef broth into the skillet and scrape up all the juices and browned bits, then pour over the meat. Add the bay leaf and thyme, cover, and simmer gently about 2 hours, or until tender.

Cook the small white onions rapidly in just enough water to cover. When they are tender, in about 15 minutes, most of the water should have boiled off; if not, turn the heat to high to evaporate. Stir in 1 tablespoon butter, sprinkle the sugar over, and sauté, tossing until browned and glazed.

If using veal kidneys, sauté the pieces in 1 tablespoon butter over quite high heat, tossing and stirring for about 5 minutes. Add to the cooked beef along with the glazed onions, making sure to scrape up all the juices to add to the casserole. Mix the cornstarch with the sherry, and stir into the beef and kidneys; bring to a simmer and let thicken. Taste and add salt and pepper as necessary. Now insert a Pyrex or metal cup, open side down, in the center of the casserole (this will catch the juices).

Meanwhile, prepare the biscuit dough. Toss the flour, baking powder, and salt together to mix, then cut in the shortening, using a pastry blender or your fingertips, until the mixture resembles fresh bread crumbs. Stir in enough of the liquid so that the dough holds together, then turn it out onto a lightly floured work surface, sprinkle the herbs on top, and knead for only a half-dozen turns. Pat or roll out to a ½-inch thickness, and with a biscuit cutter cut out circles. Arrange these all over the top of the casserole and bake in a preheated 425-degree oven for about 15 minutes, until the biscuits are browned on top. To serve, after cutting into the pie, slip your knife under the cup to release the accumulated juices (there's no need to remove the cup—just spoon up portions around it).

SERVES 6

Fresh Beef Tongue

1 fresh beef tongue
1 large onion, unpeeled
4 cloves
2 ribs celery with leaves
3 fat garlic cloves
4–5 stalks parsley with roots, if available
8 peppercorns
1 dried hot red pepper (optional)
Salt

Rinse the beef tongue in cold running water. Place in a large kettle with enough cold water to cover it by 1 inch. Add all the remaining ingredients, using approximately 1½ teaspoons salt per quart of water. Bring to a boil, cover, and simmer gently 3–3½ hours, until tender when pricked with a fork. Let the tongue cool in the cooking liquid, then remove and skin it; trim away any fatty tissue around the root end and remove any small bones. The whole trimmed tongue may be served hot or cold with mustard, relish, or Ed Giobbi's Nut Sauce (page 632).

Fried Pickled Tripe

Many of the Northeast's earliest families brought with them a taste for tripe, and there are Maine recipes for spiced fresh tripe pungent with clove and allspice, tripe casseroles similar to Philadelphia's pepper pot, as well as broiled honeycomb tripe. Today's supermarket availability of pickled tripe makes it easy to serve this variety meat in a way that is both simple and appetizing.

1½ pounds pickled tripe
2 tablespoons flour
1 tablespoon chopped fresh basil,
   or 1 teaspoon dried
Salt

Freshly ground pepper
1 egg, beaten
1 garlic clove, crushed
¼ cup corn oil

Cut the tripe into rough rectangles about 2 x 3 inches. Parboil the pieces about 5 minutes, then drain and dry thoroughly. Mix the flour with the basil and a light sprinkling of salt and pepper. Dip the tripe into the beaten egg, then in the seasoned flour. Put the garlic and oil in a wide skillet over medium heat. When the oil is hot, remove the garlic, and fry the tripe 2 or 3 minutes, just long enough to brown on both sides. Serve with mustard or tomato sauce.

SERVES 4

Parker House Broiled Tripe with Mustard Sauce

The tripe one buys today in the supermarket comes all prepared and pre-cooked, but we find it still needs simmering in an aromatic liquid to tenderize before broiling in the famous Boston Parker House manner.

About 1½ pounds tripe
2 bay leaves
12 sprigs parsley
2 sprigs celery leaves
1 sprig fresh thyme, or ¼ teaspoon
   dried

Salt
½ cup olive oil
About 1½ cups fresh bread crumbs

MUSTARD SAUCE:
6 tablespoons butter
3 tablespoons finely chopped onion
¼ cup cider vinegar

¼ cup dry mustard mixed to a
   paste with 2 tablespoons water

Put the tripe in a saucepan and cover with lightly salted water. Add the herbs, bring to a boil, and simmer gently, covered, until tender; cooking time depends on how precooked the tripe was—it can need anywhere from about 40 minutes to 1½ hours. Let the tripe cool in the cooking liquid, refrigerating overnight.

Drain the tripe, pat dry, salt lightly, and cut into pieces about 4 x 5 inches. Dip the pieces in olive oil, then dredge in bread crumbs. Broil the crumbed tripe in a preheated broiler about 8 inches from the heat for 2–3 minutes on each side, until lightly browned.

Meanwhile, make the sauce. Heat the butter in a small saucepan and sauté the onion slowly until tender. Add the cider vinegar and simmer 5 minutes. Stir in the mustard paste and simmer a few minutes longer. Strain, and serve hot—a dollop of it alongside each serving of broiled tripe.

SERVES 4

"Yanked Beef"

As unostentatious as any of life's simple pleasures is a dish composed of beef and cream. Traditionally known among Yankees of all generations as Cream Chipped Beef, the most common version is an unornamented presentation of thinly sliced beef, whether it be called chipped, dried, smoked, or in the American vernacular "jerky," served in a white sauce over potatoes, rice, crackers, or toast.

The late Eleanor Early, collector of New England lore, reported that "in the middle of the nineteenth century when chafing-dish cookery was chic, this recipe was popular in London clubs. Englishmen called it the Yankee Doodle Special, but in New England it was known as Chipped Beef de luxe." Fannie Farmer suggested that in its simple form it be served for breakfast, and there is a Maine recipe for Chipped Beef Omelet that is puffy with six eggs beaten with cream, folded over onto a hot platter, and sprinkled with grated store cheese. Our contemporary version calls for chipped beef in an Italian omelet, known as a frittata, on page 384.

Dried by cool breezes (as in Europe's *bünderfleish*) or in eddies of smoke in the American Indian method, dehydrated meat is fundamental to old-time cooking, and when made from round steak stripped of fat and gristle and cut in paper-thin pieces, then sold in convenient packages, it has achieved new popularity as a quick-energy snack that food historian James Trager credits to "its use by GIs in Vietnam." On the other hand, Innkeeper Elsie Masterton wrote recently, "To go with jonnycakes [page 377], there is nothing better, surely, than creamed chipped beef."

Creamed Chipped Beef with Biscuits

Creamed dried beef, or chipped beef as it is more often called in New England, is sometimes served over split baked potatoes or with corn bread, as well as with homemade biscuits.

Biscuits (page 494)
4–6 ounces dried beef
2 tablespoons butter

2 tablespoons flour
1½–2 cups milk, skim or whole
Freshly ground pepper

Bake a pan of biscuits, and while they are in the oven, soak the beef in boiling water only if you find it too salty to your taste. In a large skillet, melt the butter. Dry the beef, tear it into shreds, and cook it in the hot butter, stirring until the edges get a little crisp. Sprinkle the flour over the meat and stir it briskly while the flour begins to cook. Add the milk, a little at a time, stirring constantly. When the milk has absorbed the flour, bring the mixture to the boiling point then reduce the heat, and cook gently about 4 minutes. The sauce should be smooth and the thickness of heavy cream. Taste for seasoning, adding a few turns of the pepper grinder; salt should not be needed. When the biscuits are ready, split them and pour the beef and its sauce over them.

SERVES 4

LAMB

Shaker Leg of Lamb

A variation of a Hancock Village recipe from *The Best of Shaker Cooking*, one of America's best culinary volumes.

One 6½–7-pound leg of lamb
1½–2 tablespoons grated fresh
    ginger
2 tablespoons soft butter
Salt
Freshly ground pepper
Flour

1 cup chicken broth
½ cup applejack or hard cider
2 tablespoons fresh chopped mint
1½ teaspoons dried rosemary,
    crumbled
2 large shallots, chopped fine
1 teaspoon powdered ginger

Trim the lamb of excess fat and rub the grated fresh ginger into the lamb on all surfaces. Rub the butter over, and sprinkle lightly with salt, pepper, and flour. Heat the broth with the applejack or hard cider, mixing in the mint, rosemary, shallots, and powdered ginger. Put the lamb on a rack in a preheated 375-degree oven and roast for about 1½ hours for pink meat. Remove to a warm platter and let rest 30 minutes before carving. Spoon off as much fat from the pan as you can and pour in the marinade. Put the roasting pan over the heat, stir, scraping up all the browned bits, and boil hard to reduce and thicken slightly. Pour into a warmed sauceboat to pass when the lamb is carved at the table.

SERVES 8

About Herb Butters

Herb butters add verve to even the most simple dishes and are a good way to preserve your fresh herbs. It's preferable to mix small quantities to keep in the refrigerator for use at the last moment, but you can flavor ¼ pound or ½ pound of butter, form it into a log and wrap it, then put it away to freeze. Proportions are a matter of taste, but may vary between ⅓ to ½ (or more) the amount of herbs to the amount of butter, depending on the strength of the herb. Use either sweet or salted butter, depending on the seasoning of the dish.

Basil butter, for instance, zips up freshly cooked squash, just as garlic butter may please certain steak lovers. For chicken, try tarragon butter, or rosemary butter on lamb, sage butter on veal and liver, or parsley-chive butter on new potatoes, dill butter on fish. Kept in the refrigerator, flavored butters should be used in two weeks or less, and when frozen they should be used within a few months.

Mixed Herb Butter

½ cup (1 stick) butter, softened
3–4 tablespoons minced fresh herbs
2 teaspoons lemon juice (optional)
Salt
Pepper

Put the butter and the herbs in a bowl and blend with the back of a spoon. Or you may use a food processor. (If lemon juice is used, add a few drops at a time.) Add a little salt and pepper to taste. Form into a log and wrap in wax paper or foil, and chill. To use, slice and melt on each serving of meat, fish, or vegetables.

MAKES ABOUT ⅔ CUP

Sliced Lamb in Pumpkin-Honey Sauce

At his Portsmouth restaurant, The Blue Strawbery, James Haller includes several pumpkin sauces for veal and lamb among his ever-inventive repertoire. "Sometimes it's easier to slice the cooked lamb," he wrote about this recipe, "and place it in a baking and serving dish before pouring the sauce over it. The effect is just as nice, and you don't have to stand around slicing in front of everyone when it's time to sit down and eat."

1/4 pound (1 stick) butter
2 tablespoons flour
4 shallots, sliced
2 leeks, sliced
2 teaspoons finely chopped fresh sage, or 1/2 teaspoon dried
Freshly ground pepper
2 teaspoons finely chopped fresh thyme, or 1/2 teaspoon dried
1/4 cup soy sauce
1/4 cup honey

2 tablespoons ketchup
2 tablespoons moist beef base (or strong beef stock)
1 teaspoon ground nutmeg
1 teaspoon dry mustard
1 cup uncooked pumpkin, cut in thin slices
1 cup red wine
1/2 cup Cognac
12 good-size slices of roast lamb, freshly sliced

Melt the butter in a saucepan, stirring in the flour to thicken. Add the sliced shallots and leeks, the sage, pepper, thyme, soy sauce, honey, ketchup, beef base, nutmeg, mustard, and pumpkin and blend thoroughly over low heat. Blend in the wine and Cognac, and let simmer slowly for 30 minutes. Cover the bottom of a shallow baking dish with the lamb slices, and pour the sauce over the meat. Bake, covered, in a preheated 350-degree oven for 30 minutes; uncover and continue baking 15 minutes more.
SERVES 6

Roast Lamb with Minted Mustard-Honey Glaze

The idea for sealing in the juices of a lamb roast with this subtle blend of flavors began at a fashionable hostelry on Banister's Wharf in Newport, Rhode Island, but we embellished the recipe by using both a clover honey and tarragon vinegar from Vermont.

1 cup tarragon vinegar
1 garlic clove, crushed
1/4 cup dry mustard
3 tablespoons honey

1 tablespoon safflower oil
2 teaspoons dried mint
1/4 teaspoon cayenne
1 leg of lamb, about 6–7 pounds

Mix the vinegar, garlic, mustard, honey, oil, mint, and cayenne in a saucepan, and set aside at room temperature for 1 hour. Bring the mixture to the boiling point and cook over low heat at a simmer for 5 minutes. Cool. Trim the fell and almost all the fat from the lamb. Spread some of the mixture over the top and let the meat marinate at room temperature for 1–2 hours.

Roast the lamb in a preheated 350-degree oven, glazing the top with the remaining mixture every 15 minutes. After 1¾ hours, remove from the oven and let rest 20 minutes before carving. Spoon a little of the juices over each serving.

SERVES 8–10

Marinated Butterflied Lamb, Grilled

One 5–7-pound leg of lamb, boned and stretched flat
4 tablespoons maple syrup (grade B if you wish)
½ cup soy sauce
½ cup safflower oil or other vegetable oil
½ cup cider vinegar
⅓ cup lime or lemon juice
1 garlic clove, chopped

Put the meat in a dish large enough for it to lie flat. Mix the remaining ingredients in a 2-cup measuring cup and mix thoroughly before pouring over the lamb; make sure that it runs under the meat. Refrigerate for 24 hours.

For superb results, cook over a bed of hardwood coals prepared long enough for any flame to have subsided. Remove the lamb from the marinade and sear it for about 5 minutes on each side, then increase the distance between the meat and the bed of coals and continue grilling, basting several times while turning the meat; 30 minutes should be sufficient. Test with an instant thermometer; it is finished when the gauge registers 125 degrees in the thickest part. Let rest 20 minutes in a warm spot before carving (it will continue cooking and juices will become more evenly distributed). Have a hot platter and hot plates ready. Heat the remaining marinade, and serve in a sauceboat.

SERVES 6–8

Roast Rack of Lamb with Herb Coating

1 whole rack of lamb (both sides)
¾ cup fresh bread crumbs
1 tablespoon chopped fresh rosemary, or 1 teaspoon dried, crushed
½ teaspoon fresh thyme, or a pinch dried
1 tablespoon chopped parsley
Salt
Freshly ground pepper
About 1 teaspoon soy sauce
2 tablespoons mustard
2 teaspoons olive oil or melted butter

Trim the racks of lamb of any excess fat and, if you want the roast to look quite elegant, scrape about 2 inches of the bones free of fat and meat (save any good meat scraps for ground lamb). Place the racks in a small roasting pan, facing each other with the meaty chops on the bottom and the scraped bones interlocking. Roast in a preheated 450-degree oven for 25 minutes.

Roast Rack of Lamb with Herb Coating (continued)

Meanwhile, mix together the bread crumbs, herbs, and salt and pepper to taste. Pull the roasting pan tray out of the oven, shake a little soy sauce over the top of the meat, paint with mustard, and press the seasoned bread crumbs evenly over the outside surface of the chops. Drizzle olive oil or melted butter over the crumbs, and slide the meat back into the oven to roast 10 minutes more; the outside crumb coating should be lightly browned and the meat rosy. Let rest 5 minutes out of the oven before bringing to the table. Cut into chops to serve.

SERVES 4–6

Cranberry Leg of Lamb

A century and a half ago on Nantucket, sheep farming was so integrated into island life that "Sheep Shearing Days" were annual holidays. Cranberries, also, were a big Nantucket crop, because some of the largest cranberry bogs in the world are there. Here's our variation on those island themes.

1 leg of lamb (approximately 7 pounds)
2 tablespoons coarse salt (kosher or sea salt)
About ⅓ cup flour
1 large onion, chopped

1½ cups cranberries, chopped
1½ cups or more boiling water
3 tablespoons sugar
¼ cup Worcestershire sauce
½ teaspoon dried hot red pepper flakes

Trim the lamb of all excess fat—you want to have only a thin coating left. Rub it all over with coarse salt, then sprinkle flour over the surface. Place on a roasting rack in a pan and roast in a preheated 450-degree oven for 30 minutes, until nicely browned. Meanwhile, mix the chopped onion, cranberries, 1½ cups boiling water, the sugar, Worcestershire, and pepper flakes together. Remove the roasting pan from the oven when the lamb has browned, and let cool a few minutes, then splash the cranberry sauce over and around the lamb, reduce the temperature to 350 degrees, and return the lamb to the oven to roast for approximately 1–1¼ hours, or until it reaches an internal temperature of 140 degrees. Baste four or five times during roasting, and add a little more boiling water if the pan begins to scorch on the bottom. When done, remove and let rest 15 minutes before carving. Serve with mashed potatoes and turnips or parsnips (page 306), or with Scalloped Potatoes and Winter Turnips (page 305).

SERVES 8–10

1 lamb shoulder, boned and tied
    (approximately 2–3 pounds
    depending on size)
Salt
Freshly ground pepper
½ cup dry white wine or vermouth
¼ cup water
16 fat garlic cloves

2 sprigs parsley
2 sprigs fresh rosemary, or ½
    teaspoon dried, crumbled
2 sprigs fresh tarragon, or ½
    teaspoon dried
4 ounces fresh goat cheese
1 tablespoon minced chives

Lamb Shoulder with Garlic and Goat Cheese

In an ovenproof casserole, sear the lamb lightly on all sides in its own fat, then salt and pepper the meat lightly all over. Add the white wine and water and bring to the simmer. Toss in the unpeeled garlic cloves, drape the sprigs of herbs over the lamb (or sprinkle dried herbs on top), cover, and place in a preheated 350-degree oven. Baste two or three times during the cooking, and after 1½ hours remove the meat to a warm platter and keep warm. Discard the herb sprigs and remove the garlic cloves with a slotted spoon. When cool enough to handle, squeeze the tender cooked flesh of the garlic cloves into the pan juices, discarding the skins. Now mash the goat cheese into the garlicky juices, stir until smooth, and simmer long enough to heat through. Remove the strings from the lamb and pour some of the sauce over it, then sprinkle on chives. Serve the remainder of the sauce separately in a sauceboat. Serve with fresh shell beans.

SERVES 4–5

---

1 lamb shoulder, boned and tied
    (approximately 2–3 pounds,
    depending on the size of the
    lamb)
2 tablespoons vegetable oil
¾ cup dry white wine or vermouth
3 garlic cloves
Salt
Freshly ground pepper
8 small potatoes, peeled and
    parboiled 10 minutes

About 8 plum tomatoes, peeled,
    seeded, and chopped, or
    equivalent amount of canned
    plum tomatoes, drained, seeds
    removed
1 medium head cauliflower, cut in
    florets
3 tablespoons chopped fresh herbs,
    such as chives, thyme, or
    rosemary, and parsley

Lamb Shoulder with Tomatoes and Cauliflower and Roasted Potatoes

Remove excess fat from the lamb and reserve. Heat the oil in a flameproof casserole and brown the lamb on all sides. Pour out the fat from the casserole, then add the wine and bring to a boil. Smash the garlic with the flat of a large knife, remove the skins, and chop the garlic with 1 teaspoon salt, until almost puréed. Spread this over and around the lamb, and grind fresh pepper liberally over the top. Cover and cook in a preheated 350-degree oven (total cooking time will be 1 hour 40 minutes).

At the same time as the lamb is cooking, render the reserved lamb fat by putting it in a shallow pan alongside the lamb casserole until it has melted. Roll the parboiled potatoes in the fat, then sprinkle with salt and pepper, and roast them as the lamb is cooking.

After 45 minutes, add the tomatoes to the lamb, cover, and cook another 30 minutes. Finally, add the cauliflower and return the casserole to the oven again, covered, for about 25 minutes more; you want the cauliflower to be just tender, not mushy. Let the lamb rest 5 minutes before carving. Serve lamb slices on a hot platter with the hot juices poured over and herbs sprinkled on top and cauliflower arranged around. The potatoes should be served in a separate dish so they don't lose their crispness.

SERVES 4

Lamb Shanks à la Vermont

Among Vermonters whose ancestors arrived generations ago from northern France, some still know the word *brayand*—once applied to French-American farmers who love their food. The adaptation below stems from the recipe of a food-loving Green Mountain shepherd's wife. The sauce is particularly good served with grits or barley, but you could use steamed rice.

4 small lamb shanks	3–4 garlic cloves, chopped fine
Flour	2 cups beef stock
Salt	1 cup cider
Freshly ground pepper	4 tablespoons applejack
1/4 teaspoon mace	1 tablespoon chopped fresh thyme
3–4 tablespoons safflower oil	2–3 medium potatoes, peeled and
2 large carrots, sliced thick	cut in quarters
3 large onions, sliced thick	3 tablespoons chopped parsley

Remove excess fat from the shanks and season them by dredging in flour mixed with the salt, pepper, and mace. Heat the oil in a large casserole and brown the meat. Add the carrots, onions, and garlic and cook over gentle heat for about 10 minutes. Add the stock, cider, and applejack, and season with the thyme. Bring the liquid to a boil, cover the casserole, reduce heat, and cook slowly for 2–3 hours, until the meat is falling from the bones, adding the potatoes for the last 40 minutes of cooking. Baste the meat at intervals with the liquid. Remove the shanks to a warm serving platter and sprinkle parsley on top. Mash the potatoes against the sides of the casserole to thicken the liquid, then pour into a gravy boat, to be poured over coarse ground hominy (grits) or hot cooked barley.

SERVES 4

4 lamb shanks
Flour
Salt
Freshly ground pepper
5 tablespoons vegetable oil
⅔ cup white wine

¼ cup water
1 teaspoon chopped parsley
1 teaspoon chopped fresh rosemary
1 pound red chard or Swiss chard
2 tablespoons butter
1 garlic clove, chopped

Lamb Shanks with Red Chard

Dust the shanks with flour seasoned lightly with salt and pepper. Heat 3 tablespoons oil in a large pot with a close-fitting cover and brown the shanks well in it. Stir 1½ tablespoons flour into the fat, then add wine and water, a little at a time, to make a smooth paste. Coat the shanks with this mixture, and sprinkle in the parsley and rosemary. Cover the pot, turn the heat as low as possible, and cook the shanks 1½–2 hours.

Meanwhile, wash the chard in several waters, removing any grit, then pat it dry with a towel, and chop very coarsely. Heat the remaining 2 tablespoons oil with the butter in a large pot and add garlic and the chopped chard. Toss the greens to coat them with butter and cook about 8 minutes. Turn the shanks and all of their sauce into the chard. Mix lightly and serve on a hot platter.

SERVES 4

2 pounds shoulder lamb, cut in
  small chunks
2 tablespoons butter plus a little
  lamb fat
1 cup chopped onion
1 garlic clove, chopped
1 cup coarsely chopped mushrooms
¾ pound tomatoes, peeled, seeded,
  and coarsely chopped

½ cup white wine or apple cider
1 slice of lime or lemon
Salt
Freshly ground pepper
2 teaspoons chopped fresh basil or
  ½ teaspoon dried
½ teaspoon dried rosemary
1 pound cauliflower, cut in florets

Mrs. Duff's Braised Lamb and Cauliflower

Pat the lamb pieces dry and put them in a saucepan with the butter and fat. Brown the lamb; add the onion, garlic, and mushrooms and stir occasionally until the vegetables are lightly cooked. Stir in the tomatoes, wine or cider, and lime or lemon slice. Bring the mixture to the boiling point, cover, and simmer 30–40 minutes. Remove the cover and increase the heat to reduce the liquid if the lamb and vegetables seem soupy. Season lightly with salt and pepper, and add the herbs and the cauliflower florets. Cover the pan and simmer about 25 minutes, until the cauliflower is tender but crunchy.

SERVES 4–6

Yankee Shepherd Pie

1½ pounds lamb stew meat without bones, or 2½ pounds lamb neck
2 tablespoons vegetable oil
½ teaspoon salt
Freshly ground pepper
3 tablespoons flour
2 teaspoons chopped fresh dill or ½ teaspoon dried dill weed
½ teaspoon celery seed
1 cup chicken stock, heated

4–5 tablespoons sherry
½ teaspoon chopped garlic
12 small white onions, peeled
4 medium potatoes, peeled and quartered
4 medium carrots, scraped and cut into chunks
1½ tablespoons lemon juice
1 cup plain yogurt, at room temperature
3 tablespoons chopped parsley

Pat the lamb pieces dry. Heat the oil in a casserole with a tight-fitting cover and brown the lamb pieces thoroughly on all sides. Sprinkle in the salt, several turns of the pepper grinder, then the flour, a little at a time, while stirring constantly. Add the dill and celery seed. Pour in the heated chicken stock and the sherry, stirring vigorously until the sauce thickens, and add the garlic. Cover and simmer about 1 hour, or bake, after bringing to a boil, in a preheated 350-degree oven for 1 hour. Add the onions, potatoes, and carrots and continue cooking about 30 minutes, until the vegetables are tender. Stir in the lemon juice and yogurt, heat through, then sprinkle with parsley.

SERVES 4

A traditional English way of making stew that is common today among cooks who appreciate locally raised lamb.

New England Lamb Hot Pot

1½–2 pounds lamb neck or other stew cuts
2 large potatoes, peeled and thickly sliced
2 carrots, scraped and thickly sliced
1 cup sliced snap beans
2 ripe tomatoes, peeled and sliced
2 green peppers, trimmed and cut into strips

1 onion, sliced
1 tablespoon chopped fresh thyme
½ teaspoon mace
½ teaspoon freshly grated nutmeg
½ tablespoon salt
Freshly ground pepper
Butter
About ½ cup stock

Trim the lamb of skin and fat and cut in bite-size pieces. Grease a 2½-quart earthen baking dish and layer the bottom with sliced potatoes. Arrange the lamb pieces in a layer, then the carrots, beans, tomatoes, and green pepper strips interspersed with onion slices. Sprinkle in the thyme, mace, nutmeg, and salt, and some freshly ground pepper to taste. Dot the top with butter, then pour in the stock. Cover the dish with aluminum foil and put it in a preheated 350-degree oven for 1¼ hours. Remove the foil and cook 20–25 minutes longer, until the top is delicately brown and crisp.

SERVES 4

More lamb is now being produced in Vermont than at any time since the nineteenth-century era of the woolen mills that dominated villages along many rushing streams.

Stewed Beans and Lamb

2 cups dried Great Northern or navy beans, soaked overnight
3 pounds lamb neck
½ cup flour
2 teaspoons or more salt
1 teaspoon dried sage, crumbled
Freshly ground pepper
3 tablespoons bacon fat or vegetable oil

2 cups sliced onions
3 garlic cloves, finely chopped
2 cups chopped fresh tomatoes or canned tomatoes, drained
1 cup chopped celery
2 tablespoons chopped parsley
¼ pound diced salt pork
1 cup dry white wine

Put the lamb in a paper bag with the flour, 2 teaspoons salt, sage, and pepper and shake to thoroughly cover the pieces of meat. Heat the bacon fat or oil in a large iron pot and brown the meat on all surfaces. Stir in the onions and garlic and sauté about 1 minute; add the tomatoes, celery, parsley, and salt pork. Cook, stirring, for 1–2 minutes, then pour in the wine to just about cover the meat. Drain the soaked beans and add them to the pot. Put on a tight-fitting cover and simmer over low heat 3–4 hours, stirring occasionally and adding more water as necessary to keep from sticking, until both beans and meat are very tender. Taste for seasoning and add more salt if necessary.

SERVES 6–8

New England–Style Moroccan Lamb

Going from the sheep shed to the kitchen of Fern Cobble Farm, near Waterbury, Vermont, we were offered this recipe for New England–raised lamb cooked in a version of Moroccan sauce.

3 tablespoons olive oil
2 pounds lean lamb, cut into 1-inch cubes
1 medium onion, chopped
½ pound mushrooms, sliced
1 fat garlic clove, minced
1 pound tomatoes, peeled, seeded and diced

½ cup raisins
1 cup blanched almonds, slivered or whole
1–2 tablespoons sugar
1 teaspoon cinnamon
1 teaspoon salt
1 teaspoon ground allspice
About ¼ cup chicken broth

Heat the oil in a large skillet and sauté the lamb until brown on all sides. Do this in several batches, removing the batches as they are browned. Add the onion, mushrooms, and garlic and sauté for 2 minutes. Return the lamb pieces to the skillet and add the remaining ingredients except the broth—the amount of sugar depends on your taste. Bring to a simmer, cover, and cook gently, adding a little broth now and then, as needed. The lamb should be tender in 30–40 minutes. Serve with rice or orzo.

SERVES 6

Blanquette of Lamb with Sorrel

3 tablespoons butter
1 tablespoon vegetable oil
1½ pounds lamb stew meat, cut into small pieces
1 large onion, chopped
Salt
Freshly ground pepper

Pinch of thyme
1 cup warm water
2 cups sorrel, stems removed if tough, cut in shreds
2 egg yolks
½ cup heavy cream

Heat 1 tablespoon of the butter and the oil in a casserole and brown the lamb pieces on all sides. Push to the side of the casserole, add the onion, and cook, stirring, until just golden. Season lightly with salt and pepper and the thyme, and pour the warm water over. Cover and cook gently for 1¼–1½ hours, until tender. Heat the remaining butter in a saucepan and add the sorrel. Cook gently for about 2 minutes, until it has released its moisture, absorbed the butter, and turned a drab olive color. Now drain the lamb cooking liquid through a strainer into the pan with the sorrel, and heat. Beat the egg yolks with the cream, and pour a little of the hot sauce in to temper the yolks, then return them to the saucepan and heat, stirring, just to the simmer; don't let the sauce boil. Pour over the lamb, heat through again if necessary, and serve with steamed potatoes or rice.

SERVES 4

Lamb Curry

New New Englanders may have easier access to conveniently packaged spices and condiments, but Yankees of other generations have been zipping up meals with imported flavorings since before the days of the clipper ships that sailed around the Horn. This recipe has been used with meat obtained from sheep farmers in various parts of the northern tier of states. Curries invite adaptation—one recipe from the slopes of Mount Mansfield gets its special flavor because parsnips and turnips are substituted for fruit.

3 tablespoons vegetable oil
2 large onions, chopped
3 garlic cloves, chopped
1 green pepper, seeded, ribs removed, chopped
4 cups lamb cut into 1½-inch cubes (either raw or cooked rare)
2 cups lamb broth
1 teaspoon fennel seeds

2 tablespoons curry powder, or more to taste
2 tablespoons turmeric
Salt
Freshly ground pepper
2 tart green apples, peeled, cored, and cut in eighths
About 1 tablespoon fresh lemon juice

Heat the oil in a large skillet, add the onions, garlic, and green pepper, and sauté gently about 10 minutes, stirring frequently. Stir in the lamb, then add the lamb broth, the fennel, curry, turmeric, and a sprinkling of salt and pepper to taste. Cover the skillet and simmer gently for about 1 hour. Add the apples and the lemon juice and cook 6–8 minutes. Taste and add a little more curry if you like it spicy. Serve with rice and chutney.

SERVES 6

Lamb Spareribs, Chinese Style

4 racks lamb spareribs (about 3½ pounds)
4 garlic cloves, chopped
½ cup soy sauce
½ cup hoisin sauce
3 tablespoons dry sherry

1½ tablespoons ketchup, or 3 tablespoons tomato sauce
½–1 teaspoon sugar (full amount if using tomato sauce)
3 tablespoons orange juice
1 teaspoon honey

Spread the lamb ribs out in 1 or 2 pans big enough to hold them in one layer. Rub the garlic over both sides. Mix the rest of the ingredients together, and pour over the ribs. Let marinate 2–3 hours at room temperature, turning them once. Cover the pan(s) loosely with foil and roast the ribs in their marinade in a preheated 325-degree oven for 2½ hours or more, basting them three or four times—they should be very tender. Remove the foil for the last 15 minutes of cooking, making sure the marinade hasn't dried in the bottom of the pan; if so, add a little water. Scrape up any remaining marinade and spread it over the ribs before serving. Eat with your fingers.
SERVES 4

Landgrove Sautéed Kidneys

With a twentieth-century population of seventy-five, Landgrove, Vermont, is mostly famous for welcoming skiers and summering families, but once it was the home of well-known innkeepers, Simeon Leland and his progeny, who ran many U.S. hotels after leaving the Green Mountain Coffee Shop on Route 11. Here's the Landgrove Library's version of kidneys in wine, as much a Yankee specialty today as the dish has always been.

12 lamb kidneys, or 3 veal kidneys
1 small onion, chopped fine
4 tablespoons butter
1 tablespoon chopped parsley
1 bay leaf
¼ teaspoon dried thyme

½ teaspoon dried rosemary, crumbled
About 1 tablespoon flour
½ cup red wine
Salt
Freshly ground pepper

Wash, skin, and split the kidneys to cut out the fat, then run them under hot water for 2 or 3 minutes. Pat dry, and if using veal kidneys cut them into about 4 pieces each. Sauté the onion in 2 tablespoons of butter, stirring in the parsley, bay leaf, thyme, and rosemary. Add the kidneys and brown them carefully. Sprinkle in the flour, stirring until it is absorbed. Stir in the wine, a little at a time, and simmer the kidneys, covered, for 2–4 minutes. Kidneys toughen if overcooked, so watch it. As one chef says, they should cook only until the blood stops running. They should also be salted *after*

cooking, so season them with salt and pepper when done. Remove the bay leaf and serve at once on crisp buttered toast or on steamed rice.
SERVES 3–4

Lamb Kidneys on Toast Québecois

About 16 lamb kidneys
2 tablespoons butter
1 tablespoon vegetable oil
4 shallots, or 6 scallion bulbs, chopped
1 tablespoon Dijon mustard
¼ cup heavy cream

Salt
Freshly ground pepper
3 tablespoons warm Calvados or brandy
4 slices dry, nonsweet, crustless white toast

GARNISH: *chopped parsley or chives*

Split the kidneys in half lengthwise and with scissors remove the fatty membranes. Heat the butter and oil in a large skillet and, when foaming, add the kidneys and shallots or scallions. Stir and toss over high heat about 6 minutes, at which time the kidneys should have released their juices and when pricked will no longer bleed. Stir in the mustard and cream, and when it is hot, add salt and pepper to taste. Pour the heated liquor over the kidneys and set aflame. When the flames have died down, remove the kidneys with a slotted spoon and distribute even portions over the toast. Quickly boil down the sauce in the pan to reduce slightly, then pour it over the kidneys, and sprinkle on a little parsley or chives.
SERVES 4

Lamb's Liver with Onions and Juniper Berries

4 tablespoons butter
2 medium onions, sliced thin
3 tablespoons juniper berries, crushed

About ¾ pound fresh lamb's liver, sliced thin*
¾ cup plain yogurt, at room temperature

* Note: Use calves' liver if more readily available.

Heat 2 tablespoons butter in a large skillet, stir in the onions and juniper berries, and sauté over low heat, stirring now and then, until the onions are tender. Remove the onions and juniper berries with a slotted spoon to a warm bowl. Heat the remaining 2 tablespoons butter in the same skillet, then, when sizzling, add the liver slices and sauté quickly over high heat 30 seconds on each side. Return the onions and juniper berries to the skillet, stir in the yogurt, and toss together until heated through.
SERVES 4

Braised Heart, Tongue, and Kidneys of Lamb

Don't overlook these precious parts of lamb, and make a delicious feast for two.

1½ tablespoons vegetable oil
1 medium onion, chopped
1 fat garlic clove, chopped
1 lamb heart, split open
¾ cup beef broth
¾ cup red wine
1 bay leaf
2 sprigs parsley
2 sprigs thyme, or ½ teaspoon
    dried

1 lamb tongue
2 lamb kidneys, split, white
    membranes removed
1 teaspoon cornstarch
1 tablespoon port
Salt
Freshly ground pepper

Heat 1 tablespoon oil in a small heavy skillet or saucepan, then sauté the onion and garlic for 1 minute. Add the heart, turning it to coat. Pour in the beef broth and wine, put the bay leaf and herb sprigs (or dried herb, if using) over the meat, cover, and turn the heat very low to simmer.

Meanwhile, place the tongue in a separate pot with water to cover, bring to a boil, reduce heat, then simmer for 20 minutes. Remove, reserving the cooking liquid, and when cool enough to handle remove the hard skin. Add the tongue to the heart, cover, and continue to simmer another hour, or until tender, adding a little of the tongue cooking liquid as necessary (the liquid should half cover the meats). A few minutes before the heart and tongue are done, sauté the kidneys in the remaining oil over quite high heat for about 30 seconds on each side. Add them, scraping up all the cooking juices, to the braising heart and tongue. Mix the cornstarch with the port to dissolve it, then stir this into the braising sauce and bring to a boil to thicken the sauce lightly. Remove the bay leaf and herb sprigs, and season to taste with salt and pepper. To serve, halve the heart and split the tongue in half lengthwise, and arrange these halves with a kidney on 2 plates; spoon sauce over the meats, and have mashed potatoes on the side.

SERVES 2

PORK

Scandinavians and Central Europeans have perked up the old Yankee heritage by adding fruits—other than apples—to meat, and adding various spice combinations to pork. A recipe not unlike this one comes from Billerica, Massachusetts.

Roast Pork with Apricots

One 3½–4-pound pork rib roast
1 can apricots
Salt

Freshly ground pepper
½ teaspoon caraway seeds
½ teaspoon fennel seeds

GARNISH: *watercress sprigs*

Have the bones cracked, but don't separate the chops from the roast. Cut a slit with a sharp knife between each chop, which will provide a pocket into which to stuff one-half apricot. Sprinkle the meat with salt and pepper, then place it on a rack in a shallow pan. Pour in about ½ inch water, sprinkle in the caraway and fennel seeds, and splash the roast with a little of the juice from the apricots. Place the roast in a preheated 350-degree oven and cook for about 2½ hours, basting every half-hour or so with a little apricot juice and then with the juices that collect in the pan. Add a little boiling water if the liquid evaporates too fast, and reduce the heat to 300 degrees. Fifteen minutes before the meat is done—it should be very moist—place the remaining apricot halves in the pan juices. Serve the roast garnished with the apricots and a few sprigs of watercress. Braised Savoy Cabbage (page 280) is a good accompaniment.
SERVES 6

Rosemary-Flavored Roast Pork

4 pounds rib roast of pork, ribs cracked
Juice of ½ lemon
2 tablespoons finely chopped fresh rosemary, or 2 teaspoons dried rosemary, mulled
1 teaspoon salt
Freshly ground pepper
2–3 tablespoons vegetable oil
2 scallions, chopped
½ cup white wine

Rub the pork thoroughly with the lemon juice and rosemary. Sprinkle with the salt and several turns of the pepper grinder, and place on a rack in a shallow roasting pan; pour in enough boiling water to make about 1 inch in the bottom of the pan. Put the roast in a preheated 375-degree oven for about 3 hours. Meanwhile, heat 1 tablespoon oil and cook the chopped scallions 2–3 minutes. Set aside. Baste the roast occasionally with the drippings in the pan of water. Just before serving, pour the wine into the scallion pan and bring to the boiling point. Degrease the roasting pan, then add the pork drippings to the wine and scallions. Stir thoroughly while boiling the sauce and reducing it slightly. Put the roast on a hot platter, and serve with the sauce in a sauceboat.

SERVES 6–8

Pork Roast Stuffed with Dried Fruits and Walnuts in Port Wine Sauce

We had this elegant and delicious stuffed pork roast one night at the White Hart Inn in Salisbury, Connecticut, when Eric Stevens was the chef there, and he was helpful enough to work out his recipe so that it could be made successfully in the home kitchen. We have served it to very appreciative guests.

PORK STOCK:
Bones from a 4-pound pork roast (see below)
1¼ cups diced onions
1¼ cups diced celery
1¼ cups diced carrots
4 garlic cloves, peeled
6 cups water

1½ cups dried mixed fruits (apricots, prunes, apples, raisins, pears)
½ cup walnuts, chopped
1 ounce brandy
1 egg white
4 pound center loin of pork roast, boned (weight calculated after bones are removed)
Pinch each of salt, freshly ground pepper, and paprika

PORT WINE SAUCE:
2½–3 cups pork stock
2 cups port
2½ tablespoons flour

First make the stock. Place the pork bones and vegetables in a large roasting pan and broil, turning occasionally, until well browned on all sides. Remove the pan from the heat, pour off the grease, and dump the meat and vegetables into a large saucepan. Wash the roasting pan with a cup of the water, scraping up browned bits, and add this and the remaining water to the stockpot. Bring to a boil and let simmer, uncovered, 2½ hours. Skim off the fat and strain. Reserve.

Mix the fruit, nuts, brandy, and egg white together. With a long sharp knife, make an incision 1½ inches wide lengthwise from one end of the pork roast to the other. Stuff the fruit mixture into the pork as tightly as possible. Place on a rack, season with salt, pepper, and paprika, and cook in a preheated 375-degree oven 45 minutes, then reduce heat to 300 degrees and continue cooking until it reaches an internal temperature of 140 degrees—approximately 1½ hours in all (incidentally, the temperature will go up as the roast rests). Keep the roast warm while you make the sauce.

Pour off the excess grease from the roasting pan, reserving about 2 tablespoons. Place the pan over medium heat and add the 2½ cups pork stock and 1 cup of the port. Boil to reduce to 2 cups. Mix the flour thoroughly with the remaining port, and add to the pan, a little at a time, whisking until smooth. Simmer several minutes until the sauce reaches a syrupy consistency. Remove from the pan, strain, and serve over the sliced roast. Serve with Spicy Red Cabbage (page 281) and Spaetzle (page 373).

SERVES 8–10

Roast Loin of Pork with Juniper Berries and Mustard Sauce

1 loin of pork (approximately 3 pounds), bones cracked so that chops can be separated when carved
About 20 juniper berries
1 tablespoon coarse salt

¾ cup tangy preserves, such as chokecherry (page 624), beach plum (page 623), or currant
6 tablespoons Dijon mustard
½ cup water

Trim meat of excess fat. Pound the juniper berries and salt together until the berries are roughly crushed. Rub this mixture all over the pork and let stand at room temperature 1 hour, or refrigerate and let macerate overnight.

Heat the preserves and mustard in a saucepan, stirring, until melted. Place the pork in a roasting pan just slightly larger than the loin, and pour the mustard-preserves mixture over it. Pour water into the bottom of the pan and roast, uncovered, in a preheated 350-degree oven for 1½ hours. Serve with noodles or mashed potatoes.

SERVES 4–6

Marinated Loin of Pork with Prunes

As noted in the two preceding recipes, pork and fruit are good matches almost any time. In this recipe, dried prunes add just the right rich flavor and texture.

*6 pounds loin of pork, boned and
  tied*
Salt
Freshly ground pepper
*4–5 gratings nutmeg (about ⅛
  teaspoon)*
*2 tablespoons chopped fresh sage,
  or 1 teaspoon dried*
*2 tablespoons chopped fresh thyme,
  or 1 teaspoon dried*
*2 tablespoons chopped fresh
  tarragon, or ½ teaspoon dried*

2 tablespoons lard
3–4 garlic cloves, finely chopped
¼–⅓ cup chopped parsley
4 cups red wine
1 large bay leaf
2 sprigs celery leaves
1 sprig thyme
8 ounces dried prunes
2 beef bouillon cubes
3–4 tablespoons maple syrup
3–4 tablespoons brandy

Wipe the pork with a damp cloth. Mix 1 teaspoon salt, a few turns of the pepper grinder, the nutmeg, sage, thyme, and tarragon together, and rub this dry marinade into the meat on all its surfaces. Set aside for 1 hour or more. Heat the lard in a heavy skillet and sear the pork, turning it to brown well. Add the garlic and about 2 tablespoons parsley, being careful not to let the garlic and parsley burn. Transfer the pork to a baking dish in which it fits snugly, and pour in the wine with the bay leaf, celery leaves, sprig of thyme, and a little salt and pepper. Bring the wine to the simmering point on top of the stove, then put the baking dish in a preheated 350-degree oven and cook for 1 hour. Turn the pork and continue cooking for 1 hour more. Add the prunes and cook about 30 minutes longer. Remove the meat and the prunes to a hot platter and sprinkle the remaining parsley over all. On top of the stove, reduce the herb-seasoned wine by one-third, and stir in the bouillon cubes, maple syrup, and brandy. Continue simmering and taste for seasoning—the sauce should have an exotic sweet-sour flavor. Pour it into a hot gravy boat, and serve with the warm pork.
SERVES 10–12

One 6½–7-pound fresh ham
3–4 tablespoons flour
Salt
Freshly ground pepper
2–3 cups chicken or beef stock
1 medium onion, sliced
2 bay leaves
1 sprig fresh thyme, or ¼ teaspoon
  dried
1 carrot, sliced
1 small leek, sliced
8–10 or more medium sweet
  potatoes (1 per person)

Fresh Ham with Sweet Potatoes

Mix the flour with a light sprinkling of salt and pepper, and rub mixture into the pork. Put the ham on a rack in a roasting pan, pour 1 cup stock over it, and roast for 24 minutes in a preheated 425-degree oven. Reduce the heat to 325 degrees, strew the onion slices, bay leaves, carrot slices, and leek slices around the pan, and continue roasting for about 30 minutes per pound, until very tender, basting every 15 minutes with the juices in the pan and adding more stock as necessary. Almost 50 minutes before the pork is ready, prepare the sweet potatoes by peeling and quartering them, then strew them around the ham to cook for the final 40 minutes. Remove the ham to a warm platter, lift out the sweet potatoes with a slotted spoon, and arrange them around. Degrease the pan and pour in another cup of stock, scraping up all the browned bits. Serve this pan sauce with the meat.
SERVES 8–10 WITH LEFTOVERS

Pork Tenderloin with Savory

Pork tenderloin is that part of the loin, often sold separately, that is long, tapering, naturally round in shape—a well-flavored, juicy, choice morsel that weighs ⅔–¾ pound.

1 tablespoon coarse salt
2–4 tablespoons chopped fresh
  savory or 2 teaspoons dried
2 tablespoons chopped parsley
2 garlic cloves, chopped
2 tablespoons vegetable oil
2 pork tenderloins
Freshly ground pepper

Sprinkle salt over the chopped herbs and garlic on a cutting board, then chop them and mash them, using the flat of your knife until you have almost a paste. Rub 1 tablespoon oil over the tenderloins and use the other table-spoon to oil a long, shallow pan that will accommodate the 2 tenderloin strips. Rub the garlic-salt-herb mixture into the meat, and grind pepper over. Place in the pan and pour ½ cup water around. Bake in a preheated 375-degree oven for 1 hour, basting four or five times as they cook. Serve with mashed potatoes and greens; corn bread is good, too.
SERVES 4

Pork Tenderloin with Tomatoes and Cider

2 pounds pork tenderloin
2 thin slices salt pork
2 medium onions, sliced thin
1 teaspoon chopped fresh thyme
1 bay leaf

Freshly ground pepper
1 cup apple juice or cider
2–3 tomatoes, sliced
1½ cups cooked rice

Put the tenderloin and the salt pork in a flameproof serving dish and brown over high heat, turning the meat from time to time. As the fat from the salt pork accumulates, add the sliced onions and cook 3–4 minutes. Add the herbs and a few turns of the pepper grinder; salt should not be needed because of the salt pork. Pour in the cider, bring to a boil, and cook 20 minutes. Arrange the tomato slices over the meat and spread the rice over the meat and vegetables. Cover and bake in a preheated 325-degree oven for 15–20 minutes. Remove the tenderloins, cut in thin slices, then reshape and place the meat again on the bed of rice and tomatoes. Serve from the cooking dish.
SERVES 4

Caraway-Flavored Pork Tenderloin with Mushrooms

The scent of caraway, someone once said, is to New England pantries what orchids are to an evening gown, and pork and caraway are particularly compatible.

2 pounds pork tenderloin fillet
1 medium onion
1 garlic clove, finely chopped
5 tablespoons butter
1 pound mushrooms, cut in
    quarters and eighths
Salt
Freshly ground pepper

¼ teaspoon caraway seeds
1 teaspoon finely chopped fresh
    marjoram
One ¼-pound slice country ham or
    Canadian bacon, cut into strips
1 cup sour cream
2 tablespoons chopped parsley

Cut the pork into thin strips about ¼ inch thick. Peel the onion and cut it in half vertically, then in thin slices or crescents. Cook the onion and the garlic gently in 2 tablespoons of butter until the onion appears translucent. Stir in the mushrooms, season lightly with salt and pepper, and cook, tossing occasionally. Season the pork with salt, pepper, caraway, and marjoram. Heat the remaining 3 tablespoons butter in a saucepan and sauté the ham or Canadian bacon for 1–2 minutes, then increase the heat and stir in the pork. As soon as the pork browns, stir in the mushroom mixture. Add the sour cream, a little at a time, while bringing the temperature to the simmering point. Serve in a heated dish with a sprinkling of parsley.
SERVES 4

For three generations this has been our family's favorite way of doing pork chops. The secret is slow cooking, and the aromatic stuffing makes a blanket over the chops as they bake, so they remain deliciously moist. They're really good served with Fried Apples (page 251)

Stuffed Pork Chops

4 pork loin chops (about ¾ inch thick)

THE STUFFING:

3 tablespoons butter or oil or a combination
1 large onion, chopped
1 rib celery, chopped
1 small green pepper, or ½ large, ribs and seeds removed, chopped
2–3 tablespoons finely diced dry sausage or ham or dried beef (optional)

1½ cups fresh bread crumbs
1–2 teaspoons chopped fresh thyme, or ½–1 teaspoon dried
1–2 teaspoons chopped fresh rosemary, or ½–1 teaspoon dried
2 tablespoons chopped parsley
Salt
Freshly ground pepper

Trim the chops of excess fat. In a skillet, melt the butter and/or oil and sauté the onion 5 minutes. Add the celery and green pepper, along with the sausage or ham seasoning, if you are using it, and sauté 2–3 minutes more. Remove the contents of the skillet to a bowl, and toss with the bread crumbs and herbs, and season with salt and pepper to taste. Rub a little of the excess fat on the bottom of the skillet and brown the chops lightly on both sides. Turn them and season with salt and pepper, then transfer them to a shallow baking pan (unless the skillet in which you've browned them can go directly into the oven). Press equal amounts of the stuffing on top of each chop, covering the surface completely, and bake, uncovered, in a preheated 325-degree oven for 1½ hours.

SERVES 4

Cranberry-Orange Pork Chops

Early in the nineteenth century, Florida oranges and cultivated cranberries began finding their way into Yankee kitchens at about the same time. Much of the citrus fruit shipped north was processed by a transplanted Vermonter and a young man from Connecticut, who knew the New England appetites for such things.

4 thick pork chops
2 tablespoons water
½ cup port
Salt
Freshly ground pepper
1 teaspoon cinnamon

Freshly grated nutmeg
½ teaspoon ground cloves
1 tablespoon grated orange rind
2 peeled oranges, in sections
1–2 cups fresh cranberries

Cranberry-Orange Pork Chops (continued)

In a large skillet over medium heat, stand the pork chops on their fat edges and cook slowly to cover the pan with pork fat, then brown the meat on both sides. Drain off the excess fat, add the water and the port, and sprinkle the chops lightly with salt and pepper and the spices. Cover the skillet and cook over low heat for about 1 hour, until the pork is very tender. Add a little water, if necessary, to keep the meat in liquid. Add the orange rind, the orange sections, which have been picked free of pith, and the cranberries. Cook, covered, until the cranberries pop, about 10 minutes. Put the chops on a hot platter with the fruit, and pour the sauce over them. Good with Potato Pancakes (page 304).

SERVES 4

Cooked Pork and Cabbage Stew

3 tablespoons butter or oil
3–4 cups cooked pork, cut in pieces
1 onion, sliced
1 teaspoon caraway seeds
3 whole allspice
4 peppercorns

1 large bay leaf
1 head cabbage, soaked in cold water
4–8 new potatoes, peeled if desired (small ones halved; larger ones quartered)
6 tiny white onions, peeled

Heat the butter or oil in a stew pot and stir in the meat pieces. Add the aromatics—the sliced onion, caraway seeds, allspice, peppercorns, and bay leaf—and barely cover the meat with water. Simmer, covered, about 15 minutes. Meanwhile, slice the cabbage coarsely and add it to the stew along with the potatoes and onions. Continue to cook for about 30 minutes, covered, until the potatoes are tender.

SERVES 4

Pork and Parsnip Stew

3 tablespoons vegetable oil
1½ pounds lean pork, trimmed of fat, cut into bite-size pieces
2 large onions, chopped
½ cup dry cider or white wine
2 teaspoons chopped fresh savory, or 1 teaspoon dried
½ cup chicken broth or water

Salt
Freshly ground pepper
¾ pound parsnips (about 6)
2 tablespoons butter
1 tablespoon sugar
½ sweet red pepper, cut into 1½-inch strips

Heat 1½ tablespoons of the oil in a heavy saucepan or skillet, then brown the pork in several batches, not crowding the pan and removing when browned on all sides. Add the remaining oil and the onions and sauté them a few minutes, stirring, until they turn golden. Pour in the cider or wine and boil hard to reduce by half. Add the savory, then return the pork to the pan and pour broth or water over it. Season with salt and pepper to taste, cover, and simmer gently for 1 hour.

Meanwhile, peel the parsnips and cut them into even pieces about 1½ inches long, halving, then quartering the fatter pieces. Boil them in lightly salted water until just tender, about 10 minutes. Drain. Heat the butter in a skillet, then toss in the parsnips, sprinkle them with sugar, and glaze them quickly over high heat, tossing constantly. Add the red pepper strips to the stew after it has cooked 1 hour, cover, and cook about 5 minutes. Gently fold in the parsnips and cook another 2–3 minutes. Serve with steamed new potatoes.

SERVES 4

Stir-fried Pork and Cole Slaw

2–3 cups cole slaw
¾ pounds lean pork
2 scallions
3 tablespoons soy sauce
2 teaspoons sesame seeds
1½ teaspoons cornstarch
2 teaspoons peanut oil
3 tablespoons safflower oil
2 cups sliced mushrooms
1 tablespoon water

Put the cole slaw in a sieve to drain. Cut the pork into 2-inch slivers, discarding any fat. (If you put the pork in the freezer for 10 minutes, it will be easier to cut in thin, matchlike pieces.) Trim the scallions and cut both green and white parts into slivers about the size of the pork. Put the meat and the scallions in a bowl and marinate them in the soy sauce, sesame seeds, peanut oil, and cornstarch. Heat a heavy frying pan (or wok), then add 1 tablespoon of the safflower oil and swirl it around as it sizzles. Add the drained cole slaw and stir-fry for almost 2 minutes, then remove it to a bowl. Use a paper towel to wipe the pan clean, and add the remaining 2 tablespoons safflower oil. Let the oil just begin to bubble, stir in the mushrooms, and stir-fry 30 seconds. Add the water to the pork, mix thoroughly, then stir the meat, scallions and marinade into the pan, keeping the meat and mushrooms moving as they cook for about 2 minutes over high heat. Return the partially cooked cole slaw to the pan and stir-fry for about 3 minutes (the pork will become stiff and lose its pinkness and the cole slaw will be tender but crisp).

SERVES 4

Stir-fry of Strips of Pork and Broccoli Stems

A simple, fresh way of using leftover pork roast. (It may look as though there are a lot of ingredients, but many are used twice and all are readily available these days in supermarkets; get everything ready ahead, and the final preparation can be done in a matter of minutes.) The recipe may be expanded according to how much leftover pork you may have. Other vegetables besides broccoli may be added: strips of celery, green pepper, and snow peas, for example.

MARINADE:

1 egg white
1 teaspoon cornstarch

1 teaspoon dry sherry
1 teaspoon soy sauce

½ pound cooked pork, cut into long, thin strips
3 tablespoons vegetable oil
2 teaspoons chopped, peeled ginger
2 fat garlic cloves, minced

2 cups peeled broccoli stems, cut into thin strips
¼ cup sliced scallions, including tender greens

SAUCE:

2 teaspoons cornstarch
1 tablespoon water
1 tablespoon dry sherry
2 tablespoons oyster sauce
1 tablespoon soy sauce

3 tablespoons leftover pork gravy, if available, or 2–3 tablespoons chicken or pork stock
1 teaspoon sesame oil

Mix the marinade ingredients lightly with a fork. Stir in the pork strips, coating them, and refrigerate for about 30 minutes. Heat the vegetable oil in a wok or frying pan and stir-fry the pork strips over high heat 1 minute. Add the vegetables and continue to stir-fry over medium-high heat for 2 minutes. Stir the sauce ingredients together, and add them to the pan, cooking just long enough to thicken and heat through. Sprinkle on the sesame oil, and serve immediately with steamed rice.

SERVES 2

The smoked chops we used for this recipe were medium-thin pork chops, which we had smoked in our Little Chief smoker for 1 hour, using 2 pans of hickory chips. If you have any leftover pieces, chop the pork, and thin any remaining liquid with extra juice from canned tomatoes or tomato sauce. Serve over cooked thin spaghetti with strips of green, red, and even yellow tomatoes—if available—as a garnish. A sprinkling of fresh chopped oregano may be added.

BARBECUE SAUCE:

3 tablespoons oil
1 large onion
3 garlic cloves, smashed and peeled
⅓ cup honey
1 cup canned tomatoes with their juice
¼ cup cider vinegar
¼ cup Worcestershire sauce

3 tablespoons soy sauce
1–2 tablespoons raisins
1½ teaspoons dry mustard
2 bay leaves
1 sprig rosemary, or ½ teaspoon dried
Several shakes of Tabasco sauce

8 medium-thin smoked pork chops

Spin all of the barbecue sauce ingredients in a food processor or blender. Place in a saucepan and cook 15 minutes over moderate heat. Cool, and pour over the smoked chops arranged in one layer in a baking pan. Let marinate for several hours. Bake in a preheated 350-degree oven for 1½ hours.

SERVES 4–8, DEPENDING ON APPETITES AND WHETHER YOU WANT LEFTOVERS

Baked Barbecued Smoked Pork Chops

One 12–14-pound country ham, preboiled
1 cup dark brown sugar
1 cup maple syrup

Whole cloves
12 bay leaves
2 cups brandy or applejack

Trim the skin or rind from the ham and score the surface fat in a diamond pattern. Mix the brown sugar and maple syrup, then spread it evenly over the ham. Stick the center of each diamond with a whole clove and fasten the bay leaves in place with toothpicks. Put the ham in a shallow pan, pour in the brandy, and cover the pan with a closed-in tent of aluminum foil. Cook in a preheated 450-degree oven for 20 minutes per pound. After the first 10 minutes of baking, add 2 cups water. During the last hour of baking, remove the bay leaves and baste the ham frequently with the syrupy juices in the pan. Take the ham out of the oven, put it on a platter, and let it stand overnight. A fine glaze will form.

SERVES 20 OR MORE

Maple-Coated Ham with Brandy or Applejack

Ham Steak Baked with Cider and Rum

1 pound ham steak
1 cup cider
2 tablespoons brown sugar

1 teaspoon powdered ginger
4 tablespoons rum

Put the ham steak in an oval baking dish that will hold it fairly snugly. Pour the cider over it and set aside for 1 hour or more, spooning the cider over the ham occasionally. Mix the brown sugar, ginger, and rum. When ready to bake the ham steak, pour the brown sugar–rum mixture carefully over the top of the meat, and put the dish in a preheated 350-degree oven for about 1½ hours.

SERVES 4

How to Start Smoking

Smoking comes natural to rural New Englanders when pigs are ready for the market. Home-curing may have died out for a time, but there is a renewal of interest in good Yankee hams and bacon, especially among young people newly conscious of their American heritage.

Many early New England housewives had meat-curing recipes that owed something to the part of Britain from which they came. Yorkshire ham, for instance, derived special flavor from the oak sawdust over which it was smoked. Cumberland hams traditionally are dry-salted and rubbed with brown sugar; Bradenham pork should be cured with molasses and spices. And our own New England home-cured hams also vary in method and result.

Hams smoked over smouldering corncobs used to be common when most farmers raised corn, but recently they've been hard to come by. Hardwoods, sometimes augmented by apple and other fruit boughs, are most frequently the source of smoke to cure regional foods, and we know from experience how good such hams and bacon can be because of our friendship with John and Michele Mackin. The Mackins have been providing cured pork for their young family for a decade, buying the meat from a friend and neighbor. Here's how they smoke it.

For every 100 pounds of meat, they mix 5 pounds of kosher salt with 4 pounds of sugar (brown or maple or a combination; grade B or C syrup can be substituted for maple sugar). They put the ham in a large plastic pail or garbage can, packing half of the curing mixture around it and keeping the meat off the bottom with a crisscross piece of hardwood. Thus packed, the meat is left in a cool place (36–40 degrees) for about 10 days. Then the remaining curing mixture is added, and the meat is again set aside to cure. The total amount of curing time should be 1 day per pound of meat.

Bacon also requires 1 day of curing per pound of meat and can be done all at once.

1 slice country ham (about 1½
* inches thick)*
Orange juice
1 medium orange
½ cup whole cranberry sauce

Put the ham slice in a shallow baking dish not much larger than the meat, and pour in enough orange juice to cover the bottom by about ¼ inch. Bake in a preheated 325-degree oven for 45 minutes. Grate enough of the orange skin to make 1 tablespoon. Peel the orange and remove the membrane separating its sections. Chop the sections, and stir them with the

*Ham Slices
with
Cranberry-
Orange
Glaze*

Count on 4 pounds of mixture per 100 pounds of bacon, and use a ratio of 50 percent sugar to 50 percent salt. Coat the flesh side of the bacon slabs, then fold them over like a book, and place in a plastic pail with the rest of the curing mixture around.

To prepare the meat for smoking, it is removed from the brine mixture and washed for about 5 minutes in three changes of cold water. Then, using the hottest water you can stand, clean the ham with a hard-bristle brush, "scrubbing the devil out of it, to open up the pores so it will take the smoke. Do this at least the night before you start smoking, so there's time for the meat to air-dry."

Colonial New Englanders often had a smoke hole in the family fireplace for their meat, but generations of farmers have had smokehouses built for this purpose. The Mackins have a smokehouse about the size of a small closet. About an hour before bringing the ham to the smokehouse, John Mackin builds a fire of finely split maple to bring the temperature to about 90 degrees, or hot enough to force moisture out of the meat and to soften the surface so it can start taking in the smoke.

Vents in the smokehouse walls should be open to provide circulation, and a check on progress must be made every 6 hours. (If the outside temperature is very cold, this phase may take up to 12 hours.) "The best time for smoking," according to John, "is right before a big snowstorm, when you have still air and low pressure. Then I start adding wood and closing the vents. How long you keep smoking depends on the color—hams usually take two to three days, and the color of the rind turns dark mahogany, if you want it real smoky." Bacon is usually done in a day.

To age the hams and bacon well, they must be double-wrapped in cheesecloth to protect them from flies and hung up in the basement or attic. Let them hang at least 1 month before using.

grated peel into the cranberry sauce. Remove the ham slice from the oven in its dish, cover the top with the cranberry-orange glaze, and return to the oven long enough to become hot and firm.

SERVES 4 OR MORE, DEPENDING ON THE SIZE OF THE HAM

Cracker-Crumb Ham Loaf

6 common crackers (or other unsalted crackers)
2 cups milk
2 eggs, well beaten
1 pound country ham, finely chopped (about 2 cups)
1 pound lean pork, finely chopped
1 rib celery, chopped

Freshly ground pepper
10 fresh sage leaves, chopped, or ½ teaspoon dried, crumbled
2 dill pickles
1 green pepper
1 sweet red pepper
3 tablespoons rum

Spin the crackers in a blender or food processor to make fine crumbs. Scald the milk, and mix it with the crumbs. Stir in the beaten eggs, ham, pork, and celery, and season with several turns of the pepper grinder and the sage. Chop the pickles, and add them. Remove the seeds with pith from the 2 peppers, chop them, and mix them in thoroughly with the meat mixture, along with the rum. Pack into a large 9 x 5-inch loaf pan—the meat will form a rounded top. Bake in a preheated 350-degree oven for 1½ hours. Let rest at least 10 minutes before slicing.

SERVES 6–8

Maple-Apple Upside-down Ham Loaf

1 pound ground cooked ham
½ pound ground beef
½ cup dry bread crumbs
½ cup chopped celery
¼ cup chopped onion
2 eggs
¾ cup milk
1 tablespoon chopped fresh summer savory, or 1 teaspoon dried

½ teaspoon dry mustard
1 tart apple, pared and sliced in thin wedges
¼ cup maple syrup (grade-B if you wish)

GARNISH: *parsley sprigs*

In a large mixing bowl, blend the ham and beef with the crumbs, celery, and onion. Break in the eggs, add the milk, savory, and mustard, and stir until well mixed. Butter the bottom and sides of an 8-inch loaf pan thoroughly. Arrange the apple slices in a pattern on the bottom of the pan, and cover them with the maple syrup. Pack in the meat mixture. Bake in a 350-degree oven for 1 hour and 15 minutes, or until the loaf has just begun to form a crust. Remove from the oven and let rest for about 5 minutes, then turn the pan upside down on a warm platter and remove the pan. Garnish with parsley sprigs.

SERVES 4–6

In one of her cookbooks entitled *What to Have for Dinner*, Fannie Farmer suggested various croquettes to be served as part of her "Company and Formal" menus. Croquettes may be thought of now as less than formal—maybe something more appropriate for a luncheon or a light supper, or to serve as appetizers when they are shaped as small meatballs. Various croquettes can be made of ground cooked meats—lamb and poultry are particularly good—using this same formula. The addition of cheese is appealing with ham.

Ham-Cheese Croquettes

2 tablespoons butter
3 tablespoons flour
1 cup buttermilk
2 cups grated sharp cheddar
2 cups ground ham
Salt

2 scallions, including tender greens,
    chopped fine
2–3 drops Tabasco sauce
1 egg, lightly beaten
About 1¼ cups fresh bread crumbs
Oil for frying

Melt the butter in a saucepan, add the flour, and cook over low heat, stirring, for 2 minutes. Off heat, add the buttermilk, return to the heat and, whisking, bring to a boil and cook until the sauce thickens. Stir in the cheese and ham, add salt to taste, the scallions, and Tabasco. Transfer to a plate to cool, then cover and refrigerate several hours or overnight.

Form the mixture into 6 or 8 fat sausage shapes, dip each into the beaten egg, then roll in bread crumbs to cover completely. Chill again 30 minutes or more.

Heat about 3 inches of oil to 360 degrees in a skillet or frying kettle, then lower the croquettes in gently (do only half at a time if they are crowded) and fry until golden brown on the bottom; then turn and fry the other side until golden. Drain on paper towels, and serve right away.

SERVES 3–4

Ham and Kidney Pie

Madeira was not only a favorite drink but a common seasoning for Yankee cooks during clipper-ship days. It still enhances the classic mating of ham and veal kidneys.

2 veal kidneys
1 cup buttermilk or milk
½ pound baked country ham, cut into ½-inch-thick slices
2–3 tablespoons cooking oil
1 medium onion, chopped
⅓ pound mushrooms, sliced

¼ cup Madeira
2 tablespoons flour
1½ cups beef stock
2 teaspoons chopped fresh rosemary, or ½ teaspoon dried, crumbled
Freshly ground pepper

CORNMEAL CRUST:
¾ cup flour
⅓ cup cornmeal
½ teaspoon salt

⅓ cup shortening or lard
About 3 tablespoons cold water

Put the kidneys to soak in the buttermilk for 1 hour. Trim all fat from the ham slices, and render it in a large skillet. Drain the kidneys, discarding the buttermilk, and trim them of all white connective tissue and membrane, then slice them. Sauté the 2 meats in the ham fat and some of the cooking oil for 1 minute over quite high heat, then remove them with a slotted spoon to a plate. Add the remaining oil to the pan and sauté the onion gently until limp. Add the mushrooms and cook 2–3 minutes longer. Remove the vegetables and mix them with the kidneys. Now deglaze the pan by stirring in the Madeira and scraping up all browned bits. Boil down until syrupy, then sprinkle in 2 tablespoons flour and, stirring constantly, add the stock, a little at a time, and cook until smooth and thickened. Add the rosemary and some freshly ground pepper to taste (no salt should be necessary because of the ham and the prepared stock). When the sauce coats the spoon, stir in the meat and vegetable mixture and simmer about 10 minutes. Transfer the contents of the pan to a 2-quart casserole, scraping in all the sauce.

Prepare the cornmeal crust. Toss the flour, cornmeal, and salt together, then cut in the shortening, working it with your fingertips or a pastry blender, until the mixture resembles fresh bread crumbs. Stir in enough water, mixing it in with a fork, until you have a dough that holds together. Gather it up and transfer it to a lightly floured work surface. Roll it out to a circumference of about 1 inch larger than your casserole. Put a cup upside down in the bottom of the casserole with the meats (this will help to draw in the juices) and place the rolled out dough on top, folding the edges back and crimping it all around. Make several slashes in the top, and bake the pie in a preheated 375-degree oven for about 35–40 minutes, until the crust is lightly browned. When serving, cut into the pie and remove the cup so that the juices will mingle with the meats and vegetables.

SERVES 4–6

Leaner than the more typical side bacon, or the brisket characteristic of traditional boiled dinner, the so-called Canadian bacon—cured, smoked boneless pork loin—gives a *Québecois* accent to this dish when it's prepared by Yankees whose families once lived north of the border.

One 2–3-pound chunk Canadian bacon
8–12 small new potatoes
1 small cabbage, cored, cut into wedges

12–15 tiny carrots
8–12 tiny white onions, peeled
Bay leaf
Freshly ground pepper

Put the Canadian bacon in a pot and cover it with water. Add the potatoes and bring to a boil. Simmer about 15 minutes, then add the cabbage wedges, carrots, and onions. Drop in a bay leaf and sprinkle with several turns of the pepper grinder. Continue to simmer 15–20 minutes longer, until the vegetables are tender but still somewhat crisp. Remove the meat and vegetables to a hot platter, and save the broth for a soup base.
SERVES 6–8

Back Bacon with Plums

3–4 pounds Canadian bacon, unsliced
1 cup dry red wine
½ pound plums
2 tablespoons butter

1 medium onion, chopped
1 orange
2 tablespoons red wine vinegar
¼ teaspoon ground cloves
2 tablespoons honey

Marinate the whole piece of bacon for about 1 hour in the wine. Halve the plums and remove the pits. Heat the butter in a flameproof dish over low heat, then stir in the onion and cook gently until soft. Grate the rind of the orange, and squeeze its juice into the baking dish. Stir in the plums, grated rind, vinegar, and cloves, and set the marinated piece of bacon on top. Spread the top of the bacon with honey, cover the dish, and place in a preheated 325-degree oven for about 2 hours, uncovering for the last 15 minutes of cooking. To serve, slice the bacon, arrange on a warm platter, and spoon the fruit and juices over.
SERVES 8–10

Sausages with Garlic and Herbs

2 pounds pork
¾ pound pork fat
1 tablespoon coarse salt, or 2 teaspoons table salt
3 fat garlic cloves, smashed, skins removed
⅛ teaspoon ground cloves
⅛ teaspoon ground ginger
⅛ teaspoon grated nutmeg
Generous amount freshly ground pepper

1 tablespoon minced Italian parsley
2 tablespoons chopped fresh rosemary, or 1 teaspoon dried, crushed; or 4 tablespoons chopped fresh sage, or 2 teaspoons dried, crumbled
¾ cup red wine
½ teaspoon saltpeter (optional)

Put the pork and the pork fat through the coarse blade of a meat grinder (a food processor won't do for this). Sprinkle in 2 teaspoons coarse salt (or 1½ teaspoons table salt). Mince the garlic thoroughly with a knife, and then work the remaining salt into it, continuing to mince and mash until you have almost a purée. Mix this thoroughly into the meat along with the spices, herbs, red wine, and saltpeter, if desired. If you want to try both the rosemary and sage accent, divide the mixture in 2 and mix half the amount of one herb into half the meat, and half the other herb into the other half of the meat. Stuff the meat mixture into casings (see box opposite), twist every 3 inches or so, and tie with white string (use different colors if you've used 2 herbs, so you can tell them apart). Hang the sausages from a rafter in a breezy place to dry out and ripen for at least 2 days before refrigerating.
MAKES 14 SAUSAGES

1 pound pork sausage patties (see
  box below)
1 pound tart apples
½ cup flour

1 teaspoon sugar
½ teaspoon freshly grated nutmeg
¼ teaspoon ground cinnamon
Hot rendered sausage fat

Pork Sausage Patties with Fried Apples

Fry the sausage patties slowly until cooked through, about 15 minutes, turning once; they should be nicely browned. Save the fat for frying the apples. Drain the patties on paper towels and keep warm. Core the apples but do not peel; cut into ½-inch slices. Combine the flour, sugar, and spices, and dust the apple slices well with this mixture. Fry in hot sausage fat over moderate heat until browned on both sides, about 5 minutes.
SERVES 4

Your Own Sausage

Sausage meat is a wonderful, old-fashioned thing, almost as easy to make as a seasoned hamburger, and much more fun. Flavored with fresh sage, it's a part of Yankee country life, and when hibernating in a Manhattan apartment, it is often a part of ours that seems to bring back summer. The list of sausage mixtures, each differently flavored, is almost endless, but it's enough to start by calling up the aromas of an ancestral New England breakfast. The nostalgia is conjured up by the combination of pork and sage.

> 4 pounds lean pork
> 1 pound fat pork
> 2 tablespoons finely chopped fresh sage leaves, or 2 teaspoons dried
> 1 tablespoon salt
> ⅛ teaspoon cayenne
> 2–3 teaspoons freshly ground black pepper

Grind the 2 porks together in a meat grinder, or use a food processor, turning it off and on in brief spurts to avoid transforming the meat into mush. Dry the fresh herb in the oven. Use your hands to mix in the herbs (a New Hampshire variation calls for the addition of ¼ ounce each of summer savory, marjoram and/or thyme) and other seasonings. (For an Italian-style garlic sausage, see page opposite.) To taste, make tiny patties of the mixture, and sauté until cooked through; adjust the seasoning to your liking. Form into cakes, or force into casings, which you may buy from the butcher. The casings should be well salted and kept in closed containers in the refrigerator. Soak them 1 hour, then wash them thoroughly by attaching them to the faucet and running water through them before filling them with sausage meat. In casings or patties, the sausages may be frozen for future use.

Chopped Ham Patties

1½ pounds chopped country ham
4 slices bread
Milk
½ cup ground peanuts
1 garlic clove, chopped fine
1 onion, chopped fine

1 egg, beaten
1 tablespoon chopped fresh basil,
    or 1 teaspoon dried
1 tablespoon chopped parsley
Vegetable oil

Put the chopped ham in a bowl, pour a little milk over the bread slices to dampen them well, then squeeze them and crumble into the ham. Stir in the nuts, garlic, onion, and the beaten egg, and mix well. Add the herbs and continue mixing; the ham should provide all the salt you need. Pat the mixture into thin patties about 3 inches in diameter. Heat the oil in a large skillet and fry the patties about 3 minutes, then turn over to brown the other side.

SERVES 4

Cabbage and Sausage Stew

2 onions, chopped
2 garlic cloves, minced
2 tablespoons olive or vegetable oil

1 small cabbage, finely shredded
1 pound chouriço sausage, sliced
3 cups beef broth

In a large saucepan, sauté the onions and garlic in the oil for about 5 minutes, stirring occasionally. Stir in the cabbage and the sausage, and add the broth. Simmer about 30 minutes, until the cabbage is cooked but not mushy. Neither salt nor pepper should be necessary.

SERVES 4

VEAL

In the first half of this century veal was considered poor man's meat by some cooks, but a hundred years or so later in New England there were many ways to prepare various cuts, such as a roast on the bone that might be extended by the addition of oysters in a cream- and egg-enriched white sauce, known as a *velouté*, made with fish stock.

Veal Roast with Oysters

3-pound leg of veal in 1 piece
2 garlic cloves, cut in half
1 tablespoon finely chopped fresh thyme, or 1½ teaspoons dried
2–3 tablespoons finely chopped fresh dill

Salt
Freshly ground pepper
Six 4-inch-long slices salt pork
¼ cup Madeira

OYSTER SAUCE:
1 pint oysters
About ½–¾ cup fish stock or diluted clam juice (half clam juice, half water)
2 tablespoons butter

3 tablespoons flour
½ cup heavy cream
2 egg yolks
Salt
Freshly ground pepper

Wipe the meat with a damp cloth and rub it with the cut side of the garlic. Mince the garlic halves and sprinkle it and the herbs over the surfaces of the roast, then salt lightly and grind fresh pepper over. Put the veal on a rack in a roasting pan and cover the top with slices of salt pork. Pour the Madeira over the meat. Roast the meat for 2 hours or more in a preheated 325-degree oven, until its interior temperature reaches 160 degrees. Baste the meat frequently with pan juices.

When the meat is done, let it rest on a hot platter while you make the sauce. Pour the pan juices off and strain them into a 2-cup measure; spoon the fat from the surface. Drain the oysters, and add that liquid to the cup and the fish stock or diluted clam juice to bring the liquid up to 1½ cups. Melt the butter in a small saucepan, stir in the flour, and let cook slowly a minute or so, stirring. Gradually whisk in the liquid from the measuring cup, return to the heat, and let the sauce come to a boil, whisking as it thickens. Stir in the oysters and let cook slowly 1 minute. Beat the cream and egg yolks together, add a little of the hot sauce to temper them, then pour the cream-yolk mixture into the sauce. Add salt and pepper to taste, and let the sauce come to a simmer, but don't let it boil. Pour the oyster sauce over the veal roast, and be sure to include a few oysters with each serving.

SERVES 6

Veal Braised in Port

Up country, it's not uncommon to buy a side of veal at a neighbor's farm, have it butchered, and stow it away in a freezer locker. One of our ways with such veal is this adaptation of a Massachusetts Portuguese recipe.

2½ pounds boned veal loin
Flour
4 tablespoons butter
2 tablespoons olive oil
Salt
Freshly ground pepper

1¼ cups port
1 tablespoon chopped fresh
   tarragon, or 1 teaspoon dried
1 cup sour cream, at room
   temperature (optional)

Dust the veal loin with flour. In a large iron skillet, melt the butter with the oil. Sear the meat on all its surfaces. Sprinkle it lightly with salt and pepper, and add 1 cup port. When the wine begins to boil, reduce the heat, and simmer uncovered about 10 minutes, turning once or twice. Add the remaining ¼ cup port and the tarragon. Cover the skillet and simmer for 25–30 minutes, or until the veal is thoroughly tender. A cup of sour cream may be blended into the port-accented meat juices after the veal is placed on a hot platter. Heat this sauce but do not allow it to boil. Serve with hot noodles.

SERVES 6–8

Braised Shoulder of Veal

A boned shoulder of veal, neatly tied for roasting, is not easy to come by, except perhaps in Italian neighborhoods. But if you have a side of veal in the freezer or spot an unboned shoulder in the meat section of the supermarket, it's well worth the trouble of boning and tying the meat into a roll (save the bone to make a veal broth). It makes a relatively inexpensive roast that is best braised slowly with vegetables to make it succulent and flavorful. It's worth planning to have some meat left over so that you can make one of the quick and easy dishes that uses cooked veal, such as Minced Veal with Mushrooms and Sour Cream (following recipe) or Pasta with Veal Strips, Red Peppers, and Artichoke Hearts (page 353).

1 tablespoon vegetable oil
1 veal shoulder, boned, rolled, and
　tied (about 3 pounds)
Salt
Freshly ground pepper
1 tablespoon butter
1 onion, chopped
2 garlic cloves, chopped

1 rib celery, chopped
1 medium carrot, scraped and
　chopped
½ teaspoon dried thyme
2 bay leaves
¼ cup dry vermouth or white wine
1 cup or more veal or chicken
　broth

Heat the oil in a heavy casserole and brown the veal on all sides. Remove the meat and season with salt and pepper. Melt the butter in the same casserole and sauté the vegetables, stirring, until glazed and just beginning to turn color. Return the veal to the casserole, sprinkle the thyme over, lay the bay leaves on top, and pour the wine and broth around. Bring to a simmer, then cover and place in a preheated 325-degree oven for 1½–2 hours or more, turning once, until very tender. Remove the bay leaves and the strings from the meat. Purée the pan juices and vegetables in a blender or scrape through a strainer; serve the hot sauce in a sauceboat.

SERVES 4, WITH LEFTOVERS; OR 6–8

2 tablespoons butter
6 ounces mushrooms, diced
4 shallots, or 1–2 small white
　onions, minced
About 1 cup cooked veal, cut into
　small dice
Salt

Freshly ground pepper
¼ cup sour cream, at room
　temperature
2 tablespoons plain yogurt, at room
　temperature
Dusting of paprika

Minced Veal with Mushrooms and Sour Cream

Heat the butter in a medium skillet and sauté the mushrooms and shallots or onions about 5 minutes, stirring occasionally. Add the veal, season with salt and pepper, and cook 1 minute. Stir in the sour cream and yogurt and heat through. Dust with paprika, and serve with rice.

SERVES 2

Veal Scallops with Dried and Fresh Mushrooms

You don't often see scallops of veal in New England markets, unless you are in an Italian neighborhood; but if you find a leg of veal and can cut slices off it, this and the following recipe are two good ways to prepare them.

8 thin slices veal cut from the leg
Salt
Freshly ground pepper
Flour for dredging
1 tablespoon vegetable oil
2 tablespoons olive oil
1/4 pound fresh mushrooms, sliced
4 scallions, mostly white part

1/4 cup dry white wine or vermouth
About 1 dozen dried mushrooms,
   such as Italian porcini,* soaked
   in 3/4 cup hot water for 30
   minutes
1 tablespoon chopped fresh
   tarragon or savory, or 1
   teaspoon dried

* Or if you are a knowledgeable mushroom gatherer and have dried some of your own, use them.

Pound the pieces of veal lightly to flatten them. Season both sides with salt and pepper to taste, then dredge them in flour, shaking off the excess (do this only just before they are to be cooked). Heat the vegetable oil and 1 tablespoon of the olive oil in a large skillet and sauté the meat very quickly on both sides—no more than 30 seconds per side. Remove to a warm plate. Add the remaining 1 tablespoon olive oil and sauté the fresh mushrooms with the scallions for 1 minute. Add the wine, dried mushrooms and their soaking liquid, and the herb, and cook over medium-high heat about a minute or so, until the liquid is reduced a little and the mushrooms are tender. Return the veal to the pan and heat through, correct the seasoning, and serve with the pan juices poured over the meat. Serve with rice or new potatoes on the side.

SERVES 4

Veal Strips in Sour Cream with Capers, Pickles, and Onions

12 small white onions
2 tablespoons butter
2 tablespoons vegetable oil
1 medium onion, chopped fine
2 pounds leg of veal, cut in strips
   approximately 1/4 x 1/8 x 2 inches
1 tablespoon sweet paprika
1/4 cup dry vermouth
3 tablespoons chopped parsley

Salt
Freshly ground pepper
1/4 cup chicken or veal broth
1 cup sour cream, at room
   temperature
2 tablespoons capers, drained
1/4 cup garlic dill pickles (page 627),
   or commercial dill pickles cut in
   strips

Drop the small onions into boiling water to cover and boil 1 minute. Scoop out with a slotted spoon, and peel when cool enough to handle. Cut a shallow cross in the root end of each, and return to the boiling water. Cook until just tender, about 15 minutes. Drain. In a fairly large skillet, heat the butter and oil, then add the drained onions, tossing until browned. Remove with a slotted spoon and set aside. Now add the chopped onion and sauté until translucent, about 5 minutes. Toss in the veal strips and paprika, and sear, tossing, over medium heat for 1 minute. Add the vermouth, parsley, and salt and pepper to taste, cook down slightly, and then pour in the broth. Cover and cook very gently about 5 minutes, until the veal is tender. Return the browned onions to the skillet, stir in the sour cream, capers, and pickle strips, and heat through (don't let it boil). Serve immediately with steamed new potatoes or noodles.

SERVES 6

Nantucket White Stew

In colonial times, New Englanders seem to have eaten veal more often than today—although milk-fed veal is produced locally now, frequently as a 4-H project. When good veal is at hand, the pale calf meat (using the least expensive cuts) is sometimes turned into a stew that makes up in flavor and subtlety what it lacks in color. A French-American might call this a *blanquette*.

3 pounds veal shoulder
1 quart water
Salt
1 large onion stuck with 2 cloves
2 medium carrots, scraped and chopped
1 rib celery, chopped
2 bay leaves
3 sprigs fresh thyme, or 1 teaspoon dried
2 sprigs fresh summer savory, or ½ teaspoon dried

12 peppercorns
12 mushroom caps, sliced
10–12 small white onions, peeled
2 tablespoons butter
2 tablespoons flour
2 egg yolks
Juice of ½ lemon
½ cup heavy cream or condensed milk
2 tablespoons chopped parsley

Remove the excess fat and cut the veal into 1½-inch cubes. Bring the water to a boil, add the veal pieces, and simmer. As scum forms on the surface, skim it off, then put in the onion stuck with cloves, the carrots, celery, bay leaves, thyme, savory, and peppercorns. Cover the stewpot and simmer at least 1 hour, or until the veal is tender.

In another pan, sauté the sliced mushrooms and the small onions in butter, stirring frequently to avoid browning. Stir in the flour and cook 1 minute, scraping from the bottom, then stir in 1 cup of the hot liquid from the veal stewpot and let simmer until the onions are tender. Beat the egg yolks with the lemon juice, add the cream and some of the hot veal stock, then gradually stir the egg mixture into the stew. Heat gently, stirring for about 4 minutes, until the egg mixture is smoothly incorporated—it must not boil. Remove the bay leaves from the stew, then add the mushrooms and the small onions and their sauce, and heat through. Sprinkle with chopped parsley.

SERVES 4–6

Scalloped Veal and Cucumbers

2 tablespoons vegetable oil
2 pounds stewing veal, cut into
    small pieces
2 medium onions, chopped
2 teaspoons paprika
Salt
Freshly ground pepper

1¼ cups water
1 bay leaf
1 teaspoon chopped fresh dill, or ¼
    teaspoon dried dill weed
2 medium cucumbers
½ tablespoon flour
½ cup heavy cream

GARNISH: 2 tablespoons chopped fresh herbs, such as parsley, dill, and
        chives
        Paprika for dusting

In a good-size heavy casserole, heat the oil, then toss in the veal and sauté over medium-high heat a couple of minutes, stirring. Add the onions and paprika, and cook, turning and tossing 2 or 3 minutes. Sprinkle lightly with salt, grind a few turns of the peppermill over the meat, add the water and herbs, cover, and simmer for 1–1½ hours, or until just tender (it will depend on how much time the veal needs). Meanwhile, peel the cucumbers, split them lengthwise, and scoop out the seeds. Split each half in half again lengthwise, then cut the pieces into 2-inch strips. Cook in boiling salted water 4 minutes, then drain thoroughly.

Make a paste of the flour by mixing it with 2 tablespoons cold water, then stir this into the veal. Mix well, cover, and cook a minute. Stir in the cream, bring to a boil, strew the cucumbers on top, and when heated through, sprinkle with fresh herbs and a touch more paprika.

SERVES 4

4 tablespoons vegetable oil or fat
3½–4 pounds veal stew meat, cut
   up, with bone if possible
½ cup cider vinegar
1 cup boiling water
½ teaspoon salt
Freshly ground pepper
Large sprig tarragon, or ½
   teaspoon dried
Sprig thyme, or ½ teaspoon dried

2 shallots
2 small white onions
4 medium potatoes, peeled and cut
   in quarters
1 cup carrots, scraped and cut in
   even-sized logs
½ cup freshly picked and shelled
   peas
2 tablespoons rum (optional)

Farm-Style Veal Stew

Heat the oil in a large stewpot and brown the veal on all surfaces, stirring almost constantly. Stir in the vinegar, boiling water, salt, a few turns of the pepper grinder, and herbs. Bring to a boil, lower the heat, and simmer about 45 minutes. Halve the shallots and the onions, and add them along with the potatoes and carrots. Stir, add a little water if necessary, and simmer 30 minutes more. Cool and refrigerate overnight.

Return the stew to the stove and reheat. Add the fresh peas and the rum, if desired, and cook just long enough to make the peas tender.

SERVES 6

2 tablespoons butter or vegetable
   oil or a combination
1½ pounds stewing veal, cut into
   pieces 1 inch or less
2 medium onions, chopped
½ cup dry white wine
1 tablespoon chopped fresh chervil,
   or ¼ teaspoon dried
Salt

Freshly ground pepper
¼–⅓ cup chicken or veal broth or
   water
⅓ cup heavy cream
About 3 cups cleaned fresh
   fiddlehead ferns (page 44), or
   about 10 ounces frozen
   fiddleheads, thawed

Fricasse of Veal with Fiddleheads

Heat the butter or oil in a heavy casserole and sauté the veal pieces lightly for a few minutes. Add the onions and continue to sauté, stirring, until they are translucent. Pour in the wine and when it comes to a boil, add the chervil, a little salt and pepper, and ¼ cup broth. Simmer, covered, very gently for about 50 minutes, or until the veal is tender. Check, and if more liquid is needed during the cooking, add a little more broth. When done, stir in the cream.

Meanwhile, cook the fiddleheads in 1 quart boiling salted water for 5 minutes, or until almost tender. Drain, mix gently into the veal, and simmer about 3–4 minutes more. Taste and correct the seasoning, if necessary. Serve with rice, orzo, or steamed new potatoes.

SERVES 4

Veal with Swiss Chard and Potatoes

2 tablespoons butter or vegetable oil
1½ pounds stewing veal, cut into 1-inch pieces
1 large onion, diced
2 garlic cloves, minced
2 cups water

Salt
Freshly ground pepper
4 small-medium new potatoes, peeled and quartered
½ pound Swiss chard, blanched in boiling water 2 minutes
A few drops of lemon juice

GARNISH: 1 lemon, quartered

Heat the butter or oil gently in a heavy casserole, turn the veal pieces in the fat but don't brown them. Add the onion, garlic, and water, then season lightly with salt and pepper. Cover and cook gently for 40 minutes, then add the potatoes, cover again, and cook gently 40 minutes more. Drain the Swiss chard and, if the leaves are very large, chop roughly (otherwise leave whole), and add to the casserole to cook, covered, for a final 10 minutes. Taste and correct the seasoning, adding a few drops of lemon juice to taste. Serve with lemon wedges on the side.
SERVES 4

Veal in Mild Chili Sauce

6 large mild dried Mexican chilies
1½ cups boiling water
2 tablespoons vegetable oil
2 pounds stewing veal, cut into fairly small pieces
2 medium onions, chopped
3–4 garlic cloves, minced

1½ cups chicken broth
2 teaspoons chopped fresh thyme, or ½ teaspoon dried
Salt
Freshly ground pepper
12 small white onions

Break off the stems and crack the pods of the chili peppers. Shake out most of the seeds and discard. Rinse the pods, and then soak them in the boiling water 30 minutes or longer (overnight is all right). Purée them with their soaking liquid in a blender or food processor. Heat the oil in a heavy casserole and sauté the veal pieces in 2 batches on all sides until they are lightly browned. Remove the meat and add the chopped onions; stir-fry for 2–3 minutes, then add the garlic and sauté 30 seconds more. Return the veal to the pan, add the broth and thyme, and salt and pepper lightly. Now put a strainer over the veal stewpot and force the chili purée through it, leaving the seeds and tough skins behind. Cover and simmer about 50 minutes. Add the small onions and simmer, covered, another 30–40 minutes, until the onions are tender. Serve with rice.
SERVES 4

In the recipe for stuffed veal breast that follows we leave the bones in, which makes messy eating. Nothing wrong with that for a family dinner, but to make a party dish out of veal breast, it's necessary to go to the trouble of removing the bones—a tiresome but not too difficult chore, if you have a sharp boning knife. Just carefully whittle out the bones without breaking through the meat. It is important to keep the meat on the bone side intact because it forms one wall of the natural pocket that will hold the stuffing. Because you can fill these pockets so generously with a deliciously savory stuffing, the meat goes a long way to feed a good number of hungry people, and the dish looks very festive.

Veal Breast Stuffed with Mushrooms and Pepper Kasha

THE STUFFING:

4 tablespoons butter
2 onions, chopped
1 garlic clove, minced
2 medium sweet red peppers, seeds and ribs removed, chopped, or 1 sweet red pepper and 1 yellow pepper, if available
¾ pound fresh mushrooms, chopped
½ ounce dried wild mushrooms, soaked in 1 cup hot water for 30 minutes

1½ recipe cooked kasha, cooked with meat broth for 15 minutes (page 375)
1 tablespoon chopped fresh basil, or 1 teaspoon dried
2 tablespoons chopped fresh mint, or 1½ teaspoons dried
Salt
Freshly ground pepper

2 sides veal ribs (about 6½–7 pounds), boned, with pocket opened up (see headnote)
4 bay leaves

2 medium onions, sliced
2 medium carrots, sliced
8 garlic cloves, peeled
2 or more cups water

To make the stuffing, heat the butter in a large skillet, add the onions, and sauté over gentle heat for 2 minutes. Add the garlic, peppers, and fresh mushrooms, as well as the drained wild mushrooms (reserving their soaking liquid), and continue cooking 1 minute, stirring. Mix the contents of the skillet with the kasha and stir in the herbs. Season generously with salt and pepper.

Spoon the stuffing into the 2 pockets in the veal breasts, filling them as full as possible, then sew the openings closed. Salt and pepper the stuffed veal breasts on both sides, and put them in one layer in a large oiled roasting pan. Lay the bay leaves on top, strew the vegetables around, then pour the mushroom-soaking liquid and 2 cups water around. Bring to a boil on top of the stove, cover lightly with foil, and braise in a preheated 325-degree oven for 2½ hours, basting from time to time and adding more water as necessary—there should always be at least ¼ inch liquid in the pan. Uncover the meat for the last 15 minutes of cooking. Let rest on a warm platter while you make the sauce.

Veal Breast Stuffed with Mushrooms and Pepper Kasha (continued)

Drain the juices in the roasting pan into the bowl of a blender or food processor (or you can sieve them); add a little boiling water to the pan and scrape up all browned bits to include in the sauce. Before serving, remove the stitches and the bay leaves, coat the top of the meat with a little sauce and serve the rest alongside in a sauceboat. Slice lengthwise, so that each serving has a helping of the kasha stuffing surrounded by the meat.

SERVES 10

Ham-Stuffed Veal Breast

THE STUFFING:
3 ounces veal
3 ounces ham
1 medium onion
1 cup fresh bread crumbs
2 tablespoons chopped fresh herbs, such as parsley and thyme or rosemary (use half the amount if herbs are dried)
Salt

Freshly ground pepper
3 tablespoons vegetable oil or half vegetable and half olive oil
1 garlic clove, smashed, peel removed
½ pound Swiss chard, roughly chopped
About ½ cup water

1 breast of veal (about 3–3½ pounds), with pocket
4 garlic cloves, peeled
1 large onion, chopped
1 small carrot, scraped and chopped

1 cup water
Salt
Freshly ground pepper
2 bay leaves

To prepare the stuffing, finely chop the veal, ham, and onion in a food processor (or put through a meat grinder). Mix together with the bread crumbs, herbs, and salt and pepper to taste. Heat the oil in a skillet, add the garlic and the chopped Swiss chard, tossing and stirring. Add the water, cover, and let steam-cook slowly for 10 minutes, until the water is absorbed and the chard is just tender. Add to the other stuffing ingredients and, if you are using a food processor, spin together quickly. Stuff this mixture into the veal breast pocket, pressing it in securely (you won't need to sew up the opening).

Film with oil the bottom of a heavy casserole or deep skillet large enough to accommodate the veal and brown the veal on both sides. Add the garlic cloves, onion, carrot, and water, season with salt and pepper, strew bay leaves on top, cover, and cook gently about 2–2½ hours, depending on the age and tenderness of the veal.

Remove the veal and let rest 5 minutes before slicing. Remove the bay leaves, then mash the pan vegetables and cooking juices to serve as a sauce or blend in the food processor, adding a little hot water if the liquid is too reduced; be sure to scrape up all the brown bits from the pan.
SERVES 4

Veal Chops with Yogurt and Fresh Coriander Sauce

If you like the slightly musty taste of fresh coriander, try growing it in your garden or even in a window box. It is not always available in supermarkets or green markets as an herb, although the seeds have seasoned pickles for many generations. You'll find fresh coriander, however, being used more often these days by creative cooks in the Northeast. Be warned that once you've tasted it, you can easily become addicted. Here it makes a delicate green-flecked sauce when combined with yogurt and veal pan juices. Try serving the sauced chops surrounded by Pumpkin Timbales (page 307) interspersed with bright green florets of lightly cooked broccoli for color.

2 tablespoons vegetable oil
4 veal chops (about ¾ inch thick)
Salt
Freshly ground pepper
3 tablespoons chopped shallots or
   scallion bulbs

¾ cup plain yogurt, at room
   temperature
¼ cup chopped fresh coriander

Heat the oil in a large skillet and brown the veal chops on both sides. Season all over with salt and pepper, and scatter the shallots around. Cover and cook over low heat, turning once. Mix the yogurt and coriander together, and stir it into the pan, spooning some of the sauce over the veal. Heat just enough to warm the sauce through.
SERVES 4

Braised Veal Shanks

The Italians would serve this dish with *gremolada*—a mixture of lemon rind, parsley, and garlic to be passed around and sprinkled on top of the steaming aromatic veal shanks. Be sure to scoop out the marrow from the bone—that's the most delectable part of the dish.

2 veal shanks, cut into 2-inch pieces across the bone
3 tablespoons vegetable oil
2 onions, chopped
1 carrot, scraped and chopped
½ cup dry white wine or vermouth
1 sprig oregano (8–10 leaves), or ½ teaspoon dried

1 cup peeled, seeded, and chopped tomatoes
1 cup chicken broth
Salt
Freshly ground pepper

GREMOLADA (optional)
1 teaspoon minced garlic
1 tablespoon finely chopped lemon rind (pith removed)

2 tablespoons finely chopped flat-leaved parsley

In a heavy casserole, brown the veal shanks in the oil on all sides. Add the onions and carrot and cook 1 minute, stirring them in the oil. Add the wine, bring to a boil, and stir in the oregano, tomatoes, and chicken broth. Season lightly with salt and pepper, reduce the heat to a simmer, cover, and cook gently for 1½ hours. If the sauce seems too liquid, remove the shanks when tender and boil down the juices rapidly to reduce, then return the shanks to the casserole. Mix the *gremolada* ingredients together, and pass in a small bowl at the table.
SERVES 4

Garlic-Flavored Veal Balls

1½ pounds ground veal
¾ cup dry bread crumbs
3 eggs
3 tablespoons chopped parsley
4 garlic cloves, finely minced
½ teaspoon salt
Freshly ground pepper

Juice of 2 lemons
¼ cup grated Crowley cheese
Vegetable oil
2–3 cups chicken broth
1 pound pasta, such as orzo or small shells, or 1½ cups rice

Put the ground veal in a large bowl, add the bread crumbs, eggs, parsley, garlic, salt, several turns of the pepper grinder, the lemon juice, and grated cheese; mix thoroughly with your fingers. Put enough oil in a heavy skillet to cover the surface by about ⅛ inch. Shape the veal mixture into Ping-Pong-size balls, handling them very lightly. Sauté the meatballs, a batch at a time, in the oil, rolling them around to brown all over for about 6 minutes. As the balls become slightly crusty, lift them onto paper towels, and pat them free of excess oil. Add oil as needed to sauté all the meatballs. Put the cooked balls in a shallow ovenproof baking dish, cover with plastic wrap, and chill in the refrigerator.

To finish cooking, heat the chicken broth, and when it begins to boil, add the veal balls and simmer for about 5 minutes, or until they are heated through. Cook the pasta or rice, and spoon the meatballs on top with enough of the stock to make a thin sauce.

SERVES 4–6

Sweet-and-Sour Veal Riblets

Here's a dish with the mystery of green tomatoes. After making this, or other green tomato recipes (see index)—if you still have tomatoes that haven't ripened—try wrapping them in tissues or paper towels and setting them aside in a dark place. In a few days they will begin to turn yellow on the outside and, finally, almost as red as the sun-ripened fruit.

3–3½ pounds breast of veal
1½ tablespoons flour
3–4 tablespoons vegetable oil
1 large onion, chopped
1 cup, coarsely chopped green tomatoes
1 cup veal stock or chicken or beef stock
½ cup raisins
Juice of ½ lemon
¼ cup cider vinegar
2½ tablespoons sugar
1 tablespoon honey
1½ teaspoons grated ginger
½ teaspoon cinnamon
2 teaspoons dried rosemary
Salt
Freshly ground pepper
2 tablespoons tomato paste

Cut apart the riblets, which should be no more than 4 inches long, then dredge them in the flour. Brown the riblets in 2 tablespoons of the oil, remove them from the pan, and keep warm. In the remaining oil, cook the onion gently for about 10 minutes. Stir in the chopped green tomatoes with the stock, raisins, lemon juice, and cider vinegar. When this mixture is bubbling, stir in the sugar, honey, grated ginger, cinnamon, and rosemary. Add about 1 teaspoon salt and freshly ground pepper to taste, and the tomato paste. Put the riblets in a casserole, pour the green tomato mixture over them, cover, and bake in a preheated 325-degree oven for 2 hours.

SERVES 4

Mustard-Coated Fried Brains

About 1½ pounds calves' brains
(4 pieces)
Juice of 1 lemon
Salt
Freshly ground pepper

⅓ cup Dijon-type mustard
1 egg, lightly beaten
2 cups fresh bread crumbs
Oil for frying

GARNISH: 1 lemon, quartered

Soak the brains in cold water for 1 hour, changing the water occasionally or letting the faucet run slowly. Carefully remove the membrane and red strands, then place the brains in a saucepan with enough water to cover by 1 inch. Season with the lemon juice and about ½ teaspoon salt. Bring just to a boil, reduce heat, and simmer very gently for 20 minutes. Remove immediately and plunge the brains into cold water. Refrigerate for 30 minutes or longer, even overnight, with a plate on top as a weight.

Salt and pepper the brains and smear mustard liberally on both sides. Start heating enough oil in a large skillet to cover the bottom by ½ inch. Dip the brains into the egg, then roll in the bread crumbs. When the oil is hot enough so that a crumb sizzles in it and browns quickly, transfer the brains carefully to the skillet and fry over medium-high heat about 2 minutes on each side. Serve immediately, garnished with lemon quarters.

SERVES 4

Creamed Calves' Brains

In her *Woman's Home Companion* monthly column, Fannie Farmer offered guidance on such subjects as how to cook meats properly, and in her book *What to Have for Dinner,* she included menus suggesting, among other ideas, calves' brains accompanied by Swedish timbales, which were deep-fried dumplings flavored with beer. The texture of these delicately creamed brains is improved by something crunchy as contrast, and we like to serve them over crisp toast or in a flaky pastry shell. Leftover brains are also good when combined with a little bit of diced chicken or ham and/or lightly sautéed mushrooms, then used as a stuffing for thin cornmeal pancakes (page 454).

2 pounds calves' brains, prepared
as in the first paragraph of
preceding recipe
3 tablespoons fresh lemon juice
2 tablespoons butter
2 tablespoons flour
½ cup chicken broth

½ cup milk
Salt
A few gratings fresh nutmeg
Cayenne
2 egg yolks
¼ cup heavy cream
1 tablespoon minced parsley

Prepare the brains as in the first paragraph of the preceding recipe.

Heat the butter in a small saucepan, then stir in the flour and cook over low heat, stirring, for 2–3 minutes. Off heat add the broth and milk, then return to the heat and whisk until thickened. Season to taste with salt, nutmeg, and cayenne. Whisk the egg yolks together with the cream and a little of the hot cream sauce, then whisk the egg mixture into the hot sauce and heat through (don't let it boil). Cut the brains into dice, and fold them into the sauce with the remaining 1 tablespoon lemon juice. Bring just to the simmer, stirring once or twice very gently, and when heated through spoon the creamed brains over hot toast or rice or into warm pastry shells. Sprinkle minced parsley on top.

SERVES 4

Braised Sweetbreads with Honey Mushrooms

Some honey mushrooms brought to us one warm October so enhanced the delicate flavor of the sweetbreads we were cooking that we strongly recommend finding access to wild mushrooms in order to try this dish. (You can use only cultivated mushrooms, or a combination of store-bought mushrooms and a dried wild variety that you soak in warm water for 30 minutes before adding them to the sauce.)

2 pounds sweetbreads
2 tablespoons fresh lemon juice
Salt
Flour for dredging
4 tablespoons butter
4 shallots, or 1 small white onion, chopped fine
1/4 cup dry sherry

1 1/2 cups chicken broth
2 tablespoons chopped fresh tarragon, or 1/2 teaspoon dried
Freshly ground pepper
About 12 large honey mushrooms or chanterelles, or 1/4 pound cultivated mushrooms, quartered

Prepare, trim and cook the sweetbreads as in the recipe at the top of page 266. Break into bite-size pieces.

When you are ready to proceed with the braising—and only then—dredge the sweetbreads in flour, shake off the excess, and drop them into a large skillet in which the butter is sizzling. Stir and toss to brown slightly, then add the shallots and brown another 30 seconds. Pour in the sherry, boil for a few seconds, scraping any bits from the bottom of the pan, then add the broth and the tarragon, and season lightly with salt and pepper. Cover and simmer very gently for about 35 minutes, until tender. Toss in the mushrooms and cook another 3–4 minutes.

SERVES 4

Braised Sweetbreads

1¾–2 pounds sweetbreads
Salt
3 tablespoons butter
1 large onion, chopped
1 carrot, scraped and chopped
1 rib celery, strings removed, chopped
Freshly ground pepper
Flour for dredging
1 cup strong veal, beef, or chicken broth
3 tablespoons Madeira
2 tablespoons parsley

Soak the sweetbreads in ice water for about 1 hour, then put them in a saucepan with ½ teaspoon salt and water to cover; bring to a boil, reduce heat, and simmer 20 minutes. Drain, plunge into cold water, then carefully remove the membranes. Cut them in slices and sauté the onion, carrot, and celery until tender. Salt and pepper the sweetbread slices, then dredge them in flour, shaking off the excess. Add them to the skillet and cook over moderate heat, turning, until golden. Add the broth and Madeira, cover, and simmer very gently for 40 minutes. Correct the seasoning, and sprinkle chopped parsley on top.
SERVES 4

RABBIT

Rabbit in a Sweet-and-Sour Sauce

3 tablespoons butter
1 rabbit (about 2½–3 pounds) cut into 8 pieces (use lean backbone and ribs for stock)
1 large onion, sliced
2 ounces ham, chopped
1 tablespoon sugar
6 tablespoons cider vinegar
¼ cup red wine
1¼ cups rabbit stock*
Salt
Freshly ground pepper
2 teaspoons chopped fresh rosemary, or ½ teaspoon dried
1 tablespoon grated or shaved bitter chocolate
3 tablespoons raisins
3 tablespoons slivered almonds

* To make the stock, simmer the lean backbone and ribs in about 2 cups water with 1 small onion and a few parsley sprigs for about 40 minutes; then season to taste with salt and pepper.

Melt the butter in a large skillet, add the rabbit pieces, the sliced onion, and the ham. Sauté gently for about 5 minutes, then turn the rabbit and continue to sauté for another 5 minutes.

Dissolve the sugar in the vinegar, and add it to the skillet along with the wine and rabbit stock. Salt and pepper well, and sprinkle on rosemary. Transfer everything to a shallow earthenware dish or a similar vessel, and bake, uncovered, about 50 minutes in a preheated 350-degree oven. Ten minutes before the cooking time is up, spread the grated chocolate, raisins, and almonds over and around the rabbit pieces, and return the dish to the oven for 10 minutes. When the rabbit is ready, if the sauce seems too thin, remove the rabbit and boil down the juices in the dish, then return the meat to the dish and bring it to the table.

SERVES 4

Hasenpfeffer

It may have been a Hessian soldier staying on in New England after the American Revolutionary War who helped make hasenpfeffer a part of the American culinary scene; at any rate, it's still a noted Yankee dish and is served at the Lyme Inn in New Hampshire.

2 rabbits (2½–3 pounds each), cut
  up
2 cups red wine
1 cup water
½ cup red wine or cider vinegar
1 tablespoon fresh lemon juice
12 peppercorns
4 garlic cloves, peeled
½ teaspoon chopped fresh thyme or
  dried
½ teaspoon chopped fresh
  rosemary, or dried, crumbled

1 teaspoon chopped fresh
  marjoram, or ½ teaspoon dried
1 cup roughly chopped celery
  leaves
4 slices bacon, cut in squares
1½ cups chopped onions
1 cup quartered mushrooms
3–4 tablespoons butter
Salt
½ cup flour
½ cup sour cream

Two days ahead of time, marinate the rabbit pieces in a mixture of the wine, water, vinegar, lemon juice, peppercorns, garlic, herbs, and celery leaves.

Cook the bacon to release a little fat, then add the onions and mushrooms to the pan, stirring, for 2–3 minutes. Remove with a slotted spoon and reserve. Heat the butter in the same pan. Remove the rabbit from the marinade and pat each piece dry. Sprinkle a liberal amount of salt over the rabbit, and dip the pieces in the flour, then fry them in the sizzling butter (do this in several batches), removing the pieces when they are browned). When all of the rabbit is browned, return the pieces to the pan along with the onion-bacon-mushroom mixture, and strain the marinade over all. Cover the pan and simmer about 1 hour, or until tender. Lift the rabbit pieces out onto a hot platter. Stir a little salt into the sour cream, and heat it in the pan with the vegetables and cooking juices, mixing well. Correct the seasoning, if necessary, and pour this sauce over the rabbit.

SERVES 8

Marguerite Buonopane's Rabbit Cacciatore

1 small rabbit (about 3 pounds), cut into small pieces
3 ripe tomatoes, blanched
3 medium onions, sliced lengthwise
2 large green peppers, seeds and ribs removed, sliced lengthwise
2 tablespoons or more olive oil
½ pound mushrooms, cut into chunks

6 garlic cloves, chopped
Salt
Freshly ground pepper
½ teaspoon dried hot red pepper flakes, or to taste
1 teaspoon chopped fresh rosemary or oregano, or ½ teaspoon dried
1 cup fresh peas or frozen, thawed

Wash the rabbit well and soak in cold water 2–3 hours. Skin the tomatoes and chop them in coarse pieces. Sauté the onions and peppers in the oil until tender, and transfer them to a bowl. Sauté the mushrooms and half the garlic 2–3 minutes, tossing, and add them to the bowl. Now sauté the rabbit pieces, adding a little more oil if necessary, sprinkle on the remaining garlic and salt and pepper. When the meat is browned on all sides, stir the tomatoes into the pan and cover; let it boil down rapidly to dry out the juices. Add the pepper flakes, a little more salt and pepper, and rosemary or oregano. After 20 minutes, remove the cover and stir in the peppers and onions, mushrooms, and peas. Cook just long enough, partially covered, to make the peas tender, then remove from the heat and let rest for 10 minutes to combine the flavors. Serve hot with steamed potatoes or rice.
SERVES 4

Brunswick Stew

This is a good way to cook older rabbits—5–6 pounds or so.

Flour for dredging
Salt
Freshly ground pepper
1 teaspoon dried marjoram
1 dried sprig savory
One 5–6-pound rabbit, cut in pieces
4 slices bacon, cut in squares
1 onion, chopped
8 cups boiling water

1 bay leaf
2 cups canned tomatoes
1 onion, sliced
3 potatoes, peeled and quartered
2 cups fresh shelled lima beans or frozen lima beans, thawed
3–4 cups corn kernels
½ teaspoon dried hot red pepper flakes

Season the flour with salt and pepper and the herbs. Dredge the rabbit pieces in the seasoned flour. Fry the bacon in a large stewpot for 2–3 minutes. Remove the bacon, drain on paper towels, and set aside. Brown the rabbit pieces in the bacon fat, a few at a time, removing when browned. When all the meat is browned, sauté the chopped onion in the remaining fat until lightly browned. Return the rabbit to the pan and pour the boiling water over; add the bay leaf, cover, and cook gently for 2 hours. Stir in the tomatoes, sliced onion, and the quartered potatoes, and cook about 10 minutes more. Add the lima beans and corn, sprinkle on the red pepper flakes, and cook about 10–15 minutes, or until all the vegetables are tender and the meat pulls away from the bone easily. Correct the seasoning, remove the bay leaf, and crumble the reserved bacon over the top.

SERVES 6

GAME

Salmagundis or Salmis of Game (or Other Cooked Meat)

A symbolic indication of the way food is changing came to us one night at dinner in the restaurant of the New England Culinary Institute in Montpelier. The entrée called Salmagundi consisted of 2 halves of quail embellished by a classic kind of sauce. If you have no quail at hand, try this sauce for leftover duck, lamb, beef, or game.

2 tablespoons chopped shallots
1/3 cup (5 tablespoons) butter
3 tablespoons flour
3/4 cup New Hampshire Foch red
　wine or other dry red wine
1 tablespoon lemon juice
2 tablespoons orange juice

One 3-inch strip orange rind
1 cup stock*
Salt
Cayenne
About 1/2–3/4 pound sliced cooked
　game or meat

GARNISH: *chopped parsley*

* For stock, see box on page 69, using bones and trimmings of whatever game meat you are using; if not available, canned beef bouillon may be substituted.

Cook the chopped shallots in the butter until wilted. Stir in the flour and cook gently about 3 minutes, stirring, then add the wine, lemon and orange juices, the strip of rind, and stock made from the trimmings of the meat to be dressed. Sprinkle lightly with salt and a little cayenne, and boil for about 1 minute. Add the meat slices and heat through. Arrange the slices with the sauce on a hot platter, and sprinkle parsley on top.

SERVES 4

Venison Stew

2 pounds venison stew meat
2–3 tablespoons lard or vegetable oil
4 cups sliced onions
4 garlic cloves, roughly chopped
Salt
Freshly ground pepper
¾ cup beef broth
2 cups beer
1½ tablespoons brown sugar
1 bay leaf
2–3 sprigs thyme, or ½ teaspoon dried
3–4 sprigs parsley
1 tablespoon cornstarch
1½ tablespoons cider vinegar

Sauté the venison in a skillet with 2 tablespoons of the lard or vegetable oil until browned on all sides. Do this in a couple of batches so that it browns well. Remove with a slotted spoon to a casserole dish. Add a little more fat if necessary to the skillet and brown the onions. Add them to the casserole along with the garlic and season lightly with salt and pepper. Put the beef broth in the skillet and bring to a boil, scraping up any brown bits. Pour this and the beer into the casserole. Stir in the brown sugar and herbs. Place in a 325-degree oven and cook slowly, covered, for 1½–2 hours, or until tender. Mix the cornstarch with the vinegar and stir that into the bubbling stew sauce. Remove the bay leaf and herb sprigs, and serve with boiled potatoes or noodles.

SERVES 4–6

Venison Shanks

4 foreshanks
6–8 juniper berries
Salt
Freshly ground pepper
1 teaspoon nutmeg
2 tablespoons cooking oil
1 onion, sliced
4 carrots, sliced
1 large celery root, sliced
1 teaspoon Dijon mustard
Bay leaf
½ teaspoon thyme
1 teaspoon grated lemon rind
2 cloves
1 cup chicken broth
½ cup red wine
1 pint sour cream
1 tablespoon capers

Be sure all the fell is removed from the shanks. Crush the juniper berries, and mix with salt, pepper, and nutmeg, then rub the meat with this mixture. Heat the oil in skillet and brown the shanks lightly but thoroughly; add the sliced vegetables and sauté 5 minutes. Add mustard, bay leaf, thyme, grated lemon, cloves, and broth. Bring to a simmer, cover, and bake 1½–2 hours. When the meat is tender, slice it and keep it hot on a platter. Stir the wine into vegetable sauce and add sour cream, mixing until smooth. Pour the sauce over the meat, and sprinkle the capers on top. Serve with buttered noodles and cooked cranberries.

SERVES 4

1 pound very fresh venison liver
Salt
Freshly ground pepper

Flour
2–3 tablespoons butter
2–3 tablespoons minced onion

GARNISH: 1 tablespoon finely chopped parsley
            Lemon wedges

Sautéed Strips of Venison Liver

Skin the liver, cut into thin slices, trimming out the membranes, then cut into ½-inch strips. Sprinkle very lightly with salt and a few turns of the pepper grinder, then with a little flour. Heat the butter in a heavy skillet, add the minced onion, and let it cook gently just long enough to release the flavor. Drop in the liver strips and sauté over brisk heat a minute or so on each side. Be careful not to overcook. Arrange on hot plates with a sprinkling of chopped parsley and lemon wedges.
SERVES 4

Deerburgers in Tomato Sauce

In central Kennebec County during Christmas, a long-standing tradition has been the gathering of Maine game wardens and their families for a game supper. Among hostess Judy Marsh's favorite recipes is one for meatballs that mix venison and pork or pork sausage.

1 pound ground venison
½ pound ground fatty pork or
    sausage
40 common crackers, crushed

1 egg
Salt
Freshly ground pepper
About 1 tablespoon vegetable oil

SAUCE:
1 tablespoon butter
2 medium onions, chopped
2 ribs celery, chopped
2½ cups tomato juice
5 peppercorns
1 tablespoon fresh lemon juice

½ teaspoon celery seed
1 bay leaf
1 garlic clove, chopped fine
1 tablespoon sugar
2 tablespoons chopped parsley

Mix the ground venison with the pork or sausage, and stir in the crushed cracker crumbs, egg, and a generous amount of salt and pepper. Form the meat into small balls, and brown them in a heavy pan with a thin coating of oil.

To make the sauce, heat the butter in a saucepan and brown the onions. Add a sprinkling of salt and stir in the celery, tomato juice, peppercorns, lemon juice, celery seed, bay leaf, garlic, sugar, and parsley. Simmer for about 15 minutes, then pour the sauce over the meatballs and simmer very gently, covered, for about 2 hours. Remove the bay leaf before serving.
SERVES 4

Bear Fillet in Burgundy

6 cups dry white wine
1 fillet of bear (6–7 pounds)
4 ounces larding pork
5 juniper berries
Salt
6–8 medium onions, peeled

3–4 large parsnips, peeled
12 medium carrots, scraped
1 cup sliced celery
6 cups burgundy
2 cups beef stock

MARINADE:

4 cups mixed chopped onions and
  shallots
1½ cups chopped carrots
2 garlic cloves, minced

⅔ cup chopped celery
2 bay leaves
1 teaspoon tarragon

Mix together the ingredients for the marinade. Handle the well-hung bear meat gently, carefully cutting out all sinews and nerves, and marinate it in a cool place for 3–4 days.

When preparing to cook, pat the meat dry with paper towels and lard well with the pork fat. Pound the juniper berries into tiny fragments and firmly rub into the meat; salt well. Place the fillet in an ample roasting pan, and surround it with the vegetables. Pour the wine and stock over all, and put in a preheated 325-degree oven, uncovered. Cook, basting frequently, for 3½–4 hours, or until the center of roast does not bleed when pierced with a two-tined fork. Remove the meat and keep warm. Lift out the vegetables and blend to coarse pulp, using the food processor or blender, or put through a strainer or food mill. Boil the juices in the pan hard to reduce wine sauce to about 1½ cups, then add the vegetable puree, stir, and serve as gravy. Serve the roast with sauerkraut and mashed potatoes.
SERVES 10–12

PEAS
LETTUCE
TOMATOES
RHUBARB
SQUASH
SHALLOTS
FRESH DILL
BEETS
PARSLEY
HONEY

VEGETABLES

PEAS
LETTUCE
TOMATOES
RHUBARB
SQUASH
SHALLOTS
FRESH DILL
BEETS
PARSLEY
HONEY

VEGETABLES

IT'S NOT SO LONG since old Yankees considered a dining table improperly set if there weren't small individual side dishes, known by some as "bird baths," to hold the "garden sass" (a term brought over from Great Britain), one for each person at the table, while the dinner plates were reserved for meat and potatoes only. It was a time of overcooking, of drenching vegetables in slippery white gravy that made the fresh produce of the garden into a sort of sauce. Early New Englanders never served a full meal without their "garden sass."

What a lot of pride there used to be in this kind of cooking. "A stringbean, bare, by itself, is a mistake, a sad one," Robert P. Tristram Coffin of Maine wrote. "But put a half a pound of sow's belly in with about three times that weight in pole-beans, and you have something the angels will fight over. The salt pork brings out the flavors the string-beans never knew they had!"

There are virtually no strings to beans anymore, and it's a rare cook who considers it a mistake to prepare any vegetable as simply as possible—"bare by itself." We believe in cooking the produce of our gardens for as little time as it takes to lock in their individual flavors. When ham or bacon (or even salt pork) is in order, the meat serves as an accent, and vegetable sauces are admired for the contrast that enhances, rather than for any overwhelming added flavor.

In our own small New England garden, struggling toward harvestime in Northern Vermont's brief growing season, there are always rows of beans and peas, of zucchini and other kinds of squash; tomatoes, and cucumbers, carrots, parsnips, and corn, and small, thin-skinned potatoes, plus some less common vegetables such as kohlrabi, rhubarb chard, leeks, and collards. Lettuces take up nearly one-third of the garden area, and the herbs grow, more conveniently, nearer the kitchen door. Like anyone else who deals with Yankee summers, we have to work hard to live off the land as much as we can. (We've even made promises to succeed in growing salsify, despite the regional inhibitions.)

We haven't included here recipes for simple boiling or steaming of such vegetables, but have concentrated instead on new ways of cooking them in combinations, sometimes mating the fruits of the garden with the wild edibles we harvest. There is many a recipe in this section to please a vegetarian palate.

Grilled Asparagus

Credit has been given to Diederick Leertower, Esq., of Worcester County, Massachusetts, for bringing in asparagus from Holland, but the eighteenth-century cooks he knew did very little with the spiky vegetable except boil it and serve it with butter on the side for dipping (asparagus spears were eaten with the fingers—and still should be). There's nothing wrong with that traditional way of preparing asparagus, but below is a method that gives asparagus a different texture and an intensity of flavor. This is how it's done at Al Forno, a restaurant in a class by itself in Providence, Rhode Island. To make a light luncheon dish, top each serving of asparagus with a poached or fried egg, and sprinkle with freshly grated Parmesan.

½ pound trimmed asparagus per person

Virgin olive oil for brushing
Salt

GARNISH: *lemon wedges*

Prepare a medium-hot charcoal fire. Brush the asparagus on all sides with virgin olive oil. Place on the grill approximately 5–6 inches from the source of heat. With tongs, keep rotating the asparagus spears, basting as needed until they are cooked through but still firm. Salt to taste, and serve with lemon wedges.

VARIATION: Prepare fiddleheads in the same way. Use 4–6 ounces fiddleheads per person, cleaned according to the directions on page 44.

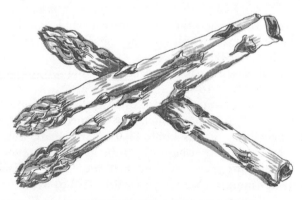

This is a good way to use up those older, larger beans that one misses when picking in the height of the bean season.

Cut Green Beans in Rosemary

1 pound mature green beans
3 tablespoons butter
3 scallions, including tender greens, chopped
1 tablespoon chopped fresh rosemary, or 1 teaspoon dried, crumbled

2 teaspoons cider vinegar
Salt
Freshly ground pepper

Break off the stem ends of the beans and cook whole in rapidly boiling lightly salted water until just tender, about 8–10 minutes. Drain, and cut into ¼-inch slices. Heat the butter in a heavy saucepan, sauté the scallions a few seconds, then add the rosemary and the beans. Stir and toss 1 minute, add the vinegar, and season to taste with salt and pepper.
SERVES 4

Puréed Snap Beans

¾ pound green or snap beans
2 large scallions, chopped
2–3 tablespoons chopped celery leaves
Salt
Freshly ground pepper

½ teaspoon curry powder
2–3 tablespoons dry sherry
2 tablespoons butter
Heavy cream (optional)

Cook the beans in water to cover for about 20 minutes, until tender. Put them in the food processor or blender with the scallions, celery leaves, a little salt and freshly ground pepper to taste, the curry, and the sherry. Scrape the purée into a saucepan with the butter and simmer about 5 minutes. Add a little heavy cream, if you choose, and serve very hot.
SERVES 3–4

Fresh Shell Beans

The term *shell beans* is more common in New England than elsewhere and is an accurate description of beans that have matured in the pod, thus needing to be shelled like common peas. To prepare them, pull down the string and squeeze the pod either at one end or between the seeds, in effect popping the pod open; split the seam and push the beans out. In this recipe, dried beans that are not too old may be substituted.

Fresh Shell Beans (continued)
3 cups shell beans
4 tablespoons (¼ cup) olive oil
2 tablespoons fresh lemon juice
Salt
Freshly ground pepper

2 tablespoons finely chopped chives
1 tablespoon chopped parsley
1 tablespoon finely chopped
  summer savory, or ½ teaspoon
  dried savory or thyme

Drop the beans into boiling water, cover, and boil gently for about 20 minutes, until just tender. The time depends on the maturity of the beans, so check frequently for tenderness. Drain and toss the hot beans with the olive oil, lemon juice, a little salt to taste, a turn or two of the pepper grinder, and the herbs.
SERVES 4

Baked Beets

A recipe from the early 1700s.

6 medium beets
1 tablespoon softened butter
Salt

Freshly ground pepper
½ cup cider vinegar

Trim the beets, leaving some of the stalk intact so they won't bleed. Put in a baking dish with a little water in the bottom or wrap them in foil and bake in a preheated 400-degree oven for about 50 minutes—a little longer for the foil-wrapped beets. Pierce them with a fork to see if they are tender. When cool enough to handle, remove the skins, and slice the beets. Toss them in butter, salt and pepper to taste, and vinegar. Serve hot.
SERVES 4

Braised Savoy Cabbage

3 tablespoons butter or vegetable
  oil or a combination
1 small onion, chopped fine
1 small carrot, scraped and
  chopped fine

1 medium head savoy cabbage
  (about 1 pound), shredded
Salt
Freshly ground pepper
½ cup chicken broth

Heat the butter and/or oil in a heavy skillet or wok and sauté the onion and carrot, stirring and tossing, for 1 minute. Rinse the shredded cabbage, and add it to the pan with the water that clings to it. Sprinkle on salt and pepper to taste, add the broth, and cook gently, covered, about 7–8 minutes, until just tender.
SERVES 4

When French-Americans we know call this dish *choux rouge aux raisins*, it seems to sound better to some New Englanders, but it's a plain, simple, and delicious way to serve cabbage in either language.

Red Cabbage with Raisins

1 head red cabbage, finely shredded
2 cups hot water
2 tablespoons butter
¾ teaspoon salt

Freshly ground pepper
Juice of ½ lemon
½ cup raisins

Put the shredded cabbage in a pot and cover it with the hot water. Add the butter, salt, and a sprinkling of pepper and bring the liquid to a boil. Add the lemon juice and raisins, cover, reduce heat, and simmer over low heat about 40 minutes. Remove the cover and boil hard to reduce the liquid.
SERVES 4–6

Cabbage in Cider

1½ pounds red or white cabbage
2 tablespoons butter
2 tablespoons sugar
Juice of ½ lemon
Salt

Freshly ground pepper
½ cup cider
1–2 cooked sausages (optional)
Grated orange rind

Shred the cabbage to make about 3 cups. Melt the butter in a 10-inch skillet and stir in the sugar and the lemon juice. Sprinkle the cabbage lightly with salt and pepper, and stir into the skillet so that the seasoned butter is thoroughly mixed in. Add the cider, bring it to a boil, and cover the pan. Reduce heat and cook over very low heat for 30 minutes, or until the cabbage is wilted and tender. If there seems to be too much liquid, uncover and increase the heat to reduce the amount. You may add 1 or 2 cooked sausages, cut sides down. Finish the cabbage by grating the skin of an orange over all.
SERVES 4

Spicy Red Cabbage

1 head red cabbage (about 1
   pound)
3 tablespoons finely chopped small
   white onion
3–4 tablespoons chicken or goose
   fat or butter
4 tablespoons dark brown sugar
¼ cup cider vinegar

¼ cup red wine
2–3 teaspoons caraway seeds
1 teaspoon dried thyme
1 bay leaf
¾ teaspoon ground mace
Salt
Freshly ground pepper

Spicy Red Cabbage (continued)

Shred the cabbage and cover it with cold water. In a large pot melt the fat or butter and cook the chopped onions gently 1 minute, then stir in the brown sugar, vinegar, and wine. Drain the cabbage, and add it to the pot along with the caraway seeds, thyme, bay leaf, and mace. Cover and simmer for 25 minutes, stirring occasionally. Sprinkle with salt and pepper to taste, and continue simmering, covered, until the cabbage is tender but not mushy.

SERVES 4

Eating on the Wild Side

April and May are the best time for wild greens, especially the delicate-flavored fiddleheads found in moist, deep woods. A revival of the traditional appreciation of these ferns, whose coiled leaves remind you of violins, has resulted in many new New England ways of serving them (see "Meat" entry in index). New popularity has come to dandelion greens, too—taste them when very young and use them in a salad if they've not become bitter. If they have, you may steam them with onions until tender. Dock, lamb's quarter, mustard, peppergrass, pigweed, purslane, wild sorrel, and watercress are among others to be identified with the help of a wildflower guide. Use them as accents in salads, or in combinations of cooked greens.

Wild milkweed has three stages of edibility. The shoots that come in late April or May in the North can be steamed or blanched and served like asparagus with butter. The sweet-smelling blossoms resemble pink broccoli buds, and before they open may be fried in batter. The spiny milkweed pods, which are easily recognizable, may be stuffed (page 19), or steamed, or fried. All milkweed parts should be cooked in several changes of water to remove any bitter taste.

Our friend Millie Owen warned us that most of the nutrient value is lost in all this boiling of the young shoots. "I like to restore some vitamins and add flavor," she wrote in *A Cook's Guide to Growing Herbs, Greens, and Aromatics.* "I put a handful of fresh spring herbs and greens in the blender, cover them with chicken stock, whirl until the herbs are finely chopped, then strain the liquid over the milkweed and boil for an additional 10 minutes. I drain the stalks (saving the cooking liquid for sauces or for boiling other vegetables), and serve the milkweed hot with lemon butter or cold with green mayonaise. Or I return the milkweed to the blender along with the cooking broth to make a puréed milkweed soup."

Many wild greens make wonderful soups. Dandelion buds, picked just before they are about to open, can be cooked in butter for 2–3 minutes, set aside, then spooned onto one side of an omelette just before it is done, and folded in as the omelette is served.

1½ pounds sauerkraut
1 onion, sliced
2 tart apples, peeled and quartered
2 cloves
1 teaspoon caraway seeds

2–3 cups meat stock
1 small potato
Salt
Freshly ground pepper

Sauerkraut with Apples and Caraway

Put the sauerkraut, sliced onion, apple quarters, cloves, and caraway seeds in a saucepan and pour in enough meat stock to cover. Simmer very gently for about 45 minutes, adding more stock, a little at a time, if needed to keep the sauerkraut damp. Peel the potato and grate it into the sauerkraut with a little salt, only if necessary, and a light sprinkling of pepper. Boil gently just long enough to allow the potato to add thickness to the sauerkraut and apples.

SERVES 4

This delicious and substantial dish could be served as a main course, particularly for vegetarians, or as an unusual first course.

Carrot Pancakes with Peppery Tomato Sauce

2 eggs
About 4 medium carrots (¾ pound), scraped and coarsely grated
2 tablespoons whole wheat flour (white may be used instead)

Salt
Freshly ground pepper
1 tablespoon chopped fresh dill
2 tablespoons olive or corn oil

SAUCE:
2 onions, chopped
2 ribs celery, chopped fine
1 green pepper, ribs and seeds removed, chopped
2 tablespoons vegetable oil
1½ cups chopped peeled, seeded tomatoes, or equivalent amount drained canned tomatoes

3 tablespoons tomato paste
2 tablespoons brown sugar
½ teaspoon dried hot red pepper flakes, or more to taste

To make the pancakes, beat the eggs lightly in a largish bowl, then mix in the carrots, flour, a light sprinkling of salt and pepper, and the dill. Heat the oil in a large skillet until a haze develops on the pan, then pour in the batter, a tablespoon at a time, to make small pancakes. Cook 3 minutes, turn them over, and brown the other side. Remove to paper towels as they are done.

Meanwhile, make the sauce. Cook the onions, celery, and green pepper in the oil until the onions are translucent. Add the tomatoes, tomato paste,

Carrot Pancakes with Peppery Tomato Sauce (continued)

brown sugar, a light sprinkling of salt and pepper, and the dried pepper flakes. Cook, uncovered, about 10 minutes, over medium to low heat, stirring often.

Pour about three-quarters of the sauce into the skillet in which you cooked the pancakes, arrange the pancakes on top, and drizzle the remaining sauce over. Cover and cook slowly for 10 minutes.

SERVES 4 AS A MAIN COURSE; 6 AS A FIRST COURSE

Carrot-Potato Croquettes

Making things stretch, today as always, is a way of life for many rural Yankees. There have been few better examples in the kitchen than this one.

*Three 6-inch carrots, scraped and
  grated*
*3 medium potatoes, peeled and
  grated*
¼ cup minced onion
¼ cup minced parsley
¼ cup milk

¼ cup flour
1 egg, lightly beaten
1½ teaspoons salt
Freshly ground pepper
Butter or oil

Put the vegetables and parsley in a mixing bowl, add the milk, and sprinkle with flour, a little at a time; stir to eliminate lumps, then blend in the egg and seasonings. Film the surface of a skillet with melted butter or oil. Drop in the croquette mixture in spoonfuls and cook 2–3 minutes on each side, turning once. Serve very hot.

MAKES ABOUT 12 CROQUETTES TO SERVE 4

Carrot Custard

4 large carrots
2 eggs
*½ cup heavy cream or condensed
  milk*
Salt

Freshly ground pepper
Freshly grated nutmeg
1 teaspoon chopped fresh tarragon
1 tablespoon melted butter
1 tablespoon chopped parsley

Peel the carrots and cut into chunks. Cook in boiling water for about 10 minutes, until tender but not soft. Drain and blend quickly in a blender until only roughly ground—don't overblend; or put through a food mill or a food processor. Beat the eggs and cream in a bowl until blended, then add the carrots and a little salt and freshly ground pepper to taste. Add nutmeg to taste and stir in the tarragon. Pour the mixture into a buttered 1-quart baking dish, and set it in a pan of hot water. Bake the custard in a preheated 350-degree oven for 45 minutes. Set aside in a warm place for about 5 minutes, then run a knife around the custard and unmold it onto a serving plate. Spoon the melted butter over the top, and sprinkle with parsley.

SERVES 4

Braised Celeriac or Celery Root

1 large celeriac or celery root (about 1½ pounds)

1½ cups chicken broth
1 tablespoon chopped parsley

Peel the celeriac and cut it into ½-inch slices, then cut the slices into eighths. Bring the broth to a boil in a large skillet and scatter the celeriac pieces over the bottom (they should fit in one layer). Turn the heat down to a simmer, cover, and cook about 20 minutes, or until just tender. The liquid should be absorbed by then; if not, turn up the heat and cook quickly, uncovered, until none remains. Scatter parsley on top and serve hot. (No salt is needed because of the natural sodium in the root vegetable.)

SERVES 4

Braised Celery with Hazelnuts or Hickory Nuts

6 cups celery, strings removed, cut into ⅛-inch slices at a diagonal slant

1½ cups or more chicken broth
2 tablespoons butter

¼ cup chopped hazelnuts or hickory nuts
About ½ teaspoon fresh lemon juice, or more to taste

Put the celery slices in a fairly large skillet and pour the chicken broth over. Dot with butter and bring to a boil, then lower the heat, cover, and cook over medium heat for 15–20 minutes, checking to make sure that the liquid has not evaporated (if so, add a little more broth). When the celery is tender but still with a little resistance, uncover, increase heat, and cook down rapidly until the liquid has evaporated and the celery sizzles in the glaze. Sprinkle the nuts on top and season with lemon juice.

SERVES 4

Winter Baked Corn and Tomatoes with Cottage Cheese

2 cups whole-kernel canned corn, drained
2 cups canned tomatoes
½ teaspoon salt

Freshly ground pepper
1 cup cottage cheese
4 tablespoons dry bread crumbs
3 tablespoons melted butter

Pour the drained corn kernels into a greased 1½-quart baking dish. Add the tomatoes with their liquid, the salt, and a few turns of the pepper grinder. Spread the cottage cheese over the tomatoes. Mix the bread crumbs with the butter, and spread the mixture over the layer of cheese. Bake in a preheated 375–400-degree oven for about 25 minutes, until the dish is bubbling and the top is moderately brown.
SERVES 4–6

Corn Fritters

4 cups corn kernels (cut from 3–4 large ears corn)
2–3 tablespoons flour
¼ teaspoon salt

Freshly ground pepper
2 eggs, separated
Vegetable oil

Mix the corn kernels with the flour—if they are very fresh and quite liquid, you will need the full amount of flour; for older corn 2 tablespoons will do. Blend in the salt, pepper, and egg yolks. In a separate bowl, beat the egg whites until they form soft peaks, then fold them into the corn mixture. Film the bottom of a large skillet with oil and heat until a drop of water sizzles and evaporates. Drop the fritter batter by large spoonfuls onto the skillet, leaving room for them to spread like pancakes. When they look firm at the edges and bubbly, carefully turn each fritter and brown on the other side. Keep warm on a platter while you fry the remaining fritters. Serve immediately.
MAKES ABOUT 14 FRITTERS

Corn Pudding

Old-fashioned corn pudding was always made simply with scraped corn, good rich top-of-the-milk, and the dish was dotted with a little butter before it went in the oven. And it is still the best of all corn puddings. The corn should be freshly picked, and if it is very milky, you might need to add a couple of teaspoons of flour to thicken the pudding. If you have a corn scraper, the job of extracting the tender flesh will be easier; otherwise, split the kernels with a sharp knife and then scrape out the flesh and milk.

8 ears corn, scraped (to make about
   2 cups)
1/3 cup heavy cream
1/3 cup light cream
2 teaspoons flour (optional)
Salt
Freshly ground pepper
1 tablespoon butter

Put the corn into a buttered 1-quart shallow casserole, stir in the cream, flour (only if the corn seems very milky), and salt and pepper to taste. Mix gently but thoroughly. Dot butter on top. Bake in a preheated 325-degree oven for 1 hour.

SERVES 4

Adele Dawson's Dandelion Tempura

4 cups dandelion flowers cut from
   stems
3 eggs
1/2 cup milk
Sea salt
Pinch of cayenne pepper
Unbleached flour
2 sprigs each oregano, thyme, and
   basil, chopped, or 1 teaspoon
   dried mixed herbs
1/2 cup finely grated New England
   cheddar or Parmesan
1 cup safflower oil

Wash the flower heads lightly in cold water, and blot them dry on paper towels. Mix the eggs, milk, a little sea salt to taste, and the cayenne pepper with enough flour to make a thin batter, and stir in the herbs and cheese. Heat the oil in a skillet until a crumb dropped sizzles and turns quickly brown. Dip the dandelion flowers in the batter, and fry until golden brown on both sides.

SERVES 4–6

Broiled Eggplant with Sunflower Seeds

1 medium eggplant
2 tablespoons olive oil
Salt
Freshly ground pepper
3 tablespoons sunflower seeds,
   finely chopped or ground

Cut the eggplant into 1/3-inch slices, leaving the skin on. Brush one side of the slices with oil, salt and pepper lightly, and place on a grill about 6 inches below a preheated broiler. Broil about 8 minutes, or until lightly browned. Turn the slices, brush the other side with oil, salt and pepper again lightly, and broil 6 minutes; then sprinkle with the sunflower seeds and broil another minute or so.

SERVES 4 AS AN ACCOMPANIMENT

Baked Eggplant with Corn Soufflé Topping

2 medium onions, sliced thin
4 tablespoons corn oil
2 garlic cloves, minced
4 large tomatoes
¼ teaspoon cayenne
1 teaspoon salt

Freshly ground pepper
½ pound eggplant
¼ cup flour
2 eggs, separated
1 ear fresh corn
Heavy cream

Sauté the onion slices in 2 tablespoons of the corn oil for about 10 minutes, adding the garlic during the last few minutes and stirring to prevent browning. Peel the tomatoes, remove the seeds, and cut them in chunks; add to the onions, and season with the cayenne, a light sprinkling of salt, and pepper, cooking over a low heat until the mixture thickens. Peel the eggplant and cut into 1-inch sticks about 4 inches long, then dredge in flour. Heat the remaining 2 tablespoons corn oil in a separate skillet and sauté the eggplant sticks for about 8 minutes, tossing occasionally to brown evenly. Arrange them in the bottom of a 2-quart casserole, cover with the thickened tomato mixture, and bake in a preheated 325-degree oven for about 15 minutes. Meanwhile, beat the egg yolks until pale yellow. Cut the corn from the cob, put in a small saucepan, and heat enough cream in the same pan to cover the corn; don't let it boil. Take the pan from the heat and carefully stir in the beaten yolks. Beat the egg whites until stiff, and fold them into the corn–egg mixture. Pour this mixture over the eggplant, return the casserole to the oven, and bake 15–20 minutes more.

SERVES 4

One 2-pound eggplant, peeled and
  cut crosswise into 1-inch slices
2 tablespoons coarse salt
¼ cup olive oil
3 tomatoes, peeled, seeded, and
  chopped, or the equivalent
  amount of canned whole
  tomatoes, drained, chopped,
  seeds removed

1 garlic clove, minced
2 tablespoons chopped fresh basil
½ cup fresh bread crumbs
2 tablespoons grated Parmesan or
  aged cheddar

Baked
Eggplant
Slices

Sprinkle both sides of the eggplant slices with salt, place on racks, and let
sweat about 30 minutes. Slap dry with paper towels, score both sides, and
rub olive oil over the surfaces and into the cut places. Place in one layer on
a large baking sheet or shallow dish and bake in a preheated 450-degree
oven for 15 minutes. Turn the slices, spread the tomatoes mixed with the
garlic and basil over them, lightly drape a piece of foil over the top, and
bake another 15 minutes. Remove the foil and distribute the bread crumbs
and cheese on top. Bake another 5 minutes, or slip under a preheated broiler
until lightly browned.

SERVES 4

Made of lightly cooked green vegetables—broccoli, spinach or chard, zucchini, beans, fiddleheads, or asparagus—these delicate timbales studded
with green look attractive unmolded around a platter of roasted or cold
meats. They are also good by themselves—2 to a serving—as a luncheon
dish.

Green
Vegetable
Timbales

3 finely minced scallions, including
  tender greens
1 cup Cream Sauce or White Sauce
  (page 629)
2 eggs, well beaten
¼ teaspoon freshly grated nutmeg
Salt
A few drops Tabasco sauce
2 cups chopped cooked broccoli,
  green beans, or asaparagus; or
  chopped cooked spinach or
  chard, squeezed dry; or grated
  zucchini salted and squeezed dry

About 2 teaspoons chopped fresh
  chervil, summer savory, basil, or
  chives, or about ½ teaspoon
  dried

Stir the minced scallions into the cream sauce and let cook gently 1 minute.
Pour the eggs into the hot cream sauce in a steady stream, beating. Add the

nutmeg and salt and Tabasco to taste, and fold in the green vegetable. Use the herb that seems to complement the vegetable you are using. Fill 6 well-buttered ½-cup molds about seven-eighths full, and place them in a pan of simmering water that comes halfway up the sides. Cover with buttered wax paper or foil. Bake in a preheated 350-degree oven for about 25 minutes, or until a straw poked into the center comes out clean. Let rest 5 minutes or so before unmolding.

SERVES 3 AS A LUNCHEON DISH; 6 AS A SIDE DISH

Jerusalem Artichoke and Mushroom Pancakes

Samuel Champlain, for whom the great border lake on New England's western rim is named, discovered this tuber when he found Indians growing it on Cape Cod, and described it as having the taste of artichokes. Later it was transplanted to European soil, where the prefix *girasole* was added because of the plant's persistent turning (or gyrating) with the sun. So English cooks re-formed the same as Jerusalem artichokes, and someone developed a bisque whimsically entitled Palestine soup, which was popular for generations in New England. A refined contemporary version is Jerusalem Artichoke Soup with watercress (page 46).

1 pound Jerusalem artichokes
3 tablespoons heavy cream
1 medium onion, grated
Salt
Freshly ground pepper
½ teaspoon Worcestershire sauce

4 tablespoons flour
2 teaspoons baking powder
2 eggs, well beaten
½ pound fresh mushrooms, finely chopped
Butter or vegetable oil

Clean the Jerusalem artichokes with a stiff brush and soak them in lightly salted water about 30 minutes. Drain, reserving the liquid, and scrape off the skin, then grate them coarsely. Mix the cream with 4 tablespoons of the soaking liquid, and add the grated onion. Season to taste with a little salt, pepper, and the Worcestershire. Mix the flour and baking powder, and stir into the beaten eggs, then stir this mixture into the cream. Stir in the grated artichokes and the mushrooms. Heat a little butter or vegetable oil in a frying pan and drop in 1 tablespoon of the mixture at a time and fry on one side 2–3 minutes, then turn and brown the other side.

SERVES 4

Kale in Madeira

This may be served as a first course. It is also "a fine accompaniment to beef, lamb, or fowl," according to Chef Albert Stockli at the Stonehenge Inn in Connecticut. He prided himself on using New England ingredients (Madeira was important to early Yankees) in new and interesting ways.

1 bunch kale (1½ pounds)
1 tablespoon vegetable oil
1 leek, or 3 scallions, washed, trimmed, and chopped fine
1 teaspoon finely chopped shallots (optional)
1 medium carrot, scraped and chopped fine
1 teaspoon cornstarch or potato starch

3 ounces Madeira
Salt
2 drops Tabasco sauce
1 medium dill pickle, chopped fine
¾ cup beef broth
1 tablespoon wine vinegar
¼ cup cooked ham sliced into long, thin strips
Freshly ground pepper

Trim the tough leaves from the kale and rinse it thoroughly in water, then drain. Heat the oil in a heavy saucepan and sauté the kale until the leaves are wilted, about 2 minutes. Mix in the chopped leek, optional shallots, and carrot. Dissolve the cornstarch in the Madeira, and add along with a sprinkling of salt, the Tabasco, chopped pickle, and beef broth, mixing well. Cover and simmer 10 minutes. Stir in the vinegar and ham strips, and season to taste with pepper and more salt, as needed. Serve hot.

SERVES 4

Stuffed Kohlrabi

8 small kohlrabi, with leaves
1 onion, chopped fine
1 tablespoon vegetable oil
2 tablespoons butter
1 teaspoon sweet paprika
1 small garlic clove, minced
1 cup ground cooked veal or half veal and half pork

½ cup bread crumbs
3 tablespoons chopped parsley
½ teaspoon dried oregano, or 1 teaspoon fresh
½ teaspoon dried thyme
Salt
Freshly ground pepper

SAUCE:
2 tablespoons butter
2 tablespoons flour
1 teaspoon sweet paprika
1 cup reserved kohlrabi cooking liquid

½ cup sour cream
1 tablespoon chopped fresh dill

Remove the leaves from the kohlrabi, chop them roughly, and boil them with the whole kohlrabi for 10 minutes in enough salt water to cover. Meanwhile, sauté the onion in oil and butter until limp; add the paprika and garlic and cook, stirring, another minute. Then add the ground meat and sauté 4–5 minutes. Stir in the bread crumbs, herbs, and a little salt and pepper to taste. Drain the kohlrabi and reserve the cooking liquid. Scoop out the insides with a knife or melon-ball scoop. Chop the insides fine, and add them to the meat mixture. Fill the kohlrabi with the stuffing, place in a baking dish that will hold them snugly, adding a little of the cooking liquid;

cover lightly with foil and bake in a preheated 350-degree oven for 45 minutes, or until tender.

Meanwhile, make a sauce by melting the butter and stirring in the flour and paprika and cooking 2 minutes. Then stir in 1 cup of the reserved cooking liquid and simmer, stirring, until thickened. Add the sour cream and dill and heat just until sauce bubbles once. Pour the sauce around the stuffed kohlrabi.

SERVES 4

Steamed Kohlrabi with Buttered Crumbs

6 small-medium kohlrabi (about 1¾ pounds)
2 cups fresh bread crumbs, not too finely crumbled

6 tablespoons butter
Salt
Freshly ground pepper
1–2 tablespoons chopped parsley

Peel the kohlrabi and cut into medium-size dice. Set in a steamer basket and steam until tender, only about 10 minutes if very young and fresh. Meanwhile, sauté the bread crumbs with the butter until they have absorbed the butter and have turned golden brown. Toss the steamed kohlrabi with the crumbs, season to taste with salt and pepper, and sprinkle parsley on top.

SERVES 4

Baked Leeks and Fresh Tomatoes

"Leeks rank with shallots as the aristocrats of the onion family," wrote the Vermont gardener Millie Owen in *A Cook's Guide to Growing Herbs, Greens, and Aromatics.* Recently in New England and elsewhere, leek harvests have multiplied astronomically, and Yankee cooks have evolved many new uses for them, including this combination with tomatoes.

4 large leeks
4 tablespoons butter
4 plump ripe tomatoes
Salt
Freshly ground pepper

2–3 tablespoons chopped fresh basil
1½ teaspoons cornstarch
½ cup heavy cream

Trim off the green part of the leeks (save for soup), wash thoroughly, and cut into 1-inch lengths. Melt the butter in a shallow baking dish, add the leeks, and put the dish in a preheated 375-degree oven for about 10 minutes. Cut the tomatoes in half horizontally, and sprinkle lightly with salt, a few turns of the pepper grinder, and the chopped basil. Put the tomatoes upside down on the partially cooked bed of leeks and turn the oven down

to 350 degrees. Bake 5 minutes, then turn the tomatoes over and bake 5 minutes longer. Mix the cornstarch with the cream, stirring until smooth. Remove the tomatoes to a hot platter, and stir the cream into the leeks, cooking until the mixture thickens slightly. With a rubber spatula, scrape the resulting leek sauce over the tomatoes.
SERVES 4

Leeks with Coriander Seeds

Sicilians in Boston's North End have introduced spicy ideas to perk up such garden vegetables as leeks. They add contrast to the old New England favorite, broiled tripe (see page 216).

6 fat leeks	Freshly ground pepper
1/2 cup olive oil	3 bay leaves
2–3 tablespoons coriander seeds	2 teaspoons chopped fresh basil, or
1 cup white wine	1/2 teaspoon dried
1 cup water	1/2 teaspoon dried oregano
Salt	Lime or lemon juice (optional)

Wash the leeks, trim away most of the green tops and the roots, and slice the stalks vertically, starting at the leaf end, halfway down. Run cold water over the leeks until they are free of all dirt and sand, then cut them horizontally into quarters. Put them in a skillet with the oil, coriander seeds, wine, and water. Heat to the boiling point, season lightly with salt and pepper to taste, and add the herbs. Simmer about 40 minutes. Remove the bay leaves, and serve hot or cold. When chilled, the flavor can be enhanced by a little lime or lemon juice.
SERVES 4

Leeks and Cider Casserole

Cider for a good many kinds of cooking should be dry, like white wine—a fact that may indicate a trip to the wines and spirits retail outlet where hard cider is sold in bottles of convenient size. This recipe makes an appropriate accompaniment for pork.

1 1/2 pounds good-size leeks	1/2 cup hard cider
2 tablespoons butter	2 tablespoons chopped Italian flat-
2 teaspoons dry mustard	leaved parsley

Trim the leeks, removing all the green part (save for soups). Cut them crosswise so that the pieces are as wide as they are long. Put the pieces in a bowl under running water for about 5 minutes, then dry them with paper towels. Heat the butter in an ovenproof dish over low heat. Add the mustard and stir 5 minutes or longer, until a thin, smooth paste is formed. Stir in the leeks, add the cider, and bring to a boil. Cover the baking dish and place in a preheated 350-degree oven for 30 minutes. Uncover, sprinkle parsley over the leeks, and continue cooking in the oven for about 15 minutes more.

SERVES 4

Milkweed Bud Fritters

Adele Dawson, who gives workshops on wild edibles and medicinal herbs and has written a book on the subject, showed us just when to pick milkweed buds—while they are still tight with a lavender-red cast before they open into flowers. The buds are broken off at the stem and used immediately. Adele dips the fritters in a sauce of half sherry and half tamari, with a few chopped scallions or chives mixed in. They are also good served simply with lemon wedges.

1 recipe for beer batter (see page 141)
Oil for frying

About 3 cups milkweed buds
Lemon wedges or tamari-sherry dipping sauce (see headnote)

Beat up the batter and heat about 1 inch of oil in skillet. When the oil is hot enough so that a crumb of bread quickly sizzles and browns when tossed in, immediately dip the buds into the batter to coat, let the excess drip off, and then slip them into the hot oil. Fry them in several batches so as not to crowd the pan. When golden on one side, turn and brown on the other. Remove with a slotted spoon to drain on paper towels and keep warm while you fry the rest. Serve immediately with lemon wedges or tamari-sherry dipping sauce.

SERVES 4–6

Viennese Mushrooms

1 cup finely chopped onions
4 tablespoons butter
½–¾ pound mushrooms
3–4 tablespoons flour
1 cup chicken stock
⅓ cup dry sherry or rum
Salt

2 teaspoons dry mustard
2 teaspoons Worcestershire sauce
½ teaspoon freshly grated nutmeg
¾ cup sour cream, at room temperature
¾ cup plain yogurt, at room temperature

Gently cook the onions in the butter until soft. Trim the mushrooms and clean them if necessary, then cut them in halves or quarters, depending on their size. Stir the mushrooms into the onions and cook gently about 5 minutes, stirring occasionally. Sprinkle the flour into the pan and stir about 1 minute to mix thoroughly with the butter. Slowly add the stock and the sherry or rum, stirring. Sprinkle lightly with salt and season with the mustard, Worcestershire, and nutmeg. Cook, stirring, until the sauce is very thick. Remove from the heat and stir in the sour cream and yogurt. Reheat but do not boil.

SERVES 4

Mushrooms

Throughout the summer we find small puffballs looking like lost golf balls in our weedy country lawn, and we sauté them often with fresh herbs. In other parts of Vermont, mushroom hunters have found as many as 300 varieties, most of which are prepared for the table in simple ways common to Yankee kitchens since settlement began. Perhaps the fact New England cooks found them so common accounts for mushrooms being ignored in most cookbooks of the past. But now there are groups meeting to learn about the morels in May and the chanterelles of midsummer in each of the states. The new cooking styles that have enlarged the regional cuisine are encouragement for gathering meadow mushrooms and experimenting with grilling oyster mushrooms or adding them to salads.

Sorrel-Flavored Mushrooms

Serve these on toast or over scrambled eggs for a light luncheon dish. They are also good as an accompaniment to meat, particularly lamb, and fish. If you are knowledgeable about wild mushrooms and you've gathered an edible variety in the woods or meadows, they may be used in this dish or included with the cultivated store-bought mushrooms.

About 1½ pounds mushrooms
2 tablespoons olive oil or butter or a combination
1 tablespoon vegetable oil
6 scallions, including tender greens, sliced

Salt
Freshly ground pepper
About 1½ cups loosely packed sorrel leaves
¼ cup heavy cream
⅓ cup plain yogurt

Trim off the woody tip end of the mushrooms stems. Wipe them with a damp cloth if they seem dirty (there's no need to soak cultivated mushrooms; only do so with wild varieties if they seem gritty). Heat the olive oil and/or butter in a large skillet, add the mushrooms and scallions and a little salt and pepper, and cook over lively heat, tossing frequently, for 3 minutes. Remove the stems from the sorrel leaves and discard them; chop the leaves roughly, and add them to the mushrooms, stirring them into the juices and cooking slowly now for 1 minute. Stir in the cream and let it thicken slightly, then blend in the yogurt. Taste and correct the seasoning as necessary.
SERVES 4

Mustard Greens and Bacon

Mustard greens are cultivated occasionally in the Northeast, and wild-food enthusiasts gather the young leaves in spring. Sometimes, as with dandelion greens, they are cooked with cornmeal dumplings (page 199).

1 bunch (1–1½ pounds) mustard greens
8 strips bacon
3 tablespoons boiled cider, or 2½ tablespoons vinegar plus 1 teaspoon sugar

Freshly ground pepper
Salt (optional)
4–6 scallions, finely chopped, including tender greens, or 1 small onion, grated

Wash the mustard greens thoroughly, then discard the hard stems and shred the leaves. Fry the bacon and remove from the pan to drain on paper towels. In the hot bacon fat, toss the shredded greens, stirring until they are wilted. Cover the pan and cook about 5–10 minutes over a moderate heat, until tender. Then add the boiled cider or vinegar plus sugar, and crumble the bacon before stirring it into the greens. Taste, and add pepper and a little salt, if needed. Sprinkle the chopped scallions or the grated onion over the top, and serve warm.

SERVES 4

Okra is ready to harvest as early as July in some Northeast gardens, and in Maine it's been cooked in a variety of ways for generations. This way is one we worked out to complement shrimp fried in beer batter (page 141).

Stewed Okra with Orzo

1 pound okra
2½ tablespoons vegetable oil
¾ cup chopped onion
2 large tomatoes, chopped

2 teaspoons ketchup, preferably
  unsweetened (see page 628)
1 teaspoon curry powder
1 cup cooked orzo or rice

Wash the okra, trim off the ends, and slice into rounds about ¼ inch thick. Heat the oil in a skillet, add the onion and okra, and cook over low heat for 6–8 minutes. Add the tomatoes, ketchup, and curry powder, and simmer for about 5 minutes. Stir in the cooked orzo and heat through.

SERVES 4

A variation on a traditional Maine recipe.

Creamed Parsnips with Mushrooms

1 pound parsnips, preferably of
  uniform size
2 onions, cut in chunks
1½ cups chicken or beef broth
Water
¾ pound mushrooms, stems
  removed

2 tablespoons butter
1½ tablespoons flour
½ cup heavy cream
1 tablespoon lemon juice
Salt
Freshly ground pepper
3–4 tablespoons chopped parsley

Peel the parsnips and cut into uniform pieces about 1 inch long. Put the parsnip chunks and the cutup onion in a saucepan and add the broth and enough water to cover. Cook for about 12 minutes, add the mushrooms, and continue cooking about 5 minutes, until the parsnips are tender. Drain the liquid from the vegetables and reserve; keep the vegetables in a warm place. Heat the butter, stir in the flour, and cook 2 minutes over low heat. Stir in the warm vegetable cooking liquid, a little at a time, and when the mixture is smooth, add the cream and blend. Add the lemon juice, and sprinkle lightly with salt and pepper to taste. Pour the sauce over the vegetables and sprinkle with chopped parsley.

SERVES 4

Puréed Parsnips with Madeira and Cream

4 pounds parsnips
3 tablespoons butter
⅓ cup Madeira
¼ cup heavy cream
⅛ teaspoon freshly grated nutmeg

Salt
Freshly ground pepper
2–3 tablespoons chopped hazelnuts
  (optional)

Trim and peel the parsnips and put them in a saucepan with lightly salted water to cover. Cook until tender, about 20 minutes, and drain. Spin the drained parsnips in a food processor, and work in the butter, Madeira, cream, and nutmeg; or put the parsnips through a vegetable mill, and beat in the other ingredients. Add salt and pepper to taste, and either reheat slowly in a heavy saucepan, stirring occasionally, for about 5 minutes to develop the flavors; or put the purée into a buttered 1-quart baking dish, sprinkle the optional nuts on top, and bake in a preheated 375-degree oven until bubbling.
SERVES 4–6

Red Peppers with Spinach

2 sweet red peppers
2 pounds young garden spinach
2 tablespoons vegetable oil
2 garlic cloves, minced

Salt
Freshly ground pepper
Lemon juice

Remove the seeds and pith and cut the peppers into ¼-inch strips. Wash the spinach and place in a colander to drain. Heat the oil, add the garlic and the peppers, and sauté, stirring frequently, until the peppers soften a bit, about 5 minutes. Be careful not to burn the garlic. Add the spinach and stir constantly, mixing with the peppers and garlic, until the leaves are wilted in the oil. Season lightly with salt and pepper and a few drops of lemon juice. Do not overcook.
SERVES 4

Sweet Red Pepper Summer Succotash

1 tablespoon corn oil
2 garlic cloves, chopped fine
1½ cups chopped onions
1 cup chopped sweet red pepper,
  ribs and seeds removed
2 cups raw corn kernels
2 teaspoons chopped fresh basil

1 teaspoon chopped fresh thyme or
  ¼ teaspoon dried
Salt
Freshly ground pepper
2 cups cooked small lima beans or
  shell beans
Chopped parsley

Heat the oil in a skillet and slowly cook the garlic, onions, and sweet red pepper until limp. Add the corn, herbs, a sprinkling of salt and pepper, and cook about 3 minutes. Stir in the lima beans and enough water to make a creamy consistency. Remove from the heat and let stand about 15 minutes. Reheat, and serve with chopped parsley sprinkled on top.
SERVES 6–8

Corn-Stuffed Green Peppers with Goat Cheese

A visit to Rawson Brook Farm's pristine goat's milk dairy in Monterey, Massachusetts, inspired this harvest-time vegetable dish—wonderful with cold slices of flank steak.

2 large green peppers
3 tablespoons butter
1 onion, chopped
2–3 cups fresh corn cut from the cob
⅓ cup heavy cream

Salt
Dash cayenne
1 teaspoon chopped fresh savory, or ½ teaspoon dried
4 tablespoons goat's milk cream cheese

Cut the peppers in half lengthwise and remove the seeds and ribs. Drop them into a pot of boiling water and boil 2 minutes, then drain. Heat the butter in a skillet and slowly sauté the onion about 4 minutes. Add the corn and cream, stir, and simmer about 3 minutes, seasoning with a little salt, a dash of cayenne, and the savory. Spoon this filling into the trimmed peppers and spread the cheese on the top of each. Bake in a preheated 350-degree oven for about 20 minutes.
SERVES 4

Stockli's Roësti Potatoes

4 good-size freshly baked potatoes, cooled

About 1 teaspoon salt
8 tablespoons (1 stick) butter

Peel the baked potatoes, reserving the peels for the recipe on page 305. Put the potatoes through the shredding blade of a food processor or grate by hand. Sprinkle with salt. Heat 2 tablespoons butter in a small frying pan and spread one-quarter of the grated potatoes over the bottom. Stir the potatoes until they are coated with butter, then press down with the flat side of the spatula and fry the potato cake until it is brown and crisp on the bottom. Turn over and fry on the other side. Remove to a hot platter and keep warm while you fry the remaining potato cakes the same way.
SERVES 4

Drying Your Garden Herbs

Harvesting should come just before blossoming because that is when the flavor of herbs is at its best. Cut perennials no later than six weeks before the first frost is expected, so they can rejuvenate before winter. If you cut back one-half to two-thirds of each lot, most will produce a second and third crop.

Pick and wash the leaves in cool water, and shake off the moisture. Blot dry. Place on trays or racks for 2½–10 hours, or until dry enough so that the herbs will crumble easily. But remember, all herbs retain more flavor when kept whole (uncrushed) until they are used.

Most common herbs for drying include: bay leaves, celery leaves, chives (chopped or snipped), marjoram, chervil, mint, oregano, parsley, rosemary, savory, sage, scallions, sweet basil, tarragon, and thyme.

There are plenty of Boston Irish convinced that this is a Southside original.

Potatoes O'Brien

1½ pounds potatoes
1 teaspoon salt
3 tablespoons vegetable oil
1 medium onion, chopped

1 large green pepper, diced
Salt
Freshly ground pepper

Peel the potatoes and cut them into ½-inch cubes, then drop them in cold salted water, bring to a boil, and cook about 2 minutes, until half done. Heat the oil in a skillet and stir in the onion and green pepper. Add the potatoes and stir thoroughly, then cook the vegetable mixture about 15 minutes over medium heat, lifting and turning occasionally with a spatula. Increase the heat and watch carefully while the vegetables turn golden brown; turn with a spatula several times. Turn out quickly to serve hot—they are delicious with fish.

SERVES 4

Infant Potatoes with Buttered Herbs

At Mountain Mowings in southern Vermont, and other New England vegetable farms, baby potatoes are dug up while the vines are still growing, all for the benefit of those who covet the fresh flavor when the new potatoes aren't much larger than marbles. When potatoes are really small, their flavor may be accented by fresh herbs in butter after they have been boiled as little as 5 minutes.

3–4 cups infant potatoes
1 teaspoon freshly chopped chives
1 tablespoon freshly chopped
  chervil and thyme or summer
  savory and tarragon or your own
  combination

2–3 tablespoons butter
Salt
Freshly ground pepper

Wash the potatoes gently but thoroughly. Put them in a wide-bottomed saucepan and pour 1 cup boiling water over them. Return the temperature quickly to the boil and cook, covered, until the potatoes are tender, with their skins intact. You must learn to judge the cooking time. Potatoes the size of golf balls are slightly large and may take 15–20 minutes. Shake the pan so that the potatoes cook evenly. Remove the pan from the heat and drain the remaining liquid. Sprinkle in the herbs, add the butter and a very little salt and a twist of the pepper grinder, only if you really want to—the flavor of the herbs and new potatoes shouldn't be counteracted. Shake the pan over low heat until the butter is melted and coats the potatoes with herbs.

SERVES 4

Potatoes in a Skillet, Seasoned with Dandelion Leaves

2 tablespoons vegetable oil
2 tablespoons olive oil
4 medium new potatoes, peeled and
    cut into 1/8-inch slices
Salt

Freshly ground pepper
1/2 cup chopped young dandelion
    leaves
1 fat garlic clove, minced

Heat the vegetable oil and 1 tablespoon olive oil in a 9-inch skillet, then arrange half the potatoes in overlapping slices to cover the bottom of the skillet, season with salt and pepper, and distribute the greens and minced garlic on top. Cover with the remaining potato slices and cook 2–3 minutes over medium-high heat. Lower the heat, cover, and cook slowly 10 minutes more. Now uncover and place a plate over the skillet that will amply cover the top and flip the skillet over onto it so that the potatoes fall in place on the plate. Slip the potatoes back into the skillet to brown the other side,

The Art of Hashed Browns

Of all ways of cooking potatoes, the style that calls for chopping and cooking them to achieve a crisp outside crust is more American than anything else, and the knack for it may have traveled across the country with railroad cooks.

It's safe to say, however, that the origin is pure Yankee, and for generations of seaboard New Englanders the name for the dish was "scootin'-'long-the-shore"—because "for years upon years," according to a Martha's Vineyard octogenarian, "Cape Cod fishermen prepared this meal while at their work." Under the more prosaic title of hashed brown potatoes, recipes appear in old regional cookbooks, including notebooks more than a century old.

Mastering the art of hashed brown cooking is tricky business. A young woman, in a serious study, wrote that she tested five different approaches before she achieved success. Salt pork fat was the original lubricant, but today the most likely formulas use bacon fat. A flavoring of onion is a matter of taste. And some cooks, including our serious student, make cold boiled potatoes the foundation of the dish. But the ultimate Yankee meal of hashed browns requires raw potatoes:

Heat about 3 tablespoons bacon fat in a skillet until the fat sizzles. Stir in 1/4 cup finely chopped onions, and while the fat is still noisy add 2 1/2 cups chopped or diced raw potatoes. Lift and turn the mixture with a spatula, immediately turning the heat to low. Cover and cook about 25 minutes. Sprinkle with salt and pepper. When the potatoes are crusty on the bottom, fold and turn like an omelet onto a serving platter.
SERVES 3–4

about 5 minutes. The potatoes probably won't stay intact, but just nudge the stray slices back into place to have a round cake. Slide onto a warm platter and serve hot.

SERVES 4

There's no alcohol left by the time the beer has boiled down—it simply makes a delicious coating for small new potatoes from the garden or farmer's market.

Small New Potatoes Steamed in Beer

7–8 tablespoons butter
⅓–½ tablespoon chopped scallions
8 small to medium new potatoes, washed and scraped

1–2 teaspoons chopped fresh rosemary, or ½ teaspoon dried, crumbled
1 12-ounce bottle or can of beer

Melt the butter in a large saucepan over gentle heat. Add the scallions and cook 3–4 minutes, until soft. Stir in the potatoes and the rosemary, turning the potatoes to coat them well with the butter and greens. Carefully pour in the beer, bring to the boiling point, cover, reduce heat, and cook very gently for about 20 minutes. (Time will depend on the size of the potatoes.) Increase the heat and continue cooking until the liquid is virtually absorbed and the potatoes are glazed, about 15 minutes more. If any residue of butter remains, scrape it onto the potatoes as they are served.

SERVES 4

Thin-skinned new potatoes, indeed, are too good in themselves to require adornment. But here's an exceptional treatment for a moment of indulgence.

Baked New Potatoes in Cream

12 small new potatoes
1 cup heavy cream
Salt
Freshly ground pepper

1 teaspoon turmeric
1 cup finely chopped scallions
3 tablespoons chopped parsley

Wash the potatoes, cover them with cold water, and bring to a rolling boil. Drain the potatoes and bake them in a preheated 350-degree oven for about 1 hour; test them after 45 minutes, and don't overcook. Cut the hot baked potatoes in quarters (leaving the skin on) and pop them into a hot serving dish. Quickly heat the cream with a sprinkling of salt and pepper, the turmeric, and the chopped scallions, and as soon as it comes to a boil pour it over the potatoes. Sprinkle the chopped parsley on top.

SERVES 4

Potato Pancakes

The only trick to making these potato pancakes is to get the grated raw potatoes into the hot pan just as soon as you grate them, before they begin to turn brown. A 9-inch pan is just right for a potato cake for two; if you want more, make additional batches.

2 tablespoons cooking oil or chicken or goose fat
2 medium potatoes (about ¾ pound)

Salt
Freshly ground pepper

Start heating 1 tablespoon of the oil slowly in a 9-inch nonstick pan while you peel and grate the potatoes (a food processor does a fast job). Immediately spread the grated potatoes evenly into the pan—they should sizzle as they go in. Press down with a spatula to make an even cake and sprinkle lightly with salt and several grinds of the pepper mill. Cook over medium heat on one side about 5 minutes or until well browned, then lift out with your spatula, drizzle the remaining tablespoon of oil into the pan, flip the cake and cook the other side about 5 minutes, seasoning the top side. Serve immediately.
SERVES 2

Cottage-Fried Potato Cakes

In northern Maine, Aroostook County's Potato Blossom Festival is a full-dress way of celebrating the region's major crop. As a popular vegetable, however, potatoes don't need a lot of gussying up, and they can be transformed as leftovers into plain but highly satisfying accompaniments for meat or fish.

2 cups creamy mashed potatoes
½ cup soft bread crumbs
1 tablespoon finely chopped fresh dill
1 teaspoon finely chopped fresh thyme

2 eggs, beaten
Salt
Freshly ground pepper
2–3 tablespoons butter

Mix the creamy mashed potatoes with the bread crumbs, the fresh herbs, and the beaten eggs, and add a little salt and pepper to taste. Heat the butter in a large skillet. When the butter gives off a slight haze, drop in large spoonfuls of the potato mixture and flatten them with a spatula. Cook over gentle heat until the undersides of the cakes are light brown, then turn over with a spatula and brown the other side. Arrange on very hot plates, and serve with pork chops, hamburgers, or other meat dishes.
SERVES 4

Scalloped Potatoes and Winter Turnip

1 very large yellow turnip or
  rutabaga (about 1¼ pounds)
2 large baking potatoes (about 1¼
  pounds)
1½ tablespoons butter
Salt

Freshly ground pepper
Freshly grated nutmeg
2 teaspoons flour
1¼ cups milk
¼ cup heavy cream

Peel the turnip, taking off quite a thick piece of peel because the outer edge of a winter turnip is apt to be bitter, then quarter it and cut it into thin slices. Peel the potatoes and cut into thin slices. Generously butter a shallow casserole and use half the the turnip slices to cover the bottom; salt and pepper them and grate a little nutmeg on top. Add a layer of half the potatoes, salt and pepper them, and sprinkle the flour over them, then dot with ½ tablespoon butter. Repeat with a layer of turnip slices, salt, pepper, nutmeg, ½ tablespoon butter, and a final layer of potatoes. Pour the milk over and let it seep down, then spread the cream over the top and dot with a final ½ tablespoon butter. Bake in a preheated 350-degree oven for 1 hour, covered loosely with foil, then remove the foil and bake another 20 minutes or so, until browned on top and tender throughout.
SERVES 6

VARIATION: PLAIN SCALLOPED POTATOES: Substitute an additional 1¼ pounds potatoes for the winter turnip and use 3 cups milk (no cream). Eliminate the nutmeg. Be sure to cook until all the milk has been absorbed.

Broiled Potato Skins

It is hard in our household to have leftover baked potato skins because our family tends to find the skins the best part of a baked potato. So one night we plan to have Albert Stockli's Roësti Potatoes (page 299), which are made with the flesh of good baked potatoes, and then save the skins to broil in this delectable way the next day. Serve these with steaks or chops.

Skins of 4 large baked potatoes
2 tablespoons vegetable oil
6 tablespoons butter
2 garlic cloves, minced

6–10 shakes Tabasco sauce, or to
  taste
Salt
About 1 teaspoon paprika

Cut the potato skins in ¼–½-inch strips. Spread the oil on the bottom of a large pan and lay the potato strips, skin side down, on top in one layer. Heat the butter and garlic until the butter is melted and sizzling. Season with the Tabasco, and pour over the potato strips. Shake a little salt to taste on top and dust with paprika. Place on the lowest rung under a broiler and let broil slowly for about 20 minutes, until browned and crisp.
SERVES 4

Mashed Potatoes with a Root Vegetable

Good mashed potatoes are a treat by themselves, but they become something special when mashed with an earthy-tasting root vegetable such as celeriac, turnips (summer or winter), Jerusalem artichokes, or parsnips. Use all-purpose potatoes for mashing—new potatoes are too waxy and russets are too mealy.

1 pound all-purpose potatoes
1 pound celeriac, white turnips or
   yellow rutabagas, Jerusalem
   artichokes, or parsnips

1–3 tablespoons butter
Salt
Freshly ground pepper

Peel the potatoes and cut in chunks. Boil in lightly salted water to cover, until tender. Peel the root vegetable and cut in chunks, then boil in a separate pot of lightly salted water to cover, until tender. Drain the potatoes and mash with a potato masher or put through a ricer. Drain the root vegetable and purée it by mashing it by hand or spinning it in a food processor. The potatoes and vegetable can be mashed together if you are doing it by hand, but not if you use the food processor because it will turn the potatoes very gluey. With a fork or whip, beat the 2 purées together, and beat in as much of the butter as conscience will allow. Season to taste with salt and pepper, and rewarm if necessary.
SERVES 4

Sweet Potatoes with Onions and Green Peppers

Sweet potatoes can be enhanced by other garden vegetables, just as is often done with white potatoes—in fact, they make a surprising vegetable dish that is not cloyingly sweet when done this way. Serve these potatoes with meat or fish.

2 tablespoons butter
4 cups cubed cooked sweet
   potatoes (not mushy)
1 cup coarsely chopped green
   peppers
1 cup coarsely chopped onion
1 teaspoon chopped fresh thyme, or
   1/2 teaspoon dried

3–4 chopped fresh sage leaves, or
   1/2 teaspoon dried, crumbled
Freshly grated nutmeg
Salt
Freshly ground pepper

Melt the butter in a skillet. Toss the vegetables with the herbs and grated nutmeg to taste, then fry them until the potatoes are brown and crisp. Sprinkle lightly with salt and pepper to taste.
SERVES 4

*2 cups mashed freshly cooked
    sweet potatoes*
½ cup hot milk
4 tablespoons New England rum
4 tablespoons melted butter

½ teaspoon salt
⅛ teaspoon mace
Freshly ground pepper
2 teaspoons grated orange rind
4 eggs, separated

Sweet Potato and Rum Soufflé

Combine the warm sweet potatoes with the hot milk, rum, melted butter, salt, mace, and a few turns of the pepper grinder, and stir until thoroughly blended. Stir in the grated orange rind. Beat the egg yolks until they are lemon-colored, and stir into the potatoes, mixing thoroughly. Whip the egg whites until they peak, and fold into the mixture. Scrape the mixture into a well-buttered 1½-quart soufflé dish, and bake for 25 minutes in a preheated 375-degree oven. Serve immediately.

SERVES 4

*2 cups mashed pumpkin, cooked
    oven-baked method (page 74)*
*½ tablespoon finely minced fresh
    ginger*
1 tablespoon maple syrup

¼ teaspoon freshly grated nutmeg
3 eggs, lightly beaten
¾ cup half-and-half
Salt
Freshly ground pepper

Pumpkin Timbales

Mix all of the ingredients together, seasoning to taste with salt and pepper. Pour the mixture into 8 lightly buttered muffin tins or custard cups, filling them two-thirds full, and place them in a pan of simmering water. Bake for 5 minutes in a preheated 350-degree oven, then lower the heat to 325 degrees and bake another 30 minutes, or until set (a skewer inserted in the center should come out clean). Let rest 5 minutes before unmolding.

SERVES 8

Butter-Steamed Radishes or Cucumbers

Here are two vegetables that we usually think of eating raw in salads, but they take on a new delicious dimension when butter-steamed this way. Actually, early New England cooks often cooked cucumbers, but they were invariably done with the ubiquitous white sauce and overcooked. You can also combine the radishes and cucumbers to make an interesting dish.

About 48 medium to large radishes,
  or 3 medium cucumbers
3 tablespoons butter
Salt
4 scallions, including tender greens,
  sliced

Several drops fresh lemon juice
1 tablespoon chopped chives and/or
  dill or flat-leaved parsley

The radishes should be washed, trimmed, and sliced quite thin. The cucumbers should be slit in half lengthwise, the seeds scooped out and discarded, and cut into pieces ½ inch wide and 1½ inches long. Melt the butter in a fairly large skillet, add the radishes or cukes, and stir-fry over medium-high heat, tossing several times to coat them. Sprinkle lightly with salt, cover, and cook over medium-low heat 3 minutes for radishes, 5 minutes for cukes. Add the scallions and cook another 4–5 minutes, or until just tender but not mushy. Season with lemon juice and fresh herbs.
SERVES 4

Scalloped Salsify

Seed catalogues tell gardeners that salsify requires 120 growing days. Its oysterlike flavor (old Yankees know it as oyster plant) inspired New England's traditional mock oysters that are made with a stiff mixture of salsify and beaten eggs, shaped to resemble oysters, and fried in butter. When cut up and baked in a sauce, salsify is equal to a scalloped seafood casserole.

4 cups cooked salsify in 1-inch
  pieces
1½ cups Cream Sauce or White
  Sauce (see page 629)
1 tablespoon chopped parsley
1 teaspoon chopped fresh savory,
  or ½ teaspoon dried
2 tablespoons chopped celery leaves

2 tablespoons finely chopped green
  pepper
2 tablespoons finely chopped onion
Salt
Freshly ground pepper
4 tablespoons melted butter
½ cup fresh bread crumbs

Mix the salsify pieces with the cream sauce, and stir in the chopped parsley, savory, celery leaves, green pepper, and onion. Season lightly with salt and pepper. Butter a 1½-quart baking dish and turn the salsify mixture into it. Mix the melted butter with the bread crumbs and spread over the contents

of the baking dish. Bake in a preheated 350-degree oven for 20–25 minutes, until the top is lightly browned.
SERVES 4

Another example of a delicious stir-fry vegetable dish when there is just a little of this and that in the garden. White turnips could be used instead of kohlrabi, and celery could certainly be substituted for the fennel, but this particular combination makes for an interesting and unusual blend of flavors.

3 tablespoons oil
1 large kohlrabi, peeled and sliced
   in sticks about ¼ inch thick x 1½
   inches long
1 fennel bulb, trimmed and sliced
   in same-size sticks

¾ pound spinach, washed, tough
   stems removed
Salt
Freshly ground pepper

Spinach, Kohlrabi, and Fennel

Heat the oil in a large skillet or wok, then sauté the kohlrabi and fennel sticks, stirring and tossing them for 30 seconds. Add the spinach with whatever water clings to the leaves, sprinkle a little salt and pepper over, and stir and toss the vegetables for 3–4 minutes, adding a few tablespoons of water if they start to stick to the pan. When just tender, the water should have evaporated; if it hasn't, boil it off rapidly.
SERVES 4

Another example of the Shakers' way with herbs and vegetables.

2 pounds fresh spinach
2 teaspoons chopped fresh
   rosemary, or ½ teaspoon dried,
   crumbled
1 teaspoon chopped parsley

1 tablespoon chopped scallions
2 tablespoons butter
Salt
Freshly ground pepper

Shaker Spinach with Herbs

Wash the spinach thoroughly, then chop it coarsely and put it with the water that clings to it into a pot. Add the rosemary, parsley, scallions, and butter, and sprinkle lightly with salt and pepper. Cover the pot and simmer over low heat for about 4–8 minutes, depending on the tenderness of the spinach.
SERVES 4

Stir-frying vegetables

It's only in the last couple of decades that New Englanders have really learned to respect vegetables. Perhaps that's because we're more health conscious and know what boiling vegetables to death does to their nutritional value, not to mention that drowning them in butter or cream or sauce to try to restore some flavor only compounds the felony. For those who have their own kitchen gardens, there is an extra pride in bringing out the good flavors of vegetables. Pleasure in their undimmed natural colors is a bonus.

Stir-frying is a relatively new cooking technique in the Western world. The trick is to cut each vegetable into small uniform sizes—usually in sticks somewhere between matchstick and pencil width and about ½ to 2 inches long—so they will cook quickly. The vegetables are seared in a pan with a little oil (a skillet will do; you don't need a wok although it is a very convenient shape for this kind of cooking) sometimes seasoned with garlic and/or ginger, and then they are fried and stirred and tossed until done. It's usually a matter of 2–3 minutes for tender vegetables like zucchini and snow peas; but for tougher vegetables like rutabaga and celery root, which require additional cooking, add a little water, cover the pan, and steam-cook until done. Unfortunately, too many restaurants have gone too far in extolling crunchily underdone vegetables. That's not the object; the vegetables should be cooked through but still have some character to them, just a touch of resistance.

One can stir-fry any of the vegetables listed below alone, but they are often more fun and colorful in combination. In trying to create a pleasing mix, nature, as always, is a help; whatever comes in season at the same time usually goes well together. Often when you find you have only a single pepper in the garden and maybe only one side shoot of broccoli and a first small yellow crookneck, you'll find that by combining them you'll have enough to feed your family or guests.

Here are some of the vegetables we like to stir-fry in varying combinations:

Summer squashes; kohlrabi; green, red, and yellow sweet peppers; young turnips; peeled broccoli stems; sugar snap and snow peas; scallions; celery; and odd stalks of asparagus.

Fall root vegetables such as rutabagas, celeriac, winter squashes, parsnips, and Jerusalem artichokes with carrots, late peppers, and broccoli stems for color contrast.

About 3 tablespoons oil is enough to stir-fry 3–4 cups vegetables, which will serve 4 (watery vegetables reduce more in cooking, so take that into consideration when calculating the yield). If you know that one vegetable is bound to take a little longer to cook than another, add it first and cook for a minute or two before adding the next one—for example, carrots or kohlrabi would need that extra time when combined with zucchini.

Use salt sparingly, particularly with root vegetables, and remember that fresh herbs are always welcome.

Stir-frying entails a little trial-and-error, but it is a simple art worth mastering.

2½ pounds fresh spinach
1 pound mushrooms, sliced
1½ tablespoons butter
1 tablespoon vegetable oil
Freshly grated nutmeg

Salt
Freshly ground pepper
4–5 tablespoons heavy cream
3 tablespoons madeira wine

Spinach with Mushrooms

Wash the spinach and cook, uncovered, in a saucepan until wilted. Drain and chop fine. Sauté the mushrooms in the butter and oil. Squeeze the spinach dry, and add to the mushrooms with the nutmeg, a light sprinkling of salt, and a few turns of the pepper grinder. Cook the spinach and mushrooms about 1 minute, then stir in the cream and the wine and serve hot.
SERVES 4–6

An unusual luncheon dish to make when your garden is full of burgeoning zucchini or yellow squash. Be sure to pick only male blossoms—the ones that have only the flower without the start of a small squash attached to it.

Squash Blossoms on Summer Squash Pancakes

2 medium summer squash (about 1 pound)
2 teaspoons salt
½ cup flour
1 teaspoon baking powder
1 egg, beaten
2 tablespoons finely chopped fresh coriander or parsley

Chili powder to taste
Oil for frying
1 tablespoon butter
About 12 squash blossoms
2 tablespoons grated aged cheddar or Parmesan

Grate the unpeeled squash, and toss with the salt in a strainer. Let drain for about 20 minutes (save the juice for soup, if you like). Squeeze the grated squash in small handfuls to extract most of the moisture, then put it in a bowl and sift the flour and baking powder over it. Stir well, add the beaten egg, fresh herb, and a dash or so of chili powder, depending on your taste. When the batter is well mixed, heat ½ inch oil in a large skillet and, when a film appears on the surface, drop the batter by tablespoonfuls, smooth each mound into a thick pancake, making 8 in all. Fry until light brown, then turn and brown on the other side.

Meanwhile, heat the butter in a second small skillet, add the squash blossoms, and flatten them with a spatula. Sauté quickly, turn and press again, salt very lightly, and fry for a few seconds. When the pancakes are done, drain them on paper towels, then arrange them on warm plates with the blossoms on top and a liberal sprinkling of cheese.
SERVES 4

Fried Green Tomatoes with Sauce

There's a saying that real New Englanders like green tomatoes better than ripe ones. True or not, in the region's north country it's a rare year when the frost fails to come before all of the tomato harvest is red. Here is a traditional foliage-season breakfast.

4 medium green tomatoes (about 1 pound)
1 cup plus 2 tablespoons flour
½ teaspoon salt
Freshly ground pepper
1 teaspoon chopped fresh savory, or ½ teaspoon dried

4 strips bacon
2 tablespoons butter
1 cup or more milk
¼ cup sour cream or plain yogurt
½ teaspoon dried rosemary

Slice the tomatoes about ¼ inch thick, and spread them out on paper towels to drain well. Put 1 cup flour on a plate, stir in the salt, a few turns of the pepper grinder, and the savory. Cook the bacon in a large skillet and put the strips aside on paper towels to drain. Dredge the tomato slices in the seasoned flour. Heat up the bacon fat in the skillet until it sizzles, and arrange the slices to cover the entire pan. Turn the heat to moderate and

Sun-dried or Oven-dried Tomatoes

An easy way of preserving an abundant crop of ripe tomatoes, particularly the meatier plum tomatoes, is to dry them. Sun-dried tomatoes have long been a staple of Italian cooking, used to intensify the flavor of sauces, but in New England, where one can't count on days of intense sun just at the time the tomatoes come ripe, oven-drying is an excellent alternative. You can, of course, use a food dehydrator, following manufacturer's instructions.

To oven-dry tomatoes: Split the tomatoes lengthwise (or quarter them if you are using a round variety) and scoop out most of the seeds. Place the tomatoes on cake racks or pieces of screen, cut side up, not quite touching. Sprinkle the cut sides lightly with salt and place in a preheated 200-degree oven for about 8 hours, or until the tomatoes have shrunk to a fraction of their size and look leathery (but not dry—they should still be flexible). Pack in jars, cover with olive oil, and seal; you can put fresh basil leaves between the pieces, if you like, and the oil will be delicious to use for salads. Store in a dark place for 4 weeks before using. Or you can store the dried tomatoes (without oil) in plastic bags and freeze them.

1 POUND FRESH TOMATOES WILL YIELD ABOUT ½ CUP DRIED

fry the slices about 6 minutes, then turn them and fry about 6 minutes more, until they are crusty and light brown. Don't hurry them. When the tomatoes are ready, put them and the bacon strips on a platter in the oven while you make the sauce.

Heat the butter in the skillet and stir in the remaining 2 tablespoons flour to make a smooth paste. Pour in the milk and let it heat before stirring it into the flour and butter mixture. Cook a few minutes, stirring until smooth, then turn off the heat and stir in the sour cream or yogurt; don't let the sauce boil. Stir in the rosemary and add a little extra milk if the sauce seems too thick. Pour the hot sauce over the hot tomatoes.
SERVES 4–6

White Turnips and Spinach

3 medium white turnips
3 tablespoons butter or vegetable oil or a combination
2 shallots, or 1 small white onion, minced
1½ pounds spinach
Salt
Freshly ground pepper
A little olive oil (optional)

Peel the turnips and cut them into pencil-thick pieces, then drop into boiling water to cover and blanch 2 minutes. Drain. Heat the butter and/or vegetable oil in a heavy pot and sauté the shallots until translucent. Remove the thick stems from the spinach leaves, tear them in pieces, and wash thoroughly. Add the turnips, then the spinach with the water that clings to it to the pot, along with salt and pepper to taste, and sauté, stirring, 1 minute. Cover and cook gently 6–8 minutes, adding a little more water if necessary. Drizzle a little olive oil over the top before serving, if you wish.
SERVES 4

Stuffed Yellow Squash

1 cup stale bread crumbs
2 summer squash (about 1 pound each)
3 tablespoons butter
3–4 tablespoons finely chopped shallots or onions
1½ cups finely chopped mushrooms
2 garlic cloves, chopped
2 cups diced ham (in ¼-inch dice)
1 teaspoon chopped fresh thyme, or ¼ teaspoon dried
1 bay leaf
Salt
Freshly ground pepper
½ cup fresh bread crumbs
¼ cup minced parsley

Soak the stale bread crumbs in water. Cut each squash into 2 equal pieces that will lie flat; scoop out the centers to leave shells about ⅛ inch thick. Chop the pulp and set aside. Melt the butter in a skillet and sauté the shallots or onions, mushrooms, and garlic. Add the chopped pulp to the skillet with the ham; stir in the thyme and bay leaf. Season mixture lightly with salt and freshly ground pepper. Stir in the soaked bread crumbs. Divide this mixture between the 4 squash shells, and sprinkle the tops with fresh bread crumbs and minced parsley. Bake in a preheated 350-degree oven for about 25 minutes.

SERVES 4

Summer Squash or Zucchini Stuffed with Ricotta

Four 6-inch-long summer squash
3 tablespoons corn oil
½ cup chopped green pepper
½ cup chopped onion
1 garlic clove, chopped fine
1 tablespoon chopped fresh basil,
    or ½ teaspoon dried

⅔ cup ricotta cheese
Salt
Freshly ground pepper
1 cup grated sharp cheddar

Blanch the squash in boiling salted water for 5 minutes. Drain and, when cool enough to handle, cut in halves lengthwise and scoop out the centers, leaving sturdy shells for the stuffing. Chop up the centers of the squash. Heat the oil in a skillet and sauté the green pepper, onion, garlic, and the chopped centers for 5 minutes over gentle heat. Mix the sautéed vegetables with the basil and ricotta cheese, and season with salt and pepper to taste. Spoon the filling into the squash halves and sprinkle on the grated cheddar. Arrange them in a greased shallow casserole just large enough to hold them in one layer. Cover with foil and bake in a preheated 350-degree oven for about 15 minutes. Remove the foil and continue baking for 25–30 minutes, until the cheddar is bubbling and lightly browned.

SERVES 4

This is a September or late-summer dish that combines yellow squash or zucchini with other vegetables to make either a meal in itself or a hearty accompaniment to cold meat or fish. You could use a layer of corn kernels, or peas and beans, and omit the mushrooms and tomatoes. Try to choose vegetables for color contrast as well as for easy availability.

Summer Squash with Vegetables and Cheese

1 pound summer squash, halved and seeded only if overgrown
3 sprigs mint
2–3 whole carrots, trimmed and scraped
8–10 scallions, chopped
2 tablespoons butter
½ pound mushrooms, sliced

1 pound tomatoes, peeled and quartered
1 tablespoon chopped fresh chervil or parsley
Salt
Freshly ground pepper
6 ounces cheddar, grated

Cut the squash halves into ½-inch pieces, then steam them with the mint and carrots for about 10 minutes. Arrange the squash in a layer on the bottom of a large shallow buttered baking dish. Cut the steamed carrots into dice. Sauté the scallions in the butter 1 minute, then add the diced carrots, mushroom slices, and tomato quarters. Season lightly with salt and pepper and stir in the chopped herb, cooking gently until the carrots are done and the mushrooms and tomatoes are lightly browned. Arrange a layer of sautéed vegetables over the squash, and sprinkle grated cheddar evenly over the top. Put the dish in a preheated 400-degree oven for 10 minutes to brown the cheese.
SERVES 4

This is the most delicious way we know to prepare butternut squash, and those tasting it for the first time are invariably charmed—and curious to know what went into the dish. It couldn't be simpler, particularly if you have a food processor with a grating blade.

Baked Grated Butternut Squash with Cinnamon and Cream

1 large butternut squash (about 2 pounds)
Salt

1 teaspoon cinnamon
¾ cup heavy cream

Peel and grate the squash. Spread half of it over the bottom of a shallow 1-quart baking dish, sprinkle lightly with salt, and dust with half the cinnamon. Repeat. Pour the heavy cream over all. Bake, covered loosely with foil, 40 minutes in a preheated 350-degree oven, uncover, and bake another 10–15 minutes, until very tender.
SERVES 6

Young Turnips with Greens

The turnips should be between the size of marbles and walnuts, and the greens should be tender and about 8 inches long.

About 24 small turnips with greens
3 tablespoons vegetable oil or a combination of vegetable oil and olive oil or butter

Salt
Freshly ground pepper
1 garlic clove, crushed and peeled

Trim the turnips, cutting off and reserving the greens. Place the turnips in boiling salted water to cover by an inch and cook for about 10–15 minutes, until almost tender. Drain and reserve the cooking liquid. Meanwhile, roughly chop the greens, rinse, and drain. In a large skillet or wok, heat the oil, oils, or oil and butter, add the crushed garlic and the greens, and sauté, tossing and stirring, for 1 minute. Add ½ cup of the reserved turnip cooking liquid, cover, and let steam along with the drained turnips over a low heat, about 5 minutes. Taste and add salt and pepper as necessary; the turnips and greens should be just tender with a little bite to them.

SERVES 4

Sautéed Turnip Greens

Fresh young turnip greens sautéed in oil with garlic make a lusty and healthful vegetable accompaniment to almost any meat, and they may also be served alone with an egg on top and a few scraps of country ham scattered around for flavor.

3 tablespoons vegetable or olive oil or a combination
3 garlic cloves, smashed and peeled
1 pound young turnip greens, washed and chopped
½–1 cup water

Salt
4 eggs (optional)
Freshly ground pepper (optional)
½ cup slivered country ham (optional)

Heat the oil in a heavy skillet or wok and sauté the garlic for a few seconds, then add the turnip greens with the water that clings to them. Stir and toss over moderately high heat for 1 minute, then add ½ cup water and a little salt, and reduce the heat and let simmer gently, covered, for 10 minutes. Check to see if there is enough water, adding more if necessary. Serve plain (and don't extract the garlic cloves if you have garlic lovers around; they are lovely just mashed into the greens). Or if you want to make a more substantial dish, with a spoon press 4 indentations on top of the greens, and crack an egg into each of them; sprinkle a little salt and pepper on top, scatter the ham slivers around, cover, and cook another 2 minutes, adding a little more water if necessary.

SERVES 4

Whether called rutabaga or swede, the big dense turnip with the soft earthy color is an old favorite of hill-country Yankees, for it's a vegetable that keeps well in a root cellar long into the winter. This is an heirloom recipe fit for contemporary vegetarian cookery, or for anyone who likes variety in vegetables.

Scalloped Yellow Turnip or Rutabaga

4 tablespoons butter
½ cup chopped onion
1 large yellow turnip, peeled and sliced (about 4 cups)
About 1 tablespoon flour
Salt

Freshly ground pepper
1 cup or more milk
½ teaspoon mace
6 strips sweet red pepper
¼ cup grated sharp cheddar

Lightly butter a 1½-quart casserole. Alternate layers of chopped onion and sliced turnip, sprinkling each with a little flour, salt, and pepper. Dot the layers with the remaining butter, and pour the milk over all, adding a sprinkling of mace. Strew the pepper strips across the top and sprinkle the cheese over all, cover the casserole, and set it in a preheated 350-degree oven for about 1 hour, or until the turnip is tender. After 30 minutes, add a little more milk if needed.

SERVES 4

Just as sweet potatoes and yams may be enhanced by the taste of maple, so the accent improves other glazed vegetables like young carrots or scraped parsnips. Mustard is used in this turnip recipe as an interesting counterbalance to the sweetness.

Maple-Flavored Baked Turnips

1½ pounds white turnips
3 tablespoons butter
2 tablespoons prepared mustard (old-fashioned seed mustard preferred)

3 tablespoons maple syrup
Salt
Freshly ground pepper
½ cup fresh whole wheat bread crumbs

Peel the turnips and slice them about ⅓ inch thick. Drop them into boiling salted water and cook about 8 minutes, until just tender. Meanwhile, melt the butter in a shallow ovenproof dish. Stir in the mustard, using less if it is particularly hot. Drain the cooked turnips and pat dry; toss the slices in the butter-mustard mixture, adding maple syrup, a light sprinkling of salt, and a few turns of the pepper grinder. Sprinkle the crumbs over the top. Bake in a preheated 450-degree oven 10 minutes, or set the dish about 8–10 inches under a preheated broiler and broil until bubbling and hot.

SERVES 4

Sweet-and-Sour Zucchini

2 pounds thin zucchini
2 tablespoons vegetable or olive oil
  or a combination
Salt

Freshly ground pepper
2 tablespoons brown sugar
2 tablespoon cider or red wine
  vinegar

Wash the zucchini and cut them in thirds or halves about 3 inches long. Cut each piece in half lengthwise, and then slice each half into 4 or 6 pieces to make long, thin triangular logs. Heat the oil in a skillet and toss in the zucchini strips. Season lightly with salt and pepper, and cook over relatively high heat, stirring and tossing to turn the pieces, for 5 minutes. Add the sugar and vinegar, and toss over heat another 30 seconds.
SERVES 4

Adele's Zucchini Pancakes

"Something is changed since yesterday," Adele Dawson writes in an enchanting volume she titled *Health, Happiness and the Pursuit of Herbs.* "Barefoot, I walk into the kitchen and flip the page of a wall calendar from May to June." It's summer for this scholarly authority on the healthy aspects of New England greens; among her garden recipes is this formula for a delicious porch or patio luncheon dish.

3 small, or 1½ large zucchini,
  grated
A few fresh basil leaves, finely
  chopped
A few fresh marjoram leaves, finely
  chopped
Sprigs savory

½ cup grated Yankee cheddar
1 cup whole wheat flour
1 teaspoon salt
1 teaspoon baking powder
1 egg, lightly beaten
Cayenne
Milk or yogurt

GARNISH: ½ cup plain yogurt blended with ½ cup heavy cream
         1 tablespoon chopped fresh parsley and chives combined

Put the zucchini in a mixing bowl and add the basil and marjoram leaves and several savory sprigs. Stir in the grated cheese, flour, salt, and baking powder. Add the egg, a dash of cayenne, and enough milk and/or yogurt to make a thick batter. When the mixture is thoroughly blended, drop by spoonfuls onto a lightly greased iron skillet or griddle and fry until lightly golden on both sides. Serve with ½ cup yogurt blended with the cream. Sprinkle with chopped fresh parsley and chives.
SERVES 4–6

1 pound zucchini
2 pounds potatoes
3 tablespoons olive or vegetable oil or a combination
1 medium onion, chopped fine
2 garlic cloves, chopped fine
¾ cup puréed tomatoes
1 tablespoon chopped fresh rosemary, or 1 teaspoon dried, crumbled
Salt
Freshly ground pepper

Baked Zucchini and Potatoes

Wash and cut the zucchini into thin slices. Peel the potatoes and cut them into thin slices, dropping them in cold water. In a skillet, heat 2 tablespoons oil and cook the chopped onion until tender, stirring occasionally; add the garlic for the last minute of cooking. Stir in the puréed tomatoes, the rosemary, and a sprinkling of salt and pepper to taste. Simmer about 5 minutes. Oil a shallow 2-quart casserole and layer the bottom with potato slices that have been drained and patted dry. Season lightly with salt and pepper. Spread the zucchini slices over the potatoes, season them, and cover with the tomato mixture. Top with the remaining potatoes, season, and sprinkle with the remaining 1 tablespoon oil. Bake in a preheated 350-degree oven for 1¾ hours, until the potatoes look like crisp pan-fries.
SERVES 4

Zucchini and Rice Gratin

1 pound zucchini
2 cups cooked rice (cooked 10 minutes and drained)
4 scallions, including some tender greens, chopped
1 tablespoon chopped fresh tarragon, or ½ teaspoon dried
1 tablespoon chopped parsley
¼ cup fresh bread crumbs
1½ tablespoons butter
2 tablespoons grated sharp cheddar cheese

Wash the zucchini and grate them, skin and all. Mix the grated zucchini with the rice, scallions, and chopped herbs. Butter a shallow 1-quart baking dish and spread the zucchini-rice mixture over the bottom. Top with bread crumbs, dot with butter, then strew the cheese over the surface. Bake 25 minutes in a preheated 400-degree oven, covered for the first 15 minutes, then uncovered so the top will brown lightly.
SERVES 4–6

Garden Vegetable Stew

Vary the vegetables in this harvest-time dish by using what is most abundant. To make a more substantial one-dish meal, add cooked chicken or turkey.

¼ pound mature pole beans
3 tablespoons vegetable oil
1 small sweet red pepper, chopped
1 small green pepper, chopped
1 medium yellow squash, cut into chunks
3 medium zucchini, cut into chunks
½ cup coarsely chopped scallions or other onions
2–3 garlic cloves, chopped
1 large red tomato, peeled, seeded, and coarsely chopped
Salt
Freshly ground pepper
1 teaspoon chopped fresh thyme, or ½ teaspoon dried
1 teaspoon fresh rosemary, or ½ teaspoon dried, crumbled
2–3 cups cooked chicken or turkey, cut into chunks (optional)

Rinse the beans, cut them diagonally into 1½-inch pieces, and blanch them in a large pot of boiling water for 2 minutes. Remove and drain. Heat the oil in a large saucepan and cook the peppers 2 minutes; add the squash, zucchini, scallions, and garlic and cook, tossing, for 1 minute. Add the tomato with its juice and the green beans. Cover and simmer 10 minutes. Season to taste with salt and pepper, and stir in the fresh herbs. Cook 1–2 minutes more, or longer if you want a "drier" stew. Stir in the optional cooked chicken or turkey and heat through.
SERVES 4

2 cups fresh cranberry or shell
    beans
3 tablespoons corn oil
1 cup chopped onion
2 tablespoons paprika
4 medium tomatoes, peeled, seeded,
    and chopped

Salt
Freshly ground pepper
1 cup hubbard squash, peeled and
    diced
½ cup fresh corn kernels
1–2 tablespoons chopped fresh
    basil or parsley

Mixed Fall Vegetables

Run water over the beans and put them in a pan with water to cover. Bring to a boil, lower the heat, cover, and simmer about 45 minutes, until the beans are tender. Drain and reserve the liquid. Meanwhile, heat the oil in a skillet and stir in the onion, sprinkling it with the paprika; cook about 2 minutes. Add the chopped tomatoes, and season with a little salt and pepper to taste. Simmer, stirring occasionally, for about 5 minutes, then add the squash. Stir in the beans and a little of the reserved liquid. Cook until the squash softens and thickens the mixture. Add the corn and cook for 5 minutes longer. Sprinkle the top with fresh basil or parsley.

SERVES 6 OR MORE

2 medium onions, sliced
4 tablespoons olive and vegetable
    oil, combined
2 garlic cloves, chopped
4 medium new potatoes, peeled and
    sliced
6–8 ounces Portuguese chouriço
    sausage, sliced fairly thin

6–8 cups chopped wild spring
    greens, such as dandelion,
    milkweed, lamb's quarters, or
    wild lettuce
1 cup water
Pepper
Salt
4 lemon wedges

Sautéed Wild Spring Greens with Potatoes

Sauté the onions in the oils about 5 minutes, tossing and stirring. Add the garlic, potatoes, and sausage slices and sauté, stirring, another few minutes. Toss in the greens, stirring until coated with oil, then add the water. Grind pepper generously all over (you probably will not even need salt—wait and taste at the end), cover, lower heat, and cook about 10–15 minutes, until everything is tender. Taste and correct seasoning, if necessary. Serve with lemon wedges.

SERVES 4

SALADS

SALADS may have come full circle. In a chapter entitled "The Sallet Bowl," the authors of *Secrets of New England Cooking* describe what's been happening. "Simple salads of early times were displaced by elaborate concoctions in the form of butterflies, candles, and geometric designs during the genteel 1860s when cooking schools and salad clubs first came into vogue. But to a real salad lover," according to these authors, "a bowl of mixed salad greens with a simple oil and vinegar dressing has no equal."

However, there may still be just as many New Englanders with a taste for fussy salads. Much of the responsibility for this, it seems dismaying to note, belongs to Fannie Farmer, who stirred a spoonful of ketchup, one day at the Boston Cooking School, into a vinaigrette, and so became a perpetrator of the misnamed reddish "French dressing" now found from coast to coast.

The increasing availability of canned pineapple and especially marshmallow (the confection composed of corn syrup, gelatin, and starch) transformed the simple, natural salad. Miss Farmer, at the turn of the century, abandoned her Boston conservatism by introducing a salad of canned Hawaiian pineapple, grapes, bits of marshmallow, and walnuts. She went further. For her monthly column in *The Woman's Home Companion*, she mixed ginger ale with gelatin, folded in some cutup grapes, apples, celery, and canned pineapple, and created the first molded salad to be based on a popular drink.

Vegetables in aspic and other jellied dishes are among foods that old New Englanders were always making, of course. But until the era of exotic packaged foods and the speedy transport of fruits and vegetables from other regions, "sallets" were composed of ingredients with which most Yankee cooks felt comfortable. "Another grand sallet," from a colonial Boston cookbook published a generation before the American Revolutionary War, goes this way: "The youngest and smallest leaves of spinage, the smallest also of sorrel, well washed currans, and red beets round the center being finely carved, oyl and vinegar, and the dish garnished with lemon and beets."

It's not so long ago that spinach salads were so much in vogue that they became a cliché, but the two-hundred-year-old salad above could be made today with lettuce in place of the spinach and not be out of place in this chapter. Now there are a dozen kinds of salad greens (arugula and *mâche*, lettuces like crisphead, butterhead, romaine, Ruby, Oakleaf, Grand Rapids, and Green Ice, for example) available year-round in New England. There are such wild greens as fiddleheads and salads of wild rice and pasta. This chapter is an effort to show some of the salads that can be served when you let your creative side have its way.

Cucumber and Fiddlehead Salad

2 cups plain yogurt
3 scallions, chopped, including tender greens
2 tablespoons finely chopped mint
Salt
Freshly ground pepper

1 medium cucumber, peeled, seeded, and diced
1 cup cooked fiddleheads (see page 44)
1 tomato, cut in wedges

Pour the yogurt in a mixing bowl and stir in the scallions and mint. Add a little salt to taste and several turns of the pepper grinder. Stir in the cucumber and fiddleheads. Place in the refrigerator for 1 hour. Fold in the tomatoes before serving.
SERVES 4

Summer Salad

4 clusters fresh broccoli (stem and florets)
A handful of fresh green beans
6–8 large leaves Oakleaf lettuce
Watercress sprigs

1 head endive
6–8 cherry tomatoes
12 Greek olives
4 large radishes, cut in fan shapes
About 12 ounces fresh goat cheese

DRESSING:
⅓ cup olive oil
2 tablespoons red wine vinegar

½ teaspoon Dijon mustard
¼ teaspoon salt

3 tablespoons, mixed to your taste, of chopped fresh Italian parsley, scallions, and a fresh herb, such as basil, tarragon, or dill

Freshly ground pepper to taste

Peel the broccoli and cook in a big pot of boiling salted water for 5 minutes. Snap the stem ends off the beans and cook them in boiling salted water until just barely tender. Drain broccoli and let beans cool. Spread the Oakleaf lettuce over a serving platter. Distribute sprigs of watercress over lettuce; separate the endive leaves and arrange them on the platter as well. Make small piles of the broccoli and green beans, interspersed with cherry tomatoes, olives, radishes, and large chunks of the goat cheese.

In a jar with a lid, shake up the olive oil, vinegar, mustard, and salt, and then pour over the greens. Sprinkle herbs and freshly ground black pepper on top of everything.

SERVES 4

Nasturtium Flower and Chervil Salad

We know a New Hampshire cook who makes a sweet batter of whole wheat pastry flour, eggs, and honey with which to coat daylilies, elderflowers, rose petals, and nasturtium blossoms before frying them in deep fat. The vibrant color of nasturtiums in this salad recipe, however, is anything but hidden when it is dappled with chervil.

1 head Boston or Bibb lettuce
1¼ cups nasturtium blossoms
   (shake down as you fill)
3 tablespoons olive oil

1½ tablespoons lemon juice
Salt
Freshly ground pepper
1 tablespoon chopped chervil

Wash the lettuce leaves, drain and dry thoroughly, and line the sides of a salad bowl with them. Wash the nasturtium flowers, drain them, and dry on paper towels. Be careful not to bruise them. Mix the oil and lemon juice with a little salt and pepper to taste and the chervil. Stir until the dressing is very well blended, then pour it over the blossoms, stirring carefully.

SERVES 4

Garden Salad of Small Zucchini, Cucumbers, and Beets

About 6 medium beets, cooked, peeled, and cut into thin slices
1 small zucchini, sliced thin
1 cucumber, every other strip peeled, sliced thin
1 young onion, including some of its tender greens, sliced thin

½ cup Vinaigrette (page 346)
2 tablespoons chopped fresh coriander or dill
Salt
Freshly ground pepper

GARNISH: *lettuce leaves and/or watercress*

Toss all the vegetables with the vinaigrette and herbs. Season to taste with salt, if necessary, and freshly ground pepper. Serve on lettuce leaves and/or watercress.
SERVES 4

Nancy Nicholas's Connecticut Gazpacho Salad

4 unpeeled (unwaxed) cucumbers
5 ripe unpeeled tomatoes
1 large purple onion

About 2 cups fresh bread crumbs
½ cup or more garlicky Vinaigrette (page 346)

Slice the cucumbers, tomatoes, and onion as thin as possible, retaining the juices. In a glass bowl arrange a layer of tomatoes and sprinkle it with bread crumbs. Add a layer of cucumbers, and another layer of bread crumbs, a layer of onions, and more bread crumbs. Continue until the bowl is filled and all the vegetables are used up. Pour enough vinaigrette over to seep down and touch the bottom of the top layer of vegetables. Put the salad in the refrigerator for at least 2 hours.
SERVES 4–6

Vegetable Salad with Sauerkraut

3 potatoes, freshly cooked, peeled, and diced (to make 2 cups)
About ¾ cup mustardy Vinaigrette (page 346)
1 large carrot, peeled and diced
1 good-size beet, cooked, peeled, and diced
½ medium cucumber, peeled and diced

2 cups loosely packed, drained fresh Maine sauerkraut
3 scallions, including tender greens, chopped
Salt
Freshly ground pepper
1–2 tablespoons chopped fresh dill

GARNISHES: *lettuce leaves and sliced red onions*

Toss the potatoes, preferably still warm, with ¼ cup of the vinaigrette, and let stand for about 15 minutes. Mix in all the remaining ingredients and toss with as much more of the vinaigrette as you wish. Season to taste with salt and pepper, and sprinkle with fresh dill. Serve on lettuce leaves, garnished with sliced red onions.
SERVES 4 OR MORE

VARIATION: For a more substantial salad, add about 1 cup diced kielbasa or about 10 slices thick bacon fried crisp and drained.

Savoy Cabbage Slaw

1 head Savoy cabbage (about 1 pound)
2 teaspoons prepared mustard
½ teaspoon salt
3 tablespoons cider vinegar
1 tablespoon sugar

2 tablespoons vegetable oil
1 small red onion, sliced very thin, or 8 scallions, including tender greens, chopped
1 medium carrot

Remove tough outer leaves from the cabbage, quarter it, and cut in fine shreds, discarding the core. In a large bowl mix the mustard, salt, vinegar, sugar, and oil. Stir in the sliced onion and the shredded cabbage. Peel the carrot and, using the large holes of the grater, grate it into the bowl. Mix everything together thoroughly and let stand to ripen at least 30 minutes before serving.
SERVES 4–6

Coleslaw

This is a lighter and less sweet version of the traditional coleslaw.

1½ pounds cabbage (1 small cabbage)
1 tablespoon sugar
1 tablespoon cider vinegar
⅔ cup Mayonnaise, preferably homemade (page 347)
⅔ cup plain yogurt
Salt

Freshly ground pepper
2–3 scallions, including tender greens, sliced thin
½ small green pepper, seeds and ribs removed and chopped fine
About 2 tablespoons chopped fresh herbs, such as parsley and chives

Finely shred the cabbage and toss with the sugar and vinegar. Let stand about 10 minutes. Mix the mayonnaise and yogurt together, then fold into the shredded cabbage. Add salt, pepper to taste and the scallions, chopped pepper, and herbs.
SERVES 6–8

Anise-Flavored Carrot Slaw

3 cups scraped, grated carrots
1 tablespoon anise seed
1 teaspoon sugar

¼ cup golden raisins
Juice of ½ lemon
4 tablespoons salad oil

Put the grated carrots, anise seed, sugar, and raisins in a bowl, and squeeze the lemon juice over them. Add the oil and toss to mix thoroughly. Chill for 1 hour or longer.
SERVES 4–6

Barley Salad

3 cups cold cooked barley
½ cup ham, cut in small dice
¾ cup chopped red and green peppers
¼ cup finely chopped red onion
½ cup cooked crisp green vegetables, such as green beans, broccoli, or zucchini, chopped

½ chopped large dill pickle
⅓ cup chopped fresh herbs, such as parsley, chives, or basil
⅓ cup mustardy Vinaigrette (page 346)

GARNISHES: lettuce leaves and black olives, preferably Mediterranean-type

Toss everything together and let stand 10–15 minutes to develop flavor. Serve on a platter garnished with lettuce leaves and olives.
SERVES 4

Tabouli

This Lebanese salad is seen often these days on New England menus, perhaps because we have come to appreciate the earthy flavor of bulgur wheat combined with the fresh taste of garden parsley and mint. There are no hard and fast rules about the making of Tabouli, but this formula from an English friend, Paule McPherson, has proved a favorite among those who've sampled it.

1 cup bulgur
1½ cups boiling water
1 cup chopped spring onions or scallions, including tender greens
2 cups chopped parsley
½ cup chopped fresh mint
½ cup olive oil

½ cup fresh lemon juice
Salt
Freshly ground pepper
2 small cucumbers, peeled, seeded, and diced
2 medium-size ripe tomatoes (when in season), cut in dice

Wash the bulgur in several changes of water and drain, then pour the boiling water over it and let stand 30 minutes. Drain and squeeze out all moisture. Put in a salad bowl with the onions or scallions, parsley, and mint. Mix the olive oil, lemon juice, and a little salt and pepper together, then pour it over the salad and toss thoroughly. Fold in the cucumbers and tomatoes, if you're using them. Taste and correct the seasoning. Let stand for a few hours before serving.

SERVES 6–8

A good dish to bring to a summer potluck supper. The mixture may be varied according to what your garden and larder offer but it is important to have some crunch, some contrasting color, plus the accent of a flavorful meat—and the inclusion of some seafood, as well, makes a particularly interesting dish. Here is a Wild Rice Salad we concocted to help celebrate a Summer Solstice party.

Wild Rice Salad

10 ounces wild rice
Salt
Freshly ground pepper
10 ounces Portuguese chouriço sausage, diced
3 ribs celery, chopped
1 large red pepper, seeded and chopped
5 scallions, including tender greens, chopped

About 1/3 cup chopped herbs, such as parsley, celery leaves, fresh basil, or tarragon
1/2 cup cooked shelled crayfish or small shrimp
1/4 cup wine vinegar
2/3 cup salad oil, part vegetable, part olive oil, if you like
Fresh lemon juice (optional)

GARNISHES: lettuce leaves, a dozen or so black olives, chopped fresh herbs, and a few whole crayfish

Cook the wild rice: Wash it thoroughly until the water runs clear. Put the rice into a saucepan with twice the amount of water and a big pinch of salt, and bring to a boil. Cover, lower the heat, and cook gently until rice is tender and water is absorbed, about 45–50 minutes (some brands may take even longer; if so, check the water and add a little more). Meanwhile fry the diced sausage a couple of minutes, shaking the pan occasionally, until the fat is released. Drain on paper towels. Toss the rice, sausage, and remaining ingredients together and season to taste with salt and pepper. Add a little fresh lemon juice to bring up the flavors if needed. Line a salad bowl or platter with lettuce leaves, mound the rice salad in the center, and garnish with olives, herbs, and if available, some whole crayfish.

SERVES 6–8, MORE IF ONE OF MANY DISHES

Celeriac and Jerusalem Artichoke Salad

½ pound celeriac
¼ pound Jerusalem artichokes
About 2 ounces country ham, trimmed of any fat (optional)
½ cup mayonnaise, preferably homemade (page 347)

½ cup yogurt
2 teaspoons Dijon-type mustard
3 tablespoons finely chopped parsley
Salt
Freshly ground pepper

GARNISHES: *lettuce leaves or watercress and paprika*

Peel and cut the celeriac into thin slices, then stack the slices and cut them into thin strips. Do the same with the Jerusalem artichokes. Cut the ham into thin strips, if you are using it (the salad is good without, but the ham makes it a more substantial dish). Beat the mayonnaise, yogurt, and mustard together, and fold the vegetables, ham, and parsley into the dressing. Season to taste with salt and pepper. Serve over lettuce leaves or watercress with a sprinkling of paprika on top.

SERVES 4

"Queerly Called Dandelions"

We should not be distressed when we see a lawn full of dandelions," a naturalist wrote, "we should smile." Often vilified today for annual invasions of carefully nurtured stretches of green grass, dandelions were considered among the best of spring tonics by our grandmothers, as well as good eating when still small and tender. Sautéed to buttery softness with a salt pork slab, they were sometimes served, hot or cold, with a generous sprinkle of assertive cider vinegar.

The paler leaves closer to the heart of the plant are best for salad, and the darker larger leaves are good for cooking. The yellow flowers that bloom early in the summer may be pulled apart and scattered over salads, or some Yankee cooks may dip the whole flowers in batter before deep-frying them. Remember, when picking your own that leaves closest to the roots are the least bitter.

Raw dandelion greens are very rich in vitamin A, along with generous amounts of the vital ascorbic acid, thiamine, calcium, sodium, and potassium. Yankees used them well before the days of vitamin pills, just as newer generations do.

"You cannot forget if you would," wrote Henry Ward Beecher (an Amherst graduate), "those golden kisses all over the cheeks of the meadow, queerly called dandelions."

Purple beans from the garden make this a lovely light lunch. The purple variety turn an olive-like green when boiled, but they have a distinctive flavor. Any other green snap bean can be used, of course. And if you don't have any of the spicy Portuguese *chouriço* on hand, use strips of salami or good country ham.

Purple Bean, Potato, and Chouriço Salad

½ pound purple snap beans
½ pound new potatoes, peeled and
  sliced in ½-inch pieces
¼ pound Portuguese chouriço
4 scallions, including some tender
  greens, chopped

⅓ cup Vinaigrette (page 346)
2 tablespoons chopped fresh herbs,
  such as parsley, basil, tarragon,
  or savory

GARNISH: *lettuce leaves*

Snap the stem tops off the beans (don't bother to tail them) and cook them in boiling, salted water to cover about 5 minutes, until just tender with a little snap to them. Remove them with a slotted spoon and add the potato slices to the same water, which will have turned green; cook until tender, about 10 minutes. Meanwhile cut the *chouriço* in fairly thin slices, then cut in strips. Fry over low heat a few minutes to release fat, then drain on paper towels. Now drain the potatoes, cut them in strips, and toss with the beans, sausage strips, scallions, and the dressing. Arrange on lettuce leaves and sprinkle fresh herbs on top.
SERVES 4

Potato Salad

3 pounds new potatoes
½ cup warm chicken broth
2 scallions, including tender greens,
  or 2 young onions, chopped
3–4 tablespoons chopped fresh
  herbs, such as parsley, chives,
  savory, or chervil

1 tablespoon wine or cider vinegar
2 tablespoons olive oil
Salt
Freshly ground pepper
1 cup Mayonnaise (page 347)

Boil the potatoes in their skins in lightly salted water to cover until tender when pierced. Drain, skin them, and cut them in generous-size dice. Pour warm chicken broth over them, add the scallions and herbs, toss gently, and let steep 15 minutes. Drizzle the vinegar and oil over them and toss again. Season to taste with salt and pepper, and fold in the mayonnaise.
SERVES 4–6

Tongue Salad

2½—3 cups diced cooked tongue
1 dill pickle, diced
½ cup diced young, fresh vegetable, such as kohlrabi, baby zucchini, or celery

About ½ cup Salad Sauce (page 346)
Salt
Freshly ground pepper

GARNISH: *lettuce leaves and/or watercress*

Toss all ingredients together, seasoning to taste with salt and pepper, and let marinate at least 30 minutes before serving. Serve surrounded by lettuce leaves and/or watercress.
SERVES 4

Leftover Meat Salad

A good luncheon salad to make when you have leftover steak or roast beef or lamb, preferably on the rare side.

2 cups cooked beef or lamb, cut in strips
¼ cup chopped scallions, including tender greens
3 tablespoons chopped fresh parsley and other fresh herbs, if available, such as tarragon, chervil, or mint

1 cup red, yellow, or green peppers, cut in strips, preferably roasted and peeled (page 25)
1 tablespoon capers, drained
⅓ cup Vinaigrette (page 346)

GARNISHES: *lettuce leaves, plus optional hard-boiled eggs, artichoke hearts, or wedges of avocado*

Toss the meat strips with the scallions, herbs, peppers, capers, and vinaigrette. Let stand at least 1 hour before serving. Toss again and garnish as you please.
SERVES 4

Ham Luncheon Salad

4 cups torn greens, such as lettuce, young spinach leaves, or watercress
1 medium red onion, sliced thin
1 cup broken pieces raw cauliflower
¾ cup ham, cut in thin strips

About ¾ cup Salad Sauce (page 346)
1 teaspoon chopped fresh thyme, or ¼ teaspoon dried
1 tablespoon chopped fresh basil, or ½ teaspoon dried
½ cup croutons

Toss the vegetables with the ham strips, adding dressing as you toss. Mix in the chopped herbs. Strew the croutons into the mixture just before serving so they remain crisp.

SERVES 4–6

Chick-pea, Sausage, and Red Pepper Salad

3 cups cooked chick-peas (canned may be used, drained and rinsed)
⅓ cup sliced scallions, including tender greens
1 small to medium sweet red pepper, seeds and ribs removed, diced
¾ cup Vinaigrette (page 346)
¼ pound Portuguese lingüiça or chouriço sausage, or kielbasa or salami, diced

3–4 tablespoons chopped fresh herbs, such as coriander, preferably, or basil or chervil mixed with Italian parsley
Salt
Freshly ground pepper

GARNISHES: salad greens and black olives

Marinate the chick-peas, scallions, and red pepper in the vinaigrette for 2–3 hours before serving. If using lingüiça, chouriço, or kielbasa, cook gently until the pieces have exuded their fat, then drain (this is not necessary with the salami). Fold the sausage into the chick-peas along with the herbs. Check seasoning, adding salt and pepper as necessary. Serve with a border of crisp salad greens and black olives.

SERVES 4–6

Uncommercial Cottage Cheese

Says a newspaper correspondent, under the date of September 1897: "At the dinner party given by the ladies of the town of Isle la Motte, on the island of that name in Lake Champlain, on the sixth of this month, to the Vermont Fish and Game League, at which dinner President McKinley and Secretary of War Alger were guests, I noticed on every table nice little cottage cheeses, about as large as a big apple, and most delicious, as I made certain as soon as dinner began. I do not see why some enterprising dairyman near every large city does not start the cottage cheese business. It would not be an expensive experiment, and there might be money in it."

Chicken Salad I

4 cups cooked chicken, cut in good-size chunks
2–3 scallions or 1 young onion, including tender greens, sliced thin
1 cup mayonnaise, preferably homemade (page 347)

2 tablespoons chopped fresh herb, preferably tarragon
Salt
Freshly ground pepper

OPTIONAL TOSS-INS:
1 cup seedless grapes, cut in half
½ cup slivered almonds
½ cup chopped celery and/or blanched peas, or slivers of snow peas or sugar snaps

OPTIONAL GARNISHES: sliced radishes, tomatoes, snow peas, black olives, halves of artichoke hearts
lettuce leaves

Toss together the first four ingredients for the salad and add salt and pepper to taste. Serve as is if you like a plain traditional salad, or toss in some of the suggested ingredients. Garnish as you wish and serve on lettuce leaves.
SERVES 4–6

Chicken Salad II

This chicken salad is lighter than the traditional mayonnaise-dressed version and makes an attractive platter. It is important that the chicken breasts are freshly cooked so that they absorb the dressing while they are still warm.

2 whole chicken breasts, deboned and skinned
2 tablespoons vegetable oil

Salt
Freshly ground pepper
¼ cup vermouth or dry white wine

DRESSING:
½ teaspoon Dijon mustard
½ teaspoon salt
3 tablespoons raspberry or blackberry vinegar (page 636)
⅔ cup olive oil, or part vegetable and part olive oil

TOPPING:
4 scallions, including tender greens, chopped
2 tablespoons chopped fresh herbs, such as tarragon, basil, or fresh coriander
2 tablespoons chopped parsley

GARNISHES: black olives, tomato wedges, lettuce leaves, and/or watercress

Split each of the 2 chicken breasts in half and, in a skillet in which they will fit snugly, brown them very lightly in the oil for 1 minute. Salt and pepper them on both sides, then pour the wine into the skillet, cover, and cook over medium heat for about 6–8 minutes, or until they are just tender. Remove them to a board, then slice them crosswise into ½-inch pieces and arrange them on a platter, re-forming them into their original shapes. Shake or beat the dressing ingredients together until thoroughly blended and pour this over the still-warm chicken and scatter the scallions and herbs on top. Let marinate for about 30 minutes, not refrigerated, then arrange the garnishes around the platter and serve.

SERVES 4–6

Rosemary Kielty, author of a lively column called "Country Cook" in the *Lakeville* (Connecticut) *Journal,* gave us this contemporary variation on a chicken salad theme from a cook in neighboring Canaan, and we find it delicious. Rosemary reported getting more requests for chicken recipes than for any other kind of main course dish.

Chicken and Noodle Salad with Sesame Soy Sauce

4 well-packed cups freshly cooked chicken, sliced or shredded

¼ cup mayonnaise
½ pound fettucine (flat noodles)

DRESSING:
1 teaspoon dry mustard
1 tablespoon sugar
4 teaspoons soy sauce

3 tablespoons sesame oil
½ cup vegetable oil
6 tablespoons white wine vinegar

TOSS-INS (use as many as you wish):
3–4 scallions, including tender greens, chopped
3–4 sliced mushrooms, marinated in a little of the dressing
1 small avocado, peeled and chopped

½ red pepper, seeds and ribs removed, chopped
3–4 cooked artichoke hearts, quartered
1 tablespoon chopped fresh coriander

Toss the chicken with the mayonnaise and chill. Cook fettucine in a large pot of boiling water until *al dente.* Meanwhile make the dressing by beating or shaking up in a jar all the dressing ingredients. Drain the pasta and immediately douse it with half of the dressing. Cover and let stand for 3 hours. Mix the chicken with the noodles, and add some or all of the toss-ins (we find lots of chopped scallions essential and we like to garnish with a little chopped fresh coriander when we have it in the herb garden). Add as much more of the dressing as you wish and toss carefully.

SERVES 6–8

Lentil and Rice Salad with Tuna

There's a saying that lentils derived their name from the Latin *lentus* (slow) because people believed the moisture in this pea made the mind heavy, and this may be why Yankees eschewed them until their globe-trotting Peace Corps offspring demonstrated that they not only tasted good but had more protein and even fewer calories than dried beans. The following recipe can be made with or without tuna.

1 cup lentils
3 tablespoons olive oil
1 tablespoon fresh lemon juice
1/2 cup chopped spring onions or
  scallions, including tender greens
1/4 cup chopped red onions
1 teaspoon ground coriander

1 cup cooked rice
1/2 cup plain yogurt
1/2 cup tuna chunks
Salt
Freshly ground pepper
2–3 tablespoons chopped fresh
  mint

GARNISH: *tomato slices*

Cook the lentils about 25 minutes, then drain. Toss the oil, lemon juice, scallions, onions, and coriander with the lentils while they are still warm. Cool to room temperature before mixing with the rice. Chill the salad. Before serving stir in the yogurt and tuna. Add salt and pepper to taste. Sprinkle fresh mint on top and serve garnished with tomato slices.
SERVES 4

Berkshires Lentil Salad

Mady Wolkenstein, chef at the Old Inn on the Green, a singular waystop in New Marlboro, Massachusetts, created this salad with the unusual goat cheese produced by Wayne Dunlop and Susan Sellew of Rawson Brook Farm at nearby Monterey.

DRESSING:
1/2 cup olive oil
2 tablespoons peanut oil
1 tablespoon lemon juice
Salt

Freshly ground pepper
8 roasted garlic cloves from a
  whole roasted head (page 161)

4 cups cooked lentils
1/2 cup finely chopped parsley
1/4 cup finely chopped cilantro
12 ounces Monterey Chèvre (or
  other fresh goat cheese)
1/4 cup olive oil

3 tablespoons chopped fresh thyme
16 oil-cured black olives
1 cup finely chopped scallions,
  including tender greens
24 roasted garlic cloves, peeled

GARNISHES: *2 roasted sweet red peppers, ribs, seeds, and skins removed,*
  cut in strips (page 25)
  1 bunch watercress

To make the dressing: Put the oils and lemon juice in a blender, sprinkle in a little salt and pepper, and add the roasted garlic cloves. Spin until smooth, taste, and adjust the seasoning as needed.

Mix the dressing with the lentils, parsley, and cilantro. Brush the cheese with ¼ cup olive oil and sprinkle on the fresh thyme. Set lentils and cheese aside for several hours. On each serving plate put a wedge of the goat cheese, a mound of lentils, a mound of chopped onions, olives, and 3 garlic cloves. Garnish with red pepper strips and watercress.

SERVES 8

Corkscrew Pasta and Vegetable Salad

½ *green pepper, cut in strips*
½ *sweet red pepper, cut in strips*
2 *tablespoons chopped fresh herbs, such as parsley, scallions, basil or tarragon, or marjoram*
1 *dozen fiddleheads, cleaned and cooked 8 minutes (page 44)*

1 *cup broccoli florets, cooked until just tender*
6 *scallions, including tender greens, sliced thin*
½ *pound corkscrew pasta, cooked al dente*

DRESSING:
2 *teaspoons lemon juice*
¼ *teaspoon salt*
Freshly ground pepper

2–3 *drops sesame oil*
¼ *cup olive or vegetable oil*

Toss all of the salad ingredients together in a large bowl. In a separate bowl or jar with a screw top, mix or shake all the dressing ingredients together. Pour the dressing over the salad, mix well, and serve; don't refrigerate.

SERVES 4

Beet, Potato, and Sardine Salad

A first-class lunch.

1 *cup cooked, peeled, and diced beets*
¼ *cup chive vinegar, or other herb vinegar*
1 *tablespoon finely chopped chives*
1 *cup cooked and peeled diced potatoes*

Salt
Freshly ground pepper
⅓ *cup mayonnaise*
⅓ *cup yogurt*
2 *tablespoons Tartar Sauce (page 633)*

GARNISHES: *lettuce leaves and 4 ounces small Maine or other sardines*

Put the diced beets in a bowl and pour the vinegar over them. Set aside for 1 hour. Stir the diced potatoes into the beets. Add the chives, a light sprinkling of salt, and pepper to taste. Mix the mayonnaise, yogurt, and tartar sauce together to blend well, then pour over the vegetables and toss to mix. Arrange lettuce leaves on 4 serving plates and divide the salad among them. Top with sardines.

SERVES 4

Riviera Shrimp Salad

A Maine cook's version of the classic shrimp salad from the south of France.

1 pound cooked shrimp
½ cup water
¼ cup cider vinegar
½ cup white wine
A few drops of fresh lemon juice
1 small chopped fresh chili pepper, seeds removed, or hot pepper flakes to taste
1 garlic clove, minced
1 tablespoon finely chopped scallions, including tender greens
1 rib celery, chopped
1 bay leaf

Salt
Freshly ground pepper
2 cloves, pounded
3 tomatoes, peeled and sliced
1 cup cooked, cutup green beans
3–4 small potatoes, cooked, peeled, and diced
8 anchovy fillets
¼ cup Vinaigrette (page 346)
½ tablespoon chopped fresh basil
½ tablespoon chopped fresh chervil
½ tablespoon chopped fresh tarragon
8 black olives

Put the shrimp in a bowl. Mix the water, vinegar, wine, and a few drops of lemon juice together. Season with the chili pepper, garlic, scallions, celery, bay leaf, salt and pepper to taste, and cloves. Mix well and pour this marinade over the shrimp until they are well covered. Set aside for at least 3 hours, stirring occasionally. Arrange the tomatoes around the edge of a salad bowl. Pile the beans and potatoes in the center, and crisscross them with anchovies. Pour the vinaigrette over the tomatoes and vegetable mounds. Sprinkle the tomatoes with basil and scatter the chervil and tarragon over the center of the salad. Drain the marinated shrimp and top the salad with them. Decorate with olives.

SERVES 4–6

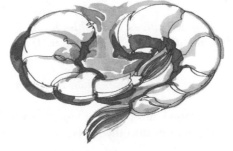

A habitué of the constantly shifting sands of Race Point, Michael Field added much to his reputation as a leading teacher of cooking techniques during his time on Cape Cod. Here is his recipe for dill-accented fish salad.

Province-town Fish Salad

1 tablespoon fresh lemon juice
½ teaspoon salt
¼ teaspoon cayenne
3 tablespoons olive oil
2 tablespoons finely chopped
   shallots or scallions
2 tablespoons finely chopped fresh
   dill
2 cups cold poached sole, cut in
   1-inch pieces

1 cup freshly made Mayonnaise
   (page 347)
2–3 cups shredded Boston lettuce
4 tomatoes, peeled and sliced
2 hard-boiled eggs, sliced
2 tablespoons capers, drained,
   washed, and dried

Mix the lemon juice, salt, cayenne, oil, shallots or scallions, and 1 tablespoon of the dill. Pour it over the cold fish and toss gently. Set aside for 1 hour, turning occasionally. Stir ½ cup of the mayonnaise into the marinated fish. Put enough lettuce in a salad bowl to make a generous bed, then arrange the fish mixture on top. Stir the remaining tablespoon of dill into the remaining mayonnaise and spread it thoroughly over the fish. Make a ring around the edge of the salad by overlapping the slices of tomatoes and eggs. Sprinkle the capers over the salad and chill.
SERVES 4

One of the first efforts to encourage the serving of "under-utilized fish" began in 1979 when many Nantucket islanders joined to invite all comers to an annual Seafest in September, on Steamboat Wharf. Of the numerous recipes devised, this one was created at Straight Wharf Restaurant.

Seafest Mako Shark Salad

2 pounds mako shark

FOR THE POACHING LIQUID:
1 whole carrot
1 onion, quartered

1 whole rib celery

1 onion, diced fine
1 rib celery, diced fine
Red wine vinegar

Mayonnaise
Salt
Freshly ground pepper

Poach the fish in simmering water to cover along with the whole carrot, quartered onion, and whole rib of celery. The shark meat is done when it separates easily as you plunge a fork into it. Don't overcook. Remove it

from the bouillon and cool. Use a fork to gently flake the fish, then mix with the diced onion and celery. Add a sprinkling of vinegar and fold in enough mayonnaise to coat the fish (don't overdo the mayonnaise or it will dominate the delicate fish flavor). Season to taste with salt and pepper, and toss lightly. Serve as a salad on a bed of lettuce. Or serve on toast or crackers as an hors d'oeuvre. Or use as a pita stuffing.
SERVES 4–6

Salt Cod Salad

4 tablespoons cider vinegar
1 garlic clove, minced
Tabasco sauce
6 tablespoons olive oil
Freshly ground pepper
1 onion, finely chopped

1 bay leaf
½ pound salt cod, soaked and
    cooked (page 89)
4 anchovies, finely chopped
8–10 black olives, pitted and sliced
½ green pepper, coarsely chopped

GARNISHES: *lettuce leaves and sliced hard-boiled eggs*

In a large bowl mix the vinegar, garlic, a drop or two of Tabasco sauce, and the oil and add a few turns of the pepper grinder. Whisk briskly until the mixture looks milky. Add the onion and the bay leaf and the codfish, flaking the fish with your fingers as you stir it in. Cover the bowl and put it in the refrigerator to marinate several hours (overnight is best). Just before serving, remove the bay leaf and add the anchovies, olives, and green pepper. Toss the mixture until it is well mixed. Arrange on lettuce leaves and garnish with hard-boiled eggs.
SERVES 4

Fish-Stuffed Tomato Salad

4 ripe tomatoes
6–7 ounces cooked fish
1 cup cooked rice
12–15 black olives, pitted and
    coarsely chopped
4–5 scallions, chopped

2 tablespoons chopped basil or
    marjoram
3 tablespoons olive oil
Fresh lemon juice to taste
Salt
Freshly ground pepper

GARNISH: *lettuce leaves*

Cut a circular opening in the tops of the tomatoes and remove the plugs around the stem. Scoop out the insides of the tomatoes into a mixing bowl; coarsely chop the pulp. Add the cooked fish, rice, olives, scallions, and herbs, and stir in the olive oil, lemon juice, and salt and freshly ground pepper to taste. Set aside to marinate. Cut the tomatoes at intervals, leaving an uncut base and spread the tomatoes flat like flowers. Arrange lettuce leaves on individual salad plates, place the tomatoes in the center, and divide the stuffing by mounding about ½ cup in the center of each tomato. Serve additional salad dressing on the side.

SERVES 4

Scallop Salad

1 pint bay or sea scallops
1 pint boiling water
Juice of ¼ lemon
Salt

6–7 tablespoons Mayonnaise (page 347)
1 large rib celery, finely chopped
1 teaspoon chopped fresh rosemary

GARNISH: *lettuce leaves*

Cook scallops 2 minutes for small, 5–6 minutes for large, in the boiling water with the lemon juice and a sprinkling of salt. Drain thoroughly and cut the sea scallops into quarters; leave bay scallops whole. Combine with the mayonnaise, chopped celery, and rosemary, and add a little salt to your taste. Chill 1 hour or more, then arrange on lettuce leaves in a salad bowl.

SERVES 4

Smoked Brook Trout and Wild Rice Salad

2–3 smoked brook trout fillets

DRESSING:
⅓ cup olive oil
Juice of ½ lemon
1 teaspoon cider vinegar

1 cup chopped celery
1 onion, chopped
1 cup finely chopped carrots (optional)

2 cups cooked wild rice

1 teaspoon unsweetened mustard
Salt
Freshly ground pepper

¼ cup chopped black olives
⅓ cup chopped parsley

Flake the fish and toss with rice. Make a dressing with the oil, lemon juice, cider vinegar, mustard, and a little salt and pepper to taste. Marinate the vegetables in the dressing for an hour or so, then add the olives and toss the mixture with the rice and fish. Chill the salad about an hour, and sprinkle it with chopped parsley.

SERVES 4–6

Shad Roe Salad

Shad lovers seem unable to wait for the first schools of spring shad to arrive in the Connecticut and other rivers, and some of them settle for earlier shad from the Hudson, the Delaware, or even the Eastern Shore. It used to be said that shad from Crisfield, Maryland, was okay but that Connecticut shad was worth the higher price. In the 1980s the king of springtime fish is celebrated annually at Essex, when the Rotary Club holds a mammoth cookout on the first Saturday in June. Shad baked at open wood fires is delicious. So is this salad of roe.

½ pound shad roe
Fresh lemon juice
2 teaspoons horseradish
¾ cup mayonnaise
2 tablespoons chopped celery leaves
1 spring onion or 3 scallions,
    minced, including tender greens

1 cup cooked fiddleheads (page 44)
½ cup dry large-curd cottage cheese
Salt (optional)
Freshly ground pepper

GARNISH: *crisp lettuce leaves*

Simmer the shad roe in lightly salted water to cover for 8 minutes, turning once. Drain and cool, using a very sharp knife to cut the roe in dice; sprinkle lightly with lemon juice. In a large salad bowl, mix the horseradish and mayonnaise, adding the celery leaves, minced onion, and the fiddleheads. Fold in the cottage cheese and roe cubes carefully so they don't break. Toss very gently. Season to taste with salt, if needed, and pepper and arrange tender lettuce leaves around the sides of the bowl. Serve chilled.
SERVES 4

Squid Salad

4 squid, cleaned
4 tablespoons olive oil
1 onion, chopped
2 garlic cloves, chopped
1 medium green pepper, or ½ green
    pepper and ½ sweet red pepper,
    chopped

Salt
About ⅛ teaspoon hot red pepper
    flakes
About 2 teaspoons fresh lemon
    juice
2 tablespoons chopped fresh herbs,
    such as parsley, chives, or chervil

GARNISHES: *lettuce leaves and small black olives*

Cut the bodies of the squid into ½-inch rings and cut the tentacles into smaller pieces. Heat 2 tablespoons of the oil in a skillet and add the squid along with the onion and garlic. Sauté over medium heat, shaking the pan often, for 2–3 minutes, then add the chopped pepper and sauté, shaking

now and then, for 2–3 minutes more. The squid should be just tender and most of the liquid absorbed. Toss with the remaining oil and season to taste with salt, pepper flakes, lemon juice, and herbs. Let cool but don't chill, and serve over lettuce leaves with a garnish of black olives.
SERVES 4

Boston Scrod Salad

2½–3 *cups cooked scrod*
½ *cup chopped fennel or celery*
½ *cup chopped red pepper*
⅓ *cup mayonnaise*
⅔ *cup plain yogurt*

4 *lettuce cups*
2 *hard-boiled eggs*
Pitted ripe olives
Paprika

Flake the cooked fish and toss it with the chopped vegetables. Stir in the mayonnaise and yogurt, and divide the mixture among the lettuce cups. Cut the eggs in wedges and arrange on each serving with olives. Sprinkle with paprika.
SERVES 4

DRESSINGS

Vinaigrette

1 teaspoon Dijon-type mustard
½ teaspoon salt
About ½ garlic clove, minced fine (optional)
2 tablespoons red wine vinegar
2 teaspoons fresh lemon juice
⅔ cup oil, preferably olive oil, or a combination of olive oil and peanut or other vegetable oil

Freshly ground pepper
About 1 tablespoon chopped fresh herbs, such as chives and tarragon, or dill, chervil, or marjoram

Mix together the mustard and salt. If you are using garlic work that into the mixture. Add the vinegar and lemon juice, and blend well. Whisk in the olive oil slowly. Season to taste with freshly ground pepper and herbs. Or put all the ingredients into a tightly capped bottle and shake. The dressing may also be made in a food processor.
MAKES 1 SCANT CUP

VARIATIONS: For a mustardy dressing, use up to 1 tablespoon mustard.
For a slightly sweet dressing, which many New Englanders favor, add 2 tablespoons maple syrup (omit garlic).

Salad Sauce

1 egg yolk
2 teaspoons of Dijon-type mustard
½ cup corn oil
¼ cup tarragon vinegar

¾ teaspoon salt
Freshly ground pepper
3 drops Worcestershire sauce

Whisk the egg yolk and mustard together. Add the corn oil in a thin, steady stream, whisking constantly. Beat in the vinegar, salt, pepper to taste, and Worcestershire. (This may all be done in the food processor.)
MAKES 1 CUP

Yogurt Dressing

3 garlic cloves
1 teaspoon salt
2 tablespoons vegetable oil
1 cup plain yogurt

2 tablespoons vinegar, preferably rice vinegar
½ teaspoon sesame oil

Smash the garlic cloves with the flat of a knife. Remove the skins and mince the bulbs, add the salt, and continue to mash until you have a purée. Work in the oil, then scrape up into a bowl. Mix the remaining ingredients into the bowl, beating thoroughly with a fork.

MAKES 1⅓ CUPS

Mayonnaise

2 egg yolks (1 egg yolk, if made in food processor)
1 whole egg (use only if made in food processor)
1 teaspoon Dijon-type mustard
¾–1 teaspoon salt

⅔ cup olive oil
⅔ cup peanut or safflower oil
About 2 teaspoons fresh lemon juice
About 2 teaspoons wine vinegar

Beat the egg yolks, mustard, and salt together for at least 1 minute. Or spin the 1 egg yolk and the whole egg with the mustard and salt in a food processor. Add the oil in a thin, steady stream, very slowly at first, beating constantly until the mayonnaise thickens, then add the lemon juice and vinegar. If using a food processor, pour the oils through the spout with the machine going, slowly at first, then more rapidly; when thick, pour in the lemon juice and vinegar and blend. Be sure to taste; you may want a bit more salt, lemon juice, or vinegar. Mayonnaise keeps very well in a covered jar in the refrigerator.

MAKES ABOUT 2½ CUPS

VARIATIONS:

Orange Mayonnaise: To 1 cup thick mayonnaise, whisk in the juice of ½ orange, a pinch of cayenne, and 3–4 tablespoons chopped fresh mint leaves.

Green Mayonnaise: This can be made by simply whisking about ¼ cup chopped fresh herbs into 1 cup mayonnaise. Or you can blend about 1 cup loosely packed herbs and watercress with the eggs when you are making the above mayonnaise, then start adding the oil when the herbs are well blended. Greens to use include watercress or young spinach leaves, plus chives and parsley and/or dill, or tarragon or chervil. Do not mix too many different herbs or you will not get a clearly defined flavor. Herb mayonnaise will keep only about 7 to 10 days.

Oriental Dressing

½ cup peanut oil
2 teaspoons sesame oil
3 tablespoons Chinese vinegar
(cider vinegar may be
substituted)

1 teaspoon minced fresh peeled
ginger
Salt
Freshly ground pepper

Whisk the first four ingredients together, adding salt and pepper to taste.
MAKES ABOUT ¾ CUP

Creamy Garlic Dressing

⅓ cup wine vinegar
½ cup half and half or milk
1 teaspoon sugar
1 teaspoon salt

½ teaspoon freshly ground pepper
1 cup vegetable oil
2 or 3 garlic cloves

Place all the ingredients in a blender or food processor and blend until very smooth. May be refrigerated; shake up thoroughly again or return to the blender before serving.
MAKES 1¾ CUPS

Maine Sardine Salad Dressing

According to the records, a $1,000 prize was awarded by the Maine Sardine Council to the creator of this recipe. As well as serving it as suggested below, it goes well on cold asparagus and on broccoli salad.

1 cup canned sardines, well drained
1 cup mayonnaise
1 tablespoon tarragon vinegar
¼ cup chopped celery

½ cup chopped parsley
4 ounces cream cheese, or Maine
goat cheese
½ cup milk

Put all the ingredients in a blender or food processor. Blend thoroughly at high speed to purée the vegetables and produce a smooth liquid. Refrigerate; if it seems too thick, the dressing may be thinned slightly with additional milk before using. Serve on greens with hard-boiled eggs, tomato wedges, and thinly sliced celery.
MAKES ABOUT 2 CUPS

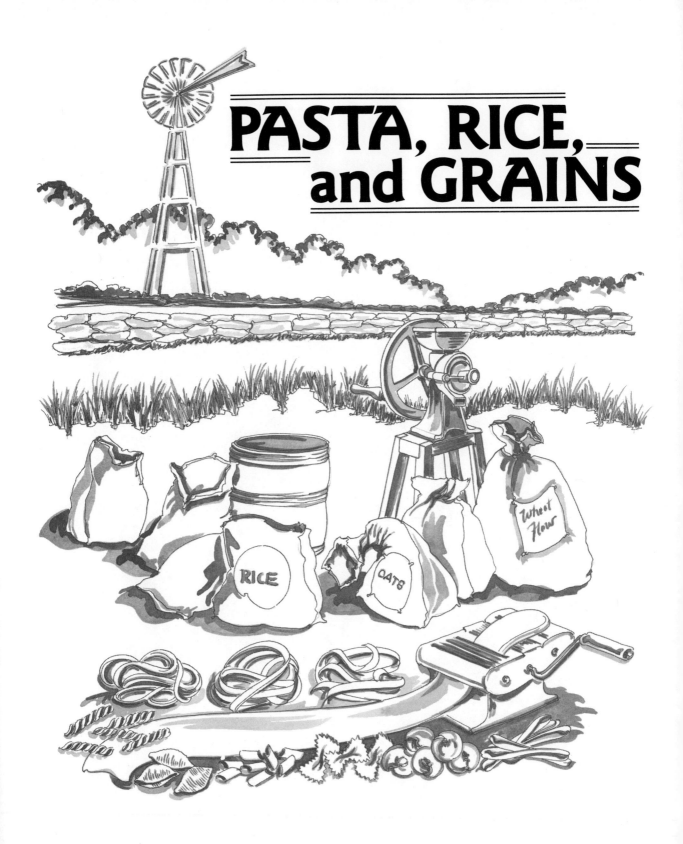

PASTA, RICE, and GRAINS

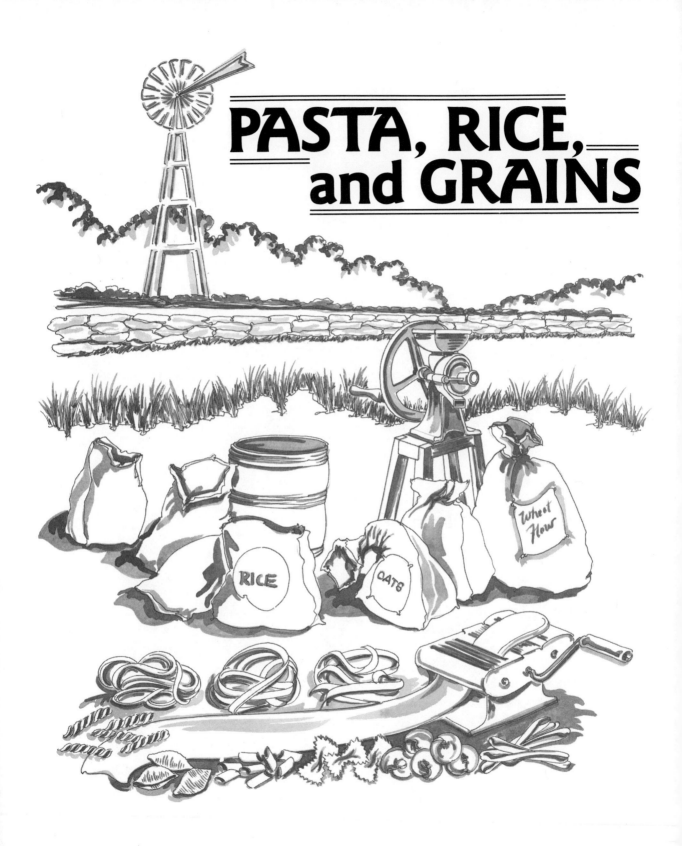

PASTA, RICE, and GRAINS

"IF I COULD EAT WHEAT in only one form other than bread," the natural foods writer Karen MacNeil said once, "it would be pasta." That statement might be the gastronomic first commandment of the young generation—thousands seem to be living off pasta and not much else. Contrary to the notion that pasta is short on nutrients and long on calories, it is considered by such authorities as Jane Brody of *The New York Times* to be a health food. When properly prepared, it fills you up with protein before you eat more calories than you really need.

Like rice and other whole grains, pasta has been prepared by New England cooks for a couple of centuries. Catherine Beecher included in her *Domestic Receipt Book* (1846) recipes for both "Macaroni Pudding, to eat with Meat," and "Plain Macaroni or Vermicelli Puddings" to serve as dessert. The latter were cooked very much in the manner of rice puddings.

Few sweet dishes based on pasta have remained popular in twentieth-century New England, but many of those adapted in Yankee kitchens to serve with main courses, along with those dependent on rice and whole grains, have been culled to include here. The baked dishes offer inspiration for cooks who know how good pasta, rice, and grains can be, and you'll find additional recipes using rice and grains in combination with other ingredients in the chapter we call "Made" Dishes.

Pasta with Basil and Lingüiça

¼ pound Portuguese lingüiça, *cut in ¼-inch slices*
1 pound spaghetti or spaghettini
2 cups loosely packed fresh basil leaves
3 fat garlic cloves, peeled
¼ cup olive oil
Salt
Freshly ground pepper
Freshly grated Parmesan

Put a large pot of salted water on to boil. Meanwhile, fry the *lingüiça* slices slowly in a skillet. When the water has come to a rapid boil, stir in the pasta. Spin the basil leaves, garlic, and olive oil with ¼ teaspoon salt in a blender or food processor until thoroughly blended. When the pasta is done *al dente,* before draining, remove ¼ cup of the cooking water and blend into the basil-garlic mixture. Then quickly drain the pasta and toss with the basil-garlic sauce and the *lingüiça* slices along with whatever fat they have exuded while cooking. Grind fresh pepper over and add salt if needed. Serve in warm bowls with Parmesan on the side.

SERVES 4

This is a simple dish that can be made with any kind of store-bought pasta. We make it when we have some veal left over from a Braised Shoulder of Veal (page 254)—it's essential that you have some of that good veal gravy for the sauce.

Pasta with Veal Strips, Red Peppers, and Artichoke Hearts

2 tablespoons olive or vegetable oil
1 red pepper, seeds and ribs removed, cut in strips
1 fat garlic clove, minced
4 scallions, including tender greens, sliced
About 1½ cups cooked veal, cut in strips
⅔ cup veal gravy, plus optional additional veal or chicken broth

6–8 frozen artichoke hearts, cooked and cut in half
Salt
Freshly ground pepper
1 teaspoon chopped fresh rosemary, or ½ teaspoon dried, crumbled
6 ounces pasta, preferably penne

Put a large pot of salted water on to boil for the pasta. Heat the oil in a skillet and sauté the pepper strips, about 2 minutes. Add the garlic and scallions and stir-fry gently 1 minute more. Add the veal, veal gravy, and artichoke hearts, and season with salt, pepper, and rosemary. Heat through and add a little broth if the sauce seems too thick. Meanwhile, when the water has come to a boil, cook the pasta until done *al dente*. Drain, toss with the sauce, and spoon onto two warm plates.

SERVES 2

Smoked Turkey Pasta

1 onion, chopped
1 tablespoon olive oil
1 tablespoon vegetable oil
¼ cup white wine
2 teaspoons chopped fresh tarragon, or ½ teaspoon dried
4 tablespoons chopped parsley
½ cup chicken broth
1 sweet red pepper, charred, peeled, and cut in strips

2 medium carrots, cut in julienne strips
3½ cups shredded smoked turkey (page 168)
¼ cup cream
1 pound thin spaghetti
Grated Parmesan

Bring a large pot of salted water to a boil. Sauté the chopped onion in combined olive and vegetable oils, and when the onion is translucent, add the wine, the tarragon, and 2 tablespoons of chopped parsley. Cook about 1–2 minutes and add the chicken broth. Add the red pepper and carrot strips to the broth, then stir in the shredded turkey and cook the mixture about 1 minute over a brisk heat. Add the cream and bring to a boil, turning down the heat and letting it reduce slightly. Stir the spaghetti into the boiling water and cook 6 or 7 minutes, until tender but not soft, then drain it and stir it into the sauce. Garnish with the remaining chopped parsley, and put the grated cheese in a separate dish.

SERVES 4

Linguine with Vegetables and Puréed Nuts

2 large carrots, peeled and sliced in thin rounds
2 large parsnips, peeled and sliced in thin rounds
3 cups broccoli florets
½ pound white button mushroom caps
3–4 tablespoons butter
½ cup chopped parsley
6 shallots, chopped fine
1 cup ground butternuts or walnuts
1 cup dry white wine
1 tablespoon paprika
Freshly ground pepper
Salt
½ pint half-and-half
1½ pounds linguine or other thin pasta

Bring 2 quarts of salted water to a boil and cook the carrots and parsnips for 5 minutes, until tender but still somewhat crisp, adding the broccoli for the last 3 minutes of cooking. Drain and hold in the strainer. Sauté the mushroom caps in butter for 3 minutes, then stir in the parsley, shallots, and nuts, and cook until the shallots are translucent and the nuts lightly browned. Stir in the wine, paprika, several turns of the pepper grinder, and a sprinkling of salt. Simmer for about 10 minutes. Stir in the half-and-half and continue to cook very gently while you cook the pasta. In a large pot of rapidly boiling salted water, cook the pasta until just done *al dente*. Reheat the vegetables by dipping them in the strainer into the boiling pasta water. Drain the pasta when done and toss with the sauce and the vegetables.

SERVES 6

Bryn Teg Pasta with Anchovies, Fiddleheads, and Sardines

½ pound fiddleheads
¼ cup safflower or other vegetable oil
3 large garlic cloves, chopped
3 shallots, chopped
½ cup raisins
½ cup pine nuts
1 tablespoon capers, washed of brine and drained
2 tablespoons chopped fresh basil
4 tablespoons chopped fresh parsley
10 anchovies, brine removed
1 tablespoon fennel seeds
¾–1 pound spaghetti
8 sardines, preserved in oil
1 cup ricotta or cottage cheese
Freshly ground pepper

Trim the fiddleheads and cook in a large pot of boiling water 6–7 minutes, until tender and slightly crisp. Remove them with a slotted spoon, set aside, and keep the water simmering very gently. Heat the oil in a large skillet, stir in the garlic and shallots, and cook gently 3–4 minutes. Stir in the raisins, pine nuts, capers, and the herbs. Chop the anchovies, add, and cook gently about 5 minutes. Increase the heat under the simmering water and toss in the fennel seeds. When the water returns to a boil, carefully add the pasta to maintain the boil; just before the pasta is done *al dente,* add the reserved fiddleheads to reheat them. Stir the sardines and cheese in with the ingredients in the skillet, season liberally with pepper (no salt needed because of the anchovies) and heat 2 minutes. Drain the pasta and the fiddleheads. Heap the pasta on a warm serving platter, spoon the sauce over, and arrange the fiddleheads on top.

SERVES 4

Pasta with Cooked Meat and Vegetables

This should be considered a very free-form dish because it is made up of leftover meats and vegetables likely to be on hand or in the garden, so use it only as a guide and take whatever liberties you wish. The recipe is designed to serve two generously, because leftovers are usually to be had in small quantities, but it can be easily doubled or tripled.

2 tablespoons vegetable oil
1 medium onion, peeled and
  chopped
2 garlic cloves, chopped
1 sweet pepper (red, green, yellow,
  or combination), seeds and ribs
  removed, sliced
1 large tomato, chopped
About ½ pound tender Swiss chard
  or spinach leaves, washed and
  cut in strips
¼ cup ham, cut in strips (with
  some fat attached)

½ cup leftover stew juices, or beef
  or chicken broth
3 tablespoons chopped fresh herbs,
  such as parsley, basil, or thyme
1 cup leftover cooked beef, cut in
  strips
Salt
Freshly ground pepper
½ pound spaghettini or vermicelli
Freshly grated Parmesan

Bring a large pot of salted water to a boil. Meanwhile heat the oil, then sauté the onion gently, stirring, for 4–5 minutes. Add the pepper, garlic, tomato, greens, ham, and the meat juices. Bring to a simmer, stir in the herbs, cover, and cook 5–8 minutes, until the greens are tender. A few minutes before the sauce is done, drop the pasta into the rapidly boiling water and cook until done *al dente.* Just before draining the pasta, stir the beef strips into the sauce and heat through. Season with salt and pepper to taste. Drain the pasta and divide it into two warm bowls. Pour the sauce over and serve with grated cheese.

SERVES 2

Fusilli with Chicken, Celery, and Leek Sauce

Pasta is made today in New England shops and in factories in a variety of shapes and is often of a quality that is admired as much as that produced in Italy.

One 3-pound chicken
1 teaspoon freshly grated nutmeg
1 teaspoon cinnamon
2–3 parsley sprigs
4 medium leeks, cleaned and sliced about 1 inch thick
2 ribs celery, cut in ½-inch slices
Water
2 tablespoons butter
2 tablespoons flour
¼ cup grated sharp cheddar
2 tablespoons chopped parsley
½ sweet red pepper cut in matchstick-size strips
Salt
Freshly ground pepper
1 pound fusilli pasta

Wipe the chicken with a damp cloth, mix the spices, and rub them into the chicken skin. Put a sprig of parsley inside the chicken and truss it. Put the chicken in a large casserole, surround it with the celery and leeks, and pour in enough water to just cover the thighs. Bring the water to a boil, cover, and lower the heat and simmer for 1 hour, until the chicken is tender. After the chicken has cooled in the broth, remove the meat from the bones and cut it into cubes. Strain the cooking broth, reserving 2 cups, and set the vegetables aside. Melt the butter in a saucepan, stir in the flour, and cook over low heat 2 minutes. Off heat, add the broth, return to the heat and cook, whisking, until the mixture comes to the boil and is smooth and thickened. Stir in the cheese and chopped parsley. Add the leeks, celery, and pepper strips. Fold in the cubes of chicken. Taste and correct the seasoning, adding salt and pepper as necessary. Meanwhile, cook the fusilli in a large pot of boiling salted water until done *al dente*. Drain and serve with the sauce on top.

SERVES 4–6

Good to make if you have a piece of cooked swordfish as a leftover—in fact, it's worth grilling a little extra so that you can have this delicious pasta the next day. It makes a full meal for two.

Pasta with Swordfish and Black Olives

2 tablespoons olive oil
1 small onion, chopped
About 1½ cups cooked swordfish, cut in chunks
1 dozen black Mediterranean olives, pitted and cut in half
½ cup fish broth, or ¼ cup clam broth and ¼ cup water

½ cup tomato purée
Salt
Freshly ground pepper
½ pound spaghetti or fettuccine
About 1 cup broccoli florets

Bring a large pot of salted water to a boil. Meanwhile heat the oil in a medium skillet, then add the onion and sauté gently until it becomes translucent. When the water comes to a rolling boil, drop in the pasta. Meanwhile, continue with the sauce, adding the swordfish and olives to the skillet. Cook and toss 1 minute, then pour in the broth and tomato purée and season with salt and pepper. Simmer very gently. After the pasta has boiled 5–6 minutes, drop the broccoli into the same water and continue cooking until done *al dente*. Drain the pasta and broccoli together and dish onto warm plates, then pour the sauce on top.
SERVES 2

Although most recipes for sea urchins use only the roe, as described on page 7, the dark liquid inside the shell has an intense, tangy taste of the sea, which when simmered a minute with freshly cooked thin pasta permeates the whole dish and makes it delicious.

Linguine with Sea Urchins

3–4 pounds very fresh sea urchins
2 tablespoons olive oil
2 tablespoons finely chopped shallots or small white onion

1 pound linguine or other thin pasta
Freshly ground pepper
3–4 tablespoons chopped parsley

With a sharp knife, cut a circle out of the top of each sea urchin, then scoop out the roe and the liquid. Put a large pot of salted water on to boil. Meanwhile, heat the olive oil and sauté the shallots or onion over low heat until tender. Drop the pasta into the water when it is boiling rapidly, and cook until not quite *al dente*. Add the sea urchins and their liquid to the pot with the shallots and heat thoroughly but don't boil. Drain the pasta and return it to its pot, then gently strain the sea urchin liquid over it. Let simmer about 1 minute until the pasta has absorbed most of the liquid and is done *al dente*. Taste; it probably won't need salt but grind over some fresh pepper. Turn into 4 warm pasta plates, arrange the sea urchin roe on pasta, and sprinkle parsley on top. Serve immediately.

SERVES 4

Michael's Seafood Extravaganza with Fresh Pasta

After boyhood days in Hartford, Michael LaCroix was trained as a chef de cuisine and performs as such at The Landing in Newport, Vermont, after closing his own restaurant in nearby Derby. As this dish shows, his inventiveness is challenged by local ingredients.

1 tablespoon butter
6 shallots, peeled and minced
2 tablespoons minced garlic
1 quart mussels (about 2 pounds), scrubbed and debearded
1 cup dry white wine
4 cups tomato sauce (page 630), or a good canned marinara
Big pinch saffron
One 4–5-pound lobster, if available, or two or three 1½-pound lobsters

¼ cup melted unsalted butter
12 littleneck clams, scrubbed
½ pound medium shrimp, shelled and deveined
½ pound Cape scallops
¼ pound squid, cleaned (page 120) and cut into ¼-inch rings
Salt
1 pound fresh pasta, preferably white or green fettuccine
¼ cup minced fresh parsley

Melt the butter in a large heavy pot and sauté the shallots and garlic a few minutes. Add the cleaned mussels and the white wine, cover the pot, and turn up the heat. Shake the pot back and forth several times while the mussels steam to encourage them to open. When they have all opened, remove them to a platter and shuck. Pour the cooking liquid and any juices from shucking into a bowl carefully, "decanting-style," i.e., leaving any grit behind. Discard the grit and clean out the pot. Pour the tomato sauce into the pot and add the reserved mussel broth and saffron. Let simmer while you tackle the lobster.

Using a large heavy knife, split the lobster(s) from head to tail. Discard the stomach sac and dark intestine. Place on a baking sheet, flesh side up, and drizzle the melted butter over. Place another large pan on top of the lobster(s), bottom side up, covering the exposed body and weighting down the tail(s). Bake in a preheated 350-degree oven until the lobster meat is just opaque, about 20 minutes for the smaller lobsters, 30–40 for the large.

Put a 4-quart pot full of water on to boil for the pasta. Meanwhile, add clams, shrimp, scallops, and squid to the simmering tomato sauce, cover, and let cook until the clams open. By now the pasta water should be boiling, add salt, and stir in the fettuccine. Fresh pasta takes only a few minutes to cook so watch and test by tasting; as soon as it is done *al dente,* drain. Now add the mussels to the seafood sauce to warm through. Scoop the meat out of the lobster(s), cut into large pieces, and crack the claws. If you have a 5-pound lobster, fill the shell with the pasta, pour the seafood sauce over, and arrange some of the lobster meat on top; serve the remaining lobster and claws in a separate bowl. If you have smaller lobsters, discard the body shells and arrange the pasta and seafood on a hot platter with lobster meat on top and claws around. Sprinkle parsley over all and serve immediately.

SERVES 4–6

Crayfish with Pasta

It will take almost 100 average-size freshwater lake crayfish to make 2 cups of crayfish meat. So roll up your sleeves and settle down in a rocking chair with a member of your family or a friend, and some newspaper to catch the drips, and enjoy this labor of love.

2½ cups Crayfish Broth (page 11)
4 ounces imported Italian pasta in small shapes (wagon wheels or shells)
2 tablespoons vegetable and olive oil combined, or butter
2 cups cooked crayfish meat (page 11)

4 scallions, including tender greens, sliced
Freshly ground pepper
Salt
1 tablespoon chopped fresh tarragon, or ½ teaspoon dried mixed with 1 tablespoon chopped fresh parsley

Reduce the crayfish broth to half its volume by boiling it down. Bring a large pot of salted water to a boil, then add the pasta. Start the sauce a few minutes after it has returned to the boil. Heat the oils or butter in a large heavy skillet or saucepan, then toss and stir the crayfish and scallions in it for a minute or so. When the pasta is almost done—a little more firm than *al dente*—drain it. Pour the reduced broth into the skillet, add the pasta, grind pepper liberally over all, taste for salt, adding it if necessary (the reduced broth may make it salty enough), cover the skillet, and simmer for a few minutes to finish cooking the pasta. Serve in warm bowls with a sprinkling of tarragon on top.
SERVES 2

Ed Giobbi's Fresh Sardines with Fennel Sauce Pasta

Some New Englanders (especially in Maine) are so busy canning sardines for inlanders that food stores seldom have an ample supply of fresh sardines. But people in the know catch them, and some Yankees with Italian leanings cook them like this.

1 pound fresh sardines
½ cup olive oil
1 garlic clove
2 cups chopped tomatoes or puréed canned tomatoes
2 tablespoons tomato paste
¼ cup warm water
1 tablespoon chopped fresh basil, or ½ tablespoon dried

1 teaspoon dried oregano
2 cups chopped fresh fennel leaves
Hot red pepper flakes to taste (optional)
Salt
Freshly ground pepper
1 pound pasta

Put a large pot of slightly salted water on to boil for the pasta. Heat half the oil in a skillet and cook the sardines gently for about 10 minutes, turning them once. When the sardines are cooked, split them and remove and discard the bones. Meanwhile, pour the remaining oil into the skillet and add the split sardines and garlic. Cook slowly, stirring, for about 3 minutes. Add the tomatoes, and tomato paste mixed with the warm water, and season with the basil, oregano, and fennel leaves, a pinch or two of hot pepper, and a light sprinkling of salt and freshly ground pepper. Cook slowly for 10 minutes while the pasta cooks. Drain the pasta when it is done *al dente*, turn out onto a warm platter, and pour over the sauce.

SERVES 4–6

Of course spaghetti squash is not a pasta, but this remarkable squash (increasingly available in New England supermarkets and featured now in seed catalogues for home gardeners) makes such a wonderful substitute for pasta when the cooked squash separates into spaghetti-like strands that we are including this recipe here. It's a boon to dieters watching their carbohydrates who might otherwise skip over the pasta offerings.

Spaghetti Squash with Seafood

1 large spaghetti squash
1 dozen littleneck clams
½ cup water
2 pounds mussels
2 tablespoons butter
2 tablespoons minced shallots

½ pound small shrimp
½ pound scallops
Freshly ground pepper
1 tablespoon chopped fresh chervil
    or tarragon, or ½ teaspoon dried
3 tablespoons chopped parsley

Split the spaghetti squash lengthwise and place cut side down in a large saucepan or roasting pan that will hold the squash in one layer. Add 2 inches boiling water to the pan, cover, and steam-boil for 20 minutes. Put the littlenecks in a heavy pot with ½ cup water, cover, and steam about 3–4 minutes, then add the mussels, cover, and steam for 3–4 minutes, or until the mussels open. Remove them as they open, and, if necessary, continue steaming the remaining bivalves until all are open. When cool enough, remove the flesh from the shells, and carefully strain broth and reserve. Sauté the butter and shallots in a skillet until soft, then add the shrimp and sauté until the shrimp turn pink. Remove with a slotted spoon and peel off and discard the shells. Sauté the scallops in the pan, tossing, for a minute. Now return the shrimp and the clam and mussel meat to the pan along with the broth in which they were cooked. When the spaghetti squash is tender, scoop out the flesh with a fork—it will separate into long strands like spaghetti—and toss in a warm bowl with the seafood sauce. Add several grindings of pepper (salt won't be needed) and the herbs, and serve immediately.

SERVES 4

Fish and Shrimp Pasta

½ pound shrimp
½ pound white fish fillets
1 large onion, chopped
1 garlic clove, chopped
1½ tablespoons vegetable oil
½ tablespoon olive oil
1 tablespoon butter
4 large tomatoes, chopped

2 tablespoons tomato purée
1 teaspoon oregano
1 bay leaf
Salt
Freshly ground pepper
½–¾ cup dry vermouth
Grated cheese
1 pound thin pasta

Shell and clean the shrimp and cut the fish into small pieces. Cook the onion and garlic in the oils and butter for about 5 minutes. Add the chopped tomatoes and the tomato paste, the oregano, bay leaf, a light sprinkling of salt and pepper, and the vermouth. Simmer the mixture, covered, for about 30 minutes, adding a little wine and water as necessary to keep the sauce fluent. Add the shrimp and fish, cover, and cook about 5 minutes. Cook thin pasta of choice until done *al dente*, drain, and combine it with the sauce.
SERVES 4

Pasta Shells with Mussels and Peas

¾ pound large pasta shells
3 tablespoons olive or vegetable oil or combination
2 medium onions, peeled and chopped
2 garlic cloves, chopped
¼ pound mushrooms, quartered
¼ cup dry vermouth
3 cups steamed and shelled mussels

1½ cups mussel cooking broth, or ¾ cup clam juice mixed with ¾ cup chicken broth
4 tablespoons chopped fresh basil, or 2 teaspoons dried
2 cups fresh peas, blanched 1 minute
Freshly ground pepper
2–3 tablespoons chopped parsley

Put a large pot of salted water on to boil, and when it comes to a rolling boil, drop in the pasta shells. Meanwhile, heat the oil in a skillet and sauté the onions slowly for about 5 minutes, until they are almost tender, then add the garlic and the mushrooms and sauté another couple of minutes, stirring. Add the vermouth and cook rapidly to reduce by half, then stir in the mussels, broth, and basil, and bring to a simmer. Drain the pasta when it is done *al dente,* and mix with the sauce, folding in the peas, and heating through. Season with freshly ground pepper (it probably will not need salt). Serve in warm bowls with parsley sprinkled on top.
SERVES 4

Yankee Doodle's Noodle and All That

The Trio family of Boston's North End, master pasta makers, shook up fettucini and spaghettini aficionados when they introduced chocolate pasta in 1982, but it was 180 years earlier that Congressman Manasseh Cutler came home to Massachusetts from a dinner at the White House. President Jefferson, he reported, had served some outlandish thing called "macaroni pie." Pasta has been familiar to Yankees ever since.

When you're fortunate enough to be near a source of well-made fresh pasta—it's made daily in many places from Boston to Barre, Vermont—it is delicious, particularly with a light sauce and fresh summer vegetables. For variety try making your own buckwheat pasta (page 367). But dried pastas made with hard semolina flour have a texture that fresh pastas lack, and they come in a variety of shapes these days that make it fun to mix and match them with different sauces and embellishments. Incidentally, there is no need to drown any pasta in a sauce, and cheese is not necessarily imperative; pasta is delicious when lightly coated in butter or olive oil, with bits of meat, seafood, and/or colorful vegetables tossed in as accents. There are no rules—at least for Americans—about what specific shape of pasta goes best with one sauce or another. We like some of the more substantial shapes like penne (quills) or fusilli (corkscrews) accompanied by chunky pieces of meat or vegetables of a similar shape. Thinner strands like angel hair or spaghettini seem to marry well with more liquid sauces. The only rule that must be observed is to cook all pasta (whole, don't break it up) in a very large pot of boiling, lightly salted water; stir it around and drain it as soon as it is tender but not mushy. The pasta should still have a little resistance when you bite into it— what Italians call *al dente*. Fresh pasta will be done in a matter of minutes after the water returns to a boil; dried can take from 7 to almost 20 minutes, depending on type and shape, so watch it, keep extracting a piece and tasting it. After draining, never leave pasta sitting in a colander. Toss it immediately with the sauce while it is still hot.

Pasta with Salmon and Fresh Peas

4 tablespoons oil, preferably part olive oil
½ cup chopped scallions, including tender greens
⅔ cup thinly sliced Italian green peppers
¼ cup dry white wine or vermouth
4 tablespoons chopped fresh tarragon, or 2 teaspoons dried
1 cup fish stock (salmon poaching liquid, if available)
2 cups cooked salmon, separated into flakes

1 cup heavy cream
Salt
Freshly ground pepper
A few dashes of Tabasco sauce (optional)
2 cups peas, cooked until just tender
3 tablespoons chopped parsley
10 ounces pasta such as fusilli or small shells

Heat a large pot of salted water and when it's boiling drop in the pasta. While the pasta cooks, quickly prepare the sauce. Heat the oil in a large skillet, then add the scallions and peppers, and sauté a few minutes. Pour in the wine, and when it has boiled hard a few seconds, add 2 tablespoons of the tarragon, the fish stock, salmon, cream, salt, pepper to taste, and optional Tabasco. Let simmer gently until the pasta is done *al dente*. Drain the pasta, and add to the mixture in the skillet along with peas. Toss gently together and serve when heated through, sprinkling each serving with remaining tarragon and the parsley.
SERVES 4

Noodles with Salt Cod and White Garlic Sauce

1 pound salt cod, soaked overnight
¼ cup vegetable oil
2 large garlic cloves, cut in half
¼ cup chopped green pepper
¼ cup chopped sweet red pepper

1 cup cold water
1 tablespoon chopped fresh tarragon, or 1 teaspoon dried
1 pound noodles, preferably fresh

Cover the soaked cod with boiling water and bring the water back to a boil over high heat, but do not continue boiling. Carefully remove the cod pieces, drain, and remove any bones before cutting the fish into bite-size pieces. Heat the oil in a large skillet and sauté the garlic halves and the chopped peppers about 3 minutes. Remove the garlic and put in the fish pieces. Pour in the water and increase the heat just to the simmering point. Sprinkle in the tarragon, cover, and simmer 30–40 minutes, shaking the skillet now and then to avoid sticking, but don't stir. Put the noodles into a large pot of boiling salted water and cook until done *al dente* (if they are

fresh they will take only a couple of minutes after the water returns to the boil). Drain. Now uncover the skillet and quickly reduce the sauce as necessary to about two-thirds. Serve very hot over the noodles.
SERVES 4

Green Pasta with Blue Cheese

3 tablespoons butter
1/3 cup ricotta cheese
3/4 cup light cream
6 ounces blue cheese
1 pound green fettuccine, fresh or
   dried

1/3 cup chopped Italian parsley
Freshly ground pepper
Salt to taste (optional)

Melt the butter in a heavy saucepan and stir in the ricotta and cream. Let simmer gently while you grate the blue cheese and put a large pot of salted water on to boil. When the water comes to a rolling boil, drop in the fettuccine. Now stir the blue cheese into the ricotta-cream mixture, and when it has melted and blended, add the parsley and remove from the fire, but keep warm. Drain the pasta when it is *al dente*. Immediately turn the drained pasta into a large warm bowl, pour the sauce over it, add several grinds of fresh pepper, and toss thoroughly. Taste and correct seasonings if necessary; it may need salt and a bit more pepper. Serve right away.
SERVES 4

Ceres Street Sage and Fiddlehead Pesto

Close to the Portsmouth waterfront, chef James Haller has turned his Blue Strawbery kitchen into an experimental studio, and his creations are often variations on well-known themes. Here's a variation on *his* variation, to be used on hot pasta. Chef Haller recommends a glass of dandelion wine to accompany the noodles enhanced with this pesto.

4 cups washed and chopped
   fiddleheads
1/2 pound North Pack cheese,
   chopped
1/2 pound mild cheddar, chopped
1 cup olive oil
1/2 cup butternuts or black walnuts
Juice of 1 lemon
4 large garlic cloves

2 tablespoons chopped fresh sage
2 tablespoons chopped fresh basil
   or marjoram
2 tablespoons chopped parsley
   (preferably Italian broadleaf)
Freshly ground pepper
1 pound fettuccine, fresh or dried

Ceres Street Sage and Fiddlehead Pesto (continued)

Put the fiddleheads and the cheeses in a food processor and add the oil, nuts, lemon juice, garlic, and the herbs. Spin the mixture until it becomes a thick paste, then grind in the pepper liberally, to your taste. Meanwhile, cook the pasta in a large pot of boiling salted water until done *al dente*. Drain, reserving a little of the cooking water to thin the sauce slightly—2 to 3 tablespoons should be enough. Toss the sauce with the pasta and serve.

SERVES 4

Cornmeal Pasta with Zucchini Meat Sauce

Noodles, macaroni, and other forms of pasta produced from cornmeal may not be commonplace in stores, but we have found them occasionally and we like the enticingly grainy texture. This simple dish, made with Vermont garden vegetables, won't be the same without cornmeal macaroni, but it can, of course, make a hearty meal with ordinary elbow macaroni.

2 tablespoons vegetable oil
1 small carrot, finely chopped
1 small onion, chopped
3 tablespoons chopped red or green pepper
1 teaspoon dried rosemary, or 2 teaspoons chopped fresh
1 pound meat, chopped
1 medium tomato, peeled and chopped

One 6-inch zucchini, peeled and sliced
1 garlic clove, minced
Salt
Freshly ground pepper
1 pound elbow corn macaroni
2 tablespoons olive or vegetable oil
1 cup grated hard Vermont cheese

In a large saucepan or skillet, heat 2 tablespoons of vegetable oil and cook the carrot, onion, and chopped pepper about 5 minutes over medium heat. Stir in the rosemary and the ground meat, and continue stirring until the meat is thoroughly seared. Add the chopped tomato, the zucchini, and the

garlic, and bring to a simmer; cook about 10 minutes. Season to taste with salt and pepper. Cook the pasta in 4 quarts of boiling water, adding the 2 tablespoons of oil, for about 6 minutes if you are using cornmeal, or follow directions for other kinds of pasta. Meanwhile, stir half the grated cheese into the vegetable mixture, mixing it in well as it melts. Drain the pasta and serve with remaining cheese sprinkled over each serving.
SERVES 4

Buckwheat Pasta

1¾ cups all-purpose flour
¾ cup buckwheat flour
½ teaspoon salt

3 eggs
1 tablespoon vegetable or olive oil
   (for machine-mixed pasta)

To mix and knead by hand: Put the flour and salt on a counter-top, mix thoroughly, then make a well in the center. Crack the eggs, one by one, and let fall into the well. Beat the eggs with a fork, incorporating little by little the surrounding wall of flour until it is absorbed. Form into a ball and let rest for a few minutes, then knead the dough with the heel of your hand, pushing it away from you and folding it back on itself. This dough will seem tough and resistant but just persist, pummeling when necessary. It will require a good 10 minutes of kneading, at which point the ball of dough will be more resilient (though never as much so as a bread dough). Form into a ball, cover with plastic wrap, and let rest about 45 minutes before rolling out.

To mix and knead in the food processor (much easier): Put the flours and the salt into the bowl of the food processor and spin a few seconds, using the metal blade. Crack the eggs and let fall through the tube, one by one, while the machine runs, add 1 tablespoon oil, and process until the dough forms a ball around the center shaft. Remove and knead for a minute by hand. Cover with plastic wrap and let rest 45 minutes.

Put the dough through a pasta cutting machine, dividing it in 3 parts, and putting each section through the roller, first at its widest opening, then tightening it a notch each time you put the portion of pasta through again. By the time you have finished, the dough will have stretched to stocking length, so cut it in two before putting through the cutting element. Repeat with the remaining portions of dough and spread the cut pasta out on trays, on a clothes rack, or over the backs of chairs to dry out. When no longer damp to the touch, it is ready to cook. Have a very large pot of boiling water ready, add a couple of teaspoons of salt, and dump in the pasta, stirring to keep it all under the water and to make sure it doesn't stick. By the time the water comes back to a rolling boil, it will be almost done. Start tasting by extracting a strand, and when it is almost tender but with still a little bite to it, it is *al dente*. Strain and sauce and serve immediately.
SERVES 4–6, DEPENDING ON WHETHER IT IS A MAIN COURSE

Crayfish, Ham, and Snow Peas with Buckwheat Pasta

About 3 dozen crayfish
Salt
Freshly ground pepper
¼ pound snow peas, strings removed
4 tablespoons vegetable and olive oil
6 scallions, including tender greens, chopped
½ large sweet red pepper, seeded and cut in 1½-inch strips
1 cup cooked ham, cut into 1½-inch strips
½ cup dry white wine
3 tablespoons chopped fresh tarragon, or 1 teaspoon dried
3 tablespoons chopped parsley
Homemade Buckwheat Pasta (preceding recipe), or ¾ pound farfalle (bow-tie), or other

Extract the meat from the crayfish according to directions on page 11. Put the shells in a saucepan, cover with cold water, and boil fairly rapidly until the liquid is reduced to 1 cup. Strain and add salt and pepper to taste. Meanwhile, boil the snow peas in water to cover for 1 minute, then drain and cut into diagonal ¾-inch pieces. Put a large pot of salted water on to boil, and stir in the pasta as you start the sauce. Heat the oil in a skillet, then add the scallions and red pepper and stir and toss for 1 minute. Add the crayfish and ham, and when hot, pour in the wine, boil rapidly, and toss in most of the tarragon (all of it if you are using dry). Add the crayfish broth, then salt and pepper to taste. The pasta should be just cooked *al dente* by now. Drain, mix with the sauce, and serve with remaining tarragon and parsley on top.

SERVES 4 AS A MAIN COURSE; 6 AS A FIRST COURSE

Lasagna

1 cup finely chopped onions
2 cloves garlic, chopped fine
3 tablespoons vegetable oil
1½ pounds ground beef
Salt
Freshly ground pepper
1 large can tomatoes with tomato purée
1 cup beef stock
2 tablespoons chopped fresh basil, or ½ teaspoon dried
½ pound lasagna pasta
¼ pound chouriço or cooked Italian spicy sausage, sliced thin
2 cups ricotta cheese
½ pound sliced mozzarella cheese
¼ pound Parmesan cheese, freshly grated

Cook the onion and the garlic in 2 tablespoons of the oil 3–4 minutes, or until almost tender. Stir in the ground beef, stirring to break it up, and brown lightly (if the meat exudes excess fat, skim to leave no more than 2 tablespoons). Season with salt and pepper to taste. Break up the tomatoes and stir them and the purée into the meat mixture along with the beef stock. Stir in the basil and simmer, covered, for about 30 minutes. Meanwhile, cook the pasta in a large pot of boiling water, adding a tablespoon of salt and the remaining oil. When pasta is *al dente*, drain and rinse in cold water. Spoon a thin layer of one-third the tomato sauce on the bottom of a shallow baking dish 13 × 9 × 3 inches. Make a layer of one-third the pasta strips and cover with half the sausage, 1 cup of the ricotta, and half the mozzarella slices. Repeat with one-third more of the sauce and the remaining sausage, ricotta, and mozzarella, and end with a final layer of tomato sauce topped with pasta. Sprinkle Parmesan over and bake in a preheated 350-degree oven for 45 minutes.

SERVES 6–8

Lasagna with Seafood

2 pounds mussels
⅓ cup dry white wine
3 chopped shallots or white part of scallions
2 tablespoons oil
1 medium onion, chopped
1½ cups peeled, chopped tomatoes, fresh or canned
¾ pound monkfish or lobster, or part monkfish and part lobster, cut in good-size chunks
Salt
Freshly ground pepper
¾ pound sea scallops
¾ pound peeled shrimp
3 tablespoons butter
3 tablespoons flour
½–¾ cup milk or light cream
9 strips lasagna, 9 inches long, 2 inches wide
5 ounces fresh goat cheese or ricotta
3–4 tablespoons freshly grated Parmesan cheese

Scrub the mussels thoroughly and remove their beards. Put the wine in a large, heavy saucepan with the shallots or scallions, bring to a boil, and simmer about 1 minute (2 minutes if using scallions instead of shallots); add the mussels, cover, and cook over lively heat a few minutes, until the mussels have opened. Remove the mussels from their shells, discarding the shells but reserving the cooking liquid.

Heat the oil in a skillet, then sauté the onion, stirring occasionally, until limp. Add the tomatoes and cook down rapidly to boil off some of the juice. Add the monkfish and/or lobster and a little salt and pepper, cover, and cook gently for 5 minutes, turning the pieces once. Add the scallops and shrimp and continue cooking 5 minutes, tossing and stirring.

Put a large pot of salted water on to boil. Meanwhile, prepare the seafood cream sauce. Melt the butter in a saucepan, then add the flour and cook over gentle heat, stirring, for 2 minutes. Off heat, strain the reserved mussel cooking liquid into the butter and flour (you should have about 1 cup) and add enough milk or the light cream to make a total of 1½ cups. Return to the heat and whisk until the sauce thickens and is smooth. When the pasta water has come to a rolling boil, add the lasagna, stirring each piece until it is immersed in the water, and cook until done *al dente*. Drain.

To assemble the lasagna, place 3 strips of the pasta on the bottom of a lightly oiled shallow 10 × 8-inch baking dish. Spoon pieces of monkfish and/

or lobster and shrimp and scallops on top. If the tomato sauce left in the pan is even a bit thin or watery, rapidly boil it down until thick, then spoon that over the seafood. Lay another 3 strips of pasta over the sauce and seafood and cover that with mussels interspersed with globs of goat cheese or ricotta. Place the final layer of pasta on top, then spread with the cream sauce and sprinkle with Parmesan cheese. Cover lightly with foil, and bake in a preheated 350-degree oven for 25 minutes (only 15 minutes if all the elements of the dish are warm when assembled), then 5 minutes uncovered. It should be bubbly inside and lightly browned on top.

SERVES 6—8

Stuffed Manicotti

These manicotti (the word means *sleeves* in Italian) are not filled with ham and ricotta, as they were in the old country, but with fresh vegetables and a little spicy sausage meat for accent. The recipe can be easily doubled or tripled for a crowd—and it makes a good party dish. Follow your own instincts about the stuffing. Sherry Golden, a Boston caterer and author of *Good Tastes*, pleases her customers with a ratatouille (eggplant, tomatoes, and peppers) filling, sometimes adding kidney beans.

½ pound diced Portuguese or Italian sausage
1 medium onion, chopped
1 medium sweet red pepper, seeds and ribs removed, chopped

2 cups freshly and lightly cooked broccoli, chopped
10 manicotti

WHITE SAUCE:
4 tablespoons butter
4 tablespoons flour
2 cups milk
Salt
Freshly ground pepper

½ pound mozzarella cheese
2 cups Quick Tomato Sauce (page 631)
¼ cup grated Parmesan cheese

Put a large pot of lightly salted water on to boil for the manicotti. In a skillet, sauté the sausage meat, and when it gives off its fat, add the onion and pepper and sauté gently for about 5 minutes. Add the broccoli, mix well, and remove from the heat. Plunge the manicotti into the boiling water while you make the white sauce.

Melt the butter in a saucepan, stir in the flour, and cook gently 2 minutes, stirring. Off heat, whisk in the milk, return to the heat, and whisk until thickened. Season to taste with salt and pepper. Mix about one-quarter of this sauce with the sausage-broccoli mixture.

When the manicotti are done *al dente*, drain them, and as soon as you can handle them, separate and stuff them with the sausage-broccoli mixture. Lay them side by side in a buttered baking dish just large enough to hold them in one layer. Slice the mozzarella and lay slices over the manicotti. Spread the remaining white sauce over, then pour on the tomato sauce, spreading it evenly over the top. Sprinkle on the Parmesan and bake the dish in a preheated 375-degree oven for 30 minutes.

SERVES 5

Shell Macaroni Ham and Cheese Casserole

1 tablespoon vegetable oil
1 large onion, chopped
½ cup chopped green pepper
1 garlic clove, finely chopped
¾ pound country ham, cubed
1 pound macaroni shells
Salt

Freshly ground pepper
1 large can (1 pound, 12 oz.) whole tomatoes
1 tablespoon dried oregano
2 cups cottage cheese
1½ cups grated cheddar cheese

Heat the oil in a skillet and sauté the onion and green pepper over moderate heat for about 5 minutes, adding the garlic the last minute. Scrape the vegetables into a large mixing bowl and add the ham cubes. Cook the macaroni in 2 quarts boiling salted water for 6–8 minutes, until tender but not soft. Drain the macaroni and stir into the mixture of ham and vegetables. Sprinkle with salt and pepper. Coarsely chop the tomatoes and add to the mixture along with the oregano and the cottage cheese. Pour the mixture into a 2-quart ovenproof casserole and scatter the cheddar evenly over the top. Bake in 325-degree oven about 25 minutes, until the casserole is bubbling and topped with melting cheese.

SERVES 4–6

Oysters and Macaroni

The Pot and Kettle Club, once an exclusive crew of amateur male cooks in Bar Harbor, Maine, staged competitions to see who could turn out the best version of "macaroni as a specialty of the house." None of them admitted to using the word pasta, but some form of the Italian specialty was often combined with seafood at their gatherings. Here a baked dish of macaroni is made interesting by the addition of oysters.

2 cups elbow macaroni
24 large fresh oysters
Salt
Freshly ground pepper
1 cup fresh bread crumbs

1 tablespoon butter
½ cup crumbled firm goat cheese or feta
1 cup milk

Cook the macaroni in boiling salted water about 8 minutes, until just tender. Drain the oysters. Cover the bottom of a greased 1½-quart casserole with a layer of cooked, drained macaroni, and add a layer of oysters loosely arranged. Sprinkle lightly with salt and pepper. Add layers of macaroni and oysters, making the top layer macaroni. Sprinkle the top layer with the bread crumbs, dots of butter, and the crumbled cheese (use Parmesan, if you prefer). Pour the milk over the top of the casserole. Bake at 425 degrees for about 20 minutes.
SERVES 4–6

Sardine and Pasta Casserole

Canned Maine sardines can be used in various cooked dishes—of which this is an appetizing lunch or supper meal.

3 tablespoons vegetable oil
2 tablespoons chopped scallions, including tender greens
3 tablespoons flour
1 cup clam juice mixed with ½ cup water or fish stock
½ cup plain yogurt
½–¾ cup grated cheddar cheese

1 large firm tomato, sliced
2 cans Maine sardines, well drained
½ pound pasta shells, cooked and drained
Salt
Freshly ground pepper
2 tablespoons chopped fresh dill, or ½ teaspoon dried dillweed

Heat the oil in a saucepan and stir in the chopped scallions. Cook about 2 minutes, until translucent, then stir in the flour. Add the clam juice or fish stock and stir until a smooth sauce is formed. Add the yogurt and stir until sauce thickens slightly. Add the grated cheese and stir thoroughly. Cut the tomato slices in quarters and drop them into the sauce as you add the pasta and broken pieces of the drained sardines. Season to taste with salt and pepper and add the dill. Pour the mixture into a greased 1½-quart casserole. Bake in preheated 350-degree oven about 20 minutes.

SERVES 4

Eric Stevens' Spaetzle

Spaetzle are tiny dumplings, much loved by the Swiss. Albert Stockli used to serve them often at his Connecticut restaurant, and Eric Stevens, who finds them the perfect accompaniment to his stuffed pork (see page 234), demonstrates how easy they are to make.

3 eggs
1 cup water
2¼ cups flour

½ teaspoon salt
¼ teaspoon nutmeg
Pinch white pepper

GARNISH: *chopped parsley and butter*

Mix the eggs and the water. Toss the flour with the salt and nutmeg, then stir in the egg and water. Bring a large pot of salted water to a boil, turn it down to a simmer, and place a colander over the pot (it shouldn't be touching the water). Dump the spaetzle dough into the colander and, with a rubber spatula, push all of the dough through the colander. Cook at a simmer about 5 minutes, until firm yet tender. Drain and toss with chopped parsley and butter.

SERVES 8–10

Kedgeree

The flavor of interesting spices has been less apparent in New England kedgeree for a couple hundred years, but younger cooks have recently been zipping up what is a tried-and-true breakfast or supper dish that is based on leftover fish and rice.

2 tablespoons butter or vegetable oil
2 tablespoons finely chopped onion
¼–⅓ cup finely chopped green pepper
½ teaspoon or more curry powder

½ teaspoon summer savory
2 cups cooked rice
2 cups flaked cooked fish
Salt
Freshly ground pepper
½ cup milk

Heat the butter or oil and quickly cook the onion and green pepper, without browning. Stir in the curry powder, savory, cooked rice, and the flaked fish, mixing thoroughly. Add salt and pepper to taste and a little more curry if desired. Stir in the milk and bring the mixture to the boiling point.

SERVES 4

Rice with Leeks

3 medium leeks
1 carrot, thinly sliced
3 tablespoons butter
Chicken stock

3 cups cooked rice
Salt
Freshly ground pepper

Trim off the green part of the leeks (save for soup). Split the leeks lengthwise, and clean under running water. Chop the leeks and put them with the sliced carrots and the butter in a saucepan. Stir thoroughly over moderate heat, add chicken stock to barely cover the vegetables, and bring the liquid to the boiling point. Cover the pan, lower heat, and simmer about 20 minutes. Add stock as necessary to keep the vegetables moist. Add the rice, stir well, and add enough more stock so that the rice is moist. Sprinkle with salt and a few turns of the pepper grinder to taste.
SERVES 4

VARIATION: This may also be made with uncooked rice. Add 1 cup of rice to the leeks and carrots, and sauté until all the grains are coated. Add 2 cups chicken stock and bring to a boil, then lower heat, cover, and simmer 20 minutes, at which point the liquid will be absorbed and the rice tender.

Wild Rice with Chicken Livers

Although the Indian bounty of wild rice has diminished, this great natural grain can be harvested in New England when sought out by wild-food enthusiasts. It can also be ordered by mail at prices often considerably less than those in specialty stores.

¾ pound chicken livers, cut up
2 tablespoons finely chopped
   scallion bulbs
⅓ cup chopped green pepper
4 tablespoons butter
¼ pound fresh mushrooms, sliced
¼ cup broken pieces butternuts, or
   other nuts

¾ cup wild rice, thoroughly
   washed
3 cups chicken broth
Salt
Freshly ground pepper

Sauté chicken livers, the chopped scallions, and green pepper in 2 tablespoons butter a minute or two. Remove the chicken livers and keep warm. Add the mushrooms and the nuts to the skillet, and cook, stirring frequently, for about 5 minutes. Stir in the wild rice and the chicken broth, mixing well, then turn into a casserole, adding remaining 2 tablespoons butter in a sprinkling of salt, and a few turns of the pepper grinder. Fold in the chicken livers. Cover the casserole and put it into a preheated oven at 325 degrees for 45 minutes, or until the rice is tender. Remove the cover and continue baking 5 minutes more.
SERVES 3–4

Whole Grains, Baked

More New Englanders are baking whole grains than ever before. Some of them are among the proliferating natural-food enthusiasts. Others with Middle Eastern backgrounds—such as Tom Azarian of Plainfield, Vermont, a candidate for governor—have influenced the new Yankee style of living. In his *Recipes from Armenia* he gives many family recipes for pilaf and other dishes produced from whole grain and recommends the top-of-the-stove method of cooking. Rich Perry, a natural-food expert from Portland, Maine, however, prefers baking as the "most foolproof" method for rice, barley, millet, bulgur, or kasha. Here is his baked rice, as an example:

2 tablespoons oil
1 small onion, chopped
1 garlic clove, crushed
¼ pound mushrooms, chopped

2 cups short-grain brown rice
4 cups boiling water or stock
Salt
Freshly ground pepper

Heat the oil in a frying pan and sauté the vegetables over medium heat until barely done. Add the rice, stirring to coat each grain with oil while the rice kernels turn light brown. Scrape the rice and vegetables into a 2½-quart casserole; add boiling water or stock and a light sprinkling of salt and freshly ground pepper. Cover and bake at 350 degrees for 1 hour.

Cooking Times and Yields for Various Grains

GRAIN	AMOUNT	LIQUID	TIME AT 350°
Brown rice	2 cups	4 cups	1 hour
Barley	2 cups	4½ cups	1¼ hours
Millet	2 cups	5 cups	1¼ hours
Bulgur	2 cups	3 cups	45 minutes
Kasha	2 cups	3 cups	45 minutes

Combinations: In all cases, 350°, 1 hour, 5 cups liquid

Rice	2 cups plus ⅔ cup wheat flakes
Rice	2½ cups plus ½ cup sesame seeds
Bulgur	2 cups plus 1½ cups kasha
Millet	1½ cups plus ½ cup kasha

Both single and combination grain dishes will fit nicely in a 2½-quart baking dish and will serve 6.

Spanish-American Rice

Sometimes called red rice and served meatless as a vegetable casserole, a baked dish of rice in tomato sauce has been the centerpiece of many a Yankee supper for generations.

2 tablespoons vegetable oil or
  bacon drippings
1 large onion, chopped
1 medium green pepper, seeds and
  ribs removed, chopped
1 large rib celery, chopped
2 garlic cloves, minced
1 pound chouriço sausage, sweet
  Italian sausage, or kielbasa, or a
  combination of sausage and
  country ham, cut in chunks

2 cups tomato sauce
Salt
Freshly ground pepper
3 cups cooked rice
2–3 tablespoons grated cheese
  (optional)

Heat the oil or drippings in a skillet and cook the onion slowly for 5 minutes. Add the green pepper, celery, and garlic, and cook another minute, then stir in the sausage chunks and sauté, stirring now and then, for another 5 minutes. Stir in the tomato sauce and add salt and pepper to taste. Bring to a simmer while you spread half of the rice in the bottom of a greased casserole. Cover it with the sausage mixture, then top with the final layer of rice. Sprinkle grated cheese on top if your wish, and bake in a preheated 350-degree oven for 20–25 minutes. Serve bubbling hot.
SERVES 4–6

Barley Ring

In early New England, oatmeal porridges called *stirabout* and *fluffin* (a gruel made of oatmeal and barley seasoned with nutmeg and brandy) were not uncommon, but contemporary cooks have widened horizons to include barley dishes among accompaniments for various meats. We often think of serving this with cold leftover flank steak.

1 cup barley
1 cup chopped celery root
½ cup chopped carrots
2 quarts water

Salt
Freshly ground pepper
½ teaspoon chervil

Rinse the barley. Put the chopped vegetables and the water in a large pot and sprinkle lightly with salt. Bring to a boil and cook about 15–20 minutes, until the vegetables are done. Lift out the vegetables with a slotted spoon, and keep them warm. Return the cooking liquid to a boil, add the barley, and cook according to directions on the package. Add the warm vegetables to the drained, cooked barley, season lightly with salt and pep-

per, and stir in the chervil. Spoon the mixture into a well-greased ring mold, set it in a pan of hot water, and bake in a preheated 350-degree oven for about 30 minutes.
SERVES 4

Wheat Pilaf

In southern reaches of the United States in which rice became an important crop early in the nineteenth century, pilafs in various guises grew in popularity as the rice harvests increased, but among early Yankees who had Middle Eastern exposure it has often been necessary to make do with wheat as a substitute grain. For pilafs, we've found that replacing rice with bulgur or cracked wheat enhances the flavor as well as adding crunchiness to the texture. (Sometimes we add local nuts, or pine nuts, garlic, almonds, raisins, or currants, and we may use lamb or pork instead of chicken, or even cubes of sharp cheddar.)

¼ cup vegetable oil
1 tablespoon unsalted butter
2 large onions, chopped
1½ cups bulgur
2½ cups chicken, beef, or vegetable broth

½ teaspoon marjoram or oregano
Salt
1½ cups quartered mushrooms
½ cup cooked, slivered chicken

GARNISH: *quartered tomatoes, chopped parsley*

Heat 2 tablespoons of the oil with the butter and stir in the onions, cooking gently for about 5 minutes. Add the bulgur and stir to coat with the oil and butter. Cook for about 5 minutes, stirring often. Add the broth and the herb and bring to the boiling point. Sprinkle sparingly with salt to taste, and turn the mixture into a casserole. Bake in a preheated 350-degree oven for about 25 minutes. Heat the remaining oil, and sauté the mushrooms for about 5 minutes, until lightly brown; stir them into the casserole along with the chicken and continue baking for about 15 minutes more. Garnish with tomatoes and parsley.
SERVES 4–6

"Jonnycake"

Spelled without an "h," jonnycake was made the official term in the eighteenth century by Connecticut and Rhode Island legislatures for the all-American fried bread made of cornmeal. In Rhode Island, purists insist only Whitecap flint corn should be used to make the unique cakes, and the Society for the Propagation of the Jonnycake Tradition in Rhode Island has been working for a couple of decades to keep things straight in the minds of wayward cooks. The several waterwheel mills devoted to grinding Rhode Island cornmeal supply mail-order customers, and until the early 1980s,

New England visitors could sample genuine jonnycakes served at the Narragansett Indian Dovecrest Restaurant, near Exeter, as well as in several other traditional eating places in the southern part of the state. When made with a proper batter (see below) of a consistency not unlike corn bread dough, jonnycakes have a brown crust and steaming hot, fluffy interior.

2 cups stone-ground Rhode Island   *¼ cup milk or cold water*
   jonnycake meal (flint cornmeal)   *Oil*
1 teaspoon salt
2 cups boiling water

Mix the cornmeal and the salt together, then pour the boiling water over it, stirring vigorously to mix. Let stand about 5 minutes. Stir in the cold milk or water. Drop large mounds of this thick batter onto a medium-hot, well-greased skillet; the cakes should spread to about 2½ inches in diameter and be about ¾ inch thick. Fry for 6 minutes without touching, then brush the tops lightly with oil and turn and fry 5 minutes on the other side. Or turn gently as soon as a crust has formed on the bottom, after about 2 minutes, and finish cooking in a preheated 450-degree oven for 10–15 minutes until very crusty and puffed up.

MAKES 12 CAKES

VARIATION: For thin jonnycakes, stir ¾ cup cold water into 2 cups meal mixed with ½ teaspoon salt. Drop enough batter onto a well-greased skillet to spread to a 3-inch cake. Fry them on one side until the edges are browned, then turn and fry the other side.

MAKES ABOUT 20 CAKES

EGGS, CHEESE, and
BREAKFAST DISHES

FROM Elm Hill Farm, in the dairy country around Brookfield, Massachusetts, Elsie the Cow traveled in 1939 to the New York World's Fair to become even better known than Plymouth Rock hens and Rhode Island Reds, which had brought earlier fame to New England chickens and the eggs they provided. The Yankee farmer is still a mainstay of rural New England, even though free-range poultry are as scarce as roadside signs that advertise eggs for sale.

In old-time New England, eggs and cheese turned out in rustic dairies could often be found side by side at the village store. As essentials in a good cook's laboratory, both were frequently substitutes for meat and fish at supper time, and both could help to make filling breakfasts—and they continue to do so. Regional cooks no longer serve pie as an expected part of breakfast, but the first meal in the morning is recognized once again as one that should provide energy rather than the briefest possible interruption between bed and an active day.

For a lot of homespun reasons, eggs and cheese and breakfast seem to us to go together, so we've gathered some ideas in all three categories. Some might come off with honors at a World's Fair. At any rate, the variation on breakfast hash created in the 1980s by The Bostonian Hotel's Chef Lydia Shire when she was devising power breakfasts not far from City Hall is just one idea we think worthy of note.

Omelets

Omelets are best made one at a time in a 7-inch skillet, preferably nonstick. Once you get the hang of it, they will go very fast. If you are planning to fill your omelets, be sure to make the filling first and keep it warm. Obviously if you are making several omelets, increase the amount of filling accordingly.

2 large eggs
1 teaspoon water
Salt
Freshly ground pepper

2 teaspoons chopped fresh herbs, such as parsley, chives, basil, savory, tarragon, and so forth (optional but desirable for a plain, unfilled omelet)
1 tablespoon butter

Beat the eggs with the water, salt (about ⅛ teaspoon or a little more if you're not using a salty filling), several turns of the pepper grinder, and optional herbs. Heat a 7-inch nonstick skillet over high heat until a drop of water will sizzle and quickly disappear, then add the butter, swirling it around. As soon as the foaming subsides, pour in the beaten eggs. Let them cook until they begin to set, about 10 seconds, then with a wooden fork stir them gently, pulling the sides in toward the center and tipping the pan so that the uncooked eggs flow toward the edge. In less than 30 seconds the eggs will be done. Place the filling, if you are using one, across the center and remove the pan from the heat. Tilt the pan downward away from you so that the omelet slides toward the edge, then quickly jerk the pan so that the far side of the omelet flips over onto the other half (or if this seems forbidding, use a spatula to flip the omelet over). Now slide the folded omelet onto a hot plate and serve immediately.

SERVES 1

OEUFS DE FERME

BACON AND MUSHROOMS:
2 strips bacon
3–4 mushrooms, sliced
Salt
Freshly ground pepper

1/2 teaspoon chopped fresh
   tarragon, or 1/4 teaspoon dried
1 tablespoon heavy cream

Fry the bacon in a skillet until crisp, remove to a paper towel, drain, then crumble. Remove all but 1 teaspoon of the bacon fat from the skillet, add the mushrooms, season lightly with salt and pepper, and cook, tossing, for 1 minute. Add the tarragon and cream and cook another minute. Just before filling, mix the bacon with the mushroom, saving a few crumbled pieces to sprinkle on top.

FOR 1 OMELET

SPINACH-RICOTTA:
1/4 cup cooked chopped spinach
3 tablespoons ricotta or strained
   cottage cheese
1/2 teaspoon chopped fresh
   rosemary, or 1/4 teaspoon dried

Salt
Freshly ground pepper
2 tablespoons freshly grated
   Parmesan cheese

Mix all the ingredients, except for 1 tablespoon of the Parmesan, and warm them in a small pan. After filling the omelet, sprinkle the remaining tablespoon of Parmesan on top.

FOR 1 OMELET

CRABMEAT:
2 teaspoons butter
1 tablespoon finely chopped green
   pepper
1 tablespoon finely chopped celery
1/4 cup crabmeat

1 teaspoon chopped fresh chives
Dash of Tabasco sauce
Salt
Freshly ground pepper
2 strips pimiento (optional)

Note: Cooked lobster, shrimp, or scallops cut in small pieces would also be good.

Melt the butter in a small skillet and lightly sauté the green pepper and celery until just tender. Mix this with the remaining ingredients. After filling the omelet, top it with 2 strips pimiento, if desired.

FOR 1 OMELET

CHEESE:

⅓ cup grated sharp cheddar cheese   ½ teaspoon chopped chili peppers, or 3–4 dashes of Tabasco sauce (optional)

Sprinkle all but a few teaspoons of the cheese over the top after the omelet has set. When omelet is done, sprinkle the remaining cheese on top of it.
FOR 1 OMELET

CHICKEN:

¼ cup cream *   Salt

2 scallions, including tender greens, finely chopped   Freshly ground pepper

¼ cup finely chopped cooked chicken   2 teaspoons chopped fresh herbs, such as parsley, chives, and/or tarragon

* If you have available 3–4 tablespoons cream sauce, use that instead. Sour cream is also good; use it at room temperature and don't let it boil hard.

Boil the cream in a saucepan until it is reduced to about 3 tablespoons, adding the scallions as it begins to thicken. Stir in the chicken, season with salt and pepper to taste, add the herbs, and heat through.

The possibilities for omelet fillings are limitless.

Frittata of Fiddleheads, Mushrooms, Red Pepper, and Chipped Beef

A frittata is an Italian version of an omelet, and good Italian cooks all over New England have been making them for generations. It is a useful dish to know about because you can enhance it, as in an omelet, with all kinds of tasty additions—a little cooked food that may be lingering in your refrigerator or something fresh from the garden or, as in this case, something you may have picked from the woods in spring. A frittata is easier than an omelet to make—the only secret being very slow cooking so the eggs don't toughen—and you can make a single one to serve 4 or many more people, depending on the size skillet you use. Frittatas are also good eaten at room temperature, so you can make them ahead and serve small slices as an easy appetizer, or take frittatas on a picnic. Vary the filling as you wish, using ham or sausage for the meat, for instance, vegetables such as blanched zucchini, beans, potatoes, and/or tomatoes; many Italian cooks like to put a sprinkling of Parmesan cheese (aged cheddar is good, too) on top.

¼ pound mushrooms, quartered
4 scallions, including tender greens,
chopped
1 medium sweet red pepper,
seeded, ribs removed, cut in
strips
3 tablespoons butter
½ cup lightly packed chipped beef,
cut in strips
8 eggs

Salt
Freshly ground pepper
2 tablespoons chopped fresh herbs,
such as parsley, chives, basil, or
tarragon
1 dozen or more fiddleheads,
cleaned and cooked (page 44)
2–3 tablespoons grated Parmesan
or cheddar (optional)

In a 10-inch skillet, sauté the mushrooms, scallions, and pepper strips slowly in 2 tablespoons of the butter for about 3 minutes. Add the chipped beef and stir-fry for 30 seconds. Set aside. Beat the eggs lightly, and season with salt and pepper. Add the remaining butter to the skillet, and when melted, turn the heat down and pour in the eggs and herbs. Distribute the fiddleheads on top and cook over *very* low heat, covered, for 15 minutes, or until barely set on top. Sprinkle the optional cheese on top and slip the pan under a hot broiler for a few seconds to finish setting and lightly brown the top. Serve hot or tepid cut in wedges.

SERVES 4

In *The Old Cook's Almanac*, Beatrice Vaughan of Thetford, Vermont, recalled that June's early asparagus spears "must be cut daily to keep roots producing well and—in our neighborhood—to get ahead of the deer, which steal out of the woods at dawn and at dusk to nibble the tender stalks." New Englanders prefer asparagus cut up in this way rather than in long awkward stalks. Like many country cooks with laying hens, she understood the affinity of asparagus for fresh eggs.

Baked Asparagus Omelet

2 tablespoons butter
2 cups cooked (preferably hot)
asparagus, cut in 1-inch lengths
6 to 7 eggs, slightly beaten

Salt
Freshly ground pepper
1 tablespoon chopped fresh dill

Preheat oven to 375 degrees. Butter liberally a 9-inch pie pan, arrange asparagus pieces in it, and pour in the eggs to cover the asparagus. Sprinkle with a little salt, some freshly ground pepper, and the dill and dot with the remaining butter. Bake about 20 minutes, until eggs are set but not hardened.

SERVES 4

Bryn Teg Eggs in Green Nests

Traditionally, regional cooks have dressed up Sunday breakfasts or suppers with eggs baked in a bed of creamy corn or in mashed potato cups. Cooked spinach enlivens the color scheme, as well as the flavors.

3 cups cooked chopped spinach
4 anchovies, finely chopped
Freshly ground pepper
4 eggs
2 tablespoons butter
2 tablespoons flour

1 shallot, minced
1/3 cup dry white wine
3/4 cup milk
2 tablespoons grated cheddar
   cheese

Mix the spinach with the anchovies and add a little freshly ground pepper. Divide the mixture among 4 greased ramekins. Break one egg carefully into each ramekin. Make a cream sauce by melting the butter in a small saucepan, stirring in the flour and shallots, and cooking slowly for 1 minute, stirring. Off heat add the wine and milk, and return to heat, stirring it until it thickens. Spoon equal portions of sauce over each of the eggs. Sprinkle each evenly with cheese. Bake at 350 degrees for about 15 minutes, until eggs are set.
SERVES 4

Squiggled Eggs

Old New England cooks gave wonderful names to egg recipes that were the basis of light lunches or suppers—"Eggernoggin" is a mixture of tomato sauce thickened with cornstarch and beaten eggs; "Frizzled Eggs" is simply eggs scrambled with chipped beef. Below is an equally straightforward combination calling for Yankee cheddar.

12 fresh eggs
Salt
Freshly ground pepper
Cayenne
Nutmeg

Sage leaves
4 tablespoons butter
2/3 cup grated sharp cheddar cheese
4 tablespoons heavy cream, scalded
6 sliced freshly made toast

Beat the eggs in a large bowl, sprinkling in a little salt, some freshly ground pepper, a dash of cayenne and nutmeg, and some crumbled sage leaves. Heat 4 tablespoons of the butter in a large saucepan. When the butter begins to foam, stir in the eggs all at once and the cheese. As the mixture cooks over gentle heat, continue stirring and pour in the heavy cream. Be careful to keep the mixture from solidifying, and when it is cooked and glisteningly moist, spoon it over the fresh toast slices on hot plates.
SERVES 6

It's easier in Portuguese neighborhoods to get traditional sausage than it is to have *presunto* ham on hand. But there is an ancestral flavor in this combination of eggs and meat, seasoned with coriander, that might provide a special Sunday brunch dish for all Yankees.

Baked Eggs with Ham, Chicken, and Tomatoes

4 tablespoons vegetable oil
½ pound country ham cut in
*   narrow strips*
½ pound dark meat of chicken cut
*   in narrow strips*
½ cup chopped onion
2 tablespoons flour
½ cup chicken stock

4 tomatoes, peeled, seeded, and
*   chopped*
2 tablespoons chopped fresh
*   coriander*
4 eggs
Salt
Freshly ground pepper

Heat the oil in a skillet, toss in the meat strips and the onion, and stir-fry for 4 or 5 minutes over medium heat. Stir in the flour and cook, until well mixed. Stir in the stock a little at a time to make a medium-thick sauce. Stir in the chopped tomatoes and the coriander. When the sauce is very hot, divide half of it among 4 shallow baking dishes, and carefully break 1 egg into each dish. Sprinkle with salt and pepper. Cover the eggs with the remaining sauce. Cover each dish with buttered wax paper, and bake 8–10 minutes at 375 degrees.

SERVES 4

Bacon and Eggs

It's a full-time job to turn out good bacon and eggs. They should be cooked in hot but not sizzling fat—and watched. Cook the bacon until crisply tender, not until it breaks into fragments when a slice has been drained on paper. As the bacon approaches doneness, tip the frying pan away from you, over moderate heat, so that there is a pool of fat at an angle. Have your eggs broken into wet saucers and slide them into the fat, side by side. Baste them by ladling the fat over the eggs with a spoon; the idea is to cook the eggs top and bottom at the same time, thereby eliminating any chance of an overly frizzled white and a leaking gelatinous top. Acceptable fried eggs are pink and white, with a thin cloudy film soothing the yolk.

—Elizabeth McLeod Jones

Shirred Eggs with Chicken Livers

4 tablespoons butter
4 eggs
2 chicken livers, cut in quarters
Salt

Freshly ground pepper
4 teaspoons dry sherry
Chopped parsley

Melt 1½ teaspoons of the butter in each of 2 shallow 6-inch-round oven-proof dishes over very low heat (use a Flame-Tamer if cooking over gas). When the butter melts, break 2 eggs into each dish. Quickly heat the remaining butter in a small skillet and, ½ teaspoon at a time, quickly baste the eggs 3 times with the sizzling butter, then continue to baste them with the butter that accumulates around the edge of each dish. Cook slowly, basting continuously for about 5 minutes until the eggs have set. Remove

Hard-boiled Eggs

Home economists have tried to change the name to "hard-cooked" because technically eggs should not be boiled hard. But who wants to change familiar terms with which we all grew up? So, although we take care to gently simmer the eggs, we still call them hard-boiled. We also take care to prick the egg at the top—a straight pin will do the trick —to release the air so the shell doesn't burst in the simmering water. And we are careful not to overcook (12 minutes is enough), and then to plunge the eggs into cold water, cracking them gently first all over, to make peeling easier.

Everyone has his or her own favorite way of making deviled eggs. Some like a lot of mustard, others favor anchovies as an accent; you can add chopped ham, olives, pickles, peppers, pimientos—whatever hits the fancy. One of the ways we like stuffed eggs best is with Maine sardines, and we give the recipe because it serves as a basic formula for you to play with:

10 hard-boiled eggs, shelled
4 fat sardines (1 can), drained
½ cup mayonnaise
3 scallions, including tender greens, chopped
1–2 tablespoons chopped fresh herbs—parsley, chives, or dill
A few drops fresh lemon juice
Salt
Freshly ground pepper

Slice the hard-boiled eggs lengthwise and scoop out the yolks. Mash them with the sardines and work in the mayonnaise, scallions, and herbs. Season with a little lemon juice and salt and pepper to taste.

from the heat. Now quickly sauté the chicken livers with the shallots in the butter remaining in the skillet, tossing and turning, for about 3 minutes. Remove, arrange a liver around each serving of eggs, and season both with salt and pepper. Pour the sherry into the skillet, boil down for a few seconds, then pour the pan juices over the eggs. Quickly slip the dish under a preheated broiler and leave just long enough to set the tops of the eggs— no more than 1 minute. Sprinkle parsley on top and serve sizzling.
SERVES 2

Ham and Cheese Strata

A layered casserole of country ham and Yankee cheese that is a rural New England heritage.

6 slices Italian white bread
1 cup diced cooked ham
5 ounces sharp cheddar cheese, cubed
½ cup cooked sliced mushrooms

3 large eggs
1½ cups milk
1 teaspoon dry mustard
Salt
Freshly ground pepper

Put a layer of bread in a greased 1½-quart casserole and alternate with layers of ham, cheese, and mushrooms to fill the dish. Cheese should be the top layer. Beat the eggs with the milk and mustard and stir in salt cautiously, depending upon the cheese, and add a few turns of the pepper grinder. Pour the mixture carefully over the contents of the casserole. Bake at 350 degrees for 45–50 minutes, until the liquid has set and is lightly browned.
SERVES 4

Spiedini alla Boston's North End

Country ham and mozzarella from a Vermont cheese maker helped us turn this traditional Italian recipe for a sizzling snack into an American treat with ethnic lineage.

About 6 ounces ham (preferably country ham), cut in 1-inch squares
About 6 ounces mozzarella, cut in 1-inch cubes

2 eggs, lightly beaten
1½ cups fresh bread crumbs
Vegetable oil for frying

Thread alternate pieces of ham and cheese onto four 8-inch skewers. Put the lightly beaten egg in a large soup dish and spread the crumbs on a plate or sheet of wax paper. Dip the skewers in egg, one by one, turning to coat all sides. Then roll the skewers in the bread crumbs. Repeat to give them a double coating. In a large skillet, heat to 375 degrees enough oil to cover the skewers by 1½ inches. Lower the skewers into the hot oil and fry about 2 minutes, turning once, until the crumbs are deep golden and the cheese is molten. Drain on brown paper and serve at once.

SERVES 4

Pepper-Cheese Fried Sandwich

½ cup chopped onion
½ cup chopped green pepper
½ cup chopped sweet red pepper
2–3 tablespoons sliced jalapeño pepper, seeded
2 tablespoons olive or vegetable oil

Soft butter
2 slices rye bread with caraway seeds
¼ pound Green Mountain Jack or mild cheddar cheese, shredded
Salt

Sauté the onion and three kinds of peppers in the oil gently until just soft. Butter both sides of the two slices of bread, liberally on the outside, and place half the cheese on the inside of one slice. Spread the onion/pepper mixture over it, salt lightly, and distribute the remaining cheese on top. Press the other piece of bread on top, liberally buttered side up, then fry over moderate heat in a lightly oiled skillet, placing a plate on top to weight the sandwich. When lightly browned, turn and fry the other side. Serve hot.

SERVES 1

Welsh Rabbit

2 tablespoons melted butter
2 egg yolks
½ cup beer
½ teaspoon dry mustard
1 teaspoon Worcestershire sauce

½ pound sharp cheddar cheese, shredded
Cayenne or Tabasco sauce
4 slices toast

Have all the ingredients at hand and use a double boiler, a chafing dish, or a very heavy cooking pot set over a Flame-Tamer. Melt the butter in the pan, set over barely boiling water or very low heat. Beat the egg yolks, beer, mustard, and Worcestershire sauce together and stir into the butter. As soon as the mixture gets hot, start adding the cheese in handfuls, stirring constantly in one direction with a wooden spoon. When all the cheese has been added and the mixture is creamy and smooth, correct the seasoning, adding as much cayenne or Tabasco as you like, then spoon over warm toast. Serve immediately.

SERVES 4

Yankee Cheeses

====

Gone is the time when the cheddary "store cheese" was all that a New England cook could find to call her own. Among numerous cheddar types churned out in all six states are Vermont's Plymouth, a so-called stirred curd loaf, and Crowley, a version of Colby cheese. There are good Americanized Camemberts and Bries produced in Maine and Vermont, and New England's roadside creameries make a great deal of cottage cheese as well as ricotta and variations on mozzarella and pizza cheese. The farmer cheese made by hand at Butterworks in Westfield, Vermont, has been described by a restaurateur as "a kind of cross between a ricotta and cottage cheese, but with more flavor."

New Hampshire's "North Pack" is considered unique, although it has antecedents in Quebec's Oka and the other monastery cheeses of Europe.

Production of goat cheese throughout the region began mushrooming in the 1980s, with very good versions of log-shaped Montrachet coming from Letitia Kilmoyer of Westfield Farm, Hubbardston, Massachusetts, and Monterey Chèvre in logs (with and without herb seasonings) produced by Wayne Dunlop and Susan Sellew at Rawson Brook Farm in the Berkshires.

Cheese Charlotte

3 tablespoons butter
6 medium-thick slices homemade-type white bread
1 pound sharp cheddar cheese, grated
6–8 scallions including tender greens, finely minced
1 tablespoon olive or other vegetable oil

1 teaspoon salt
Freshly ground pepper
½ teaspoon dry mustard
2 cups milk
2–3 drops Tabasco sauce
4 eggs, lightly beaten
1–2 Ortega green chilis, or 3–4 Salonica green peppers in brine, cut in slivers

Butter each slice bread on one side and cut into smallish cubes. Butter a shallow 2-quart casserole, and arrange a layer of bread cubes on the bottom. Place about one-half of the cheese on top, then cover with a final layer of bread, and sprinkle the remaining cheese on top. Sauté the scallions in the olive oil until limp. Mix the salt, pepper, and dry mustard with the milk and Tabasco, stir in the eggs, scallions, and peppers, and pour over the bread and cheese. Let stand 15 minutes or so. Place in a pan of hot water that comes halfway up the sides of the casserole and bake for about 1 hour, until browned on top and firm.
SERVES 4–6

North Pack Cheese Tartlets

North Pack cheese is made on a Monadnock farm by Ellen and Lowell Reinheimer, who developed the recipe below.

PASTRY:
1½ cups all-purpose flour
½ teaspoon salt
6 tablespoons chilled butter

1½ tablespoons chilled lard or shortening
2–3 tablespoons ice water

FILLING:
2 egg yolks
2 whole eggs
⅔ cup rich milk or cream
1 cup freshly grated aged North Pack cheese *

A few drops of Tabasco sauce
Salt
Freshly ground pepper

* Cheddar may be substituted.

Mix the flour and salt together and either cut in the butter and lard or spin in short spurts in a food processor about 8 times, until the mixture resembles cornmeal. Mix in the water, using just enough so that the dough holds together; if using the processor, again do it in spurts about 8 times. Now,

with the heel of your hand, smear the dough, about ½ cup at a time, just once on your working surface, then gather it together into a cohesive flat patty. Wrap it in paper and refrigerate for 30 minutes. Roll the dough out into a piece large enough to cut out 4 circles, each 6 inches in diameter, to fit into 4 individual quiche pans with removable rims. Press the dough securely into the sides, trim, if necessary, leaving ½ inch above the rim to fold over and press in around the edge.

To make the filling, beat the egg yolks and whole eggs together with the milk or cream. Fold in the grated cheese, and add Tabasco and salt and pepper to taste. Divide the filling among the 4 tart shells. Place these on a baking sheet and bake in a preheated 350 degree oven for 20 minutes. Remove the tarts from the forms by placing each one on a glass, slipping the rim down, then easing the tart back onto the baking sheet (you may need to use a spatula to lift it from the bottom of the form). Return the tarts to the oven and bake 5 minutes more, free of the forms.
SERVES 4

VARIATION: For hors d'oeuvres, these tarts can be made in small molds, boat-shaped, scalloped, or even in small brioche tins filled only three-quarters full. Bake for 12–15 minutes. Other kinds of cheese may also be used.

Three-Cheese Soufflé

4 tablespoons (½ stick) butter
¼ cup all-purpose flour
1¼ cups milk
¼ teaspoon salt
Freshly ground pepper
Freshly grated nutmeg

8 egg yolks
¾ cup grated aged cheddar
¾ cup grated Swiss cheese
¼ cup freshly grated Parmesan cheese
9 egg whites

Preheat oven to 400 degrees. In a heavy saucepan, melt the butter. Blend in the flour and cook over low heat a few minutes. Off heat, stir in the milk, then whisk again over low heat until mixture is very thick and smooth. Add salt, pepper, and nutmeg to taste, then one by one, beat the egg yolks into the sauce, and, with the pan again off heat, stir in the first two cheeses and half of the Parmesan.

Butter a straight-sided 2-quart soufflé dish and sprinkle the remaining Parmesan over the bottom and sides. Beat the egg whites until they form soft peaks. Stir one-quarter of the yolk and cheese sauce into the egg whites, then carefully fold the remaining sauce into the whites. Pour the batter into the prepared dish and place on the middle rack of the oven, turning down to 375 degrees as soon as the soufflé is in. Bake 25 minutes for a slightly runny interior, 30–35 for a firmer soufflé.
SERVES 4–5

Cheese Cushion

BREAD DOUGH:

2 packages (2 tablespoons) active
  dry yeast
1 cup warm water
2 teaspoons granulated sugar

¼ cup nonfat dry milk
2 teaspoons salt
About 3⅓ cups unbleached flour
8 tablespoons butter, softened

CHEESE FILLING:

2 pounds mild cheddar or Green
  Mountain Jack cheese, shredded
2 tablespoons butter, softened

2 eggs, beaten
¼ cup chopped fresh coriander, or
  Italian parsley

In a large bowl, dissolve the yeast in the warm water. Stir in the sugar, nonfat dry milk, salt, and as much of the white flour as can be absorbed to make a firm but pliable dough. Now beat in the butter, 1 tablespoonful at a time, until it is all absorbed. Turn the dough out on a floured working surface, and knead, adding more flour as necessary, for at least 10 minutes, until the dough is smooth and elastic. Clean and grease the bowl lightly. Return the dough to it and cover with plastic wrap. Let rise until it has doubled in volume—about 1–1½ hours. While the dough is rising, prepare the filling. Beat together the cheese, butter, all but 2 tablespoons of the beaten egg (reserve the rest for glazing), and the coriander or parsley until smooth, or spin in a food processor.

Butter a 9-inch cake pan or round earthenware casserole 1½–2 inches deep. When the dough has doubled, turn it out on a lightly floured surface, punch it all over, then roll it out into a circle about 20 inches in diameter. Roll the dough over the rolling pin and unroll it over the cake pan. Press it firmly into the sides of the pan. Mound the cheese filling in the middle. Pull the sides of the dough up, pleating them as you do so (you should have

Rhode Island's May Breakfasts

On May 4, 1776, Rhode Island became the first colony to declare independence from Britain, and ever since there have been spring celebrations, the most consistent of which are the May breakfasts staged around the state like church suppers for early risers. Breakfast menus may be as traditional as those that include clam fritters ("a Yankee version of hush puppies," someone said), ham and scrambled eggs, and apple pie; or anything from baked beans to pancakes, doughnuts, berry muffins, sausage, French toast, hash-brown potatoes, jonnycakes baked on a griddle, coffee—and pie. At Belcourt Castle in Newport, for $12 per breakfaster (in the 1980s), the menu offered champagne, blintzes, and crêpes but no meat because Defenders of Animals are the organizers.

about 10 loose pleats in all), then gather the top together and twist the dough firmly to make a topknot. Let rest for 10 minutes while you preheat the oven to 375 degrees.

Paint the top of the "cushion" with the remaining beaten egg, and bake in the center of the oven for 1 hour. If the top seems to be getting a bit too brown, cover loosely with foil. Transfer to a rack and let settle for about 10 minutes before serving.

VARIATION: To make small cushions, divide the risen dough in half, covering one half while you work with the other. Roll the first half out on a lightly floured surface to an 18-inch square. Using a 4- or 4½-inch cookie cutter, cut out 8 circles. Place a generous tablespoonful of the cheese filling in the center of each circle, then draw up the two opposite sides and pinch them together firmly in the middle. Do the same with the other two sides. Pinch together all the seams and be sure they are secure, otherwise the filling will ooze out. Drizzle a little of the remaining beaten egg along the seams, then pinch again with well-floured fingers. Place 2 inches apart on a greased baking sheet. Repeat with the other half of the dough to make 16 cushions. Let cushions rest, uncovered, for 20 minutes, until beginning to swell slightly. If any seams have opened up, pinch them back together. Just before baking, paint the tops of the cushions again with the beaten egg and sprinkle a little grated Parmesan over them. Bake for 20 minutes in a preheated oven at 375 degrees.

MAKES 1 CUSHION 9 INCHES IN DIAMETER, OR 16 SMALL CUSHIONS.

Cheese and Egg Patties

2 eggs
¾ skim milk
½ cup crushed common or soda
   crackers
¼ cup grated sharp cheddar cheese
1 garlic clove, chopped very fine
1 tablespoon olive oil
¼ cup grated onion, or scallions,
   chopped fine

3 tablespoons grated green pepper
½ cup chopped ham or salami
Salt
Freshly ground pepper
A dash of cayenne
1 tablespoon or more olive or
   vegetable oil for frying

Beat the eggs thoroughly. Add the milk and the remaining ingredients, except the frying oil, seasoning lightly with salt (depending on the saltiness of the ham) and with the two kinds of pepper according to your taste. Heat the oil in a large skillet over medium heat. Drop heaping spoonfuls of the batter, which should be the consistency of thin pancake batter, and let it spread to about 3 inches in diameter. When the edges begin to brown, turn the patties and brown the other side. Drain on paper toweling and repeat with the rest of the batter.

MAKES ABOUT 12

Breakfast Custards

Make these individually according to the number of people you have for breakfast.

1 egg
½ cup milk or half-and-half
Salt
3 tablespoons grated cheese,
  preferably smoked

A dash of cayenne or a grating of
  nutmeg

Beat the egg lightly with the milk. Season with a little salt and stir in the cheese. Pour into a buttered 6- or 8-ounce custard cup and either top with a dash of cayenne or a grating of nutmeg. Place in a dish with enough boiling water to come about one-third to halfway up the cup, and place in a preheated 350-degree oven for 20 minutes. Serve in the cup.
SERVES 1

VARIATION: Add 2 tablespoons ground ham along with the cheese.

Tofu Breakfast Scramble

The first time we ate "scrambled eggs" in which tofu, substituting for the real thing, passed the blindfold test was at a coveside Bridgeport, Connecticut, restaurant called Bloodroot. Vegetarians from all over the Northeast have discovered ideas for meatless dishes here. This is one of our adaptations.

1½ pounds tofu
3 tablespoons brewers yeast
3 tablespoons white miso
Soy sauce
Water
¼ teaspoon turmeric

2 tablespoons vegetable oil
2 sweet red peppers, sliced thin
1 small onion, sliced thin
2 tablespoons port wine
Salt
2–3 tablespoons chopped parsley

In a saucepan, break up the tofu with a fork to resemble scrambled eggs. Mix together the yeast and white miso with a few drops of soy sauce, 3 tablespoons of water, and turmeric, then gently fold this mixture into the tofu curds. Cover the saucepan and cook over very low heat, adding a drop or two of water to prevent burning and keep the mixture creamy. Heat the oil in a frying pan and cook the vegetables, stirring often, until they are lightly brown. Sprinkle lightly with salt and add the port, scraping the pan as the wine mixes with the vegetables. Fold the vegetables into the warm tofu and sprinkle with parsley.
SERVES 4

The Good Egg

In the mistaken notion that one color is better than another when it comes to eggs, Boston markets used to insist on brown eggs, letting the white ones go on to New York. Among Yankee chickens, Rhode Island Reds for generations have been favored as prolific layers of brown eggs, and also as good mothers. But the truth as we've found it is that you can't get better eggs (color no matter) than those you buy when you see a rustic FRESH EGGS sign on a country road. These tend to be dark of yolk and rich in flavor and therefore better either cooked by themselves or used in batters, or as one of a combination of ingredients in various dishes.

But supermarket eggs are reliable, usually surprisingly fresh, and less expensive. Commercial eggs are graded in a range of sizes from jumbo to pullet, based on weight per dozen and according to U.S. Department of Agriculture standards and grades: AA and A to B and C. For all the recipes in this book we have used standard large eggs. They weigh 3 ounces (2 ounces for the white, 1 for the yolk). If you have smaller (or larger) eggs, crack them into a measuring cup and compensate accordingly. In most recipes, a few grams off won't make much difference, but it could if you're making an angel food cake or a soufflé.

To be sure any egg is fresh, see if it floats in water; if it does, or tips noticeably upward, an air sack has formed as the interior has shrunk away from the shell, an aging process that takes about three weeks at room temperature. In a really fresh egg, the yolk and the white will cling together tightly when you crack open the shell. The older it gets, the more the yolk flattens and the runnier the white becomes. Always refrigerate eggs as soon as you bring them home. They lose freshness quickly if left at room temperature.

Souffléed Sausage-Cheese Dish

Nancy Rogers serves meals family style, and she and her husband, Jim, provide farm vacations for guests who come to stay with them near West Glover, Vermont. Nancy's cooking has been described as being "at least as appealing as barnyard chores are for city folks," and one of the dishes most appreciated is this breakfast soufflé.

Soft butter	Salt
12 slices bread, crusts removed	Freshly ground pepper
4 eggs	1 pound sausage
3 cups milk	1 cup grated cheddar cheese

Butter the bread and cut it into cubes. Mix together the eggs and milk and add salt and pepper to taste. Brown the sausage, breaking it up, and when it has given off all its fat, drain. Place 6 of the bread slices in the bottom of a greased 9 × 13-inch pan. Spread half of the cheese and half of the sausage over the bread. Pour all of the milk and egg mixture on top and mash it down with a potato masher or spatula. Put the rest of the bread pieces, cheese, and sausage on top. Cover and refrigerate the dish overnight. In the morning bake in a preheated 350-degree oven for 1 hour.
SERVES 6–8

Kennebec Scrapple

When produced from scraps of pork, the American sausagelike mixture is usually associated with the Pennsylvania Dutch. But German colonists also moved to Maine a generation before the Revolutionary War, and their influence on Down East cooking is considerable.

1 cup white cornmeal	2 cups cooked or canned salmon
1 quart boiling water	Flour
1 teaspoon salt	Butter, or bacon or ham fat for
1 teaspoon chopped fresh thyme, or ¼ teaspoon dried	frying
1 teaspoon chopped fresh sage, or ¼ teaspoon dried	

Stir the cornmeal slowly into the boiling water, add the salt, thyme, and sage; mix well. Cook over hot water, covered, for about 1½ hours, stirring frequently. Pick out any bones or skin for the salmon, flake it with a fork, and stir it evenly into the hot cornmeal mush. Pour the mixture into a loaf pan and chill about 2 hours, until firm. Slice the scrapple in thin rectangles, flour the slices, and fry them in butter, or bacon or ham fat, until brown and crisp. Serve with eggs.
SERVES 4–6

Here are the secrets to making good French toast: (1) Try to use thickish slices of a good homemade white bread, a little stale; (2) use less milk than the usual recipe calls for, and (3) cook over a slow fire to build up a crust.

French Toast

1 egg
¼ cup milk
½ teaspoon sugar
Pinch salt

Several gratings fresh nutmeg
2 slices good white bread
1 tablespoon butter

Mix the egg, milk, sugar, salt, and nutmeg together. Soak the bread slices about 5 minutes, turning once and making sure that all sides are exposed to the batter. Melt the butter slowly in a skillet large enough to accommodate the bread slices, then lift them, one at a time, from the batter, shaking off any excess, and slip them into the warm butter. Fry over low heat until golden brown on one side, about 5 minutes, then turn and brown the other side, 5 minutes more. Serve with warm maple syrup.
SERVES 1

VARIATION WITH BERRIES: Before turning the slices, press about a dozen berries (blueberries, raspberries, blackberries) into the uncooked side, then flip the bread over and fry the berry-studded side about 1 minute.

8 slices cinnamon raisin or other
   bread
4 eggs
1 cup evaporated milk
2 tablespoons rum

2 teaspoons sugar
½ teaspoon cinnamon
Freshly grated nutmeg
Salt
Cooking oil

FOR THE SYRUP:
½ cup grade B maple syrup

6 tablespoons rum

Yankee French Toast for Brunch

Put the bread slices in a shallow baking pan large enough (9 × 13 inches) to hold them flat. Beat the eggs in a bowl, adding the evaporated milk, the rum, sugar, cinnamon, a few gratings of nutmeg, and a light sprinkling of salt. When the mixture is well-blended, pour it over the bread slices and let stand about 1 hour in the refrigerator. Cover the bottom of a large skillet with ¼ inch of oil and heat until haze rises. Sauté the soaked slices in the oil until they are golden on the bottom, then turn and sauté the other side. To make the syrup mixture, heat the maple syrup and the rum in a saucepan, stirring occasionally. When it is bubbly, pour it into a hot pitcher, and arrange the sautéed toast on hot plates; serve immediately.
SERVES 4

French Toast, Anyone?

With new BED AND BREAKFAST signs proliferating in every corner of New England, the interest in morning menus had good cooks scrambling for ideas in the 1980s. Sweet breads and muffins are more varied than ever before, cereals and pancakes are served up in new combinations, and there's more accent on meat and fish.

The evolution of French toast takes its own ecumenical course. For colonists this soothing breakfast dish was first known as "poor Knights of Windsor," and later as *pain perdu,* meaning "lost bread," or specifically stale bread restored to life. In Fannie Farmer's era day-old bread slices were cooked in a sweet batter, and for some reason called "German toast;" when maple syrup was substituted for the sugar in the batter, the name was changed to "Yankee toast." The ideal enhancement for New Englanders may be a pitcher of warm maple syrup for each breakfaster to pour himself.

The imaginative cook at Ashley's Bed and Breakfast in Lexington, Massachusetts, adapted the recipe for *croque monsieur* to make a French-toast morning sandwich filled with cream cheese; another in Essex, Connecticut, designed her "Crescent French Toast" by wrappping a croissant around a grilled sausage, then dipping it in batter before frying.

All kinds of breads have been transformed into versions of French toast: for instance, day-old brioche slices dipped in a rum-laced mixture of equal parts of egg yolk and heavy cream, sautéed in butter, and accompanied by Grade A maple syrup.

Here's a breakfast celebration worth the hoarding of that gift of maple sugar you may have received; if butternuts are hard to come by, you may substitute walnuts (another member of the *Juglans* family).

Maple Butternut Toast

4 slices homemade whole wheat
  bread
¼ cup melted butter

3 tablespoons soft maple sugar
4 teaspoons finely chopped
  butternuts

Toast one side of the bread slices under the broiler, then pour the butter evenly over each untoasted side and sprinkle with sugar to cover. Return the slices to the broiler just long enough to melt the sugar, and just before serving, while the sugar is still bubbling, sprinkle finely chopped nuts over the top.

SERVES 4

Here's one of the principal items that Jim Ledue devised when he made up his breakfast menu for The Good Egg, a small restaurant in Portland, Maine, with loyalties so steadfast that people wait in line morning after morning for their first meal of the day. The look of beetless hash reminds some Yankees of calico corn.

Note: Jim's secret for a good hash is to use the flesh of freshly baked potatoes.

Calico Corned Beef Hash

2 cups finely chopped cooked,
  peeled potatoes (see note above)
3–4 tablespoons vegetable oil
½ cup chopped onion
1½ cups ground cooked corned
  beef
½ cup finely chopped cooked carrot
2 teaspoons dried rosemary,
  crumbled

2 tablespoons finely chopped
  parsley
Salt
Freshly ground pepper
1 cup broth in which the corned
  beef was cooked

Heat enough oil to cover the bottom of a large skillet, add the chopped onion, and cook over low heat, stirring, until straw-colored. Mix the corned beef with the potatoes and carrot, scrape the cooked onion into the mixture, stir in the herbs, a light sprinkling of salt and pepper, and the corned beef cooking broth. Turn the hash mixture into the skillet, but don't mash it down. Cook over the lowest possible heat about 40 minutes. With a spatula, loosen the hash around the edges. Make a deep crease across the hash

Calico Corned Beef Hash (continued)

at right angles to the handle. Tip the skillet and fold this half of the hash over its lower half. Loosen the bottom with the spatula to be sure it comes free of the pan. Hold a hot platter over the pan, invert the skillet and platter together. Let the hash drop out like an omelet—it should be well browned and crusty on top.

SERVES 4

Lydia Shire's Chicken and Corned Beef Breakfast Hash

As the chef as Seasons restaurant in Boston, Lydia Shire created this hearty breakfast fare for chilly weekend mornings and gave us the recipe.

One 2½-pound whole chicken
1 head garlic, separated into cloves
1 bunch fresh thyme, or 1½ teaspoons dried
1 bunch fresh tarragon, or 1½ teaspoons dried
1½ teaspoons salt
¾ teaspoon freshly ground pepper

1 pound red-skinned potatoes
1 cup clarified butter
1 large onion, sliced
2 medium sweet red peppers, cut lengthwise into ½-inch strips
¾ pound corned beef, thinly sliced
½ cup chopped parsley
6 poached eggs

Stuff the chicken with the garlic, thyme, and tarragon. Sprinkle it inside and out with ½ teaspoon of the salt and ¼ teaspoon black pepper. Place the chicken, untrussed, on a rack in a roasting pan and roast in a preheated 400-degree oven until the meat is just a bit underdone, about 40 minutes. Let cool. Using your fingers, remove the chicken meat from the bones in large (1–2 inch) pieces.

Meanwhile, boil the potatoes until tender but still firm, about 15 minutes. Let cool, then cut into ¼-inch slices.

In a large heavy skillet, heat half of the clarified butter over high heat for about 1 minute. Arrange half of the potato and onion slices in an even layer over the bottom of the pan and place half of the peppers on top. Cook until the potatoes begin to brown, about 20 minutes. Turn and continue to cook until the potatoes are browned and the peppers are soft, about 15 minutes. Sprinkle with ½ teaspoon of the salt and ¼ teaspoon pepper. Transfer the vegetables to a piece of aluminum foil, cover loosely, and keep warm in the oven. Repeat with the remaining potatoes, onions, and peppers, seasoning as before.

Combine the 2 batches of potatoes, onions, and peppers in the skillet, and toss with the chicken and corned beef. Cook over moderate heat until the meat is warmed through and the chicken is fully cooked, about 5 minutes. Add the parsley and toss. Divide the hash among 6 warmed plates and top each serving with a poached egg.

SERVES 6

Leftover fish chopped with vegetables and cooked gently to form a crust can become a good breakfast or lunch dish. When it is made with freshened smoked herring, no salt is required.

Smoked Herring Hash

2 cups coarsely chopped smoked
  herring
2 tablespoons vegetable oil
1/4 cup chopped onion

2 1/2 cups chopped cooked potatoes
1/2 cup chopped cooked beets
1/2 cup unsweetened condensed milk
1 tablespoon chopped parsley

Freshen the herring by pouring boiling water over it and draining it two successive times. Heat 1 tablespoon oil and cook the chopped onion a minute to wilt. Mix together the fish, potatoes, and beets, then add the wilted onion and the condensed milk and toss the mixture well. Add the remaining 1 tablespoon oil to the skillet and spoon the hash mixture in, pressing it down with a spatula. Cook over very low heat for about 30 minutes, until a crust forms. Sprinkle chopped parsley over the top. A poached egg may be placed in the center of each serving, if you like.
SERVES 4

One of the treats at the Inn at Sawmill Farm in West Dover, Vermont, is the breakfast pancakes. They are large and crisp and delicious—quite unlike anyone else's pancakes. One morning we begged Brill Williams to let us watch him make them and learn his secret. Here's how he does it. The yield is large but the amounts can easily be reduced if you don't have a crowd. Or you can refrigerate the batter and make more the next day and the next.

Brill Williams's Pancakes

4 cups flour
4 eggs
4 teaspoons baking powder
1 cup sugar
4 1/2 cups milk

2 tablespoons vegetable oil
1/2 teaspoon salt
Butter
Maple syrup

Mix all the above ingredients (except the butter and maple syrup) together thoroughly. Be sure to have your griddle very hot and grease it only lightly. Once you've greased it, work quickly or the grease will burn. Wipe off any excess. Pour on enough batter so that each pancake spreads to a circle about 4–4 1/2 inches in diameter. Cook about 45 seconds on one side, turn and cook the other side just about 45 seconds. Serve with butter and warm maple syrup.
MAKES ABOUT 40

Our Basic Pancakes

We've found after years of pancake making that the secret to making light pancakes is to separate the eggs, folding in the beaten whites at the last. If you won't want to go to this extra effort, you can use the same recipe simply beating 2 whole eggs in with the milk, but the pancakes won't be as delicate. For more flavor, try using part whole wheat or buckwheat flour.

1⅓ cups all-purpose flour, or 1 cup
  flour plus ⅓ cup stoneground
  whole wheat flour or ⅓ cup
  buckwheat flour
2 teaspoons baking powder
3 tablespoons sugar

¾ teaspoon salt
2 eggs, separated
1¼ cups milk
3 tablespoons melted butter
Maple syrup, or blueberry or apple
  syrup

Toss the flour, baking powder, sugar, and salt together. Beat the egg yolks with the milk until just blended. Mix with the dry ingredients and add the melted butter. In a separate bowl beat the egg whites until they form firm peaks, then fold them into the batter. Drop about 2 tablespoonfuls of batter onto a hot, lightly greased griddle or an ungreased soapstone, and bake until bubbles appear on the surface. Turn and bake the other side about 30 seconds. Serve with warm maple, blueberry, apple, or beach plum syrup.
MAKES ABOUT 18 PANCAKES

VARIATION FOR BERRY PANCAKES: Add about 2 tablespoons blueberries, raspberries, currants, or blackberries to the pancakes after the first side has baked and bubbles appear, pressing the berries into the batter, then turn them, and bake on the other side about 30 seconds.

Buttermilk Wheat Germ Pancakes

2 cups buttermilk*
¼ cup butter, melted
2 eggs
2 cups flour
½ cup wheat germ

¼ cup sugar
1 teaspoon salt
1 teaspoon baking soda
Warm butter
Maple syrup

  * If buttermilk is very thick, you may need a little more.

Whisk the buttermilk, melted butter, and eggs to blend well. Mix together the dry ingredients, then add to buttermilk mixture, stirring until fairly smooth. Drop one large mixing spoonful at a time onto a hot greased griddle and cook until browned on one side, then turn and cook until browned on the other. Keep the pancakes warm while making the remainder on the hot griddle, regreasing lightly as necessary. Serve with butter and warmed maple syrup.
SERVES 6, ABOUT THIRTY 3-INCH PANCAKES

1 cup flour
½ teaspoon baking soda
¼ teaspoon salt
1 egg
1 cup buttermilk
2 tablespoons maple syrup

About 1 cup blueberries, roughly
  chopped
2 tablespoons melted butter
Confectioners' sugar
A pitcher of melted butter
A pitcher of maple syrup

Poker Chip Blueberry Pancakes

Mix the flour, baking soda, and salt together thoroughly. Beat the egg, buttermilk, maple syrup, and melted butter together, then stir in the dry ingredients. Drop the batter by the level tablespoon onto a hot soapstone (preferably) or lightly greased iron skillet, allowing room for the batter to spread between each small cake. When bubbles appear all over the surface, press about a teaspoon of chopped berries on top of each pancake, then turn and bake another minute on the other side. Serve at least 6 to a plate sprinkled with confectioners' sugar, with a pitcher of melted butter and one of maple syrup on the side.

MAKES ABOUT 48 SMALL PANCAKES

1½ cup rolled oats
2 cups or more milk
3 eggs, lightly beaten
3 tablespoons melted butter
⅔ cup unbleached flour

⅓ cup whole wheat flour
2 teaspoons baking powder
Pinch salt
About 1 cup cranberries
Maple syrup

Oatmeal Pancakes with Cranberries

Soak the oats in the milk 10 minutes. Stir in the eggs and melted butter. Mix the flour, baking powder, and salt together, then add them to the oats mixture. Add a little more milk if you don't like too thick a batter. Drop large spoonfuls onto a hot griddle, preferably soapstone, and bake until bubbles form on the top, then press several cranberries into the uncooked side, turn the cakes and bake another minute. Serve with warm maple syrup.

MAKES ABOUT 24 PANCAKES

Susan Cunningham's Pumpkin Pancakes

One of the imaginative breakfast menus served by Susan Cunningham at her Inn on Goodwin Park in Portsmouth, New Hampshire, includes the soothing pancakes whose ingredients depend on some leftover cooked pumpkin, squash, sweet potatoes, or parsnips.

1 cup whole wheat flour
⅔ cup white flour
2 teaspoons baking powder
¼ teaspoon salt
⅔ cup puréed cooked squash,
  pumpkin, sweet potatoes, or
  parsnips*

2 eggs, separated
1 cup milk
2 teaspoons melted butter
Maple syrup

* The vegetable can be leftover pumpkin or squash that has been baked with maple syrup, honey, or, some other sweetener and butter, or sweetened sweet potatoes or perhaps the parsnips in madeira on page 298. Remove any skin and purée the vegetable in a food processor or put through a vegetable mill.

Toss or sift the flours, baking powder, and salt together. Beat the vegetable purée with the egg yolks, milk, and butter, and mix with the dry ingredients. Beat the egg whites until they hold firm peaks and fold them into the batter. Ladle about ¼ cup of batter at a time onto a preheated, lightly greased griddle. Bake until bubbles appear on the surface, then turn and bake the other side until lightly browned. Serve with warm maple syrup.

SERVES 4–6

2 cups all-purpose flour
1 teaspoon baking soda
1/2 teaspoon salt
2 eggs
3/4 cup cottage cheese

3/4 cup plain yogurt
1 cup milk
1/4 cup molasses
Maple or apple syrup

Molasses Cottage Cheese Pancakes

Toss the flour, baking soda, and salt together. Separate the eggs, and mix the yolks with the cottage cheese, yogurt, milk, and molasses. Combine this with the dry ingredients. Beat the egg whites until they form soft peaks, then fold them into the batter. Drop the batter by heaping spoonfuls onto a hot greased griddle or a soapstone, and bake until bubbles form on the top. Turn and bake the other side until lightly browned. Keep them warm as you continue to bake the rest. Serve with warm maple or apple syrup.

MAKES 24 PANCAKES

1 1/2 pint jar beach plum jelly
1/4 cup water
2 tablespoons orange juice

1/3 cup sugar
3–4 strips of orange peel

Beach Plum Syrup for Pancakes

Put all of the ingredients in a saucepan and simmer for 30 minutes. Skim off the foam. Remove the orange peel and serve in a pitcher to pour over pancakes and waffles (it's also good as a glaze for duck).

MAKES ABOUT 2/3 CUP

4 eggs
1 cup flour
1 cup milk or half-and-half

1/4 teaspoon salt
4 tablespoons melted butter
Confectioners' sugar

Giant Puffy Oven Pancake

Place a 10-inch cast-iron or heavy nonstick pan in a preheated 450-degree oven to get hot, about 10 minutes. Meanwhile, mix the batter. Beat the eggs, then add the flour, milk or half-and-half, salt, and 2 tablespoons of the melted butter and continue beating until smooth. Remove the hot skillet from the oven, swirl the remaining butter around in it, and quickly pour the batter in. Bake on the lower rack for 10 minutes, then lower the heat to 350 degrees and bake another 10 minutes. Serve immediately with a dusting of confectioners' sugar over the top.

SERVES 4

Blinis

1 package (1 tablespoon) active dry
  yeast
2¼ cups warm water
1 cup all-purpose flour

1 cup buckwheat flour
½ teaspoon salt
1 tablespoon melted butter
¼ teaspoon baking soda

GARNISH: *1 cup sour cream and ½ cup flaked smoked fish*

The night before you plan to make these, dissolve the yeast in ¼ cup of the warm water. When dissolved, stir in 1½ cups warm water, the two flours, and salt. Cover with plastic wrap and leave in a warm place overnight.

    Just before baking the blinis, stir in the remaining ½ cup warm water, the melted butter, and the baking soda. Heat a small greased iron skillet until you see haze rising from the pan, then pour in just enough of the batter to cover the bottom of the pan, tilting the pan so that it spreads evenly all around. When bubbles appear on top of the pancake, turn it and bake until lightly browned on the other side. Remove to a warm plate and keep warm while baking the remaining blinis, greasing the skillet lightly before adding more batter. Serve with sour cream and smoked fish.

MAKES ABOUT TEN 8-INCH BLINIS

Joan Ashley's Cream Cheese Sandwiches with Apricot Sauce

This special treat, served some mornings at Ashley's Bed and Breakfast in Lexington, Massachusetts, is bound to start your day off right.

8 ounces cream cheese
½ cup chopped walnuts

1 teaspoon vanilla
6 slices outdated soft bread

BATTER:
4 beaten eggs
¾ cup milk
1 teaspoon vanilla

A pinch of nutmeg
3 tablespoons butter

SAUCE:
1 cup apricot preserves

⅓ cup orange juice

About 1 cup sliced bananas or blueberries or other fruit

Mix the cream cheese, walnuts, and 1 teaspoon vanilla together and spread on the 6 slices of bread. Slap together 2 slices, filling side in, to make sandwiches, 3 in all. Beat the batter ingredients together until well mixed, then dip the sandwiches into the batter, coating both sides. Melt the butter in a large skillet and fit in the sandwiches in one layer. Fry on one side over medium heat, pressing down lightly, until golden, then flip and fry the other side until golden. Meanwhile, warm the apricot preserves with the orange juice and beat to mix. When the sandwiches are done, cut each into 4 triangles and serve 3 per person with a sprinkling of fruit over and around and the apricot sauce drizzled over the top.

SERVES 4

Raised Waffles

1 tablespoon (1 package) active dry
   yeast
¼ cup warm water
2¼ cups warm milk
10 tablespoons butter, melted
1 teaspoon salt
1 teaspoon sugar
2 cups flour
2 eggs
⅛ teaspoon baking soda
Butter
Maple syrup
Berries, in season

The night before, or at least 4 hours before you are planning to serve the waffles, dissolve the yeast in the warm water in a medium-size bowl, then add the milk and melted butter, salt, and sugar. Stir in the flour and beat for a minute. Cover and set aside at room temperature. When you are ready to make the waffles, beat the eggs lightly and then beat them into the batter along with the baking soda. Bake the waffles in a waffle maker according to the manufacturer's instructions. Serve with soft butter and warm maple syrup and perhaps a small handful of whatever wild berries may be in season.

MAKES 6 WAFFLES

Cornmeal Waffles

1 cup cornmeal, preferably stone
   ground
1 cup boiling water
1 cup flour
1 teaspoon baking soda
2 teaspoons baking powder
2 tablespoons melted butter or
   vegetable oil
2 tablespoons brown sugar
1½ cups buttermilk
3 eggs, separated

Put the cornmeal in a bowl, pour the boiling water over it, and let stand 10 minutes. Toss the flour, baking soda, and baking powder together to mix, then add to the cornmeal along with the melted butter and brown sugar. Beat in the buttermilk and the egg yolks. In a separate bowl beat the egg whites until they form firm peaks, then fold them into the batter. Bake in a waffle iron according to manufacturer's directions.

MAKES 6–7 WAFFLES

Maple Biscuits

These were made for breakfast. They can be served at other hours of the day but they won't be appreciated as much.

4 tablespoons melted butter
½ cup maple syrup
1 cup flour
2 teaspoons baking powder

½ teaspoon salt
3 tablespoons cold butter
⅓ cup milk

Pour the melted butter and maple syrup into a 9-inch cake pan, swirling it around to mix well. Toss the flour, baking powder, and salt together, then cut in the cold butter, mixing, with your fingertips until the texture is like soft bread crumbs. Stir in the milk. Turn the dough out and knead it gently about 6 turns—just enough for it to hold together. Either pat the dough or roll it out to ½-inch thickness, then cut it into 9 rounds. Arrange the rounds in the cake pan on top of the maple-butter mixture, and bake in a preheated 375-degree oven 12–15 minutes, or until the biscuits are lightly browned and the syrup is bubbling up around them. Serve hot from the pan and eat them all—they don't keep.
SERVES 3–4

Oatmeal Cakes

Many of the twenty-odd million Americans of Scottish heritage have lived in New England for generations and many of them are responsible for the continuing popularity of such hearty fare as finnan haddie. In Vermont's Northeast Kingdom, where the weather isn't unlike Scotland's, the gloom of a rainy morning is often dispelled by making a batch of oatmeal cakes for breakfast to go with with a cup of hot tea or coffee.

1½ cups flour
1½ cups rolled oats
1 cup sugar
1 teaspoon salt

¼ teaspoon baking soda
2 cups shortening
6 tablespoons cold water

Toss the dry ingredients by hand or with a fork to mix and lighten. Add the shortening and mix with your fingertips or a pastry blender until the mixture resembles coarse bread crumbs. Add the water. On a lightly floured surface, roll out the dough to a rectangle about 8 × 10 inches. Cut into approximate squares, making 5 cuts on each side, and transfer them to a lightly greased baking sheet. Bake in a preheated 350-degree oven for 15 minutes.
MAKES 25 SQUARES

There have been French influences in New England cooking since the first Huguenots arrived in Rhode Island in the seventeenth century, and even today French-Americans mark the Christmas holidays with ethnic treats. *Boudin blanc* (white pudding) makes a festive addition to a *reveillon* spread or a holiday breakfast or lunch.

Christmas White Sausage

3 medium onions, chopped
2 tablespoons butter
½ pound pork fat
½ pound sweetbreads, trimmed of
  membranes
½ pound chicken or turkey breast
2 teaspoons salt
⅛ teaspoon allspice
⅛ teaspoon ground cloves
⅛ teaspoon freshly grated nutmeg

¼ teaspoon freshly ground white
  pepper
½ teaspoon dried savory
2 egg whites, lightly beaten
¾ cup fresh bread crumbs
¼ cup heavy cream
Sausage casings
About 1½ cups chicken broth
  mixed with equal amount of
  water

FOR SAUTÉING:
1 tablespoon butter

1 tablespoon chicken fat or
  vegetable oil

Sauté the onions slowly in the butter until very tender. Grind together the pork fat, sweetbreads, and poultry breast. Mix the onions and the ground meat with all the ingredients down to sausage casings, and beat until thoroughly mixed and light. Stuff the mixture into sausage casings, which you have soaked for 30 minutes (see page 251), and twist every 3 inches to make sausage links. Refrigerate until ready to use but be sure to cook them within 24 hours. To cook, prick the sausages in several places and poach them very gently, covered, for 30 minutes in a mixture of enough chicken broth and water to cover them. Drain and sauté in butter and chicken fat or oil until lightly browned on all sides, about 5 minutes. Serve with red cabbage and/or fried apples and skillet-fried potatoes.
SERVES 6–8

2 smoked kippered herrings (about
  ½ pound each)
Lemon slices

Parsley sprigs
Prepared mustard

Pan-Broiled Kippers

Place the kippers (head and tail removed, if desired) in a non-stick skillet. Cover and cook over low heat for 10 minutes; turn the fish and cook another 10 minutes. Serve on very hot plates with lemon slices, parsley sprigs, and a pot of spicy mustard.
SERVES 2

Finnan Haddie Soup

Served with chilled Sakonet chardonnay from Rhode Island, this smoked haddock bisque has been recommended as a breakfast for lovers by Lu Lockwood, a kitchen artist known to restaurant goers in Essex, Connecticut, and Cape Cod.

2 pounds smoked haddock
4 cups water
2½ cups heavy cream
2 tablespoons safflower oil
2 medium carrots, scraped and
    chopped fine
2 leeks, cleaned and chopped fine
1 medium onion, chopped fine
2 teaspoons chopped fresh dill or
    dried dillweed

Salt
Freshly ground white pepper
1 garlic clove, crushed
2 sprigs parsley
1 teaspoon dried thyme
¼ cup vermouth
Lemon wedges

In a large saucepan, put the fish, water, and 2 cups of the cream, and simmer for about 20 minutes. Drain the fish and keep warm, reserving the cooking liquid. Heat the oil in a skillet over low heat and cook the chopped vegetables until soft, stirring occasionally. Stir in the fish liquid, the dill, a light sprinkling of salt and pepper, and the garlic, parsley, and thyme wrapped in cheesecloth. Simmer for 30 minutes, then stir in the remaining ½ cup cream and the vermouth. Add the fish and purée in a blender or food processor. Reheat and serve with lemon wedges.

SERVES 4

"MADE" DISHES

VARIETY is implicit in the term *"Made" Dishes,* and there is much variety in this chapter. "A dish composed of several ingredients," is the OED's definition; it's an expression that has been around since colonial housewives were using Robert May's *The Accomplished Cook: or, The Art and Mystery of Cookery,* a seventeenth-century compendium that gave assorted recipes ranging from orange-flavored lobster to stuffed sheep's maw.

The "made" dishes in this chapter sometimes make use of leftover ingredients and sometimes are composed of fresh meats or seafood with garden vegetables. Many of them derive from the technique of cooking *en casserole* (in a baking dish), *au gratin* (crusted with bread crumbs or grated cheese), and the preparation of fish or vegetables in sauces to make what we call scalloped dishes. Here there are one-dish meals, a category that includes various combinations that show how simple and good genuine "hamburger helpers" can be when cooked at home from scratch instead of from a package.

Casseroles called "hot" dishes (one-dish meals) are not exclusively Yankee inventions, but such combinations owe much to the early New England institutions of barn-raisings and church suppers. Baked beans and sometimes succotash were among covered dishes traditionally brought to community feeds. Today the spectrum of meals based on casseroles is as variegated as the distribution of all kinds of ingredients in New England markets. From the village church suppers that tempted women to compete with each other in providing portable food there evolved what is often called the "progressive dinner," a meal that moves, to be true to its name in nonpolitical terms, course by course, from one home to another. Each participating hospitable cook can't avoid hoping her contribution will be the hit of the evening, can she? The recipes that follow are not competitive choices, but they make good eating nevertheless.

Stuffed Artichokes

Artichokes enhanced by a flavorful stuffing can make a very satisfying main course. As with other stuffed vegetables, the filling can be made from leftovers just as well as from fresh ground meat.

4 medium artichokes
½ lemon
3 tablespoons olive or other
 vegetable oil
1 medium onion, chopped
1 fat garlic clove, minced
1 cup ground beef or lamb or
 cooked leftover meat

Salt
Freshly ground pepper
1 cup fresh bread crumbs
2 tablespoons chopped fresh sage,
 or 1 teaspoon dried, crumbled
⅓ cup grated Parmesan cheese

Trim away the stems of the artichokes so that they will sit upright. Remove any discolored leaves and snip off with scissors the prickly ends of the leaves. Slice off about ½ inch of the top evenly. Rub all the cut parts with lemon. Set the artichokes upside down on a steamer basket and steam for 30 minutes. Remove, and when cool enough to handle, pull out enough of the center leaves to get at the choke, then with a spoon, dig down into the center and scrape out all the thistly choke.

Heat the oil in a skillet, add the onion, and sauté gently until tender, adding the garlic the last half minute of cooking. Stir in the meat and if uncooked, sauté it, breaking it up with a fork, until it has lost color. Season liberally with salt and pepper and stir in all but 3 tablespoons of the bread crumbs, the herbs, and all but 2 tablespoons of the Parmesan. Spoon equal amounts of stuffing into the area of the artichokes from which you removed the choke; also open up some of the leaves and dribble a little stuffing down between them. Place in a pan that will hold the stuffed artichokes upright, sprinkle on the remaining bread crumbs and Parmesan, then cover loosely with foil and bake for 1 hour in a 350-degree oven, removing the foil the last 5 minutes to brown the tops slightly.

SERVES 4

Stuffed Cabbage Rolls

1 medium head red or white
 cabbage
¼ cup cracker crumbs
¾ cup cooked rice

SAUCE:
½ cup chopped onion
Freshly ground pepper
Juice of 1 lemon
½ cup packed dark brown sugar

1 egg
⅔ cup ground pork
⅓ cup ground country ham

1 cup tomato sauce, canned or
 fresh (page 630)
½ cup water

Cut the cabbage core at its base, then loosen the leaves and drop them into a pot of rapidly boiling water. Lift them out when they are tender, after 3–4 minutes. Choose 8 large whole leaves and lay them out flat. (Reserve the remaining cabbage and refrigerate to use in soup or to cook further for a dish such as braised or creamed cabbage.) Mix the cracker crumbs, rice, egg, and ground meats (country ham will eliminate the need for salt and provide plenty of flavor). Spoon into the center of each cabbage leaf 2–3 tablespoons of the filling. Fold the upper end of the cabbage leaf over the filling, then fold in the sides, and roll the filled leaf up. Put the rolls side by side, seam side down, in a saucepan or large skillet. Mix the onion with the pepper, lemon juice, brown sugar, tomato sauce, and water and pour this over the cabbage rolls. Cover the pan and simmer for 1½ hours, basting occasionally with the sauce.

SERVES 4

Peppers Stuffed with Rice and Herbs

Growing peppers in New England takes patience for the required three months of sunny weather, but many Yankee gardeners raise them and cook them in a variety of styles.

4 medium green peppers
1 cup cooked rice
3 tablespoons chopped fresh herbs, such as parsley, thyme, fennel, or chives, or green part of scallion, finely chopped

Vegetable oil
Lemon juice

Cut off the pepper tops and chop fine, scrape out the seeds, then parboil the hollow peppers for 5 minutes. Drain and place in an oiled baking dish of a size that will let them stand upright fairly snugly. Mix the rice with the chopped pepper tops and a blend of three or four herbs. Spoon the stuffing into the peppers, squeezing in a little lemon juice and dribbling in some of the oil. Cover the baking dish loosely with foil and bake in a preheatd 375-degree oven about 30 minutes, basting the peppers with the oil in the dish from time to time to prevent having a hard crust on top of the rice stuffing. Serve hot or tepid.

SERVES 4

Meat-Stuffed Green Peppers

4 large green peppers
2 tablespoons butter or vegetable oil, or combination of both
1 medium onion, peeled and chopped
2 garlic cloves, minced (optional)
2 cups cooked pot roast or lamb stew, chopped fairly fine
About 1/3 cup leftover pot roast or stew gravy
1 1/2 cups cooked barley

Salt
Freshly ground pepper
3–4 tablespoons chopped parsley
2 teaspoons fresh chopped thyme, or 1 teaspoon dried
2 teaspoons fresh chopped rosemary, or 1 teaspoon dried, crumbled
4 tablespoons fresh bread crumbs
2 tablespoons grated aged cheese

Slice the tops off the peppers, remove the seeds inside, and trim the ribs. Parboil the peppers in boiling water for 5 minutes, then drain.

Meanwhile heat the butter or oil and sauté the chopped onion over low heat until limp, adding the optional garlic for the last minute of cooking. Mix the onions with the meat, gravy, barley, salt and pepper to taste, and the herbs. Fill the peppers with equal amounts of the stuffing and arrange them in a baking dish that will hold them snugly upright. Sprinkle the bread crumbs and then the cheese on top, and bake in a preheated 375-degree oven for 30 minutes.

SERVES 4

Baked Green Peppers with Crabmeat Stuffing

This can also be served as an appetizer.

4–6 medium green peppers, cut in half vertically, seeds and ribs removed
2 tablespoons butter
1/2–3/4 cup cucumber, peeled, seeded, and cut in small cubes
1 tablespoon finely chopped shallots

2 tablespoons flour
1 cup half-and-half or milk
Salt
Freshly ground pepper
6 tablespoons chopped pimiento
1/2 cup chopped cheddar cheese
1/2 pound crabmeat, or crabmeat substitute

Parboil the green peppers in lightly salted water for 10 minutes. Drain and prepare the stuffing. Heat the butter in a skillet and sauté the cucumber with the shallots over low heat for about 5 minutes. Stir in the flour and cook for a minute, then add the half-and-half and stir until thickened. Season lightly with salt and pepper and stir in the pimiento, cheese, and crabmeat. Stuff the green pepper halves and lay them in a buttered dish that will hold them snugly. Bake in a preheated 375-degree oven for about 20 minutes, until the tops are brown and the stuffing bubbling.

SERVES 4–6

2 eggplants, about 1 pound each
2–3 tablespoons oil
1 medium onion, chopped
1 cup sliced mushrooms
2 cups ground ham

½ cup pine nuts
1 teaspoon curry powder
¼ cup currants or raisins, soaked in
    hard cider or sherry
1 cup cubed dry white bread

GARNISH: *toasted sesame seeds*

Curried Ham-Stuffed Eggplant

Bake the eggplants in a preheated 400-degree oven for 30–40 minutes, until they have just begun to turn tender. Cut the eggplants in half lengthwise. When cool, remove the pulp, leaving about ½ inch of flesh next to the skin. Chop the pulp coarsely. Heat the oil, then sauté the onion until it turns translucent. Add the mushrooms and sauté another minute. Mix the chopped eggplant, mushrooms, onions, ham, pine nuts, curry powder, and currants together with the bread cubes. Divide this stuffing among the eggplant shells, and bake about 40 minutes in a 350-degree oven until tender. Sprinkle the toasted sesame seeds over the tops.
SERVES 4

There was a time when Yankees either sliced and fried eggplant or boiled it and turned it into fritters. Many ways to stuff this purple fruit of the nightshade family have developed since, and this is one from our kitchen, using butternuts when we have them, or pine nuts, or pecans for a less New England accent.

Eggplant Stuffed with Ground Meats and Nuts

2 medium eggplants
2 medium onions, chopped fine
4 tablespoons butter or vegetable
    oil, or a combination
3 tomatoes, peeled and chopped, or
    1 cup drained canned whole
    tomatoes
1 cup minced cooked pork or other
    meat
1 cup chipped beef, soaked if very
    salty, minced

½ cup roughly chopped butternuts,
    or pine nuts or pecans
1 teaspoon Worcestershire sauce
About 2 tablespoons fresh herbs,
    such as parsley, thyme, or
    marjoram
1 cup fresh bread crumbs
2 tablespoons melted butter or
    olive oil

Prick the eggplant and bake in a preheated 425-degree oven for 40 minutes. Remove, split in half lengthwise, scoop out the pulp, and chop it. Sauté the onions in the butter or vegetable oil about 5 minutes, add the chopped eggplant and the tomatoes, and cook until the liquid has almost evaporated and the vegetables are tender. Add the minced meats, the nuts, and the seasonings, and heat through. Place the eggplant shells in a shallow pan, skin side down, and fill each with equal amounts of the stuffing. Top with bread crumbs and drizzle melted butter or olive oil on top. Bake at 400 degrees for 25 minutes, until nicely browned on top.

SERVES 4

Stuffed Boston Lettuce with Red Wine Sauce

This makes a handsome presentation. The moist meat filling has the taste and texture of a good pâté, and it is delicious served cold.

¼ pound ground beef
¼ pound ground pork sausage, cooked, fat drained off
¼ pound chicken livers, lightly cooked and finely chopped
¼ pound ground veal
1 cup fresh bread crumbs
1 egg
1 medium onion, chopped fine
½ cup chopped green pepper
½ cup chopped spinach, lamb's quarters, or watercress

¼ cup bourbon
Salt to taste
Freshly ground pepper
1 large head Boston lettuce
2 cups beef broth
¾ cup dry red wine
1 tablespoon cornstarch
2 tablespoons water
3 tablespoons chopped fresh herbs, such as parsley, chives, marjoram, or savory

Mix together the meats, bread crumbs, egg, onion, green pepper, greens, and bourbon, and season liberally with salt and pepper. Remove the tight heart from the head of lettuce, keeping the leaves attached to the core. Chop the heart and add it to the stuffing. Put the lettuce on a large piece of cheesecloth and spread out the outer leaves enough to make a cavity for the stuffing. Form the stuffing into a ball and place it in the center of the lettuce, pressing the inner leaves against the stuffing and drawing the outer ones over to cover the stuffing. Wrap the cheesecloth closely around the stuffed lettuce and tie the ends together, maintaining the ball shape. Place the stuffed lettuce in a deep saucepan that is just slightly larger, pour in the beef broth and wine, and bring to a boil. Lower heat, cover, and simmer for 50 minutes.

Lift out the stuffed lettuce, let rest for 5 minutes, then remove the cheesecloth. Meanwhile reduce the wine stock by boiling furiously until it is reduced by half. Dissolve the cornstarch in 2 tablespoons water and stir into the sauce. Pour a little of the sauce over the stuffed lettuce and sprinkle with chopped herbs. Slice at table and pass the remaining sauce separately.

SERVES 6

Lydia Marie Child, who deeply influenced Yankee cooking more than a century before the contemporary Mrs. Child, told cooks that "the lower part of a squash should be boiled half an hour and the neck pieces fifteen or twenty minutes longer." Her butternut or crooked neck squash was usually mashed with butter and salt. This is a recipe that offers a contrast of both texture and flavor.

2 medium butternut squash
6 tablespoons softened butter

Salt
Freshly ground pepper

STUFFING:
2 cups diced cooked lean pork
1 large apple, peeled and diced
8 cooked chestnuts, roughly chopped

3 scallions, including tender greens, chopped
1 teaspoon crumbled sage leaves

Split the squash, scoop out the seeds and fibers, and rub the insides with some of the butter. Fill the centers with about 1 teaspoon of butter, and sprinkle lightly with salt and freshly ground pepper. Bake the squash for 40 minutes at 350 degrees. Meanwhile, mix the stuffing ingredients in a bowl. Remove the squash from the oven and pour the butter from the hollows into the filling mixture. Scoop out the partially cooked flesh from the shells, chop roughly, and fold into the stuffing mixture. Add a little salt and pepper to taste. Pile the stuffing evenly into the shells, dot remaining butter on top, and cover the squash with aluminum foil. Bake 30–35 minutes at 350 degrees.
SERVES 4

Butternut Squash Stuffed with Pork, Apples,and Chestnuts

4 large red onions
2 ounces (4 tablespoons) goat cheese or cream cheese
3 tablespoons heavy cream
2 cups finely chopped cooked chicken
½ cup finely chopped celery
1 tablespoon chopped fresh sage, or ½ teaspoon dried, crumbled

2 teaspoons chopped fresh savory, or ½ teaspoon dried
3 tablespoons chopped parsley
3 tablespoons chopped sweet red pepper
Salt
Freshly ground pepper
3 tablespoons buttered fresh bread crumbs

Boil the onions in a large pot of salted water for 12 minutes. Meanwhile, mash the cheese and heavy cream together. Drain and shave off the root ends of the onions, then slip off the peel and the tough outer layer of skin.

Red Onions with Chicken Stuffing

Red Onions with Chicken Stuffing (continued)
Slice off the other end, and using a grapefruit knife, remove the center of the onion, leaving a wall of about 2 layers all around. Mix together all of the remaining ingredients, except the bread crumbs, adding salt and pepper to taste. Stuff equal amounts of this mixture into the 4 hollowed-out onions, sprinkle the bread crumbs on top, and place in a casserole that will hold them snugly upright. Bake in a preheated 350-degree oven for 1 hour —covered for the first 40 minutes, then uncovered—until very tender.
SERVES 4

Mrs. Cooney's Stuffed Tomatoes

As Grandma's cook on Bailey Avenue, Mrs. Cooney produced meals that were seldom first rate, but her sausage stuffing inspired us to devise our own version one day when our garden was heavy with ripe tomatoes.

4 good-size tomatoes
½ pound sausage meat
1 small onion, chopped
1–2 garlic cloves, minced (optional)
1 cup cooked rice or barley
3 tablespoons chopped fresh herbs, such as parsley and basil or chervil or sage

Salt
Freshly ground pepper
¼ cup fresh bread crumbs
2–3 tablespoons grated sharp cheese

Cut the tops off the tomatoes and scoop out the seeds and juice and most of the interior (save for sauce or soup), leaving ample flesh around the skin to make a thick, sturdy shell. Cook the sausage meat until it gives off fat, then add the onions and optional garlic and continue cooking until the onions are soft. Mix with the rice or barley and herbs, and add salt and pepper to taste. Fill the tomato cases, and sprinkle bread crumbs and cheese on top of each one. Bake in a preheated 400-degree oven for 15 minutes.
SERVES 4

Maine Stuffed Potatoes

A pioneer of frozen foods who grew up in Maine, Frederic Starret was all set when he got a chance to introduce frozen baked potato skins to Yankee restaurants and eventually to the rest of the country. Skins became a hit as an adorned nibble with drinks, but when they are repacked with steaming potato flesh mixed with well chosen additions, they make a delicious meal in themselves.

4 large baking potatoes	2–3 tablespoons butter
6 frankfurters, chopped	Hot milk
¾ cup chopped celery	4 thin slices Yankee cheddar
1 medium onion, chopped	

Bake the potatoes in a hot oven until tender inside. Meanwhile, sauté the frankfurters, celery, and onion in the butter until the onions are tender. Make a slash in the baked potatoes and scoop out the flesh. Mash it with enough hot milk to make smooth, moist mashed potatoes and stir into the sautéed vegetables and frankfurters. Divide this mixture into four parts and stuff the potato skins. Top each filled potato with a slice of cheese, and bake just long enough for the cheese to melt and brown.
SERVES 4

Stuffed Pumpkin

This makes a very handsome and delicious party dish.

1 perfectly shaped pumpkin, about 6 pounds	¼ pound mushrooms, chopped fine
	2¼ pounds ground lamb
4 tablespoons butter	1 teaspoon cinnamon
1 cup bulgur wheat	⅓ cup chopped parsley
1 cup water	¼–⅓ cup fresh chopped mint (depending on the strength)
Salt	
3 tablespoons vegetable oil	1 tablespoon chopped fresh coriander (or, if available, parsley)
2 medium onions, peeled and chopped	
4–5 garlic cloves, minced	2 eggs, lightly beaten
½ large sweet red pepper, seeded, ribs removed, chopped	Freshly ground pepper

THE SAUCE:

3 cups seasoned chicken broth	½ cup lemon juice
1½ tablespoons cornstarch	4 egg yolks

Cut a lid out of the pumpkin large enough to enable you to scrape out all the seeds and strings from the inside thoroughly with a large spoon. Sprinkle a little salt inside and set upside down to drain while you prepare the stuffing.

Melt the butter in a heavy saucepan and add the bulgur wheat, stirring to coat the grains. Pour the water on top, salt lightly, cover, and cook gently for 20 minutes.

Heat the oil in a large skillet and sauté the onions until they are limp, adding the garlic for the last minute of cooking. Add the red pepper, mushrooms, and ground lamb, and sauté, stirring occasionally, for 5 minutes. Stir in the cooked bulgur wheat, all the spices and herbs, the eggs, and salt and pepper generously, tasting to make sure that you have a highly seasoned stuffing. Spoon this mixture into the scooped-out pumpkin shell,

Stuffed Pumpkin (continued)

cover with foil and then with the pumpkin lid, and place in a pan with about 1 inch of water in the bottom. Bake in a 375-degree oven for 3 hours, or until tender, adding more water to the pan as necessary.

A little before serving, prepare the sauce. Heat the chicken broth. Dissolve the cornstarch in the lemon juice, then stir into the hot broth. Beat the egg yolks and gradually stir in about ½ cup of the hot, thickened broth to temper them, then whisk the eggs into the sauce. Keep over hot water until ready to serve.

Present the whole pumpkin (with the foil removed) at the table. To serve, cut slices from top to bottom, keeping the stuffing intact, and spoon some of the sauce over each wedge.

SERVES 8–10

Ham Timbales

These timbales can also be baked in pasta-lined molds (page 426).

3 tablespoons butter
1 cup milk
½ cup fresh bread crumbs
1½ cups minced or ground ham
3 eggs, lightly beaten
1 tablespoon chopped parsley

1–2 teaspoons chopped fresh sage, dill, or chervil, or ½ teaspoon dried
½ teaspoon curry powder
Salt
Freshly ground pepper

Melt the butter in a saucepan, then stir in the milk and bread crumbs. Cook gently over low heat 5 minutes. Stir in the ham, eggs, and seasonings, tasting carefully before adding any salt (the saltiness of the ham may be sufficient). Pour into 8 buttered muffin tins or pyrex dishes and set these in a pan of hot water that comes about two-thirds of the way up the sides of the molds. Bake in a preheated 350-degree oven for 20 minutes. Remove and let stand out of the hot water for 5–6 minutes before unmolding. You can serve these plain or with Mushroom Sauce (page 629), or a little Hollandaise Sauce (page 632).

SERVES 4

Timbales

The first really special things I learned to make as a child were timbales. I was intrigued watching the way my Auntie Marian—the one person in my family who loved cooking—would put the liquid custard in small molds, bake them in a gentle water bath, and then take them out of the oven, turn them upside down, and, plop, they would emerge in perfectly shaped mounds. It seemed a small miracle. The timbales would quiver slightly as she carried them out onto the flower-bordered terrace of her house in Montpelier, and she would often pick a few leaves or blossoms to decorate the plate. And then the first bite of that tender custard spiked with tiny granules of country ham—it seemed to me that timbales spelled magic.

It was many years before I started making timbales again. Now they are on menus everywhere—they seem to be part of the new-found interest in regional American food, just as the simple instinctive touch of putting a few flowers on a plate has now become something "nouvelle."

I always loved the word *timbale*—it means kettledrum. It seems that in the nineteenth century many households used to have timbale irons that were plunged into hot fat to heat them up, then dropped into a cup about ¾ full of batter. The batter would adhere to the hot iron, which was then immersed again in hot fat until the batter turned brown and crisp and could easily be slipped off the iron. The resulting crisp cases were filled with creamed oysters, chicken, or sweetbreads, or even strawberries. There is a picture of the irons in the first edition of *Fannie Farmer* and instructions on using them. As well, there is a recipe for halibut timbales souffléed with egg whites and baked in "Dario moulds," and one for timbale molds lined with strips of macaroni and filled with "force-meat." Pretty fancy stuff for the ladies of Boston. The 1920 revised edition carried some twenty-three different timbale recipes, from lobster to carrot timbales, and most of these were the kind that I learned to make in my aunt's cozy Vermont kitchen. To celebrate the return of timbales on the New England scene, we have Auntie Marian's original ham version and several made with vegetables in the vegetable chapter. We also tried the pasta-lined timbale, filled it with a leek-lobster custard (it could be oysters or sweetbreads or chicken), and we recommend it highly.

J·J·

Lobster and Leek Timbales in Pasta Mold

10 pieces of lasagna
2 tablespoons butter
2 leeks, washed, trimmed of green leaves, and chopped
3 eggs
3/4 cup light cream
Dash of cayenne

1/8 teaspoon freshly grated nutmeg
1 teaspoon chopped fresh dill (optional)
Salt
1/2 pound cooked lobster, broken into bite-size pieces
Fresh lemon juice

Cook the lasagna in a large pot of boiling salted water until done *al dente*. Drain and run cold water over them. Pat dry. Using 2 of the strips, cut out 8 circles exactly the size of the bottom of the molds you will be using (muffin tins are fine). Fit the circles into the bottom of 8 well-buttered molds. Cut the other strips in half lengthwise, then fit them around the sides of the molds, trimming off the excess. Melt the butter in a medium-size skillet and sauté the leeks slowly, covered, until tender, about 10 minutes; if there is any danger of them drying out and browning, add a little water to the pan. Beat the eggs and mix in the cream, the cooked leeks, and seasonings, adding salt to taste. Distribute equal amounts of lobster in the pasta-lined molds, pushing the meat against the sides to help keep them in place, and sprinkle a few drops of lemon juice over each. Pour equal amounts of the egg-cream-leek mixture on top of the lobster—the pasta will protrude above the edge of the custard (don't worry if a little leaks out). Place the molds in a pan of boiling water, enough to come about two-thirds up the sides of the molds. Bake in a preheated 375-degree oven for 20–25 minutes, or until the custard has set. Let rest 5 minutes. Unmold by running a knife around the edges of the mold and lifting the pasta cup out.
SERVES 4

Cheese and Fish Casserole

Mild jack is among the cheeses made throughout New England, and it combines well in this casserole with such Atlantic fish as sole or haddock.

2–3 tablespoons butter
2 tablespoons flour
1 1/2 cups milk
Salt

Freshly ground pepper
3/4 cup grated cheese
1 pound fish fillets
Freshly grated nutmeg

Heat the butter in a saucepan, stir in the flour, and cook over gentle heat 2 minutes. Off heat whisk in the milk. Return to the heat, and whisk until smooth and thickened. Season lightly with salt and pepper and stir in the cheese. Arrange the fish fillets in a buttered baking dish, alternating with the sauce sprinkled lightly with nutmeg. Bake at 450 degrees for 45 minutes.
SERVES 4

When fresh sardines aren't available, Maine cooks know how to make the best of those preserved in cans.

A Maine Casserole of Canned Sardines

Two 4-ounce cans Maine sardines
2 tablespoons light vegetable oil
1 small onion, finely chopped
2 tablespoons flour
1 teaspoon salt

Freshly ground pepper
2 cups milk, heated
1 cup grated Sebago cheese
4–5 medium new potatoes, cooked
Paprika

Drain the sardines on paper towels. Heat the oil in a pan and cook the onion until translucent, then stir in the flour and the seasonings, and cook, tossing, 1 minute. Stir in the milk, a little at a time, to make a smooth sauce. Add the cheese and stir until it melts and blends into the sauce. Slice the cooked potatoes and arrange half in a 1½- or 2-quart baking dish. Arrange the sardines on top, then the remaining potatoes. Pour the cheese sauce into the dish to cover the contents, and sprinkle the top with paprika. Bake in a 350-degree oven about 25 minutes, until bubbling.
SERVES 4

Hasty Pudding and Seafood Casserole

If, as has been said, there are as many ways to make hasty pudding as ways to bake bread, this is one of the most satisfying contemporary one-dish meals based on cornmeal and descended from the pudding that symbolized early New England. Shrimp is the seafood called for here, but fresh oysters make an interesting substitute.

1 cup cornmeal
1 cup water
Salt
1½ cups milk, scalded
¼ pound (1 stick) butter
¾ cup chopped green pepper

1 medium onion, chopped
½ pound shrimp
Freshly ground pepper
1 egg, well beaten
2 tablespoons chopped parsley

Mix together in a saucepan the cornmeal, water, and ¼ teaspoon of salt. Add the scalded milk and cook over low heat for about 15 minutes, stirring occasionally. Meanwhile, heat 2 tablespoons of butter and sauté the chopped green pepper and the onion for about 2 minutes, then add the shrimp and sauté 2 minutes longer. Season to taste with pepper. Set aside to cool slightly, and remove the shells from the shrimp. Mix the remaining butter and the egg with the cornmeal. Pour into a greased 1½-quart casserole or baking dish and stir in the pepper-onion-shrimp. Bake in a preheated 350-degree oven for 40 minutes. Sprinkle with chopped parsley.
SERVES 4

Cape Codfish and Chick-pea Casserole

Canned chick-peas, or garbanzos, have become a kitchen staple for many cooks, and you'll find this Cape Cod fisherman's casserole an interesting way of using them, the salt cod and beans making an unusual flavor combination.

1½ pounds dried codfish, soaked 24 hours in several changes of water
6 tablespoons vegetable oil or combination vegetable and olive oil

2 large onions, chopped
3 garlic cloves, chopped
2 cups cooked tomatoes, chopped
1 teaspoon dried marjoram
Freshly ground pepper
2 cups cooked chick-peas, drained

Cut the softened codfish in small rectangles. Heat the oil in a skillet until a haze forms, then fry the fish to brown both sides. Remove the fish to a paper towel and cook the chopped onions until they are translucent, stirring in the garlic for the last minute of cooking. Add the tomatoes, the marjoram, and a few turns of the pepper grinder, but do not add salt. Stir in the cooked chick-peas and simmer for about 20 minutes. Put the codfish pieces in a 1½–2-quart casserole and pour in the tomato and chick-pea mixture. Cover and bake in a preheated 350-degree oven for about 20 minutes. Portuguese-Americans in New England serve cruets of oil and vinegar to season each helping as individuals may choose.
SERVES 4–6

Chicken, Eggplant, and Corn Casserole

1 medium eggplant
1 cup corn kernels, fresh or frozen
4 scallions, including tender greens, chopped
½ cup chopped red or green pepper
1 cup chopped cooked chicken
Salt

Freshly ground pepper
4 eggs
2½ cups milk
⅛ teaspoon mace
2 tablespoons grated hard tasty cheese

Cut the eggplant in half lengthwise, and score deeply in a crisscross pattern. Steam for 15 minutes, adding the corn to the steamer for the last 2 minutes. Scoop out the eggplant in chunks following the scoring lines. Mix gently with the corn, scallions, peppers, and chicken and season to taste with salt and pepper. Place in a buttered casserole. Beat the eggs lightly with the milk, season with mace and a little more salt and pepper to taste, then pour over the mixture in the casserole. Bake in a preheated 350 degree oven for 40 minutes, sprinkling the cheese over the top the last 5 minutes of baking.
SERVES 4

Church Suppers

One New England institution that remains in spite of changes everywhere else is the church supper. No other occasion is apt to bring so many cooks together, nor such an array of one-dish meals that could take the place of a meat-and-potatoes course, requiring little else than a crisp side dish like coleslaw, plenty of rolls, lots of relishes, and pies, cakes, and ice cream, all homemade.

Of course the menus are not insistently dominated by combination dishes, but church suppers generally may have added to the reasons a Yankee cook worked hard to perfect one dish she might call her own invention. As a report from New London county in Connecticut has it, "The congregation assembled as a gustatory jury. Many a housewife's reputation was established and many others went home to try harder. What came out of this evening was the perfection of plain and fancy New England cooking."

At such an event there was always the likelihood of a secret ingredient in a classic dish of baked beans and salt pork. There was often, when warm weather prevailed, a chicken salad—or a chicken pie with a new-fangled crust. Certainly, the church supper as an institution was responsible for the evolution of macaroni and cheese (which in southeastern Connecticut was known for a while as macaroni pudding). Much as it may be an occasion of fellowship and sharing, supper in a church basement offers a chance to be well fed at bargain prices.

Not long ago, we heard a big man laugh out loud as he poised a fork over his plate—it was crammed with potato pudding, dabs of macaroni, pickled peaches, dill pickles, split Parker House rolls oozing molten butter, trencherman's slices of ham loaf. All this lovingly cooked supper, plus cakes and pies for dessert, had cost four and a half dollars for grownups, half price for children.

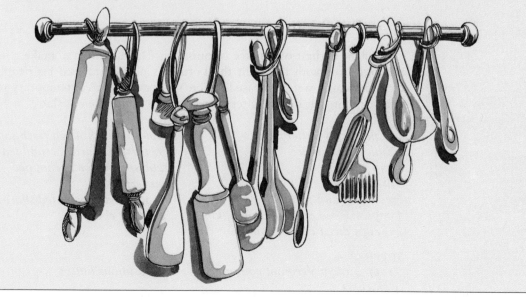

Chicken and Spinach, Act II

"Leftover" was not a term in common use among New England's Shakers, instead they used yesterday's cooked ingredients in flavorful combinations like this, from Hancock Shaker Village in the Berkshires.

4 cups diced cooked chicken
Salt
Freshly ground pepper
3 cups chopped cooked spinach
1 teaspoon fresh rosemary, or ½
    teaspoon dried, crumbled
1 cup chopped cheddar cheese
3 tablespoons butter

3 tablespoons flour
½ cup half-and-half
1½ cups milk
1 teaspoon dry mustard
1 teaspoon grated onion
4–5 thick slices stale bread
Soft butter

In a greased 3-quart baking dish, arrange layers of the diced chicken seasoned with salt and pepper and the spinach seasoned with the rosemary. Spread ½ cup of cheese over the chicken-spinach mixture, poking some of the cheese into it. Heat the butter and stir in the flour to make a smooth paste. Stir in the half-and-half and the milk a little at a time, and when it is smoothly blended, stir in the seasonings. Add the remaining cheese and simmer about 4 minutes. Trim the bread slices to fit the top of the baking dish and toast them on one side. Fit the bread, untoasted side up, over the casserole contents and spread the pieces liberally with soft butter. Bake in a preheated 350-degree oven for about 20 minutes, or until the bread lid becomes crusty.
SERVES 4–6

Vermont Pumpkin Casserole

One of the earliest of Yankee colonists wrote, "Let no man make a jest of pumpkin, for with this fruit the Lord was pleased to feed his people till corn and cattle were increased." Here's a version of a contemporary recipe whose originator said he often served it with pineapple coleslaw.

2 tablespoons butter
2 tablespoons flour
1 cup milk
Salt
Freshly ground pepper
4 cups mashed or puréed pumpkin
1½ cups diced cooked ham

1 tablespoon chopped fresh sage, or
    ½ teaspoon dried, crumbled
3 tablespoons finely chopped
    butternuts
1⅓ cups coarsely grated sharp
    cheddar cheese

TOPPING:
½ cup broken Vermont common
    crackers

2 tablespoons butter

Prepare a white sauce by melting the butter in a saucepan, stirring in the flour, and cooking gently over low heat a couple of minutes. Off heat pour in the milk, return to the heat, and stir until thickened. Season with salt and pepper to taste. In a large bowl, mix the pumpkin purée with the white sauce (or if you are puréeing the pumpkin in a food processor do the mixing in that) and the ham, sage, butternuts, and 1 cup of the cheese. Correct seasoning if necessary. Transfer to a buttered 2-quart casserole, sprinkle the remaining cheese on top, and dot with butter. Bake in a preheated 350-degree oven for about 30 minutes, until bubbling on the surface. Bring to the table very hot.

SERVES 4

Eggplant, Zucchini, and Ground Meat Casserole

1 good size eggplant
Salt
Freshly ground pepper
2 small zucchini
About ½ cup vegetable oil
1 large onion, chopped
1 large garlic clove, minced
2 cups minced cooked meat, such as beef, lamb, or veal

2 tablespoons chopped parsley
1 teaspoon chopped fresh thyme or oregano, or ½ teaspoon dried
¾ cup ricotta
1 large tomato, chopped
½ cup chicken or beef broth
¾ cup fresh bread crumbs
1 tablespoon olive oil or melted butter

Peel the eggplant and cut it into ½-inch slices. Salt both sides of the slices liberally and spread out on a counter with a board or other weight on top. Let the eggplant sweat for 30 minutes, then dry the slices, slapping them between paper towels to absorb excess salt. Heat about ¼ cup of the oil in a large skillet and fry half the eggplant slices on both sides, pressing down on them with a spatula so they release their moisture. Trim the zucchini and cut into the same size pieces and add half of them to the eggplant skillet. Toss and cook for 5 minutes, then transfer to a shallow casserole, making a single layer of the vegetables. If there is no oil left in the skillet, add 1 more tablespoon and sauté the onions. When they turn limp, add the garlic and sauté another minute, then spread over the eggplant and zucchini. Now make a layer of the minced cooked meat and season with salt and pepper and herbs. Distribute the ricotta on top and salt and pepper again. Cook the rest of the eggplant and zucchini slices in the same way, using up the remaining oil, and make a final layer of the vegetables, interspersing the slices with the chopped tomatoes. Pour the broth over, sprinkle bread crumbs on top, and drizzle the olive oil or melted butter over. Bake casserole in a 350-degree oven for 50 minutes. Serve when browned and bubbling. Also good cold.

SERVES 4

Turkey on Broccoli au Gratin

In this recipe, broccoli, which is cooked only briefly in lots of water to keep it green, provides a colorful complement for sliced turkey, a favorite dish at the White Turkey Inn, on Connecticut's Danbury Road, a half century ago.

4 cups broccoli florets, cooked until just tender

6 large slices cooked turkey

SAUCE:
1 cup crumbled cheddar
1 tablespoon butter
Salt
Freshly ground white pepper
¼ teaspoon paprika

1 cup half-and-half
¼ teaspoon prepared mustard
4 tablespoons buttered bread crumbs

Strew the broccoli florets on the bottom of a buttered 1½-quart shallow baking dish and arrange the turkey slices on top. To make the sauce, put the cheese and butter in the top of a double boiler, add a sprinkling of salt and pepper, the paprika, half-and-half, and mustard. Stir over simmering water until the mixture thickens. Pour the sauce over the turkey slices and sprinkle the top with the buttered bread crumbs. Bake for 15–20 minutes in a preheated 350-degree oven until bubbling.

SERVES 6

Cooked Veal and Mushroom Casserole

1 pound fresh mushrooms
2 cups diced cooked veal
1 chopped onion
2 tablespoons butter
2 tablespoons Dijon mustard

½ teaspoon summer savory
Freshly grated nutmeg
2 teaspoons flour
Salt
1 cup heavy cream

Slice the mushrooms and put a layer on the bottom of a buttered 1½-quart casserole, then add a layer of veal cubes. Cook the onion about 3 minutes in 1 tablespoon of the butter, then mix in the mustard, savory, and several grindings of nutmeg. Add the remaining butter and sprinkle in flour and a little salt. Spread half of this mixture over the contents of the casserole, then make a layer of the remaining mushrooms and another layer of the remaining meat. Pour the cream over all and put the casserole in a 350-degree oven for 1 hour.
SERVES 4

Mushroom, Lamb, and Barley Casserole

Returning to favor, barley is particularly good flavored with mushrooms and lamb. This is a dish to make when you have some leftover lamb stew or a roast with some remaining pan gravy. But it's also worth stewing up some shoulder of lamb, and perhaps a shank, if you have some odd pieces in your freezer. If you do the lamb from scratch, be sure to add a chopped onion and a couple of whole garlic cloves to the braising liquid so that you'll have some flavorful juices to use when making this dish.

1½ cups barley
3½ cups water and lamb broth or
    gravy
Salt
10 ounces mushrooms, quartered
2 tablespoons butter and/or oil
1 small onion, or 3 shallots,
    chopped fine
2 cups cooked lamb cut in small
    pieces

Freshly ground pepper
2 tablespoons chopped herbs, such
    as parsley, savory, dill, or
    marjoram
3 tablespoons bread crumbs
1 tablespoon olive oil or melted
    butter

Cook the barley in the water, lightly salted, augmented with lamb broth or gravy, reserving about ¼ cup of the lamb cooking juices to season the casserole later. In 35–40 minutes the water should be absorbed and the barley tender. Sauté the mushrooms in the butter or oil along with the onion or shallots for 3–4 minutes, tossing now and then. Fill a 2-quart casserole with a layer of half the barley, season with salt, pepper and herbs, then add a layer of mushrooms and lamb, seasoned, plus remaining gravy, and a final layer of barley. Sprinkle the bread crumbs over the top and drizzle a little olive oil or melted butter over it. Bake, uncovered, in a 350-degree oven for 30 minutes.

Some Spicy Remarks

As Connecticut is proud to call itself the "Nutmeg State," Chelsea, Massachusetts, is the hometown of David and Levi Slade, two teenage boys who in 1837 conceived the idea of pulverizing large amounts of cinnamon in their father's gristmill, thus eliminating the chore of grinding the bark in kitchen mortars.

The processing of all kinds of spices helped to make them so common in the nineteenth century that Yankee food—the good and the bad—became known for its spiciness. When used to excess, spices brought complaints from some well-traveled New Englanders, including Harriet Beecher Stowe, whose opinions embraced things culinary as well as domestic politics. Only after a year of living in France was she able to forget, she wrote, "the taste of nutmeg, clove, and allspice, which had met me in so many dishes in America."

In the twentieth century, skill in seasoning has changed in subtle ways some fixed ideas about regional flavors. No longer is the food either bland or too redolent of the condiment shelf. Just as Portuguese palates have added cumin seed and spicy sausage to clam chowder, some Oriental inspirations have changed other standard fare. Flavor counts in contemporary New England cooking, so you must give yourself the leeway your own sense of taste suggests.

And remember to buy only the amounts of spices you can use in a short time. Check them every few months and throw out any that smell like dust. Buy whole spices and grind them yourself, using a small coffee grinder; use a blender or food processor for cinnamon sticks, and a fine grater for nutmeg. Keep them in screw-top jars, away from the heat and moisture of the stove.

Lamb with Eggplant

Another dish to make with leftover leg of lamb, particularly if the meat hasn't been overcooked and is still rosy at the bone. But it also can be made from fresh lamb, in which case use stew meat and cook it with the onions and garlic and just enough water to keep it moist, until almost tender, finishing the cooking with the eggplant.

1 very large or 2 medium eggplant
2 tablespoons vegetable oil
2 large onions, sliced
2 garlic cloves, minced
About 3 cups cooked lamb,
   preferably rare, cut in chunks

Salt
Freshly ground pepper
About 16 cherry tomatoes
2 tablespoons chopped fresh
   coriander or flat-leaved parsley

Split the eggplant in half lengthwise and make deep slashes in the cut flesh about 1 inch apart to make a crisscross pattern. Place in a steamer and steam for about 15 minutes, until just tender.

Meanwhile, heat the oil, add the onions, and sauté them gently until almost tender. Add the garlic and sauté another minute.

Put the meat in a casserole, season with salt and pepper, and spread the sautéed onions and garlic on top. Scoop the eggplant flesh from the shell in 1-inch chunks and tuck in around and on top of the meat. Distribute cherry tomatoes on top, season again, and bake, uncovered, in a preheated 350-degree oven for about 25 minutes until bubbly. Sprinkle chopped coriander or parsley on top.

SERVES 4

Lamb and Vegetable Casserole

A change from the usual grilled chop, this lamb casserole can be varied in a number of ways according to what's in season. You can also use leftover cooked chops instead of fresh meat, simply eliminating the first step.

3 tablespoons vegetable oil
4 loin lamb chops, about 1-inch thick, trimmed of excess fat
Salt
Freshly ground pepper
2 large onions, peeled and sliced
2 fat garlic cloves, chopped
1 medium eggplant (about ¾ pound), peeled and cut in large dice
1 green pepper, seeds and ribs removed, cut lengthwise in slices
1 sweet red pepper, seeds and ribs removed, cut lengthwise in slices.

1 semi-hot small green pepper, seeds and ribs removed, cut in strips
2 small zucchini, cut in ½-inch slices
¾ cup lamb or chicken broth
About 6 medium new potatoes, peeled and cut in ¼-inch slices
1 tablespoon chopped fresh rosemary, or 1 teaspoon dried, crumbled
3 tablespoons chopped parsley, preferably flat-leaved

Heat 1 tablespoon of the oil in a large skillet and brown the chops about 2 minutes on each side. Remove them, salt and pepper them on each side, and keep them warm. Add the remaining oil to the skillet and sauté the onions, stirring, over medium heat for 2–3 minutes. Stir in the garlic and cook 1 more minute. Add the eggplant, peppers, zucchini, and salt and pepper to taste; cook for several minutes, tossing, then with a slotted spoon remove all the vegetables to a bowl. Add the broth to the skillet and boil vigorously a few seconds, scraping up any browned bits.

Spread half of the potatoes over the bottom of a large casserole, pour half the broth over, spoon half the vegetable mixture on top, and nestle the

chops in among the vegetables, sprinkling them with some of the rosemary and parsley. Now make a layer of the remaining vegetables and end with the remaining potatoes. Sprinkle salt and pepper and the rest of the herbs on top, pour the rest of the broth over, and bring to a simmer on top of the stove. Cover and bake in a preheated 350-degree oven for 30 minutes, then uncover and cook another 15 minutes. Serve from the casserole.
SERVES 4

Reuben Casserole

A zesty casserole from Ethelyn Morse, who runs a family company that has produced sauerkraut in Waldoboro, Maine, since soon after World War I. The basic formula goes back to the arrival Down East of German immigrants in 1748.

3 cups Morse's fresh sauerkraut, drained
8 fairly thick slices corned beef
10 ounces Swiss cheese, grated
¼ cup chicken broth or dry white wine

4 slices rye bread, made into coarse bread crumbs
2 tablespoons butter

In a 2-quart casserole, make a layer of one-third of the sauerkraut. Lay 4 of the corned beef slices on top, then sprinkle with one-third of the grated cheese. Repeat, then add a final layer of sauerkraut and top with cheese. Pour the broth or wine over and bake, covered, in a preheated 350-degree oven for 30 minutes. Uncover, sprinkle the rye crumbs on top, and dot with butter. Bake another 15 minutes, uncovered, until the crumbs are browned.
SERVES 4

Broccoli is no longer an oddity, but in 1849, when Henry David Thoreau was gathering observations for his book on Cape Cod, he was surprised to find that broccoli was growing in the garden of a Wellfleet oysterman and that it had been planted with seed found in the wreck of a London schooner. Italian Yankees may have made broccoli popular, as you can see from the number of times it shows up in this book, but the New England meal below has the Scandinavian heritage of immigrants living in the Boston area.

North Country Broccoli Casserole

1 pound fresh broccoli, coarse
    stems peeled and stems and
    florets chopped
1 egg, lightly beaten
½ cup creamed cottage cheese
1 cup milk
Juice of ½ lemon

Salt
Freshly ground pepper
½ teaspoon grated nutmeg
½ pound frankfurters, coarsely
    chopped
2 tablespoons melted butter
12 Vermont crackers, crumbled

Cook the broccoli in a little salted water for about 5 minutes, until tender but not soft. Drain and pour into a greased casserole. Mix the beaten egg with the creamed cottage cheese, the milk, and the lemon juice. Sprinkle in a little salt, several turns of the pepper grinder, and the nutmeg. Stir in the chopped frankfurters, and pour the sauce over the broccoli. Mix the butter and crumbled crackers, and spread the mixture over the contents of the casserole. Bake at 350 degrees about 30 minutes, until browned.
SERVES 4–6

Canadian Bacon and Potato Casserole

6 medium potatoes, peeled
Salt
1 tablespoon vegetable oil
1 medium onion, chopped
½ medium sweet red pepper,
    chopped

1 cup diced Canadian bacon
3 tablespoons butter
¼ cup hot milk
2 eggs, beaten
⅔ cup grated cheddar cheese
Freshly ground pepper

Cook the potatoes in salted water. Heat the oil in a skillet and sauté the onion for 2 minutes, then add the red pepper and bacon and sauté another minute. Drain the potatoes when tender and put through a potato ricer or mash them, then beat in the butter, hot milk, eggs, and cheese. Add the sautéed onion and pepper and Canadian bacon, and mix well. Season with salt as needed and freshly ground pepper. Turn into a greased casserole and bake in a preheated 350-degree oven for about 30 minutes, until lightly colored on top.
SERVES 4–6

Ham and Sweet Potato Casserole

1 pound sweet potatoes
Grated rind of 1 orange
Freshly ground pepper
1/8 teaspoon grated nutmeg
1/2 pound cooked ham, cut in pieces
   about 1/8-inch thick

1–2 teaspoons prepared mustard
1 1/2 cups milk
2 tablespoons sesame seeds

Peel the sweet potatoes and either slice them very thin or grate them. Spread half the potatoes over the bottom of a shallow 1 1/2-quart casserole, sprinkle half of the grated orange rind over, and season with some pepper and nutmeg (if you are using country ham, you probably won't need salt; otherwise season lightly with salt). Arrange overlapping pieces of ham over the potatoes, spread mustard on top, then finish with the remaining potatoes and a little more the pepper and nutmeg. Pour the milk over all. Cover lightly with foil and bake in a 375-degree oven 40 minutes, remove the foil, sprinkle sesame seeds over the top, and bake another 15–20 minutes until the potatoes are tender and all the liquid has been absorbed.
SERVES 3–4

Tim Kielty's Main Course Potatoes

This vegetarian main dish was devised by a Canaan, Connecticut, bachelor, who is a limnologist dedicated to the study of freshwater insect life and who is dedicated as well to "cooking as an art and a hobby."

4 large baking potatoes
1 medium onion, chopped fine
1/2 pound mushrooms, sliced
2 tablespoons butter
1/2 head fresh broccoli

1/2 head fresh cauliflower
1 1/2–2 cups cream cheese
1 cup sour cream
1 1/2–2 cups grated cheddar cheese
Grated Parmesan cheese

Cut a shallow lengthwise slash in the potatoes and bake about 45 minutes in a 400-degree oven. While they are baking, sauté the onion and mushrooms in the butter, and set aside. Steam the broccoli and cauliflower just enough to leave them crunchy and the broccoli bright green (about 3–5 minutes). Remove the potatoes from the oven when they are soft and cut them in half lengthwise. Scoop out the potato pulp, leaving the skins intact, and mash the pulp with the cream cheese and sour cream to produce a light, fluffy mixture. Stir in the cooked onions and mushrooms, fold in the broccoli and cauliflower, and divide the mixture in four parts. Stuff the potato skins and nestle them closely in a shallow baking dish. Sprinkle them with a generous layer of cheddar and lightly top this with Parmesan. Bake at 350 degrees for 20 minutes, until the cheese is bubbly and lightly browned. A green salad makes a good accompaniment.
SERVES 4

Another way to use up leftover roast lamb.

2 tablespoons butter	Freshly ground pepper
3 fat leeks, cut in ½-inch slices, white part only	¼ cup heavy cream
	1 teaspoon lamb fat or vegetable oil
3 medium new potatoes, peeled and cut in ¼-inch slices	About 1½ cups pieces cooked lamb
	2 tablespoons chopped parsley
Salt	3 tablespoons fresh bread crumbs

Lamb, Leek, and Potato Gratin

Melt the butter in a skillet and add the leeks and potatoes. Salt lightly, grind some pepper over, and pour about ⅓ cup water in, cover tightly, and cook over low heat, adding a little more water if the pan becomes dry, for about 15–20 minutes, until the leeks and potatoes are tender and all the water is absorbed. Pour in the cream and bring to a boil. Film the bottom of a flameproof shallow dish with fat or oil and toss the lamb pieces in it just long enough to heat through. Season with salt and pepper, cover with the leek-potato mixture, sprinkle parsley over, and top with the bread crumbs. Place a good 8 inches under the broiler until brown on top, about 10 minutes.
SERVES 3–4

A favorite way or turning out this simple supper dish calls for Portuguese sausage, *lingüiça* or *chouriço*, but you may like trying kielbasa or something similar, instead.

4 cups medium diced, peeled potatoes	2–3 tablespoons flour
	Milk
⅔ cup chopped leeks, white part only	¾ pound sausage, coarsely chopped
	4 tablespoons butter
Salt	Bread crumbs
Freshly ground pepper	

Potato and Sausage Casserole

The potatoes should be in small dice and the leeks chopped rather fine. Spread half the vegetables in the bottom of a 1½-quart casserole, sprinkle lightly with salt, pepper, and flour, then scatter the chopped sausage over and add the remaining vegetables. Pour milk over until it can be seen just below the top layer. Dot the surface with butter, and sprinkle amply with bread crumbs. Cover the casserole, and bake at about 375 degrees for about 1½ hours, until the potatoes are tender. To brown the crumbs, remove the cover 15 minutes before the casserole is fully cooked.
SERVES 4

Sausage and Pasta Casserole

A good one-dish meal to be made with almost any form of small pasta. We prefer orzo.

4 Italian sausages (about ½ pound total)
2 tablespoons olive or vegetable oil
¼ pound mushrooms, quartered
1 scallion, including tender greens, chopped

1 garlic clove, chopped
2 cups canned tomatoes
1 teaspoon dried marjoram
¼ pound orzo, or other small pasta, cooked
1 cup cooked peas

Cook the sausage until it has released its fat, remove from the pan, and slice it. In the same pan heat the oil and cook the mushrooms about 10 minutes, then add the scallion and garlic and cook gently 2–3 minutes. Stir in the tomatoes and marjoram and continue cooking over very low heat for 10 minutes. Stir in the sausage, cooked pasta, and peas. Turn into a lightly greased 1½-quart casserole and bake about 30 minutes in a preheated 350-degree oven until the casserole begins to bubble.
SERVES 2–3

Yankee Cheddar Enchilada Casserole

Vacationing in the Southwest, says a friend who wants to be nameless, inspired the combination of sharp cheddar cheese with hot peppers, garden tomatoes, and ground beef.

2 tablespoons corn oil
2 onions, chopped
2 garlic cloves, chopped
2 cups ground beef
2½ cups tomatoes, peeled and chopped
2 dried hot red peppers, seeded and chopped

1 dozen tortillas, fresh, frozen, or canned
Oil for frying
2 cups half-and-half
6 beef bouillon cubes
½ pound sharp cheddar cheese, grated

Heat the corn oil and cook the chopped onions and garlic gently until soft, about 2–3 minutes. Stir in the ground beef and cook until it changes color, breaking it up with a fork. Add the tomatoes and crush with a spoon to mix with the meat, then add the crushed red peppers. While the meat and tomato mixture is simmering, separate the tortillas and heat about 1 inch of oil in as large a skillet as you have and fry the tortillas, turning them over when they bulge. When they have cooked about 1 minute, remove the tortillas and drain on paper towels. Heat the half-and-half to the simmering point and dissolve the beef cubes in it. Dip each tortilla in the hot milk and let it cook there for about 30 seconds. Place 1 tortilla, folded, in a shallow baking dish, lift the top half, and fill with 2–3 tablespoons of the meat mixture, then cover with the top half of the tortilla. Repeat, arranging the folded tortillas snugly next to each other so they fill the dish. Spoon any leftover meat mixture on top of the tortillas, then cover with the grated cheese. Bake in a preheated 350-degree oven for about 30 minutes, until the cheese bubbles.

SERVES 4

Fiddleheads and Chipped Beef Casserole

¼ pound sliced chipped beef
2 cups cooked fiddleheads (page 44)
2 cups Cream Sauce (page 629)
½ cup grated sharp cheddar
4 tablespoons rum or dry sherry

Taste the beef and soak it about 10 minutes in hot water only if it is highly salted. Drain and tear in pieces. Arrange the cooked fiddleheads in a buttered baking dish and spread the shredded beef on top. Blend all but 2 tablespoons of the grated cheese into the sauce and stir until it is thoroughly blended. Stir in the liquor. Pour the sauce over the meat and vegetable layer, sprinkle the remaining cheese on top, and bake in a preheated 350-degree oven for about 25 minutes, until delicately browned.

SERVES 4

Broccoli and Ham Gratin

2 cups lightly cooked broccoli
4 tablespoons butter
4 tablespoons flour
1 tablespoon Dijon-type mustard
2 cups milk
8–10 leaves fresh sage, chopped, or a few dried leaves, crushed
Salt
Freshly ground pepper
8 slices ham (about ½ pound)
½ cup fresh bread crumbs
2 tablespoons freshly grated Parmesan or aged cheddar cheese

Cut the broccoli in florets and the stems in 1-inch pieces and spread both on the bottom of a shallow baking dish to make a single layer. Melt the butter in a saucepan, stir in the flour, and cook slowly a minute or so, stirring, then blend in the mustard. Off heat, add the milk and the sage, and whisk well. Return to the heat and let the sauce thicken, stirring constantly. Add salt and pepper to taste, but remember to go lightly on the salt because of the saltiness of the ham. Cover the broccoli with the slices of ham, then pour the sauce over all. Top with bread crumbs and cheese. Bake in a preheated 350-degree oven for 25 minutes. Then slip under the broiler to brown the top.

SERVES 4

Bean-Hole Beans

Professionally at times, and always for his own pleasure, our friend Jim Beard cooked indoors and out, in virtually every part of America, including Cape Cod. No single recipe does justice to his love of food in all its glory. But the art of alfresco cooking, of which he was also a master, resulted in his *Complete Book of Outdoor Cookery,* from which we learned how to bake Yankee beans on our slope of Stannard Mountain (we like to use part maple syrup instead of molasses). Jim would say this would feed 6 hungry people but it might serve 8.

> 1 pound navy or pea beans
> Two ¼-pound slices salt pork
> 1 teaspoon salt
> ½ cup molasses, or ¼ cup molasses and ¼ cup maple syrup
> Freshly ground pepper

Soak the beans overnight in water to cover. Put them in a large pot, bring to a boil, and cook until the skins burst when two or three are spooned out and blown upon. Pour off the liquid and save. In a heavy pot with a tight-fitting lid, put 1 thick piece of salt pork. Add the cooked beans, the reserved liquid, salt, molasses, and several turns of the pepper grinder. Put the remaining slice of salt pork on top, skin side up. Cover the pot, and put it in the hole you have prepared as follows:

Dig a hole about 6 inches deeper and wider than the bean pot, and line it with small stones embedded in the earth. Build a fire of hardwood in the hole, and let it burn for about 2 hours. Use a shovel to remove the fire, but leave a layer of hot coals on the bottom. Put the filled bean pot in the hole, cover with the remaining hot coals, then top with a layer of earth about 4 to 6 inches thick. Leave the hole and its contents for about 6 hours, or, better yet, overnight. (A fire built on top of the hole and its covering of earth will hasten the underground baking.)

1 medium cauliflower
2 cups diced cooked ham
4 tablespoons butter
1 cup mushroom caps
2 tablespoons flour

1 cup milk
3/4 cup cottage cheese
1 cup cheddar cheese, shredded
1 cup fresh bread crumbs

Cauliflower Baked with Ham

Break cauliflower into pieces, keeping the small florets intact as much as possible. Cook them about 5 minutes in boiling water. Drain and mix with the ham. Heat 3 tablespoons butter and cook the mushrooms about 4 minutes, then stir in the flour and cook over low heat 2 minutes. Off heat, add the milk, return to the stove, and cook, stirring, until thickened. Stir in the cottage cheese and the cheddar, and blend thoroughly into the sauce. Stir in the cooked cauliflower and the ham, then pour the casserole mixture into a greased 2-quart baking dish. Melt the remaining butter, mix the crumbs with it, and spread the crumbs over the top of the casserole. Bake, uncovered, about 20 minutes in a 375-degree oven.

SERVES 4

Meat and Cabbage Pudding

"Ladies' Cabbage," simply creamed shredded cabbage that was often browned in the oven, is an old New England tradition that can become a sturdy casserole meal when combined either with ground pork or with chopped corned beef.

5 cups finely shredded cabbage
1 small onion, chopped
2 eggs, separated
2 cups chopped cooked corned beef
1/2 cup milk

Salt
Freshly ground pepper
1 teaspoon chopped fresh thyme or
   1/4 teaspoon dried

Cook the cabbage and the onion for 10 minutes in boiling water to cover. Drain. Beat the egg yolks with the milk and stir into the cabbage mixture. Stir in the meat and add a very little salt and pepper to taste. Whip the egg whites until they peak, and fold into the cabbage and meat mixture, adding the thyme. Butter a 1½-quart casserole and turn the mixture into it. Bake for about 1 hour at 375 degrees.

SERVES 4–6

Cooking with Alex Delicata

In the village of Durham, Maine, community suppers are often perked up when Alex and Irene Delicata arrive with their contribution of a pot of beans to add to the cooperative menu. They cook together in their own kitchen, and Alex teaches the tricks of outdoor cooking in classes sponsored by L. L. Bean. Both are Yankees who believe in New England dishes that reflect changing times. Delicata baked beans are best, Alex tells friends, when they start with a combination of Jacob's cattle beans, pole beans, or maybe some cannelini. Salt pork may be replaced by a little olive oil, and the subtle aroma emanating from the pot comes from light seasoning with fried basil, parsley, and a touch of garlic.

Whether cooking indoors or over an open fire in the woods, Alex Delicata is a fervent believer in preserving the best of Yankee culinary ingenuity with modifications that concentrate on health factors. With his own family background that brought over the taste of Italy, along with his wife's Slovak influences, he points out the enhancements of Yankee cooking resulting when traditional regional dishes take on various ethnic accents.

And he himself often adds innovations that prove how "creative" New England cooking can be. For instance, with squid, which he may have dipped on a spring night in Maine waters, instead of slicing it in rubbery ringlets, he cuts it lengthwise, then fries it gently so, as a friend describes it, "it curls up like beautiful wood shavings" (see his recipe, page 120). His Snuff Box Duck consists of duck breast marinated in buttermilk overnight and sautéed in a mixture of onion, green pepper, and celery, to be topped by crumbled bacon and a dollop of marmalade. He's a cook with a high regard for natural flavors emphasized by imagination.

Alex Delicata's Baked Beans

If you dry your own garden beans, as Alex does, you know they are fresh and there's no need for overnight soaking, unless you have stored them for more than a year.

1 cup Jacob's cattle beans, cannelini, or romano pole beans
Water
1 chopped onion
2 tablespoons olive oil
2 big garlic cloves, crushed and skins removed

1 tablespoon chopped fresh basil, or 1 teaspoon dried
1 tablespoon chopped parsley
¼ cup molasses
¼ cup honey
1 tablespoon dry mustard
¼ teaspoon cayenne

Put the beans in a pot with water to cover. Set them on the back of a wood stove or over very low heat, covered. The beans can also be baked in a slow oven or in a crockpot. Add more water as necessary to keep them from sticking. Sauté the chopped onion in the olive oil until soft, add the garlic cloves and the basil and parsley, and fry gently together a few minutes. Stir this into the bean pot along with the molasses, honey, mustard, and cayenne and continue cooking until the beans are ready (about 4 hours). You'll know they're done when you blow on them and the skin cracks.

SERVES 6

Canadian Cassoulet

2 pounds Great Northern beans
3 medium onions, chopped
Ham bone (optional)
1 bay leaf
3 garlic cloves
Water
2 tablespoons butter
1 carrot, peeled and chopped
1 rib celery, chopped
½ cup dry white wine
¼ teaspoon dried thyme
½ cup goose or chicken broth or water

1 Canada goose (about 5–6 pounds)*
Salt
Freshly ground pepper
1½ pounds homemade garlic sausage (page 250)
Ham jelly† (optional)
3 tablespoons fresh winter savory, chopped, or 1 teaspoon dried
3 cups country ham, cut in chunks
1½ cups bread crumbs
¼ cup chopped parsley

* If wild Canadian goose is not available, a good-size duck can be substituted, but be sure to remove most of the fat braising. (Canadian wild goose is relatively fat free.)
† When you have baked country ham, jelly will accumulate on the plate on which it chills; use this salty jelly for seasoning.

Soak the beans overnight in a large bowl of cold water. The next day, drain them and put them in a large saucepan with 2 of the chopped onions, the optional ham bone, the bay leaf, whole garlic cloves, and cold water to cover by a couple of inches. Bring to a boil, then lower the heat, cover, and simmer about 1½ hours, until the beans are tender but not falling apart. Drain, reserving the cooking liquid. Meanwhile, in a heavy casserole or roasting pan large enough to hold the goose, sauté in the butter and the remaining onion along with the carrot and celery. Add the wine, bring to a boil, then add the thyme, broth or water, and the goose. Turn the goose in the braising liquid, salt and pepper it all over, drape with foil, then cover the pot and braise in a preheated 325-degree oven about 1½ hours, until tender. Remove, reserving the braising liquid, and when cool enough to handle, cut into generous bite-size pieces (the 2 legs and 2 thighs, and breast and other parts will make about 18 to 20 pieces). Make sausage into cakes and fry lightly about 5 minutes on each side, reserve cooking fat.

To assemble: Spread one-third of the beans across the bottom of a large casserole. If you have any ham jelly, spread some across the beans, as well as salt, pepper, and some of the savory to season well. Distribute a layer of ham and goose pieces evenly on top, then another layer of beans, seasoned as before, a layer of sausage, and a final layer of seasoned beans. Strain 1½ cups of the bean cooking liquid into the goose braising liquid and pour that over the casserole, poking to let it seep down. Mix the bread crumbs and parsley together and spread over the top of the beans. Drizzle the sausage fat over and bake the casserole in a preheated 350-degree oven, covered, for 1 hour, then uncovered for 30 minutes more.

SERVES 10

Martha's Vineyard Lima Beans and Sausage

It may be that migrants have always needed dried legumes to ensure themselves food, and newly arrived Yankees have done as much as any regional people to prove the versatility of a variety of legumes. It's said that after Captain John Harris, U.S. Navy, early in the nineteenth century brought some back from Peru, they became popular in America; but lima beans had already been used widely in places such as Portugal, where other transatlantic sailors had introduced them. Iberian fishermen, long established on the New England coast, preferred them to other beans, and their wives, most of whom remained good Portuguese cooks, adapted a number of old-country recipes, like this one employing *lingüiça* or *chouriço* sausages.

1 cup dried lima beans (yellow eye or soldier beans may be substituted)
2–3 tablespoons vegetable oil and butter combined
1 large onion, coarsely chopped
1 garlic clove, chopped

1 pound lingüiça or chouriço or other garlic sausage
½ teaspoon dried thyme
½ teaspoon dried savory
Salt
Freshly ground pepper

Soak the beans overnight in water to cover. Drain, put in a large saucepan, and add 3 cups of fresh water. Bring to a boil, then reduce heat, and simmer very slowly about 1 hour. (The time needed for soaking and cooking dried beans depends on how long they have been kept on a grocer's shelf, so continue simmering until the beans have begun to split their skins.) Heat the oil and butter in a heavy skillet and when a slight haze rises, add the onion and garlic and the sausage, cut in thick disks. Cook gently, stirring, while the sausage browns and the onion and garlic cook. Drain the beans, add them to the sausage with the thyme and savory. Cook a minute or two while stirring. Add salt to taste and a few turns of the pepper grinder. Cook until flavors are well blended, and serve.

SERVES 4–6

"Beans, Beans, the Musical Fruit..."

If Boston beans are accepted as a prototype of New England Baked Beans, it's time once again to remember that the recipe comes straight from Indian cooks encountered almost immediately by the pioneers of the Plymouth Colony. The Massachusetts natives flavored beans with maple syrup and bear's meat, a formula to be only slightly altered when the colonists found salt pork to be a more convenient ingredient than wild meat and, later on, molasses to be more easily obtained than maple syrup. (The latter, however, is still used by many who are lucky enough to have access to sugarbush.)

Yankees thrive on dried beans—cranberry beans, Jacob's cattle, marrow-fats, navy, pea beans, soldier, and yellow eyes. Soaked beans are cooked in soups, made into salads, and baked with bacon or spareribs, or, in the State of Maine, with coot breasts that have been acidulated in lemon or lime juice.

And though there's much affection for New England beans, and children still sing that "the more you eat, the more you toot," some people are embarrassed by the flatulence that results from eating beans. Legumes, including peas and beans, contain large amounts of carbohydrates that aren't absorbed by the body, and thus small quantities of intestinal microbes can generate larger amounts of hydrogen and other gases. Gas created in the colon can cause much abdominal distress and, worse, a lot of social embarrassment.

Three decades ago, Dr. Sara M. Jordan of Boston's Lahey Clinic listed, among "notoriously indigestible foods," corn, radishes, tomatoes, cucumbers (a "burpless" cuke is now common), and hot breads of all kinds. Nevertheless, navy and lima beans are generally the most offensive, and it's been suggested that future astronauts may be culled from among candidates with "low flatus production." Indians, for their part, had no such social problem.

1½ pound escarole
2 tablespoons butter
½ teaspoon rosemary
½ teaspoon thyme

½ pound chipped beef, loosely
  shredded
Freshly grated nutmeg
Juice of ½ lemon

Escarole in Black Butter with Chipped Beef

Trim and wash the escarole, then put the leaves in a saucepan with only the water that clings to them after washing. Cover the pan and cook over moderate heat, stirring occasionally, for 2 or 3 minutes. If all the water has not evaporated, increase the heat to boil away the remainder. In a frying pan melt the butter and cook it over moderate heat until it turns dark brown. Stir in the herbs, add the escarole and the beef, and stir to absorb the herbs and butter. Stir in the nutmeg and lemon juice.
SERVES 4

Stove-Top Lentils and Ham, Portuguese-Style

Seafaring folk appreciate lentils, just as they've turned the baked bean into a Yankee icon. And some Portuguese cooks along the coast may know that a cup of lentils provides about as much healthy protein as a fast-food burger —without the grease.

1 cup chopped onion
1 large garlic clove, chopped
2 tablespoons vegetable oil
4 medium tomatoes, peeled and
    seeded, or equivalent canned

½ pound cooked ham, in chunks
1 cup cooked lentils
½ teaspoon celery seed
1 tablespoon chopped fresh basil,
    or 1 teaspoon dried

Sauté the onion and garlic in the oil about 4 minutes, then cut up the tomatoes and stir them into the vegetables, continuing to cook for about 5 minutes. Add the ham and cooked lentils, with some of their liquor, and the seasonings, and simmer, covered, about 15 minutes.
SERVES 4–6

Ham-Spinach Custard Ring Filled with Mushrooms

½ cup chopped cooked spinach
    (about ½ pound fresh)
1¼ cups ground ham
4 eggs
⅓ cup fresh breadcrumbs
1 cup half-and-half or milk
Freshly ground pepper
⅛ teaspoon freshly grated nutmeg
2 tablespoons butter or oil, or a
    combination

½ pound mushrooms, quartered
2 scallions, including tender greens,
    sliced
Salt
2 tablespoons sherry or port
2 teaspoons chopped fresh chervil
    or tarragon, or ½ teaspoon dried
½ cup heavy cream (optional)

Mix the spinach and ham together. Lightly beat the eggs and stir them, along with the bread crumbs and half-and-half or milk, into the spinach-ham mixture. Season with pepper and nutmeg (you probably won't need salt because of the ham). Turn into a lightly buttered 4- or 6-cup ring mold. Place the mold in a pan filled with enough boiling water to come about three-quarters of the way up the mold, and bake in a preheated 325-degree oven for 35 minutes, or until the custard is set. Let rest 10 minutes before unmolding.

Meanwhile, heat the butter or oil in a skillet, and sauté the mushrooms along with the scallions, tossing occasionally, for 5 minutes. Season with salt and pepper, add sherry or port to the pan, sprinkle on the herbs, and let the wine boil up until it is a little syrupy. Pour in the optional cream, and let that boil to thicken. When the custard has rested, unmold it onto a warm platter and spoon the mushrooms into the center.
SERVES 3–4 AS A LIGHT LUNCH DISH.

3 tablespoons butter
1 medium onion, chopped
½ large green pepper, chopped
1 rib celery, chopped
3 eggs, separated
One 15½-ounce can salmon
½ cup fresh bread crumbs
Salt

Freshly ground pepper
⅛ teaspoon hot pepper flakes, or
    dash of pepper sauce
1 tablespoon lemon juice
1 tablespoon chopped parsley
2 teaspoons chopped fresh tarragon
    or dill, or ½ dried

Salmon Ring or Loaf

Melt the butter in a skillet and sauté the onion gently until translucent. Add the green pepper and celery, and sauté another 2 minutes. Beat the egg yolks lightly in a bowl and add the drained salmon, broken up in pieces, the bread crumbs, salt and pepper to taste, and the other seasonings. Add the sautéed vegetables and mix throughly. Beat the egg whites in a separate clean bowl until they form firm peaks, then fold them into the salmon mixture. Turn it into a buttered 4-cup ring mold or an 8-inch loaf pan or casserole, and set in a larger pan of boiling water that comes halfway up the sides. Bake in a preheated 350-degree oven for 45 minutes. Let rest 10 minutes before unmolding, then unmold (unless baked in a casserole) first onto a cookie sheet, then reverse onto a platter so that it is served browned side up.

SERVES 4–6

1 large eggplant, peeled and cut in
    cubes
Salt
3 tablespoons oil
2 medium onions, peeled, halved,
    and sliced
4 medium tomatoes, peeled, seeded,
    and diced
¼ teaspoon hot pepper flakes

1¾ pounds shrimp, peeled and
    deveined, if necessary
½ chicken breast, cut in thin strips,
    or about 1 cup cooked chicken,
    cut in strips
Freshly ground pepper
4 tablespoons mixed fresh herbs,
    such as parsley, chives, or basil

Stir-Fry of Shrimp, Chicken, Eggplant, and Tomatoes

Put the eggplant pieces in a colander and sprinkle salt over them. Let stand, tossing occasionally, for 20–30 minutes. Heat 1 tablespoon of the oil in a skillet, and sauté the onion until limp and lighlty brown. Squeeze the eggplant pieces gently in paper towels to rid them of excess juice, then add the remaining oil to the pan, toss in the eggplant, and stir-fry over medium heat 5 minutes. Add the tomatoes and hot pepper flakes, cover, and cook 2–3 minutes. Fold in the shrimp, enveloping it in the sauce in the pan, cover, and simmer 5 minutes. Add the chicken strips, salt and pepper lightly, cover, and cook 5 minutes. Sprinkle on the herbs.

SERVES 4

Quiche Formula

In a generation, the wonderfully simple dish called *quiche lorraine,* consisting of a custard pie studded only with bits of bacon or ham (no cheese), has not only become generally Americanized but has been aggrandized in a Vermont cookbook (the recipe is credited to a French-American Yankee whose surname is Gauthier) under the title, "Unbelievable Quiche." The ingredients that distinguish this quiche from the original in Alsace-Lorraine include 2 cups cooked broccoli, ⅓ cup chopped onions, ¼ cup shredded cheddar cheese and ¾ cup of shredded Swiss cheese, a cup of small-curd cottage cheese, and a cup of milk beaten with 3 eggs and ½ cup of biscuit mix from the convenience food section. This is heavy stuff.

Somewhat like omelets, New England quiches are worthy of enhancement (below), but the foundation is important to achieve the right consistency:

For one 8- or 9-inch pie pan or quiche mold, 3 eggs broken into a measuring cup and enough milk and/or light cream to make 1½ cups. Any desired embellishments should not add up to more than an additional 1½ cups.

Tip: Partially bake the crust before pouring in the filling.

If you use ingredients that give off water, i.e., vegetables such as zucchini, eggplant, tomatoes, mushrooms, and so forth, cook them first until the liquid has been exuded.

Let quiches rest 10 minutes before cutting in wedges.

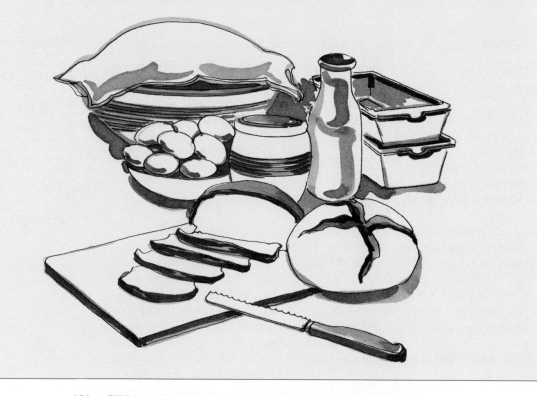

Zucchini and Country Ham Quiche

3 cups grated raw zucchini
Salt
1 small white onion or 3 scallion
   bulbs, chopped fine
2 tablespoons olive oil or butter
3–4 mushrooms, chopped
   (optional)
2 tablespoons chopped fresh basil
Freshly ground pepper

½ cup chopped country ham
3 eggs
⅔–¾ cup milk or light cream, or a
   mixture of both
One 8- or 9-inch partially baked
   pie shell (see Basic Pie Dough,
   page 564)
3–4 tablespoons mild grated
   cheddar cheese

Sprinkle the grated zucchini with about ½ teaspoon salt and let it drain in a colander for about 15 minutes. Squeeze the zucchini dry in your hands, a handful at a time. Sauté the onion in the olive oil or butter for 1 minute, then add the zucchini and optional mushrooms, and stir-fry for 2 minutes. Season with basil and freshly ground pepper and stir in the ham. Beat the eggs with the milk or cream until blended, then add to the zucchini mixture and turn into the partially baked shell. Sprinkle cheese on top and bake in a preheated 350-degree oven for 35–40 minutes, or until set. Let rest 10 minutes before serving.
SERVES 6–8

Yankee Fiddlehead Pie (or Quiche)

In Bangor, Maine, one day, we were talking at the Docket Deli with Joline Brayley when her enthusiasm for fiddlehead ferns surfaced, and she gave this way of using them in a hearty but light luncheon dish.

4 eggs
1 cup milk
1 cup chopped cooked fiddleheads
2 tablespoons chopped cooked
   leeks
1–2 tablespoons chopped parsley
1 cup shredded mild Maine cheddar
Salt

One 9- or 10-inch partially baked
   pie shell (see Basic Pie Dough,
   page 564)
8 whole cooked fiddleheads

Beat the eggs with the milk until blended. Fold in the chopped fiddleheads, leeks, and parsley, and half of the grated cheese. Season with salt to taste. Turn into the partially baked shell and sprinkle on the remaining cheese. Decorate the edge with the whole fiddleheads. Bake in a preheated 350-degree oven for 40 minutes, or until set. Let rest 10 minutes before serving.
SERVES 8

Smoked Fish Quiche

2 egg yolks
2 whole eggs
3/4 cup milk
1/2 cup heavy cream
1 1/4 cups smoked salmon or other smoked fish

1/8 teaspoon mace
Salt
Freshly ground pepper
One 9-inch partially baked pie shell (see Basic Pie Dough, page 564)

Beat the yolks and eggs with the milk and cream until blended, then stir in the salmon and mace, and add salt and pepper to taste. Turn into the partially baked pie shell, and bake in a preheated 350-degree oven for 35–40 minutes, or until set. Let rest at least 10 minutes before serving.
SERVES 6–8

Autumn Winds' Mustard Scampi Crêpes

As a partner and chef of the Brattleboro, Vermont, restaurant named Autumn Winds, Marsha Heller was known by her clientele as a talented hostess. She gave us this recipe one evening in 1981 as we sat at a window overlooking a splash of moonlight on the water fifty feet below.

CRÊPE BATTER:
1 egg
1 egg yolk
2/3 cup milk

1/2 cup flour
1/8 teaspoon salt
1 tablespoon melted butter

MUSTARD SAUCE:
1/2 pound butter
1/4 cup chopped fresh tarragon, or 2 teaspoons dried
1/8 teaspoon red wine vinegar
1 1/2 tablespoons Dijon mustard

3–4 drops Tabasco sauce
1 1/2 tablespoons Worcestershire sauce
Juice of 1/2 small lemon

1 1/4 pounds large shrimp

Salt

Prepare the crêpe batter by beating together all the ingredients for the batter. When thoroughly blended, let rest for 1 hour or more.

Make 12 small (6–7 inches in diameter) crêpes by heating a small greased skillet that size, spooning in just enough batter to make a thin layer, tilting the pan to spread the batter evenly to the edges, and cooking the crêpe about 1 minute on one side over medium heat, then turning and cooking it another 30 seconds on the other side. Repeat until you have made 12 crêpes.

Make the mustard sauce by melting the butter, then whisking in all the remaining sauce ingredients.

Peel the shrimp and butterfly them. Spread them out in a pan in one layer, season lightly with salt, and drizzle about ⅓ of the mustard sauce over them. Bake in a preheated 425-degree oven for 5–6 minutes, until the shrimp have turned opaque and are just lightly cooked. Place about 3 shrimp in the center of each crêpe (put them on the side cooked last as it is the less attractive) and roll up. Arrange seam-side down on 6 ovenproof plates, 2 per serving. Spoon the remaining sauce over them and put the plates in the oven for 3 minutes, until the edges of the crêpes turn a little brown.

SERVES 6

Thin Buckwheat Crêpes

1 egg
½ cup beer
⅓ cup flour

2 tablespoons buckwheat flour
½ teaspoon salt
1 tablespoon melted butter

Mix all of the above ingredients together until well blended (a blender or food processor will do the job well). Let stand 30 minutes or longer before using, then stir well. Heat a 5–6-inch skillet, preferably nonstick, until hot but not smoking, brush lightly with oil, then pour about 3–4 tablespoons batter into the pan. Immediately tilt on all sides to spread the batter evenly over the surface, and bake over medium-high heat until bubbles appear on the surface. Turn and bake on the other side for about 30 seconds. Remove, cover with foil, and keep warm while baking the rest.

MAKES ABOUT SIX 6-INCH CRÊPES

Crêpes, or Thin Pancakes

With their usual jaunty aberrance, old New Englanders were comfortable with the French terms such as *croquettes* and *omelettes,* but steered away from the word *crêpe*—perhaps because it had already become part of local speech in the form of *crepe de chien* and *crepe paper.* Whatever the name, thin pancakes nevertheless were made and often wrapped around a sweet stuffing as a dessert. Nathaniel Hawthorne described a New Hampshire evening at which party pancakes filled "a silver tub, of the capacity of four gallons, holding a pyramid of pancakes powdered with white sugar." The recipe of the period called for a sweet batter enhanced by wine and nutmeg.

Thin cakes, unsweetened as well as sweetened, are often served today. Stuffings of finely chopped cooked chicken, or some of spinach and mushroom, along with other kinds of vegetables, are the most common, usually baked with a white sauce and cheese. We like to use a thin cornmeal or buckwheat crêpe for variety in taste and texture.

Pheasant in Buckwheat Crêpes

A good way to use up any leftover game bird meat—or chicken.

Double recipe for buckwheat crepes (page 453)
4 tablespoons butter
1 small white onion or 3 shallots, minced
2½ cups cooked pheasant or other game bird or poultry, bones removed and cut in small pieces
1½ cups kohlrabi or broccoli stems, peeled and cut in matchstick pieces
½ ounce dried mushrooms, soaked in ½ cup hot water for 30 minutes

4 scallions, including tender greens, cut in matchstick
1 cup strong chicken or game bird broth
1 tablespoon cornstarch
3 tablespoons dry sherry or madeira
Salt
Freshly ground pepper
¾ cup sour cream

Make twelve 5- to 6-inch crêpes, stack them, and keep them warm. Heat the butter in a skillet, then sauté the onion or shallots until tender. Add the pheasant, kohlrabi or broccoli, the drained mushrooms (reserving the soaking liquid), and the scallions, and sauté, stirring, for 3–4 minutes. Mix the mushroom soaking liquid with the broth. Dissolve the cornstarch in the sherry and stir that in, then add this liquid to the pheasant mixture. Cook over gentle heat, stirring, until the sauce is lightly thickened and the vegetables are just barely tender. Salt and pepper to taste. Using a slotted spoon, distribute equal amounts of this filling in the center of each crêpe, spoon a little of the sauce over, and roll up the crêpes. Place them, seam-side down, in a shallow baking dish so that they fit snugly. Stir the sour cream into the remaining sauce, heat through, then spoon over the crêpes. Bake in a 375-degree oven about 10 minutes, until the dish just beings to bubble.
SERVES 6

Cornmeal Crêpes

⅔ cup cornmeal
½ cup flour
¾ teaspoon salt
2 eggs

1 cup skim milk, or 2 parts milk and 1 part water
4 tablespoons corn oil

Mix all the above ingredients together and let stand 30 minutes or longer. Film the bottom of a 6-inch skillet, preferably nonstick, with a little oil or butter, and heat until hot but not smoking (a drop of water should sizzle and quickly disappear). Pour in just enough batter to cover the bottom of the pan, tilting it in all directions so the surface is completely but lightly covered; if you have added too much batter, just pour out the excess. Bake the crêpe over medium-high heat until bubbles appear on the surface, then turn (or flip) it over and bake the other side less than 30 seconds. Stack on foil in a warm place while you bake the remaining crêpes. As you get to the bottom of the bowl, the batter is bound to have settled and become thicker so beat in a little water to thin it to its original consistency.

MAKES SIXTEEN 6-INCH CRÊPES

IDEAS FOR FILLINGS: Goat cheese mashed with a little cream and seasoned with fresh herbs. Grated mozzarella with chopped country ham, rolled up in the crêpes while they are still warm so the cheese melts. Leftover creamed chicken or turkey, chipped beef, seafood, salmon mousse, and so forth.

Chicken Pie

One 2½–3-pound chicken
About 8 cups water
Salt
1 small scraped carrot
1 rib celery with leaves
1 medium onion
2–3 leeks (optional)

Small white onions (8–10 if using leeks, otherwise, about 16)
4 tablespoons butter
4 tablespoons flour
½ cup light or heavy cream
1 tablespoon chopped fresh tarragon or parsley and chives

BAKING POWDER BISCUIT CRUST:
1½ cups flour
1 tablespoon baking powder
½ teaspoon salt

6 tablespoons vegetable shortening or fresh lard
About ½ cup milk

Wash the chicken and remove all fat. Bring the water to a boil with a teaspoon of salt, the carrot, celery, onion, and, if you are using leeks, the cleaned green tops, along with the chicken neck and gizzard. When the water comes to a boil, lower the chicken into it (if there is not quite enough water to cover, add more boiling water), cover and turn down to a lively simmer. Cook until done—about 50–60 minutes; you can tell by lifting the chicken out and making sure that the juices that run out of the cavity are no longer pink. Plunge the chicken into a bowl of water filled with ice cubes (this makes the juices retreat into the chicken so that it is very succulent).

When the chicken is cool enough to handle, pull all the flesh off the bones and cut into generous pieces. Return the bones and any juices to the water in which the chicken was simmered, and cook over moderate heat to reduce to a tasty broth—about 1 hour.

Meanwhile, cut the leeks into ¾-inch slices and peel the small onions. Put them in a pan with chicken broth to cover and cook until just tender and the broth has boiled away.

To make the sauce, melt the butter in a saucepan and stir in the flour. Cook over moderate heat, stirring, for 2 minutes. Off heat, whisk in 2 cups of the hot chicken broth and return to the heat, stirring until thickened. Add the cream, season to taste with salt, and let simmer to reduce slightly. Add the chicken, leek and onions, and herbs to the sauce, heat through, and keep warm until ready to assemble.

To make the biscuit crust: Toss the flour with the baking powder and salt, then work in the shortening until the mixture resembles fresh bread crumbs. Stir in just enough milk so that the dough holds together. Turn it out on a floured board and knead it lightly 4 or 5 turns. Roll or pat it out into a circle the same circumference as the baking dish you plan to use (a shallow 6-cup dish is preferable). Spread the chicken mixture into the baking dish, placing a ½-inch metal cup, open-side down, in the middle to catch the juices. Transfer the circle of dough to the top, pressing it to the edges of the dish. Make several slashes in the top and bake in a preheated 425-degree oven for 20 minutes. To serve, cut a slice and remove the cup to release the juices.

SERVES 4–5

Josephine Reilly's Corn-Puff Chicken and Oyster Pie

A Yankee friend gave us a copy of a cookbook from St. Andrew's Church in Hanover, Maine, and in it we found this variation on the traditional way to turn out a delicious casserole. The addition of the oysters and the oyster liquor to the sauce is also common, but this dish could be made with chicken alone.

One 3–4-pound chicken, boiled and steamed (page 455)
4 tablespoons butter
4 tablespoons flour
1 cup chicken broth or cooking liquid
1¼ cups oyster liquor

Salt
Freshly ground pepper
Few drops lemon juice
1 tablespoon chopped fresh tarragon, or ½ teaspoon dried
1 dozen fresh oysters

TOPPING:
½ cup flour
1 tablespoon baking powder
1 teaspoon salt
¾ cup cornmeal, preferably stone ground

1 egg
1 cup milk
¼ cup melted butter

Remove all the chicken meat from the bird and cut it in good-size pieces. Melt the butter in a saucepan, stir in the flour, and cook over low heat, stirring, for a few minutes. Off heat, pour in the chicken broth and oyster liquor, then return to the heat and stir until thickened. Season with salt, pepper, lemon juice, and tarragon. Stir in the chicken pieces and heat through, then add the oysters. Pour into a shallow baking dish and keep warm.

Toss the flour, baking powder, salt, and cornmeal together. Beat the egg with the milk, then stir into the dry ingredients along with the melted butter. Pour this over the chicken-oyster mixture. Bake in a preheated 400-degree oven for 25 minutes.

SERVES 4–6

Ground Beef, Rice and Cheese Pie

To combine an old-fashioned Yankee respect for the common cracker with today's appetite for seasoned ground beef, this formula makes a hearty supper.

1 cup rice
2 cups cold water
¾ pound ground beef
1 onion, finely chopped or grated
½ medium green pepper, seeded, trimmed, and finely chopped
Salt
Freshly ground pepper
1 tablespoon chopped fresh basil, or 1 teaspoon dried

4 tablespoons butter
4 tablespoons flour
½ teaspoon Tabasco sauce
2½ cups milk
3 cups finely diced sharp cheddar cheese
½ cup crushed common or soda crackers

Steam the rice: Put it in a saucepan, pour the cold water over, bring to a boil, then cover and simmer 15 minutes. Let stand, covered, 5 minutes, then fluff up with a fork. Mix the beef, onion, and green pepper with about ½ teaspoon salt, a few turns of the pepper grinder, and the basil. Spoon the meat mixture onto the inside surface of a 9-inch pie pan, pressing it lightly all over to make a shell of even thickness. Put the meat shell in a preheated 325-degree oven to bake, removing after 10 minutes to pour off fat; bake and remove fat at least once more to leave the shell lightly cooked and dry. Meanwhile, melt the butter in a saucepan, stir in the flour, and cook 1 minute, stirring, over low heat. Sprinkle in a little salt, pepper, and the Tabasco sauce. Add the milk a little at a time and stir until the white sauce is very smooth. Stir in the cheese; when it is thoroughly melted, stir in the rice. Pour this mixture into the baked meat shell, and sprinkle the top with crushed crackers. Increase the oven to 375 degrees, and bake the pie about 15 minutes, until the top is golden brown. Remove it from the oven and let it rest for 5 minutes. Cut into wedges.

SERVES 4

Ham and Ricotta Pie with Raisins

Of numerous variations on pizza brought to New England, one of the most unusual originated in Basilcata, and this elegant adaptation of that region's *pizza rusticata* originated, in turn, at Boston's Gardner Museum Café as a luncheon dish.

⅓ cup butter
¼ cup chopped onion
½ pound smoked country ham, diced
½ cup chopped flat-leaf parsley
1½ cups golden raisins
5 tablespoons applejack
½ cup heavy cream
1½ pounds ricotta

2 eggs, beaten
¾ teaspoon cinnamon
¼ teaspoon ground cloves
½ teaspoon allspice
Salt
Freshly ground pepper
1 partially baked 9-inch pie shell (see Basic Pie Dough, page 564)

Heat the butter over low heat, and cook the onion for about 5 minutes, then stir in the ham, parsley, and raisins, cooking 1 or 2 minutes more. Stir in the applejack and cream, and simmer while beating the cheese with the eggs and the seasonings. Mix in the ham, raisins, onions, and cream. Turn the filling into the pie shell, and bake in a preheated 350-degree oven for 30 to 35 minutes.

SERVES 4–6

Turkey and Leek Deep-Dish Corn Bread Pie

CORN BREAD TOPPING:
¾ cup white cornmeal
¾ cup flour
2 teaspoons baking powder
1 tablespoon sugar
½ teaspoon salt

1 egg
½ cup milk
1 tablespoon melted butter
2 tablespoons chopped parsley and chives

4 leeks, trimmed and washed thoroughly
6 tablespoons butter
6 tablespoons flour
1½ cups turkey or chicken broth
1½ cups milk

Salt
Freshly ground pepper
⅛ teaspoon freshly grated nutmeg
4 cups cooked turkey, cut in large dice
¼ cup heavy cream

Toss the cornmeal, flour, baking powder, sugar, and salt together. Beat the egg and add the milk and melted butter. Mix the dry and wet ingredients together, and stir in the herbs. Butter an 8- or 9-inch pie plate (it should be the circumference of the casserole you will use for the turkey base) and spread the corn bread batter evenly into the pan. Bake in a preheated 400-degree oven for 20 minutes.

In the meantime, cut the leeks into ½-inch pieces and cook in water to cover until just tender. Prepare the sauce: Melt the butter in a heavy saucepan, add the flour, and cook slowly for about 2 minutes over low heat, stirring. Off heat, whisk in the broth and milk, return to the heat, and cook, stirring constantly, until thick and smooth. Season with salt and pepper to taste and nutmeg. Fold in the turkey meat, the leeks with a little of their cooking juices, and the cream. Heat through.

Place the turkey filling in an ovenproof casserole about 8 inches in diameter. When the corn bread is done, carefully remove it from the pan and place on top of the turkey filling. Return the casserole to the oven and bake 5–10 minutes until bubbling.

SERVES 6–8

Seafood Pie

2½–3 pounds littleneck clams
2½–3 pounds mussels
½ cup water
¾ pound small or medium shrimp
4 tablespoons butter
1 pound small scallops
2 tablespoons minced shallots or
  scallion bulbs
4 tablespoons flour

1 cup milk
3 tablespoons chopped parsley and
  chives
Fresh lemon juice
Freshly ground pepper
Salt (optional)
Pie dough for 9-inch crust (see
  Basic Pie Dough, page 564)

Scrub the clams and mussels thoroughly and put them in a large heavy pot with ½ cup water—clams on the bottom as they open more slowly, mussels on the top. Cover the pot and set over moderately high heat. Check after 2–3 minutes and start extracting the shellfish that have opened up, covering the pot again and continuing to cook the unopened seafood until the shells open. When cool enough to handle, extract all the meat, discarding the shells but reserving the cooking liquid. Strain carefully, leaving the sediment behind, and use about ½ cup of the liquid and enough water to cover the shrimp in a saucepan. Cook the shrimp until they turn pink—about 1–2 minutes, depending on their size. Strain them, pouring the cooking liquid into a measuring cup, then peel the shrimp and put them with the clams and mussels. In a skillet, heat 1 tablespoon of the butter, then add the scallops and shallots. Cook, stirring and tossing them, over high heat for about 2 minutes, then mix the scallops in with the other seafood.

Make the sauce by heating the remaining butter in a small saucepan, then stir in the flour. Cook gently, stirring for a minute. Off heat, add the milk and ½ cup of the shrimp-cooking broth. Over moderate heat, whisk until the sauce is smooth and thick (this will be a very thick sauce but it will be thinned out because the seafood continues to release juices as the pie cooks). Mix the sauce with the seafood, add the parsley, chives, a few drops of lemon juice and several turns of the pepper grinder—it's unlikely it will need salt because of the seafood broth, but taste critically and adjust the seasoning. Turn this mixture into a shallow casserole 8 to 9 inches in diameter, or into 6 small individual baking dishes. Roll the pie dough out and cover the casserole or small baking dishes with the dough, leaving a border so that you can fold the dough over and crimp the edges. Cut several decorative slashes in the top of the dough and bake in a preheated 400-degree oven for 30 minutes, until lightly browned on the top.

SERVES 6 AS A FIRST COURSE, 4 AS A MAIN COURSE

Salmon and Cottage Cheese Pie

½ cup sesame-flavored cracker crumbs
½ cup common or soda cracker crumbs
¼ pound butter
1 tablespoon chopped fresh summer savory, or ½ teaspoon dried

One 7¾-ounce can salmon, drained, boned, and flaked
1 cup cottage cheese
3 eggs, separated
½ cup heavy cream
2 tablespoons flour
Freshly ground pepper
1 tablespoon fresh lemon juice

Mix the crumbs, butter, and savory together until smooth (this may be done in a food processor), then press the mixture into a 9-inch pie pan to make a shell of even thickness. In a large bowl stir the flaked salmon, cottage cheese, and egg yolks until thoroughly blended. Add the cream and flour, stirring vigorously to mix well, then sprinkle with a few grinds of the pepper grinder (salt should not be necessary) and the lemon juice. In a separate bowl, beat the egg whites until peaks form and fold gently into the fish mixture. Turn into the cracker shell and set in a preheated 350-degree oven for 40–45 minutes, until the center of the pie is firm.

SERVES 4 AS A MAIN COURSE, OR 6 AS A FIRST COURSE

Crayfish and Tuna Pie

6–8 ounces cooked crayfish meat (see page 11) or shrimp
One 6½-ounce can tuna
½ cup chopped onion
¼ cup chopped celery
¼ cup chopped green pepper
2 tablespoons butter

1 tablespoon flour
¾ cup milk, heated
2 teaspoons curry powder
½ teaspoon salt
Freshly ground pepper
Dough for 12 baking-powder biscuits (page 494)

Toss the crayfish with the tuna in a mixing bowl. Cook the onion, celery, and green pepper in the butter for about 5 minutes, but don't let the vegetables brown. Stir in the flour and cook about 1 minute, then stir in the milk, a little at a time. As the sauce begins to thicken, season with the curry powder, salt, and a few turns of the pepper grinder. Add the seafood and warm gently, while mixing the biscuit dough. Turn the curried fish into a 9-inch pie dish and arrange 12 rounds of ½-inch thick biscuit dough on top. Bake 12–15 minutes in a preheated 450-degree oven, until the biscuits are golden brown.
SERVES 4

New England Greek Pie

In southern New Hampshire and other industrial regions there are many Greek-Americans who combine supermarket conveniences with their culinary heritage to enrich the so-called Yankee repertoire. Here's just one recipe that provides a fine luncheon dish, or that can be doubled or enlarged even more to make a party dish to be served with drinks.

⅓ cup pine nuts
¼ cup raisins
3 pounds fresh spinach or 2 packages frozen spinach
1 medium onion, minced
4 tablespoons olive oil
Jucie of ½ lemon
Salt

Freshly ground pepper
4 eggs, lightly beaten
½ pound feta or goat cheese, crumbled
6 ounces filo dough at room temperature
¼ cup melted butter

Put the pine nuts in a skillet and dry-roast until slightly brown, shaking the pan frequently to prevent burning. Cool the pine nuts and mix them with the raisins. Wash thoroughly and remove tough stems from the spinach, then boil in water to cover 2 minutes. Or thaw the frozen spinach and cook 1 minute in water to cover. Drain well. Sauté the minced onion in 2 tablespoons of the olive oil until tender, then add the spinach and cook 2 minutes, stirring. Remove from the heat, stir in the pine nuts and raisins, and add the lemon juice, a little salt to taste, freshly ground pepper, the beaten eggs and the crumbled cheese. Mix well. Butter an 8 × 10-inch baking dish and line the bottom with 5 sheets of the thin filo dough, brushing each sheet with the melted butter mixed with the remaining 2 tablespoons olive oil as each layer is arranged. Turn the spinach-cheese mixture into the baking dish, spreading it over the filo layers. Cover this filling with the remaining sheets of dough, brushing each with butter and oil. Bake 45 minutes at 350 degrees. Remove and cool.
SERVES 4

Ham, Cheese, and Tomato "Pie"

1 pound ripe, firm tomatoes, peeled
    and sliced
Salt
1 cup chopped country ham
2 teaspoons finely chopped
    scallions
2 tablespoons applejack

2 tablespoons chopped fresh basil
Freshly ground pepper
1 cup soft, fresh bread crumbs
1 cup grated cheddar cheese
⅓ cup heavy cream
Finely chopped parsley

Layer the bottom of a buttered pie pan with sliced tomatoes that have been salted. Add a layer of chopped ham and the scallions. Sprinkle with 1 tablespoon of applejack, a little chopped basil, and a few turns of the pepper grinder. Sprinkle with bread crumbs and cheese. Repeat the layers, topping with cheese. Bake at 300 degrees for 30 minutes. Pour the cream over all and sprinkle with a little chopped parsley. Bake 15 minutes more.
SERVES 4

Turnip and Pork Pie

Jacques Cartier, the French navigator who discovered the St. Lawrence River in 1536, brought the turnip to the New World five years later and they were soon one of the commonest of American garden plants. French-American cooks have perked up Yankee meat pies by playing the flavors of turnips and pork against each other in this version of a *tourtière*, which in our version uses only a top crust accented by cornmeal to make a somewhat lighter dish.

1½ pounds small white turnips
8 slices Canadian bacon, cut in
    squares
1½ pounds pork with some fat,
    diced
2 medium onions, chopped
2 fat garlic cloves, chopped fine
½ cup diced celery

2 tablespoons flour
2 cups boiling chicken broth
Salt
Freshly ground pepper
1 tablespoon chopped fresh chervil
    or savory, or 1 teaspoon dried
¼ teaspoon mace
2 bay leaves

CORNMEAL PIE CRUST:
⅔ cup four
⅓ cup cornmeal
¼ teaspoon salt

4 tablespoons lard or vegetable
    shortening
3 tablespoons ice water

Peel the turnips and cut them into ½-inch cubes. Put the bacon and the pork in a skillet over low heat and cook long enough to melt the fat, then stir in the onions, garlic, and celery, and cook for 3 minutes. Stir in the turnips, sprinkle the flour evenly over them, and work the flour into the pork and vegetables. Gradually add the hot broth and stir until the sauce thickens. Season lightly with salt and pepper and the remaining seasonings. Cover and simmer for 30 minutes. Remove the bay leaves and turn the stew into a shallow casserole, placing a ½-cup metal measuring cup, open side down, in the center to catch the juices.

Make the pie crust: Toss the flour, cornmeal, and salt together, then cut in the lard or vegetable shortening and blend until the mixture resembles coarse bread crumbs. Stir in the water gradually, and mix. Gather the dough together and on a lightly floured work surface roll out into a circle about ½ inch larger in circumference than your baking dish. Drape the dough over the top of the dish, crimp the edges, and make several slashes in the top. Bake in a preheated 400-degree oven for 20 minutes.
SERVES 6

Chances are that the parsnips available in many New England stores come from Bowdoinham, Maine, where Harry Prout became known when still a young farmer as the "Parsnip Prince"—because his "Merrymeeting Gardens" could produce as much as 360,000 pounds of fragrant parsnips annually.

Parsnip Pie with Peas and Onions

1 pound parsnips, scraped and cut
   in small chunks
½ pound potatoes, cut in quarters
   with skins left on
¾ pound fresh peas
2 tablespoons cornstarch
1 cup light cream or whole milk
4 tablespoons finely chopped onion
Fresh grated nutmeg

Salt
Freshly ground pepper
⅓ cup grated New England
   cheddar cheese
1 prebaked 9-inch pie shell (see
   Basic Pie Dough, page 564)

In a large saucepan, cover the parsnips and potatoes with water, bring to a boil, and cook 15–20 minutes, until just tender. Pour off 1 cup of the cooking water and reserve. Drain the vegetables, and skin the potatoes when cool, cutting them into smaller pieces. Meanwhile, cook the peas just long enough to make them tender; do not overcook. Blend the cornstarch with the cream or milk and put the mixture in a pan with the reserved cup of cooking liquid. Add the onion, plenty of nutmeg, a little salt and pepper, and stir until a thickish sauce forms. Stir in the parsnips, potatoes, and peas, and taste for seasoning. Pour the sauce and vegetables into the prebaked 9-inch pie shell and sprinkle the top with the grated cheddar. Brown the pie in a preheated 450-degree oven for about 10 minutes.
SERVES 6

Tourtière de Violette LeCours

2½–3 pounds lean pork, ground
1 cup water
½ cup finely chopped onions
1 teaspoon cinnamon

¼ teaspoon ground cloves
Salt to taste
Freshly ground pepper to taste

CRUST:
¾ cup lard
2½ cups flour

½ teaspoon salt
7–8 tablespoons water

On the day before baking, brown the meat in a large skillet, stirring with a fork, while slowly adding the water and onions. Cook about 1 hour, until moist but not watery. Add seasonings and refrigerate overnight.

To make the crust: Cut the lard into the flour (Mrs. LeCours says to use a silver knife), add the salt, then work in the water with your fingers to make a smooth dough. Divide dough into two parts. Roll out one part and line a 9-inch pie pan. Fill with the refrigerated pork. Cover with remaining dough, making a vent for the release of steam. Bake at 450 degrees for about 45 minutes, until the crust begins to turn golden.
SERVES 8

Christmas Goose Pie

Not long ago on a Christmas day at Bryn Teg, when we were snowed in, this dish was made with ingredients at hand. We'd had a roast stuffed goose (see Roast Goose, page 182) on Christmas Eve, and there was enough meat left to make another festive dish.

⅛ ounce dried mushrooms
2 cups hot water
One 8-inch lard crust (see Basic Pie Crust, page 564)
6–8 small white onions, boiled or braised
6–8 braised chestnuts (page 171)
About 3 cups goose meat from the bones, cut in small pieces

3 tablespoons goose fat or butter
3 tablespoons flour
1½ cups goose broth or leftover gravy, or combination
Salt
Freshly ground pepper
2 tablespoons dry sherry
1 teaspoon chopped fresh rosemary, or ½ teaspoon dried

Cover the mushrooms with the hot water and let soak for 30 minutes. Meanwhile, prepare the pie dough and refrigerate it.

Arrange the onions, chestnuts, and goose meat in the bottom of a casserole (about 1½ quarts) with a cup in the center open side down. Heat the fat in a saucepan, stir in the flour, and cook over low heat for a minute or two. Pour in the goose broth and return to the heat, stirring until thickened. Add the mushrooms and their soaking liquid to the sauce, season with salt and pepper, sherry, and rosemary, and cook down, stirring, until smooth and about as thick as heavy cream. Sprinkle a little salt and pepper on the ingredients in the casserole and pour the sauce over. Roll the pie dough out to a circle 1 inch larger than the casserole, then drape the dough over the top. Crimp the edges and make several slashes in the top of the dough. Bake in a preheated 400-degree oven for 25–30 minutes, until lightly browned on top. Remove the cup after you cut into the dough for the first serving (the cup will then release most of the sauce that it has drawn in). SERVES 3–4

Miners, like the Welsh quarrymen who settled in Vermont's western slate towns, are addicted to the handy, succulent meat pies known as pasties. Various meat and vegetable combinations are used in pasty recipes. In Landgrove, Vermont, one variation calls for lining the cups in a muffin pan with pastry to contain a filling of corned beef, onion, and cooked tomatoes. Each cup-shaped pastry is covered with a pastry top, like an ordinary-size pie.

Slate Quarry Pasties

WHOLE WHEAT DOUGH:
½ cup whole wheat flour
½ cup white flour
1 teaspoon salt

6 tablespoons cold butter
3 tablespoons ice water

MEAT FILLING:
1 pound round steak, cut in ¼-inch cubes
1 onion, chopped
1½ tablespoons flour
1 tablespoon finely chopped celery leaves
1 tablespoon finely chopped parsley

1 tablespoon finely chopped summer savory, or 1 teaspoon dried
1 teaspoon salt
Freshly ground pepper
1 tablespoon butter, melted

To make whole wheat dough: In a large mixing bowl blend the flours and salt, then work in the cold butter, using your finger tips or a pastry cutter, until the mixture resembles meal. Blend in the ice water and form the dough into a ball. Flatten the dough, cut, fold in half, and push it out with the heel of your hand. Repeat 3 times. Reform the dough into a ball, dust it with flour and wrap it in wax paper; chill 30 minutes.

To make meat filling: In a large bowl, mix the steak cubes and the chopped onion and sprinkle with flour. Stir in the celery leaves, parsley, and savory, and sprinkle the mixture with salt and pepper. Divide the chilled dough in 6 equal parts, and, on a lightly floured surface, roll each piece into a thin round about 10 inches in diameter. Spoon the filling in equal amounts onto one half of each round, leaving a ½-inch margin around the edges. Moisten the edges and pull the unfilled half over the filling to cover it neatly. Seal the edges together by pressing them with the tines of a fork. Slash the top surface of the dough to allow steam to escape. Butter a large baking sheet and arrange the pasties on it. Bake in a preheated 375-degree oven for 45 minutes, until the pasties are golden brown. Remove from the oven and immediately brush the pasties with melted butter.

MAKES 6 PASTIES

YEAST BREADS, QUICK BREADS, and MUFFINS

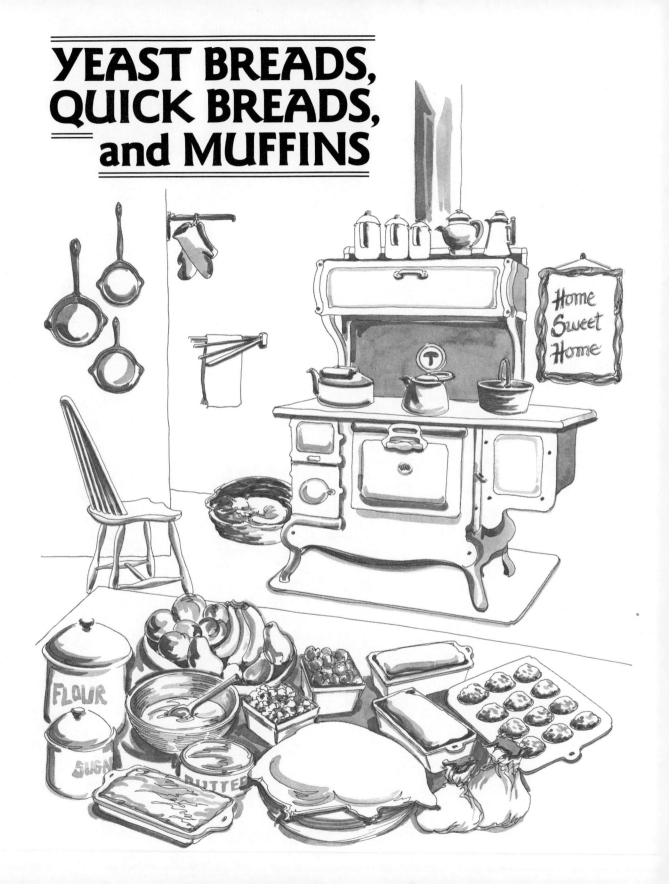

T WICE A WEEK, in the afternoons," a Berkshire visitor said in a letter home, "Clara's aunt dons a long starched apron—lace trimmed, if you please—and with her mending sits in the kitchen to watch the bread rise. She actually appears to enjoy it. . . ."

A couple of generations later, there is a return to the appreciation of homemade bread throughout the Northeast. Men and women in considerable numbers recognize the mystical satisfaction to be found in kneading and shaping and baking your own aromatic loaves. And the variety of breads that can be created seems almost limitless. The ethnic influences that changed the old Yankee culinary style generally also changed the kinds of bread coming out of ovens, whether modern or traditional in their capacities; everyone began to like the variety of breads available.

Throughout the region, the renewed interest in bread was reflected in the proliferation of fledgling shops, started by young escapees from big-city lives, that changed the kind of baking offered in restaurants and made it possible for cooks who didn't produce their own to buy long, crusty French and Italian loaves, Middle Eastern "pocket breads," crescent twists, and airy brioche, not to mention bagels. And the number of home bakers finding pleasure in using the oven to create grew far larger, in the 1980s, than it had ever been. Young New England cooks can produce anything—from pepperoni bread to corn tortillas for their own versions of tacos, a formidable exhibit among the evidence of changing baking styles.

However, we're neither wiser nor more inventive about the uses of bread than we were in the past—we're simply different. In grandmother's day, quick meals were often "invented," morning, noon, and at the end of the day. In the Connecticut Valley hill country, Beatrice Vaughan recalled, "Jonnycake was not only a bread but was often also used as the heartier part of a meal—with dried beef or salt-pork gravy spooned over a hot square; or split and buttered, with a fried egg and a strip of bacon laid between the halves, or sometimes the yellow corn bread was just crumbled into a bowl of milk for Sunday night supper." (See page 377 for Jonny-cakes.)

Contemporary cooks may be equally resourceful when it comes to stretches of imagination through which they adorn the fillings for home baked pizzas, or the stuffings worked into croissants. The times call for muffins studded with berries of the season, or for elegant crêpes of cornmeal wrapped around creamy fillings of chicken or fish. Baking on top of the stove or in the oven is no less fascinating than it was for Clara's aunt. Bread comes in many guises, more than ever before, for the Yankee cook.

No-Knead Brook Farm Bread

Long before communal living became a Yankee commonplace in the twentieth century, Brook Farm at West Roxbury, south of Boston, was a haven from 1840 to 1846 for philosophic probing that attracted Ralph Waldo Emerson, Nathaniel Hawthorne, and others. One of them was a Mrs. Butterfield, who shared her recipe for no-knead loaves with another proper Bostonian family in whose archives it was preserved.

2 cups hot water
2 teaspoons salt
¼ cup butter or lard, plus
    additional butter for glazing
2½ tablespoons molasses

1 package active dry yeast
3 tablespoons warm water
7½ cups all-purpose or unbleached
    flour

Put the hot water in a large mixing bowl and stir in the salt, butter or lard, and molasses, stirring until the fat has melted. In a small bowl, dissolve the yeast in the 3 tablespoons warm water and let stand a few minutes, then stir into the large bowl, making sure that the water in it has cooled to lukewarm. Add the flour and beat until smooth (you should really beat for a whole minute). Cover the bowl with a towel or plastic wrap and let the dough rise in a warm place until tripled in volume.

Now turn the dough out onto a lightly floured work surface. Do not knead, but using lightly floured hands, handle the dough quickly and lightly to divide it in half. Shape each half into a loaf and place them in greased 9-inch bread pans. Cover and let rise in a warm place until the dough is well above the tops of the pans. Brush the risen loaves with melted butter and bake in a preheated 375-degree oven for 45 minutes. Remove from the pans and cool on racks before slicing.

MAKES TWO 9-INCH LOAVES

Braided Buttermilk Bread

6 tablespoons butter or shortening
1½ cups buttermilk
2 tablespoons (2 packages) active
    dry yeast
½ cup warm water

2 tablespoons sugar
2 teaspoons salt
3 eggs
6–7 cups flour, preferably
    unbleached

Heat the butter or shortening in the buttermilk until melted. Let cool enough so that you can hold your finger comfortably in it. Dissolve the yeast in the warm water in a large mixing bowl. When dissolved add the cooled buttermilk and beat in the sugar, salt, and the eggs, but as you crack the last egg into the bowl, reserve half the yolk in a cup for glazing the loaves later. Now stir in about 5–6 cups of the flour until you have a fairly stiff dough. Turn the dough out onto a floured working surface and let rest while you clean out the bowl.

Knead the dough for about 5–8 minutes, until it is smooth and elastic, adding more flour as necessary to keep it from sticking. Butter the cleaned bowl and return dough to it, turning to coat. Cover with plastic wrap and let rise until double in volume, about an hour.

Turn the dough out onto your floured work surface and punch down thoroughly. Divide the dough into three equal parts, then divide each third into 3 parts and roll these out into strands about 12 inches long. Pinch the ends of 3 of the rolls together, and braid strands, pinching the other end of the braid together and tucking the ends under. Either place in a greased 8-inch bread pan, or if you wish a more crusted loaf, place free standing on a greased baking sheet. Repeat the process two more times. Cover lightly with a towel and let stand until double in volume. Add an equal amount of water to the reserved egg yolk and mix until blended. Paint the loaves with this glaze and bake them in a preheated 375-degree oven for 45 minutes. Remove and cool on racks.

MAKES 3 LOAVES

Potato Pumpernickel Bread

1½ tablespoons active dry yeast
2 cups lukewarm potato water *
1 tablespoon salt
1¼ cups mashed potatoes
1½ cups pumpernickel or rye flour

1½ cups whole wheat flour
½ cup yellow cornmeal
2 tablespoons caraway seeds
About 2½ cups unbleached flour

GLAZE:
1 egg yolk beaten with 1 teaspoon water

* Potato water is simply water in which potatoes were boiled.

Put the yeast in a large bowl and pour the lukewarm potato water over it. When the yeast has dissolved, beat in the salt, mashed potatoes, pumpernickel and whole wheat flours, cornmeal, caraway seeds, and a little of the white flour—just enough to make a fairly stiff dough that begins to leave the sides of the bowl. Turn the dough out onto a floured work surface and let rest while you clean out the bowl. Knead the dough for 10 minutes, adding more of the white flour as necessary to keep it from sticking; it will absorb a good deal of the flour. Lightly butter or oil the clean bowl and return the dough to it, turning to coat all over. Cover with plastic wrap and let stand at room temperature until the dough doubles in volume, about 1–1½ hours.

Turn the dough out on a floured surface. Punch it all over and knead in more of the remaining white flour until dough is no longer sticky. Return the dough to the bowl, cover again, and let rise until doubled in volume, about 45 minutes to 1 hour. Turn the dough out again onto a floured surface and punch all over. Now grease your pans—either two 8-inch loaf pans or 7- to 8-inch shallow casseroles (cake pans will do), or one of each. Divide the dough in half and shape each half to fit the pans you are using. For the round loaves, form balls a few inches smaller than the round pans you are using; the dough will spread. Place in the pans and cover lightly with a towel. Let rise again until doubled in volume—about 35–45 minutes.

Paint the tops of the loaves with the egg glaze and, using a sharp knife or razor blade, slash each loaf three times across the top. Bake in a preheated 350-degree oven—1 hour for the pan loaves, 1 hour and 10 minutes for the round loaves. Turn out and cool on racks.
MAKES 2 ROUND LOAVES (ABOUT 7 TO 8 INCHES IN DIAMETER) OR TWO 8-INCH LOAVES OR ONE OF EACH

Note: Pumpernickel flour is coarsely ground, unsifted dark rye flour including the husk; it is not easy to find, although some mail-order places that specialize in flours carry it. If not obtainable, simply use dark rye flour (or whatever rye flour you can get) and substitute ¾ cup bran flakes for ¾ cup whole wheat flour called for. Or, even better, if you have an electric coffee grinder, grind about ½ cup of either rye berries or wheat berries to a coarse texture and substitute this home-milled flour for an equivalent amount of the rye or whole wheat flours called for here. Of course, if you have your own flour mill that grinds to a fairly coarse texture, you can prepare all the whole grain flours called for in this recipe this way.

Sourdough Rye

Vermont's Bread and Puppet Theater is internationally famous, and a high-light of the annual pageant in the Northeast Kingdom is the bread, baked in an outdoor oven, that is engraved with an ancient symbol of the sun and served to all comers with garlic mayonnaise.

STARTER:
3 cups dark rye flour
3 cups warm water

1 teaspoon active dry yeast
   (optional)

DOUGH:
1 package (1 tablespoon) active dry
   yeast
⅔ cup warm water
1 tablespoon salt

2 cups dark rye flour
3½–4 cups all-purpose or
   unbleached flour
Cornmeal

GLAZE:
1 egg white beaten with 1 teaspoon
   water

For the starter: In a bowl or 1½- to 2-quart glass jar, mix 3 cups rye flour with the 3 cups warm water to blend. Cover with cheesecloth and place in a larger bowl of warm water and set in a warm place (on the top of the stove with a pilot light is a good idea; don't put it in a closed oven). If bubbles have not started to appear after 24 hours, stir in the optional teaspoon of yeast. Leave for another day or two.

For the dough: In a large bowl, mix the tablespoon of yeast with the ⅔ cup warm water and let stand until dissolved. Stir in 2½ cups of the starter, the salt, the 2 cups dark rye flour, and as much of the white flour as can be absorbed to make a fairly stiff dough. Turn the dough out onto a floured work surface and let rest while you clean out the bowl. Knead the dough for 10 minutes, adding more flour as necessary; you will find that it absorbs quite a lot. Grease the clean bowl lightly, return the dough to it, cover with plastic wrap, and let stand at room temperature until the dough doubles in volume, about 2½ or more hours.

Turn the dough out onto a floured work surface, work in a little more flour if it seems tacky, and divide in half. Shape each half into an oval about 8 inches long. Sprinkle a baking sheet with cornmeal and place the 2 loaves, far apart, on the sheet. Cover lightly with a towel and let rise until doubled in volume—about 1 hour.

Just before baking, paint the loaves with the egg white glaze and, with a sharp knife, carve the sun symbol on top of each—a circle with rays extending. Bake in a preheated 400-degree oven for 10 minutes, then turn the heat down to 350 degrees and bake another 40 minutes. Remove and cool on racks. Freeze the second loaf when cooled if you're not going to be eating it soon; this bread dries out more quickly than most. Wrap well in plastic wrap for storage.

MAKES 2 OVAL LOAVES ABOUT 8 INCHES LONG.

Note: Refrigerate the remaining starter in a tightly closed jar. To keep the starter alive, feed it every 5 days by mixing in another ½ cup rye flour and ½ cup warm water; then leave in a warm place overnight to ferment. Return it to the refrigerator until you use it or feed it again.

VARIATION: For the traditional "Bread and Puppet" loaves, use no yeast when mixing the dough (you rely completely on the starter for leavening) and use all rye flour. If you mill your own flour and grind to a coarse texture, the bread will be more authentic, or grind half the total amount of rye flour you'll be using in a coffee grinder to get that chewy coarse texture. You will probably use almost 1 additional cup of flour, as rye tends to remain moist. If you find you like this chewy, rather crude bread and want to make it often, reserve about one-fourth of the dough and set aside to incorporate into the next batch when you make the bread again; the bread will develop more and more wonderful sour flavor. Put the reserved dough —known in French as the *levain*—in a plastic container and refrigerate or freeze if you won't be using it for a new batch within 10 days. Try serving the bread with garlic mayonnaise.

Three-Grain Bread

1 package (1 tablespoon) active dry yeast
3¼ cups warm water
½ cup honey
½ cup nonfat dry milk
2 teaspoons salt
½ cup buckwheat flour
½ cup cornmeal
¾ cup bran
½ cup safflower oil
3 cups whole wheat flour
3–4 cups unbleached all-purpose or bread flour

In a large bowl dissolve the yeast in ¼ cup of the warm water. After a minute or so stir in the remaining water, the honey, dry milk, salt, the buckwheat flour, cornmeal, bran, oil, whole wheat flour, and enough of the white flour to make a stiff dough. Turn out onto a floured work surface and let rest while you clean out the bowl. Now knead the dough, adding more flour as necessary to keep it from sticking, until it is smooth and resilient—about 5–8 minutes. Grease the clean bowl lightly and place the dough in it, turning to coat. Cover with plastic wrap and let rise until doubled in volume, about 1½ hours.

Turn the risen dough out, punch down thoroughly all over, and divide in half. Form 2 loaves and place them in 2 greased 8-inch bread pans. Cover lightly with a towel and let rise until almost doubled, about 30–40 minutes. Bake in a preheated 400-degree oven for 10 minutes, then lower the heat to 350 degress and continue baking for 40 minutes. Turn out on racks to cool.

MAKES TWO 8-INCH LOAVES

Poppy Seed Bread

Poppy seed bread seems to have become the rage of the 1980s, but what you get is invariably the sweet cakelike quick bread, not something to be eaten with a good meal. This yeast bread, made with poppy seeds, is much more to our liking as a bread to accompany savory dishes.

1 package (1 tablespoon) active dry
  yeast
2¼ cups warm water
2 tablespoons soft butter
2 tablespoons honey

1 teaspoon salt
1 egg
6–6½ cups unbleached all-purpose
  or bread flour
About 1 cup poppy seeds

GLAZE:
1 egg yolk beaten with 1 teaspoon water

In a large bowl, dissolve the yeast in ¼ cup of the warm water. After a minute, stir in the remaining water, the soft butter, honey, salt, egg, and enough of the white flour to make a stiff dough. Turn the dough out onto a floured work surface and let it rest while you wash out the bowl. Knead the dough, adding more flour as necessary to keep it from sticking, until it is smooth and elastic, about 6–8 minutes. Grease the clean bowl and put the dough into it, turning to coat. Cover with plastic wrap and let rise until the dough is doubled in volume, 1–1½ hours.

Turn the dough out onto the floured surface, punch it down all over and flatten it, then sprinkle some of the poppy seeds over, fold the dough, sprinkle more on, and repeat, until you have used up all but 1 tablespoon of the seeds and distributed the poppy seeds evenly through the bread. Divide the dough in half and form 2 loaves. Place them in 2 greased 9-inch bread pans (8-inch will do but you will get a very high loaf, which some people like), and let rise until almost doubled in volume, about 30 minutes. Paint the tops of the loaves with the glaze and sprinkle on the remaining poppy seeds. Bake in a preheated 350-degree oven for 45 minutes. Turn out on racks to cool.

MAKES TWO 9-INCH LOAVES

Pepperoni Bread

1 tablespoon active dry yeast
1 tablespoon granulated sugar
1¾ cups warm water
About 3½ cups unbleached all-
    purpose flour

7 ounces pepperoni
3 tablespoons olive oil
1 teaspoon salt

Put the yeast and sugar in a large bowl and add 1 cup of the warm water. Let stand until dissolved. Beat in 1 cup of the flour, then cover the bowl with plastic wrap and let sit for anywhere from 1 to 3 or 4 hours. This is the sponge and it will foam up, then settle down.

Meanwhile, chop the pepperoni into fine dice or shreds (a food processor does a good job if you process quickly, turning on and off). Heat the olive oil in a skillet and add the finely chopped pepperoni. Sauté over low heat a few minutes, then let cool. Add the remaining ¾ cup warm water to the sponge and stir in the salt, the cooled pepperoni and oil, and as much of the remaining white flour as the dough will absorb easily. Because you want a soft dough, you should now knead it with a dough hook for about 1 minute or scrape it into a food processor and process for about half a minute; otherwise beat the dough about 100 strokes with a wooden spoon. Cover the bowl with plastic wrap and let rise until doubled in volume, about 1½ hours. Turn the dough out onto a floured work surface and divide it into 3 equal pieces. Roll each piece out very lightly to about 12 inches, using only your well-floured hands. Then pick up the rope, twist it five or six times quickly, form it into a circle—pinching the ends together—and place on a greased baking sheet. Repeat with the other pieces. The dough should have a rough-hewn, uneven look, and you should widen the hole once each piece is on the baking sheet so that the center doesn't close up completely. Let rise, uncovered, for 20 minutes.

Bake the loaves in a preheated 400-degree oven for 40 minutes. Cool on racks but serve the bread warm. What you don't eat right away, freeze, wrapped in foil, and reheat in the foil.

MAKES 3 ROUND LOAVES

Banana-Maple-Sesame Bread

1 package (1 tablespoon) active dry
    yeast
1 cup warm water
2 very ripe bananas, mashed
⅓ cup maple syrup
1 teaspoon salt

2 tablespoons safflower oil
2½ cups whole wheat flour
About 3 cups unbleached all-
    purpose or bread flour
3 tablespoons sesame seeds

In a large bowl dissolve the yeast in ¼ cup of the warm water. After a minute, add the remaining water, the mashed bananas, maple syrup, salt, oil, whole wheat flour, and stir in enough of the white flour to make a stiff dough. Turn out onto a floured work surface and let rest while you wash the bowl. Now knead the dough, adding more flour as necessary to keep it from sticking, until it is smooth and elastic, about 8–10 minutes. Grease the clean bowl lightly and place the dough in it, turning it to coat. Cover with plastic wrap and let rise until doubled in volume, about 1½ hours.

Meanwhile, roast the sesame seeds by heating them in a small skillet, shaking the pan frequently, until they begin to turn color and smell toasted. When the dough has risen, turn it out onto the floured work surface, punch it down all over and flatten, sprinkle the sesame seeds on top, then knead long enough to distribute the seeds evenly throughout. Divide the dough in half, form into 2 loaves, and place in greased 8-inch loaf pans. Cover lightly with a towel and let rise until almost doubled in volume, about 30 minutes.

Bake in a preheated 350-degree oven for 45 minutes. Turn the bread out onto racks and let cool.

MAKES TWO 8-INCH LOAVES

Banana-Nut-Marmalade Bread

1 tablespoon (1 package) active dry yeast
2 cups warm water
1 teaspoon salt
1 cup whole wheat flour
2 ripe bananas, mashed

¼ cup orange marmalade
2 tablespoons oil
6–7 cups all-purpose flour
¾ cup finely chopped nuts
    (walnuts, almonds, or butternuts)

GLAZE:
1 tablespoon beaten egg mixed with ½ teaspoon milk

In a large bowl dissolve the yeast in ¼ cup of the warm water. When dissolved, stir in the remaining water, the salt, whole wheat flour, mashed bananas, marmalade, and oil. Stir in enough of the white flour to get a cohesive dough, then turn it out onto a lightly floured surface. Let rest a minute while you wash out the bowl.

Now knead the dough, adding more flour as necessary, for about 10 minutes, or until the dough is smooth and elastic. Grease the cleaned bowl and return the dough to it, turning to coat. Cover with plastic wrap and let rise until double in volume, about 1½–2 hours, depending on the warmth of the room.

Turn the dough out again, punch it vigorously to deflate it, cut it in half, and form 2 loaves. Place in 2 buttered and greased 8-inch long bread pans, cover lightly with a towel, and let rise again until double in volume, about 45 minutes. Bake in a preheated 375-degree oven for 45 minutes. Remove from the oven and turn the loaves out onto a rack to cool.

MAKES TWO 8-INCH LOAVES

Portuguese Sweet Bread

1 tablespoon (1 package) active dry
  yeast
3/4 cup warm water
3 tablespoons nonfat dry milk
2 eggs at room temperature, lightly
  beaten

1/2 cup sugar
1/4 teaspoon salt
About 3 1/4 cups bread flour
4 tablespoons soft butter

In a large bowl, dissolve the yeast in 1/4 cup of the water. Mix the remaining water with the dry milk, eggs, sugar, and salt. Stir into the dissolved yeast along with 1 cup of the flour. Beat in the butter 1 tablespoon at a time, adding the next after each has been incorporated. Stir in most of the remaining flour until you have a manageable dough, then turn it out onto a floured work surface. Let it rest while you clean out the bowl, then knead the dough about 8 minutes, adding more flour as necessary to keep it from sticking. When you have a smooth, elastic dough, place it in the cleaned, buttered bowl, cover it with plastic wrap, and let rise until it has tripled in volume.

Turn the dough out again onto a lightly floured work surface, punch it down thoroughly, and then form it into a round, stretching the dough and pulling it downward; pinch it together on the bottom and place in a buttered 9- or 10-inch shallow pan, cover loosely with a towel, and let rise again until doubled in volume. Bake in a preheated 350-degree oven for 45 minutes. Turn the bread out onto a rack to cool.

MAKES 1 LARGE, HIGH LOAF

Note: If you want a large, less high loaf, put it in a 12-inch pan or larger—it will be less spectacular but possibly easier to slice. You can also bake it free form, in which case the loaf will spread out more.

Christmas Mincemeat Bread

1 1/2 packages (1 1/2 tablespoons)
  active dry yeast
3/4 cup warm water
3 tablespoons honey
1 cup mincemeat
1 teaspoon salt
2 eggs

1/2 teaspoon cinnamon
1/8 teaspoon each allspice, cloves,
  and mace
4–4 1/2 cups all-purpose flour
1/2 cup chopped walnuts
Confectioners' sugar

In a large bowl, dissolve the yeast in 1/4 cup of the water, then stir in remaining water, honey, mincemeat, and salt. Beat in the eggs, spices, and enough of the flour to make a cohesive dough. Turn dough onto a floured working surface and knead 8–10 minutes, until elastic and no longer sticky, adding more flour as necessary. Clean and butter the mixing bowl and return the dough to it, turning to coat. Cover with the plastic wrap and let rise until double in volume, about 1–1½ hours.

Turn the dough out onto the floured work surface, punch it down, work in the walnuts, and shape into a roll about 15 inches long. Butter a Bundt pan liberally and fit the roll of dough in, pinching the ends together. Cover loosely and let rise for 30 minutes. Bake in a preheated 350-degree oven for 45 minutes. Turn out on a rack and dust generously with confectioners' sugar. Serve warm or slice and toast lightly.

MAKES 1 LARGE RING

Leslie Wagstaff's Coffee Cake

½ pound butter
½ cup milk
2 packages (2 tablespoons) active
  dry yeast
¼ cup warm water

3 egg yolks
2½ cups flour
¼ teaspoon salt
1 cup sugar

FILLING:
3 egg whites
1 cup sugar
½ cup brown sugar

½ cup raisins
½ cup chopped nuts
2 teaspoons cinnamon

Heat the butter and milk together until the butter is melted. Cool slightly. In a large bowl, dissolve the yeast in the warm water and let stand a few minutes, then beat in the egg yolks. Stir in the flour, salt, and sugar, along with the butter and milk. The dough will be soft. Cover with plastic wrap and refrigerate until the dough has doubled in volume, several hours.

Just before the dough is ready, make a meringue by beating the egg whites until they form soft peaks, then adding the 1 cup sugar and continuing to beat until very thick.

Turn the dough out onto a floured work surface and divide in half. Roll each half out into a rectangle about 14 inches long and 6 inches wide. Spread each piece with half of the meringue, then sprinkle on half the brown sugar, raisins, nuts, and cinnamon. Roll the pieces of dough up over the filling as you would a jelly roll and seal the edges. Fit one of the rolls into a buttered 9-inch tube pan, pinching the edges together where the ends meet, then place the second ring of dough on top. Bake in a preheated 350-degree oven for 1 hour, rotating the pan halfway through the baking; if the top seems to be browning too much, place foil loosely over it. When done, unmold and cool on a rack (may be reheated).

MAKES 1 HIGH 9-INCH RING TO SERVE 12

Bessie Blake's Sweet Rolls

Having marked with her husband, Clarence, their sixty-fourth wedding anniversary, Mrs. Blake was still baking cookies and other good things for her great-grandchildren when she gave Connecticut cooking editor Rosemary Kielty this recipe for rolls: "Her most famed . . . wonderfully light rolls with a delicate flavor and perfect with almost any food . . ."

1 package (1 tablespoon) dry yeast,
  or 1 cake compressed
¼ cup lukewarm water
1 cup milk
¾ cup butter or margarine

½ cup sugar
2 teaspooons salt
3 eggs
5–5¼ cups King Arthur flour
Soft butter for glazing

Soften the yeast in the lukewarm water. Scald the milk and let it cool to lukewarm. Cream the butter or margarine with the sugar, add the salt and whole eggs, and beat until the mixture is light and fluffy. Add the yeast mixture and the lukewarm milk, then stir in about 4¾ cups of the flour. (At this point, according to Mrs. Blake, use only this amount of the flour and spread ¼ cup onto the work surface to be kneaded into the dough.) When the flour is thoroughly mixed with the liquid ingredients, turn dough out of the bowl and knead, adding more flour as necessary, until it is satiny but not stiff and does not stick to the surface. Put the dough in a greased bowl and grease the top of the dough, then set it in a warm place, covered, to double in bulk, usually about 1½ hours.

Turn the dough out on a floured surface, knead a few times, and break off pieces to make round rolls, cloverleaf shapes, or crescents (see Pumpkin Rolls, page 481, for shaping). Put the rolls in greased pans, cover, and let rise in a warm place until double in volume. Bake in a preheated 400-degree oven for 15 minutes. Spread the tops with butter as you take them from the oven.

MAKES ABOUT 42 SMALL ROLLS

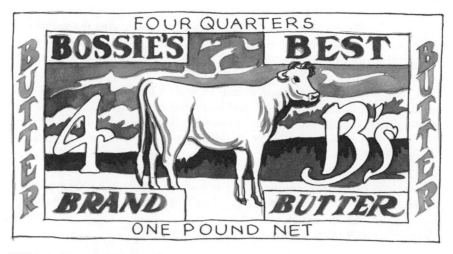

1 package (1 tablespoon) active dry
   yeast
¼ cup warm water
3 tablespoons honey
2 eggs, at room temperature
1¼ cups cooked puréed pumpkin
   or winter squash, or one 12-
   ounce package frozen, thawed

1 teaspoon salt
¼ cup sunflower meal (optional) *
2 tablespoons melted unsalted
   butter
4–4½ cups unbleached all-purpose
   flour

Pumpkin or Squash Rolls

GLAZE:
1 egg beaten with 1 teaspoon water

TOPPING:
sunflower seeds (optional)

   * Spin sunflower seeds in a blender or coffee grinder to make the meal.

Put the yeast in a large bowl and pour the warm water over it. Stir in the honey and let stand until yeast is dissolved. Beat the eggs, one at a time, into the yeast-honey mixture, then stir in the puréed pumpkin or squash, salt, sunflower meal, if available (if not, just use an extra ¼ cup flour), the melted butter, and enough flour to make a cohesive dough that starts to leave the sides of the bowl (you'll use only about 3 or so cups of the flour at this stage).

Turn the dough out onto a floured work surface and let rest while you clean out the bowl. Now knead the dough, adding more flour as necessary to keep from sticking; it will absorb almost another whole cup of flour as you knead for a good 10 minutes. Grease the clean bowl and return the dough to it. Cover with plastic wrap and let rise at room temperature until doubled in volume, about 1½ hours.

Turn the dough out onto a large floured work surface and punch down all over. To shape simple round rolls, tear off pieces of dough about the size of golf balls. Flatten slightly; then, using your cupped, lightly floured hands, ease the edges of the dough under, at the same time plumping up the ball of dough, taking care that you stretch the gluten cloak, not break it. Pinch together the dough where it meets on the bottom. *For soft rolls,* place side by side in 3 buttered 8-inch cake tins so that they just touch. *For crisper rolls,* set 1 inch apart on greased baking sheets. *For cloverleaf rolls,* tear off three marble-size pieces of dough, roll into balls, and place together snugly in the bottom of a greased muffin cup.

For Parker House rolls, tear off pieces of dough the size of golf balls, flatten each, make a crease down the middle with a floured spatula or chopstick, brush with melted butter, and fold one half over the other to make a half moon. If you like, sprinkle with about ½ teaspoon chopped sunflower seeds before folding. Press the edges together securely. Place 1½ inches apart on greased baking sheets.

For rolled crescents, pat a portion of the dough into a circle about 7 inches in diameter. Cut 12 even wedges (as though cutting a pie), brush each with melted butter, then roll up, starting at the base of the triangle and rolling toward the point. If you like, sprinkle first with ½ teaspoon or so of chopped sunflower seeds. Place 1½ inches apart on greased baking sheets.

Cover the rolls, whatever shape, with a towel and let rise until doubled in volume, about 45 minutes. Just before baking, paint the tops of the rolls with egg glaze. Slash some if you want with a cross or a curve and sprinkle chopped sunflower seeds on top. Bake in a preheated 400-degree oven about 18 minutes for rolls baking on a sheet, and about 20 minutes for rolls in a pan or muffin tin. Remove and let crisper rolls rest on racks a few minutes, but serve warm. They may be reheated, of course.

MAKES ABOUT 32 ROLLS

Potato Buns

3 smallish potatoes
2 tablespoons (2 packages) active
   dry yeast
¾ cup buttermilk
2 eggs

2 tablespoons melted butter or
   vegetable oil
1 teaspoon salt
About 4½ cups bread flour
Melted butter for glazing

Boil the potatoes in water to cover until they are tender. Drain, saving the potato water. Put the potatoes through a ricer (you should have about 1½ cups). Put ⅓ cup of the potato water in a large bowl and when it has cooled to lukewarm, sprinkle the yeast over it. Stir and let stand to dissolve. Add the cooled riced potatoes, buttermilk, eggs, butter or oil, and salt, and mix well. Stir the flour in, a cup at a time, and when you have a manageable dough, turn it out on a floured work surface, and knead until it is smooth and elastic, adding more flour as necessary, about 5 minutes. Place the dough in the cleaned, greased bowl, and cover with plastic wrap. Let rise until the dough has tripled in volume, about 2 hours.

Punch the dough down and roll out on a floured surface to about ½-inch thickness. Cut into circles with a 2-inch round cookie cutter and place on greased baking sheets 1½ inches apart. Cover lightly with a towel and let rise until doubled in volume and light to the touch, about 50 minutes. Bake in a preheated 400-degree oven for 15–20 minutes until the tops are lightly browned. Remove from the oven, brush the tops with melted butter, and serve warm.

MAKES ABOUT 18 ROLLS

Back in the 1930s a resident of Wethersfield, Connecticut, found a hot cross bun recipe in an old hand-written cookbook that had been noted by her grandmother as "Goes good at church suppers." On a spring day in the 1980s we came across the news of a baked goods sale in the *Ellsworth* (Maine) *American*. "An innovation this year," we read, "among the usual baked goods was an old-fashioned hot cross bun, which is going to be a standard Easter item at sales in the future." The hot cross bun seemed to these regional cooks to have come full circle. The recipe below is a good one for the Easter holidays anywhere.

Hot Cross Buns

1 cup milk
2 tablespoons (2 packages) active
　dry yeast
¼ cup warm water
1 teaspoon salt
3 tablespoons light brown sugar
1 teaspoon cinnamon
¾ teaspoon freshly grated nutmeg
¼ teaspoon allspice

¼ teaspoon ground cloves
¼ cup chopped candied orange or
　citron (optional)
2 eggs
3½ cups unbleached all-purpose
　flour
2 tablespoons softened unsalted
　butter
½ cup dried currants

GLAZE:
½ cup confectioners' sugar mixed with 2 tablespoons warm milk

Scald the milk and let cool to lukewarm. Place the yeast in a large bowl and pour warm water over it. Let stand until yeast is dissolved. Stir the cooled milk, salt, brown sugar, spices, and orange or citron peel into the yeast-milk mixture, then beat in the eggs, one at a time. Now stir in enough of the flour to make a soft dough. Beat in the butter and continue to beat for a full minute. Cover the bowl with plastic wrap and let rise until the dough doubles in volume, about 2 hours. Turn the dough out onto a floured work surface and knead briefly, working in the currants as you do so. Lightly roll the dough out under your hands into a cylinder, and with a knife, cut off 18 even-size pieces. Shape these into buns by rounding them with two cupped hands, tucking under the sides, and pinching the seams at the bottom. Place them on greased baking sheets 2 inches apart. Cover the buns lightly with wax paper and let them rise in a warm place until double their size, about 30 minutes. When ready to bake, slash a cross in each bun, first one way, then the other, with a very sharp knife or a razor blade. Bake immediately in a preheated 425-degree oven for 12 to 15 minutes, until golden on top.

　Remove buns and cool slightly on racks before applying glaze. Dip a chopstick or the handle end of a wooden spoon into the mixture of confectioners' sugar and milk and drizzle a little over the buns, following the line of the crosses, which will have opened up somewhat during baking. Serve warm.

MAKES 18 BUNS.

Maple Sticky Buns

1 package (1 tablespoon) active dry yeast
1/4 cup warm water
1 1/4 cups warm milk or water mixed with 1/4 cup nonfat dry milk

1/4 teaspoon salt
3/4 cup sugar
1/4 cup (1/2 stick) melted shortening or butter
About 4 1/2 cups flour

FILLING:
1/4 cup (1/2 stick) soft butter
3/4 brown sugar or maple sugar
1/2 teaspoon cinnamon (use only with brown sugar)

1/2 cup raisins
1/3 cup chopped pecans

GLAZE:
3 tablespoons soft butter
3/4 cup maple syrup

9 tablespoons pecans, broken up

In a large bowl, dissolve the yeast in the warm water. Add the warm milk, salt, sugar, and melted shortening or butter. Stir in the flour, a cup at a time, beating thoroughly. Cover with plastic wrap and let rise in a warm place for 1 hour or more, until the dough doubles in volume.

Turn the dough out onto a floured work surface and roll it out 1/4-inch thick into a rectangle about 30 × 8 inches. Spread the soft butter over the surface, then sprinkle on the brown or maple sugar, optional cinnamon, raisins, and chopped pecans. Roll up like a jelly roll. Pinch the edges together to seal. Cut into 3 pieces, then cut each roll into 8 slices.

Spread 1 tablespoon butter over the bottom of three 8-inch cake pans. Pour 1/4 cup maple syrup into each, swirl it around to cover the bottom, then scatter 3 tablespoons broken pecans over. Arrange 8 slices of the filled dough in each pan, cut-side down, and cover lightly with towels. Let rise to double in size. Bake in a preheated 375-degree oven for 25–30 minutes, until golden. Let rest in the pans 10 minutes, then turn upside down onto plates and serve warm.
MAKES 24 BUNS

English Muffins with Raisins

1 tablespoon (1 package) active dry yeast
3/4 cup warm water
1 tablespoon brown sugar

About 2 1/4 cups all-purpose flour
1/4 teaspoon baking powder
1 teaspoon salt
1/2 cup raisins

Dissolve the yeast in 1/4 cup of the warm water along with the brown sugar. If you are using a food processor (and it is very convenient for this amount of dough), spin the flour, baking powder, and salt together, then pour the dissolved yeast and remaining water through the tube and spin until the dough starts to form a ball. Add the raisins and spin another few seconds to mix them in. Remove and knead a few turns by hand.

If preparing by hand, put the dissolved yeast and sugar and remaining water into a mixing bowl. Mix 1½ cups of the flour together with the baking powder and salt and stir into the liquid, adding a little more flour until you have a fairly stiff dough. Turn this out onto a floured board, sprinkle on the raisins, and knead about 8 minutes, adding more flour as necessary, until the dough is smooth and elastic. Put the processed or kneaded dough into a buttered bowl, cover with plastic wrap, and let rise until double in bulk, about 1–1½ hours.

Turn out onto a floured surface and punch down thoroughly. Slap the dough out into a thickness of about ½ inch, then use a cutter or an empty tuna fish can to cut rounds about 2½ inches in diameter. Heat a soapstone griddle or a heavy iron skillet until hot enough so that a drop of water sizzles and disappears. If using an iron skillet, brush with shortening (soapstone shouldn't be greased). Transfer as many of the rounds as the baking surface will accommodate without touching, and bake, turning the heat down to moderate, for 5 minutes, at which point the bottoms will be lightly browned. Turn and bake another 5 minutes. Let cool on racks. To serve, split and toast the muffins.

MAKES ABOUT 10 MUFFINS

Violette LeCours' French Twists

Violette LeCours is a French-American octogenarian and mother to a baker's dozen of sons and daughters, all of whom grew up to be educators and thrived, in the interim, on their mother's home baking. She shared this recipe with us one snowy Christmas. See page 464 for her traditional tourtière.

1 cup sour cream
2 tablespoons vegetable shortening
3 tablespoons sugar
⅛ teaspoon baking soda
1 teaspoon salt

1 tablespoon (1 package) active dry yeast
1 large egg
About 2½ cups flour

FILLING:
6 tablespoons very soft butter
½ cup dark brown sugar

½ teaspoon cinnamon

GLAZE:
½ cup confectioners' sugar
1–2 tablespoons warm milk

2 teaspoons vegetable shortening

Bring the sour cream just to a boil, stirring. Add the shortening, sugar, soda, and salt, mix well, then turn into a bowl and let cool to tepid. Add the yeast and stir until dissolved, then beat in the egg. Stir in gradually enough of the flour to make a dough that holds together. Turn out onto a floured work surface and knead about 10 turns, adding more flour as necessary. Form the dough into a ball, cover with a damp towel, and let stand 5–10 minutes.

Roll the dough out into a rectangle 6 × 18 inches. Spread the soft butter over the dough, mix the brown sugar and cinnamon together, then sprinkle that over the buttered surface. Fold the dough lengthwise to make a rectangle 3 × 18 inches. Seal the edges, using a little water to make them stick. With a sharp knife, cut 1-inch-wide strips. Line 2 jelly roll pans or cookie sheets with foil and grease well. Twist each strip twice and place the twists 1½ inches apart on the foil-lined pans. Let rise in a warm place, covered with a towel, about 1 hour, or until almost double in size. Bake in a preheated 375-degree oven for 15 minutes, or until just beginning to brown. Mix the ingredients for the glaze together and, using a decorator tube or just a toothpick, decorate the tops of the twists after they have cooled somewhat. Serve warm with fresh butter.

MAKES 18 TWISTS

Pizza Bread with Garlic and Rosemary

1 teaspoon active dry yeast
1½ cups warm water
½ teaspoon salt
¾ cup whole wheat flour, preferably coarsely ground
2½–3 cups unbleached all-purpose flour

3–4 tablespoons olive oil
1–2 garlic cloves, slivered (about 2 teaspoons)
2–3 tablespoons rosemary
About 2 teaspoons coarse salt, such as kosher
Freshly ground pepper

Put the yeast in a large bowl and pour the warm water over it. Let it stand until dissolved. Stir in the salt, whole wheat flour, and enough of the white flour to make a cohesive dough that begins to leave the sides of the bowl. Turn the dough out onto a floured work surface and let rest while you clean out the bowl. Knead the dough for a good 10 minutes, adding more flour if necessary, until it is smooth and bouncy. Oil the bowl lightly with some of the olive oil and return the dough to it. Cover with plastic wrap and let it rise until doubled in volume, about 1½–2 hours.

Turn the dough out, punch it down well, and return it to the bowl for a second rising, about 50 minutes to 1 hour. Turn the dough out again on a floured surface, punch it all over, and roll it out into a circle 14 inches in diameter. Using more of the olive oil, oil the bottom of a pizza pan that size, then drape the dough over your rolling pin and transfer it to the pizza pan. Pat out any uneven areas so that the dough fits the pan evenly. Cover tightly with a towel and let rise about 25–30 minutes, until about doubled in size and puffy. Now, using a skewer or sharp, pointed knife, prick holes about 1½ inches apart all over the surface of the dough. Insert the slivers of garlic into the holes, making sure that the slivers do not protrude above the surface of the dough. Then into each hole insert 3 or 4 twigs of rosemary. Let rise another 15 minutes. Just before baking, drizzle the remaining olive oil (about 2 tablespoons) over the surface of the dough and then rub with your fingers lightly so that the whole top of the dough is smeared with oil. Sprinkle the coarse salt evenly over all, and grind fresh pepper liberally on top. Bake in a preheated 400-degree oven for 20 minutes. Remove and let rest on a rack. Serve warm, if convenient, but it is also good cold on a picnic.

MAKES 1 FLATTISH ROUND, 14 INCHES IN DIAMETER

Cheddar Pizza

DOUGH:

1 package (1 tablespoon) active dry yeast
1¼ cups warm water
1 teaspoon salt

2 tablespoons plus 1 teaspoon olive oil
3¼–4 cups all-purpose flour

FILLING:

¾ cup tomato sauce, homemade or a good canned variety
½ teaspoon very finely chopped garlic
¼ pound mushrooms, sliced
About 8 black olives, pitted and sliced

Salt
Freshly ground pepper
1 teaspoon chopped fresh oregano, or ½ teaspoon dried
3 cups grated cheddar cheese

In a large bowl, dissolve the yeast in ¼ cup of the warm water. Let stand 5 minutes, then add the remaining water, salt, olive oil, and about 3 cups of the flour. Mix well, then turn out onto a lightly floured working surface and knead, adding more flour as necessary, until the dough is smooth and elastic—about 6–8 minutes. Wash and dry the bowl and oil it lightly. Return the dough to it, cover with plastic wrap, and let rise until doubled in volume, about 1–1½ hours.

Punch the dough down thoroughly. It is now ready to be rolled out for pizza. If you are making only one 12-inch pizza as called for below, you can make a loaf of bread with the remaining dough (following final rise and baking instructions opposite), or you can freeze the dough. To make 2 or 3 pizzas, simply double or triple the filling ingredients.

Roll out one-third of the dough with a heavy rolling pin in as large a circle as you can manage (it tends to want to retract), then pick it up and, placing it on the knuckles of your two fists, stretch it, by turning and stretching it lightly, until you have a 12-inch circle. Place this on a lightly greased pizza pan or baking sheet. Spread the bottom with the tomato sauce, leaving a ½-inch border, scatter garlic over, then the sliced mush-

Cheddar Pizza (continued)

rooms and olives. Season with salt and pepper and oregano, then scatter the grated cheese over. Bake in a preheated 450-degree oven about 12 minutes, until slightly brown at the edges and bubbly. Serve immediately.

MAKES ONE 12-INCH PIZZA

Mushrooms and Ham Pizza

8 ounces pizza dough (either of the two preceding recipes *)
Olive oil
1/4 pound mushrooms, thinly sliced
2 ounces country ham, cut in thin strips
1/2 medium red pepper, cut in thin strips

4 ounces mozzarella
Salt
1 teaspoon chopped fresh savory, or 1/2 teaspoon dried
1/8 teaspoon red pepper flakes

* If you prefer, the dough may be made with white flour only.

After the pizza dough has had its first rise, punch it down and roll and stretch it out into a circle 10–11 inches in diameter. Brush the surface all over with olive oil, then distribute the sliced mushrooms evenly on top, arrange alternate strips of ham and red pepper like the spokes of a wheel. Pull off small pieces of mozzarella, and dot the top with them. Season with salt, savory, and red pepper flakes. Drizzle a little more olive oil over the surface and bake in a preheated 450-degree oven for 12 minutes, until bubbling and lightly browned at the edges.

MAKES ONE 10–11-INCH PIZZA

Millie Owen's Tomato and Green Oregano Pizza

An inventive Vermont career woman, growing her own herbs and vegetables, created this gardener's pizza one day in haying season.

DOUGH:
1 package (1 tablespoon) dry yeast
1 cup warm water
2 cups all-purpose flour

1 cup whole wheat flour
Salt
4 tablespoons olive oil

FILLING:
4–5 ripe tomatoes, sliced
4 large mushrooms, thinly sliced
2 tablespoons chopped fresh oregano leaves

1/2 pound mozzarella cheese, sliced
1/2 cup grated Parmesan cheese

Stir the yeast into 1 cup of lukewarm water. While it is dissolving, place both kinds of flour in a large bowl, make a well in the center, and add about 1 teaspoon of salt and 1 tablespoon of the oil. Work the liquified yeast into the flour with your fingers a little at a time. When the mixture holds together, turn it out on a floured surface and knead until the dough is plastic and shiny. Form it into a ball, and place it in a well-oiled bowl, turning to coat the surface. Let rise until doubled in volume.

Punch the dough down and roll it out to the size of the pan, then lift it into the greased pan, stretching the edges with your fingers to cover. Brush it with the remaining oil and put it in a 500-degree oven for 5 minutes. Leaving on the oven heat, remove the pizza crust and cover it with tomato slices, overlapping. Arrange the mushroom slices on top (you may also add pizza meat, if desired). Sprinkle with fresh oregano, scatter with sliced mozzarella and Parmesan. Return to the oven. Bake for about 15 minutes, until cheese bubbles.

MAKES ONE LARGE PIZZA

Yankee Pita Pizza

Like other eaters-on-the-run, New Englanders are street food addicts—this is a thrifty home combination of two favorites.

2 pita or pocket breads
2–3 tablespoons oil
1½ cups chopped onions
1 cup chopped mushrooms
½ pound Polish sausage, sliced

1½ cups chopped canned tomatoes, drained
1 teaspoon oregano
2 cups grated mozzarella
1 tablespoon chopped fresh basil

Use a sharp pointed knife to separate the two layers of pita bread to make two matching rounds. Heat two tablespoons of the oil in a skillet and add the onions, the mushrooms, and sausage slices. Cook, stirring occasionally, until the onions are translucent, the mushrooms tender, and the sausage slices lightly browned. Stir in the tomatoes and oregano, and simmer about 3 minutes. Put the pita rounds on a cookie sheet, smooth side down, and spread the tomato-sausage sauce evenly over each piece. Cover the sauce with cheese and sprinklings of basil. Drizzle with about 1 tablespoon of oil. Bake at 375 degrees for 12–15 minutes.
SERVES 2

Rhubarb–Hickory Nut Bread

1 cup coarsely chopped rhubarb
1 cup sugar
1½ cups flour
1½ teaspoons baking powder
½ teaspoon baking soda
½ teaspoon salt

1 egg
2 tablespoons milk
4 tablespoons (½ stick) melted butter
½ cup coarsely chopped hickory nuts

Let the rhubarb steep in ½ cup of the sugar for 1 hour or more—even overnight—stirring once or twice. Toss the remaining sugar and all of the dry ingredients together to mix thoroughly. Beat the egg lightly and stir into it ¼ cup of the juice that the rhubarb will have exuded after steeping, as well as the milk and melted butter. Mix the dry ingredients into the wet, stirring just enough to mix. Fold in the rhubarb (if there is still more juice, drain it off) and the nuts. Scrape the batter into a buttered 8-inch loaf pan and bake in a preheated 350-degree oven for 1 hour. Let the loaf rest in the pan 10 minutes before unmolding, then cool it on a rack.
MAKES ONE 8-INCH LOAF

Records indicate that the first commercial cranberry cultivation was begun at Dennis on Cape Cod in 1816. The pumpkins were beginning to grow fast as the cranberry harvest turned red.

Cranberry-Pumpkin Corn Bread

2 cups flour
3 tablespoons baking powder
½ cup sugar
1 teaspoon salt
1 cup yellow cornmeal
½ teaspoon cinnamon

½ teaspoon allspice
⅓ cup corn oil
2 eggs
¾ cup puréed pumpkin
½ cup milk
1 cup cranberries, chopped

Sift the flour with the baking powder, sugar, salt, cornmeal, and the spices. In a bowl beat the oil with the eggs, pumpkin purée, and milk until thoroughly mixed. Add the seasoned flour to the eggs, pumpkin, and milk and stir well. Stir in the chopped cranberries, and when blended, turn it into a greased 9-inch loaf pan. Bake in a preheated 350-degree oven for about 1 hour, until a tester comes out clean. Cool the loaf on a rack for about 10 minutes before removing from the pan. Serve warm or cold.

MAKES ONE 9-INCH LOAF

Green Tomato Bread

2¾ cups all-purpose flour
1½ teaspoons baking powder
1 teaspoon baking soda
½ teaspoon salt
¾ teaspoon cinnamon
½ teaspoon ground ginger
¼ cup chopped crystalized ginger

¾ cup chopped walnuts
2 eggs
⅓ cup maple syrup
⅓ cup melted sweet butter
⅔ cup apple cider
1 large or 2 small green tomatoes, chopped (to make 1–1¼ cups)

Mix the flour, baking powder, baking soda, salt, cinnamon, and ground ginger together, tossing to mix thoroughly. Toss in the crystalized ginger, then the walnuts, separating and coating each piece. In a medium-size bowl, beat the eggs until light and slightly thickened. Add the maple syrup, butter, and cider, mixing well. Now fold the dry ingredients into the bowl, add the green tomatoes, and stir until just mixed. Pour the mixture into a buttered 9-inch loaf pan and bake in a preheated 350-degree oven for 60–65 minutes, until the edges are browned and start to leave the sides of the pan. Cool in the pan for 10 minutes, then turn out onto a rack. It's better to let this bread settle, so wait until the next day to slice it.

MAKES ONE 9-INCH LOAF

Pumpkin Sweet Bread

2 cups all-purpose flour
1 teaspoon baking powder
¼ teaspoon baking soda
½ teaspoon salt
1 teaspoon cinnamon
1 teaspoon freshly grated nutmeg
½ cup shortening

1 cup brown sugar
1 egg
1 cup puréed cooked pumpkin
2 tablespoons molasses
1 teaspoon vanilla
1 cup shredded coconut

Sift the flour, baking powder, and baking soda with the salt and spices. In a separate bowl cream together the shortening and the sugar, and stir in the egg, puréed pumpkin, molasses, and vanilla. Stir the dry ingredients into the pumpkin mixture, and stir until just blended. Add the coconut. Spread the batter in a greased 10 × 13-inch shallow baking pan. Bake in a preheated 350-degree oven for about 30 minutes. Cut when slightly cool.
MAKES 24 SQUARES

Boston Brown Bread

Mr. Latly Gee and Mrs. Bennett have gone down in local history as the makers of the best Boston brown bread in the eighteenth century. In her first cookbook, Fannie Farmer gave a recipe not only for the steamed loaf (which we have adapted to bake in a 1 pound coffee can) but another for Brown Bread Ice Cream and one for Brown Bread Sandwiches to be filled with "finely chopped peanuts seasoned with salt, or grated cheese mixed with chopped English walnut meat. . . ."

½ cup rye flour
½ cup yellow cornmeal
½ cup graham or whole wheat
   flour

1½ teaspoons baking soda
½ teaspoon salt
6 tablespoons molasses
1 cup sour milk or buttermilk

Toss the rye flour, cornmeal, graham or whole wheat flour, baking soda, and salt in a large bowl. Add the molasses and sour milk or buttermilk and mix well. Butter a 1-pound coffee can, and pour in the batter. Cover tightly with a double piece of aluminum foil placed firmly over the top and partially down the sides, then tied with a string to hold secure. Place in a deep saucepan. Add enough boiling water to come halfway up the can. Cover the pan and steam for 1½ hours, or until a straw inserted in the middle of the bread comes out clean. Remove and cool on a rack, then unmold and serve warm.
SERVES 8–10

Our friend Marian Morash of Nantucket and Lexington, Massachusetts, is the inventor of this bread, which appears in her splendid *Victory Garden Cookbook*.

Marian Morash's Winter Squash Corn Bread

¾ *cup yellow cornmeal*
¾ *cup flour*
4 *teaspoons baking powder*
½ *teaspoon cinnamon*
¼ *teaspoon allspice*
½ *teaspoon salt*
½ *cup soft butter*

¼ *cup dark brown sugar, packed*
2 *eggs*
1½ *teaspoons lemon juice*
1 *cup puréed steamed winter squash*
¼ *cup milk*

Mix the cornmeal, flour, baking powder, spices, and salt together. In a separate bowl mix the soft butter and the brown sugar, and beat until light. Stir in the eggs, lemon juice, squash, and milk and beat well. Gradually add the dry mixture, blending thoroughly. Pour the dough into a buttered 8-inch loaf pan. Bake in a preheated 350-degree oven. After 50 minutes insert a skewer into the center of the loaf, and remove from the oven if the skewer comes out clean; otherwise continue baking for 10 minutes more. Cool in the loaf pan for 10 minutes, then remove the loaf and cool on a rack.

MAKES ONE 8-INCH LOAF

Basic Baking Powder Mixes

Long before these things were packaged and found on supermarket shelves, our Yankee culinary ancestors used to make their own convenience mixtures of flour, baking powder, and shortening to be stored without refrigeration for up to several months or more, then used to prepare biscuits, muffins, pancakes, and so on. A standard batter results when eggs, milk, or sour cream are added.

Storage Formula

12 cups sifted flour   6 teaspoons salt
6 tablespoons baking powder   3 cups shortening

Sift the dry ingredients together two or three times. Cut in the shortening. Stir and mix until you have granular texture, like corn meal. Put the mixture in glass jars and cover lightly.

MAKES ABOUT 4 QUARTS

BISCUITS: To 2 cups of the above mixture, add ½–¾ cup milk or sour cream to make a soft dough. On a floured surface, knead lightly, then roll to ½-inch thickness and cut into biscuits. Bake on an ungreased cookie sheet 12–15 minutes in a 450-degree oven.

MAKES 1 DOZEN 2-INCH BISCUITS.

MUFFINS: Add 1 well-beaten egg, 2 tablespoons sugar, and ¾ cup milk to 2 cups of the above mixture. Blend lightly, and fill greased muffin tins two-thirds full. Bake in a 450-degree oven for 20 minutes.

MAKES 10 MUFFINS

Suppertime Corn Bread

This is especially good as an accompaniment to chicken chowder or other hearty soups.

¾ cup flour   1 tablespoon sugar
¾ cup cornmeal   1 egg
1 tablespoon baking powder   ¾ cup milk
¼ teaspoon salt   3 tablespoons melted butter

In a large bowl, mix the flour, cornmeal, baking powder, salt, and sugar. Crack the egg into the dry mixture, add the milk, and stir thoroughly until

the batter is smooth. Add the melted butter and continue stirring until blended. Pour the batter into a well-greased 8 × 8-inch shallow baking pan. Bake in a preheated 425-degree oven for 25 to 30 minutes. Cool and cut into 2-inch squares.

MAKES 8 SQUARES

Orange-Flavored Carrot Bread

6 tablespoons butter
1 cup sugar
¼ cup honey
½ teaspoon cinnamon
¼ teaspoon freshly grated nutmeg
¼ teaspoon allspice
1 tablespoon coarsely grated
  orange peel

1 egg
1¼ cups grated carrots
⅓ cup orange juice
1½ cups all-purpose flour
1 teaspoon baking powder
1 teaspoon baking soda
⅛ teaspoon salt
¾ cup chopped hazelnuts

Cream the butter with the sugar in a food processor or with a mixer, beating until thoroughly incorporated. Add the honey, spices, orange peel, egg, grated carrots, and orange juice. Thoroughly mix the dry ingredients and the nuts, then blend with the liquid mixture until all the flour is moistened. Turn the batter into a buttered 9-inch loaf pan and bake in a preheated 350-degree oven for 1 hour. Let rest in the pan 15 minutes before turning out on a rack.

MAKES ONE 9-INCH LOAF

Beer Bread

This is a good, easy quick bread to make when there is leftover beer in the refrigerator. It is coarse-textured, not sweet, and goes with almost anything.

3 cups all-purpose flour
2 teaspoons baking powder
½ teaspoon baking soda
½ teaspoon salt
½ cup bran

2 eggs
1½ cups beer
6 tablespoons butter
1 tablespoon honey

Mix the flour, baking powder, baking soda, salt, and bran together. Beat the eggs and add them to the dry ingredients along with the beer. Melt the butter, stir in the honey, and add to the batter. Beat for about 30 seconds, then pour into a buttered 9-inch loaf pan. Bake in a preheated 450-degree oven for 10 minutes, then lower the heat to 375 degrees and bake another 35 minutes. Cool in the pan for 5 minutes, then turn out onto a rack and cool thoroughly before slicing.

MAKES ONE 9-INCH LOAF

Blueberry Coffee Cake

¾ cup sugar
¼ cup butter
1 egg
2 cups all-purpose flour
½ teaspoon freshly grated nutmeg

½ teaspoon salt
2 teaspoons baking powder
½ cup milk
2 cups fresh blueberries

CRUMB TOPPING:
½ cup sugar
⅓ cup flour

½ teaspoon cinnamon
¼ cup soft butter

Cream the sugar, butter, and egg together. Sift or toss the dry ingredients together to blend them. Add the dry ingredients to the creamed butter in 3 parts alternately with the milk. Mix only enough to incorporate the ingredients without overbeating them. Carefully fold in the blueberries. Pour the batter into a greased and floured 9-inch-square pan. Mix the sugar, flour, cinnamon, and soft butter together with your fingertips or a pastry blender, or mix briefly in a food processor. Sprinkle this crumb topping evenly over the cake. Bake in a preheated 375-degree oven for 45–50 minutes. Check with a cake tester or straw to see if it comes out clean. Serve warm from the pan.

MAKES ONE 9-INCH-SQUARE CAKE

Berry Bundt Cake

3 cups all-purpose flour
1½ teaspoons baking powder
½ teaspoon baking soda
¼ teaspoon salt
¾ teaspoon cinnamon
¾ cup soft butter

1½ cups sugar
4 eggs
1 teaspoon vanilla
¾ cup sour cream
¼ cup plain yogurt

BERRY FILLING:
2 cups berries (blueberries,
   raspberries, blackberries)

1½ tablespoons flour
¼ cup dark brown sugar

TOPPING:
3 tablespoons confectioners' sugar

Toss the flour, baking powder, baking soda, salt, and cinnamon together. In a bowl, cream the butter and sugar together, then add the eggs, one at a time, beating after each addition until well mixed. Add the vanilla. Mix the sour cream and yogurt together. Now beat the dry ingredients alternately with the sour cream–yogurt mixture into the butter-sugar-egg mixture. Toss the berries with the flour to coat lightly, then toss them with the brown sugar. Scrape one-third of the batter into a buttered Bundt pan or tube pan, distribute ½ of the berries on top, add another layer of batter, another layer of berries, and finish with the last of the batter. Bake in a preheated 350-degree oven for 1 hour. Let rest 15 minutes before unmolding. Using a shaker or a strainer sprinkle confectioners' sugar over the top.

MAKES 1 LARGE ROUND CAKE

Corn Sticks

½ cup all-purpose flour
½ cup cornmeal, preferably stone-ground
1 teaspoon baking powder
¼ teaspoon baking soda
2 tablespoons sugar
¼ teaspoon salt

½ cup sour cream
¼ cup milk
2 tablespoons melted butter
2 eggs, separated
½ cup corn kernels, scraped from cob, cooked or uncooked *
Oil or bacon fat for brushing molds

* If you use uncooked corn, heat the kernels in 1 tablespoon butter for about 30 seconds before adding to the batter.

Place a traditional corn stick mold (which usually has 7 indentations) in a 425-degree oven to heat while you prepare the butter. Stir the flour, cornmeal, baking powder, baking soda, sugar, and salt together in a bowl to mix thoroughly. Mix the sour cream, milk, melted butter, and egg yolks together, then stir into the dry ingredients. Beat the egg whites until they form soft peaks and fold into the batter along with the corn kernels. Brush the heated cornstick molds with oil or bacon fat, and pour equal portions of the batter into each mold. Bake in the preheated 425-degree oven 20 minutes.

MAKES 7 CORNSTICKS

Skillet Corn Bread

Cooked in colonial days over an open fire, this staple is sometimes enhanced today with the south-of-the-border accent of chilis and fresh coriander.

1 cup all-purpose flour
½ cup yellow stone-ground cornmeal
2 tablespoons sugar
½ teaspoon baking soda
½ teaspoon salt
1 egg

¾ cup buttermilk
2 jalapeño chilies or other hot pepper, chopped (optional)
1 cup cooked corn
3 tablespoons chopped fresh coriander or parsley
2 tablespoons butter

Toss the flour, cornmeal, sugar, baking soda, and salt together. In a separate bowl beat the egg with the buttermilk, then mix the dry ingredients with this mixture. Stir in the optional chilies, the corn, and the fresh herb.

Melt the butter in a 9- or 10-inch skillet and pour in the batter, spreading it evenly. Cover the skillet and cook over very low heat for 20 minutes, being very careful not to burn the bottom of the bread. Turn the bread over, using 2 spatulas or flipping it onto a flat round plate and then slipping it back into the skillet, and brown the other side about 5 minutes.

SERVES 6–8

Matt Lewis's Buckwheat Corn Bread with Cheese

New England born and a highly knowledgeable student of food, Matt Lewis developed this recipe for "one of the breads," as she says, "which can be a lunch or supper in itself, with a little salad or other green thing, a piece of fruit, and a glass of wine."

1 tablespoon corn oil
½ cup stone-ground cornmeal,
  yellow or white
¼ cup buckwheat flour
1 teaspoon baking powder
½ teaspoon salt
¾ cup buttermilk
1 egg
2–4 ounces cheddar cheese, sliced
  or shredded

Pour the corn oil into an 8-inch skillet, preferably nonstick, with an oven-proof handle, and place it on the top rack of a preheated 450-degree oven. Sift the dry ingredients into a bowl. Whisk the buttermilk and egg together, then whisk them gently into the dry ingredients. Remove the skillet from the oven, swirl the oil around, and pour the excess off into the batter, and stir it around. Scrape the batter into the hot skillet. Return the pan to the oven, and bake 15–20 minutes, until cooked through but only lightly browned on top. Remove the pan and turn the bread out onto a cutting board. Slice the bread in half vertically and then horizontally. Spread the cheese out over the bottom halves, then quickly cover with the warm top halves so the cheese will melt.

SERVES 2–4

Cranberry Muffins

1 cup all-purpose flour
½ cup sugar
1 teaspoon baking powder
½ teaspoon baking soda
½ teaspoon salt
½ teaspoon grated orange rind
¾ cup orange juice
1 egg, beaten
2 tablespoons melted butter
½ cup coarsely chopped cranberries
¼ cup chopped nuts

Toss or sift together the dry ingredients. Mix together the orange rind, orange juice, and egg. Stir the liquid ingredients along with the melted butter into the dry ingredients, mixing only enough to moisten. Fold in the cranberries and nuts. Pour the batter into greased muffin tins, and bake in a preheated 350-degree oven for 20–25 minutes.

MAKES 10 MUFFINS

Buckwheat Muffins

If you like the pure flavor of buckwheat, you'll love these muffins. For a little less purity you could add about ½ cup golden raisins.

1 egg
1 cup milk
3 tablespoons honey
1 cup buckwheat flour

⅓ cup all-purpose flour
½ teaspoon salt
2½ teaspoons baking powder

Whisk the egg, milk, and honey together until blended. Toss the two flours, salt, and baking powder together, then stir them quickly into the liquid ingredients until just blended. Pour the batter into well-greased muffin pans, filling them two-thirds full, and bake in a preheated 350-degree oven for 20–25 minutes.

MAKES 8 MUFFINS

Rich Nutmeg Muffins

3 cups all-purpose flour
1½ cups brown sugar
¼ pound butter
½ teaspoon salt
2 teaspoons baking powder

½ teaspoon baking soda
2 teaspoons freshly grated nutmeg
1 cup buttermilk
2 eggs, lightly beaten

In a bowl mix together 2 cups of the flour and the brown sugar, then cut in the butter as you would for biscuits or pie dough. Measure out ¾ cup of the mixture and set aside to use later as topping. Sift the remaining cup of flour with the salt, baking powder, baking soda, and nutmeg, then combine with the flour-brown sugar-butter mixture remaining in the bowl. Stir in the buttermilk and eggs, and mix until just blended. Pour into lightly buttered muffin tins, filling them three-quarters full, and sprinkle equal amounts of the reserved topping over each muffin. Bake in a preheated 350-degree oven 20–25 minutes.

MAKES ABOUT 14 MUFFINS.

Muffin Country

Muffins may be as characteristically Yankee as either baked beans or Boston brown bread, and they have a way of bringing New England right to the table—even when breakfast is served as far away from the rocky Atlantic coastline as San Francisco. (The blueberry muffins we devoured there come from a New Hampshire formula.) Across the country, muffins in their infinite variety remind people of "back home"—among those included here are Maple Muffins, Parsnip Muffins, Rich Nutmeg Muffins, Oatmeal-Maple-Raisin Muffins, and Sticky Rhubarb Muffins.

To make any of them, remember, don't overmix the batter. You may eliminate greasing the muffin pan if you use paper baking cups. To have a crisp crust, use old-fashioned cast-iron gem pans that get very hot. If you like lots of crust, try baking any of these muffins in small cake tins.

Any muffin may be glazed by brushing the top with egg white; sprinkle with poppy or sesame seeds, if you like. To gild the lily, so to speak, sprinkle a streusel topping on just before you bake the muffins: It may be made with ¼ cup flour mixed with 1 teaspoon of cinnamon, ¼ cup butter, and ⅓ cup brown sugar. For an extra flourish, you might add ½ cup finely chopped nuts.

Maple Muffins

2 eggs
½ cup maple syrup, preferably grade B
½ cup plain yogurt
2 tablespoons melted butter
1 cup rolled oats
1 cup whole wheat flour
½ teaspoon salt
1 tablespoon baking powder
1 cup roughly chopped walnuts

Beat the eggs with the maple syrup, yogurt, and melted butter. Toss the oats, flour, salt, and baking powder together. Add the dry ingredients to the liquid ingredients and stir until just blended. Fold in the nuts. Fill 10 buttered muffin cups. Bake in a preheated 350-degree oven for 25 minutes.
MAKES 10 MUFFINS

Carrot-Ginger Muffins

1 cup finely grated carrots
¼ cup finely chopped candied ginger
¼ cup brown sugar
½ teaspoon salt
¾ cup milk
2 tablespoons melted butter or vegetable oil
1 egg
1½ cups all-purpose flour
½ cup bran
2 teaspoons baking powder

Mix the carrots, ginger, brown sugar, and salt together. Whisk the milk, butter or oil, and egg together until blended, then mix in with the carrots. Stir and toss the dry ingredients together, then quickly mix them with the wet mixture until just blended. Pour the batter into well-greased muffin cups, filling them two-thirds full, and bake in a preheated 400-degree oven 20 minutes.
MAKES ABOUT 12 MUFFINS

Parsnip Muffins

1 egg
1 cup mashed parsnips
3 tablespoons honey
½ cup buttermilk
1 cup all-purpose flour
1 cup oatmeal flour
½ teaspoon baking soda
½ teaspoon salt
About ¼ teaspoon freshly grated nutmeg

Beat the egg lightly, then mix the parsnips, honey, and buttermilk in with it. Toss the two flours, baking soda, and salt together, grate about ¼ teaspoon nutmeg in, and mix. Stir the dry ingredients into the liquid and spoon into buttered muffin tins. Bake in a preheated 400-degree oven for 20–25 minutes.
MAKES 9 MUFFINS

Rutabaga Muffins

1 egg
1 cup cooked, mashed rutabaga
2 tablespoons melted butter or
  vegetable oil
½ cup milk
⅔ cup light brown sugar
1½ cups all-purpose flour
2 teaspoons baking powder

½ teaspoon salt
½ teaspoon cinnamon
¼ teaspoon freshly grated nutmeg
¼ teaspoon ground ginger
⅛ teaspoon ground allspice
⅔ cup raisins, or ½ cup finely
  chopped candied ginger

Beat the egg lightly, then add the mashed rutabaga, the butter or oil, milk, and brown sugar. Toss the dry ingredients together, then stir them into the first mixture. Fold in the raisins or candied ginger. Pour the batter into greased muffin tins. Bake in a preheated 400-degree oven for 20 minutes. Serve warm.

MAKES 8 GOOD-SIZE MUFFINS

New Hampshire Blueberry Muffins

New England chefs turn up all over the country, just as do Yankee recipes for blueberries, among other good things. Jim Dodge, a New Hampshire boy who became the pastry chef at San Francisco's Stanford Court Hotel, adapted his very special, almost cakelike blueberry muffin recipe for use in this book. Follow his directions carefully and you will produce blueberry muffins that people dream of long after they have breakfasted on them at Stanford Court.

10 tablespoons unsalted butter
2 cups sugar
½ cup milk
2½ cups cake flour
1 tablespoon baking powder *

1 tablespoon kosher salt, or 1½
  teaspoons table salt
4 large eggs
1⅔ cups blueberries †

  * Rumford, Jim Dodge says, is best.
  † If you don't have fresh blueberries, frozen work very well. When you buy them, make sure they are loose in the bag, like marbles. Do not defrost before using.

Preheat the oven to 400 degrees. Line muffin tins for 24 muffins with paper baking cups. Let the butter stand at room temperature until it is soft and warm to the touch. Combine the butter and sugar in the bowl of an electric mixer and cream until light. Warm the milk lightly, just enough to remove the chill, and add it slowly to the creamed butter, mixing at medium-low speed.

  Sift the flour, baking powder, and salt together. With your mixer on low speed, stir in one egg, then a quarter of the flour mixture. Stop the mixer and scrape down the sides of the bowl. Repeat three more times, until all the eggs and flour have been incorporated into the batter. Mix at medium-low speed for 7 minutes.

Pour 2 tablespoons of batter into each muffin cup and top with 1 tablespoon of blueberries. Bake about 30 minutes, until the tops of the muffins are golden brown and the centers spring back when lightly touched.

MAKES 24 MUFFINS

Oatmeal Muffins with Fresh Berries

1¾ cups hot milk
1 cup rolled oats
2 cups all-purpose flour
4 teaspoons baking powder
1 teaspoon salt
⅓ cup brown sugar
1 egg, beaten
¼ cup melted sweet butter
About 1 cup fresh berries

Pour 1 cup of the hot milk over the rolled oats and let stand for 10 minutes. Butter muffin tins—this batter should be enough to fill 14 medium-size 2-inch cups. Sift together the flour, baking powder, salt, and brown sugar. Combine the egg, melted butter, and remaining milk, then add to the flour mixture alternately with oatmeal mixture. Do not overmix; stir only long enough to moisten flour. Fill each cup of the prepared muffin tins two-thirds full of batter. Tuck about 6 or 8 berries into the batter of each filled cup, distributing them evenly. Bake in a preheated 375-degree oven for 20–25 minutes, until lightly browned on top.

MAKES 14 MUFFINS

VARIATION: To make muffins with raisins, first soak ½ cup of raisins in 3 tablespoons of sherry or hot brewed tea for 30 minutes. Then drain and fold them into the batter before filling the individual cups, instead of adding the berries after.

Banana-Pecan Muffins

2 very ripe bananas
1 egg
⅓ cup dark brown sugar
1½ cups all-purpose flour
½ cup bran
2 teaspoons baking powder
A pinch of salt
½ cup roughly chopped pecans

Mash the bananas and beat in the egg and brown sugar (this may all be easily done in a food processor). Toss the flour, bran, baking powder, and salt together, and stir into the banana mixture, blending just enough to mix. Fold in the pecans. Turn the batter into greased muffin tins, filling them three-quarters full, and bake in a preheated 375-degree oven for 20–25 minutes, until lightly browned.

MAKES 10 MUFFINS

Fig and Orange Muffins

2 cups flour
⅓ cup bran
1 tablespoon baking powder
½ teaspoon salt
1 egg

1¼ cups orange juice
Grated rind of 1 orange
2 tablespoons vegetable oil
1¼ cups chopped figs

Toss the flour, bran, baking powder, and salt together to mix. Beat the egg lightly with the orange juice and rind and oil. Mix the liquid ingredients with the dry, then fold in the figs. Pour the batter into buttered muffin tins and bake in a preheated 400-degree oven for 25 minutes.
MAKES 12 MUFFINS

Grape-Nuts— Raisin Muffins

1 cup all-purpose flour
2 teaspoons baking powder
¼ teaspoon salt
1 cup Grape-Nuts cereal with raisins

1¼ cups brown sugar
1 egg
1 cup milk
3 tablespoons safflower oil
½ cup raisins

Mix the flour, baking powder, and salt together thoroughly. Toss in the Grape-Nuts and brown sugar and mix again. Beat the egg lightly and stir in the milk and oil. Stir the liquid ingredients into the dry ingredients just long enough to blend. Fold in the additional raisins. Turn the batter into greased muffin tins, filling them three-quarters full. Bake in a preheated 375-degree oven for 25–30 minutes, until lightly browned.
MAKES 10 MUFFINS

Oatmeal- Maple- Raisin Muffins

1 cup boiling water
¾ cup rolled oats (not quick cooking)
2 tablespoons butter
1 cup flour

2 teaspoons baking powder
¼ teaspoon salt
1 egg
¼ cup maple syrup
½ cup raisins

Pour the boiling water over the oats, add the butter, and let stand until cool to the touch. Mix the flour, baking powder, and salt together in a bowl. In a separate bowl beat the egg and mix in the maple syrup. Now combine the three mixtures, stirring only enough to mix together. Fold in the raisins. Spoon the batter into well-buttered 8-cup muffin pan and bake in a preheated 375-degree oven for 25 minutes.
MAKES 8 MUFFINS

Prune-Pecan Muffins

1 ½ cups all-purpose flour
½ cup whole wheat flour
1 teaspoon baking soda
¼ teaspoon salt
1 egg
1 cup buttermilk

¼ cup melted butter
¼ cup sugar
1 cup pitted and roughly chopped prunes
¾ cup roughly chopped pecans

Mix the two flours, baking soda, and salt thoroughly together. Beat the egg lightly and stir in the buttermilk, melted butter, and sugar. Add the dry ingredients to the egg-buttermilk mixture, stirring just long enough to mix the two. Fold in the prunes and the pecans. Turn the batter into greased muffin tins, filling them about three-quarters full. Bake in a preheated 400-degree oven for 25 minutes.

MAKES 10 MUFFINS

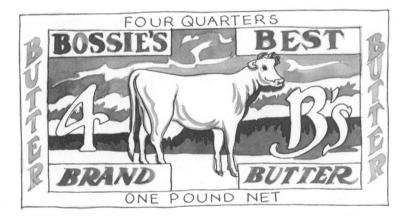

Spoon Bread Muffins

½ cup stone-ground cornmeal
1 ½ teaspoons baking powder
1 teaspoon salt
1 teaspoon sugar

1 ½ cups milk
1 egg
4 tablespoons butter or shortening

Stir and toss the dry ingredients together. Add the milk and beat in the egg. Drop 1 teaspoon butter or shortening into each of 12 medium muffin cups (cast-iron if available). Place the pan in a preheated 475-degree oven until smoking hot. Remove the pan quickly and fill each muffin cup half full. Bake 25–30 minutes. Serve immediately, blistering hot.

MAKES 12 MUFFINS

Sticky Rhubarb Muffins

THE STICKY GLAZE:

4 tablespoons butter

6 tablespoons dark brown sugar

1 cup rhubarb, cut in small dice

THE MUFFIN DOUGH:

4 tablespoons butter, softened

1/4 cup sugar

1 egg

1 1/2 cups all-purpose flour

1 teaspoon baking powder

1/2 teaspoon baking soda

1/4 teaspoon salt

1/2 teaspoon nutmeg

1/2 cup milk

Grated rind of 1 orange

Using your fingertips or a pastry cutter, mix the butter into the brown sugar roughly. Stir in the rhubarb. Distribute this mixture evenly into 12 greased muffin cups. Cream the softened butter and the sugar together, then beat in the egg. Mix the flour, baking powder, baking soda, salt, and nutmeg together thoroughly, then add to the butter-sugar mixture alternately with the milk. Don't overmix. Stir in the orange rind and pour equal amounts of the batter into the muffin cups. Bake in a preheated 350-degree oven 25 minutes. Let cool in the pans 5 minutes, then invert the muffin tins and ease the muffins out so that the sticky glaze remains intact. Serve warm, with glaze topside.

MAKES 12 MUFFINS

Cream Scones

Lots of New England cooks with Scottish background—and without—make good scones, most often served for tea. One good cook, Aristene Pixley, used unadorned cream scones in place of baking powder bicuits to make strawberry shortcake. These scones are made according to Martha Geffen's recipe.

3 cups all-purpose flour

1/2 cup sugar

4 teaspoons baking powder

1/4 teaspoon salt

6 tablespoons minced crystalized ginger

2 cups heavy cream

2 tablespoons melted butter

2 tablespoons dark brown sugar

Sift together the flour, sugar, baking powder, and salt. Mix in the ginger. Beat the cream to soft peaks, then fold it into the dry mixture. Knead just until the dough holds together. Pat it out into a 10-inch round, and place on a lightly greased baking sheet. Brush with butter. Put the brown sugar in a strainer and sieve it evenly over the top. Score in 8 wedges. Bake in a preheated 375-degree oven for 45 minutes, until slightly browned.

MAKES 8 WEDGES

Ruda Kesselhut, who serves afternoon tea in her big white clapboard house —one of a handful that makes up the village of East Craftsbury, Vermont —prepares these scones fresh every day for her customers. Scones are traditionally cut in wedge-shaped pieces, as in the preceding recipe, but she prefers them shaped in "stubby rounds. . . . They are neater to eat that way with tea."

Ruda's Scones

2 cups all-purpose flour
3 teaspoons baking powder
2 tablespoons sugar (more or less according to taste)

½ teaspoon salt
1 stick (¼ pound) butter
⅔ cup light cream
1 egg

FOR THE TOPS:
Melted unsalted butter   Sugar

Sift the flour, baking powder, sugar, and salt together. Cut in the butter and mix lightly. Beat the cream and egg together, then stir that into the flour-butter mixture. Knead a few turns—just long enough to hold the dough together. Roll or pat out to ½-inch thickness. Cut into rounds with a 1½-inch cutter. Cup your fingers around each piece and plump it up, then place the scones about an inch apart on an ungreased baking sheet. Brush the tops with melted butter and sprinkle on a little sugar. Bake in a preheated 425-degree oven for 15 minutes.
MAKES 16 SCONES

Popovers

1 cup all-purpose flour
1 teaspoon coarse salt, or ½ teaspoon table salt

3 eggs
2 tablespoons melted butter
1 cup milk

Put the ingredients into the container of a blender or a food processor. Blend slowly until thoroughly mixed, scraping down any flour sticking to container walls. Or mix the flour and salt in a bowl, making a well in the center, then add the remaining ingredients and beat until smooth. Fill well-greased 5-ounce Pyrex cups between half and two-thirds full. Place them in a cold oven, turn the heat to 400 degrees, and bake 35 minutes. Run a knife around the edges of the cups to loosen popovers and serve immediately with butter and jam or preserves.
MAKES 8 POPOVERS

Note: If you have a stove with a timer that can start the oven automatically, prepare the batter the night before, put it in well-greased cups, set the timer, and in the morning make breakfast a golden treat by serving piping hot puffy popovers.

"A Mess of Biscuit"

Miss Ruby Hemenway, once described as the oldest newspaper columnist on earth, continued to share her thoughts about Yankees and old-time cooking until she was more than 100 years old. Readers of her contributions to the *Greenfield Recorder* in the Berkshires were sometimes told the traditional methods of making Plum Duff (page 522) or farmer's pudding sauce—or how to "whack up a mess of biscuit." Old New England cooks often used buttermilk and a combination of baking powder and baking soda for biscuits that are "lighter and more feathery."

2 cups all-purpose flour
1 teaspoon baking powder
½ teaspoon baking soda
1 teaspoon salt

4 tablespoons shortening
1 cup buttermilk
24 cooked, pitted prunes

In a large mixing bowl, stir the flour, baking powder, baking soda, and salt together. Cut in the shortening and mix until you have a crumbly dough. Stir in the buttermilk. Turn the dough out and knead lightly, then roll it out to a thickness of about ¼ inch. Cut in 2½-inch circles, and place a prune in the center of each one. Pinch the dough upward and over the prunes, pressing together at the top. Put the uncooked biscuits, bottom side up, on a greased baking sheet, and bake in a preheated 400-degree oven for 20 minutes. Serve hot with butter.
MAKES 24 BISCUITS

Note: These, of course, can be made without the prunes.

Cider Doughnuts

2 eggs
1 egg yolk
1 cup fresh apple cider
⅓ cup brown sugar
⅓ cup sugar
4 cups unbleached all-purpose flour
1 teaspoon baking powder
½ teaspoon baking soda

½ teaspoon salt
1 teaspoon cinnamon
½ teaspoon freshly grated nutmeg
2 tablespoons melted sweet butter
Frying oil, lard, or vegetable
*   shortening*
Confectioners' sugar

Beat the eggs and egg yolk together in a large bowl, then gradually add the cider and two kinds of sugar. Sift the flour, baking powder, baking soda, salt, and spices together, and stir into the egg mixture along with the melted butter. Stir only enough to mix. Turn the dough out onto a work surface, floured just enough so that the dough won't stick as you roll or pat it out. When the dough is ½-inch thick, cut out doughnut shapes, using a well-floured doughnut cutter, and let them rest for 5 minutes on a lightly floured surface. (Remove the holes but save them to fry along with the doughnuts —they're delicious.)

Heat enough oil, lard, or shortening to fill your frying kettle to a depth of 2–3 inches. When it reaches 365 degrees (and if you are not using an electric fryer, test with a frying thermometer), drop in 3 or 4 doughnuts, depending on the size of your pan—they should not be crowded. As soon as they float to the top and are holding their shape, turn them. Fry until golden on both sides, 2–3 minutes. Remove doughnuts as they are done and drain on absorbent paper. Dust with confectioners' sugar when they have cooled a little. Let the frying oil temperature return to 365 degrees before frying a new batch.

MAKES ABOUT 24 STANDARD-SIZE DOUGHNUTS, OR 14 LARGE DOUGHNUTS

VARIATION: To make doughnuts with fresh berries, cut the spices to less than half the given proportions. After you roll the dough out, trace with the doughnut cutter the shape of each doughnut, then press about 6 or 8 fresh berries into the circle of dough before cutting it. Let rest at least 5 minutes, then proceed with the frying.

White Mountain Doughnuts

The Philbrook family, innkeepers in the White Mountains near Shelborne, New Hampshire, for more than a century, is known for the excellence of its traditional meals. The Philbrook cooks have been producing these doughnuts for generations on a ten-burner kitchen range that's black as a wood stove should be, and beautiful, too. They say the secret to good doughnuts is using sour milk or buttermilk in the batter, seasoning it with a little bacon fat, taking care not to add too much flour, and cooking the doughnuts in lard. They also have at hand a well-worn small wooden dowel that they stick into the hole of each doughnut as the batter hits the hot fat, swirling it around just long enough to make sure the hole doesn't close up. Their chocolate doughnut variation is a great hit with the farm's guests.

1 cup sugar
2 eggs
A dash of nutmeg
3 teaspoons bacon fat
1 cup sour milk or buttermilk
1 teaspoon baking soda

1 teaspoon baking powder
About 3½ cups flour
Lard for frying
Confectioners' sugar for dusting
  (optional)

Beat the sugar and eggs together, then add the nutmeg, bacon fat, milk, baking soda, baking powder, and just enough flour to be able to handle the batter. Turn the dough out onto a lightly floured surface and pat it out gently to a thickness of about ½ inch. Cut the dough into doughnut shapes with a well-floured doughnut cutter. Heat enough lard to fill a frying kettle to a depth of at least 3 inches. When it reaches 360 degrees, pick the doughnut pieces up carefully and drop them one by one into the hot fat. You may want to use a wooden implement, as the Philbrook women do, to keep the hole intact. As soon as the dougnuts float to the surface and are holding their shape, turn them. Fry until golden on both sides, about 2–3 minutes in all. Drain on absorbent paper and dust with confectioners' sugar, if you like, when they have cooled a little.

MAKES 25–30 DOUGHNUTS

VARIATION FOR CHOCOLATE DOUGHNUTS: Add 3 squares melted unsweetened chocolate to the dough before adding the flour.

DESSERTS, PIES,

CAKES, and COOKIES

COME FOR DESSERT,'' a phrase full of tempting prospects, was as much an invitation to sociability in the nineteenth century as it is among some of our Northeast Kingdom friends today. The end of the meal is apt to be seen as a celebration, no matter whether or not company arrives.

And the desserts offered haven't changed that much. In truth, there seems to be more of an appreciation than ever today of the old-fashioned homely desserts and puddings that most of us grew up on, and that is a blessing. For almost a generation or so one feared that supermarket mixes with their synthetic flavors were going to wipe out the memory of those lovely, comforting desserts that graced the end of any home-cooked meal, desserts made of a little milk, eggs, butter, sugar, flour or often leftover bread, and whatever fruit might be in season, sometimes served warm from the oven, sometimes chilled, and invariably with a pitcher of rich cream. But with the new interest in regional American cookery, a lot of those dishes have been restored to their proper place, and a younger generation is learning not only what they were missing but how simple they are to prepare. Even restaurants today are proud to feature a cobbler or an Indian pudding over Continental pastries.

As youngsters both of us took for granted the simple goodness of a properly made bread pudding or an apple crunch, and we used to celebrate the progression of the summer with berry puddings, starting with blueberries and ending with late-season wild blackberries. In later years the nostalgia of such dishes, as the fruit bursts in one's mouth and the simple goodness of a warm dumpling topping mingles with the juices, can bring tears to the eyes.

So we celebrate here many of the desserts that we learned at a mother's or aunt's or grandmother's side. Many of the pies and cakes and cookies are the same, too, except that good fresh lard is not as readily available these days so that pie crusts may not have quite the same flaky magic (but then vegetable shortening may not be quite as lethal). Also, a fruit tart, being on the lighter side, quite often replaces the two-crust pie, and we feature a few of those. Ices and sherbets or sorbets using fresh seasonal fruits are often more welcome than a rich ice cream so you'll find a wide variety of those to choose from. And the proliferation of good small bakeries or luncheon-tea parlors like Rainbow Sweets in Marshfield, Vermont, have brought some new-style tortes, cheesecakes, and meringuelike confections to the dessert scene, and we have wrested some recipes from their creators.

But the biggest difference is in how these wonderful confections are put together. Seldom does one hear in the kitchen the plop-plop of a cake batter being beaten rhythmically in a brown ceramic bowl with a big wooden spoon or the steady churn of an ice cream freezer being turned by hand on the back stoop. Today it's the shrill whizz of a food processor or an electric beater or ice cream freezer that pierces the air. But that's a small price to pay for the speed these machines have brought us, in putting together a three-layer filled and frosted cake or having a fresh fruit sherbet whipped up while we eat the first part of dinner. So there's little excuse for not baking your own cakes, pies, and cookies from scratch. For the money you'd save buying your own good, fresh ingredients rather than mixes, you can easily put away enough to equip yourself with first-rate appliances. And you can celebrate the end of the meal as your grandmother did with a sense of pride in her own creation.

MOSTLY PUDDINGS

Honey-Baked Apples

Mid-July is the time in the Green Mountains when clover combines with blossoms of wild raspberry and blackberries to give Vermont honey "a very delicate, delicious bouquet" that is coveted by many connoisseurs. Bees in their turn are essential in the pollination of fruit trees, and New England cooks long ago recognized the close affinity of honey and apples by devising many simple culinary combinations.

4 large tart apples
4 tablespoons honey
3 tablespoons orange juice
1 tablespoon chopped butternuts or
  walnuts

Sugar
Freshly grated nutmeg
Heavy cream

Core the apples, being careful not to cut all the way through; trim off a ½-inch band of skin around their equators. Combine the the honey, orange juice, and nuts, and divide equally to fill the apple centers. Set the apples in a baking dish, pouring in boiling water to ¼-inch depth. Bake at 400 degrees for 50–60 minutes, or until the apples are tender. Sprinkle the tops with a little sugar and freshly grated nutmeg, then put the apples under the broiler to glaze. Bring to the table hot, with heavy cream to pass.
SERVES 4

Mrs. John Haynes's Apple Dessert

Are there ever enough good apple desserts? This one from Hartford, is a very simple, satisfying one.

1 cup sugar
2 tablespoons flour
⅛ teaspoon salt
1 teaspoon baking powder
1 egg, beaten
2 cups chopped apples, peeled and
  cored

½ cup chopped nuts, such as
  walnuts, butternuts, or hickory
  nuts
Heavy cream, whipped cream, or
  custard (page 518—with or
  without rum)

Mix the sugar, flour, salt, and baking powder together. Stir in the beaten egg, chopped apples, and nuts. Place in a shallow buttered baking dish and bake in a preheated 350-degree oven for 40 minutes, until a browned crust forms on the top. Serve warm with rich farm cream, whipped cream, or custard. It is also good cold.
SERVES 4

Flaming Bananas

4 bananas
Juice of ½ lemon
4 teaspoons maple sugar

2 teaspoons butter
¼ cup hard cider, applejack, or
  rum

Peel and split the bananas and place them side by side in a lightly buttered shallow baking dish. Pour the lemon juice over them, sprinkle on the maple sugar, and dot with butter. Bake in a preheated 425-degree oven about 5 minutes, until the bananas are tender and the sugar is bubbling up. Heat the liquor and bring it to the table in a small pitcher to pour over the bananas and set them aflame. Spoon some of the sauce over the bananas as you serve them.
SERVES 4

Baked Bananas and Pears

2 bananas
1 large fresh pear, peeled and cored
4–5 tablespoons brown sugar

½ cup orange juice
1 tablespoon butter
2–3 tablespoons applejack

Peel the bananas and cut them in 1-inch disks. Cut the pear in eighths, then in 1-inch pieces. Arrange bananas and pear pieces attractively in a buttered baking dish. Sprinkle the fruit liberally with brown sugar. Pour the juice in at one side of the dish so that it seeps evenly under the fruit. Cut up the butter and distribute it evenly over the brown sugar. Bake at 350 degrees for about 10 minutes, then sprinkle the applejack over all, and bake another 5 minutes, until the sugar is bubbling.
SERVES 4

Mystery Banana Trifle

4 ripe bananas
⅔ cup orange marmalade
⅓ cup liqueur de Chambord or
    other sweet liqueur

1 envelope gelatine, softened in ¼
    cup cold water
1½ cups heavy cream
1½ tablespoons toasted almonds

Purée the bananas in a food processor and add the marmalade and liqueur and the prepared gelatine. Spin about 1 minute and pour the mixture into a glass bowl. Set aside to chill. Just before serving, whip the cream stiff, and dollop the top of the dessert with it. Sprinkle with toasted almonds.
SERVES 4

Mary Whitcher's Orange Sponge Custard

This Shaker recipe is very much like our old family favorite lemon pudding. We like to make this in individual ovenproof dishes or custard cups and serve it with rich cream, or with a fresh raspberry sauce in summer.

1½ tablespoons butter
¾ cup sugar
1 tablespoon grated orange rind
3 eggs

3 tablespoons flour
⅓ cup fresh orange juice
1 cup milk

Cream the butter, sugar, and orange rind together until well blended. Separate the eggs and beat in the yolks one by one, putting the whites in a very clean mixing bowl. Stir in the flour alternately with the orange juice and milk. Beat the egg whites until they form peaks that hold, then fold them

into the pudding mixture. Butter 6 custard cups and fill them equally, then set them in a pan filled with an inch of hot water. Bake at 325 degrees for 45 minutes. You may also bake this dessert in a 1½-quart baking dish, in which case bake for 1 hour. Serve warm, although leftovers are good cold.
SERVES 6

VARIATION FOR LEMON PUDDING: Use 1 tablespoon of lemon rind instead of orange rind and ¼ cup fresh lemon juice instead of ⅓ cup orange juice.

A Scallop of Sweet Potatoes and Apples

3 medium sweet potatoes (about 2½ pounds)
1 large tart apple
1 teaspoon soft butter
1 teaspoon cinnamon
¾ cup honey
1 cup cider
½ cup heavy cream, whipped

Peel the sweet potatoes and cut into thin slices. Peel and core the apple and cut into slightly thicker slices. Butter the bottom of a shallow baking dish and place a layer of sweet potatoes on the bottom. Sprinkle with some of the cinnamon, spoon about ⅓ of the honey over, cover with apple, repeat the cinnamon and honey, and top with sweet potatoes and rest of the cinnamon and honey. Bake in a 400-degree preheated oven for about 2 hours, or until the potatoes are soft and caramelized on top. Serve warm with whipped cream on top.
SERVES 4

Pumpkin Pudding

2 cups pumpkin purée
4 eggs
2 cups heavy cream
½ cup amaretto liqueur
½ cup water
1 cup honey
½ cup raisins
½ cup currants
4 tablespoons flour
Heavy cream

Put all the ingredients except the cream in a food processor or blender and mix thoroughly. Put the batter in a shallow, lightly buttered baking dish, and place the dish in a pan containing about 1 inch hot water. Bake in a 350-degree oven for 50–60 minutes. Serve hot or at room temperature with heavy cream to pass at the table.
SERVES 6–8

Baked Prune Whip with Rum Custard

1 pound prunes
2 slices lemon
2/3 cup sugar
4 egg whites

RUM CUSTARD:
1 cup milk
2 egg yolks
2 tablespoons sugar

1/8 teaspoon cream of tartar
1/8 teaspoon salt
1/2 cup walnuts (preferably black
   walnuts)

Pinch salt
1 tablespoon rum

Cook the prunes with the lemon slices in water to cover for about 10 minutes, or until tender. Drain, cool, and then remove the pits. Mash either by putting through a vegetable mill or pureeing in a food processor. Stir in the sugar. Beat the egg whites until frothy, then add the cream of tartar and salt and beat until they hold soft peaks. Stir a couple of spoonfuls of the whites into the prune mixture to lighten it, then fold the remaining whites in. Stir in the nuts and place in a buttered baking dish. Bake in a preheated 325-degree oven for 15 minutes.

Meanwhile, make the rum custard: heat the milk to the boiling point. Beat the egg yolks lightly, then add the hot milk in a steady stream. Stir in the sugar and cook the custard in a heavy saucepan or double boiler, stirring, over low heat, until the sauce coats the spoon and has thickened slightly. Remove from the heat, stir in the salt and rum, and chill.

Serve the prune whip cold with the rum custard in a pitcher alongside.
SERVES 6

Peach Cobbler

We remember when James Beard shared this recipe with us. He used bourbon, feeling that bourbon and peaches had a natural affinity, but we've found that applejack is equally pleasing. It is certainly a cobbler that beats any cobbler we've ever tasted.

8–9 large peaches
2–3 tablespoons sugar

DOUGH:
1 1/2 cups all-purpose flour
3 teaspoons baking powder
1 teaspoon salt

TOPPING:
2 tablespoons melted butter

Heavy cream

3 tablespoons applejack

1/2 cup soft butter
3 tablespoons sugar
About 1/2 cup light or heavy cream

2 tablespoons sugar

Peel the peaches (dropping them first into boiling water for a minute makes the job easier). Halve them, remove the pits, cut into thick slices, and sprinkle 1–2 tablespoons sugar over them, depending on how sweet they are. Scatter them on the bottom of a large, fairly shallow buttered baking dish, and sprinkle another tablespoon of sugar over them and the applejack. Toss the flour, baking powder, and salt together, then work in the butter. Stir in enough of the cream to make a very soft dough. Plop spoonfuls or handfuls of this dough on top of the peaches; don't smooth it out, you want that cobbled look. Refrigerate the dish for at least 30 minutes. Just before baking, drizzle melted butter over the top and sprinkle on sugar. Bake in a preheated 425-degree oven 25–30 minutes, until puffy and lightly browned. Let cool to tepid and serve with a pitcher of cream alongside.
SERVES 6–8

Fresh Peaches in Maple Yogurt

If maple syrup seems a luxury to be closely hoarded, this dessert offers a healthy consolation in that it will provide a surprising climax to a festive meal.

1 pint plain yogurt
1 cup maple syrup

8 peaches, cut in wedges

Stir the yogurt and maple syrup thoroughly enough to cause the syrup to disappear. Chill the mixture several hours. Just before serving, gently stir in the fruit wedges and divide the dessert among stemmed sherbet glasses.
SERVES 4

Rhubarb-Strawberry Cobbler

TOPPING:
¾ cup all-purpose flour
1 teaspoon baking powder
2 tablespoons sugar

A pinch of salt
4 tablespoons vegetable shortening
2 tablespoons milk

1 pint strawberries
1¼ cups sliced rhubarb, about ½-inch thick
1 tablespoon cornstarch, dissolved in 1 tablespoon water

⅓ cup sugar
Heavy cream

Make the topping by mixing the flour, baking powder, 1 tablespoon of the sugar, and salt together, then work in the vegetable shortening, mixing it with your fingertips or with a pastry blender, until it is just coarsely blended. Moisten the batter with the milk.

Rhubarb-Strawberry Cobbler (continued)

If the strawberries are large, cut them in quarters; otherwise, halve them and strew them in the bottom of a baking dish along with the rhubarb. Pour the dissolved cornstarch and the sugar over them and mix well. Pinch off good-size pieces of the dough and plop them on top of the berry mixture; don't make too smooth a top, it's supposed to have a cobbled look. Sprinkle the remaining tablespoon of sugar on top and bake in a preheated 350-degree oven for 40 minutes. Serve warm or cool with a pitcher of heavy cream alongside.

SERVES 4–6

Blackberry Buckle

¼ cup soft butter
¾ cup plus 2 tablespoons sugar
1 egg
2 cups all-purpose flour
2 teaspoons baking powder

½ teaspoon salt
½ cup milk
½ teaspoon vanilla
2 cups freshly picked blackberries

TOPPING:
3 tablespoons soft butter
⅓ cup sugar
¼ cup flour

½ teaspoon cinnamon
¼ teaspoon nutmeg

Heavy cream or whipped cream

Sweet Words

The language of Yankee kitchens must be said to be well seasoned in every category. Desserts, especially. Take a buckle, for instance—it's a biscuity proposition that bulges over an under layer of cooked fruit that is apt to "buckle" in the middle as it bakes in a hot oven. A cobbler might once have been known by a seafaring man as a fruit drink found in the West Indies, but when its fruity character was covered by a shell the word became a common term for New England deep-dish pie, even though a true cobbler is topped with dollops of biscuit dough, giving it a cobbled look. The word *duff*—as in apple duff—used to be a dried-fruit boiled pudding and was spelled "dough," which sailors pronounced as if it were meant to rhyme with rough, as in hazardous crossings.

The etymology of "grunts" and "slumps" may be even more arcane. Both words, in Maine or on Cape Cod, have been used interchangeably as local parlance for the desserts sometimes known as flummeries. Harriet Beecher Stowe so liked the image an edible slump evokes that she named her house in Concord, Massachusetts, Apple Slump.

Cream the butter with ¾ cup of sugar, then beat in the egg. Sift the flour, baking powder, and salt together, and add to the batter alternately with the milk. Stir in the vanilla. Sprinkle the blackberries with the remaining sugar and fold them into the batter. Spread evenly into a buttered 8-inch cake pan.

Make the topping: Using your fingertips, mix the butter, sugar, and flour until they are crumbly. Stir in the spices and sprinkle the topping evenly over the cake batter. Bake in a preheated 350-degree oven for 35 minutes. Serve warm with heavy cream or whipped cream.

SERVES 8–9

Banana Rum Soufflé

2 ripe bananas
½ cup sugar
3 tablespoons dark rum
1 teaspoon butter

4 egg whites, at room temperature
A pinch of salt
⅛ teaspoon cream of tartar

Peel and mash the bananas thoroughly (the food processor does a good job). Beat in ¼ cup of the sugar and the rum. Prepare the soufflé dish: Cut a long sheet of foil, enough to go around the top of a 6-cup soufflé dish. Fold it over so that it will stand 4 inches high. Butter the inside of the soufflé dish and one side of the foil. Place the foil around the top of the soufflé dish, butter side in, so that it stands about 3 inches above the dish. Sprinkle 1 teaspoon of the sugar over the buttered bottom and sides of the dish.

Beat the egg whites until they foam. Add the salt and cream of tartar, and continue to beat until the egg whites form soft peaks. Slowly add the remaining sugar and beat until you have firm shiny peaks. Spoon in the mashed bananas and fold the egg white into the bananas gently. Pour into the prepared soufflé mold, and bake in a preheated 400-degree oven for 30 minutes.

SERVES 4

Currant Flummery

A flummery may be made with wild blackberries, raspberries, elderberries, or gooseberries, adjusting the amount of sugar if the wild berries are particularly sour. This one, made with fresh ripe currants, is a treat.

2 cups fresh currants
2¼ cups water

3 tablespoons cornstarch
½ cup sugar

GARNISH: *about ½ cup heavy cream*

Pick over the currants and put them in a saucepan. Cover them with 2 cups of the water, bring to a boil, and simmer the berries until tender. Dissolve

the cornstarch in the remaining water and stir this into the currants. Simmer another 2 minutes, then stir in the sugar. When cool, spoon the flummery into sherbet glasses and serve with heavy cream poured on top.
SERVES 4

Plum Duff

4 tablespoons soft butter
½ cup brown sugar
1 egg, beaten
1 cup mashed, pitted plums
⅓ cup cake flour
¼ teaspoon baking powder

¼ teaspoon baking soda
A pinch of salt
1 tablespoon cream
Whipped cream or Foamy Sauce
  (page 534) or Rum Custard
  (page 518)

Cream the butter and sugar together. Mix in the egg and the plum mash. Sift the dry ingredients over the moist ingredients and stir in the cream. Distribute the batter evenly among 6 buttered Pyrex cups or muffin tins, and bake in a preheated 325-degree oven for 25 minutes. Turn out of the molds and serve the duffs with whipped cream, Foamy Sauce, or Rum Custard.
SERVES 6

Colonial Parsnip Pudding

1½ pounds parsnips
3 tablespoons butter
2 eggs
½ cup heavy cream
¼ cup maple syrup
¼ cup rum

1 teaspoon lemon juice
About ¼ teaspoon freshly grated
  nutmeg
⅛ teaspoon mace
½ cup raisins
Heavy cream

Trim and peel the parsnips. Cook in a pot of rapidly boiling water until tender, then drain. Mash either by hand or in a food processor. Beat in the butter, eggs, cream, 3 tablespoons of the maple syrup, the rum, lemon juice, and spices, then fold in the raisins. Spoon into a lightly buttered shallow baking dish and drizzle the remaining maple syrup on top. Bake in a preheated 350-degree oven for 30 minutes, until set. Serve warm with a pitcher of heavy cream alongside.
SERVES 6

If you are lucky enough to have a quince bush in your backyard, as many New Englanders have had for generations, here's one of the many things you can make with the ripe fruit.

Quince Scallop

3 large quinces
⅔ cup water
⅓ cup sugar
1 cup coarse bread crumbs
4 tablespoons melted butter

2 tablespoons maple sugar or
  brown sugar
2 tablespoons coarsely chopped
  walnuts or black walnuts
Heavy cream

Peel, quarter, and slice the quinces. Arrange in a shallow round baking dish, overlapping the slices. Add the water and the sugar and bake, uncovered, in a preheated 350-degree oven for 40 minutes. Spread the bread crumbs on top, pour the melted butter over, and sprinkle on the maple or brown sugar and walnuts. Bake another 15–20 minutes, until browned on the top. Serve warm with a pitcher of cream.
SERVES 4

"Serve with a Pitcher of Heavy Cream"

Good old-fashioned New England desserts end with that instruction, and the image conjures up a pitcher filled with yellowy cream so heavy that you can almost hear the plops it makes when it is poured. Only dairy farmers still enjoy that kind of good cream. Most of us have to settle for what is on the supermarket shelves.

But there is a way of giving store-bought cream some of the character it once had. The French call this kind of cream *crème fraîche,* and it is not only thick, it has a little tang to it. Furthermore, it keeps well—at least 10 days in the refrigerator—so you don't have to resort to buying the synthetic-tasting "ultra-pasteurized" cream for longer keeping. We like to whisk about one part crème fraîche into one part regular heavy cream when "serve with a pitcher of heavy cream" is called for. It almost makes you feel you are back on the farm.

To make crème fraîche: Whisk 2 tablespoons sour cream or buttermilk into 1 cup heavy cream, beating until it is completely smooth. Put in a jar and leave at room temperature, uncovered (you may put cheesecloth over it but not plastic wrap, it needs to breathe), 8–12 hours. When it has thickened so that it is hard to pour, cover tightly and refrigerate.
MAKES ABOUT 1 CUP

Rhubarb-Apple Crunch

2 pounds rhubarb
2 large firm apples

TOPPING:
4 tablespoons butter
¾ cup sugar

Heavy cream

¾ cup sugar
2 tablespoons water

¾ cup flour

Chop the rhubarb into 1½-inch pieces. Peel, core, and cut the apples into ¼-inch slices. Mix together with the sugar and water and place in a baking dish. For the topping, rub the butter, sugar, and flour through your fingertips until the mixture is crumbly. Sprinkle this topping over the rhubarb and apples, and bake in a preheated 375-degree oven for 1 hour. Serve warm or cold with a pitcher of heavy cream.
SERVES 6

VARIATION FOR APPLE CRUNCH: Use all apples (about 3 pounds) instead of rhubarb, and reduce the sugar to ⅓ cup.

VARIATION FOR PEAR CRUNCH: Use about 3 pounds pears, peeled and cut in slices, and bake them in ½ cup sugar and ⅓ cup water. The topping may be varied by using dark brown sugar and 1 part oatmeal to 1 part sugar.

Dealing with Rhubarb

Rhubarb is one of the first delights of spring, and you'll find many ways to use it in these pages (see Index). If you have an abundance of rhubarb in your garden, it will freeze successfully. After you have cut rhubarb up and discarded the leaves, steeping it overnight has several advantages. You don't need to use as much sugar as the average recipe calls for, the rhubarb will then cook quickly, and you have the dividend of pure rhubarb juice (no water added) to use as a cooling drink.

To cook rhubarb: Use a proportion of 4 cups sliced rhubarb cut in ½-inch pieces to 1 cup sugar. Toss the rhubarb and sugar together and let steep overnight (you will be amazed at how much juice the rhubarb gives off). Pour off ¾ cup of the liquid and use for a drink. Cook the rhubarb slices in the remaining liquid until just tender but still holding their shape—less than 5 minutes. The rhubarb is ready to eat as is, to freeze in containers, or to use in recipes.

Blackberry Slump

1 quart blackberries
1 cup sugar
⅛ teaspoon freshly grated nutmeg

2 tablespoons lemon juice
3 tablespoons water

TOPPING:
2 cups Basic Baking Powder Mix
   (page 494)

½–⅔ cup water
Confectioners' sugar

Heavy cream

Put the blackberries, sugar, nutmeg, lemon juice, and water in a 1½-quart baking dish and place in a preheated 350-degree oven for 20 minutes. Moisten the Baking Powder Mix with enough water to make a soft dough. Scoop up tablespoonfuls of the dough and scrape it off onto the hot blackberries, dropping mounds of dough all over the top of the dish. Return to the oven and bake for 25 minutes. Sprinkle confectioners' sugar on top and serve with heavy cream.
SERVES 6

Summer Berry Pudding

A dish cherished in childhood that has come back into favor. And no wonder. What better way to enjoy the procession of summer berries—blueberries, raspberries, currants, blackberries, and combinations of them when their seasons overlap—tasting of the essence of summer in this simple, colorful bread pudding?

1 quart blueberries, raspberries,
   currants, or blackberries, or a
   combination of 2 of these berries
¾ cup water
⅔–¾ cup sugar, depending on the
   sweetness of the berries

Soft unsalted butter
9 slices homemade-type white
   bread, crusts removed
Heavy cream

Pick over the berries and rinse them. Cook them in water and sugar, covered, until they soften but have not started to burst, stirring them several times. Butter all but 2 slices of the bread lightly. Press the slices in a round bowl (1½–2 quarts) butter side out, placing one on bottom center, 4 slices around the sides, then cutting triangles from some of the remaining slices and fitting them into the interstices so that the bowl is completely lined. Pour the hot berries and their juice over the lined bowl. Place an unbuttered slice on top and fill in any gaps with remaining pieces of bread. Place a plate on top that will fit down into the bowl and press lightly so that the juices ooze through the top layer. Refrigerate with a small weight, such as

a couple of tuna fish cans, on top for several hours or overnight. This can be served from the bowl but it is prettier unmolded onto a round dessert platter, with a pitcher of heavy cream alongside.
SERVES 6

Wild Berry Summer Pudding

Crowley Island, off Corea, Maine, is a good place to see a heron fly "like a slow arrow," as the painter Marsden Hartley observed, and a nearby island, says Anita Seay, another painter who summers here, is covered with "the most exquisite tiny little wild blueberries that I use in everything." One of her uses for the wild berries she picks is an artist's variation on a New England classic (see the preceding recipe).

1¾ *cups wild blueberries*
1 *pint raspberries*
¾ *cup sugar*
Juice of ½ lemon

½ *teaspoon cinnamon*
1 *loaf French bread*
Heavy cream

Put the berries with the sugar and lemon juice in a stainless steel frying pan, and sprinkle with cinnamon. Bring gently to the boiling point and boil for 2 minutes, keeping the berries whole. Line an ovenproof glass pie pan with slabs of French bread, from which you have cut off the crusts; trim the slices to fit, entirely covering the bottom and sides of the dish. Pour the cooked berries over the bread, spreading them evenly and reserving a little of their juice. Thoroughly cover the top of the berry filling with more slices of bread. Cover the dish with plastic wrap and weight down with a heavy pan that fits snugly into the dish, then chill overnight. To serve, invert the pudding onto a platter and spread the reserved juice over the top as a glaze. Cut the pudding in wedges. Pour cream into dessert plates and arrange a wedge of pudding on each plate. Garnish with uncooked berries. (The pudding improves with age, and can be made up to 2 days in advance.)
SERVES 6

Impy's Bread Pudding

2½ *cups milk*
2 *tablespoons butter*
1½ *cups rough bread crumbs or*
  cubes, crusts removed
¼ *cup raisins or currants*
½ *teaspoon fresh lemon juice*

Grated rind of ½ lemon
3 *eggs*
3 *tablespoons sugar*
Freshly grated nutmeg (about ⅛
  teaspoon)

About 1½ tablespoons sugar,   *Heavy cream*
preferably raw or crushed sugar
cubes

Heat the milk with the butter, stirring, until the butter melts. Remove from the heat, add the bread crumbs and raisins or currants, and let cool to lukewarm. Mix in the lemon juice and rind. Separate the eggs, and beat the yolks into the milk mixture along with the sugar. Beat the whites until they form soft peaks, then fold them into pudding mixture. Season with nutmeg and pour into a lightly buttered shallow baking dish. Sprinkle the sugar on top. Set the dish in a pan of simmering water and bake in a 325-degree oven for 1 hour. Serve warm or cold with a pitcher of cream.

SERVES 6

---

4 small winter squashes, about 5½   *A pinch of salt*
  × *4½ inches*   *¼ teaspoon nutmeg*
¼ cup plus 1 tablespoon sugar   *A pinch of allspice*
½ teaspoon cinnamon   *⅓ cup raisins*
4 slices good homemade-type bread *2 tablespoons brandy*
1¾ cups milk   *½ pint vanilla ice cream*
2 eggs

Bread Pudding in Small Squashes

Cut ½ inch off the top of each squash. Trim the bottoms so that they sit securely. Scrape out the insides, leaving ¼ inch wall all around; discard the seeds and save the meat for another use (such as squash fritters or squash soup). Sprinkle 1 tablespoon of the sugar around the interior walls of the squashes, then sprinkle the insides with a little of the cinnamon. Let stand about 1 hour.

Tear the bread into rough pieces and place in a bowl. Beat the milk and eggs together and pour over the bread. Stir in ¼ cup sugar, the salt, and the spices, and let stand 30 minutes. Meanwhile, soak the raisins in the brandy for 30 minutes.

Drain the squashes of any excess water. Stir the raisins into the bread mixture, then spoon equal amounts of it into the four squashes, mounding the bread pudding over the top slightly (if you have too much, bake the remaining pudding in a buttered Pyrex cup alongside the squash). Bake the squashes in a preheated 325-degree oven for 1 hour, covered, and for an additional 30 minutes, uncovered. Serve hot with dollops of ice cream on top.

SERVES 4

Sugar from the Trees

I t's true that maple syrup is produced in other parts of the East as well as in the Midwest, but no flavor seems more characteristically New England than the taste of maple. The boiled down sap of the rock maple or sugar maple is another gift of Indian cooks to early colonists. The ritual of sugaring-off remains virtually unchanged, as much a part of the early spring scene for Yankees as is the foliage season in autumn.

Some time between mid-February and mid-April, when temperatures range between 28 degrees and 40 degrees, farmers throughout the Northeast tap their maples, hoping for a yield of twelve gallons of sap per tree, as an average. Depending upon the quality of the untreated sap, which is very watery, the best yield may produce one gallon of syrup from twenty gallons of sap; the worst may take eighty gallons of the natural liquid to boil down to one gallon fit for kitchen use.

Most syrup available for retail sale is grade A, an amber product with distinct maple flavor. Those who have easy access use grade B, which is dark and less refined for cooking, and they reserve the best of the year's harvest for the incomparable combination of pancakes or waffles with warmed maple syrup. Maple sugar is produced in small quantities and, when substituted, adds appealing flavor to dishes requiring either white or brown sugar.

Here are two recipes we were given one day in Chelsea, Vermont:

Norma Gillman's Maple Cream

Cook maple syrup to 220 degrees (232 degrees is usually called for but that's too much). Cool the syrup until you can almost put a finger into it, then stir it gently. Keep stirring and stirring until it is all creamy.

Win Bacon's Maple Butter

1 cup maple syrup
½ stick butter (4 tablespoons) butter

Cook the maple syrup and the butter together to the soft ball stage (240 degrees). That's it. Store in the refrigerator.

A dessert you might want to make for a dinner party, it's so good. The recipe can easily be doubled or tripled.

Rhubarb-Maple Toasted Bread Pudding

4 slices good white bread
3/4 cup milk
3 tablespoons butter
2 eggs
1/4 cup maple syrup

1/4 cup plus 1 tablespoon sugar
A pinch of salt
1 cup rhubarb, chopped
Whipped cream flavored with
  maple syrup

Remove the crust from the bread and toast the slices. Tear into small cubes and place in a bowl. Heat the milk with 2 tablespoons of the butter and pour over the bread cubes. Use the remaining butter to coat a 1-quart casserole. After the toast has soaked for 10 minutes, beat together the eggs, maple syrup, 1/4 cup sugar, and salt, then stir in the rhubarb and combine with the bread mixture. Pour into the buttered casserole, sprinkle remaining sugar on top, and bake for 40 minutes in a preheated 325-degree oven. Serve warm with maple-flavored whipped cream.

SERVES 4

Lord Jeffrey Amherst Pudding

Whether or not the undergraduates who sing Lord Jeffrey Amherst's praises have proprietary rights to this crunchy, thoroughly Yankee dessert has not been established, but our favorite Amherst College alumnus long ago raised his voice in tribute to all such good things.

7–8 slices homemade-type white
  bread, crusts removed
3 tablespoons soft butter
1 pound firm apples
About 3/4 cup brown sugar

1 tablespoon cinnamon
1 teaspoon ground cloves
1 tablespoon sugar
1 tablespoon maple syrup
Hard sauce

Line a deep 1 1/2-quart baking dish with buttered slices of bread, butter side out, fitting the pieces together snugly so there are no gaps in the casing. Peel, core, and slice the apples and layer them into the bread-lined dish, sprinkling each layer liberally with brown sugar, and some of the cinnamon and cloves (the amount of the brown sugar may vary, depending on the sweetness of the apples). When filled, fold toward the center any overhanging pieces, then lay strips of bread, buttered on both sides, over the top. Sprinkle the top with the sugar, the remaining spices, and drizzle the maple syrup over. Bake in a 300-degree oven for 2 hours. Unmold onto a platter and serve with Hard Sauce (page 533).

SERVES 6

Chocolate Bread Pudding

2 cups milk
1/4 cup unsweetened cocoa
3 tablespoons sugar
1 cup torn pieces good homemade-type bread

2 eggs
Pinch salt
1/2 teaspoon vanilla
Several gratings nutmeg

TOPPING:
1/2 cup heavy cream whipped with 2 tablespoons sugar

Dusting of cocoa

Heat the milk and whisk in the cocoa and sugar until dissolved. Remove from the heat and stir in the bread. Lightly beat the eggs and mix into the cocoa along with the salt, vanilla, and nutmeg. Pour into a buttered mold and bake in a preheated 325-degree oven for 50 minutes. Serve warm with whipped cream spread on top, dusted with cocoa.
SERVES 4

Applesauce-Maple Bread Pudding

1 pound apples, peeled, cored, and cut in chunks
1/3 cup water
4 cups cubed, crustless good white bread

6 tablespoons butter, melted
1/3 cup maple syrup
1 1/2 tablespoons sugar mixed with 3/4 teaspoon cinnamon

GARNISH: whipped cream, vanilla ice cream, or custard sauce

Put the apples and water in a saucepan, and cook over moderately high heat until the apples are soft and the liquid has boiled away. Beat with a fork to make a relatively smooth purée. Toss the bread cubes with the melted butter and maple syrup in an 8-inch pie plate. Stir the applesauce into the bread mixture and sprinkle cinnamon sugar evenly over the top. Bake in a preheated 375-degree oven for 30 minutes. Serve warm with any of the suggested garnishes.
SERVES 4

As this pudding bakes, the batter rises to the top and the sweet, dark sauce stays on the bottom. It is delicious warm but it also mellows with age and can be refrigerated for several days and served cold.

Cottage Pudding

BATTER:
3/4 cup dark brown sugar
2 tablespoons butter
2 teaspoons baking powder
1 1/4 cups flour
1 teaspoon salt

1/2 cup milk
3/4 cup raisins, preferably, large
  seedless
1 teaspoon vanilla

SAUCE:
1 cup dark brown sugar
1 tablespoon butter

1/4 teaspoon freshly grated nutmeg
2 1/2 cups boiling water

For the batter, cream the brown sugar and butter together. Toss the baking powder, flour, and salt together to mix, then add them alternately with the milk to the butter and sugar, stirring until smooth. Stir in the raisins and vanilla. Spread the batter into a greased 9 × 9-inch cake pan. Make the sauce by putting the brown sugar, butter, and nutmeg in a bowl, and then stirring in the boiling water. Pour this sauce over the batter and bake in a preheated 375-degree oven for 45 minutes, until the top is golden brown.
SERVES 8

Creamed Rice with Maple Syrup

1/2 cup rice
1 1/2 cups milk
3–4 cardamom seeds (optional)
1 cup heavy cream

1/4 cup sugar, preferably superfine
1/2 teaspoon vanilla
About 3/4 cup maple syrup

Put the rice in a small heavy saucepan, pour 1 cup of the milk over, and drop in the optional cardamom seeds. Bring to a boil, then turn down the heat, cover, and simmer gently for about 15 minutes, or until the milk is absorbed. Stir with a fork gently, add the remaining milk, and simmer again, covered, for 15–20 minutes, or until the milk is absorbed; if it isn't, simmer uncovered, stirring occasionally, until it has all evaporated. Fluff the rice up with a fork and let cool completely, first at room temperature, then in the refrigerator. Whip the cream, preferably over a bowl of ice cubes, until it thickens, then add the sugar and continue to beat until it forms firm peaks. Stir in the vanilla and fold the whipped cream into the cooled rice. Pack the mixture into 4 individual molds and chill thoroughly. To serve, unmold onto plates and pass the maple syrup in a jug to pour on top.
SERVES 4

Traditional Indian Pudding

This is the traditional slow-baked Indian Pudding—with no eggs and only one spice (sometimes it was cinnamon, sometimes ginger). If you like to serve it as a sauce for ice cream, rather than the other way around with ice cream as the accompaniment, take it out of the oven after 2 hours when the pudding will still be loose.

4 tablespoons cornmeal
2 cups boiling milk
½ cup molasses
½ teaspoon salt
3 tablespoons sugar

2 tablespoon butter
1 teaspoon cinnamon or ginger
3 cups cold milk
Heavy cream, whipped cream, or
   vanilla or coffee ice cream

Add the cornmeal to the boiling milk in a thin stream, stirring, and cook it slowly in a heavy saucepan for 20 minutes, continuing to stir from time to time. Add the molasses, salt, sugar, butter, and spice. Transfer to 1½-quart buttered baking dish and pour 2 cups of the cold milk on top. Bake for 30 minutes at 275 degrees, then pour the remaining cup of milk on top—don't stir—and bake for another 2½ hours. Serve with heavy cream, whipped cream, or ice cream.
SERVES 6–8

Marmalade Indian Pudding

Yankee ideas have traveled as far west as the Pacific and have influenced the cooking in many regions in between. In this traditional dessert, molasses is accented by orange marmalade, and the interesting result is served regularly by Andy and Jan Coulson at the White Gull Inn at Fish Creek, Wisconsin—a state settled by many New Englanders.

⅓ cup yellow cornmeal, preferably
   stone-ground
⅓ cup molasses
½ cup orange marmalade
4 cups milk

1 egg, well beaten
½ teaspoon salt
½ teaspoon ground ginger
½ teaspoon cinnamon

In a saucepan, mix together the cornmeal, molasses, marmalade, and 2 cups of the milk. Cook, stirring constantly, over low heat until the mixture bubbles and thickens slightly. Beat the remaining milk with the egg, salt, and spices. Stir into the cornmeal mixture. Pour into 8 custard dishes and place in a preheated 350-degree oven to bake for 1 hour. Serve warm with freshly whipped cream.
SERVES 8

Deacon Porter's Hat

Many graduates of Mount Holyoke College, in South Hadley, Massachusetts, have celebrated the birthday on February 28 of founder Mary Lyon, to whom a fitting tribute has been the serving of a suet pudding called "Deacon Porter's Hat." Andrew W. Porter was a college trustee who wore a stovepipe hat, similar in shape to the pudding mold, and the likeness inspired the young undergraduates of 1837 to name the favorite Mount Holyoke dessert in his memory. "Unlike many schools," a South Hadley alumna wrote as recently as a couple of years ago, "our food was really good—especially the desserts." The steamed pudding that keeps the deacon's name alive is perky with spices and dappled by puffy raisins, and is served with a fluffy rum-flavored sauce.

Deacon Porter's Hat

The original recipe from the steward of Mount Holyoke College called for ground suet. In an effort to make a less heavy dessert, we've substituted a light oil and found the steamed pudding much more appealing for today's taste. The recipe may be doubled for a holiday feast, using a 2-quart mold —preferably a tall one to resemble a deacon's hat.

1/2 cup molasses
1/2 cup safflower or other light oil
3/4 cup milk
1 1/2 cups flour
1 teaspoon baking powder
1/8 teaspoon salt
1/2 teaspoon ground cloves
1/2 teaspoon cinnamon

1/8 teaspoon ground ginger
1/8 teaspoon freshly grated nutmeg
1/2 cup raisins
1/2 cup currants
1/2 cup chopped nuts, such as walnuts, butternuts, and/or hazelnuts

HARD SAUCE:
4 tablespoons soft unsalted butter
1 cup confectioners' sugar
1 tablespoon heavy cream

2 teaspoons rum, brandy, or vanilla extract

Stir together the molasses, oil, and milk. Toss or sift the flour, baking powder, salt, and spices to mix, then add them to the liquid ingredients. Fold in the raisins, currants, and nuts. Pour into a 1-quart mold (preferably a tall one), set it on a rack in a large pot, and pour enough boiling water in to come halfway up the mold. Cover and steam for 2 hours.

Meanwhile, prepare the Hard Sauce by whipping the butter until light,

Deacon Porter's Hat (continued)

then adding the confectioners' sugar gradually, continuing to beat until fluffy. Stir in the cream and rum or brandy or vanilla. Unmold the pudding onto a platter and serve warm, passing the Hard Sauce in a bowl.

SERVES 6–8

Chocolate Steamed Pudding

2½ squares unsweetened chocolate
4 tablespoons butter
2 eggs
¾ cup sugar

⅔ cup milk
2 cups flour
1 tablespoon baking powder
¼ teaspoon salt

FOAMY SAUCE:
½ pound unsalted butter
2 cups confectioners' sugar
2 eggs, well beaten

⅛ teaspoon salt
4 tablespoons dry sherry

Melt the chocolate with the butter in a saucepan set over simmering water. Beat the eggs until lemon-colored, then beat in the sugar and the milk. Toss the flour, baking powder, and salt together to mix thoroughly. Stir the melted chocolate into the egg mixture, then stir in the dry ingredients. Pour into a lightly buttered 1½ or 2-quart mold, cover tightly, and set over boiling water to steam for 1¾ hours.

Meanwhile, prepare the Foamy Sauce: Beat the butter until soft and creamy. Gradually add the confectioners' sugar and when well blended, transfer the mixture to the top of a double boiler (unless your mixing bowl fits over a pot of simmering water without touching). Add the well-beaten eggs and salt, and beat for 5 minutes over simmering water. Stir in the sherry and serve warm.

Unmold the pudding and serve warm with Foamy Sauce.

SERVES 8–10

Steamed Cranberry Pudding

1⅓ cups all-purpose flour
1 teaspoon baking soda
¼ teaspoon salt
½ cup maple syrup
½ cup orange juice

1¼ cups cranberries
½ cup coarsely chopped black
    walnuts or walnuts
Hard Sauce or whipped cream

Toss or sift the flour, baking soda, and salt together. Stir the maple syrup and orange juice together, then mix into the dry ingredients. Fold the cranberries and nuts into the batter. Transfer to a well-buttered 6-cup mold for steaming, cover securely, and steam over boiling water for 2 hours. Unmold the pudding onto a platter. Serve with Hard Sauce (page 533) or whipped cream.
SERVES 5–6 (MAY BE DOUBLED, USING A 3-QUART MOLD)

Maine Goat Cheese Honey Dessert

At her small goat farm near Dixmont, Maine, Camilla Stege adapted this Greek recipe as a surprising, delicious way to end a meal.

1 pound crumbled goat cheese
4 tablespoons honey
1½–2 tablespoons Cointreau, or
    other liqueur

¼ cup butternut meats, ground fine

Mix the cheese, honey, and liqueur until it is a smooth consistency. Lightly butter a 2-cup mold. Sprinkle the ground butternuts evenly to line the mold. Scrape the cheese mixture into the mold. Cover with plastic wrap, and put the mold in the refrigerator to chill for 24 hours. Dip the mold into hot water and then unmold by turning upside down onto a decorative plate. Garnish with fresh seedless grapes or other fruit.
SERVES 4

Crowdie Cream with Toasted Oats

Vermont old-timers in the Connecticut Valley not far from us like to remind the curious that oats were introduced to the region a couple of centuries ago by Ryegate farmers from Scotland. Some of these Green Mountain Scots celebrate the beginning of lent with this unusual old-fashioned dessert.

⅓ cup rolled oats
1 cup heavy cream

3 tablespoons powdered sugar
2 tablespoons dark rum

Preheat the oven to 400 degrees. Spread the oatmeal over the bottom of a shallow 8 × 10-inch pan, and put it in the center of the hot oven. Toast for about 15 minutes, shaking the pan occasionally, until the flakes are uniformly light brown—watch for any sign of burning. Set aside to cool. In a chilled bowl, whip the cream until it begins to thicken. Gradually beat in the sugar, and continue beating the cream until stiff peaks form. Gently stir in the rum, one drop at a time. With a rubber spatula, carefully fold in the toasted oats; do not stir, but fold the flakes thoroughly into the stiff cream. Divide the resulting crowdie cream into individual serving dishes or parfait glasses that have been well chilled, and set them in the refrigerator until dessert time.

SERVES 4

Maple Custard

½ cup plus 2 tablespoons maple syrup
2 cups light cream, or 1 cup milk and 1 cup light cream

5 eggs
¼ teaspoon salt
2 tablespoons dark rum
¾ cup heavy cream

In a heavy saucepan, heat ½ cup maple syrup and the light cream. Beat the eggs lightly, then pour them into the hot syrup and cream along with the salt and the rum. Lightly butter a 1½-quart baking dish and pour the custard into it. Set the dish in a pan of hot water that comes halfway up the sides and bake in a preheated 325-degree oven for 1 hour. Remove and chill. Whip the heavy cream and flavor it with the remaining 2 tablespoons of maple syrup and serve a dollop on each portion.

SERVES 6

Fresh Cheese and Apple Crêpes, Flamed

Thin pancakes, sometimes called *cresps* or *crisps* by English colonists, were often served as sweet desserts in much the way they appear on French menus. Stuffed and rolled, adorned with an apple sauce, these have a modern Yankee resonance.

CRÊPE BATTER:
½ cup all-purpose flour
⅛ teaspoon salt
½ cup milk
¼ cup water

2 eggs
2 tablespoons melted butter
½ teaspoon vanilla

FILLING:

1 cup drained cottage cheese

½ cup sour cream

2 teaspoons sugar

Grated rind of 1 lemon

½ teaspoon lemon juice

⅛ teaspoon freshly grated nutmeg

SAUCE:

4 medium apples, peeled, cored, and sliced

4 tablespoons maple or brown sugar

2 tablespoons butter

3 tablespoons warm applejack or brandy for flaming

Beat all the ingredients for the crêpes together until very smooth (a blender or food processor will do a good job). Let rest 30 minutes or more.

Using about 3 tablespoons batter for each crêpe, drop the batter onto a hot greased griddle, about 8 inches in diameter, and spread evenly by tilting immediately and swirling the batter all around to the sides of the pan. Cook over medium heat until the surface looks dry and little bubbles appear, then turn and lightly brown the other side. Scoop the finished crêpe up and place on a rack. Continue until you have made 6 crêpes.

Make the filling by blending all the filling ingredients together in a food processor or beat smooth with an electric mixer. Spoon one-sixth of the filling onto the center of each crêpe, roll up, and arrange on a flameproof serving dish, seam side down.

Make the sauce by sautéing the sliced apples and brown or maple sugar in the butter, tossing, until barely tender, about 3 minutes. Pour the hot sauce over the crêpes, then drizzle the warm applejack on top and set aflame.

SERVES 6

---

3 large firm apples

½ cup raisins

1 teaspoon cinnamon

1 cup sugar

4 eggs

A pinch of salt

A pinch of nutmeg

3 cups milk

Heavy cream

Bird's Nest Pudding

Peel the apples and cut them evenly in half horizontally. Cut out the cores and set the apple halves, cored side up, in one layer in a shallow dish so they fit quite snugly. Fill the cored-out hollows with equal amounts of raisins and cinnamon and a sprinkling of the sugar. Beat the eggs and mix in the remaining sugar, salt, nutmeg, and milk. Pour this over and around the apples and set the dish in a preheated 325-degree oven to bake 45 minutes. Serve warm with a pitcher of cream, if you wish.

SERVES 6

Wild Rice and Maple Pudding

Outdoorsmen who know the Northeast region as well as Euell Gibbons did confirm his conviction that the combination of maple syrup and wild rice, often found in the same location, is "pure bliss." One of our favorite combinations of the two results in a delectable dessert that can be served with whipped cream or ice cream.

1½ cups cooked wild rice
1 cup day-old whole wheat bread cubes
3 eggs, lightly beaten
2 cups milk

¼ cup maple syrup
¼ cup maple or brown sugar
Salt
2½ tablespoons melted butter

Put the wild rice and the bread crumbs in a 1-quart buttered casserole and mix well. Stir the eggs, milk, and maple syrup in a bowl, blending in the maple or brown sugar and a shake of salt. Pour the melted butter over the mixture of rice and bread so that it is evenly distributed. Pour the egg-milk mixture over and set the casserole in a pan of hot water, then put in a preheated 350-degree oven for 1 hour, or until the custard is set.
SERVES 4

Here is another pudding—like Cottage Pudding—that makes its own sauce while it bakes.

Fudge Pudding

1 cup flour
2 teaspoons baking powder
¾ cup sugar
6 tablespoons unsweetened cocoa
2 tablespoons melted butter

½ cup milk
1 teaspoon vanilla
¾ cup broken walnut meats
¾ cup brown sugar
1¾ cups boiling water

Sift together the flour, baking powder, sugar, and 4 tablespoons of the cocoa. Stir the melted butter into the milk, along with the vanilla. Beat this into the flour mixture and stir in the walnuts. Pour into a well-greased 9-inch square pan. Now mix the brown sugar with the remaining 2 tablespoons of cocoa. Sprinkle this mixture on the top of the pudding. Pour the boiling water over it, and bake in a preheated 350-degree oven for 40 minutes. Cut it into squares and serve it upside down on serving plates, spooning over each square some of the pudding sauce. It should be served warm.

SERVES 4–6

This is a favorite recipe. Our ninety-three-year-old mother still makes it regularly in her Vermont kitchen for whatever occasion arises, a gathering of the great-grandchildren, even high tea—a ritual she favors.

Phyllis's Chocolate Roll

5 eggs
1 cup confectioners' sugar

5 tablespoons unsweetened cocoa
½ cup heavy cream

Separate the eggs, dropping the whites into a large clean bowl and the yolks into another. Beat the yolks until thick and lemon colored, then beat in the sugar and cocoa. Clean and dry the beaters thoroughly, then beat the egg whites until they form soft peaks. Lighten the yolk-sugar mixture by stirring in a little of the egg whites, then fold the remaining whites into the batter. Butter a 10 × 15-inch jelly roll pan, fit it with wax paper, and butter the top of the paper. Spread the batter in the lined pan. Bake in a preheated 350-degree oven 8–10 minutes, until the edges have started to shrink slightly. Turn out onto a floured kitchen towel and peel off the wax paper. Let the cake cool. Beat the cream until almost stiff, then spread it over the cooled cake. Roll the cake up lengthwise, using the towel to help, and turn it onto a serving platter.

SERVES 8

Cold Lemon Soufflé

From Dana Jennings in Canaan, Connecticut, a lovely cold soufflé that you can garnish with violets from your garden or candied violets.

1 tablespoon gelatine
¼ cup cold water
3 eggs
1 cup sugar
Grated rind of 2 lemons

⅓ cup lemon juice
1½ cups heavy cream
1 tablespoon confectioners' sugar
Fresh or candied violets (optional)

In a measuring cup set in a pan of simmering water, soften the gelatine in ¼ cup cold water. Separate the eggs and beat the yolks with the sugar until thick. Beat in the lemon rind and juice, then stir in the softened gelatine. Whip 1 cup of the cream until it forms soft peaks. Beat the egg whites until they form soft peaks. Then fold the egg whites into the lemon mixture, and finally fold in the whipped cream. Turn the mixture into a deep bowl, preferably glass, and refrigerate for at least 3 hours. Whip the remaining cream with confectioners' sugar until firm. Put into a pastry bag and make small rosettes around the edge of the dish with a larger one in the center; or if you don't want to fuss with a pastry bag, just place dollops of whipped cream on top. Decorate with violets, if you wish.
SERVES 6–8

Old-fashioned Strawberry Shortcake

The filling for this shortcake can, of course, be raspberries, peaches, blueberries, blackberries—whatever is in season. The directions here are for one large cake that lends itself to a handsome presentation, decorated with a ring of fresh berries, but you can easily make individual shortcakes from this dough, cutting them out with a biscuit cutter and baking them only about 12 minutes.

2 cups cake flour
½ teaspoon salt
2 teaspoons baking powder

½ teaspoon baking soda
1 cup sour cream
3 tablespoons milk

THE FILLING AND TOPPING:
2 teaspoons unsalted butter, softened
2 cups heavy cream
½ cup superfine sugar that has been

steeped with a vanilla bean, or ½ cup sugar and 1 teaspoon vanilla extract
2 pints strawberries

Measure out the two cups of flour by sifting the flour directly into the cup and sweeping off the excess. Resift twice with the salt and baking powder. Stir the soda into the sour cream, then add to the flour, mixing lightly with a fork. Add the milk and blend lightly. Scrape the dough out onto a lightly floured working surface and pat into shape to fit a generously buttered 9-inch springform pan. Bake in a preheated 425-degree oven 20–25 minutes, until nicely golden. When cool enough to handle, slice the cake in half horizontally. Scoop out a little of the soft interior and discard, and spread both cut surfaces with butter.

Whip the cream, adding the vanilla sugar (or the sugar and vanilla extract) as it thickens. Select about a dozen handsome strawberries for the top and mash the rest roughly with a fork, and then stir in about half the whipped cream. Spread the whipped cream-strawberry mixture over one of the buttered shortcake halves, place the second piece on top, buttered side down, and spread the whole cake with the remaining whipped cream. Slice the dozen strawberries in half and make a border of them, leaving one nice strawberry for the center.

SERVES 8

Strawberry Short Cake and Milk White Bread

Kate Douglas Wiggin's *Rebecca of Sunnybrook Farm* may be little known today, but the author had an idea to be long remembered when she asked readers: "Who would not rather make a delicious strawberry shortcake than play 'The Maiden's Prayer' on the piano? Where is the painted table scarf that can compare with an honest loaf of milk-white bread?"

FROZEN DESSERTS

Maple Butternut or Walnut Ice Cream

2 cups heavy cream
1 cup light cream
1 cup maple syrup

½ cup coarsely chopped butternuts
or walnuts or black walnuts

Mix the two creams and the maple syrup together. Place in the container of your ice cream maker and freeze according to directions. When the ice cream has thickened almost to the desired consistency, toss in the chopped nuts and continue to churn until ready.

MAKES ABOUT 1 QUART

Peppermint Candy Ice Cream

When Vrest Orton decided it was time to revive the concept of an authentic old-fashioned Vermont country store, he said he wanted to create "atmosphere redolent with an evocative potpourri of wood smoke from the pot-bellied stove . . . peppermint sticks, freshly cut cheese . . . nutmegs, cinnamon sticks . . ." The nostalgia boom that has thrived since he began includes much that is authentic, such as this ice cream, rich with the aromas of the candy counter.

12 wheel-shaped peppermints
½ cup water
1½ pints heavy cream

½ pint milk
⅔ cup crushed peppermint candy
canes

Melt the peppermint wheels in the water, stirring constantly to make ½ cup simple syrup that should be just barely pink. Mix the heavy cream and the milk in a bowl and stir in the syrup. If using ice trays in the refrigerator, freeze the mixture, add the crushed candies and freeze again, stirring to mix well. If using a crank freezer, stir in the crushed candies after about 20 minutes of cranking.

MAKES ABOUT 1½ QUARTS

Fresh Strawberry Ice Cream

If freshly picked strawberries are not quite as sweet as they might be—and those grown in northern New England aren't always—the best way to bring out the flavor is to add some lemon juice along with sugar and a few drops of vanilla. You must taste critically when you mix in the lemon juice and sugar and vanilla with the mashed strawberries, so do not add everything at once.

2 cups mashed strawberries *
   (approximately 1½ pints fresh)
⅓–½ cup sugar
2–4 teaspoons fresh lemon juice
   (optional)

Up to ⅛ teaspoon vanilla
   (optional)
1 cup heavy cream
½ cup light cream

* If you use a food processor to mash the berries, do not purée them completely.

Mix the strawberries and ⅓ cup sugar together. Taste critically and add more sugar plus lemon juice and vanilla, if needed. Stir in the creams, put the mixture in an ice cream freezer and follow the manufacturer's directions for freezing.
MAKES ABOUT 1 QUART

Chocolate Ice Cream

3 squares unsweetened chocolate
1 cup sugar
2 cups heavy cream

1 cup light cream
⅛ teaspoon salt
1 teaspoon vanilla

Melt the chocolate and then beat together with the sugar, creams, salt, and vanilla. Freeze in an ice cream freezer following manufacturer's directions.
MAKES ABOUT 1½ PINTS

Rhubarb Soft Ice "Cream"

This rhubarb sherbet has a surprisingly creamy taste—it is almost like a frozen mousse and it doesn't contain an ounce of cream.

1 pound rhubarb, cut in rough
   chunks (don't peel)
1¼ cups sugar
1 cup water

2 tablespoons port, elderberry
   wine, or red currant liqueur
1 egg white

Boil the rhubarb, sugar, and water together until the rhubarb is soft, about 10 minutes. Purée in a food processor or blender, then blend in the wine and egg white. Allow to cool, then freeze the mixture in an ice cream freezer according to the manufacturer's directions.
MAKES ABOUT 1 QUART

Emperors of Ice Cream

It's not so strange to speak of New England and ice cream in the same breath—Cote's dairy farm in Maine has long been a mecca for aficionados of a non-factory-made version, just as Steve's of Boston and Ben and Jerry's of Vermont, in the 1980s, began to share their personalized ice creams with the rest of the world.

America's favorite dessert has owed much to enterprising Yankees since 1853, when the White Mountain Freezer Company turned out the first hand-crank machine from New England pine and cast-iron from its own foundry. It's difficult to imagine neighborhood lawn parties and ice cream socials of the past without the ice-packed wooden buckets and their slatted dashers that children got to lick. "Sometimes my arm ached as I turned the creaking White Mountain Freezer in the welcome shade of the woodshed," a New Hampshireman recalled, adding enthusiastically that sucking what adhered to the paddle made it all worthwhile. There was a regal feeling in making one's own.

There are abundant recipes for homemade frozen desserts, and the variety of manufactured flavors grows longer each year. But the various types fall into three categories: churned ice creams, churned ices and sherbets (or sorbets), and still-frozen mixtures. With all of them, modern technology has eliminated the need for "aching arms."

Churned mixtures are prepared from custard bases or from sweetened cream with the flavoring of fruits and berries and other enhancements. Vanilla ice cream is distinguished as "Philadelphia" when made from sweetened cream and vanilla, and when prepared from a custard base it's often called "New York." Churned water ices and sherbets

---

Custard Ice Cream: Vanilla, Cinnamon, or Ginger

1½ cups milk
3 egg yolks, lightly beaten

½ cup sugar
½ teaspoon salt

FOR VANILLA ICE CREAM:
1 vanilla bean plus 1 teaspoon vanilla extract (optional)

FOR CINNAMON ICE CREAM:
1 stick cinnamon

FOR GINGER ICE CREAM:
⅔ cup finely chopped crystallized ginger

1½ cups heavy cream

require a syrup base. Milk sherbet may be made with milk or buttermilk. Mousses and parfaits, and other still-frozen desserts, are made in the freezer and don't require churning or beating.

It is useful to have a jar of simple syrup on hand, particularly in summer, so that you can make an ice or a sherbet on the spur of the moment with whatever fruits or berries may be ripe—sometimes using just a handful of fruits that need to be used up immediately before they're too ripe (it's a good way of preserving them).

To make simple syrup: The usual formula is 2 parts water to 1 part sugar. Mix the water and sugar together in a saucepan and bring to a boil. Boil, stirring, until the sugar has melted, then chill. Store the syrup in a closed jar in the refrigerator.

Note that most of our recipes for ice creams, ices, sherbets, and sorbets yield relatively small amounts—a quart or less—because many of the new ice cream makers are limited in their capacity (and if you're using freezer trays, you don't want to preempt too much space). Any of the mixtures can be doubled or tripled according to the capacity of your machine.

To make ice cream in the freezer compartment of the refrigerator, put your ice cream mixture into ice trays. Freeze for about 1 hour, or until the mixture has frozen about 1 inch around the sides of the trays, then remove and beat thoroughly. Return to the freezer and let freeze completely.

Heat the milk to the boiling point. Add the hot milk to the lightly beaten egg yolks in a slow steady stream, beating. Clean out the pan in which the milk was heated and return the milk-egg mixture to it, then stir in the sugar and salt. Add the vanilla bean, crushing it slightly, or the cinnamon stick or the candied ginger. Cook over gentle heat, stirring until the custard begins to thicken; as soon as steam begins to rise around the sides of the pan, that is a sign that the custard is ready. Remove from the heat and put the pan in a pan of ice water to stop the cooking, stirring until the custard begins to cool. Chill thoroughly. When the custard is very cold, stir in the heavy cream and freeze in your ice cream freezer according to manufacturer's directions or in ice trays in the freezer following the directions above.
MAKES ABOUT 1 QUART

Raspberry Tofu Ice Cream

1 cup tofu
1 cup soy milk
1 cup frozen raspberries
Juice of 1/2 lemon
1/2 cup buckwheat honey

1/4 cup safflower oil
1/2 teaspoon vanilla extract
Whole frozen or fresh raspberries
   (brought to room temperature)

Put all ingredients except the extra raspberries in a food processor and spin until smooth. Pour into 1 ice cube tray and freeze 1 hour. Stir well or beat again in the food processor and return the mixture to the freezer. Stir and add whole raspberries and freeze.
MAKES 1 1/2 PINTS

Black Walnut Ice Cream

2/3 cup sugar
4 egg whites, beaten stiff

1 pint cream
1/2 cup finely chopped black walnuts

Carefully fold the sugar into the stiffly beaten whites. Whip the cream and fold into the egg whites along with the finely chopped nuts. Freeze according to manufacturer's directions.
MAKES 3 PINTS

Oatmeal Ice Cream

In the 1980s imaginative ice cream makers such as Charles Cox of Big Alice's in Providence began making ice creams of cookies and cakes, usually leftovers. An older idea calls for the use of crumbs of bread, or in this case, flakes of oatmeal, and is sometimes known as Caledonian ice cream. (You may also try toasting Boston brown bread crumbs to substitute for the oatmeal.)

1/3 cup oatmeal
1 cup heavy cream
1 cup light cream
3/4 cup vanilla sugar *

1/4 cup sugar
1/3 cup water
1 egg white, beaten stiff (optional)

   * To make vanilla sugar: Put a vanilla pod in a large screw-top jar with 2–3 cups of superfine sugar, and leave for 1–2 weeks or more. Add more sugar as you use it.
   * Jane Grigson suggests the possibility of using syrup from a jar of preserved ginger instead of the vanilla sugar.

Spread the oatmeal in a thin layer on a large baking sheet and put it in the oven at the lowest possible temperature, stirring occasionally, leaving it until the oatmeal is hard and crunchy and lightly brown. Whip the creams together with the vanilla sugar until light and thick. Put the mixture into refrigerator trays and freeze, turning the sides to the middle when it begins to harden. Boil the granulated sugar with the water to make simple syrup. When the syrup is cool, mix it with the dried oatmeal and stir immediately into the ice cream, beating thoroughly. The stiffly beaten egg white may be mixed in at this point. Refreeze the ice cream, and serve with oatmeal cookies.

MAKES ABOUT 1 QUART

Apple Syrup Yogurt "Ice Cream"

The best Vermont farm-made apple syrup we know (it may be so red in color it reminds you unfortunately of maraschino cherries) is not only good on pancakes, but it makes a terrific ice cream, as we discovered when we worked out this formula, based on Windy Wood's patented product.

4 eggs
1 cup Windy Wood apple syrup
1 quart plain yogurt

Beat the eggs until very light and fluffy. Pour in the apple syrup a little at a time and continue to beat until pale red and airy. Fold in the yogurt. Freeze in an ice cream freezer following manufacturer's instructions, or put into freezer trays and follow the directions in the box, page 545. Beat once again, and then freeze until firm throughout.

MAKES ABOUT 1 QUART

Frozen Maple Mousse

1 cup maple syrup
2 egg whites
Pinch salt
1 cup heavy cream

Put the maple syrup in 1-quart pan over medium heat. Meanwhile, beat the egg whites with the pinch of salt until they hold firm peaks. Watch the syrup carefully now; as the large bubbles start to turn into smaller bubbles and when you lift a spoon with syrup in it 8 inches or so above the pan and the falling syrup spins a thread, remove immediately from the fire (it should be about 260 degrees). With an electric beater going, pour the hot syrup in a thin, steady stream into the egg whites. In a separate bowl beat the cream, preferably over a bowl of ice to get greater volume, until it forms soft peaks, then fold it into the maple-egg white mixture. Turn into a pretty bowl or sherbet glasses and freeze 2 hours or more before serving.

SERVES 6

Rhubarb Mousse

¾ cup sugar
¼ cup water
3 egg whites at room temperature
A pinch of salt
⅛ teaspoon cream of tartar

1 cup heavy cream
2 tablespoons raspberry liqueur, or other fruit-flavored liqueur
2 cups cooked, drained, puréed rhubarb

GARNISH: *a handful of strawberries, blackberries, or raspberries*

Cook the sugar and water until it forms a thick syrup (the temperature should be 238 degrees). Beat the egg whites and when they foam, add the salt and cream of tartar, and continue to beat until they start to form soft peaks. Add in a slow steady stream the hot sugar syrup, beating constantly, and continue to beat until the mixture has cooled and is thick. Beat the cream in a separate bowl until almost stiff, then beat in the liqueur. Fold the whipped cream into the egg white–sugar syrup mixture and freeze for 2 hours.

Remove the bowl from the freezer and stir in the puréed rhubarb. If you are not serving immediately, hold the mousse in the freezer. Serve in a glass bowl or in sherbet glasses, decorated with berries.
SERVES 8

Strawberry Ice with Mint

½–¾ cup sugar
3 cups mashed fresh strawberries (see footnote page 543)
⅛ teaspoon vanilla

2 tablespoons lime juice
2 tablespoons lemon juice
4–5 tablespoons chopped mint

Mix ½ cup sugar with the mashed strawberries, then stir in the vanilla, citrus juices, and mint. Taste critically to determine whether it needs more sugar. Freeze in an ice cream freezer according to manufacturer's directions.
MAKES ABOUT 1 QUART

Cantaloupe-Rum Sherbet

1 cantaloupe, pared and seeds removed
⅓ cup water

3 tablespoons sugar
2 tablespoons dark rum
2 tablespoons grated lemon rind

Cut the cantaloupe into small pieces. Make a syrup by boiling the water and the sugar just long enough to dissolve the sugar. Put the cantaloupe pieces in a blender or a food processor, add the other ingredients, and purée. To freeze in the refrigerator, pour into a shallow container and freeze. Remove the partially frozen mixture to the blender or food processor and beat until it is smooth. Repeat when the sherbet firms up again and then freeze for about 3 hours, or until it is firm. Follow manufacturer's directions to freeze in home freezer.

SERVES 4

Honeydew and Lime Sherbet

About 3 pounds very ripe honeydew melon (to make 3½ cups puréed)
Grated rind of 1 lime
¾ cup sugar syrup—see box, page 545
1–2 tablespoons lime juice
Sprigs of mint

Scoop out the flesh of the melon and purée it in a food processor or blender with the grated lime rind and sugar syrup. Add lime juice to taste, being careful not to overpower the delicate taste of the honeydew. Freeze in ice cream freezer following manufacturer's directions. Decorate servings with sprigs of fresh mint.

MAKES 1 QUART

Plum-Peach Sorbet

6 red plums
1 cup water
2 tablespoons sugar
2 ripe peaches, peeled and pitted
1½ cups sugar syrup (page 545)

Cook the plums in the water and sugar until soft, about 10 minutes. Let cool until you can handle them, then remove the pits (not the skins; they give good color), and put them in a food processor or blender along with their cooking liquid and the peaches. Blend until very smooth. Stir in the sugar syrup and cool. Then freeze in an ice cream freezer according to the manufacturers' instructions.

MAKES ABOUT 1 QUART

Grapefruit Sherbet

2 cups grapefruit juice, freshly squeezed
2 cups simple syrup—see box, page 545
2 tablespoons coarsely grated grapefruit rind
2 tablespoons grenadine or cassis
Sprigs of mint

Mix together all the ingredients except the mint and freeze in an ice cream maker according to manufacturer's directions. Top each serving with a sprig of mint.

MAKES ABOUT 1 QUART

Blackberry-Peach Sherbet

1 cup blackberries, picked over and washed
3 medium-size ripe peaches, peeled, pitted, cut in chunks

¼ cup raspberry liqueur
¾ cup simple syrup (page 545)
Fresh lemon juice to taste

Spin the blackberries and peaches in a food processor until puréed, or mash through a sieve. Add the liqueur, sugar syrup, and a few drops of lemon juice. Freeze in an ice cream freezer following manufacturer's directions.
MAKES ABOUT 1 PINT

Two-Melon Sorbet

2 cups puréed ripe cantaloupe
2 cups puréed watermelon
1 cup simple syrup (page 545)

Grated rind of 1 lemon
Juice of 1 lime

GARNISH: *sprigs of fresh mint*

Mix all the ingredients together and chill. Freeze in ice cream maker according to manufacturer's directions.
MAKES 1½ PINTS

Mrs. Platt's Blueberry Ice

The author of the *June Platt Cook Book* and *June Platt's New England Cook Book* spent a couple score of summers in a house built into an old barn foundation in Little Compton, Rhode Island, where she gathered recipes from all the New England states. Here is her formula for a frozen dessert that often causes guests to ask what the basic fruit is.

2 cups blueberries
1 cup sugar
Cold water
1 tablespoon plain gelatine

1 cup boiling water
½ cup fresh lemon juice
1 egg white

Put the blueberries and ¼ cup of the sugar in a bowl and mash together with a wooden potato masher or some similar tool. (Today we would use a food processor.) Force the mixture through a fine sieve, and discard any particles of skin that remain. Measure the blueberry juice and add enough cold water to make 1½ cups. Soak the gelatine in 2 tablespoons cold water for 5 minutes. Bring 1 cup of water to the boiling point, and stir in the remaining ¾ cup of sugar. Remove from the heat and stir in the softened gelatine, the blueberry juice, and the lemon juice and let cool. Beat the egg white until peaks are formed, then fold it into the cold berry mixture. Freeze in an ice cream freezer according to manufacturer's instructions, or pour the mixture into a freezing tray and freeze according to the directions in the box, page 545.

SERVES 4

One of New England's most tempting places to sample frozen desserts is Big Alice's ice cream parlor near Brown University on Providence's East Side. Proprietor Charles Cox recommends the combination of Yankee cranberries and rough-cut marmalade.

1 quart whole fresh cranberries
1½ cups rough-cut orange marmalade

2 whole cinnamon sticks
2 cups sugar

Rinse and clean the berries and put them in a saucepan with water to cover. Cook gently over low heat until the water begins to boil, then mash the berries and skim off the skins. Add the marmalade, the cinnamon sticks, and the sugar. Stir until the mixture thickens. Remove from the heat, cover the pan, and let the sauce stand 15 minutes or longer, until it is room temperature. Remove the cinnamon sticks, and pour the sauce over vanilla ice cream.

MAKES 3–4 CUPS

Big Alice's Cranberry Sauce for Vanilla Ice Cream

We first tasted this one Sunday afternoon in spring at Big Alice's Ice Cream Parlor. It was magnificent simply on top of vanilla ice cream, but as its creator insists, it is "wonderful on coffee ice cream with lots of whipped cream."

½ pound unsalted butter
3 cups diced tart apples
1 cup dark brown sugar

½ cup raisins (optional)
2 tablespoons cinnamon
1 cup apple juice

Slice the butter and cover the bottom of a baking pan with it. Arrange the diced apples in a layer over the butter, and sprinkle the sugar, raisins, and cinnamon evenly over the apples. Add the apple juice, then put the pan in a preheated 350-degree oven and bake for 15 minutes, stirring frequently, until the apples are soft and break apart; if the apples are too dry, add up to 1 cup water. Spoon the hot mixture on top of ice cream and add whipped cream, if desired.

MAKES 1 QUART

Charles Cox's Hot Spiced Apple Topping for Ice Cream

Vermont Honey Sauce for Ice Cream

In the score books of those who keep track of such things, Vermont rates as the top producer of honey in New England—the best recent figures tally 1,700 beekeepers who own almost 12,000 beehives. Somewhat like the wine-growing valleys of California where vintages have different characteristics, Yankee honeys have different distinctions depending upon local plant life. Along the Connecticut River in the southern part of the state the honey has a minty flavor (sometimes compared to tupelo or sourwood). In the Northeast Kingdom, the flavor comes from wildflowers. Honey from the Champlain Valley, whence comes the greatest volume, has the delicate flavor of alfalfa, trefoil, vetch, and clover. Raspberry honey, much coveted by connoisseurs, enhances vanilla ice cream—as does this nutty, gingery grape-accented sauce.

½ cup chopped butternuts
¼ cup seeded raisins
6 white grapes, chopped
A small piece preserved ginger,
  chopped

1 cup strained honey
Juice of ½ lemon

Combine the ingredients, mixing well, and pour over ice cream.
SERVES 4

Plain Honey Sauce

2 tablespoons butter
2 tablespoons cornstarch

½ cup honey
Water

Heat the butter and stir in the cornstarch to make a smooth mixture; be careful that it doesn't burn. Stir in the honey and 1 or 2 tablespoons of water, a little at a time. You can regulate the consistency to your taste. Cook over low heat about 3 minutes.
MAKES ABOUT ⅔ CUP

1/3 cup sugar
A pinch of salt
1 tablespoon cornstarch

3 tablespoons water
1 tablespoon lemon juice
2 cups blueberries

Blueberry Sauce

Mix the sugar, salt, cornstarch, water, and lemon juice in a nonaluminum saucepan. Stir in the blueberries and bring to a boil. Boil just 1 or 2 minutes —the liquid should be clear.
MAKES 1½ CUPS

VARIATION: To make blackberry sauce, add an additional 2 tablespoons sugar and use 2 cups blackberries instead of blueberries. You will need to boil the blackberries about 3 or 4 minutes in all to soften. Strain, if you wish, as blackberries are very seedy.
MAKES 1 CUP, STRAINED

PIES

This is not really a cream pie in the traditional Bostonian sense; the lightly flour-thickened cream poured over the open-faced pie for the last 15 minutes of baking simply makes a light, creamy liaison for the cooked berries. We use the richer, more cookielike crust found on page 566 for this luscious pie.

Blueberry "Cream" Pie

Shortcrust Sweet Tart Dough for
   single-crust 9-inch pie (page 566)
6 tablespoons sugar

1 quart blueberries, picked over
1 cup heavy cream
3 tablespoons flour

Roll out the pastry dough and fit it into a 9-inch tart or pie pan, fluting the edges. Sprinkle 2 tablespoons of the sugar on the bottom, then scatter the blueberries over, and sprinkle with another 1 tablespoon of sugar. Bake in a preheated 425-degree oven for 12 minutes. Beat the cream, flour, and remaining sugar together, then pour this over the berries. Lower the heat to 375 degrees and continue baking about 15 minutes until the cream is bubbly. If the crust shows signs of browning too much, drape foil over the edges. Remove from the oven, let the pie settle and cool a bit, but serve it warm.
MAKES ONE 9-INCH PIE

The Proverbial American Apple Pie

"Thy breath is like the steame of apples pyes," an Elizabethan wrote, and the first New Englanders brought the same admiration with them on the *Mayflower*. Apple trees were planted almost immediately, including an orchard on the slope of Beacon Hill. In more rustic times there were Yankees who liked to recite the names of old-time apples, just for the sound of them: Baldwins, Black Gillflower, Duchess, Fameuse, Rhode Island Greenings, Jonathans, Northern Spy, Pippins, Red Astrachans, Roxbury Russets, Westfield Seek-No-Furthers, Spitzenburgs, Sweet Paradise, Tompkins King, Williams Nothead, Winter Bananas, Winesaps, Yellow Transparent. In fact, a "museum orchard" was established in Massachusetts to make sure that old apple strains are preserved.

"The best of all physicians," according to Eugene Field, "is apple pie and cheese." It's hard to believe, but records show that some housewives often baked as many as one hundred pies at a time, stacked them in crocks, and stored them in the shed where they'd freeze. When a pie was wanted, it was put in the pie cupboard in the fireplace chimney and thawed out. In one grandmother's dog-eared receipt book a note was appended: "Here is a good pie to go with fried potatoes for breakfast." "What is a pie for?" Emerson exclaimed, and nobody challenged him.

In Vermont, where the 1986 harvest yielded 1,250,000 bushels, there's no current trend toward reviving apple-pie breakfasts, but apple pie is still the number-one favorite at church suppers, and every harvest season local newspapers are full of the latest variations on the classic dessert, such as apple pizza pies and tarts with lemon zest and caramelized apples. There are arguments about which apples make the best pie, whether spices should be included. Some like the filling mushy (there is even a century-old recipe from the Union Station in Connecticut that calls for resting the top crust gently over the pie so that it can be removed when the apples have baked tender, then the apples are forked to a purée and the top is replaced) and others insist on an apple that holds it shape.

We find that freshly picked, tart fall apples need no enhancement—in fact, that it is part of the pleasure to let the particular apple variety declare itself—and also we often enjoy crab apples from the trees that edge our woods. But in winter when only storage apples can be used, spices and butter are welcome in a pie. The Shakers sprinkle on a tablespoon of their own rosewater for an elusive flavor.

To make a pure apple pie: Use 5 cups sliced apples and as you scatter them over an 8-inch pie pan lined with a dough made of lard or vegetable shortening (page 564), sprinkle on about ½ cup sugar or less, depending on the sweetness of the apples (considerably more if they are crab apples), and 1 scant tablespoon of flour, piling the apples high in the middle. Drape the top layer of dough over, crimp the edges, and slash in several places. Bake in a preheated 425-degree oven for 20 minutes, then lower the heat to 350 degrees and bake another 40 minutes.   SERVES 6–8

Basic Pie Dough for double-crust
  9-inch pie (page 564)
3 cups fresh currants, cleaned and*
  stemmed
3 cups fresh blueberries, cleaned
  and stemmed

3 tablespoons flour
A pinch of salt
1 1/4 cups sugar
1 tablespoon butter

* If unavailable, use all blueberries or any other berry.

Currant and Blueberry Lattice-Top Pie

Divide the dough in 2 pieces—one slightly larger than the other. Roll out the larger half and line 9-inch pie pan, then trim the overhang to about 1 inch all around. Roll out the remaining dough into a circle and cut it into strips about ½ inch wide.

Toss the currants and blueberries together with the flour, salt, and all but 1 tablespoon of the sugar, then pile them into the lined pie plate, letting them dome in the center. Dot with butter. Now place the strips on top, interweaving them. Press the ends of the strips into the overhanging dough, then fold the overhang over and crimp all around. Sprinkle the remaining sugar on top, and bake in a preheated 425-degree oven for 20 minutes, then lower the heat to 350 degrees and bake another 25–30 minutes. Be sure to place a pan or foil below to catch any juices that will probably bubble over. Remove from the oven and cool on a rack. This pie is good served still slightly warm.

MAKES ONE 9-INCH PIE, SERVING 8

3 pounds parsnips
2 tablespoons unsalted butter
1/3–1/2 cup maple syrup
Grated rind of 1 orange
2 eggs, lightly beaten
1/2 teaspoon allspice
1/2 teaspoon cinnamon

1/2 teaspoon mace
1/4 teaspoon ground cloves
1/2 teaspoon or more fresh lemon
  juice
One 9-inch partially baked pie
  shell, page 564

Parsnip Pie

Peel the parsnips and cut them into equal-size chunks. Boil in water to cover until they are tender, then drain thoroughly, and purée them in a food processor or put them through a vegetable mill. Beat the butter into the parsnip purée while still hot, then stir in ⅓ cup maple syrup, the orange rind, eggs, spices, and ½ teaspoon lemon juice. Taste; you may want to add a little more syrup or a few drops more lemon juice. Turn the parsnip filling into the partially baked shell and bake in a preheated 375-degree oven for 10 minutes, then turn the heat down to 350 degrees and bake another 50 minutes, or until set. Cool on a rack and serve at room temperature with whipped cream or vanilla ice cream, if you like.

SERVES 8

Rum-Flavored Pumpkin Pie

The author Maud Howe Elliott, whose New England roots were manifold, brooked no compromises in regard to one of the oldest of American pastries. "No squash or pumpkin pie," she wrote her friend Julian Street, "is eatable unless made with brandy. Perish the thought!" Another perishable thought suggests a liberal splash of orange liqueur as the accent. But far more Yankee than either of the above is a pumpkin pie flavored with the mainstay of Down East winter toddies.

1½ cups cooked winter squash or
   puréed pumpkin
1 cup sugar
1 tablespoon brown sugar
1 cup heavy cream or evaporated
   milk
3 eggs
2 tablespoons rum

1 teaspoon cinnamon
1 teaspoon nutmeg
½ teaspoon ginger
½ teaspoon salt
⅛ teaspoon ground cloves
⅛ teaspoon ground allspice
Basic Pie Dough for single-crust
   9-inch pie (page 564)

In a large mixing bowl, mix the squash or pumpkin with the sugars and the cream or evaporated milk. Beat well, adding 1 egg at a time, until the mixture is well blended. (Before adding the last egg, remove a little of its white and set aside for use in painting the pastry.) Season the filling with the rum and the spices and stir until they are blended in. Line a 9-inch pie pan with the pastry and brush it with egg white. Fill it with the squash or pumpkin filling, and bake in a preheated 450-degree oven for 10 minutes; lower the heat to 300 degrees and bake about 45 minutes, until firm.
MAKES ONE 9-INCH, OPEN-FACED PIE SERVING 6–8

James Beard's Cranberry Raisin Pie

We remember when James Beard worked out this pie and shared it with us. He had had a less good version of a cranberry raisin pie at what he called an "Amerindian" dinner and he had to go right home and improve on it. He describes his version as tasting a little like mincemeat but with a wonderfully different taste and texture.

2 cups raisins
About ¾ cup Grand Marnier
½ cup water
4 cups cranberries, picked over and
   washed
1 cup sugar

2 tablespoons flour
1 tablespoon grated orange peel
Basic Pie Dough (made with lard)
   for a 9-inch double-crust pie
   (page 564)

GLAZE: 1 egg yolk beaten with 2 tablespoons milk

Cover the raisins with equal parts of water and Grand Marnier (½ cup should be enough, reserve the other ¼ cup for later). Let steep for 2 hours. Strain the raisins and mix them with the cranberries, sugar, flour, grated orange peel, and ¼ cup Grand Marnier. Toss until well mixed.

Roll out half the dough and line a 9-inch pie pan with it. Fill with the cranberry-raisin mixture, mounding it toward the center. Roll out the top crust and fit it onto the top, trimming and crimping the edges. Make several slashes in the top and brush with the egg glaze. Refrigerate the pie for 1 hour, then brush it again with the glaze. Bake in a preheated 400-degree oven for 15 minutes, then turn the oven down to 350 degrees and cook another 45 minutes. Cool on a rack.

SERVES 8

Light and Airy Summer Squash Pie

Because early Yankees more often stewed garden vegetables instead of conceiving new ways of preparing them, they were often served as side dishes—see the discussion of "garden sass" (page 277). It seems to have taken black cooks—many of whom were freed in New England before the Revolutionary War—to come up with ideas such as this dessert based on yellow crooknecks.

5–6 medium yellow squash (about 1½ pounds)
¼ cup water
Salt
2 tablespoons butter
½ cup light brown sugar
3 eggs, separated
⅓ cup milk or light cream

¼ teaspoon cinnamon
⅛ teaspoon freshly grated nutmeg
⅛ teaspoon allspice
Basic Pie Dough or Shortcrust Sweet Tart Dough for 9-inch single-crust pie (pages 564, 566)
¾ cup heavy cream
3 tablespoons maple syrup

Wash the squash and cut it up in small pieces. Put it in a heavy saucepan with the water and a light sprinkling of salt, and cook, covered, over low heat, stirring occasionally, until very tender, about 15 minutes. Uncover and boil away any remaning liquid, then stir in the butter until melted. Remove from the heat and mash the squash thoroughly or spin in a food processor. Blend in the sugar, egg yolks, milk or cream, and spices. Beat the egg whites in a separate bowl until they form peaks, then fold them gently into the squash. Line a 9-inch pie pan with the dough and pour in the squash mixture. Bake in a preheated 450-degree oven for 10 minutes; reduce the heat to 350 degrees and bake until firm, about 45 minutes. Remove and let cool slightly. Whip the cream until thick. Pour the maple syrup carefully in a fine stream over the whipped cream, turning the cream and folding in the syrup, then spread in swirls over the pie.

SERVES 8

Concord Grape Pie

Basic Pie Dough for 9-inch double-crust pie (page 564)
About 5 pounds Concord grapes
1 cup sugar

Grated rind of 1 lemon
2 teaspoons lemon juice
1½ teaspoons quick-cooling tapioca

Line a 9- or 10-inch pie plate with part of the pie dough and chill. Meanwhile, squeeze the grapes into a saucepan to extract their flesh. Add the sugar and bring to a boil, then simmer for 5 minutes, stirring now and then. Press through a vegetable mill or strainer to remove the seeds. Mix the skins with this purée and stir in the lemon rind and juice. Let cool to tepid. Sprinkle tapioca over the bottom of the dough-lined pie plate and pour in the filling. Roll out the remaining dough and cut into ½-inch strips. Make a latticework top crust with the strips and crimp the dough around the edges. Bake in a preheated 425-degree oven 15 minutes, then lower the heat to 350 degrees and bake another 25 minutes. Serve, if you wish, with whipped cream.

MAKES ONE 9- OR 10-INCH PIE

Green Tomato Pie

Basic Pie Dough for double-crust 9-inch pie, (page 564)
6 medium green tomatoes
2 tablespoons butter
1 cup sugar

½ teaspoon allspice
½ teaspoon cinnamon
½ cup cider vinegar
1 teaspoon all-purpose flour

Divide the pie dough in half, roll out one half and line a 9-inch pie pan, leaving a 1-inch overhang. Slice the green tomatoes paper-thin. Dot a little of the butter on the bottom of the dough-lined pan, then spread layers of tomatoes, topping each layer with some of the sugar, spices, vinegar, and flour; repeat until all the ingredients are used. Roll out the remaining dough and lay it over the filling; trim the edges and crimp all around. Slash the top in several places and bake in a preheated 425-degree oven for 20 minutes, then reduce the heat to 375 degrees and bake another 35–40 minutes. Serve slightly warm.

MAKES ONE 9-INCH PIE, SERVING 6–8

Maple-Butternut Pie

3 eggs
1 cup maple syrup
½ cup melted butter
½ cup dark brown sugar
⅛ teaspoon salt

1 teaspoon vanilla
1 tablespoon flour
1½ cups butternuts, halved
1 prebaked 9-inch pie shell made with lard (page 564)

Beat the eggs until they turn lemon colored, at least 1½ minutes. Add the maple syrup, melted butter, brown sugar, salt, vanilla, and flour (if you are using a standing electric mixer add them with the beaters running). Beat another minute. Turn the butternuts into the baked pie crust and spread them out evenly, then pour the liquid mixture on top. Bake in a preheated 425-degree oven for 10 minutes, then lower the heat to 375 degrees and bake another 30 minutes.

SERVES 8

Spalding Inn's Maple-Nut Chiffon Pie

1 tablespoon unflavored gelatine
¼ cup cold water
¾ cup milk
½ cup maple syrup
A pinch of salt

2 eggs, separated
1 teaspoon vanilla
1 cup heavy cream
1 prebaked 9-inch pie shell made
    with Basic Pie Dough (page 564)

GARNISH:
¾ cup whipped cream

⅓ cup chopped walnuts

Sprinkle the gelatine over the water and let stand until softened. Mix together in a saucepan the milk, maple syrup, salt, and egg yolks, then add the gelatine and place over medium heat. Stir until slightly thickened. Remove from the heat and add the vanilla. Chill until the mixture starts to thicken.

Whip the egg whites until they form firm peaks, then fold them into the maple mixture. Beat the cream until stiff and fold that into the filling. Spread into the baked pie shell and decorate the top with whipped cream and nuts.

SERVES 6

Marlborough Pie

Food historians trace this apple-lemon custard confection to an old British recipe that is also sometimes known in New England as Deerfield Pie and has a number of versions popular in Massachusetts.

About 3 medium fresh tart apples
    (to make 1½ cups grated)
4 tablespoons butter
½ cup sugar
1 lemon
3 eggs

1 cup heavy cream
¼ teaspoon mace
2 tablespoons applejack or brandy
1 pie shell, prebaked in an 8-inch
    pie pan or 9-inch quiche pan

Peel the apples and grate them on a grater or cut them in chunks and spin in a food processor until reduced to small pieces. Melt the butter in a skillet,

Marlborough Pie (continued)

add the apples, and the sugar. Grate the lemon into the apples and squeeze about 1 tablespoon of the juice into the pan. Mix thoroughly and let cook about 10–15 minutes, stirring occasionally, until the liquid has cooked off.

Beat the eggs lightly, stir in the cream, mace, and applejack, and then beat in the cooled apple mixture to blend. Pour into the prebaked pie shell, still in its pan, and slide onto the middle rack of a preheated 375-degree oven. Bake 35–40 minutes, covering lightly with foil if the crust seems to be getting too dark. Remove when the custard is set and slightly puffy. Let rest at least 20 minutes before slicing, but serve warm.

SERVES 6–8

Butter Pecan– Pumpkin Ice Cream Pie

As a talented cook and hostess of Three Mountain Inn in Jamaica, Vermont, Elaine Murray has pleased many visitors to New England with her imaginative combination of two regional favorites, pumpkin and butter pecan ice cream.

1 quart butter pecan ice cream

CRUST:
1½ cups graham cracker crumbs   *4 tablespoons melted butter*
¼ cup sugar

FILLING:
One 16-ounce can pumpkin, or   *½ teaspoon salt*
*   2 cups cooked mashed pumpkin*   *1 teaspoon cinnamon*
½ cup brown sugar

TOPPING:
4 tablespoons butter   *2 tablespoons water*
½ cup dark brown sugar   *½ cup pecans, broken up*

Before preparing the shell, take the butter pecan ice cream out of the freezer and put in a large bowl to melt partially. Mix together thoroughly all of the ingredients for the crust and press into a 9-inch pie pan. Bake in a preheated 350-degee oven for 8–10 minutes, until lightly browned, then remove from the oven and let cool.

Mix together all the filling ingredients and stir them into the partially thawed ice cream, mixing well. Spread the filling into the cooled graham cracker crust and freeze 4–6 hours before serving.

Meanwhile, make the topping by melting the butter, then adding the brown sugar, water, and pecan pieces. Drizzle on individual wedges of the pie when serving.

SERVES 6–8

Alexina Mercier has a reputation in her Northeast Kingdom parish for the perfect meringue pie, which she often makes for church suppers.

Grated peel of 2 lemons
Juice of 2 lemons (about ½ cup)
1 cup sugar
2 egg yolks
¼ cup cornstarch

1½ cups boiling water
1 tablespoon butter
1 prebaked 8-inch pie shell made
  with Basic Pie Dough (page 564)

MERINGUE TOPPING:
2 egg whites
⅛ teaspoon cream of tartar

2 tablespoons sugar

Alexina Mercier's Lemon Meringue Pie

In a saucepan, beat the grated lemon peel and juice, the sugar, egg yolks, and cornstarch together. Gradually add the boiling water, stirring constantly. Bring to a boil, stirring, then lower the heat and simmer 1 minute. Stir in the butter and let cool. Pour the cooled filling into the prebaked pie shell. Make the topping by beating the egg whites with the cream of tartar and sugar until they form firm peaks. Spread the meringue over the filling, making sure it reaches to the edge of the pie crust, and swirl the meringue into peaks. Bake in preheated 350-degree oven 10–12 minutes until golden.
MAKES ONE 8-INCH PIE

1½ ounces unsweetened chocolate
  (1½ squares)
1 cup hot water
3 tablespoons unsalted butter
1 tablespoon vanilla extract
1 cup sugar

3 egg yolks, well beaten
2 tablespoons cornstarch, dissolved
  in 2 tablespoons cold water
One 9-inch prebaked pie shell
  made with Basic Pie Dough
  (page 564)

MERINGUE TOPPING:
4 egg whites
1 teaspoon cream of tartar

½ cup sugar
1 teaspoon vanilla extract

Helen Budd's Chocolate Meringue Pie

Grate the chocolate and put it in a heavy saucepan or the top of a double boiler. Add the hot water, butter, vanilla, sugar, and egg yolks, and mix thoroughly. Stir in the dissolved cornstarch. Place over boiling water and cook, stirring constantly, until the mixture has thickened (this will take about 8 minutes). Cool thoroughly, stirring from time to time.

Meanwhile, make the meringue topping. Beat the egg whites and when they turn frothy, add the cream of tartar and beat until they form peaks. Beat in the sugar gradually, add the vanilla, and continue to beat until very stiff. Spread the cooled chocolate filling into the pie shell and heap the meringue on top, swirling it into peaks and making sure that it is spread onto the pie crust all around the edge (we've called for extra meringue so you will have plenty—no danger of shrinking). Bake in a preheated 350-degree oven for 10–12 minutes, until golden brown all over. Serve cool but do not refrigerate.

SERVES 6–8

Raspberry-Chocolate Tart

This tart is deceptively simple to make. The pastry can all be prepared in a food processor, and the chocolate is nothing more than melted semisweet chocolate. It was inspired by a dessert served by Cynthia Giarrasputo in Peacham, Vermont, at the height of the raspberry season, and it was so exquisite, with the thin layer of chocolate setting off the juicy raspberries, that it warranted working out a way to reproduce it at home. So this is our version.

SWEET PASTRY DOUGH:
1 1/3 cups all-purpose flour
1/3 cup cake flour
1/8 teaspoon salt
2 tablespoons sugar

3/4 cup butter (1 1/2 sticks)
1 egg yolk
3–4 tablespoons cold water

3 squares semisweet chocolate
1 quart raspberries

TOPPING:
3/4 cup heavy cream
1 tablespoon sugar

1 teaspoon vanilla

Spin the two flours, the salt, and sugar together in a food processor. Cut the butter in small pieces and dump them in, then start the processor. Count to 5 slowly, stop the motor, and start again, counting to 5. Do this about 6 times. Beat the egg yolk with 3 tablespoons of the water just enough to blend, then, with the motor running, pour the liquid through the tube. The dough should start to ball up; if it doesn't do so, add a little more water. (If you don't have a food processor, follow the mixing directions for Short-crust Sweet Tart Dough, page 566.) Remove the dough, pat it into a circle, flour lightly, and wrap it in wax paper; refrigerate for at least 1 hour.

Remove the pastry dough to a lightly floured board and give it a few whacks with your rolling pin to relax the dough, then roll it out into a circle large enough to fit a 9-inch tart pan (or, if you haven't one, use a pie plate) with a slight overhang. Cut the edges so they are even, then make a decorative finish with the tines of a fork or scallop the edge all around. Prick the bottom all over. Butter a large piece of foil and fit it into the pastry, butter-side down, then fill the foil with dried beans or small pebbles to prevent the pastry from swelling up. Bake in a preheated 425-degree oven 8 minutes, then remove the foil and beans, prick the bottom here and there again, and bake another 10 minutes until lightly browned. Remove from the oven and let cool.

Meanwhile, melt the chocolate in a small saucepan set over barely simmering water. When the tart is cool spread the melted chocolate over the bottom. Fill with raspberries. Beat the cream, adding the sugar and vanilla as it begins to thicken, and continue to beat until stiff. Put the whipped cream into a pastry tube and pipe a decorative pattern on top of the berries. Or simply spoon mounds of whipped cream on top.

MAKES ONE 9-INCH TART

McIntosh Apple and Currant Tart

Just north of Dartmouth College, on Route 10, is a restaurant called D'Artagnan, which served on the night of our first dinner there a splendid variation on the apple pie theme. We couldn't wait to get Rebecca Cunningham's recipe, and rushed home to work out a Bryn Teg version—you may be tempted just as we were. These may be made either in individual tart molds with fluted edges and removable bottoms, or you can make them free form if you don't have the fancy molds. They must be served as soon as they come out of the oven.

1 recipe Shortcrust Sweet Tart
    Dough (page 566)
2/3 cup currant jelly, melted

3 firm McIntosh apples
3 tablespoons unsalted butter
About 1/3 cup sugar

Roll out the pastry to about 1/8-inch thickness. Cut out circles to fit the tart molds you are using, or cut the pastry dough into rounds about 6 inches in diameter. Fit the dough into 6 molds, or place the circles on an ungreased baking sheet and roll the edges in all around about to make a slight border, pressing down with the tines of a fork all around to make the border hold. Brush the bottom of the tarts with melted currant jelly. Peel and core the apples and cut them into 1/4-inch slices. Lay overlapping slices on the center of pastry and fill in the sides with extra slices. Paint the apples with the remaining currant jelly, dot them with butter, and bake in a 425-degree oven for about 20 minutes, until the apples are cooked and the pastry is lightly browned at the edges. Sprinkle on sugar and run the tarts quickly under the broiler to glaze. Serve hot with whipped cream.

SERVES 6

Peach Shortbread Tart

3½ tablespoons quick-cooking
  tapioca
¾ cup sugar
¼ teaspoon salt
About ¼ teaspoon freshly grated
  nutmeg

½ cup water
4 cups sliced, ripe peaches
1½ tablespoons fresh lemon juice

SHORTBREAD CRUST:
1 stick (½ cup) soft butter
¼ cup sugar

1 cup flour
¼ cup cake flour

Put the tapioca, sugar, salt, nutmeg, water, and 1½ cups of the sliced peaches in a saucepan and bring to a boil over medium heat, stirring. Remove from the heat and let stand 15 minutes. Stir in the lemon juice and remaining peaches and cool.

Meanwhile, make the crust. Mix the butter and sugar together with a fork. Work in the flour until you have a crumblike consistency, then mix thoroughly with your hands to form a soft dough (all this may be done in the food processor, using short pulses). Press evenly into the bottom and sides of an 8-inch round cake pan. Prick the bottom all over with a fork and bake in a preheated 325-degree oven, until lightly browned, 35–40 minutes. Let cool. Remove gently from the pan; if the shell sticks, warm it up a little over gentle heat. Fill the crust with the peach mixture just before serving.

SERVES 6

Basic Pie Dough

2 cups flour
½ teaspoon salt
⅔ cup good lard or vegetable
  shortening

6 tablespoons cold water

Toss the flour and salt together, then work in the lard or vegetable shortening, using your fingertips or a pastry blender, until the mixture resembles fresh bread crumbs. Add the cold water, a little at a time, stirring with a fork, until you have a dough that is just moist enough to hold together. Gather up half of it firmly in your hands and shape it into a ball. Place on a floured work surface and, with a heavy, floured rolling pin, roll the dough out into a circle, starting at the center and rolling out almost to the edge, then turning and rolling again. Reflour the surface and your rolling pin as necessary. When you have a circle about 1½ inches larger than an 8-inch pie pan, roll the dough up onto your rolling pin and unroll it over the pie pan. Press it evenly all around, patching if your have any tears, and trimming the edges. After filling the pie, repeat the same procedure with remaining half of dough. Leave a slight overhang, then trim, and crimp all around the edges.

MAKES ENOUGH FOR DOUBLE-CRUST 8-INCH PIE

For a single-crust 8-inch pie: use 1 cup flour, ¼ teaspoon salt, ⅓ cup shortening or lard, and 3 tablespoons cold water.

For a double-crust 9-inch pie: Use 2½ cups flour, ¾ teaspoon salt, ¾ cup shortening or lard, and 6–7 tablespoons cold water.

For a single-crust 9-inch pie: Use 1½ cups flour, ⅓ teaspoon salt, ½ cup shortening or lard, and 3–4 tablespoons cold water.

To prebake or partially bake a pie shell: Press a sheet of buttered foil into the dough-lined pie pan, butter-side down, and bake shell in a preheated 425-degree oven for 5 minutes, then remove the foil and bake another 5 minutes, for a partially baked shell, and another 10–12 minutes for a fully baked shell (total time 15–17 minutes).

Tart Shells

Use the Basic Pie Dough, opposite, or one of the Tart Dough recipes on pages 562 or 566, eliminating the sugar that is called for if you are going to have a savory filling; if you are filling with berries or a sweet mixture, add 2 tablespoons sugar to the Basic Pie Dough when mixing. Roll the dough out as thin as possible. Cut into circles about 2 inches larger than the tart molds you plan to fill, or lacking those, use Pyrex baking cups or muffin tins and cut the dough into circles about 2 inches larger than the bottom circumference. Fill the molds, pressing the dough all around and trimming it at the edges. Or turn the muffin tins or Pyrex cups upside down and fit the dough circles onto the outside of the cups, pressing firmly to hold the dough in place, then trim evenly so that the form will be 1½ inches deep. Prick the dough around the bottom and sides with the tines of a fork, place the molds or muffin tins or cups on a baking sheet, dough side up, and bake in a preheated 400-degree oven for 15–16 minutes until lightly browned. If you are using muffin tins or cups, carefully remove the individual tarts, turn them right side up and bake another 1–2 minutes standing free on the baking sheet until lightly browned inside.

ONE RECIPE FOR AN 8- OR 9-INCH PIE WILL YIELD ABOUT 4 TART SHELLS

Shortcrust Sweet Tart Dough

This dough can be done in a food processor if you are careful not to overblend it. It has a delicious buttery flavor and holds up well for unmolded tarts and small pastry shells. If you use it for a savory filling, omit the sugar.

1⅓ cups all-purpose flour
3 tablespoons cake flour
¼ teaspoon salt

2 tablespoons sugar
1½ sticks unsalted butter (¾ cup)
2–2½ tablespoons ice water

Toss the flours, salt, and sugar together to mix. Cut in the butter and work it with your fingers or with a pastry blender until it resembles fresh bread crumbs. Mix in the ice water with a fork, using just enough for the dough to hold together. Turn the dough out onto a floured work surface.

To make in the food processor: Spin the dry ingredients to mix. Cut the chilled butter into 10–12 pieces and add all at once with the motor going. Count to about 4 and stop. Then repeat 4 or 5 times more. Add the water and process in the same short spurts about 6 times. Don't let the dough ball up around the shaft. Turn the dough out onto a floured work surface.

Gather the dough together firmly to form a ball. Smear the dough with the heel of your hand in 4 or 5 pushes until you have smeared it all, then scrape it up and form into a flat round. Wrap in wax paper and refrigerate for 15–20 minutes.

Roll the dough out on a floured surface, using a good heavy floured rolling pin. Start from the middle of the dough and roll out toward the edges, not going quite out to the edges. Turn the dough every few times you roll it, using a dough scraper and reflouring the surface, if necessary. Roll the dough up around the rolling pin and unroll it over a pie pan or tart mold or small tart molds. Press it all around to fit it snugly into the pan. Patch wherever necessary if the dough tears. Trim the dough, leaving a ½-inch border around the edge, then roll the edge under and flute.

To prebake or partially bake: Prick the bottom of the dough all over with a fork and bake in a preheated 425-degree oven for 12 minutes, for a partially baked tart; for a fully baked tart shell, continue to bake for another 10 minutes.

MAKES ENOUGH FOR ONE 10-INCH PIE OR TART

This is a dessert to put together when you have collected enough leftover pie dough to line several small tart molds—which is, incidentally, an easy and thrifty way to save scraps of dough to put to good use later. You can freeze the small molds after you have lined them with dough or refrigerate them, covered with plastic wrap, if you plan to make use of them in a week or so. The formula below will do for 3 small molds (such as heart-shaped) or 2 larger ones. Simply multiply it if you have more tarts to fill.

Custard–Berry Preserves Tarts

2 medium (about 3 inches in
    diameter) or 3 small tart molds
    lined with unbaked pie dough
3 tablespoons blackberry,
    raspberry, or other berry
    preserves

1 egg
1/3 cup light cream
1 tablespoon sugar
Freshly grated nutmeg

Line the bottom of the dough-lined molds with the berry preserves, letting a little of the liquid run off the spoon if the jam is not very thick (sometimes one's homemade preserves are apt to be less thick and you don't want any wateriness in these tarts). Beat the egg lightly and mix with the cream and sugar. Pour this over the tarts in equal amounts and bake in a 375-degree oven 20 to 25 minutes, or until set and puffy and golden on top. Grate a little nutmeg over and serve warm.
SERVES 2–3

Dining on Deck is not only the title of a cookbook by Linda Vail of Charlotte, Vermont—it's a fact of life for many New England sailing families with both saltwater and freshwater inclinations. On Lake Champlain, Mrs. Vail serves these aboard the 33-foot sloop, *Magnifique*.

Blueberry Turnovers

1 pint blueberries, picked over and
    washed
1/4 cup sugar
3 tablespoons flour

1/4 teaspoon freshly grated nutmeg
16 sheets phyllo dough
1/2 cup (1 stick) butter, melted
Bread crumbs

Drain the blueberries well after washing and mix with the sugar, flour, and nutmeg. Spread out 1 sheet phyllo dough (keep the rest covered with a damp towel while you are working) and brush melted butter on top, then sprinkle lightly with bread crumbs. Add a second layer of phyllo, butter, and crumbs. Repeat until you have 8 sheets stacked up. Form another stack of 8 sheets in the same way. Cut each stack in half, crosswise. Now across each stack of phyllo, draw an imaginary diagonal line. Place one quarter of the blueberry mixture on one side of the line on each of the 4 stacks of dough. Fold in half diagonally and crimp the edges. Place the triangles on a greased baking sheet and bake in a preheated 350-degree oven 35 minutes, or until golden brown. Serve hot.

MAKES 4 TURNOVERS TO SERVE 4 VERY GENEROUSLY

CAKES

New England Apple-Cranberry Cake

2 eggs
1 1/4 cups sugar
1/3 cup vegetable oil
3/4 cup all-purpose flour
3/4 cup oatmeal
1/2 teaspoon salt
1 teaspoon baking soda
1 teaspoon cinnamon
1/4 teaspoon freshly grated nutmeg

1/8 teaspoon allspice
1/2 cup coarsely chopped cranberries
2 medium apples, peeled, cored, and grated
1 medium pear, peeled, cored, and grated
1 cup coarsely chopped walnuts
Whipped cream or Cinnamon Ice Cream (page 544)

Lightly beat the eggs, then beat in the sugar until creamy. Stir in the oil. Toss together the flour, oatmeal, salt, soda, and spices, and mix thoroughly with the eggs and sugar. Fold in the fruits and walnuts. Scrape the batter into a greased 9 × 9-inch cake pan and bake in a preheated 350-degree oven for 45 minutes. Serve warm with whipped cream or Cinnamon Ice Cream.

MAKES ONE 9 × 9-INCH CAKE

Apple-Topped Cake

1 1/2 cups all-purpose flour
1/2 cup cornmeal
3/4 cup sugar
1 1/2 teaspoons baking powder
1/2 teaspoon salt

1/4 teaspoon freshly ground nutmeg
1/4 cup shortening
2 eggs
1/2 cup milk

TOPPING:
1 large apple
3 tablespoons melted butter

1/3 cup sugar
1/2 teaspoon cinnamon

Sweetened whipped cream

Toss together the dry ingredients to mix thoroughly. Work in the shortening. Beat the eggs lightly and add the milk. Mix the liquid ingredients with the dry, then pour the batter into a buttered 8-inch square pan.

Peel the apple and cut into 15 even-size wedges, then remove the cores. Roll the slices in the melted butter, then dip them in the sugar mixed with the cinnamon. Make even rows of the apple slices on the top of the cake batter—3 across and 5 down and sprinkle the remaining sugar and cinnamon on top. Bake in a preheated 400-degree oven 35 minutes. Serve warm with sweetened whipped cream.

MAKES ONE 8-INCH SQUARE CAKE

Blueberry Cake

6 tablespoons soft butter
1 cup sugar
2 eggs
1 teaspoon vanilla
1½ cups all-purpose flour
1 teaspoon baking powder
¼ teaspoon salt
⅓ cup milk
1½ cups blueberries
¼ teaspoon mace
Whipped cream

Cream the butter with all but 3 tablespoons of the sugar. Separate the eggs and add the yolks and the vanilla to the butter and sugar. Beat until creamy and light. Sift the flour with the baking powder and salt, then add alternately with the milk to the creamed butter and sugar. Beat the egg whites, adding 1½ tablespoons of the remaining sugar as they thicken and continue to beat until they form peaks. Fold the beaten whites into the batter and then gently stir in the blueberries. Grease and flour an 8 × 8-inch cake pan and spread the batter evenly into the pan. Mix the mace and remaining 1½ tablespoons sugar together and sprinkle this over the top. Bake 50 minutes in a preheated 350-degree oven. Serve warm with whipped cream, if you like.

SERVES 8

Molasses Blueberry Cake

½ cup sugar
2 eggs
½ cup soft butter
1 cup molasses
2 cups all-purpose flour
1 teaspoon baking soda
1 teaspoon allspice
1 teaspoon nutmeg
1 cup boiling water
2 cups blueberries, dusted with flour
Whipped cream

Beat the sugar, eggs, butter, and molasses together until smooth, or put in food processor. Mix the flour, baking soda, and the spices together, and add a little at a time to the wet ingredients while beating or while the food processor is turning. Stir in the boiling water and floured berries. Bake in a

buttered 9 × 13-inch pan in a preheated 325-degree oven for 35–40 minutes, or until a straw inserted in the center comes out clean. Cut into 24 squares when cool. Whipped cream makes a good accompaniment.
MAKES 24 SQUARES

1887 Gingerbread

This old family recipe remains the best of all gingerbreads, in our opinion.

¼ cup shortening
½ cup sugar
¾ teaspoon baking soda
½ cup molasses
1½ cups all-purpose flour
¾ teaspoon baking powder

1 teaspoon cinnamon
1 teaspoon ground ginger
¼ teaspoon ground cloves
A pinch of salt
¾ boiling water
1 egg, lightly beaten

GARNISH: *1 cup cream, whipped*
1–2 tablespoons minced candied or stem ginger (optional)

General Directions for Making a Cake

Tie up your hair so that none can fall, put on a long-sleeved apron, have the kitchen put in order, and then arrange all the articles and utensils you have occasion to use. . . .

It saves much trouble to have your receipt book so arranged that you can *measure* instead of weighing. This can be done by weighing the first time, and then have a small measure cup, and fill it with each ingredient you have weighed. Then note it down in your receipt book, and ever after use the same measure cup.

Always sift your flour, for neither bread nor cake should be made with unsifted flour, not merely because there may be dirt in it, but because packing injures its lightness, and sifting restores it. . . .

An oven, to bake well, must have a good heat at bottom, and not be too hot on top, or the cake will be heavy. As these receipts have all been proved, if they fail to make a good cake, the fault is probably in the baking. . . .

—Catharine E. Beecher, Hartford, 1846

Cream together the shortening and sugar. Beat ½ teaspoon baking soda into the molasses until fluffy and light; add it to the sugar mixture. Sift together the flour, baking powder, cinnamon, ginger, cloves, and salt. Mix together the boiling water and the remaining ¼ teaspoon baking soda, then gradually add this liquid, alternately with the dry ingredients, to the molasses mixture. Stir until well mixed, then stir in the egg. Butter and flour an 8-inch square cake pan, and pour in the batter. Bake in a preheated 325-degree oven for about 25 minutes, or until a straw inserted in the center comes out clean. Let cool in the pan on a wire rack. Serve warm with whipped cream, with optional minced ginger folded into it.
SERVES 8

Rhubarb Cake

2 tablespoons soft butter
¾ cup light brown sugar
1 teaspoon vanilla
1 egg
1¼ cups all-purpose flour

½ teaspoon baking powder
¼ teaspoon salt
½ cup sour cream
2 cups chopped rhubarb

TOPPING:
About 6 lumps sugar

½ teaspoon mace

In a bowl beat together the butter, brown sugar, vanilla, and egg. Mix the flour, baking powder, and salt in the top of the sifter, set over the butter-mixture bowl, then sift it into the bowl alternately with the sour cream. Blend well, then fold in the rhubarb. Spread the batter into a greased 8-inch square pan. Crush the sugar lumps and mix with the mace. Sprinkle over the top of the batter and bake in a preheated 350-degree oven for 45 minutes.
MAKES ONE 8-INCH SQUARE CAKE

Butternut Squash Cake

1 butternut squash (about 1 pound)
4 eggs
1½ cups sugar
1 cup vegetable oil
2 cups all-purpose flour
2 teaspoons baking powder

1 teaspoon baking soda
1 teaspooon salt
2 teaspoons cinnamon
½ teaspoon freshly grated nutmeg
Confectioners' sugar

Split the butternut squash lengthwise and scoop out the seeds. Set in a steamer and steam until very tender—30–40 minutes. Scoop out all the flesh and mash or purée it in a food processor, then measure it; you will need 1¾ cups. Beat the eggs in a large bowl until lemon-colored, then add the sugar. When blended, add the oil and squash and beat thoroughly. Toss the flour, baking powder, baking soda, and salt together, then add them to the first mixture, mixing well. Stir in the spices. Pour the batter into a buttered Bundt pan and bake in a preheated 350-degree oven for 45 minutes. Let cool in the pan 10 minutes, then turn out onto a cake rack. Dust all over with confectioners' sugar.

MAKES 1 ROUND BUNDT CAKE

Carrot Cake

This makes an 8-inch square cake—fine for a small family. But if you want to make carrot cake for a picnic or a party, double the recipe and bake it in a Bundt pan or 9- or 10-inch tube pan.

1 cup all-purpose flour
1 teaspoon baking powder
1 teaspoon baking soda
1 teaspoon cinnamon
1/4 teaspoon grated nutmeg
1/2 teaspoon salt
1/2 cup sugar
1/3 cup brown sugar
1/2 cup vegetable oil
2 eggs

1 1/2 cups grated carrots
1 teaspoon grated lemon or orange rind
1/4 cup coarsely chopped hazelnuts or walnuts
1/3 cup raisins
Cream Cheese Frosting (page 592) or Lemon or Orange Frosting (page 593)

Sift or toss the flour, baking powder, baking soda, spices, and salt together. Beat the two sugars, oil, and eggs together, then stir them into the dry ingredients. Fold in the grated carrots, lemon or orange rind, nuts, and raisins. Butter and flour an 8-inch square cake pan and pour the batter in. Bake in a preheated 325-degree oven for 30 minutes (if doubling the recipe, bake 50 minutes). Let cool in the pan and frost with Cream Cheese Frosting or Orange or Lemon Frosting, using half the amount called for in those recipes. Let cool in the pan on a rack.

MAKES ONE 8-INCH SQUARE CAKE

Leslie Jones's Oatmeal Cake

1½ cups boiling water
1 cup rolled oats
1 stick butter (¼ pound)
1 cup sugar
1 cup dark brown sugar
1 teaspoon vanilla

2 eggs, beaten
1½ cups all-purpose flour
1 teaspoon baking powder
½ teaspoon salt
¾ teaspoon cinnamon
¼ teaspoon freshly grated nutmeg

TOPPING:
¼ cup melted butter (½ stick)
½ cup dark brown sugar
3 tablespoons half-and-half or
  evaporated milk

⅓ cup chopped nuts
¾ cup shredded coconut

Pour the boiling water over the oats and let stand for 20 minutes. Beat the butter until creamy. Gradually add both sugars and beat until fluffy. Blend in the vanilla and eggs, then stir in the oats. Sift together the flour, baking powder, salt, cinnamon, and nutmeg. Add to the creamed mixture and beat thoroughly. Pour the batter into a greased 9-inch square cake pan. Bake in a preheated 350-degree oven for 50–55 minutes. Remove from the oven and let rest in the pan.

Make the topping. Combine the butter, brown sugar, cream, nuts, and coconut, and blend until smooth. Spread evenly over the top of the cake, then put it under the broiler just long enough to glaze. The cake is good either hot or cold.

MAKES 9 SERVINGS

Spice Cake

1 cup granulated sugar
2 cups all-purpose flour
½ teaspoon salt
1 teaspoon baking soda
1 teaspoon cinnamon
1 teaspoon freshly grated nutmeg
¼ teaspoon mace
⅛ teaspoon allspice

1 teaspoon ground cloves
½ cup melted shortening
1 cup buttermilk
1 egg, lightly beaten
1 cup raisins
Confectioners' sugar, Lemon
  Frosting (page 593), or Cream
  Cheese Frosting (page 592)

Toss the sugar, flour, salt, baking soda, and spices together to mix well. Stir in the shortening, buttermilk, egg, and blend thoroughly. Fold in the raisins. Pour the batter into a greased 9-inch square cake pan, and bake in a preheated 350-degree oven for 35–40 minutes until done in the center when tested. Remove, sprinkle confectioners' sugar on top (or frost with a Lemon or Cream Cheese Frosting) and let cool in the pan.

MAKES ONE 9-INCH SQUARE CAKE

Peach and Blueberry Upside-Down Cake

Peaches and blueberries have a natural affinity and they are in season at the same time. But you can vary this upside-down cake with other kinds of fruits and berries. It can be made in a round dish or in individual custard cups, unmolded on separate plates.

3 medium peaches
6 tablespoons light brown sugar
½ cup blueberries, or other berries
1 cup all-purpose flour
1½ teaspoons baking powder
¼ teaspoon salt

½ stick butter (4 tablespoons)
½ cup sugar
1 egg
1 teaspoon vanilla
¼ cup milk
Whipped cream

Butter a round baking dish (we use a glazed clay dish about 8 inches across the top with a 5½-inch bottom, but an 8-inch cake pan would do) or 6 custard cups. Peel and slice the peaches, then arrange the slices on the bottom of the dish(es), coming up the sides slightly, and sprinkle the brown sugar on top and in the interstices. Scatter the berries on top. Toss together the flour, baking powder, and salt. Cream the butter and sugar together, then beat in the egg and the vanilla. Add this mixture to the dry ingredients alternately with the milk, stirring until smooth after each addition. Spread the batter over the fruit, taking care not to disturb the arrangement but covering completely, and bake in a preheated 375-degree oven 40 minutes for the larger dish, 25–30 minutes for the custard cups, or until a straw comes out clean when poked into the center. Let cool for 5 minutes, then turn out onto a cake platter or individual dessert plates. Serve with whipped cream.

SERVES 6

Pound Cake

2 cups (1 pound) unsalted butter
2 cups sugar
9 eggs
1 teaspoon vanilla extract

4 cups sifted cake flour
½ teaspoon cream of tartar
½ teaspoon salt

Cream the butter, then add the sugar, and beat until light and fluffy. Add the eggs one at a time, beating well after each addition. Stir in the vanilla. Sift the measured flour with the salt and cream of tartar. Add the dry ingredients to the liquid ingredients in several parts, mixing only enough to blend. Do not overbeat.

Prepare either two 7-inch loaf pans by greasing them lightly and lining them with parchment paper, leaving enough paper hanging over the top edge to help remove the loaves after baking, or grease and flour a 10-inch tube pan with removable bottom, shaking off the excess flour. Pour the batter into the pan(s) and bake in a preheated 325-degree oven for 1 hour. Test by inserting a cake tester or straw in the middle to see if it comes out clean. Let rest in the pan(s) 5 minutes before turning out onto a rack to cool.

MAKES TWO 7-INCH LOAVES OR ONE 10-INCH TUBE CAKE

VARIATIONS:

Lemon Pound Cake: Use 1 teaspoon lemon extract instead of the vanilla and add the grated rind of 1 lemon.

Almond Pound Cake: Use 1 teaspoon almond extract instead of the vanilla and add ¾ cup chopped almonds.

Walnut Sponge Cake with Coffee Frosting

12 ounces walnuts, ground with 1 scant tablespoon flour *
10 eggs, separated
2 teaspoons baking powder

1¼ cups sugar
1 teaspoon vanilla
⅔ cup all-purpose flour

FROSTING:
1 stick unsalted butter (8 tablespoons)
3 cups confectioners' sugar
3 tablespoons strong black coffee

1–2 tablespoons coffee liqueur or other liqueur, or light cream

* Finely grind in several batches 12 ounces of walnuts in a nut grinder, blender, or food processor, adding a scant tablespoon of flour to each batch so that the nuts don't become too oily. Put the ground nuts in a medium (not fine) strainer and shake them over a bowl, using the finer consistency of nuts in the cake. Use the remainder in the frosting.

Beat the egg yolks, baking powder, and sugar together until smooth. Add the vanilla, flour, and 1 cup finely ground walnuts and mix well. In a separate very clean bowl beat the egg whites until they form firm peaks. Mix several large spoonfuls of the egg whites into the yolk mixture to lighten it a little, then gently fold the rest of the beaten egg whites into the batter. Pour the batter into a greased and floured 9 × 13-inch pan. Bake in a preheated 350-degree oven for 30–35 minutes until a cake tester or straw inserted in the middle comes out clean. Loosen the edges with a knife and turn the cake out onto a wire rack to cool.

Meanwhile, make the frosting. Beat the butter until it is fluffy. Gradually beat in the sugar and the black coffee. As it becomes very thick, stir in the remaining ground nuts. Add enough of the liqueur or light cream to make a spreadable consistency. When the cake is cool, transfer it to a platter and spread the frosting all over.

MAKES ONE 9 × 13-INCH CAKE

Mrs. Beattie's Basic Cake

This best-of-all simple basic cake owes its quality to an hour we spent in the kitchen of Mr. and Mrs. Harold Beattie of Danville, Vermont. An instinctive cook, Kate Beattie rarely writes down her recipes, but the measurements she pulls out of her memory seem to have magic of their own.

4 eggs
2 cups sugar
2 cups all-purpose flour
2 teaspoons baking powder
⅛ teaspoon salt
1 cup milk

½ stick butter (4 tablespoons)
1 teaspoon vanilla
Aunt Lucy's Vermont Maple
  Frosting (page 592) or Chocolate
  Frosting (page 591) or Mocha
  Frosting (page 591)

Beat the eggs until lemon colored, then add the sugar and continue beating until fluffy. Sift the flour with the baking powder and salt. Add to the butter-sugar mixture and beat until smooth. Heat the milk and melt the butter in it, bringing almost to the boil and stirring until smooth. Beat the milk and butter into the batter. Stir in the vanilla and turn the batter into 2 greased and floured 9-inch cake pans or into one large 13 × 9 × 2-inch pan. Bake in a preheated 350-degree oven for 25 minutes. If you're making a layer cake, let rest in the pans 5 minutes before unmolding. Fill and frost with Maple Frosting or Chocolate Frosting. Try the Mocha Frosting for the rectangular cake.

MAKES TWO 9-INCH LAYERS OR ONE 13 × 9 × 2-INCH CAKE TO SERVE 12–16

Yankee Chocolatiers

Chocolate became a Northeasterners' pantry staple a decade before the Revolutionary War when James Hannon persuaded Dr. James Baker to sponsor a chocolate mill on the Neponset River in Massachusetts. Soon there were villages named Chocolatetown in Rhode Island and on other New England streams, and in 1780 Baker was in full control of the Dorchester factory that grew to supply cooks and cakemakers throughout the United States.

Chocolate has been used by Yankees to make "temperance drinks"—as well as a "Chocolate Wine," compounded of a "pint of Sherry, or a pint and a half of Port, four ounces and a half of chocolate, six ounces of fine sugar," and so forth.

We find no date for the first use of the word "chocoholics," but it was considerably after Fannie Farmer offered her first recipe for "Chocolate Cream Candy" in 1896, and there has been plenty of time for addicts in all regions to blame New Englanders for perfecting a way to make chocolate easily available—for all kinds of candies, cookies, and cakes, as well as addictive liqueurs, which might be said to be doubly dangerous.

Michele Mackin makes this luscious cake only on special occasions—her children's birthdays. She advises the inexperienced cook not to try to make the tricky buttercream frosting without using a candy thermometer.

Michele's Very Special Chocolate Birthday Cake

1 cup unsweetened cocoa
2 cups boiling water
2¾ cups sifted all-purpose flour
2 teaspoons baking soda
½ teaspoon salt

½ teaspoon baking powder
1 cup (2 sticks) soft butter
2½ cups sugar
4 eggs
1½ teaspoons vanilla

FILLING:
1 cup heavy cream, chilled
¼ cup confectioners' sugar

1 teaspoon vanilla

RICH BUTTERCREAM FROSTING:
1½ cups sugar
¾ cup water
7 egg yolks

¾ pound (3 sticks) soft unsalted butter
1 tablespoon vanilla

In a small bowl whisk the cocoa and boiling water together until smooth. Cool completely. Meanwhile, sift together the flour, baking soda, salt, and baking powder. Grease well and lightly flour three 9-inch cake pans. Beat the butter, sugar, eggs, and vanilla at high speed with an electric mixer for at least 5 minutes. At low speed, beat in the flour mixture (in four takes) alternately with the cooled cocoa (in three takes), beginning and ending with the flour. Be careful not to overbeat. Divide the batter evenly into the 3 prepared pans, smoothing the tops with a spatula. Bake in a preheated 350-degree oven for 25–30 minutes, or until the surface springs back when pressed gently with your fingertips. Remove from the oven and cool the layers in the pans for 10 minutes, then loosen the sides carefully with a spatula and turn the layers onto racks.

To make the filling: Whip the cream with the sugar and vanilla until quite firm. Refrigerate until needed.

To make the buttercream frosting: Put the sugar and water into a 2-quart saucepan and set over medium heat. Stir until the sugar dissolves and the syrup comes to a boil. Let the syrup boil, washing down with a pastry brush dipped in cold water any sugar crystals that form on the side of the pan. When the syrup reaches 218–220 degrees on a candy thermometer, remove the pan from the heat and dip it into a bowl of cold water just long enough to stop the cooking. Meanwhile, in a large bowl, beat the egg yolks until they are pale yellow, at least 4–5 minutes. Cream the butter in a separate bowl. Now, whisking or beating vigorously, pour the hot syrup into the egg yolks in a thin stream, and continue to beat until fluffy and cooled. With a wooden spoon beat the cooled mixture into the creamed butter. Add the vanilla and beat well again.

To assemble the cake, spread half of the filling over two of the layers, then stack them one on top of another. Spread the buttercream frosting over the top and sides of the cake.

MAKES ONE 9-INCH 3-LAYER CAKE TO SERVE 12

Three-Layer Fresh Coconut Cake

"The success of this recipe is the selection of a fine fresh coconut," according to Brill Williams, chef at his family's Inn at Sawmill Farm in West Dover, Vermont. Shake it to make sure there is still liquid inside.

CAKE:

1 cup (2 sticks) unsalted butter
2 cups sugar
4 eggs, separated
1 teaspoon vanilla extract

3 cups cake flour
3 teaspoons baking powder
1 cup fresh coconut milk *

FROSTING:

2 egg whites
1/8 teaspoon cream of tartar
1/4 teaspoon salt
1/4 cup sugar

3/4 cup light corn syrup
1 teaspoon vanilla extract
1 cup whipped cream
1 coconut, grated *

FILLING:

1 cup heavy cream
1 tablespoon sugar

1/2 teaspoon vanilla

* Heat a coconut in 400-degree oven for 15 minutes. Crack open with a hammer, or drop forcefully on a hard surface. Drain and reserve the liquid. Pry out the coconut meat and thin brown skin, then peel away the skin. Chop the coconut pieces roughly, then put them in a food processor to grate. Or you can grate large pieces with a hand grater. Pour 2/3 cup of boiling water over the grated coconut, and add the reserved coconut liquid. Let steep 30 minutes or more. Stain through a cheesecloth-lined strainer and twist the cheesecloth to squeeze out as much milk as possible. This will be your coconut milk. Use the grated coconut meat for decorating the cake.

Cream the butter and sugar together. Beat the egg yolks with the vanilla and add to the butter-sugar mixture. Sift the flour and the baking powder and add to the moist ingredients alternately with the coconut milk, a little at a time, beginning and ending with the dry ingredients. Beat the egg whites until they form firm peaks and fold them into the batter. Spread equal amounts of the batter into three 8-inch cake pans that have been buttered and floured. Bake in a preheated 350-degree oven for 30 minutes. Remove, let rest in the pans 5 minutes, then turn the cakes out to cool in racks.

While cakes are baking, prepare the frosting. Beat egg whites to form peaks, sprinkling in the cream of tartar and salt as you beat. Slowly add sugar, and continue beating to a smooth satin finish. Add the syrup and vanilla very slowly, and beat until stiff.

While cakes are cooling, whip the cream with the sugar and vanilla until quite stiff. Divide whipped cream and spread on the tops of two of the cake layers; put them together and top with the third layer. Spread frosting all over the top and sides of the layered cake. Sprinkle evenly with grated coconut.

MAKES 8-INCH ROUND 3-LAYER CAKE

Devil's Food Cake with Fudge Icing

This is an old-fashioned chocolate cake, dense and quite chocolaty. It is one of the few cakes that tastes better after it has settled for a day with the fudge icing permeating the cake; in fact, it will keep well through the week if you know where to hide it. Cakes like this were often made with leftover milk that had turned sour, but today with pasteurization milk doesn't go naturally sour—it simply gets rancid. So unless you have access to a dairy farm, the simplest way to sour supermarket milk is to stir 1 tablespoon vinegar into 1 cup of milk and let it stand at room temperature for 15 minutes.

¾ cup sour milk (see above remarks)
5 tablespoons unsweetened cocoa
2 tablespoons brown sugar
¼ pound butter (1 stick)
1 cup sugar

2 eggs, separated
1 teaspoon vanilla
1 cup all-purpose flour
½ teaspoon cream of tartar
½ teaspoon baking soda
½ teaspoon salt

ICING:
2 cups sugar
2 tablespoons corn syrup
3 tablespoons unsweetened cocoa, or 3 squares unsweetened chocolate

½ cup half-and-half
2 tablespoons butter
½ teaspoon baking powder
1 teaspoon vanilla

GARNISH: butternut halves

Butter and flour two 8-inch cake pans, shaking off the excess flour. In ¼ cup of the sour milk, dissolve the cocoa with the brown sugar over very low heat or in a pan of water. Cream the butter and sugar together, then stir in the egg yolks, the cocoa mixture, and the vanilla. Mix and toss together the flour, cream of tartar, baking soda, and salt, then add alternately with the remaining sour milk to the batter. Beat the egg whites until they form peaks that hold, then fold the whites into the batter. Divide the batter between the two pans and bake in a preheated 350-degree oven for 30 minutes. Let sit in the pans for 5 minutes, then turn out onto cake racks.

Meanwhile, prepare the icing. Cook the sugar, corn syrup, cocoa or chocolate, and half-and-half together until it reaches the soft ball stage (240 degrees). Remove from the heat and beat in the butter and baking powder.

Cool slightly, then add the vanilla, and beat thoroughly. When the fudge frosting thickens, spread it over one layer of the cake, top with the other and spread frosting on top and all around. Decorate with halves of butternuts around the edges.

MAKES ONE 2-LAYER 8-INCH CAKE

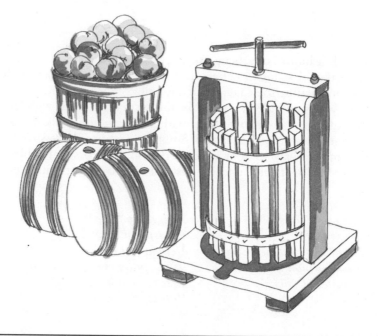

Barbara's Austrian Chocolate Cake

There are many Austrian cooks in ski areas who have been delighting New Englanders with rich chocolate confections, of which this recipe is an example—a far cry from the traditional New England chocolate cake

4 tablespoons soft unsalted butter
¾ cup sugar
2 eggs, separated
2 squares unsweetened chocolate, melted

½ teaspoon vanilla
⅓ cup sifted all-purpose flour

FILLING:
4 tablespoons unsalted butter
½ square unsweetened chocolate
½ cup confectioners' sugar

1 egg yolk
2 tablespoons currant jelly, melted

ICING:
2 teaspoons butter
2 squares unsweetened chocolate, melted

6–7 tablespoons confectioners' sugar
1 tablespoon or more water

Cream the butter and sugar, add the egg yolks, and beat until lemon colored. Add the melted chocolate and beat thoroughly, then stir in the vanilla. In a separate bowl beat the egg whites until they form firm peaks but are not dry, and fold them into the chocolate mixture a little at a time alternately with the flour. Pour into a small buttered jelly roll pan (13 × 7 inches), spreading the batter to cover the bottom evenly. Bake in a preheated 350-degree oven for 12 minutes. Remove and cool in the pan while you make the filling.

Make the filling: Mix together the butter, chocolate, sugar, and egg yolk in a small saucepan or double boiler, and stir over simmering water until thickened. Let cool. Remove the cake from the pan and cut it lengthwise in 3 strips of even width. Spread half of the filling on top of one strip, place a second strip on top and the remaining filling, then put the third strip on top, and spread the currant jelly over the surface.

Make the icing: Stir the butter into the melted chocolate and as much of the confectioners' sugar as can be absorbed. Add 1 tablespoon or more water to smooth. When smooth spread a thin coat on the top and sides of the cake. Refrigerate the cake for an hour or longer. To serve, cut into 1-inch slices.

SERVES ABOUT 10

Butternut or Walnut Torte

If you are lucky enough to have a cache of butternuts, make this delicious torte—a cake using nuts ground to a meal and very little flour. Walnuts will make a good substitute if butternuts aren't available. In either case, be sure the nuts are fresh tasting and be careful not to grind so many at once that they pack down and become oily.

7 eggs
1 cup sugar
2 teaspoons vanilla
2 tablespoons all-purpose flour
1/8 teaspoon cinnamon

1/8 teaspoon freshly grated nutmeg
1 teaspoon rum or brandy
1/2 pound butternuts or walnuts
1/4 teaspoon cream of tartar

GARNISH: *Dusting of confectioners' sugar or 1 cup heavy cream, whipped*
Fresh strawberries or raspberries and/or whole nuts

Separate the eggs, putting the whites into a very clean bowl (not plastic). In another bowl, beat the yolks until lemon colored, then add the sugar, beating continuously until the sugar is absorbed. Stir in the vanilla and put the flour into a small strainer and sift it in. Beat well and add the cinnamon, nutmeg, and rum or brandy. Pulverize the nuts in a hand nut grinder or in a blender or spice/nut grinder, in three or four batches. When very finely ground, stir small amounts into the batter, crumbling the nuts through your fingers to loosen them; beat well into the batter. Beat the egg whites with the cream of tartar until they form firm peaks. Mix one-fourth of the beaten whites into the batter to lighten it, then turn the batter into the bowl of remaining egg whites and carefully fold the whites into the batter; don't over-fold. Butter a 10-inch tube pan on the bottom only and sprinkle it with flour, knocking out the excess. Pour the batter into the pan and bake in a preheated 325-degree oven for 1 hour. Let the cake cool in the pan, then turn it out onto a rack. To serve, slip onto a cake plate and either sprinkle well with confectioners' sugar or heap with whipped cream. Garnish with berries and/or additional whole nuts.

MAKES 10 SERVINGS

Rainbow Sweet's Blueberry Whipped Cream Meringue Torte

FOR THE BATTER LAYER:
½ cup butter (1 stick)
½ cup confectioners' sugar
4 egg yolks
1 cup cake flour

1 teaspoon baking powder
½ teaspoon salt
3 tablespoons milk
1½ teaspoons vanilla

FOR THE MERINGUE LAYER:
4 egg whites
½ teaspoon cream of tartar
1 cup sugar

1 teaspoon cider vinegar
1 teaspoon vanilla

FILLING:
2 cups heavy cream
1 cup yogurt

1 pint fresh blueberries, washed, stemmed, and dried

Grease two 10-inch springform pans and dust them with flour.

To make the cake batter: With an electric mixer, beat the butter in a bowl until it is light and fluffy. Gradually add the confectioners' sugar, then the egg yolks, one at a time, beating constantly. Combine the cake flour, baking powder, and salt, and sift them twice. Add the sifted ingredients to the butter and egg mixture alternately with the milk. Stir in the vanilla. The batter will be stiff. Divide it evenly between the two prepared cake pans.

For the meringue: In another bowl combine the egg whites with the cream of tartar, and beat until the egg whites are stiff. Gradually add the sugar, and continue to beat until the whites stand up in stiff peaks. Beat in the cider vinegar and the vanilla. Then put equal amounts of the meringue into the two cake pans, smoothing it with a rubber spatula evenly over the batter. Bake the layers in a preheated 325-degree oven for 30 minutes. Carefully remove from the pans and cool, meringue side up.

Make the filling: Beat the cream until stiff. Spoon about ½ cup of it into a pastry bag, fitted with a fluted tip, if you have one; if not, simply set aside

to chill. Gently fold the yogurt into the remaining whipped cream. Spread half of this mixture on top of one of the cake layers. Scatter half the blueberries on top. Place the second cake layer on top of the first. Cover with the remaining cream and blueberries. Use the reserved whipped cream to decorate. Chill until ready to serve.
SERVES 10–12

Chocolate Cookie Pie Cake

As a specialty of Nickerson Tavern at Searsport, Maine, a first helping of this uncommon variation on the chocolate theme was described by a ten-year-old as "a cross between a brownie and a cake."

1 cup sugar
1½ teaspoons baking powder
5 egg whites, at room temperature
8 ounces semisweet chocolate chips, ground in a food processor

1¼ cups graham cracker crumbs
1 cup ground toasted pecans

GLAZE:
4 ounces semisweet chocolate chips
1 tablespoon corn syrup

1 tablespoon butter

TOPPING:
3 tablespoons instant coffee
3 tablespoons Amaretto, coffee liqueur, or rum

1 pint heavy cream
½ cup confectioners' sugar

GARNISH:
About 16 toasted almond halves

4 ounces bitter chocolate

Sift the sugar and the baking powder together. Beat the egg whites on high speed, and when they have foamed and begun to thicken, add the sugar–baking powder mixture, sprinkling it on as you continue to beat the whites until they become stiff and glossy. Toss the ground chocolate chips, graham cracker crumbs, and ground toasted pecans together in a bowl to mix them well, then stir in several spoonfuls of the beaten whites to lighten. Pour this mixture down the side of the egg white bowl and then carefully fold the rest of the egg whites into the mixture. Pour into a buttered, fluted baking dish, 2 inches deep and 9 inches across, or use a springform pan, and bake in a preheated 350-degree oven for 30 minutes. The cake should be pale golden. Invert it while it is still hot onto a flat cake plate.

While the cake is baking, prepare the glaze. Melt the chocolate chips, the corn syrup, and the butter in a small saucepan set over a pan of barely simmering water. Whisk until smooth. Spread the glaze over the top and sides of the cake while it is still hot. Now chill the cake.

Just a little before serving, prepare the topping. Dissolve the instant coffee in the liqueur. Beat the cream and as it begins to thicken, add the dissolved coffee and the confectioners' sugar, and continue beating until fairly stiff. Spread this over and around the chilled cake.

Garnish with toasted almond halves. Make chocolate curls by melting the bitter chocolate on a cookie sheet in a low oven, and then scraping up ribbons of the chocolate with a putty knife just before it really hardens; as it curls around the knife, scrape the curls off onto the cake at even intervals. And there it is.

SERVES 8–10

Twice Butternut Cheesecake

CRUST:
1/3 cup all-purpose flour
1 1/8 teaspoon salt
4 tablespoons butter

6 ounces butternuts
1 tablespoon honey
1/2 teaspoon vanilla

FILLING:
One 8-ounce package cream cheese
2 eggs
1 egg yolk
1 1/2 cups puréed cooked butternut squash, at room temperature

1/2 cup maple syrup
2 teaspoons vanilla

TOPPING:
3/4 cup sour cream

8 butternut halves

To make the crust, toss the flour and salt together, then cut in the butter and work it with your fingertips until the texture resembles fresh bread crumbs. Grind the butternuts in a blender or coffee grinder in several batches; if you grind too many at a time they pack down and become oily (or you can chop them very fine with a knife). Stir them into the butter-flour mixture, then add the honey and vanilla and mix well. Pack the crumb crust into the bottom of a 9-inch springform pan, cover with plastic wrap, and refrigerate for 30 minutes or longer.

Prebake the crust for 10 minutes in a preheated 400-degree oven while you make the filling. Beat the cream cheese until soft or spin it in a food processor. Beat in the eggs, one at a time, and the egg yolk (you can continue to use the processor), then the butternut purée, maple syrup, and vanilla. Remove the crust from the oven—it should have browned a little —spoon in the filling and smooth the top. Return the cheesecake to the oven and bake 10 minutes, then turn the heat down to 325 degrees and bake another 30 minutes. Turn off the oven and let the cake rest there with the door open for 30 minutes, then cool at room temperature. It may be eaten at this point or chilled. Before serving, remove from the mold, spread the sour cream on top, and decorate with butternut halves around the edge.

SERVES 8

Cheesecake

CRUST:
1½ cups graham cracker crumbs
½ cup finely chopped walnuts

¾ teaspoon cinnamon
½ cup soft butter

FILLING:
1 pound cream cheese
3 eggs
1 cup sugar
¼ teaspoon salt

1 teaspoon vanilla
Grated rind of 1 lemon
3 cups sour cream

Mix the ingredients for the crust together and reserve about ¼ cup. Press the remainder firmly into a 9-inch springform pan, pressing it ½ inch up the sides all around. Chill for 1 hour.

With an electric mixer beat the cream cheese until fluffy. Beat the eggs thoroughly in a separate bowl, then add them to the cream cheese along with the sugar, salt, vanilla, and lemon rind, beating thoroughly until well blended. Stir in the sour cream. Pour the filling into the crust and sprinkle the reserved crumb mixture on top. Bake in a preheated 350-degree oven for 50–60 minutes, until firm. Turn off the oven and let the cake stand in the oven with the door open for about 45–60 minutes. Let cool completely, then chill in the refrigerator before serving.

MAKES ONE 9-INCH CAKE TO SERVE AT LEAST 12

Maple Cheesecake

CRUST:

1/3 cup maple sugar
2 cups pulverized graham crackers
   (about 1/2 pound crackers)

1 1/4 sticks butter, melted (10
   tablespoons)

FILLING:

1 pound cream cheese
3/4 cup maple syrup
1 cup sour cream

1 tablespoon flour
6 eggs, separated
6 tablespoons sugar

To make the crust, mix the maple sugar with the cracker crumbs. Pour in the melted butter and mix with a fork. Press into a 10-inch springform pan and bake in a preheated 350-degree oven for 10 minutes.

Meanwhile make the filling. Beat the cream cheese, maple syrup, sour cream, flour, and egg yolks together (this can be done in a food processor). In a separate bowl, beat the egg whites until they start to form peaks, then add the sugar, continuing to beat until they form very firm peaks. Fold into the maple-cream cheese mixture. Spread the filling over the crumb crust, and bake in a preheated 325-degree oven for 1 hour and 10 minutes. Turn off the oven, and leave in the oven with the door open for about 45 minutes, then let cool on a counter. Chill in the refrigerator for at least 1 hour and unmold.

SERVES 10–12

Maple Butternut Tea Cake

So pure and delicious that it doesn't really need a frosting, this tea cake needs only a light dusting of confectioners' sugar to dress it up. But if you want to ice it for a special occasion, try using Aunt Lucy's Vermont Maple Frosting (page 592) for both a filling and frosting to make a two-layer cake.

1/2 cup (1 stick) butter
1/2 cup sugar
2 eggs
2 1/2 cups flour
2 teaspoons baking powder
1/2 teaspoon baking soda

1 cup maple syrup
1/2 cup hot water
1/2 teaspoon vanilla
1 cup finely chopped butternuts
Confectioners' sugar

Cream the butter and the sugar together, then beat in the eggs. Sift the flour, baking powder and soda together. Combine the maple syrup and the hot water. Add the dry ingredients alternately with the diluted maple syrup to the butter-sugar-egg mixture, beating thoroughly. Stir in the vanilla and butternuts. Grease and flour two 8-inch cake pans, shaking off the excess, and pour the batter evenly into the two pans. Bake in preheated 350-degree oven for 30 minutes, until lightly browned on top and a toothpick inserted in the center comes out clean. Cool 5 minutes in the pans, then turn out onto racks. Sprinkle confectioners' sugar on top.

MAKES TWO 8-INCH CAKES

Hartford Election Cake

Sermons were common on election days throughout colonial New England, but so was good food. "Weeks of preparation went into getting ready for this June celebration. It was a day of parades . . . of feasting and drinking, with tables groaning . . ." say the authors of *Secrets of New England Cooking.* "But no matter how many rich viands were served, Election Day was not complete without its time-honored raised cake, full of raisins and thin slices of citron, and topped with a sticky coating of treacle." In *Domestic Receipts,* Catharine Beecher, who grew up in Litchfield, Connecticut, gave a recipe for Old Hartford Election Cake, which she said was 100 years old in 1857. Here is our version.

½ cup yellow raisins
½ cup dark raisins
4 teaspoons dried coriander seeds
¼ cup brandy
2 packages active dry yeast
  (2 tablespoons)
2½ cups warm water
½ cup nonfat dry milk
7 cups all-purpose flour

¾ cup sugar
½ pound butter (2 sticks)
¾ cup brown sugar
4 eggs
1 teaspoon salt
1 teaspoon cinnamon
½ teaspoon freshly grated nutmeg
½ cup sliced citron
Molasses

Soak the raisins and coriander in the brandy for 3–4 hours.

In a large bowl, dissolve the yeast in ½ cup of the warm water and let stand a minute. Add the remaining water, the dry milk, 4 cups of the flour, and ¼ cup of the sugar and beat well, about 100 strokes by hand or 3 minutes on the electric beater. Cover with plastic wrap and let this sponge rise for about 3 hours.

Cream the butter with the remaining sugar and the brown sugar, then beat in the eggs, salt, cinnamon, and nutmeg. Turn this mixture into the sponge, stir in the remaining flour, cup by cup, using enough to form a soft dough. Add the citron and the raisins and coriander, along with their juices, and a little more flour, if necessary to make a cohesive dough. Cover with plastic wrap, and let rise again until double in volume.

Beat down the dough, adding a little more flour again if it is too sticky. Divide in half and place in two greased 9-inch cake pans, cover lightly with a towel, and let rise again for 30 minutes. Bake in a preheated 350-degree oven for 55 minutes. Turn out of the pans onto a baking sheet. Drizzle molasses over the tops and slip the cakes under the broiler until the glaze bubbles. Let cool on racks.

MAKES TWO 9-INCH CAKES

Boston Cream Pie

6 tablespoons butter
1 cup sugar
2 large eggs
1¾ cups flour

½ teaspoon salt
2 teaspoons baking powder
½ cup milk
½ teaspoon vanilla

FILLING:
⅔ cup sugar
⅓ cup flour
A pinch of salt

2 cups milk
2 egg yolks
½ teaspoon lemon extract

TOPPING:
Confectioners' sugar

Cream the butter with all but 2 tablespoons of the cup of sugar. Beat the eggs until lemon colored, then beat in the remaining sugar. Add to the creamed butter and sugar and beat until fluffy. Sift together the flour, salt, and baking powder. Add the dry ingredients alternately with the milk to the batter and beat until all is blended. Finally mix in the vanilla. Turn into two well-buttered 8-inch cake pans and bake in a preheated 375-degree oven for 25 minutes. Turn out on racks to cool while you prepare the filling.

Make the filling: Mix the sugar, flour, and salt together in the top of a double boiler. Heat the milk just to the boiling point, then slowly blend it into the sugar-flour-salt mixture and let cook slowly in the double boiler, stirring from time to time until thick, about 15 minutes. Beat the egg yolks, mix in a little of the hot custard, and then stir the yolks into the custard in the double boiler and cook gently, stirring for 3 to 4 minutes. Season with lemon extract. Let the filling cool, then spread it thickly between the cake layers. Sprinkle the top with powdered sugar and cut into pie-shaped wedges to serve.
SERVES 8–10

Maple Tea Cakes

There are those who remember, as did Dorothy Canfield Fisher, being sent as children to the cellar "with an old chisel and a hammer, to chip off a week's supply of sweetenin' from the big barrel." The recipe below makes striking use of the "sweetenin'."

1 cup granulated maple sugar
¼ cup white sugar
⅓ cup soft unsalted butter
1 egg, well beaten
2 cups sifted cake flour

2 teaspoons baking powder
¼ teaspoon salt
½ cup milk
Confectioners' sugar

Cream the 2 sugars and the butter together, beating thoroughly until the sugar has been well absorbed. Beat in the egg. Mix the sifted cake flour with the baking powder and salt and add to the batter alternately with the milk. Butter a 12-cup non-stick muffin pan or line the cups with cupcake papers and fill the cups with batter about ½ to ⅔ full. Bake in a preheated 350-degree oven for 18–20 minutes until lightly browned on top. Let rest in the pan 5 minutes before removing carefully—these cakes are fragile. Dust the tops with confectioners' sugar.

MAKES 12 CUPCAKES

Linda Sayer, who caters parties and weddings around Stannard, Vermont, says that these cupcakes are a favorite among those Northern Yankees who appreciate her food. Perhaps it's because of the wonderful textures as you bite into these small cakes—the surprise grains of solid chocolate and the nugget of rich filling in the center.

Linda Sayer's Cupcakes

1¼ cups shortening
1 cup granulated sugar
1 egg
2 cups all-purpose flour
¾ cup unsweetened cocoa

2 teaspoons baking soda
1 teaspoon salt
1½ cups milk
One 6-ounce package mini
    semisweet chocolate chips

FILLING:
Two 3-ounce packages cream
    cheese
⅓ cup granulated sugar

1 egg
¼ cup coconut

FROSTING:
1 pound confectioners' sugar
½ cup shortening
¼ teaspoon salt

½ teaspoon lemon extract, or 1
    teaspoon fresh lemon juice
2–3 tablespoons milk or water

Cream the shortening and the granulated sugar together, then beat in the egg. Mix and toss the flour, cocoa, baking soda, and salt together, and add to the shortening and sugar alternately with the milk. Stir in the mini chocolate chips.

To make the filling, beat the cream cheese, granulated sugar, and egg together until smooth, then stir in the coconut.

Fill 24 greased muffin or cupcake pans with half of the cake batter. Make a little well in the center of each batter-filled cup and spoon a heaping ½ teaspoon of the filling in. Cover with the remaining cake batter. Bake in a preheated 350-degree oven 20–25 minutes, or until a skewer plunged in the center comes out clean. Remove from the oven and let sit 5 minutes before turning the cakes out onto racks. Make the frosting by beating the confectioners' sugar with the shortening, salt, and lemon extract. Add enough milk or water to make a spreadable icing, and frost the tops of the cakes.

MAKES 24 CUPCAKES

Date and Nut Cakes

3 eggs, separated
3 tablespoons sugar
1 cup chopped pitted dates

1 cup chopped walnuts
1 tablespoon fresh bread crumbs

GARNISH: *1 cup cream, whipped*

Beat the yolks with the sugar until lemon colored. Add the dates, walnuts, and bread crumbs. In a separate bowl, beat the egg whites until they form firm peaks, then fold them into the first mixture. Butter 10 muffin tins and fill them three-quarters full of batter. Bake in a preheated 375-degree oven for 12 minutes. Remove from the pans, let cool slightly, but serve warm with big dollops of whipped cream on top.

MAKES 10 CAKES

1½ cups sugar
4 tablespoons water
¼ teaspoon cream of tartar

2 egg whites
1 teaspoon vanilla

Seven-Minute Frosting

Place everything except the vanilla in the top of a double boiler over boiling water. Immediately start beating at high speed (it will be easier with a hand-held electric beater) and continue at moderate speed as the mixture cooks. In 7 minutes the frosting will be thick enough to stand in a peak as you hold the beater in the air. Remove from the heat, add the vanilla, and beat for 1 minute. Spread on the cake right away.

ENOUGH TO FILL AND FROST A 9-INCH LAYER CAKE

2 squares unsweetened chocolate
½ cup unsalted butter (1 stick)
2¾ cups confectioners' sugar, sifted

2 egg yolks
1 teaspoon vanilla

Chocolate Frosting

Put the chocolate in a small pan over simmering water and let melt. Beat the butter until fluffy, then beat in the confectioners' sugar a little at a time, adding the egg yolks as it gets thick. When all the sugar has been incorporated, stir in the melted chocolate and the vanilla.

ENOUGH TO FILL AND FROST A 9-INCH LAYER CAKE

¼ cup butter at room temperature
2 tablespoons unsweetened cocoa
1½ teaspoons instant coffee
   (powdered)

1 teaspoon vanilla
3 cups confectioners' sugar
3–4 tablespoons milk

Mocha Frosting

Beat the butter until fluffy, then beat in the cocoa, instant coffee, and vanilla. Put the confectioners' sugar in a sifter or strainer and sift a little into the butter mixture alternately with drizzles of the milk, beating continuously. Use just enough milk to get the consistency you want.

ENOUGH TO FILL AND FROST AN 8-INCH LAYER CAKE

Aunt Lucy's Vermont Maple Frosting

1½ cups maple syryp
2 egg whites

A pinch of salt

Boil the maple syrup until it spins a thread (230 degrees). Beat the egg whites with the salt until they form soft peaks. Add the maple syrup gradually and keep beating until the frosting is smooth and of a spreadable consistency.

ENOUGH TO FILL AND FROST A 9-INCH DOUBLE LAYER CAKE

Cream Cheese Frosting

4 tablespoons unsalted butter (½ stick), at room temperature
½ pound cream cheese, at room temperature

2 cups confectioners' sugar
1 teaspoon vanilla extract

Beat the butter and cream cheese together until fluffy. Gradually add the confectioners' sugar through a sifter or strainer and the vanilla, beating well. The frosting may be mixed in a food processor.

ENOUGH TO FILL AND FROST AND 8-INCH LAYER CAKE

Lemon or Orange Cake Filling

⅓ cup sugar
2 tablespoons flour
½ cup lemon or orange juice
¼ cup water

1 egg yolk
2 tablespoons unsweetened butter
1 teaspoon grated lemon or orange rind

Mix the sugar, flour, citrus juice, and water together in a saucepan, stirring until smooth. Cook over medium heat, stirring until thickened. Beat the egg yolk in a small bowl and gradually beat in a little of the hot mixture to temper the yolk. Now turn the yolk into the rest of the hot mixture and stir in the butter and rind. Cook, stirring, for about 2 minutes. Let cool before spreading onto the layer of a cake.

ENOUGH TO FILL A 9-INCH LAYER CAKE

3/4 cup fresh orange or lemon juice
1 1/2 teaspoons grated orange or
    lemon rind

2 cups confectioners' sugar

Lemon or Orange Frosting

Warm the juice and rind, then beat in the confectioners' sugar (through a strainer or sifter if it is lumpy).

ENOUGH TO FILL AND FROST AN 8-INCH LAYER CAKE

COOKIES

6 tablespoons butter (3/4 stick)
1/2 cup sugar
2 egg whites

1/8 teaspoon salt
1/3 cup flour
1 cup broken butternuts

Butternut Cookies

Cream the butter and the sugar together. Using a wooden spoon, beat in the egg whites, salt, and flour; don't overbeat. Fold in the butternuts. Drop by the teaspoonful onto greased cookie sheets, leaving about 1 1/2 inches between. Bake in a preheated 400-degree oven for 10 minutes, or until the cookies are browned at the edges and lightly golden in the middle. Remove with a spatula while still warm, and place on cookie racks to crisp.

MAKES ABOUT 30 COOKIES

1 cup butter (2 sticks)
1 1/4 cups sugar, plus extra for
    sugaring the tops
2 eggs

2 teaspoons vanilla
2 cups flour
2 1/2 teaspoons baking powder
1 teaspoon salt

Phyllis's Sugar Cookies

Cream the butter and sugar together. Beat in the eggs and the vanilla. Mix thoroughly the flour, baking powder, and salt, then mix in with the butter-egg-sugar mixture. Pinch off small balls of dough, no more than 1 teaspoon, and drop onto lightly greased baking sheets about 1½ inches apart. Now grease lightly the bottom of a glass, then dip it into sugar, and press it onto each mound to flatten. Repeat, regreasing and resugaring the glass for each cookie. Bake in a preheated 375-degree oven 8–10 minutes until just lightly brown at the edges.

MAKES ABOUT 50 COOKIES

Maple Pecan Cookies

2 cups flour
2 teaspoons salt
½ teaspoon baking powder
3 eggs
1 cup maple sugar

4 tablespoons melted butter
½ teaspoon baking soda
½ cup warm water
⅔ cup pecans, broken
⅔ cup yellow raisins

Toss the flour, salt, and baking powder together. Beat the eggs lightly, then stir into the dry ingredients along with the maple sugar and melted butter. Dissolve the baking soda in the warm water and stir into the batter. Fold in the pecans and raisins. Drop by heaping teaspoonfuls onto greased cookie sheets and press down the top of each mound with your fingers, which should be dipped into cold water now and then to keep them from sticking. Bake in a preheated 375-degree oven 11–12 minutes, until lightly browned.

MAKES ABOUT 40 COOKIES

Rhubarb Cookies

¼ pound butter (1 stick)
1 cup light brown sugar
1 egg
1 cup cooked rhubarb (page 524), drained
2 cups flour
¼ teaspoon salt
1 teaspoon baking soda

1 teaspoon freshly grated nutmeg
1 teaspoon cinnamon
½ teaspoon ground cloves
3 tablespoons finely chopped crystallized ginger (optional but delicious)
½ cup chopped walnuts
1 cup raisins

Cream the butter and sugar together. Add the egg and beat until light, then stir in the rhubarb. Stir the flour, salt, baking soda, and spices together and toss until thoroughly mixed. Stir the dry ingredients into the rhubarb mixture until the two are blended, then fold in the optional ginger, the walnuts, and the raisins. Drop the batter by tablespoonfuls onto greased baking sheets about 1½ inches apart, and bake in a preheated 350-degree oven for 12 minutes, until lightly browned at the edges.

MAKES ABOUT 30 COOKIES

½ cup butter (1 stick)
½ cup shortening
1 cup light brown sugar
1 cup honey
1 egg

4 cups flour
½ teaspoon baking powder
¼ teaspoon salt
1 cup chopped walnuts or hazelnuts

Honey Cookies

Beat the butter, shortening, and brown sugar together until smooth. Beat in the honey and the egg. Toss together the flour, baking powder, and salt to mix, then add to the butter-sugar mixture, and blend thoroughly. Fold in the chopped nuts. Drop by the teaspoonful onto greased baking sheets, leaving about 1½ inches between, and bake in a preheated 350-degree oven, until the cookies are lightly browned at the edges. Remove to a rack to cool.

MAKES ABOUT 60 COOKIES

Nutcracker Suite

They're a disappearing species, but there remain nutcrackers in the Berkshire and Green Mountains who are rightly proud of their craft. One of them, who said he's not found a good modern tool for the job, wrote a few years back, "Cracking nuts with a hammer is an art, one does not become an expert overnight. It requires considerable experience and practice. Over the years I have learned how to bring out halves in hickories, black walnuts, and butternuts almost every time—but I started cracking them some 70 years ago. . . .

"Let's take a butternut. First of all, you remove the outer shell after it becomes well dried out.* You will then notice that one end of the nut is more pointed than the other. Stand the nut so that the more pointed end rests in a small depression (a cement block with a small gouge in it is excellent for this purpose). Naturally you will be cracking someplace where the problem of shells does not have to be considered.

"Now start tapping the blunt end with the hammer. Not too hard at first until you get the sound and feel of it. Don't be hasty! It should not crack before at least four or five taps. Often as many as a dozen taps are necessary. A hard bash and you end up with crushed nut meats. Every single nut is different in the texture and strength of its shell, so each one has to be treated separately. Properly tapped, the nut will break so the two meat halves easily come out of their intricate structure.

"You use the same procedure for black walnuts. Here again you will find one end more pointed than the other. Keep the pointed end down."

* Most experts agree that butternuts should be stored through the winter in a cool, dry place with lots of air circulation for their husks to dry out properly.

Schrafft's Butterscotch Cookies

This wonderful, big, crisp cookie with the delectable flavor of butterscotch and finely ground pecans has been a favorite since the childhood of one of the authors, and was missed by many other fans when the Schrafft's baked goods and candy shops were closed. But we managed to track down the original recipe, and it has appeared heretofore only in Marion Cunningham's *The Fannie Farmer Baking Book*.

2 tablespoons butter, at room temperature
3/4 cup shortening, at room temperature
1 1/4 cups dark brown sugar
1 egg
2 tablespoons nonfat dry milk

1 tablespoon vanilla
1 3/4 cups flour
1/2 teaspoon baking soda
1/2 teaspoon salt
1 cup finely chopped pecans
Flour for coating glass

Cream the butter and shortening with the brown sugar. Beat in the egg, dry milk, and vanilla. Mix and toss the flour, baking soda, and salt, then add to the creamed mixture. Stir in the pecans. Drop the batter by heaping tablespoonfuls onto cookie sheets, leaving 2 inches between. Dip the bottom of a glass about 3 inches in diameter into flour and press each mound of dough into a circle of that size. Reflour the glass and continue to press out into circles the rest of the cookies. If the dough sticks a little to the glass, just scrape it off and pat it back into place. Bake in a preheated 375-degree oven 8–10 minutes, until lightly browned. Remove and carefully scrape up the cookies with a spatula and place on racks to cool.
MAKES ABOUT THIRTY 3-INCH COOKIES

Scottish Shortbread

As the pride of Scottish cooks everywhere, shortbread is turned out in more than one Yankee kitchen. "I bake it for the Morrisville and Barre Farmers Markets," a Vermont woman wrote, "and always sell out, never can make enough." Shortbread can be made in cookielike shapes, or in round flat loaves, as below.

4 cups flour
1 cup sugar

1 pound butter

Put the ingredients in a large bowl and mix with a pastry cutter, then knead the mixture thoroughly. When it forms a ball, divide into four flat cakes and press them into four 9-inch cake pans. Prick the surfaces with a fork, making evenly distributed perforations. Bake at 375 degrees for about 1 hour, until the cakes are delicately brown. To serve, cut in wedges.
MAKES 32 WEDGE-SHAPED PIECES

¼ pound butter (1 stick)
½ cup confectioners' sugar
1 cup cake flour
¼ teaspoon salt

½ teaspoon baking powder
2 teaspoons grated lemon rind
½ teaspoon vanilla

Lemony Shortbread

Cream the butter until soft, then add the confectioners' sugar gradually until thoroughly blended. Mix and toss the cake flour with the salt and baking powder, then add to the butter and sugar, mixing well. Stir in the grated lemon rind and vanilla. Spread evenly into an 8-inch pie pan, with a fork make light cross-hatch marks on top, and bake in a preheated 350-degree oven for 25 minutes, watching carefully the last 5 minutes to make sure that it doesn't brown too much (if you bake in a Pyrex pan, 20 minutes will be long enough). Cool slightly, and then cut into wedges.

MAKES 16 WEDGE-SHAPED PIECES

Founded in Boston in the nineteenth century, the gastronomic enterprise known as Schrafft's soon had stores and restaurants scattered throughout New York City and a reputation for various kinds of delicious candies, ice creams, and especially—for aficionados—cookies. So zealous were some Manhattan cookie lovers that they would entrain for Schrafft's Yankee headquarters, so the story goes, in the belief that the Boston cookies had the edge over those made elsewhere—particularly the oatmeal cookies. The original formulas produced 10-pound batches, but we have reduced the amounts in the recipe below (as well as in the Schrafft's Butterscotch cookies) for more practical use in the kitchen.

Schrafft's Oatmeal Cookies

¼ pound (1 stick) butter
1 cup sugar
2 eggs
1 teaspoon vanilla
1½ cups oatmeal
1½ cups flour
½ teaspoon baking powder

½ teaspoon baking soda
½ teaspoon salt
1 teaspoon cinnamon
½ teaspoon allspice
¼ cup milk
1 cup raisins
1 cup chopped walnuts

Cream the butter and sugar together. Add the eggs and vanilla and beat until light and fluffy. Stir in the oats. Mix and toss the flour, baking powder, baking soda, salt, cinnamon, and allspice, then add to the butter-sugar-egg mixture along with the milk. Beat until well blended. Stir in the raisins and nuts. Drop by full tablespoonfuls onto greased baking sheets, about 1½ inches apart. Bake in a preheated 350-degree oven for 12 minutes. Remove and cool on racks.

MAKES 40 COOKIES

Butternut and Cocoa Brownies

1 cup butter (1/2 pound)
1 2/3 cups sugar
1 teaspoon vanilla
4 eggs

1 cup flour
1/2 cup plus 1 tablespoon powdered
  cocoa
3/4 cup butternut pieces

Cream the butter, adding the sugar gradually until the mixture is thoroughly blended. Stir in the vanilla and break in the eggs and blend thoroughly. Sift the flour and cocoa together, then stir the mixture into the butter-sugar batter. Add the nut meats and stir thoroughly. Butter a 9 × 9-inch baking pan and pour in the brownie batter. Bake at 350 degrees about 35 minutes; do not overbake—brownies should be moist inside. Cut into squares.

MAKES ABOUT 24 BROWNIES

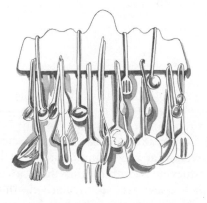

Caraway Cookies

Mrs. Norma Roberts of Bristol, New Hampshire, preserved this recipe, along with many others, from her grandmother's time. "Caraway cookies are to New England butteries," she wrote, "what orchids are to an evening dress. Full of the flavor of June fields (be sure your seeds are fresh and pungent), starred with daisies, and washed with golden sunshine. They cling to a man's memory all the days of his life."

1/2 cup shortening
1/2 cup sugar
1 egg, lightly beaten
1/8 teaspoon salt

1/2 teaspoon baking soda
2 cups flour
1/2 cup sour cream
2 teaspoons fresh caraway seeds

Cream the shortening and the sugar together. Add the egg, salt and baking soda, then gradually sift in the flour and mix well. Stir in the sour cream and caraway seeds. Chill the dough 1 hour. Roll it out to 1/8-inch thickness. Cut the cookies in small rounds and transfer to greased baking sheets, 1 inch apart. Bake in a preheated 375-degree oven for 10–12 minutes.

MAKES ABOUT 40 COOKIES

Chocolate Chip Oatmeal Cookies

1/2 cup shortening
1/2 cup dark brown sugar, firmly packed
1/2 cup granulated sugar
1 egg
1 tablespoon water
1/2 teaspoon vanilla
3/4 cup flour
1/2 teaspoon baking soda
1/2 teaspoon salt
1 1/2 cups oatmeal
1/2 cup semisweet chocolate chips

Beat the shortening, then add both sugars, and continue to beat until creamy. Beat in the egg, and add the water and vanilla. Toss together the flour, baking soda, and salt, then blend this mixture with the creamed sugar. Stir in the oatmeal and chocolate chips, mixing thoroughly. Drop by the heaping teaspoonful onto greased cookie sheets, 1 1/2 inches apart, and bake in a preheated 375-degree oven 12 minutes.

MAKES 36 COOKIES

Naomi Morash's Hermits

Some like their hermits made like drop cookies; others insist on baking them in a pan like brownies. It all depends on what kind of hermit you grew up with. Done the way Naomi Morash suggests, you combine something of both methods—and they're about the best hermits you'll ever taste.

3/4 cup butter or margarine (1 1/2 sticks)
2/3 cup sugar
3/4 cup dark brown sugar
2 eggs, beaten
3 cups flour
1/2 teaspoon salt
1 teaspoon baking powder
1 teaspoon cinnamon
1 teaspoon cloves
1/2 teaspoon ginger
1/4 cup molasses mixed with 1/8 cup warm water
1 cup raisins
1 cup chopped nuts

GLAZE: 1 beaten egg

Cream the butter or margarine with the sugars, then beat in the eggs. Toss the flour, salt, and baking powder, and spices together, then add them to the butter-sugar mixture along with the molasses. Fold in the raisins and nuts. Spread the batter into greased cookie sheets, shaping with floured hands into strips about 10 × 3 inches, spaced several inches apart. Paint the tops of the 4 strips with egg glaze. Bake in a preheated 350-degree oven for 15–20 minutes, depending on how crisp you like your hermits. While still warm, cut each strip into about 9 bars.

MAKES 36 BARS

Spicy Molasses Cookies

One old-fashioned variation on this theme was published under the title "Crybaby Cookies," and another was called "Joshua Cookies," as baked by lumber camp cooks in Vermont's Northeast Kingdom. Here's our version of the latter.

1 cup butter (2 sticks)	½ teaspoon cinnamon
1 cup sugar	¼ teaspoon allspice
1 cup molasses	¼ teaspoon grated nutmeg
½ cup sour cream	Salt
½ cup plain yogurt	3½ cups flour

Cream the butter with the sugar and gradually beat in the molasses. Stir the sour cream and yogurt together. Mix the spices and a light sprinkling of salt with the flour, then sift into the molasses mixture alternately with the mixed sour cream and yogurt, stirring until blended. Drop the batter by the teaspoonful onto greased cookie sheets in mounds 1 inch apart. Bake in a preheated 350-degree oven for about 30 minutes.

MAKES ABOUT 48 COOKIES

Cookies Called Joe Froggers

The Publick House in Sturbridge, Massachusetts, still serves Joe Froggers on a Sunday night with a pitcher of milk. The cookies were real favorites not only at the hotel in Sturbridge but at many other Yankee places, including Marblehead where they originated. According to Eleanor Early in *New England Cookbook* (1954) and Lillian Langstreth-Christiansen in the *Mystic Seaport Cookbook* (1970), their creator was a black man called Uncle Joe who lived on the edge of a pond in Marblehead that was called Uncle Joe Frog's Pond. His cookies got their name, Miss Early reported, "because they were as plump and dark as the fat little frogs that lived in the pond. Marblehead fishermen would give the old man a jug of rum and he would make them a batch of Froggers to take to sea. But he wouldn't tell how he made them." A woman named Mammy Creasey, who said she was Joe's daughter, revealed the secret, however, and soon they were sold in a local bake shop for a penny apiece. At least one Massachusetts family lays claim to possessing the recipe for 150 years or so.

½ cup shortening	4 cups flour
1 cup plus 2–3 tablespoons sugar	1 teaspoon baking soda
1 teaspoon salt	1½ teaspoons ginger
1 cup dark molasses	½ teaspoon ground cloves
6 tablespoons water	½ teaspoon freshly grated nutmeg
2 tablespoons rum	¼ teaspoon allspice

Mix the shortening and 1 cup sugar together thoroughly, and stir in the salt, molasses, water, and rum. Toss the flour with the remaining dry ingredients and then stir it into the shortening mixture. Chill the dough thoroughly. On a lightly floured work surface roll the dough out to ⅛-inch thickness, then cut into 3-inch circles. Transfer the rounds to a greased cookie sheet, and sprinkle the remaining sugar over the tops. Bake in a preheated 375-degree oven for 10–15 minutes. This is the kind of cookie that becomes rather dry and hard after a couple of days, but they are wonderful to dunk into milk, cocoa, tea, or coffee.

MAKES 36 COOKIES

These "bars" are more like tarts with a custard-fruit filling and a meringue topping than they are like old-fashioned cookie bars. They make a fine dessert, best served fresh.

Laura's Strawberry-Rhubarb Bars

THE CRUST:
1¾ cups flour
2 tablespoons powdered sugar
½ cup margarine or butter

THE FILLING:
1½ cups sugar
¼ cup flour
¼ teaspoon salt
6 egg yolks
1 cup heavy cream
4 cups sliced rhubarb
1 cup sliced strawberries
½ teaspoon lemon juice

THE TOPPING:
6 egg whites
½ cup sugar

To make the crust, mix the flour and sugar together. Cut in the margarine or butter. Press into a lightly greased 9 × 13-inch pan. Bake in a preheated 350-degree oven for 10–12 minutes, until golden. Remove and let cool while you prepare the filling.

Toss the sugar, flour, and salt together. Lightly beat the egg yolks and cream together, then stir into the sugar mixture. Fold in the rhubarb, strawberries, and lemon juice. Spread over the baked crust and bake at 350 degrees for about 1 hour, until firm.

Beat the egg whites until foamy. Beat in the sugar, 1 tablespoon at a time, until stiff peaks form. Spread this meringue over the rhubarb mixture and return to the oven 10–15 minutes, until lightly browned. Cool and then cut into squares.

SERVES 8–10

Hazelnut-Date Bars

FILLING:
2 cups pitted dates
1/2 cup sugar
1/4 cup water

Coarsely grated rind of 1 orange
1/2 cup roughly chopped hazelnuts

BATTER:
1 cup flour
1/2 teaspoon salt
1/2 teaspoon baking powder

1 cup dark brown sugar
1/2 cup melted butter
1 cup rolled oats

Cook the dates, sugar, water, and orange rind in a small saucepan over gentle heat, stirring, until thickened. Remove from the heat, fold in the hazelnuts, and let cool.

Mix and toss the flour, salt, and baking powder. Mix the brown sugar, melted butter, and oats together, then stir in the flour. Spread two-thirds of this mixture into a buttered 8-inch square pan and pack it down tightly. Spoon the filling evenly on top, then cover with the remaining batter, packing it down lightly all around. Bake in a preheated 350-degree oven 30 minutes. Cool and cut into bars.

MAKES 36 BARS

Lemon Pie Bars

CRUST:
3/4 cup (1 1/2 sticks) butter, at room
    temperature

1/2 cup confectioners' sugar
1 1/2 cups flour

FILLING:
5 lightly beaten eggs
5 tablespoons flour

2 cups sugar
6 tablespoons lemon juice

Confectioners' sugar

Mix the ingredients for the crust thoroughly by beating or spinning them in a food processor. Press into the bottom of a 13 × 9-inch pan. Bake in a preheated 350-degree oven for 20 minutes. Meanwhile, beat together the ingredients for the filling. Pour this mixture onto the crust when it has baked and return to the oven to bake another 20–25 minutes, or until the filling is set. Let cool, then cut into bars or fancy shapes. Sprinkle confectioners' sugar over the tops of the bars.

MAKES 25–30 SMALL BARS

½ cup melted butter
1 cup dark brown sugar
1 egg
1 cup flour

1 teaspoon baking powder
½ teaspoon salt
1 teaspoon vanilla
⅔ cup roughly chopped walnuts

Butterscotch Bars

Mix the butter and brown sugar together, then beat in the egg. Toss the flour with the baking powder and salt, then stir into the first mixture. Add the vanilla and stir in the nuts. Spread the batter into a buttered 8 × 8-inch pan and bake in a preheated 325-degree oven for 30 minutes. While still hot, cut into bars, making 6 slices one way across the pan and 3 slices down. Let cool before removing from the pan.

MAKES 18 BARS

PASTRY BASE:
½ cup butter (1 stick)
¼ cup sugar
1 egg

¾ teaspoon vanilla
1¼ cups flour
⅛ teaspoon salt

FILLING:
2 eggs, well beaten
1⅓ cups dark brown sugar
1 cup chopped pecans
½ cup dried coconut *

½ teaspoon baking powder
2 teaspoons salt
2 tablespoons flour
1 teaspoon vanilla

Pecan Bar Cookies

* If you prefer not to use coconut, increase the amount of chopped pecans from 1 cup to 1½ cups.

To make the pastry base, cream the butter and sugar together, then beat in the egg and vanilla. Incorporate the dry ingredients into the butter mixture until just absorbed, but not sticky. All this may be done in the food processor. With lightly floured fingers, pat the pastry into an ungreased 9 × 13-inch pan, making sure it is evenly distributed. Bake in a preheated 350-degree oven for 15 minutes.

Meanwhile, make the filling by stirring together all the filling ingredients until well mixed. Pour the filling onto the hot pastry crust and return it to the oven to bake for 25 minutes more. Cool the cookies in the pan and then cut them into bars or squares.

MAKES 48 BARS OR 36 SQUARES

Betsy's Connecticut Spice Cookies

½ cup shortening
½ cup sugar
½ cup molasses
1 egg
1 tablespoon cider vinegar
2 cups flour
¼ teaspoon ground cloves

¼ teaspoon allspice
1 teaspoon cinnamon
½ teaspoon ginger
½ teaspoon salt
1 teaspoon baking soda
½ cup chopped dates

Cream the shortening and sugar together. Beat in the molasses, egg, and vinegar until well mixed. Toss the flour, spices, salt, and baking soda together, then mix the dates with them to coat thoroughly. Stir these ingredients into the creamed mixture. Drop the batter by heaping tablespoonfuls onto lightly greased cookie sheets. Bake in a preheated 350-degree oven 12–15 minutes.

MAKES ABOUT 36 COOKIES

Cornmeal Hazelnut Cookies

¾ cup butter (1½ sticks)
1 cup dark brown sugar
1 egg
1 cup flour
1 cup cornmeal, preferably stone-ground

1 teaspoon salt
1½ teaspoons baking powder
1 teaspoon vanilla
1 cup chopped hazelnuts

Cream the butter and sugar together, then beat in the egg. Mix and toss the flour, cornmeal, salt, and baking powder together and then blend into the creamed mixture. Stir in the vanilla and nuts. Form on sheets of wax paper 2 rolls about 1 inch in diameter. Wrap up each piece and chill for several hours or longer. Cut into ¼-inch slices and place on greased baking sheets. Bake in a preheated 400-degree oven 10–12 minutes until lightly browned. Remove and cool on racks.

MAKES ABOUT 80 SMALL COOKIES

Lemon-Cardamom Cookies

½ cup butter (1 stick)
¾ cup light brown sugar, lightly packed
1 egg
2 cups flour

½ teaspoon salt
¼ teaspoon baking powder
¼ teaspoon ground cardamom
1 tablespoon lemon juice
1½ teaspoons grated lemon rind

Cream the butter and sugar together. Beat in the egg. Mix and toss all of the dry ingredients including the cardomom together, then blend them into the creamed mixture. Stir in the lemon juice and rind. Chill the dough well. Press the dough into molds that have been oiled and floured. Or if you don't want to bake the cookies in molds, shape the dough into 2 rolls about 1 inch in diameter, chill. Cut off ¼-inch-thick slices and place on greased cookie sheets. Bake 10–12 minutes in a preheated 375-degree oven, until the edges start to brown.

MAKES ABOUT 8 LARGE SHAPES OR 40 SMALL COOKIES

Peanut Cookies

½ cup butter (1 stick)
½ cup sugar
1 egg
½ teaspoon baking soda
¼ teaspoon cream of tartar

1 cup flour
¼ teaspoon salt
1 cup finely chopped peanuts, preferably unroasted with skins
1 teaspoon lemon juice

Cream the butter and sugar together. Beat in the egg until the mixture is light. Mix and toss the baking soda, cream of tartar, flour, and salt together, then add to the creamed mixture. Stir in the peanuts and lemon juice until well mixed. Drop the batter by tablespoonfuls onto a lightly greased cookie sheet, leaving about 1½ inches between. Bake in a preheated 350-degree oven 10–12 minutes, until lightly browned. Cool on racks.

MAKES ABOUT 24 COOKIES

Double Peanut Cookies

2 tablespoons butter
¼ cup light or dark brown sugar
½ cup sugar
6½ ounces peanut butter
1 egg

2 tablespoons milk
1 cup flour
1 teaspoon cream of tartar
¼ teaspoon baking soda
¾ cup chopped peanuts

Soften the butter in a bowl and blend in the two sugars and peanut butter. Beat in the egg and milk. Toss together the flour, cream of tartar, and baking soda, then blend into the creamed mixture. Fold in the peanuts. Drop by the heaping teaspoonfuls onto greased baking sheets, leaving 1½ inches between, and press down lightly on each mound to flatten. Bake in a preheated 325-degree oven for 12–15 minutes, until lightly browned at the edges. Remove to a rack to cool.

MAKES ABOUT 36 COOKIES

Welsh Currant Cookies

These seem to be an Americanized version of the cookies made for fairs in Wales and brought to the States by miners' wives, some settling in Fairhaven, Vermont. Sometimes the cookies were about 6 inches long, 3 inches wide, and ¼ inch thick. Beer was originally kneaded into the dough in place of milk, and the cookies were dotted with currants to look like dominoes. For the fun of it, this recipe could be turned out in similar fashion.

2 cups flour
½ cup sugar
2 teaspoons baking powder
½ teaspoon salt

½ cup shortening
1 egg
½ cup milk
½ cup currants

Mix and toss the dry ingredients together and then work in the shortening as you would for pie dough. Beat the egg and milk together and stir them into the dry ingredients. Fold in the currants. Pat the dough out into approximately ⅓ inch thickness. Cut out shapes with a cookie cutter, scrape them up with a spatula, and place them on greased cookie sheets. Bake in a preheated 350-degree oven about 10 minutes, until lightly browned. Remove to racks to cool.

MAKES ABOUT 40 COOKIES

Thumbprint Cookies

⅔ cup butter
⅓ cup sugar
2 eggs
1 teaspoon vanilla
½ teaspoon salt

1½ cups sifted flour
¾ cup finely chopped walnuts
About ½ cup strawberry,
  raspberry, or other preserves

Cream the butter and sugar together until smooth and fluffy. Separate the eggs, reserving the whites in a shallow bowl, and beat the yolks into the butter and sugar along with the vanilla and salt. Gradually incorporate the flour. Shape the dough into balls ¾ inch in diameter. Beat the egg whites until just mixed, and spread the chopped walnuts on wax paper. Dip the balls first in the egg whites, then roll them in the walnuts. Place them 1 inch apart on greased cookie sheets and press down the middle of each cookie to make an indentation. Bake in preheated 350-degree oven for 15–17 minutes, watching carefully—they should be just lightly browned. Remove and cool on racks. Before serving, fill the center of the cookies with preserves (incidentally, Chokecherry Jelly, page 624, is delicious in thumbprints).

MAKES 36 COOKIES

½ cup maple syrup
½ cup butter (1 stick), melted

½ cup flour
½ cup oatmeal

Maple Lace Cookies

Stir together the maple syrup and butter, then add the flour and oats, mixing thoroughly. Drop by 2 teaspoonfuls onto greased baking sheets, leaving plenty of space in between as they will spread (only 6 cookies to a baking sheet). Bake in a preheated 350-degree oven for 7–8 minutes. Remove and let cool about 1 minute, then scrape up with a spatula. You can now transfer the cookies to a rack to cool, or you can roll them one by one, while they are still warm, around a broomstick, or mold them onto the bottom of cups to make a saucerlike shape; as soon as they have hardened into the form you want, place them on a rack. If the cookies harden too quickly so you cannot remove them easily, put the baking pan back in the oven for about 30 seconds to warm up again. Fill the shapes, if you like, with whipped cream or ice cream just before serving.

MAKES ABOUT 18 COOKIES

Snicker-doodles

New England cooks had a penchant for giving odd names to their dishes—apparently for no other reason than the fun of saying them. Snickerdoodles come from a tradition of this sort, which includes Graham Jakes, Jolly Boys, Brambles, Tangle Breeches, and Kinkawoodles.
—*The American Heritage Cookbook*

1 egg
1 cup sugar
2 tablespoons soft butter
2 cups flour
2 teaspoons baking powder

½ teaspoon salt
⅛ teaspoon freshly grated nutmeg
½ cup milk
2 teaspoons vanilla

TOPPING:
3 tablespoons sugar

2 teaspoons cinnamon

Beat the egg, then mix it into the sugar. Stir in the butter and beat until everything is thoroughly blended. Toss the flour, baking powder, salt, and nutmeg together, then add to the butter-sugar mixture alternately with the milk. Stir in the vanilla and beat the batter well. Drop by the heaping teaspoonful onto greased cookie sheets, leaving 2 inches between the mounds. Press lightly with wet fingers to flatten slightly and sprinkle the sugar mixed with the cinnamon on top. Bake in a preheated 350-degree oven for 8–10 minutes, until browned at the edges. Cool on racks.

MAKES ABOUT 24 COOKIES

Brambles

1 egg
1 cup chopped raisins
1 cup sugar

Rind and juice of 1 lemon
Basic Pie Dough for 8-inch shell
  (page 564)

Beat the egg in a small saucepan, then add the raisins, sugar, lemon rind, and juice. Cook slowly until thick, stirring often, about 5 minutes. Let cool.

Roll out the pie dough to ⅛-inch thickness. Cut pieces about 4 × 5 inches. Wet the edges all around and place about 1 teaspoonful of the filling in the center, then fold the long sides over. Seal the edges all around with the tines of a fork and prick the top. Bake in a preheated 425-degree oven for 10 minutes.

MAKES ABOUT 30 COOKIES

Thin Pecan Cookies

1 cup dark brown sugar
½ cup flour
⅛ teaspoon salt
2 tablespoons soft butter

1 egg, lightly beaten
1 teaspoon vanilla
1 cup pecans, each broken in
  several pieces

Sift the brown sugar, flour, and salt into a bowl. With your fingertips, work the soft butter in, then stir in the egg and the vanilla to make a smooth batter. Fold in the pecans. Drop by the teaspoonful onto lightly greased cookie sheets, leaving several inches between each cookie, as they will spread. Bake in a 375-degree preheated oven 7 minutes. Let the cookies cool a bit before you try to scrape them from the pans with a spatula. The cookies may rumple and stick a little but you can straighten them out. Cool on racks.

MAKES ABOUT 24 COOKIES

Hazelnut-Orange Snowballs

1 cup butter (2 sticks)
⅓ cup sugar
2 cups flour
2 cups finely chopped hazelnuts

2 tablespoons grated orange rind
1 teaspoon vanilla extract
About 1½ cups confectioners' sugar

Cream the butter and the sugar until light and fluffy. Stir in the flour, nuts, orange rind, and vanilla. Chill for 1 hour.

Shape the cookies into small balls—you should have about 36. Bake on ungreased cookie sheets in a preheated 300-degree oven for about 30–35 minutes. Cool the cookies slightly on wire racks, then roll them in confectioners' sugar. Put them back on the racks to finish cooling. The cookies can be rolled again in confectioners' sugar when cooled, or store as they are in an airtight container.

MAKES 36 COOKIES

Lewis Hill's Maple Butternut Fudge

Lewis Hill is a friend whose books for gardeners and cooks include *Fruits and Berries for the Home Garden;* another of his more specialized achievements is the recipe below.

3 cups maple syrup
1 cup milk

½ cup chopped butternuts or
walnuts

Put the syrup and the milk in a saucepan and boil the mixture to the soft ball stage (when ½ teaspoon dropped into a cup of water can be shaped into a soft ball with your fingers), or about 236 degrees. Remove from the heat and cool to lukewarm before beating until the mixture is creamy. Add the nuts to the maple cream and pour the mixture into an 8-inch square buttered pan. When it spreads out evenly, score the fudge with a knife to make 16 squares and center one nutmeat in each square.

MAKES 16 SQUARES

DRINKS, PRESERVES and RELISHES, and SAUCES

IN FRONT OF the General Samuel McClellan Inn, on the village green of South Woodstock, Connecticut (on land once owned by the great grandfather of Justice Oliver Wendell Holmes), a well was dug expressly, so the story goes, to provide water for the flips imbibed daily by General Sam, a hero of the Battle of Lexington.

Sometimes rendered *phlippe*, a flip was a popular Yankee drink for several generations, usually requiring an egg or two, and furnishing nourishment as well as alcohol to warm the cockles of the heart. Lacking central heating, old New Englanders drank intoxicants for protection against the cold as well as insurance against the diseases they believed were bound to strike those who depended upon water alone. All sorts of mixed drinks, such as flips, compounded of rum or sherry sweetened by molasses or dried pumpkin, have been produced in Yankee kitchens.

Regardless of the season, mixtures of fruit and alcohol are a part of life in the region, and those called shrubs are gaining new popularity. "My grandmother," a letter from Old Orchard Beach, Maine, says, "got thirsty now and then even as you and I, and so she made raspberry shrub. She used to cool it in a well." In the twentieth century, commercial versions of such fruit drinks are simply called coolers.

Pumpkins may no longer be a common ingredient in alcoholic drinks, but cooks transform such vegetables, as well as every imaginable fruit, into relishes, preserves, and sauces of many kinds. In addition to carrot and cucumber marmalades, pumpkin marmalade, and meat sauces, the modern cooks' kitchens manufacture sundry good things, from green tomato mincemeat to old-fashioned raspberry vinegar (much in vogue in the 1980s). A few ideas follow.

DRINKS

Blueberry-Yogurt Shrub

Served chilled, this is intriguing in flavor combinations when made with wild Maine blueberries, now on hand among supermarket frozen foods throughout the year.

1⅓ cups skim milk
1⅓ cups plain yogurt
1⅓ cups blueberries, preferably wild

1⅓ tablespoons strained clover honey
½ teaspoon vanilla extract

Place all ingredients in the canister of a blender or food processor and spin 1 minute, or until the blueberry skins have been reduced to pinpoints of color. Chill thoroughly.
SERVES 4

Rhubarb-Yogurt Cooler

½ cup cooked rhubarb (page 524)
1 cup plain yogurt

1½–2 cups seltzer

Put the rhubarb in a blender or food processor and spin about 30 seconds until puréed. Add the yogurt and the seltzer water, spin until smooth, and chill the mixture in the refrigerator.
SERVES 3–4

Cantaloupe-Lemon Cooler

1 cup ripe cantaloupe chunks, chilled
¼ cup fresh lemon juice
3 tablespoons superfine sugar

1 cup fresh orange juice
1 cup ice cubes
About 2 dozen fresh mint leaves

Put the cantaloupe chunks, lemon juice, sugar, and orange juice in the container of a blender, and spin until the fruit is puréed. Add the ice cubes

and all but about 6 of the mint leaves, and and blend on high speed until icy and frothy. Pour into glasses filled with ice and garnish with a mint leaf.
SERVES 6

Cantaloupe-Yogurt Shake

1 ripe cantaloupe
1/4 cup milk
1/2 cup plain yogurt
2 teaspoons or more fresh lime juice

1 tablespoon sugar
2 tablespoons orange- or almond-flavored liqueur
1 pint vanilla ice cream or cantaloupe sherbet

Peel and seed the cantaloupe, cut it into chunks, and put them in a food processor, adding the milk, yogurt, and about 2 teaspoons of lime juice; add the sugar and the liqueur, and spin the mixture just long enough to reduce it to a thick liquid. Taste and adjust flavor if necessary. Spoon in the ice cream or sherbet and spin until smooth. Pour into chilled glasses.
SERVES 4–6

Peabody Punch

"No punch is better than the palate of the person who tastes it," the connoisseur Julian Street wrote one day from his hideaway in the Housatonic Valley. "Taste as you go along. The object is to achieve a blend without obtrusive flavor." Peabody Punch, named for Joseph Peabody, the celebrated West Indies merchant who lived in Salem, Massachusetts, is typically Yankee in that regard—his recipe, often revised, blended green tea with as many as four wines and spirits, including two ports bottled for S. S. Pierce of Boston. Nonalcoholic flavor derived from Caribbean fruits were brought north by his schooners in the early nineteenth century. Below is a simplified version of an estimable party libation.

12 large limes, or 24 small limes
Sugar
1 jar guava jelly
1 pint boiling water
1 pint green tea

1 bottle best Jamaica rum
6 wine glasses port
3 wine glasses Madeira
Orange slices

Rub the limes with sugar to get the essential oil diffused into the sugar. Cut the limes in half, and add their juice to the impregnated sugar. Dissolve the guava jelly in the boiling water, and add the dissolved jelly to the lime juice. As you stir the mixture, taste for the right degree of sweetness, and add the tea. Stir in the rum, port, and Madeira. Let the punch stand overnight, or longer. Pour it over a large block of ice in a punch bowl to dilute as it matures.
MAKES ABOUT 1 GALLON

Hot Mulled Cider

If you do not have your own homemade cider keg—most current New England cider is simply apple juice—ask your wine retailer to supply hard cider from New England's West Country, or from Normandy. In earlier days (John Adams drank a tankard of hard cider before breakfast every day of his life) hard cider was available throughout New England.

2 quarts hard cider
12 whole cloves
1 stick cinnamon

1 tablespoon finely grated lemon
  rind
Lemon slices

Put the cider, spices, and grated lemon rind in a saucepan, heat it to the simmering point and continue heating the mixture for about 15 minutes. Strain and pour into heated mugs, topping each with a lemon slice.
SERVES 8 OR MORE

The Brethren's Cider

1 fifth applejack

½ gallon fresh apple cider

GARNISH: *twists of lemon peel*

Mix the applejack and cider in a punch bowl. Add lots of ice and chill thoroughly. Serve straight up with a twist of lemon.
SERVES 15

Herb Teas and Tisanes

Herb tea mixtures are a matter of experiment and individual taste. Try borage, lemon balm, marjoram, thyme, or lemon verbena in various proportions. Add rose blossoms for color. For storage, dry the leaves in an airy place. Mint leaves are, or course, the most traditional for making infusions, and the flavor will vary with the species—spearmint, orange, or pineapple mint.

One of the rewards of summer is to be able to pinch off a half-dozen leaves of your choice of herb and crush them in the bottom of a teacup or mug (glass preferred to show the color), then pour boiling water over them and let the tea steep a minute or two.

To make a pot of herb tea, use a china, earthenware, or porcelain teapot (stainless steel and enameled metal pots lose the heat quicky). Heat the pot with boiling water. Pour off the water and drop the leaves into the pot. If using fresh herbs, the ratio is one tablespoon per cup; for dried leaves, 1 to 2 teaspoons per cup will usually do, depending upon the variety.

Maple Coffee

A warming, soothing after-dinner cup in winter or a cooling stimulant for a hot day.

8 cups strong coffee
1/3 cup maple syrup
8 cloves
1 stick cinnamon
8 whole allspice berries

8 tablespoons heavy cream
2–3 tablespoons confectioners' sugar
1/2–1 teaspoon vanilla extract

Strain the coffee and pour it into a large saucepan with the maple syrup and the spices. Heat the coffee to the barest simmer—it should do no more than "smile"—and keep it at this temperature for about 15 minutes. Combine the heavy cream with the confectioners' sugar and vanilla, and whip until peaks form. Strain the simmering coffee into demitasse cups or mugs, and top each with the whipped cream. In hot weather, chill the spiced and simmered coffee in the refrigerator several hours before serving. Pour it over ice in chilled glasses and top with the whipped cream.
MAKES 8 CUPS

PRESERVES and RELISHES

Beatrice Vaughan's Red Pepper Jam

In her kitchen in North Thetford, Vermont, Mrs. Vaughan turned out a number of Vermont cookbooks, including *The Old Cook's Almanac* in which she gave this midwinter advice: "These are days when friends drop in casually and are asked to take potluck, so keep a jar of this old-fashioned garnish handy. It's dark red, delectable and wonderful with meats as well as for sandwiches when combined with cream cheese."

12 large sweet red peppers   *2 cups sugar*
1 tablespoon salt   *2 cups cider vinegar*

Remove seeds and pith from the peppers, cut in pieces, and grind in a food processor or meat grinder. Add the salt, mix well, and set aside in the refrigerator overnight. Turn the ground peppers into a sieve and let the mixture drain 15–20 minutes. In a large saucepan mix the drained peppers with the sugar and the vinegar, then bring the mixture to a boil. Simmer about 30 minutes, until the consistency is that of marmalade. Pour into screw-top jars.

Blackberry Jam

2 lemons   *1½ quarts blackberries (6 cups)*
1½ cups water   *7 cups sugar*

Coarsely grate or chop the lemon—peel, seeds, and all (the food processor does a very good job). Combine with the water in a nonaluminum pot and boil gently 20 minutes, covered. Add the blackberries and sugar, and cook, uncovered, over medium heat, stirring occasionally, for 20 minutes, at which point the syrup will have thickened; if not, boil 2 or 3 minutes more. Remove from the heat and pour into sterilized jars and seal.
MAKES ABOUT 2 HALF-PINT JARS

Berry Jams

For each cup of prepared berries—blueberries, strawberries, raspberries, gooseberries, elderberries, or blackberries—use ¾–1 cup of sugar (the larger amount for more acidic fruit). Work with only 4–6 cups of prepared fruit at a time. The berries can be chopped coarse, sliced (as with strawberries), crushed slightly, or left whole. If left whole, crush the bottom layer as you put it into a saucepan (a large enough one to avoid boiling-over problems) in order to draw some juices out as the berries begin to cook. If necessary, a small amount of water—no more than ½ cup—can be added.

Simmer the fruit to soften it a little before adding the sugar. Take care not to let it stick to the pan by stirring often and keeping the heat moderate. Add the sugar and stir until it is dissolved. Bring to a boil and continue to stir frequently. Now reduce the heat and cook until the jam has thickened.

Determining when the jam is ready can be tricky. Be sure to stir it up well, as it will be thick near the bottom of the pan; if you have a candy thermometer, it should be 214 degrees. When done, the jam should round up nicely on a spoon. Another good way to tell when it's done is to spoon a small amount onto a dish that has been chilled in the refrigerator or freezer. Tip the dish a little: the liquid should be syrupy, not runny. If you are still not sure, rather than risk overcooking the jam, turn the heat off and set a small amount in the freezer to cool. When chilled, you will be able to tell what the consistency of your jam is going to be. If it is still too runny, cook a bit more and retest.

Pour the boiling hot jam into hot screw-top jam or jelly jars that have been sterilized in a boiling water bath. Place sterilized lids on top, first wiping the edge of the jar to remove any drips. Apply screw bands firmly. Invert the jars for a few seconds, then place them upright on a wire rack to cool completely. Because of the high sugar content of jams, jellies, and the watermelon pickles recipe on page 628, most people do not bother to process after they are well sealed, but to be on the safe side, process in a water bath for 10 minutes.

If any jars have not sealed—because of a chip in the glass, a tear in the rubber seal, or because you have left some drips on the rim—empty the contents, reheat, and pack again into hot sterilized jars. Be sure to process such jars in a water bath for 10 minutes or store in the refrigerator.

Frozen Jams from Berries and Fruits

For those who have ample freezing space, making jams for the freezer is so easy—no need to stand over the hot stove cooking down the fruit and to process the jars. Moreover, you can make freezer jams in small batches with just a few pounds of berries or fruits as they ripen in the summer. And the frozen preserves seem to have a much fresher taste. Here's the formula:

2 pounds fresh fruits or berries
1 lemon, freshly squeezed (about 3–4 tablespoons)
One 2-ounce package powdered pectin
¾ cup light corn syrup
3½ cups sugar

For fruits, peel them and remove the pits, then finely chop them (you can use the food processor but be careful not to overprocess). For berries, crush them. Put the fruit or berry pulp in a large saucepan with the lemon juice and stir in the powdered pectin and corn syrup. Let stand about 30 minutes. Stir in the sugar and heat just enough for the sugar to dissolve. Pour into sterilized jars, screw on the lids, and store in the freezer. You may keep freezer jams in the refrigerator for up to 4 weeks.

MAKES 4 HALF-PINT JARS

Peach Jam

If it hasn't been a very good peach season and the fruit is not flavorful, be sure to add the optional crystalized ginger and lemon juice. Otherwise, you may want to let just the pure peach with citrus flavor shine through.

2 pounds peaches
1½ pounds sugar
1 whole orange, sliced thin,
  including peel, seeds removed

½ lemon, seeds removed, sliced
  thin (skin on)

OPTIONAL:
½–¾ ounces crystallized ginger,
  minced (½–2 tablespoons)

1 tablespoon fresh lemon juice

Blanch the peaches in boiling water a few at a time for 1 minute, then drop them into cold water. Remove the skins, which will come off easily. Split the peaches and remove the pits, then chop the fruit fine. Cook the peaches for a few minutes in a large pan to soften them slightly. Add the remaining ingredients and bring to a boil, stirring, until the sugar is dissolved. Reduce the heat enough to maintain a medium boil, and cook, stirring frequently to prevent sticking. The length of cooking time will vary according to the juiciness of the peaches. Test for doneness and put in jars following the directions in the Berry Jam box (page 619).

MAKES 6 HALF-PINT JARS

Tomato Marmalade

1½ quarts ripe tomatoes, peeled and chopped
3 cups sugar
1 orange, including peel, chopped fine, seeds removed
1 lemon, including peel, chopped fine, seeds removed
½ cup chopped walnuts
1 cup water
2 sticks cinnamon, broken into pieces
1 teaspoon whole cloves
15 ounces raisins, dark or golden, or a combination (about 2 cups)

Put all of the ingredients into a large saucepan—the spices may be tied in cheesecloth to remove later, or added loose to be left in the jam, if you prefer. Place over medium heat and stir frequently, until the sugar dissolves. After the mixture comes to a boil, reduce the heat to a simmer, and cook, stirring often to prevent sticking, for about 45 minutes, or until thickened (see Berry Jam box for test). Place boiling hot marmalade into hot, sterilized jars, then close, invert to test seal, and cool, following the same technique as for Berry Jams, page 619.

MAKES 7–8 HALF-PINT JARS

Carrot Marmalade

Chef Louis De Gouy, who knew more about American cooking than most, wrote wisely about many foods, and he was in top form when he called carrots "more sinned against than sinning." Carrot marmalade is a neglected favorite of old-time Yankeee kitchens.

2 pounds carrots
2 lemons
2 cups water
1 cup orange juice
3 cups sugar

Scrape the carrots, cut in chunks, and spin in the food processor while you count slowly to ten, or else grate coarsely. Cut the lemons in quarters and spin in the food processor while you count to ten. Combine the carrots and the lemons in a large saucepan, adding water and orange juice. Bring to a boil and cook, bubbling, about 45 minutes. Add the sugar, and simmer about 1 hour, until the mixture stands in a spoon. Pour hot into sterilized glass jars.

MAKES ABOUT 4 PINTS

Green Tomato Marmalade

Berkshire Shakers often added preserved ginger to green tomato marmalade, while other New Englanders are apt to stick to spices most readily at hand. Here is an aromatic breakfast spread that is not too sweet and is a variation on two themes.

3 pounds green tomatoes
1 pound sugar
3 lemons
½ teaspoon salt
½ cup water

One 1-inch piece stick cinnamon
½ teaspoon ground ginger
1 tablespoon crystallized ginger
  slices

Wash tomatoes and chop them coarsely. Put them in a large bowl and stir in the sugar. Cut the lemons in thin slices, removing the seeds, and sprinkle

Beach Plums

Known as *Prunus maritima* by botanists, beach plums aren't exclusively confined to Yankee coastlines, but it's likely that the thriftiness of New England has done much to romanticize the pinkish jams and jellies that are made for sale to visitors as much as for home consumption.

People marvel that beach plums seem to thrive in sand so barren of nourishment it's unbelieveable anything could grow. Not surprisingly, beach plums are naturally bitter, but they combine the good qualities of grapes, cherries, and other plums, although they are in comparison tiny in size, and range in color from purple to bright red.

Along the beaches of Cape Cod and Martha's Vineyard beach plum pickers agree that the shrublike trees literally covered in billows of white blossoms offer one of the most beautiful sights of New England springtime. The ripened fruit is often so abundant that the weight bends the whole bush to the ground.

"There is something peculiarly remindful of human life in the beach plum, its bush and fruit," as a writer for the *Vineyard Gazette* once put it. "The blending of bitter and sweet in the flavor of the fruit, the obvious fight against odds . . . in order to maintain life and bear fruit. And the tinge of bitterness that is noticeable in the ripest of the plums is as though the bush were conscious of having always labored under the most serious of handicaps, beaten by winds, undernourished. . . ."

The gathering of beach plums has become commercially successful, and full appreciation of New England food remains incomplete until you've had a taste. It's been said that clear beach plum jelly goes with soft-shell crab as cranberry sauce goes with turkey. The juice itself has true Yankee pungency.

them with salt. Put the slices in the water, and cook 5 minutes. Add to the tomatoes and sugar, along with the cinnamon stick and ground ginger, place in a large saucepan, and cook, stirring continually, until the boiling point is reached. Reduce heat to the lowest point possible, and cook about 2 hours, until the syrup is very thick. This should have the consistency of thick cut marmalade. Remove the cinnamon stick and stir in ginger slices. Place in hot sterilized jars and seal according to directions in the Berry Jam box, page 619.

MAKES 4 HALF-PINT JARS

Nancy Nagel's Beach Plum Jelly

5 cups whole beach plums, washed
   and cleaned of leaves (don't
   bother about the stems)
1 cup water
6 cups sugar
3 ounces liquid pectin

Crush the plums with a potato masher in a big pot, add the water and simmer, covered, for 20 minutes. Continue to mash them now and then during the cooking. Filter the mixture through a really fine jelly bag. Don't mash or try to force it through—just let it drip slowly if you want a clear jelly. If the plums were juicy, you will have about 3½ cups when finished.

Stir the 3½ cups juice (if you don't have quite that much cut down on the sugar and pectin accordingly) and sugar together in a large pot and bring to a rolling boil—it should be boiling so hard you can't stir down the bubbles. Add the pectin, stirring constantly, and boil for 1 minute. Remove from the heat and let sit for a minute, then skim off all the foam. Pour into hot, sterilized jars, and seal.

MAKES 7 HALF-PINT JARS

Red Pepper Jelly

3 sweet red peppers (1 pound)
1 large onion
4 fresh red chili peppers (about 2–
   2½ inches long), or 1 teaspoon
   dried red pepper flakes
1 tablespoon salt
4½ cups sugar
1¼ cups white vinegar
½ cup lemon juice
6 whole cloves
One 6-ounce bottle liquid pectin

Quarter the sweet red peppers and remove the seeds and ribs. Peel and chop the onion in quarters. Using gloves, remove the seeds from the chili peppers. Put all three through the meat grinder using the coarse grinding blade. As they are ground, transfer them to a strainer and toss them with 1½ teaspoons of the salt. Let them drain for 3 hours. Squeeze the vegetables dry gently with your hands. In a large cooking pot, mix the drained vegetables with the remaining 1½ teaspoons salt, the sugar, vinegar, lemon juice, and cloves. Bring to a boil, and cook for 10 minutes. Add the liquid pectin, and continue to boil for 1 minute, skimming off with a large spoon any foam that rises to the surface. Pour immediately into hot, sterilized jars with 2-piece caps and follow the directions in the Berry Jams box (page 619).

MAKES 5–6 HALF-PINT JARS

Chokecherry Jelly

Chokecherries may be poisonous if you try to eat them raw. And who would after the first mouth-puckering taste? But cooked, they are benign and have an unusual and delectable flavor—just one more of nature's surprises.

2 quarts chokecherries
1 quart water

3 tablespoons pectin
2 cups sugar

Boil the chokecherries gently in the water, covered, for 20 minutes. Mash the cooked fruit by hand or in a food processor, and put the mash in a jelly bag. Hang from a hook or a faucet with a bowl underneath and let drip for about 24 hours, or until all the juice is extracted. Measure the juice (you should have 1½ cups) and pour into a saucepan. Add the pectin to the juice, bring to a boil, then stir in the sugar and simmer until just dissolved. Pour into sterilized jelly jars and seal.

MAKES ABOUT 2 HALF-PINT JARS

Green Tomato Mincemeat

4 cups finely chopped green tomatoes*
Salt
½ orange
4 cups chopped apples, peeled, seeded, and cored
1½ tablespoons salt
1½ cups dark brown sugar
   * May be done in food processor.

½ pound seeded raisins
1 teaspoon cinnamon
½ teaspoon ground cloves
½ teaspoon allspice
¼ teaspoon freshly grated nutmeg
¼ teaspoon cider vinegar
2 tablespoons margarine

Sprinkle the chopped tomatoes with salt and let them stand 1 hour. Drain them thoroughly. In a large heavy saucepan, mix the remaining ingredients with the tomatoes and boil gently about 2 hours, until tender. Pour into hot, sterilized 1-pint jars, leaving ½ inch space at the top. Process in a boiling water bath for 25 minutes.

MAKES 3 PINT JARS

Ever since New England Indians showed what affinity there is between cranberries and roasted meat, there have been refinements of cranberry concoctions that give a lift to meals of many kinds. With its touch of applejack, this relish is decidedly Yankee.

Cranberry Relish

1 pound cranberries (4 cups)
2 tart apples
2 oranges
½ lemon

¼ pound chopped butternuts or walnuts
About ¾ cup sugar
Applejack

Wash and pick over the cranberries, discarding any damaged ones. Chop them coarsely—it's easy to do in a food processor in on and off spurts. Peel, core, and chop the apples. Using the food processor or a meat grinder, coarsely chop the oranges and lemon, skins as well. Mix the nuts in with the berries and fruit, and stir in sugar and a little applejack to taste. Set aside to marinate for 24 hours or more. Store in the refrigerator. Serve cold.
MAKES ABOUT 1½ QUARTS

½ cup dark brown sugar
½ cup cider vinegar
1 teaspoon mustard seeds
1½ teaspoons curry powder
¼–½ teaspoon red pepper flakes, according to taste
½ teaspoon salt

1 cup diced onion
1 cup diced green pepper, membrane and seeds removed
3 cups diced, peeled peaches
¾ cup coarsely chopped black walnuts, if available, or English walnuts

Fresh Peach Chutney

Mix the brown sugar, vinegar, spices, pepper flakes, and salt together in a pot, and heat, stirring, until the sugar is dissolved. Add the onion and green pepper and simmer 2–3 minutes. Cool to lukewarm. Stir in the peaches and black walnuts. Transfer to jars and seal. Store in the refrigerator.
MAKES 5 HALF-PINT JARS

Aunt Ida's Apple Chutney

15 large sour or tart apples
2 large onions
2 garlic cloves
1 tablespoon salt
1 ounce mustard seeds

1 pound light brown sugar
1 pound golden raisins
1 tablespoon ginger
3 cups cider vinegar

Pare and slice the apples and onions. Mince the garlic. Stir all the ingredients together in a large pot and cook over medium heat, stirring often, until thick. This will take 1½–2 hours. Pour while hot into hot, sterilized jars.

MAKES ABOUT 7 PINT JARS

Bread-and-Butter Pickles

6 quarts thinly sliced unpeeled cucumbers (not *waxed*)
1 quart sliced onions (or more to taste)
½ cup pickling salt
1½ pints white vinegar

6 cups sugar
¼ cup mustard seeds
2 tablespoons whole cloves
1 tablespoon celery seeds
1 teaspoon turmeric (optional)

Put the sliced cucumbers in a large shallow pan along with the onions. Sprinkle the picking salt over the vegetables and mix well with your hands. Cover with ice (coarsely cracked or cubes) and let stand for 3 hours. Drain well.

Make a brine by bringing the vinegar, sugar, and spices to a boil. Add the drained vegetables and bring the mixture just to a boil. Stir very little. Pack immediately into hot, sterilized jars with canning lids and process in a boiling water bath canner for 15 minutes. Store for 3–4 weeks before eating.

MAKES 4–5 QUARTS

Late Harvest Pickles

2 pounds green tomatoes
2 pounds onions
1 sweet red pepper
2 pounds McIntosh apples
2 pounds dark brown sugar

1½ tablespoons salt
1 pint cider vinegar
1½ teaspoons cinnamon
½ teaspoon allspice
1½ teaspoons ground cloves

Chop the vegetables and apples and mix them in a pot, adding the seasonings. Bring to a boil and cook gently for 1½ hours, or until thick. Pour into hot, sterilized jars and seal.

MAKES ABOUT 4 PINT JARS

We first encountered these dill pickles when we stopped by one day at our friend Michael LaCroix's restaurant in Derby Line just over the border from Canada. As he was "prepping" the evening meal, listening to baroque music on Vermont Public Radio, he was munching on Julie Carter's wonderful garlicky dill pickles and he invited us to dip into the barrel. Here is her recipe:

Julie Carter's Dill Pickles

About 16 small cucumbers (4 inches long) or 12 larger, but slim cucumbers (enough to fill 4 pints)

12 large garlic cloves, peeled
4 heads fresh dill
2 hot red peppers or 1 teaspoon crushed hot red pepper flakes

BRINE:
2½ cups vinegar
2½ cups water

¼ cup salt

Wash the cucumbers. Leave the small ones whole or chunk the larger ones. Pack into 4 pint jars that have been sterilized. To each pint add 3 cloves garlic, 1 head dill, ½ hot red pepper or ½ teaspoon pepper flakes. Make the brine: put the vinegar, water, and salt in a saucepan and heat to the boiling point. Pour hot over the cucumbers in the jars. Seal and place in a water bath that is barely simmering, not boiling, for 5 minutes, marking the time as soon as you put them in—if you leave them longer, they will get soft. Store for several weeks before using.

MAKES 4 PINTS

Sweet Pickle (Hot Dog) Relish

4 cups finely chopped or ground cucumbers, not waxed*
2 cups chopped onions*
1 cup chopped green pepper*
1 cup chopped sweet red pepper*

¼ cup salt
2 cups cider vinegar
3½ cups sugar
1 tablespoon celery seeds
1 tablespoon mustard seeds

* All of the vegetables may be prepared by putting them through a meat grinder or food processor, using a coarse grinding blade.

Mix the chopped vegetables with the salt in a large bowl. Add enough cold water to just cover them. Let stand for 2 hours, then drain, in several batches, through a strainer, pressing down to force out all the excess liquid. In a large pot, heat the vinegar, sugar, and spices to the boiling point, stirring until the sugar is dissolved. Add the drained vegetables and simmer for 10 minutes. Pack immediately into hot, sterilized canning jars with 2-piece lids, leaving ¼-inch head room. Process for 10 minutes in a boiling water bath. Store the relish for at least 4 weeks before using.

MAKES ABOUT 4 PINTS

Watermelon Pickles

7 pounds watermelon rind
Brine made from ¼ cup pickling
   salt to 1 quart water
7 cups sugar

2 cups white vinegar
½ teaspoon oil of cloves*
½ teaspoon oil of cinnamon*

* These are *not extracts*. The oil of cloves and cinnamon can be found among candy-making supplies in some supermarkets; if not available, stores specializing in candy-making equipment will have them and maybe drugstores.

Use the rind of firm, slightly under ripe watermelon. Trim off the dark green skin with a vegetable peeler and discard. Cut the fruit off the slices (use, if you wish, for another purpose), but leave a very thin rim of pink. Cut the rind into 1-inch cubes. Soak for 2 hours in enough brine to cover the rind. Drain and quickly rinse off the rind. Place in a large saucepan, cover with cold water, and bring to a boil. Cook rapidly until tender but not soft, about 10 minutes. Drain thoroughly. Combine the sugar, vinegar, and spice oils in a saucepan and heat to the boiling point, stirring to dissolve the sugar. Put the cooked rind into a large glass or pottery bowl and pour the hot syrup over it. Let the pickles stand for 1 day at room temperature, covered with wax paper or a glass cover.

Drain off the syrup, heat it to the boiling point, and pour it back over the rind. Let the pickles stand again, covered, overnight.

On the third day, heat the rind in the syrup to the boiling point. Pack hot in hot, sterilized jars, following the directions in the Berry Jam box (page 619).

Be sure to let the pickles stand for a few weeks before using.

MAKES 7 PINTS

Yankee Sugarless Tomato Ketchup

As Yankee novelist Kenneth Roberts put it, "Ketchup is important to many Maine dishes, particularly in families whose manner of cooking comes down to them from seafaring ancestors . . . A sweetened ketchup in those families is regarded as an offense against God and man . . ."

1½ pecks very ripe tomatoes
3 cups cider vinegar
2 teaspoons crumbled dried basil
3 tablespoons dry mustard
4 tablespoons salt

⅓ cup allspice
1 tablespoon ground cloves
1 teaspoon freshly ground pepper
1 teaspoon ground ginger
1 teaspoon paprika

Wash, trim, and cut the tomatoes in pieces over a large bowl, catching all the juices. Scrape the tomatoes and their juices into a pot and simmer, stirring frequently for about 30 minutes, until soft. Purée the tomatoes in a

food processor or blender until smooth. Put the purée and the remaining ingredients into a heavy iron kettle and simmer 3–4 hours, stirring frequently. Pour into sterilized bottles, insert corks, and seal with sealing wax.
MAKES 12 PINTS

SAUCES

Cream Sauce or White Sauce

2 tablespoons butter
2 tablespoons flour
1 cup milk

Salt
A few gratings nutmeg
Freshly ground pepper (optional)

In a heavy saucepan melt the butter, then stir in the flour, and cook over low heat, stirring, for 2 minutes. Remove from the heat and let the bubbling die down. Immediately pour in the milk, whisk well, and then return to the heat. Continue whisking as the sauce thickens. Let cook gently about 1 minute, season to taste with salt, nutmeg, and optional pepper. If the sauce is too thick for your purposes, stir in a little more milk.
Makes 1 cup

Mushroom Sauce

¼ ounce dried mushrooms (3 to 4 medium mushrooms)*
½ cup hot water
2 tablespoons butter
3 tablespoons minced shallots or scallion bulbs or small white onion
¼ pound mushrooms, chopped
2 tablespoons flour

1 cup or more chicken or beef broth
2 tablespoons Madeira or sherry
2 teaspoons chopped fresh tarragon or chervil, or ½ teaspoon dried
Salt
Freshly ground pepper
¼ cup heavy cream (optional)

* If you do not have dried mushrooms, use 3 or 4 more medium-size fresh mushrooms and in place of the mushroom soaking water, use another ½ cup chicken or beef broth.

Soak the dried mushrooms in the hot water for 30 minutes. Melt the butter in a heavy saucepan and sauté the shallots or scallions slowly for 2 minutes. Add the chopped mushrooms. Drain the dried mushrooms (reserving the soaking water), chop them, and add them to the pan. Sauté, stirring, for 2 to 3 minutes, then stir in the flour and cook over low heat for 1 minute. Pour in the mushroom water and broth and cook, whisking, until the sauce thickens. Add the wine, herb, and salt and pepper to taste, add optional cream and simmer 1 minute.

MAKES 1½ CUPS

Homemade Tomato Sauce

This is the best way to preserve garden tomatoes for the winter: put up pint-size containers of fresh tomato sauce and freeze them. The sauce tastes better if the seeds are removed, and this can be done either before cooking by peeling and seeding the tomatoes by hand—a tiresome chore—or putting them through an excellent gadget designed for seeding and skinning tomatoes, which you set on the counter and as you feed the tomatoes into it and crank by hand, the seeds and skins are separated from the pulp and juice. Another alternative is to remove the seeds and skin after cooking by putting the cooked sauce through a vegetable mill. The carrots give extra sweetness, which most New England-grown tomatoes need.

3 tablespoons olive oil
2 medium onions, chopped
2 good size carrots, scraped and chopped
1 rib celery, chopped
2–3 fat garlic cloves, chopped
4 pounds ripe tomatoes
Salt
Freshly ground pepper
¼ cup chopped fresh basil, or 1 teaspoon dried, or 1 teaspoon chopped fresh oregano, or ½ teaspoon dried
A pinch of sugar (optional)

Heat the oil in a heavy pot and sauté the onions, carrots, and celery slowly, stirring now and then, for 5 minutes, adding the garlic for the last minute of cooking. Meanwhile, peel and seed the tomatoes by dropping them into boiling water for 1 minute, then skinning; cut in half and squeeze out the seeds. Or put them through the above-mentioned gadget. (If you choose to seed and peel later by putting them through a food mill, simply chop them.) Chop the skinned and seeded tomatoes in rough pieces and add them to the pot along with a little salt and pepper. Cook for 15 minutes, covered, over moderate heat, then uncover, add the basil or oregano, and cook 25–30 minutes more, until the vegetables are tender. Put the sauce into the food processor and spin, turning on and off, so you retain a fairly coarse texture, or put the sauce through a vegetable mill. (If you have not peeled and seeded the tomatoes, they must be put through a vegetable mill at this stage.) Taste and correct the seasoning. If the tomatoes are quite acid, the sauce may need a little sugar.

MAKES ABOUT 5 CUPS

Quick Tomato Sauce

One 16-ounce can tomatoes
1 onion, chopped
1 large carrot, chopped
1 garlic clove, skin removed
¼ cup water

Put all the tomatoes, onion, carrot, and garlic together in a heavy saucepan and cook, covered, over a medium heat for 25 minutes, stirring occasionally to make sure the sauce isn't sticking, and adding water if sauce gets too thick. Purée in a food processor or blender. Taste and add salt and pepper.
MAKES ABOUT 1¼ CUPS

Chili Sauce

3 quarts ripe tomatoes, peeled and chopped
2 large green peppers, seeds and ribs removed, chopped
8 medium onions, chopped
1 cup chopped celery
1½ cups cider vinegar
1½ cups dark brown sugar
1½ teaspoons cinnamon
½ teaspoon ground cloves
½ teaspoon nutmeg

Put the vegetables in a large cooking pot and simmer for 1 hour. Add the vinegar, sugar, and spices, and continue to cook for about 30 minutes or more, depending on how watery the tomatoes are (you want most of the juice to cook off). Put immediately into hot, sterilized canning jars with 2-piece lids, leaving ¼ inch head room, and process in a boiling water bath for 10 minutes.
MAKES ABOUT 3½ QUARTS

Hot Sauce

Juice of 2 lemons or 3 limes, or a combination of lemon and lime juice
2 hot red peppers, seeds removed
2 fat shallots, peeled and roughly chopped
2 fat garlic cloves, peeled and roughly chopped
½ cup fresh coriander, torn in pieces

Put the lemon and/or lime juice, the peppers, shallots, garlic, and coriander leaves in a food processor and spin until thoroughly minced. Or chop the solids very fine and blend in the citrus juice. A little of this goes a long way.
MAKES ABOUT ⅔ CUP

Basil and/or Parsley Pesto

Because basil grown in New England, particulary in the northern regions, is apt to have a harsh flavor, this Italian specialty is apt to taste better and look greener if made in part with flat-leaved parsley. It can be made entirely with parsley—the flat-leaved variety. The sauce is usually used with pasta, thinned a little with the pasta-cooking water, but if you wish to use it instead as a sauce for fish, meat, or poultry, leave out the nuts.

2 cups basil and/or parsley leaves, packed down
2 fat garlic cloves, peeled and chopped with salt (page 161)
6 tablespoons olive oil

1/3 cup pine nuts or walnuts (optional)
Salt
Freshly ground pepper

Spin all the ingredients, except salt and pepper, in a food processor until puréed. Taste and add salt and pepper as needed. If storing, put in a jar and film the top with a little more olive oil.
MAKES ABOUT 1 CUP

Ed Giobbi's Nut Sauce

This sauce does wonders for a New England boiled dinner and is also good with cold meats.

1 cup fresh bread crumbs
4 tablespoons chicken or beef broth
6 walnuts, shelled
1 garlic clove, chopped
1 tablespoon safflower oil

2 or more tablespoons olive oil
Juice of 1 lemon
2 tablespoons flat-leaved parsley
Salt
Freshly ground pepper

Soak the bread crumbs in the broth until soft, then transfer to a food processor along with the rest of the ingredients. If you haven't a food processor, chop the walnuts very fine, then work in the soaked crumbs and remaining ingredients. Blend until creamy, adding salt and pepper to taste. Add a few more drops of olive oil if the sauce is too thick—it should have the consistency of heavy cream.
SERVES 4–6

Hollandaise Sauce

2–3 teaspoons lemon juice
2 egg yolks
1/4 pound cold unsalted butter (1 stick)

Salt
Freshly ground pepper

In the top of a double boiler over simmering heat, or in a very heavy saucepan over low heat, whisk 1 teaspoon of the lemon juice with the egg yolks for about half a minute, until they begin to feel thick. Immediately start adding the cold butter one tablespoon at a time, whisking after each addition, until the butter is well incorporated. When all the butter has been used up and the sauce is thick, season with more lemon juice and salt and pepper to taste. If the sauce starts to curdle while you are making it, remove it from the heat and whisk in a tablespoon of cold cream. If it seems to have curdled beyond redemption, start over again with 1 egg yolk and a little cold butter, then start whisking in the curdled sauce—it should smooth out again.
MAKES ABOUT 1 CUP

Ground Peanut Sauce

Peanuts enhance lots of Yankee recipes, including this sprightly sauce that goes well with chicken.

1 onion, chopped fine
2 tablespoons corn oil
2 tomatoes, peeled and chopped
1–2 teaspoons curry powder
¾ cup ground peanuts

2–3 cups water
Salt
1½ cups cooked, chopped spinach, fresh or frozen (one 10-ounce package)

Cook the onion in oil until translucent, then add the tomatoes and the curry powder, and continue cooking about 5 minutes. Add the peanuts, ground as fine as possible, and the water. Bring the mixture to a boil and simmer, stirring constantly, for 10–12 minutes, until the sauce is reduced by about one-third. Sprinkle lightly with salt. Stir the spinach into the sauce.
SERVES 4

Tartar Sauce

Once the result of blending hard-boiled egg yolk with oil and adding accents of pickles or olives, this sauce now based on mayonnaise is good for cold meats as well as many kinds of fish dishes.

1 cup mayonnaise, preferably homemade (page 347)
1 teaspoon finely chopped shallots
1 teaspoon minced parsley
½ teaspoon chopped onion

1 teaspoon finely chopped gherkins
2 teaspoons chopped pickled capers
1 teaspoon chopped black olives (optional)

Spoon the mayonnaise into a 2-cup mixing bowl, add the other ingredients, and stir until all is evenly distributed.
MAKES ABOUT 1¼ CUPS

Salsa

This is our version of the salsa served at Christopher's Pub on Porter Street in Cambridge, Massachusetts.

½ cup finely chopped onion
2 teaspoons red wine vinegar
1 jalepeño pepper, cored, seeded, and chopped
2 cups peeled, seeded, and diced ripe tomatoes, or, if not in season, one 16-ounce can tomatoes, drained

2 tablespoons chopped fresh parsley, preferably flat-leaved
2 tablespoons chopped fresh coriander
About ½ teaspoon salt
Freshly ground pepper

Toss together all of the ingredients. Refrigerate for 24 hours before serving, then taste and correct the seasoning as necessary.
MAKES ABOUT 2 CUPS

Cucumber-Radish Sour Cream Sauce

½ cup grated cucumber, peeled, split in half, and seeded by scooping out center
3 fat radishes, grated
2 teaspoons minced fresh dill
2 minced scallions, including tender greens

1 cup sour cream, or 1 part plain yogurt to 1 part sour cream
Salt
3–4 shakes Tabasco sauce

After you have grated the cucumber and radishes, squeeze them dry in a towel. Then mix all of the ingredients together, salting to taste. Refrigerate for an hour so before serving.
MAKES ABOUT 1½ CUPS

Shaker Vegetable Sauce for Ham or Pork

The cooks in the Shaker Villages of New England were among the most imaginative in devising palatable vegetable combinations. Among the recipes collected at Hancock Shaker Village near Pittsfield, in the Berkshires, is a sweet-sour combination of tomatoes and cider. Heat cooked slices of meat in the sauce.

3–4 tablespoons chopped onions
2 tablespoons butter or vegetable oil
2 cups peeled, seeded, and chopped tomatoes

1 tablespoon dark brown sugar
1 tablespoon capers
1 tablespoon lemon juice
1 tablespoon cornstarch
1 cup apple cider

Sauté the onions in the butter or oil. When they are tender, stir in the tomatoes, the sugar, and the capers. When the mixture is blended, add the lemon juice and cornstarch, and stir thoroughly, cooking as the mixture thickens. Add the cider and continue cooking until the cider blends with the vegetables.

MAKES ABOUT 3 CUPS

Kit Osgood's Homemade Mustard

Catharine Osgood Foster of southern Vermont was both college teacher and gardener, and the author of *The Organic Gardener*, which has become a classic. Here's how she taught the art of prepared mustard, redolent of her herb patch.

1 tablespoon chopped fresh parsley
1 tablespoon chopped fresh
 tarragon
1 teaspoon chopped fresh chervil
½ cup mustard seeds (the black is
 more pungent than the brown)

1 tablespoon corn oil
1 tablespoon vinegar or currant
 juice

In a mortar, pound all the chopped herbs with the mustard seeds. (The grinding can also be done in a blender, but the flavor may seem more dull.) Put this through a sieve and save the powder that comes through. Slowly add to the powder the oil and the vingar, stirring. Keep covered but use quickly because it doesn't keep well.

MAKES ABOUT ¾ CUP

Raspberry Vinegar

Restaurant chefs often dress up their menus by calling attention to their own berry vinegars, sometimes made with New England fruit—doing what Yankee cooks have done for generations without fanfare. In fact, a delicious old-fashioned summer cooler, using 2 tablespoons of raspberry vinegar to 6 ounces of ice water, has been traditional in the hills. Some generations ago, a cook might add an ounce or so of brandy to each quart of juice.

4 quarts fresh black or red
 raspberries

⅔ quart cider vinegar
Sugar

Cover the berries with the vinegar and set aside in a cool place for about 24 hours. Strain, squeezing the liquid from the berries. Measure the result and add about one cup of sugar for each 2 cups of liquid. Bring to a boil and simmer for about 15 minutes. Cool and keep refrigerated in lidded jars.

MAKES ABOUT 1½ QUARTS

Your Own Vinegars

It's simple enough to make your own vinegars, especially in berry season. To make blackberry or raspberry vinegar, for instance, use about 1 cup of fruit to 1 cup of white vinegar. Wash the fruit, and heat the vinegar, then put the fruit in a jar, and cover with the warm vinegar. Let cool before screwing on the top. Keep in a cool, dark place for 7–10 days before tasting. If you can recognize the flavor of the fruit, the vinegar is ready; if it tastes weak, set it aside for a few more days. You can either leave the fruit in the vinegar, or strain it out through a piece of cheesecloth. Keep stored in a cool dark place —it should last indefinitely.

B.J.'s Mint Vinegar

According to a friend who knows more about wild foods than anyone we know, "This is a good vinegar to use with fruit salad or any green salad that includes pieces of orange or grapefruit, or in any vegetable dish calling for vinegar in which a minty flavor would be welcome."

2 cups packed spearmint leaves, chopped coarse

1 cup sugar
1 quart cider vinegar

Place mint leaves in the bottom of an enameled or stainless steel kettle and crush them thoroughly. Add sugar and vinegar, bring to a boil, and simmer for 5 minutes. Cool, then strain through cheesecloth and pour into sterile bottles. Cap or cork well.

MAKES ABOUT 1 QUART

ACKNOWLEDGMENTS

We're enormously in debt to many New Englanders, as well as to other friends, family members, and acquaintances. Among those who have helped are the following: Joan Ashley, Tom Azarian; Win Bacon, Phyllis H. Bailey, Kate Beattie, Bessie Blake, Bloodroot Collective, Peter and Raquel Boehmer, Sally Bole, Henry Borel, Jolene Brayler, Marguerite Buonopane; Ginny Callen, Angus Cameron, Julie Carter, Rene Chardain, Christine Cotsibos, Andy and Jan Coulson, Charles Cox, Dorothy Crandall, Marion Cunningham, Rebecca Cunningham, Susan Cunningham; Ellen Darrow, Adele Dawson, Alex Delicata, Antoinette and Oscar DeStefano, Ann Dixon, Jim Dodge, Jane Doerfer, Wayne Dunlap, Bronwyn Dunne; Carole Evans; John Farrell, Michael Field, Carol Fielders, Perley Fielders, Sheila Finney, Des Fitzgerald, Catharine Osgood Foster, Amelia and Tim Fritz, Robert Fuller; Peter Gaylor, Martha Geffen, George Germon, Cynthia Giarrasputo, Edward Giobbi, Sherry Golden, Dan Gore, Megan Goss, Jane Grigson, Linda Guica; James Haller, Patricia Halloran, Daphne Hamead, Marcia Heller, Gretchen Higgins, Lewis and Nancy Hill; Bill and Flora Ingram; Dana Jennings, Sheryl Julian; Ruda Kesselhut, Rosemary Kielty, Tim Kielty, Johanne Killeen, Letitia Kilmoyer; Michael LaCroix, Jim LaDoux, Gale Lawrence, Violette LeCours, Ann Leger, Matt Lewis, John and Pat Lincoln, Marie Lombardo; John and Jane Mahoney, John and Michele Mackin, Pietrina Maravigna, Judy Marsh, Rux Martin, Alexina Mercier, Anita Mercogliana, John and Susan McCarthy, Kathy McGee, Paule McPherson, Edward Meyer, Joseph Miles, Amy Bess Miller, Leslie Miller, David Miskell, Marian Morash, Naomi Morash, David Morrison, Ethelyn Morse, Charles and Elaine Murray; Nancy Nagel, James Nassikos, Nancy Nicholas; Vrest Orton, Bill Osgood, Millie Owen; Melendy Paine, John Palmer, Chris Pardou, Rose Paul, Richard Perlman, Gloria Pepin, Ralph Persons, June Platt, Nancy Potter; Ralph Ray, Edith and Lowell Rheinheimer, Howard and Peg Reinhardt, Lillian Ricketson, Mrs. Norma Roberts, John O. Robertson, Claudia Roden, Nancy Rogers, Tom Roussel; Linda Sayer,

Anita Seay, Susan Sellew, Penny Schmidt, Valarian D. Schmokel, Mildred Schrumpf, Lydia Shire, Judy Siemans, David and Wilhelmina Smith, Joan Smith, Randolph Smith, Thomas Spaulding, Camilla Stege, Eric Stevens, Albert Stockli, Richard David Story, Frank Susi; William Tecoskey; Mary Louise and Ron Thorborn, Anthony and Genevieve Trio, Dennis and Sally Turpin; Linda Vail, Beatrice Vaughan, Janice Vogan, Jeanne Voltz; Bradford and Leslie Wagstaff, Jonathan Walker, Tom Weiner, Helen Wilbur, Brill Williams, Mady Wolkenstein, Diane Rossen Worthington, Bill and Judy Wolf; Sharon Zacchini, Judy Zagoren.

Special thanks to our editor, Jason Epstein, whose gastronomic memories of Maine have been inspiring; and to a long-time friend and advocate Robert Lescher—once more a source of strength and wisdom.

INDEX

ABOUT THE AUTHORS

JUDITH JONES has for many years been an editor at Alfred A. Knopf, where she has shepherded the work of some of the best contemporary cookbook writers. EVAN JONES is the author of a number of books including *American Food: The Gastronomic Story* and *The World of Cheese.* Together they wrote *The Book of Bread,* which won the Tastemakers' Best Cookbook of the Year award in 1982. Judith Jones learned to cook in her aunt's Vermont kitchen, and she and Evan spend a good part of each year living off the land at Bryn Teg (Welsh for "beautiful mountain") in Vermont's Northeast Kingdom.